THE DIARIES OF JOHN BRIGHT

John Bright (1883)

THE DIARIES
OF JOHN BRIGHT

WITH A FOREWORD BY
PHILIP BRIGHT

John Bright.

EDITED BY
R. A. J. WALLING

ILLUSTRATED

NEW YORK   MCMXXXI
WILLIAM MORROW & COMPANY

KRAUS REPRINT CO.
New York
1971

KRAUS REPRINT CO.
A U.S. Division of Kraus-Thomson Organization Limited

Printed in U.S.A.

EDITOR'S NOTE

JOHN BRIGHT kept Diaries for fifty years, mostly in little oblong note-books which he filled from cover to cover with his firm, neat handwriting. With some exceptions he intended the entries merely as aids to his own memory, for he spent on them little of the care in composition and arrangement that he would give to even the least of his speeches, letters or newspaper articles. The exceptions are his records of foreign travel and the accounts of memorable experiences (e.g. his interviews with Queen Victoria) written at the request of his family. Their informality enhances rather than diminishes the personal interest of the main body of the Diaries; they are the frank private notes of a singularly simple, candid and noble mind upon the men and the events of the Victorian Age.

In the selection of these passages from the great bulk of a journal reaching from 1837 to 1887 the purpose kept in view has been to intervene as little as possible between the reader and John Bright. To make out of the Diaries an historical biography was both impossible and unnecessary, for a great historian had already written a beautiful "Life" which admirably synthesized Bright's career and his era. Some ellipses here and there, however, called for brief statements of biographical or historical fact to bridge them and make the whole intelligible. They have been provided as simply as might be. The largest of these spaces is the period of the Anti-Corn-Law campaign, whose arduous and continuous labours left Bright little time for diary writing. For the rest, such references and explanations as appeared necessary will be found in footnotes.

The Memoir of his youth with which the book opens, written in his old age, contains a remarkable picture of the life of a Quaker family at the beginning of the nineteenth century. It provides the key to Bright's character. He broke completely away from that austere quietism in the Quaker system which frowned upon a career of public activity and especially of political strife; but no understanding of his life is possible without realization of the profound and abiding influence upon it of the characteristic Quaker doctrine of the Inner Light.

The co-operation of Mr. Philip Bright, the statesman's youngest and only surviving son, has ensured the closest possible accuracy in personal detail. Invaluable aid has also been given by many others, among whom I desire to mention Mr. Herbert Putnam, the Librarian of Congress at Washington, and Sir Charles Hyde, the proprietor of the *Birmingham Daily Post*, and (for references to Hansard) Mr. Isaac Foot, M.P.

R. A. J. WALLING.

PLYMPTON,
July, 1930.

CONTENTS

LIST OF PLATES

FOREWORD

SOME surprise may be felt that these diaries have not seen the light before, and that their publication should have been delayed until forty-one years after the death of their writer. When my father died in 1889 all his papers became the property of my eldest brother, Albert Bright, who placed the letters and diaries at the disposal of Mr. G. M. Trevelyan when he was engaged on "The Life of John Bright," which was published in 1914 by Messrs. Constable. Numerous extracts from the diaries appear in that admirable work, some of which, by the courtesy of the author and publishers, are reproduced here. Unfortunately many of the earlier diaries are missing, and all efforts to trace them have been unsuccessful.

At my brother's death the diaries became the property of his daughter, Mrs. Darbishire, who at the date of her grandfather's death was a child.

I was aware of their existence, but I had not read them all until three years ago. On so doing I formed the opinion that they contained much which would interest the public, and I therefore obtained the consent of my niece to their publication.

I proposed, and she readily assented, that any profit which might result from their publication should go to objects on behalf of which my father's friend and colleague, Richard Cobden, laboured so strenuously during his useful and unselfish life, and accordingly it is proposed, so far as may be possible, to support financially the Dunford House (Cobden Memorial) Association, whose head-quarters are at Midhurst, Sussex, in the house where Cobden lived for many years, and near West Lavington Church where he is buried. Since this Association was founded it has been generously assisted by the Carnegie Endowment for International Peace, and several conferences have been held at Dunford House in furtherance of the objects of the Association.

Although I never heard my father mention religious questions in our home, he was a deeply religious man, as his speeches abundantly prove. That he had abiding faith in a future life is shown by the following extract from a letter which he wrote in August, 1846, to my mother—then Miss Leatham—"I was struck with the beauty of our Meeting House yard this morning—the grass was so green, and yet shining bright under the morning sun—the graves even looked less gloomy than usual. Within that small plot of ground there lie my mother, sister, brother, wife—all in one small portion of it. How much of what was good and lovely is there entombed! And yet the good and lovely cannot perish, and now is not there—it is, we humbly trust, where the good of all ages meet for ever."

My father when at Rochdale invariably read the Bible to our household before breakfast, and so greatly did we delight in his reading that we were always down in time to hear him.

He had a remarkable gift for reading and reciting poetry, and often made use of it for our benefit.

The diaries afford many examples of my father's merciful attitude towards persons in trouble: although he was opposed to capital punishment and harsh sentences, he never hesitated to administer corporal punishment to his children when he thought they deserved it. He was eminently just, and for this we all admired him and never questioned his decisions. He was loved and revered by his household and by his work-people, and when the end came on March 27, 1889, we felt that the world would never be quite the same again.

PHILIP BRIGHT.

July 24, 1930.

THE DIARIES OF JOHN BRIGHT

CHAPTER I

JOHN BRIGHT'S MEMOIR OF HIS YOUTH[1]

MY dear children have often asked me to write some of the incidents of my youth and of my life, and I attempt to do it in the belief that they may interest them in years to come.

I have before me at this moment what in the registration system of our religious society is called my "Birth Note." It is as follows:

> On the Sixteenth day of the Eleventh Month, One Thousand Eight Hundred and Eleven, was born at Green Bank near Rochdale in the Parish of Rochdale in the County of Lancaster unto Jacob Bright, Cotton Spinner and Martha his wife, a son who is named John. We who were present at the said Birth, have subscribed our names as Witnesses thereof.
> James Dunlop.
> Margaret Wood Junr.
> Esther Wood.

On the back of this note is the following, in the handwriting of my dear mother: "John was born about 8 o'clock on 7th day evening;" and then follow these words, and this loving and pious wish: "May he indeed love his Creator in the days of his youth, and continue steadfast unto the end."

My dear father was born in Coventry in the year 1775 on the 24th of August. His father and mother were Jacob and Martha Bright. He, my grandfather, was in his later days in bad health and in humble

---

[1] The Memoir, which covers in varying degrees of fullness his first thirty years, was written in old age. He began it in 1880, dropped and resumed it several times, and wrote the last pages, describing the death of his first wife and the beginnings of his association with Cobden, in 1888, little more than a year before his death. It fills with his minute script two of the small oblong note-books in which most of his diaries were entered.

circumstances. My father was sent to Ackworth School when about nine years of age, and remained there about five years. From Ackworth he came to Lowlaton, near New Mills in Derbyshire, where he was apprenticed to a Friend, William Holme, who had a small farm, and had a few looms employed in weaving fustians. Here he learned to weave, and afterwards became familiar with cotton-spinning, being employed in a small mill at a place called The Torr, at New Mills, where the business was carried on by John and William Holme, the sons of his master. In the year 1802 these sons removed to Rochdale, and, assisted by capital provided by some of their friends in Rochdale, built a good mill, called then and now The Hanging Road Mill. My father was with them, and assisted in starting the machinery in the mill; and he also afterwards attended the market at Manchester, delivering the produce of the mill with invoices to the different customers. My father some time after this married Sophia Holme, one of the daughters of his master, but she did not live long; I have not the date of her death.

In the year 1809 two Friends in Manchester, Roger Merrick and Joseph Flintoff, doing business with the firm, and discovering his industry and good conduct, proposed to my father to join them in the cotton business—they to provide the capital, and he the knowledge of the business. His brothers-in-law were not disposed to take him into partnership, although John was in very delicate health and William had small capacity for business. He therefore felt at liberty to accept the proposal made to him by Merrick and Flintoff, and they provided the sum of £6,000 as capital for the new firm, Jacob Bright and Co.

They engaged a small mill, adjoining Green Bank, on the north side of the town of Rochdale, which had been a worsted mill but was then unoccupied. It was on Christmas Day in the year 1809, that their steam-engine began to work. It was an engine made by Boulton and Watt of Birmingham. Its beam was of wood, and its arrangements altogether were of a very primitive character. In this year, 1809, my father and mother came to live at Green Bank, soon after my father had married again. My dear mother was the youngest daughter of John and Margaret Wood, of Bolton. The business was prosperous. My father had one-third of the profits for seven years, at the end of which time he was able to conduct it on his own capital; but he felt grateful to the partners for the help they had given him, and he consented to go on with them for seven years more—with half the profits—till the year 1823, when the partnership was dissolved, and he took the business into his own hands.

Green Bank, Rochdale, in 1865

My dear mother was a delicate woman, much less robust than her sisters; but she had an excellent natural capacity, a logical mind, and qualities of head and heart rarely excelled. She was only about twenty years of age when she married my father, who was then thirty-four. They had eleven children—seven sons and four daughters. The eldest boy was named William. He died when only four years old of a sudden attack of croup. I was the second child, then about three years old, and became then the eldest of the family.

I remember little of my younger years beyond the unceasing care and tenderness of my parents. Of my dear mother I have the idea that she was wiser and kinder and better than all other women whom I met with during my early years: this, doubtless, multitudes of men and women can say and have said of their mothers. With so many young children, our house was well filled. Those of us who were old enough to learn were sent to a cottage near the house, where a nursery governess had charge of us and taught us. From the cottage we could see the kitchen window, and when the blind was let down, we knew that dinner was ready, and we were expected to run across the field to join the rest of the family at home.

It was in the year 1820, when I was nearly nine years old, that I first went to a regular school. This was Townhead School, for boarders and day scholars, and was kept by William Littlewood, then a very young man to have the responsibility of conducting a considerable school. His father had but recently died, and the son succeeded him. He lived with his mother, Sarah Littlewood, of whom I stood in much awe, for she was a stately lady, and my mother had a great regard for her. Townhead School was at the top of Yorkshire Street in Rochdale, at the distance of half a mile from my home. I walked down after an early breakfast—came home to dinner, and went back to school for the afternoon. I can well remember as I went out at the back door of our house, and round to the front, to go out by the little garden gate, my dear mother would often meet me at the front door with a piece of cake for me to eat as I walked down the four or five fields through which I passed before I reached Yorkshire Street. I must have been one of the youngest and smallest boys in the school; and it was on this account, probably, that I was sometimes sent by the other boys into the parlour to ask for a holiday for myself and them. The master was popular with the boys, for he was kind and worthy of our good opinion. I remember that he often took his coffee for breakfast at a small table whilst the lessons were going on, and, when he had finished it, he sometimes told me to carry the small tray into the house, and I was allowed to indulge in the toast which was left on the plate.

William Littlewood was not only my first schoolmaster, but he was, whilst he lived, one of my best and kindest friends; and, not infrequently in after years, I have spent pleasant evenings at his house with his wife and daughters and friends who were visiting him.

It was during the time I was at this school that my father met with a serious accident which had nearly cost him his life. He had taken a small mill at Rakewood, just beyond Hollingworth Reservoir, and went frequently to visit it. On the day of the accident he was riding a new and young horse for the first time. My dear mother was with him on a safe and favourite horse. They were going down a very narrow lane by Dearnley Colliery, and turned into the open space where carts were loaded with coals to allow a cart coming up the narrow lane to pass. In this open space the young horse reared, and, I understand, fell over. My father came down on the ground, and the horse crushed him on the hip joint. My mother was at his side in a moment. He told her he thought or feared he was killed. He was taken into the little cottage or hut belonging to the colliery, and a carriage or chaise was sent for, to take him home. I was at school, when Reuben Harrison, who was in some sort manager in the mill at Green Bank and who lived very near the school, called on his way to his dinner and told me of the accident. I immediately went home, and can remember the excitement and terror which seized me as I hastened up the fields to know what injury my dear father had suffered. He was some weeks confined to his bed, and for some months was only able to move with the help of crutches; but ultimately his recovery was so complete that no lameness was noticeable in his walk.

In the summer of 1821 I was sent to a school at Penketh near Warrington. The school was in part of, or adjoining, the Friends' Meeting House. The master was Joseph Edmundson. There were not many scholars, and amongst them were a few girls. I lodged with John Davies, a Friend and a farmer. His family consisted of a wife, his sister Ruth, and two sons and a daughter. Several boys and girls who attended the school lodged with them. John Davies was a very kind man, rather stout in figure—a good specimen of a farmer. His wife, too, was kind, and we had a very comfortable home. Behind the house was a good garden and orchard, and a vinery where grapes were abundant; and beyond the garden were cornfields through which we walked daily to the school. Adjoining the house was a small cottage or wing, in which apples and pears were stored, and in the evening we often sat round the fire in the lower room, amusing ourselves with stories, some of which, being in the nature of ghost stories, sometimes frightened me very much. We were well fed and cared for. We had Scripture reading in the family, and I remember how I found a place for some of the New Testament narratives on or about the premises of our kind friend and host. Among them I particularly remember two. The vineyard mentioned in the 13th Chapter of Luke I pictured as just like our vineyard—and I fancied I could see the discontented brother of the Prodigal Son returning from the field down the short lane which led from the house to the neighbouring cornfield. These imaginings of my boyhood have remained with me ever since. Our schoolmaster was not well qualified for his office. His temper was not good, and the school was much less pleasant than our home with the kind and generous farmer.

The Meeting House and school were on the border of a common, called Sankey Common, and we had abundant room for playing; but we were sometimes annoyed by boys from the neighbouring school in the village of Sankey. We had much amusement in fishing in a small brook not far from the farm-house,—not with rod and line or nets, but we diverted the stream just above a small pool frequented by the small trout, and then we ladled the water from the pool and took the fishes, the "little quivering things," we found in it. I remained at Penketh School for a year, and after that I was sent to Ackworth School, near Pontefract in Yorkshire.

My parents, my father especially so, were rather strict in the observance of the customs of the religious Society to which they belonged, and they thought that Ackworth School afforded the most careful training for the children of Friends. It was in the summer of 1822 that I went to Ackworth. My dear mother went with me. I think we stopped a night at Halifax at the house of Mary Witchal, afterwards Mary Wright, a Friend who for some years lived near us in one of the houses belonging to my father. She spent her last years in Leeds and died at the age of 103 years. We went to Ackworth the next day, and I remember the feeling of sadness which oppressed me as we came in sight of the great buildings of the school. There was a look of gloom about them which almost made me shiver when I contrasted them with my own pleasant home.

I remained at Ackworth only for one year, and it was a year of much discomfort to me. The superintendent was Robert Whitaker,

5

an elderly man, small in stature, but of a kind expression of face. He was not well qualified for his office, and much of what I had to complain of might have been remedied by a person of more force of character. Still I have only a kindly feeling towards him, for in his dealing with the children at the school he was always kind.

In the school there were 180 boys and 120 girls,—one wing for the boys and the other for the girls. I found the provisions insufficient in quantity and inferior in quality. Our breakfast was good—hot milk and bread, but never more than half [as much as] I could have eaten with pleasure and advantage. Our dinners were much to be complained of. I will not describe them further than to say that on half the days of the week they were to me simply intolerable. The four masters— for the whole school of the boys was divided into four schools—were invariably kind to me, and I believe, generally so to all the boys; but in each school there was an apprentice or assistant master, not much older than the oldest boys, and entrusted with an authority wholly beyond what was proper for his years; and it was from this unfortunate arrangement that I suffered much annoyance and injustice which seemed almost like persecution. The masters were Henry Brady for reading, John Donbavand for grammar, Thomas Brown and William Doig for writing and arithmetic—for beyond these branches education at Ackworth did not then much extend. I will not mention the names of the apprentices, for their faults were the faults of their youth.

I was a timid and docile boy, and with older and wiser control I should have escaped much of the unhappiness I suffered whilst at Ackworth. One source of misery to me was the custom of taking us, I think once in the week during summer, to a dismal cold bath at some distance from the school. We were up early, soon after 6 o'clock, and hurried off to the bath. The water was cold as from a spring, and I cannot describe the terror which seized and afflicted me on the mornings when I had to undergo the inevitable plunge. On one occasion as I was clinging to the side of the bath, and about to come out, shuddering with the intense cold, one of the apprentices, a man for whom in after years I have had much respect, supposing I had not been overhead in the water, thrust me backwards into the bath by pushing me with a common besom, so that my face was miserably scratched and disfigured.[1]

In those days—now nearly sixty years ago—schools were very

[1] Bright often told his son Philip that the wielder of the besom was John Newby. Among his schoolfellows at Ackworth was John Howe, the actor, who played for many years with Irving at the Lyceum.

6

different from what they are now. Even this great school, maintained by a religious society in many things in advance of public opinion in gentleness and kindness and justice, was in many respects grievously mismanaged. In the matter of food it was insufficient in quantity and in quality; in the matter of punishments it was harsh if not barbarous; and the comforts of the children were very inadequately attended to. What I suffered induced my father to make inquiries of other great schools and of other public institutions, and he placed before the Committee of Management facts to prove that a thorough reform was needed; and from the part he took in regard to this may be dated the commencement of improvements which have been made from that time to the year in which I am now writing. Now the school is good, so far as I know, in all respects. The masters are better paid; the children are better fed; their education is much more complete; and the superintendent is worthy of the confidence that is placed in him.

I left Ackworth at the time of the General Meeting in the summer of 1823; and, soon after this, I was sent to a school at York kept by William Simpson. It was the first house on the left-hand side, as we passed out of Walmgate Bar. The master was a kind and pleasant man, and he had generally two assistants, young men from Edinburgh University. The journey to York outside the coach was a fresh experience, and I enjoyed it much. The ancient City interested me, and we had much more of reasonable freedom than at Ackworth.

The Meeting at York, too, was attractive. Among the ministers was Samuel Tuke, a superior man of high character and cultivation and an eloquent speaker. He lived very near the school, and sometimes I visited at his house. He had a large family, and his children were lively and intelligent. Among the boys at the school was one named Gorwood Rigg, whose father was a nurseryman and gardener. Of his family, several, if not nearly all his children were drowned by the upsetting of a boat in the River Ouse. They are buried in the churchyard outside Walmgate Bar, not far from the house in which Samuel Tuke then lived, and in the church is an epitaph written, I believe, by James Montgomery.

I must mention one of our Scotch teachers, John Macmillan, for many years afterwards classical master at the High School in Edinburgh. He was a good teacher, I think the best of the many I have had. I remember the first time I went up to say my lesson to him. It was my first lesson in Latin: "singular nominative, *musa*, a song; genitive, *musæ*, of a song." I said it so imperfectly that he was disappointed and addressed me very seriously: "If this is the way in which you intend to learn Latin, I cannot advise you to go any further." I was humiliated at this rebuke, which I felt to be deserved; and I took care in future he should never have occasion to complain of my carelessness and idleness.

During the two years I spent at York, I learned more than in any other two years of my school life. I was keen at my studies, and ran, I think, even with William Harvey, of Barnsley, for the place in reputation of first in the school. We had plenty of play in the ground adjoining the school. "Prison Bars," or as we called it "Prisoners' Base," was the favourite game, and I was not too studious to be less active at it than others.

York did not suit my health very well. The school was not in a good situation. It was low, and near the Foss River, which often overflowed, and there was much of a swamp in the neighbourhood of the school. It was chiefly on this account that I did not remain at York more than two years. They were years that I can look back upon with pleasure. We had a reasonable freedom and were well treated. We were invited out to tea occasionally to the houses of Samuel Tuke, of Benjamin Horner and other Friends, some of whose names I fear I have forgotten; and we had pleasant walks in the neighbourhood. I more than once visited The Retreat, a lunatic asylum under the care of Friends, and have since had to admire the wisdom and kindness which have always marked the conduct of that institution. Some of the patients, when in their best state, came to York Meeting, and we became acquainted with them and interested in them. I remember one of them, whose name has passed from my mind, engaging in prayer on one occasion, and I was much struck with the force and beauty of his language. In an impassioned manner he said, "Oh that mine eyes could pierce that blue ethereal concave by which thou art surrounded, and behold the purity of thine Almighty Godhead." Their behaviour in the Meetings was generally orderly and in all respects becoming.

After leaving York, I was sent to a school at Newton-in-Bowland, a village six or seven miles from Clitheroe. The master was Francis Wills, an Irishman and a Friend. He had a wife and three daughters. He was a little man, well informed, of a lively disposition and somewhat hot temper, but kind and generous, and anxious to make the boys comfortable. There were about thirty boys in the school, besides six who lived in the village, the sons of villagers, and who were taken, I believe, free, as a condition of a small endowment of £40 a year which the master enjoyed. The school building and the house were not large; they were very unpretending. There was a small garden and a humble Meeting House, and near it a little brook ran merrily down towards the river. A short distance above the school was an ancient burial ground belonging to Friends in which were graves, but without tombstones or anything to mark who, of past generations, had been buried there. This went by the name of The Sepulchre.

The village of Newton was small and there were few indications of prosperity about it. At the bottom of the village flowed a pleasant little river called the Hodder, which, a few miles lower down, ran into the Ribble. In the village were two inns, two or three shops—a blacksmith's shop, a tailor's and a shoemaker's—and the cottages of a few labourers. In coming from Clitheroe we had to ascend a long hill called Waddington Fell, and then to descend a steep hill to the river, which was crossed by a good bridge just as we entered the village. About a mile or a little more up the river was the quaint old village or small town of Slaidburn, in which was the parish church. Below, five miles down the river, was Whitewell, where was a comfortable inn and some charming scenery.

Our school studies and tasks were not hard and we had plenty of liberty for play and amusement. The Hodder afforded us as much fishing as we liked to have, and in it we bathed during the summer, and here I learned to swim, as did many others of the boys. We took long walks up the hills among the remains of lead mines that had once been worked, and occasionally we made excursions to Clitheroe and to Whitewell, where we wandered among the woods and visited some small caves in the hill-sides which were called "Fairy-holes." We had a good deal of bird-nesting, and had no lack of anything which tended to promote health.

More than once I spent a pleasant time at Slaidburn, at the house of Mr. Leonard Wilkinson, who was the great man or squire of the place, and once I think we visited Bronsholme Hall, the seat or house of Mr. Parker. In those days angling was an occupation with uncertain result, as I have since often proved. The most noticeable of the village fishermen was a little man, a shoemaker by trade, and by name Bob ———. We often met him returning from the river, and we always asked him what sport he had met with. Almost his invariable answer was, as he spoke with a half growl, "Thunner,"—thunder being, as all anglers know, very unfavourable for fishing.

I made some progress in my studies whilst at Newton. But the great advantage I gained was in the improvement of my health. The year and a half I spent there seemed to work a complete change in me, and I have always attributed much of the generally good health I have since enjoyed to the fine air and healthful occupations of the valley of the Hodder. I left Newton on the 16th of February, 1827, and, at the age of fifteen years and three months, my school education terminated. I came home and soon began to be employed in my father's mill and to take an interest in the business. I had learned some Latin and a little French, with the common branches then taught in such schools as I had been placed in—reading, writing, arithmetic, grammar and geography; no mathematics and no science.

I began my business work by helping in the warehouse, by going through all the rooms of the mill, and by making out invoices of goods, and trying to make myself generally useful. My father was rather strict in some things, and required me to pay attention to the matters which by degrees were committed to my charge. In the warehouse were two men whom I may notice, one of whom, Nicholas Nuttall, took in the work from the mule spinners, and the other, Isaac Sladen, attended to the warps, to the receiving of bales of cotton from the canal or carriers, and to the waste which had to be sold. Isaac came to our house every morning about half-past five o'clock for the keys of the mill, and it was my duty to get up and give them to him. In those days there were no lucifer matches, and I have not forgotten the trouble I had to strike a light with the old tinder-box and flint and steel. I had a room over the counting-house, which I fitted up for my own use with a comfortable chair, a desk, and a small cupboard with shelves for a few books. The door into the office was just opposite the furnace of one of the boilers, and the old "steam-tenter," Josiah Lee, or "Old Siah" as he was commonly called, brought a shovelful of fire from his furnace and carried it into the grate in my room, and thus I had a good fire made in a few minutes. Here I often read a good deal before breakfast, and was undisturbed.

Nicholas Nuttall was a great politician of the Radical type. About this time Henry Hunt, sometimes called "Radical Hunt," or "Orator Hunt," was very prominent as a leader of the politicians of the working classes. In the year 1830, he was a candidate at an election in the Borough of Preston, and the contest excited great interest, especially in Lancashire. His opponent was Lord Stanley, afterwards Earl of Derby and for many years leader of the Tory Party, though at the time of this election he was not reckoned among the Tories. His family had long had great influence in Preston, and it was thought a daring step for anyone to enter the field against him. In those days elections were held for many days, I think for fourteen days, and the constituency of Preston was a large one, it being composed of what were called "pot-wallopers," that is of all men in the borough who had a hearth and warmed a pot: it answered to a wide interpretation of what we now call the household suffrage. There were then no railways and no telegraphs, and news did not travel very rapidly; but each day we learned the state of the poll at Preston on the preceding day. Day by day I heard from Nicholas the progress of the contest. His interest in it was extra-ordinary and he communicated to me some of his enthusiasm, and through him I became something of a politician.

The son of the great peer was defeated, and Hunt became Member for Preston, to the great joy of Nicholas and to my entire satisfaction. At that time I knew little of the questions in dispute, but I sympathized with the multitude who supported the Radical candidate. In fact, I could not be otherwise than Liberal. My father was Liberal, though we had no elections in our town and there was rarely a contest for the county.

I was, as I now am, a member of the Society of Friends. I knew something of their history and of the persecutions they had endured, and of their principles of equality and justice. I knew that I came of the stock of the martyrs, that one of my ancestors, John Gratton of Monyash, in Derbyshire, had been in prison for several years because he preferred to worship in the humble Meeting House of his sect rather than in the church of the law-favoured sect by whom he and his friends were barbarously persecuted. John Gratton's granddaughter was my father's grandmother. Among the biographical literature of the Society is a life of John Gratton. He was a man of influence in the part of the country where he lived, and I observed, many years after the time of which I am now writing, in a Parliamentary return for which I moved, that when Nonconformist places of worship were legalized by the Protection Act, all the Meeting Houses of Friends in Derbyshire were registered by, and in the name of, John Gratton.

I have said that my father was Liberal in his views of political affairs. He took in the *Manchester Guardian*, a weekly Liberal paper. There were then no daily papers in Lancashire, and few, if any, in the kingdom out of London. The *Guardian* was published on Saturday, and on the evening of that day my father read his paper, or I read it to him. The Parliamentary reports were very brief, and as I read the scraps of speeches in the House of Commons, he would ask me, "What did Joseph Hume say?" Joseph Hume was then, as he was during all his Parliamentary career, distinguished for his Liberal views, and especially for his anxiety to prevent any waste of public money. I have known him intimately in later years, and may have to speak of him when I come to the time when I sat near him in the House of Commons.

This year, 1830, is memorable as that in which we suffered, as a family, our first great sorrow by the loss of my dear mother. Her health had been failing for a year past, or more. She was about forty-one years of age. She had had eleven children, and was never robust, and now we had the grief to witness a gradual decline. I remember driving her out in my father's gig in the hope that the fresh air might be useful to her, and I went over to Southport on one occasion to see her when she was staying there for the hoped-for benefit of the sea air. As the summer drew nigh, her weakness increased, and we lost hope of her recovery. A few days before her death, perhaps a week or ten days before it, I went in the morning, as was my custom, to inquire as to her state, and was struck with the light and the cheerfulness that were upon her worn and pallid countenance. I asked if she had heard something that pleased her; she said, looking earnestly at me, "It is because I am so happy." She was about to leave her loving husband and her ten children, and yet the sorrow of this was overcome by the faith which upheld her, and by the sense granted to her of the greater joys which awaited her in the immortal life on which she was about to enter.

It was on the 18th of June that she passed from her family on earth to one of the "many mansions" prepared for such as she was. It was late in the evening, and we stood round her bed as her spirit left her poor wasted form. During that last day, when only partially conscious, she often mentioned my name. Though not her first-born child, I am her eldest living one, and I have a feeling that her mother's sympathy with me was even more than usually strong. The loss of this dear mother was a calamity to my father and to all his children which cannot be measured, and which I will not attempt to describe. From it sprang many troubles and disappointments which disturbed us in after years. She had all the qualities of help and guidance for a family, and her removal from amongst us was a loss which could never be repaired.

The years 1831 and 1832 are memorable for the great agitation which produced the Reform Bill. I was too young to take much part in it, but I well remember the London papers bringing the news to

Rochdale of the great Bill as it was first introduced in the House of Commons, and the sensation which it caused throughout the country. Rochdale was not included in the first list of new boroughs, and a public meeting was held in the news-room to memorialize the Government to grant a member to our town. I think John Roby was in the chair, and the best speech was made by W. W. Barton, the cabinet-maker, who afterwards was very useful in the Liberal politics of the town.

The Bill did not pass till 1832. On the night it passed the House of Lords, I was on my way from Manchester on my first visit to London, outside the "Peveril of the Peak" fast coach. We spent twenty-two hours on the journey, and during the morning we met two post-chaises, with four horses each, coming at full gallop with the news for the provinces. From the chaises handbills were thrown, giving particulars of the division in the Lords with a majority of nine in favour of the Bill. This majority was only gained by the danger of revolution, from which the country had a narrow escape. The Lords yield to menace and peril—rarely, and in questions affecting their power and position—never to reason and a sense of justice.

The passing of this Bill was itself a revolution, for it broke down the absolute power of the aristocracy and of the borough-mongers, and introduced into the House of Commons a large element of popular opinion and control which has made great changes possible in the half century which has since passed over us. The Government from that time has been, with the exception of about twelve years, Liberal in name, and has steadily become more and more Liberal to the great advantage of the nation.

In the year 1833 I made my first visit to the Continent. With me were Chas. Cumber, of Manchester, Thos. Midgley, of Rochdale, and Thos. Ashworth, of Bolton, who afterwards became my brother-in-law by marrying my dear sister Sophia. We left London on the 22nd of June at ten in the morning, and reached Ostend at two the following morning after a rough and uncomfortable passage. I was too ill to leave the deck much of the time, and few if any of the passengers escaped the usual misery of a sea voyage. We went on to Brussels, Antwerp, Cologne, Frankfort, Mayence, and down the Rhine to Rotterdam. At Antwerp we went over the citadel which had lately been besieged by the French and given over to the Belgians, who had made war and renounced the connexion with Holland.

Coming down the Rhine at Arnheim we found our passports of no avail. On the Dutch frontier they would not admit Belgian passports. We were directed to go to Nimwegen, and went before a Dutch general officer, who gave us passports for Rotterdam, where we obtained fresh passports for our stay in Holland. On going to the Consul's office, we learned from him that cholera was in the city and that forty or fifty persons were daily carried off by it. I had not been well for two days past, and, on returning to our hotel, sent for Dr. Sanders, an eminent doctor there. He gave me medicine, *"pour fortifier l'estomac,"* as he said. We went for a day to The Hague, but I was too ill to see much of the city. Returning to Rotterdam, Thos. Midgley and I went on board the *London Merchant* steamer on the 12th of July, and came to London, a passage of twenty-nine hours, losing some hours at the mouth of the Thames waiting for daylight.

My first excursion was cut short by this slight illness, but it gave me a new and a real pleasure. The cities I saw were full of interest, and the Rhine pleased me much.

For two years I remained mostly at home giving such help as I could give to my father's business.

But two events happened during this period which I may mention. In the month of August, 1831, there occurred a terrible accident by the loss of the vessel the *Rothesay Castle* on her voyage from Liverpool to Beaumaris. Amongst her passengers were four of our friends, William Bottomley, a partner with my father in a small mill at Rakewood, near Hollingworth Reservoir, his brother-in-law, Alexander Wheeler, from Birmingham, George King, the brother of my father's great friend James King, and Robert, or Benjamin, Lees, one of the sons of Esther Lees, of the colliery near Bacup.

On hearing of the shipwreck James King urged me to go with him to the scene of the catastrophe, and I went with him to Liverpool and thence by the mail to Conway. The vessel had struck upon the Dutchman's Bank, close to Puffin Island, not far from the entrance to the Menai Straits. We went from Conway to Beaumaris, and there we found in the Court House many bodies of the drowned passengers,—I think fifteen or seventeen of them. It is said only about twenty-two passengers were saved out of probably 130. More than 100 perished, and among them were our four friends. Many bodies were cast up, but, during our stay, not one of the four. We moved up and down the coast, and saw many of the drowned, but of our friends not one.

After we left, the body of Alexander Wheeler was found, and he was brought to Liverpool to be buried; and it was said the clergyman objected to his being buried in a churchyard, as, being a member of the Society of Friends, he had never been baptized!

A fortnight after the day of the wreck, my father and some of our family were at Blackpool when, one morning, an object was observed nearing the shore, and a boat going out found it to be a human body, and on bringing it to land, it proved to be that of one of our lost friends, that of William Bottomley, my father's partner. He was fully clothed, except for the loss of his hat. His overcoat was closely buttoned, and in his pocket was his memorandum book with particulars of his business transacted on Tuesday, the day before he left Liverpool. His watch had stopped at five minutes past three. His body was brought to Rochdale and was buried in the graveyard of our Meeting House. The body had passed the Ormes Head, had passed the mouth of the Dee, and of the Mersey, and lastly of the Ribble, and had come ashore opposite the hotel where my father and some of my sisters were then staying. The bodies of Geo. King and R. Lees were never found or were never recognized.

During this period, I think in 1832, I made my first visit to Ireland in company with James Crosland whose father had married my mother's sister, Esther Wood. He was a card maker, and went to Ireland on business. We sailed from Liverpool to Dublin. From Dublin we travelled outside the mail-coach to Belfast. What I most remember of our journey was the crowd of beggars that gathered round the coach at every place where we stopped to change horses. Nothing like it could be seen in England. From Belfast we crossed over to Glasgow, and had a very rough and unpleasant passage. From Glasgow we came home by coach.[1]

---

[1] At this point Bright's Memoir melts into the diary of his tour in the Near East in 1835–36, which he had written fifty years before.

CHAPTER II

THE NEAR EAST

I

BRIGHT was a young man of twenty-four when he set out in August, 1835, on a journey which almost exactly reproduced the route if not the adventures of another young man of twenty-four who had preceded him by five years. Disraeli brought back from the Near East the material of "Tancred" and the ideas about Oriental policy which coloured his career. Bright returned with no mystic conceptions of the place of the Oriental mind in civilization and no literary work of the imagination, but with a large cargo of facts and a very definite dislike of the Turkish system. Disraeli's letters and Bright's diaries, written within a few years of each other and showing their reactions to the same circumstances, startlingly foreshadow the antagonisms which were to be fought out at Westminster forty years later.

Bright took his Grand Tour in the company of James King, son of his father's friend of that name. They visited the Peninsula, Greece, the Holy Land, Egypt, Turkey, and Italy. The diary hardly fails of a daily entry for eight months.

The young Quaker, with his handsome face, his sanguine spirit, his sense of fun and his love of human intercourse, seems to have charmed every being with whom he had contact during this high adventure. His notes reveal an avidly observant mind and an exhaustless curiosity, but also a good deal more than the lively interest of youth in novel surroundings. In this first self-record it is, indeed, almost possible already to see John Bright whole. Here is his personality in embryo—its apposition of extensive interest and intensive feeling, its downright frankness and its immense reserves, its limitless concern for humanity and its ineffable inwardness. There is surprising maturity in his reflections, certainty in his judgments, decisiveness in his conduct in emergency. At twenty-four he has thought more and probed his mind more deeply than most men at their climacteric. When

Bright in his old age re-read these impressions of men and things, he found nothing he wished to alter as a record of opinion or even to correct in temper.

When he sailed on the steamer *Crescent* from the Brunswick Dock, Liverpool, on August 17, 1835,[1] he had savoured only the one brief taste of foreign travel two years before in Belgium and the Rhineland, from which he came back "speaking French with much greater facility." This protracted Mediterranean and Near East excursion was therefore an event. Indeed, a hundred years ago such a journey was a considerable adventure even for experienced voyagers.

Bright was the worst sailor in the world. But, in the intervals of his sufferings, he made a sunny companion and entered with great zeal into the diversions of shipboard. Less various then than now, they consisted chiefly of such intellectual exercises as capping verses and supplying *bouts-rimés*, singing songs, telling stories, and discussing politics. He was then full of Byron—as most young men were about that time. His fervour for Milton came later. Every scene reminds him of some Byronic couplet. At Cintra, his mind dwells on *Childe Harold*. On the voyage from Rhodes to Beirut he reads *The Giaour*, *The Bride of Abydos*, *The Corsair*, and *Lara*. In Athens he goes to "visit Black, whose wife is the lady to whom Byron addressed the lines—

> Maid of Athens, ere we part,
> Give, oh give me back my heart.

She has a very pleasing appearance, with the fine eyes of her country: has a fine boy and girl." He is too busy sightseeing, inquiring, storing his mind with impressions, generalizing on his observations, to do a prodigious amount of reading. But he records having got through "The History of the Ottoman Empire in Two Volumes," and (as light relief) "Ivanhoe" and "Old Mortality." He played billiards when the opportunity offered, once went shooting small birds—without much enthusiasm —read *Galignani* for the home news when he could get it, played écarté to while away long evenings at sea, studied female beauty on shore when it was available (and complained to his diary when it was not). He also displayed a young man's healthy interest in bagatelles. But the great preoccupation of his days was to acquire information, assimilate it, and apply it. His journal of the tour is a kind of philosophical Baedeker.

[1] The *Crescent* was due to sail on the 16th; but "the 1st steward and cook being absent, the captain postponed his departure till to-morrow noon."

The *Crescent* was a small steamer going out from Liverpool for service in the Black Sea. With a defective piston, she made slow progress, and as her coal failed to last out the voyage to her first regular port of call, Gibraltar, she unexpectedly put into Lisbon. A seasick company welcomed the change from agitated weather in the Bay to the serene placidity of the Tagus—Bright not least among them: he had been ill on and off for four days. Landing at Lisbon on August 23, he spent three days ashore, doing the usual tripper's round. The excursions *de rigueur* from Lisbon do not seem to have altered much from that day to this—except that one then went slowly up to Cintra on a donkey's back instead of being jolted up quickly in a motor-car as now, and that instead of rumbling along on the shores of the Tagus in a little narrow-gauge tramcar one glided past them in a boat.

The *Crescent* anchored off Belem on the evening of August 22:

"[*August* 22.] All is quiet, and the change from the continual turmoil of the engine is exceedingly pleasant. We have had tongue and fowl; also port wine and water, very weak, to drink; and really the sudden change is so delightful that I cannot describe it. After having eaten nearly nothing for several days (and what little I have eaten has come back again), I have enjoyed this late dinner or lunch or supper very much. The Director of Customs has been on board. He speaks French. Barton and I managed the conversation, though Barton is the better linguist. The Director is a fat, jolly-looking man, very much like Hutchinson in Liverpool, but not so large quite. He drank 3 or 4 glasses of porter or ale and was very obliging and communicative. It is a beautiful night—now 12 o'clock. The stars shining, and we on board the *Crescent* at anchor in the Tagus, a noble river, placid as possible, the lights beaming on the shore and the boats sleeping around us."

The first day ashore was a Sunday. He spent it walking about Lisbon, admiring the planning and building of the city, noting its occasional "abominable stenches" and their unfailing olfactory background of garlic and onions. He compared manners, customs and prices—he was always deeply interested in prices. He sat at a market stall, "eating grapes and water melon for half hour," and talking to its ancient keeper. One is irresistibly reminded of young Lavengro conversing with the old apple woman on London Bridge. But unfortunately Bright had no time to record the talk; he contents himself

with remarking that the market-woman "speaks all languages—more
or less." He met with a moustachioed Irish soldier of Donna Maria,
"a regular dreadnought." This person, in spite of his animated description of battle scenes, seemed to his hearer "a despicable specimen of our
countrymen." Bright could never tolerate bombastical persons. Towards the end of the day, he went up to the aqueduct to see the famous
view of city and river, "a splendid panorama, surpassing almost all I ever
saw in loveliness."

"[23rd.] Observed the bonnet trade must be bad, as the women
to-day (First Day), and other days the same, wear only a muslin starched
white handkerchief over a very high comb. . . . Saw a few drunken
men; but, during the hot weather, lemonade, sherbet, etc., are the
principal drinks. The coffee is splendid. Soldiers abundant. Rob-
beries very frequent after sunset. Englishmen alone, or in companies
of two, sure to be marked because they are supposed to have most money.
We went in a party of seven—had pistols, but were not attacked. Byron
is extremely happy in his description of Lisbon and its people: fine
country, but degraded people. Prospect of improvement under the
new Govt."

It was curious that, though thrilled by the beauty of the scene
from the hills close to Lisbon, he was disappointed with the stark splendour of Cintra, to which he climbed on horseback on the Monday.
Perhaps it was that, at Mr. Bento's hotel where he stayed, he slept in
one of four beds in a room, all damp, and had to lie on the blanket with
his trousers on for fear of rheumatism. One is jaundiced against
rugged grandeur after such a night. He saw Donna Maria walking
about in the palace grounds, "a stout and rather fine woman, or girl, in
black mourning. She bowed very politely, and the gentlemen who were
with her." The people in Cintra village struck him as infinitely poorer
than the labourers in England, "and apparently very ignorant, though
there is a certain degree of sharpness about them which tells what they
would be with a good government and with the benefits of education."
Byron was much in his thoughts at Cintra; but if he agreed with the
poet's estimate of the people, he could not endorse his panegyric of
Cintra itself:

"Cintra does not display those beauties which seem calculated to
call forth the poetic feeling and the admiration of a Byron in so high

a degree as appears to have been the case from the stanzas in Canto 1st of *Childe Harold*.[1] The country is extremely mountainous and sterile, the hills covered with detached blocks of stone which seem to have been thrown into all sorts of fantastic shapes by some dire convulsion of nature, and rising to a great height upon the tops are seen the remains of a convent or castle."

It is interesting to compare these sentences with the famous passage about Cintra in George Borrow's "Bible in Spain." Borrow saw it for the first time three months later than Bright. "If there be any place in the world entitled to the appellation of an enchanted region," he began, "it is surely Cintra; Tivoli is a beautiful and picturesque place, but it quickly fades from the mind of those who have seen the Portuguese Paradise. . . ."

Nevertheless, Bright had great fun out of his excursion to the mountain-tops and to the Convent of Nostra Senhora de Pena and the Convent Cortesa (Cork Convent) to see the cave where

> Honorius long did dwell
> In hopes to merit Heaven by making
> Earth a Hell.

His party went on donkey-back, a method of progression involving much chaff and laughter. The asses threw two of his companions—although they were "excellent animals, and endowed with less obstinacy than their brethren in England."

"[*25th.*] Expecting the *Crescent* will sail to-night, are intending to start for Lisbon immediately. . . . At one, started for Lisbon, I on a black horse about 15 hands high and one of the best and pleasantest horses I ever rode: excellent walk, no trot; but its canter would have made it truly welcome at home. Stopped twice on the way to eat grapes and arrived in Lisbon at five.

[1] Poor paltry slaves, yet born 'midst noblest scenes—
Why, Nature, waste thy wonders on such men?
Lo! Cintra's glorious Eden intervenes
In variegated maze of mount and glen.
Ah me! what hand can pencil guide, or pen,
To follow half on which the eye dilates,
Through views more dazzling unto mortal ken
Than those whereof such things the bard relates,
Who to the awe-struck world unlock'd Elysium's gates?
—*Childe Harold*, Canto I.

"Lady Church was on board. She has been in lodgings for one night in Lisbon at a house kept by an old Irish woman, and, by her account, she had suffered miserably. She was but five minutes in bed, for she was immediately attacked by multitudes of bugs, and her chief occupation during the night was killing them."

His interest in things American, one of the most constant loyalties of his life though he never crossed the Atlantic, manifests itself thus early in his journals. He cannot meet an American without putting down his characteristics and his conversation. In the inn at Cintra, he encountered two gentlemen, one, if not both, American:

"The one who owned himself an American had travelled much, and owned Trollope had done them good. In the theatre pit between the acts, if a person turned round standing with his back to the stage, the people called out 'Trollope! Trollope!' and made him turn and sit down.[1]

"He told us of an American stonemason now in Constantinople who had invented a gun shooting thirty or forty rounds a minute to be applied to cannons. Rather an American tale, we thought. Perhaps possible,—but, knowing how many American patents had fallen through, I doubted this account."

He sums up in a few notes his general impressions of the visit to Lisbon:

"In Portugal there is everything to be observed which is likely to render one more attached to one's own country. The Govt. is not in a very settled state, nor very economical. The people seem to have no spirit nor industry. They lie about in the roads asleep in the daytime, and travelling is by no means safe in the evening. . . .

"About the streets are great numbers of dogs; but we were told that 2 or 3 yrs. ago these were much more numerous, the Govt. having given orders to kill them. They are not private property, but run loose and feed upon what is thrown out of the houses. So many having been killed ought to have bettered the condition of the rest, according

[1] See Mrs. Trollope's "Domestic Manners of the Americans," the only fruit of the queer enterprise undertaken at the instance of her eccentric husband, when she went out to start a fancy bazaar in Cincinnati for the benefit of the untutored natives of the Middle West.

to the saying 'Fewer, the better;' but they are without exception the dirtiest, lousiest, most emaciated, forlorn-looking creatures I ever beheld, without an atom of spirit and never uttering a growl. The streets are filthy, owing chiefly to the habit here of emptying everything from the windows during the night. When about to throw they call out '*Agoa via*,' or 'here goes water,' and woe to the unfortunate wight upon whom the present descends." [1]

A long swell with a northerly breeze during the voyage down the coast greatly discommoded Bright: he seemed never to grow accustomed to the motion of a steamer. But the weather moderated as the *Crescent* approached the Strait of Gibraltar, and he recuperated his exhausted frame with great daring at dinner on the second day—"had soup, roast mutton and fowl and ham, with dessert of melon, grapes and champagne. Had a good dinner, and quite well all the evening, being in smooth water." During dinner they were abreast of Cape Trafalgar:

"[*27th.*] Passed over the scene of Nelson's great victory. Melancholy reflections crowd upon the mind while traversing scenes where man has thus proved himself the greatest enemy of man, where have found graves thousands, each of whom has left a gap which future years can perhaps never close. When will the happy times arrive when the nations will learn that their interest is to be at peace, when that saying will not be borne out by the fact, that man's inhumanity to man makes countless thousands mourn?

"[*28th, at Gibraltar.*] Bought a carpet bag for 13/–, a scent-bottle, and a cross made of the rock stone. In the last purchase was considerably jewed. Entered the King's Arms Hotel, where our party were, and had a very excellent dinner along with Captain Tudor: vermicelli soup, red mullet (see Garrick as to this fish), mutton and beef steaks, etc. Afterwards went thro' the market place and bought a straw hat for 2/6 and abundance of grapes, etc., to bring aboard. Came on board at ½ past 6, and immediately stripped and bathed out of the *Crescent's* boat.

"I am decidedly pleased with Gibraltar. As a town it combines the lightness and elegance of continental with more than the cleanliness of English cities, whilst the strange mixture of its population, being

[1] The *Crescent* coaled at Lisbon. He notes that the coal "cost 12 milreis the pipe = ⅘ 10 tons, being about 25*s*. 9*d*. per ton alongside the steamer. This is Newcastle coal, and the duty in Lisbon is 30 per cent."

composed of people of almost all countries, gives a liveliness and a novelty to the scene which is highly pleasing. The Jews are particularly remarkable, and the sharpness of their features agrees well with the idea generally entertained of their shrewdness in commercial matters. The Moors from Barbary are fine powerful men, and the countenances of the Spaniards convince one that they only require a good govt. and diminution of the number of their sleek priesthood to render them one of the finest nations in the world."

The voyage from Gibraltar to Malta took five days, and at Valetta they were ordered to do five days in quarantine. It was between Gibraltar and Malta that he finished with the Ottoman Empire and took up with Scott. The ship sailed again before the quarantine period had expired, and he saw very little of Malta, but found opportunity to discuss with various people the general economic and social state of the island. Cotton naturally interested him. He obtained specimen pods and statistics of the Maltese crops: the island was growing four million pounds a year, and its price, then $9\frac{1}{4}d.$ per lb., was expected to fall 25 per cent. He notes:

"[*September* 4.] This cotton is principally used here for making sail cloths, and considerable quantities are exported to Trieste and some even to England. About the end of this month is crop time, but a kind of red cotton is grown here which is not ripe so early as the end of this month."

The prosperity of Malta had declined since the war; the Neapolitan Government's heavy duties on goods from the island led to smuggling; and there was much petty annoyance of British traders.

". . . In the article of ice which is here quite a necessary of life, there is a monopoly, a Maltese being allowed the whole trade, being under a penalty to keep the place well supplied. A short time since an unfortunate Yankee arrived here with a cargo of ice from Boston, unconscious of the monopoly existing here. He had thus only one customer and realized very little from his adventure."

The *Crescent* weighed anchor and pointed eastward on September 4. The weather being good, Bright enjoyed the warmth, and sat on deck and "read Greece in the modern 'Traveller and Anastasius'." The approach to the Archipelago thrilled him profoundly.

"[*6th.*]   All on board in health and spirits and enjoying the delight-ful sensations which a first approach to the classic soil of Greece can never fail to awaken; but, alas,

"'Tis Greece but living Greece no more.'

Our Greek captain, now acting as pilot, seems delighted with the view of his native land and becomes very loquacious.   He has sung us several war songs, and in him seems to burn a *spark* of that fire which once burned so brightly in the bosoms of his ancestors and raised his country to the highest pitch of glory.

". . . Then Sparta and Greece were in all their glory, giving laws to nations, and ruling with uncontrolled sway; England not known to the civilized world, and inhabited only by rude and barbarian tribes. Now, how different, how changed!   Sparta is known no longer but as what she has been; Greece scarce rising from the dreary darkness of Turkish despotism, endeavouring to cast off the bonds which have so long fettered her, and turning to the once barbarian Britain, now reaching near the zenith of her power, as her only friend.   May England dili-gently preserve her own freedom and exert her power in the glorious task of liberating the world."

In such exalted mood, he gazed on Egina, "impatient to arrive, anxious to be inspecting the ruins of august Athens," when the engine (or the boiler) of the erratic *Crescent* chose an inauspicious moment to break down.   The delay sorely irritated his impetuous spirit.

But even the *Crescent* came in at last: he set foot on Grecian soil for the first time at the Piræus at half-past twelve on the 7th.   Before he sat down that night to write his diary, he had rushed through a tourist's hectic first day—ridden to Athens on a small horse (uncom-fortably saddled) at a fare of two shillings; paid eightpence for a permit to view the antiquities; done the Acropolis; found the temples surpassing everything he had expected; drunk in the beauty of the view from the "immense rock;" deplored the dilapidation and squalor of the modern city; and eaten a not very good dinner at the Royal Hotel—"the wine bad and the whole not very much beyond a second-rate inn in England."

Next day was very hot.   The first rapture over, he was "not industrious in seeing the antiquities," contenting himself with many shops and one temple.

"[*8th.*]   Went alone strolling thro' the city and bought a walk-ing stick 2/–; 2 portraits of Otho, King of Greece, 8*d*. each; a red cap with blue silk tassel 2/–; a sash of silk and cotton 8/8; antiquities; alabaster drinking cup and ancient lamp 5/–, the former from Marathon, the latter from Acropolis. There are here abundance of cafés, and I called in one and had a cup of coffee for a little less than 1*d*. Breakfasted at 9 and strolled about city. Played billiards and read the papers, which appear here to be Oppositionists and speak very freely of Otho's Govt. They are printed 1 side Greek and 1 French, and are respectably got up. . . . At noon bought the head of a statue which I suspect had been stolen from the Acropolis; gave 18/– for it. Engaged horses and rode up to the Temple of Theseus, which is the most perfect remaining of Ancient Athens."

He spent the night on the ship, retiring at midnight "after a long argument, religious and political, with the Captain," and the last day of his first stay at Athens was occupied in a visit to the marble quarries at Pentelicos. As a final act of remembrance he "strolled up to the Acropolis and brought away three pieces of marble." He was to return to Athens for a much longer sojourn before the end of the year.

"[9*th.*] Greece, so far as my limited view of it goes, does not offer any high station even to its King. It seems almost depopulated and presents in the immediate neighbourhood of Athens nothing but an uncultivated waste. To a private individual it offers but little allurement. Everything now is very dear, and most things are infinitely below England in comfort. There are but few Europeans here, excepting Bavarians, and the Greek language is very difficult to acquire. For some weeks past a fever has been raging here, called the malaria, which has attacked almost all the inhabitants, but which has not been very fatal. We seem to have escaped and trust we shall have none of it on board.

"The antiquities of Athens are splendid and these would give an intense interest to the place if it were now a barren heath; and so long as the Parthenon exists so long will Athens be worth visiting.

"I leave Greece with hearty wishes for its prosperity, and I shall look back with considerable pleasure on the many things I have seen during our short stay here. The dress of the Albanians is particularly fine: a beautifully braided coat and waistcoat, with cotton petticoat made very full, and gaiters worked in an expensive way; colours, blue or crimson.

"The Greeks are remarkably straight, and walk with a majestic air, and they are decidedly the finest race of men I have ever seen. We saw very few women, but many of those who were visible had excellent profiles.

"Six months ago Athens was little more than a heap of ruins;[1] now, however, it is fast recovering and houses are rising on every side. Money is very scarce, bearing 15 and 20 per cent. interest; rents tremendously high, double the actual worth of the houses in fact. Owing to the population increasing faster than the means to accommodate them, everything is extremely dear."

The next port of call was Syra, where he saw the son of Admiral Miaullis, the famous Greek commander during the revolution,—"a fine, tall, handsome Greek."

"[10th.] The Greeks here seem possessed of an intense curiosity. During the whole day the vessel was literally crowded with them, the boatmen charging them so much each to bring them off; and it was very amusing to observe the astonishment depicted on their countenances when looking at the different parts of the vessel.

"The Consul-general, Mr. Wilkinson, came on board with his family. One of his daughters is very pretty, and decidedly the most interesting girl I have seen since leaving England.

"There were many vessels in the Bay. The *Smyrna*, an English brig, a trader, was here (Capt. Cornish), and several others. Capt. Cornish was attacked by a pirate some years ago, his ship taken, himself and men forced below, everything valuable taken out of her, and then scuttled. The carpenter, however, contrived to get upon deck and opened a passage for the rest, and they happily escaped in the boat. The pirate was afterwards taken, and some 5 or 6 of the men hanged and gibbeted at Gibraltar."

2

The Gulf of Smyrna disappointed Bright much as Cintra had done. Gaunt grandeur seemed not to appeal to him: "the scenery, tho' rather bold, is not beautiful, owing to the barrenness of the rocks." But Smyrna itself, seen from the sea, entranced him: "We beheld Smyrna

---

[1] In the three sieges of the revolutionary war the greater part of the city was destroyed. The Greeks invested it twice in 1822, the second time successfully, and the Turks in their turn captured it in 1826. Its population of 12,000 had dispersed to the ends of the archipelago. It had been declared the capital of the new Kingdom in 1834, a year before Bright's visit.

in the distance looking like a city floating upon the waters. The view now becomes very fine." . . . He was to see a good deal of Smyrna during the next month, as he made it his head-quarters for excursions to Jerusalem, Alexandria, and Constantinople. Though he found the city itself at close quarters an unattractive place, with narrow, ill-paved dirty streets, he spent some interesting days in the neighbourhood, entertained by Mr. H. R. Barker, head of a commercial house, who had a country residence at Bootgea. In this, his only taste of the intimacy of family life since leaving England, he was able to get into closer touch with everyday social conditions than the ordinary sightseer. Smyrna was his first Moslem city. It interested him highly if critically, and he made time for full entries in his diary.

"[11*th*.] I found Mr. Barker's family to consist of 8 children, 4 boys and 4 girls, the eldest about 11 yrs. of age. Mr. Barker does not speak English, but French, Italian and Greek.

"There is also here a young lady, who is a native of Scio, who was taken prisoner by the Turks at the Massacre of Scio in 1823. She was offered for sale in Smyrna and H. R. Barker ransomed her, with whom she has resided ever since. At that time about £200 was sent by Friends in England to H. R. Barker to rescue the unfortunate Greeks, and many were thus saved from a horrible slavery. The English merchants here ransomed great numbers of these poor creatures.

"At 12 I retired to my bed and found it covered with a muslin curtain under which I had to creep into bed. This curtain falls down at all sides without any opening except at the bottom, and is used as a net and defence against the mosquitoes, tho' in Bootgea there are very few.

"[13*th*.] The family are all going to Chapel down in the village. Last evening they had family worship, and I think my host is a truly religious character. It was very grateful to the feelings to hear the little children joining in singing hymns last night and performing worship in this land where the false religion of Mahomet has so long prevailed. At 12 they returned from Chapel where a Mr. Jetter (a German missionary) had preached from the 33rd of Isaiah: 'Who is this that cometh from Edom, with dyed garments from Bosrah?'

"[15*th*.] In the afternoon took donkeys—Miss Thespina, Miss Slith,[1] a young American lady, M. Barker, Junr., and self (Mr. Jameson

---

[1] A month afterwards he took another excursion with Miss Thespina and Miss Slith, of whom he remarks that she is about 16 years of age "and very pretty."

walking), and rode out a couple of miles to see Great and Little Paradise, so called from their beauty. At the former is an old stone aqueduct, but all the water to be seen was running under and not over the arches. Here were sitting a Turk and a Greek. The former cut up a melon and gave it to us with some *Rakia* (a sort of spirit), and the latter lent us his pipe to have a whiff with.

"[16th, *during a ride in the country.*] Passed on to Bonarbish. Had coffee and a pipe in a Turkish café in which were some of the reputed descendants of the Prophet, distinguished by wearing green turbans. At Boonabat played billiards, and had a miserable dinner at the hotel, for which, with straw for 3 donkeys, and the guide, they charged 2 dollars—4/4. We protested against this exorbitant demand and offered 1 dollar, which was taken, and we left the place. From Boonabat we came on to Smyrna by 4 o'clock, having travelled about 20 miles on donkey-back. In this excursion we passed over hill and dale,—the former barren, the latter very fertile, tho' not generally well cultivated. We entered a Turkish dyeing-house where were some large earthenware vessels fixed upon or between mud walls. Under the vessels was a wood fire, and the smoke came out at the mouth. In the vessels was a dye mixture of madder root, and in this was boiling a quantity of hanks of strong woollen yarn. After being boiled they are dried and then washed in the river.

"[18th.] Went with Barton and J. King to see the slave market. But few there, but they were tall athletic men, and did not seem, with the exception of one, at all unhappy.

". . . The bazaars are extensive but not splendid. Each trade has its own street or bazaar, and to this the people know to go when they want anyone connected with any particular trade. The bazaars are merely streets over which is thrown a sort of awning or matting, stretching the short distance from house to house. Along these are the principal shops where may be seen the Turks sitting, with the most extraordinary gravity, smoking their pipes or argillas. The cafés (of which there are many) are crowded with people lounging about smoking and drinking coffee. The Turks appear to be a very quiet, orderly race of people, tho' having in their gait all the stateliness which we imagine to be characteristic of the followers of the Prophet. All people coming in from the country are armed—large pistols and dagger in their belt, which gives them rather a ferocious appearance. In travelling in the interior it is much the best to wear pistols, because the people everywhere pay much greater respect to a man armed than to one unarmed. Benjamin Barker (agent here to the British and Foreign Bible Society) always travels with pistols, but without powder and shot.

"The Greek women go with their faces uncovered, and the Turkish never. The latter ride on horseback astride. They cover their faces with a dark shade over the eyes, and up to the nose with a white hand-kerchief, and look, thus equipped, hideous creatures. The Greek women are generally interesting looking, but soon fade. They and the Turkish also marry at 12 to 14 yrs. of age often, and mere girls in appearance are seen nursing their own children.

"Fires are extremely frequent, owing chiefly to the houses being built in great measure of wood. So frequently do these disasters occur that insurance cannot be effected, and individuals are often reduced from competency to poverty in a single night.

"Of late some attempts have been made to provide a remedy against the devouring element, and a fire-engine has been employed. It will be happy for the Turks when they become thoroughly dispossessed of the notion that all things which do happen would have happened in spite of all precautions to prevent them. This appears to be accomplishing with respect to the plague, from which they have not been accustomed to provide any method of escape save that of leaving the places where it broke out. Now, however, they are becoming convinced that care and cleanliness will go far to rid them of this scourge. The Europeans have no anxiety for their own safety during the prevalence of this scourge. The infection can only be taken by touch of something infected; therefore when the plague breaks out the Franks establish a strict quarantine about their houses, which are built so as to be rendered quite secure. There is a court-yard with a pair of large doors. These doors, being closed, prevent all ingress and egress. In the door is a small door which is opened to receive the provisions, etc., for the family, and these, on being put thro' the hole, fall into a tub of water which effectually removes any danger. The persons who supply and carry the articles are those who have recovered from the plague on former occasions and who never have it again with severity. These men, however, are anything but respectable. But necessity compels the sufferers from the plague to have them as attendants when their friends fly from them, and it is believed that many die who might recover were it not for the sake of the valuables or goods they possess, which fall into the hands of these wretches in the absence of the rightful heirs."

3

Having said good-bye to the Barkers, he set forth with his friend King, on the night of the 18th, on a pilgrimage which to him was of the deepest and devoutest interest. His copious notes leave no doubt that he had anticipated with much inward fervour the journey to Jerusalem, and the month which passed before he came back to Smyrna made an ineffaceable landmark in his life.

They sailed for Jaffa in a crowded little tub ("the *Levant* is a small steamer of 106 tons and 50 horse power—very strong"), threading the archipelago to Rhodes, thence to Cyprus, and so to Beirut and Jaffa.[1] Bright was ill when the sea was rough and well when it moderated. But he never lost interest in the things seen or in the people about him. He enumerates with the greatest care his fellow-passengers, who included "1 Greek and 1 Armenian bishop," and presents a lively view of existence on the *Levant*:

"The boat on which our lives and fortunes are embarked is small and consequently somewhat unpleasant. We are rather crowded and there is but little room for walking about. The chimney and the caboose (a cooking shop) are so near the quarter-deck that it is impossible to escape the odours which are continually proceeding from them. We have good living on board, but not such expensive wines as we had on the *Crescent*; but this is no matter to me, as I am not particularly fond of strong wines.

"We have an Armenian bishop on board, and to-night he supped on his usual fare—brown bread, olives, and oil; and he now reposes upon deck. This forms a strong contrast with the state of the Right Revds. in England. My remarking this, adding that I should like to see our bishops for once supping in like style, provided a long discussion on Church Establishments, etc. The principles of Temperance Societies and of the doctrine of Peace were also warmly discussed. Mr. Brown is an American total abstainer and seems a very excellent man.[2]

"To-day during breakfast the skylight was open and a spaniel dog presumed to leap over the casement and come down on the breakfast table. At dinner he played the same freak and found himself in a

---

[1] He records the payment of "185 dollars Spanish" for his fare from Smyrna to Jaffa.

[2] Mr. Brown was a man after Bright's own heart. He flits out of the story when the ship reaches Alexandria.

large tureen of hot soup, to the no small amazement of our dinner party
—and to the annoyance of those who had not recd. any soup."

He read Byron, as already recorded, during these days, but he was
also moved to improve a nodding acquaintance with Wordsworth, as
appears from the entry: "This morning read in the *Quarterly Review*
of 11th Month, 1834, a review of Wordsworth, with which am much
pleased, and intend on my return to England to pay more attention to
the writings of this poet."

At Beirut he spent a day "in the very calm employment of gazing
upon the walls and town and the sea over which we had been wafted."
But the calm of his mood was incontinently disturbed by the indifferent
conduct of the British consul. It thoroughly stirred up the fundamental Englishman in Bright. "Our English consul, Moore," he
writes indignantly, "has not yet come off to us [they were in quarantine]
though the American and French consuls have showed us every civility.
Moore is said to be a puppy, so puffed up with his consular dignity that
he can scarcely look down on common people, and certainly our experience tells us nothing in his favour. I feel ashamed that our country
should be represented by such a coxcomb, and that English bounty should
be expended upon objects so unworthy." He whiles away the tedium
of quarantine as best he may. He describes a young Turk, a pilgrim
on his way to Mecca, who "had no appearance of a pilgrim, being as
fat, jolly, unthinking, good-humoured a fellow as ever believed in the
Prophet." He employs one of the ship's firemen to cut his hair. "He
did it well, but wished to know how it should be done—for running,
jumping or fighting? I said, 'For sailing.' Many an accomplished
West-End barber would have given one more thrusts with the scissors'
point."

They got pratique at last, though even then (as he is particular to
observe) the consular puppy did not in person bring them their emancipation, but sent his brother-in-law. It was on shore at Beirut that he
made his first acquaintance with the Arabs:

"They are not so tall, not so strongly built, as the Turks, but have
a quickness of eye and a cunning expression of countenance, combined
with considerable determination, which I have not remarked amongst
any other class of men. They are dressed very slightly and seem to
know very little of what we term the comforts of life.
"Passing thro' one of the gates, which was only about 6 feet wide, a

sort of barren piece of ground was before us where grew a few trees, principally mulberry. Here we noticed a gallows standing as a terror to evil-doers. It was merely an upright post with a cross-piece at the height of about 10 feet, into the end of which cross-piece was inserted a pulley round which runs the rope which suspends the unfortunate wretch who happens to offend the capricious rulers of the Mahommedan World."

The *Levant* anchored off Jaffa on October 1, and the last stage of Bright's journey to Jerusalem began the same day. He does not indicate how many there were of the party, but it included King and one Abro, an Armenian. They rode up on horseback with an armed janissary for guide.

"[*October* 1.] Here and there we met a single horseman or an Arab on his ass, but nothing to make us think we were traversing a land flowing with milk and honey except that the sky was clear without a cloud, the sun intensely hot, and the air pure. All that here might be seems to languish under a heavy curse and to be suffering from the blight of a withering despotism. My saddle was about 3 feet long and 2½ feet wide, and raised me a foot from the back of my wretched horse: no stirrups, and a halter without a bit in the mouth. The ride was therefore excessively laborious, and I was truly glad when we arrived at Ramla, the ancient 'Ramah.'"

They fed at Ramleh, smoked a pipe and rested till the evening; then took fresh horses and resumed the journey, this time with two janissaries in attendance:

"The sun was down, and after passing along a plain thro' a lane lined with the prickly pear, etc., we had the moon to befriend us, and a lovely night it was. After two hours we came to the foot of the mountains. The janissaries who carried muskets, pistols, and yataghans, desired us to keep together for fear of banditti. My horse was a very good one and I got on with pleasure.

"At 20 mins. after 10 we halted at a small village and entered a sort of poor mosque, or rather stone shed, where was a good spring or fountain; also in the yard was a fine palm tree. The horses were tied outside, and, after eating biscuits and drinking of the spring, we lay down, some under the shed, and others (myself included) under the shade of the palm tree, on a sort of raised terrace. My carpet bag served as a pillow, and the blue star-bespangled sky as our only canopy. The moon looked down smilingly, and all wore an air of cheerfulness and novelty."

Mr. Abro, the Armenian, had undertaken to call them at four in the morning, but alas! his watch being two hours fast, he routed them out at two. They kindled a fire, and spent the two hours warming themselves, smoking and drinking coffee:

"The scene was quite new to me and I rather regretted that my friends could not at that moment see what we were doing. Imagine a blazing, crackling fire under a fine palm tree, whose branches spread majestically from the top of the stem and tell us that we are in an Eastern country; two Arabs and a Nubian (almost black) bending over the fire, watching its progress, or drawing the embers round the pot wherein the coffee is boiling; myself and 1 or 2 more puffing away with long Turkish chibouks; others lying stretched upon their hard couch; the stars shining with a brilliancy, in reality or in fancy, much greater than they ever vouchsafe to afford to us in my native land; and add to this that we were in Palestine, the Holy Land, and within 2 hrs. ride of Jerusalem, once the 'joy of the whole earth'—the heart must be cold indeed that would not feel somewhat of interest in such a situation."

Bright's "very good" horse outstripped his companions, and it was he who, at six o'clock, sun-up, had the first view of the Holy City. A great moment. But he would always be as perfectly honest with himself as with others, even in the greatest moments:

"I cannot say that on the first view of the City I was overpowered with those sensations which so many travellers have professed to have felt, and which they have attempted to describe in many a glowing paragraph. There is but little in its appearance which merits the title of grand or magnificent. From the Jaffa road nothing is seen but a few hundred yards of fortification, the wall so high that the houses inside are hardly visible. At 4 mins. past 6 I beheld the City, and at 18 mins. past 6 entered the gates."

In the two days of his stay at Jerusalem, he visited all the holy places, and he describes them in detail, just as a thousand tourists have

33

done, but with a special reverence of his own and from a special point of view. It is unnecessary to follow him in the itinerary with which he illustrated for himself the Bible story. A youth trained in the quiet Quaker tradition could not fail to conceive distaste for much that he saw in Jerusalem. His feelings about the condition and the exploitation of the holy places may be judged by his comment on the visit to the Tomb:

"[*2nd.*] We enter a small low doorway, and are in the place of the Tomb. This room is about 7 ft. long by 6 broad, and against the wall lengthway in the room is a tomb of white marble 6 ft. long × 3 ft. broad × 2½, or nearly 3 ft., high. The slab which forms the top is cracked or broken across about the middle. This tomb is said to stand in the very place where Jesus was laid. About it are burning continually 50 or 60 lamps, and pilgrims are continually coming in to kiss the Tomb and to pray. It is, however, almost impossible to feel those sensations which such a place is calculated to awaken whilst around, on every side, we behold the manner in which the simplicity of Christianity is departed from. Everything is covered with trumpery pictures and gaudy colouring, and nothing exists but the outward show of veneration for the Holy Place. To feel rightly the emotion which more or less cannot fail to arise, one ought to be alone, undisturbed by the mummery of reading in a whining tone long Latin prayers and imposing upon the poor ignorant creatures who bring offerings to the priests.

"Notwithstanding all this, objectionable and revolting as it is, I felt what I can never describe on gazing on the place where was laid He who had suffered for us, He who had left the glory of the Heavens to offer Himself a propitiatory sacrifice for all mankind. My eyes filled with tears, and I thought, 'a moment here is better than a thousand sermons.'"

At Bethlehem, they stayed at the Catholic Convent at the Church of the Nativity.

"We were ushered into a room 8 yds. × 5, set round with sofas. The Padre Superiore received us and about 12 monks bowed very politely as we entered. There was a strong smell of rakia (a sort of spirit) and after a short time some of it was handed round. The conversation was carried on in Italian, Maraccini acting as interpreter.

Coffee was brought, and in a few minutes wax tapers, and we went to survey the Church of the Nativity, some of the monks accompanying us.

". . . We returned to our room in the convent and had supper. Being 6th day, no meat to be had, so had first boiled eggs, then a sort of bread pudding done up with oil and not bad, then omelet, then anchovies, then cheese and fruits with a wine rather sour. The monks soon retired, except the Padre Superiore, and the servant of the convent brought in beads and boxes, etc., made of mother-of-pearl, of which we purchased some. Retired to our room, which was 12 yds. long at least and 6 broad, with sofas all round and a recess at one end. Three beds were made up on the sofas, and I had one in the recess, which is the same that Ibrahim Pacha slept in when at the convent two years ago."

Having ridden eighty miles during two nights, with only five hours' sleep, he got back to Jaffa in time to board the *Levant* which sailed for Alexandria on the evening of October 3. In the intervals of seasickness and exhausted sleep, he put down some notes on his experiences:

"[5*th.*] The reflections caused by a visit to Palestine are of the most sorrowful kind. When we behold a country, pre-eminently favoured by nature and once chosen by God for his favoured people to dwell in, reduced in many parts to a desert, its people sunk into the lowest depth of ignorance, suffering under the tyranny of the Turks, and without one ray of hope to point to happier days, we feel a sadness of the soul and wish that the curse might depart from the ill-fated land. Here, indeed, we see the human species almost under its worst form. The women are more than ordinarily ugly, and at 20 look old. They have a haggard look; the bottom lip seems to fall upon the chin; many of them have a complaint in the eyes; and altogether they have the appearance of being what in reality they are, slaves. All seem poor, their cabins wretched, their children badly cared for, and the whole has an appearance of the most abject misery."

During the excursion King had fallen ill of a fever, and his condition gave Bright great anxiety, for cholera had just broken out in Jaffa. Happily, King proved not to be infected, and a long course of quinine, doctoring by the English physician at Alexandria, and careful nursing by Bright put him right for the time.

Bright gave the tourist's conventional attention to Pompey's Pillar and the antiquities within reach of Alexandria. He even "brought away a piece of stone" from Cleopatra's Needles. But it was the Alexandria of Mehemet Ali rather than the Alexandria of the Ptolemys that chiefly concerned him: he found it detestable and the heat "insupportable."

"[12th.] The bazaars are poor, the people are half naked, vast numbers of them suffering from ophthalmia, and very many quite blind. The huts of the poor an Irishman would scarcely turn a pig in. Went thro' the Pacha's arsenal, and were astonished at the exertion he is making—three 100-gun and one 50-gun ships on the slips; thousands of men at work rope-making, etc. etc. etc. From this it is easy to perceive that all the wealth of the country flows into his coffers to support his enormous expenditure, and consequently the country is miserably poor and oppressed. This year he exports 97,000 bales of cotton and sells for 25 dolls. what he pays but 7 dolls. for. He monopolizes all the grain and produce of the country, paying for it what will just keep the grower alive, and selling it out at his own price. He even formed a design to monopolize all the British manufactures imported, and a *Frenchman* recommended him to *buy them all* as they arrived. . . . In the words of a late author, 'Mehemet Ali is a rebel to his sovereign, a traitor to his faith, a tyrant to his people, and so selfish that everything sinks into insignificance when put in comparison with his own aggrandizement.' He is 66 yrs. old and his son, Ibrahim Pacha, who has more of the soldier than the statesman, is reputed exceedingly intemperate."

The year before, twenty thousand people had died of plague. Mrs. Hume, a widow who kept the lodgings which he and King occupied, told him that so strict was the quarantine of private houses during the epidemic that for six months she was alone in her house and never left it. Everything she received was passed to her through water. "During two months of this most awful period, incessant howlings and wailings were heard day and night around her dwelling. One unbroken line or procession of funerals was nearly all that was to be seen in the streets, and it seemed as if offended Heaven were again pouring its vial of wrath upon this devoted country. . . . I can safely say I never quitted a city or a country with less regret."

He was back in Smyrna on October 16, after a voyage with only two incidents. First at Rhodes he discovered the complete Turkish official when he called on Schuchurn Pacha, the Governor of the island:

"We found him a stout good-sized man, apparently 55 to 60 yrs. old, sitting cross-legged upon a sofa or divan. The room was about 8 yrds. $\times$ 5½; sofas round 3 sides of it about 18 ins. high. Muskets hung the room, and swords and pistols. The old Turk was smoking his chibouk, and recd. us *graciously*. We sat down opposite to him and were immediately furnished with a pipe each, about 7 ft. long, with a brass dish to place the bowl in. These were brought in by his attendants, young men, of whom there were 8 or 10 in waiting. After the pipes, coffee was handed as usual in very small cups, which cups were carried in a small silver vessel exactly the shape and size of an egg-cup. The Pacha asked many very sensible questions. He is one of the most powerful Pachas of Anatolia, and has every reason to look forward to being created Capitan Pacha before long."

Next, on the night of the 13th, he saw "the comet which had been expected for so long a time. I was the first to discover it . . . in the north western part of the heavens, and its tail stretched out towards the zenith. In Alexandria and Rhodes the heat has been excessive for several days, and this is attributed by many to the influence of the comet." [1]

At Smyrna, the Barkers welcomed him again with open arms, and he was "truly glad to be under a hospitable roof." He stayed a week with them, during which his chief diversions were a Greek funeral and a Turkish bath. He describes the bath (his first in that mode) with gusto and particularity, and adds: "The operation of a Turkish Bath has nothing in it at all disagreeable, and I would recommend everyone to take one who visits Turkey."

"[18*th*.] Saw a Greek funeral, so followed into the church. The Greeks always carry their corpses in the coffin without lid or cover, adorned with flowers and dressed in white, and with shoes on the feet. On entering the church, in which went a great crowd, along with the corpse, the frame upon which the coffin was carried was set down, and a man belonging to the church began to distribute great numbers of small wax tapers among the bystanders. I, of course, took one, and having lighted it, stood equally interested with the rest. The priests

[1] Halley's Comet.

37

sung for several minutes the service in Greek, and soon after one of them came in at a door very near, reading from a book, in a half singing tone, what I supposed to be a mixture of prayer and benediction. On the conclusion of the ceremony perhaps 39 or 40 people rushed to the corpse to kiss it, everyone kissing the hands and the forehead. The deceased was a young lady lately married.

"[23rd.] H. Barker went down with us to the beach and took leave of us there. I know not that I have ever met a more worthy man. He is pious and endeavours to bring up his family in a religious manner. He is agreeable in his manners, generous and hospitable to his friends, and in every way worthy of esteem. Thro' his kindness and that of his amiable family my abode in Smyrna has been rendered extremely pleasant, and I shall never look back upon my stay there with any other feelings than those of the purest satisfaction."

4

His next objective was Constantinople. Reaching the Sultan's capital by the Austrian steamer, *Maria Dorothea*, on the 24th, he put up with King (better, but still shaky) at Mr. Roboli's "sort of private boarding house where we are to pay one dollar a day and trust we shall be pretty comfortable."

"[24th.] The view of Constantinople has been often praised but I should think never in too high colours. I imagined nothing could be much more beautiful than the approach to Lisbon. Lisbon, however, is all on one side of the river, and so far as it goes, is really very magnificent; but, in entering the capital of Turkey, we are in a sort of circle, and on whichever side we turn a scene of almost unrivalled beauty meets the eye. The whiteness of the buildings, the size of the mosques, the height of the minarets, and the cypress trees, rearing their tall and sombre figures in contrast with the light of everything around, whilst are seen the Bosphorus right before and the port to the left, traversed by innumerable caiques skimming along the surface with amazing rapidity, all combine to fill this panorama of surpassing splendour and magnificence.

"[25th.] Took a boat for an excursion. This boat was long and narrow, but a beautiful boat. We had 3 watermen and we were obliged all four to sit in the bottom of the boat in a space of little more than 4 feet. We were rowed up the Bosphorus and landed to pay a *pop* visit to an Armenian who formerly was S. Barker's broker. We

were shown into a room with sofas or divans round it and were served
with pipes. Then the attendant brought a glass vessel with preserves
and a silver spoon, and each person took a spoonful. Then a glass of
water was handed to each, and after this coffee."

A slight relapse befalling King, Dr. Millingen, "who was formerly
physician to Lord Byron in Greece, I believe," [1] advised him to have
leeches on the pit of the stomach and to eat very little: an Armenian
barber applied them. King was somewhat relieved; but there was
plague in the city—sixty or seventy people died of it daily—and they
cut short their visit, taking passage in the *Crescent* for Smyrna once
more.

Bright had now been travelling about the Turkish dominions for
several weeks. As usual, he spent some of his time on shipboard in
putting down on paper, not panegyrics of scenery, records of antiquity
or historical speculations, but practical observations on the condition
of the communities through which he had passed. In the indictment
of the Turkish system which he wrote on board the *Crescent* can be
detected the first flashes of that lightning which descended upon the
Ottoman with such terrible force twenty years later in the famous letter
to Absalom Watkin about the Crimean War: [2] "We are not only at
war with Russia, but with all the Christian population of the Turkish
Empire, and we are building up our Eastern Policy on a false foundation—namely on the perpetual maintenance of one of the most immoral
and filthy of all despotisms over one of the fairest portions of the earth
which it has desolated, and over a population it has degraded but has
not been able to destroy."

"[28*th*.] It is much to be regretted that we had so short a time
to see the beauties of this celebrated capital which is ere long likely to
become the theatre of great events. On beholding it we are astonished
at the extraordinary excellence of its situation and perceive at once that
under favourable circumstances it might become, nay it must become,
perhaps the first city in the world. Nature has done everything for it.

---

[1] The Dr. Millingen who, two days before Byron's death, persuaded him, much
against his prejudices, to be bled. When he could no longer bear to be pestered,
Byron, "throwing out his arm, said in the angriest tone, 'There—you are, I see, a
d——d set of butchers; take away as much blood as you like, but have done with it.'
We seized the moment and drew about 20 ounces." (Millingen's account, quoted by
Moore.)

[2] "Letter to Mr. Absalom Watkin," *The Times*, Nov. 4, 1854.

Its climate is salubrious, neither suffering from the excessive heats of Syria nor from the intense cold of Russia, but preserving that equality which is found most conducive to health; notwithstanding which, Constantinople is one of the most unhealthy cities in the world.

"The plague, that dire scourge of Eastern countries, seems to have seated itself here with a firmness which nothing has yet been able to overcome, and every year, scarcely without exception, it carries off its victims. The existence of this evil is a drawback which goes far to counterbalance the great natural advantages which this city possesses. It renders it impossible to enjoy the pleasures of society in their full extent, and imprints an air of suspicion and distrust on every countenance during its continuance. The friend meets his friend, but dare not hold out the right hand of friendship. Each man walks the streets as if the pestilence in all its horror were rioting on every individual he meets, and he draws his coat close around him and edges his way with the utmost caution thro' the crowd, as if the slightest touch of his fellow townsmen or their garments would inevitably give him the plague.

"If you enter a warehouse or office on matters of business, the paper you bring must be smoked and held at a considerable distance while it is read. If you take a recipe to an apothecary, he holds it at arm's length almost whilst he deciphers the Latin of the physician. If a person call at your house, you inquire what part he comes from and if there be plague in his neighbourhood before you dare to admit him. And should an accident of plague occur in your house, you must be shut up in it and keep rigorous quarantine for 35 or 40 days. At the present moment these precautions are being taken in Constantinople in general.

"The Turks unfortunately still possess so much of the doctrine of fatalism that they take few measures against this dreadful invader of their peace. It will be perceived at once that in a state of uncertainty like the one I have attempted to describe, when every day adds new victims to the list of the dead, and he who least suspects it may be the next, life can have few pleasures and its purest joys must be embittered.

"If I might venture an opinion on such a subject, I would say that the recurrence of the plague might be prevented. Unfortunately the Govt. of Turkey is so bad that its very tendency is to prevent improvement amongst its subjects. The will of the Sultan, and after him, that of his great officers, being Law, the most extraordinary oppressions are practised upon the people with impunity.

"If a man have property he is made the subject of gross exaction.

If he die without children, the Govt. seizes all he leaves without reference to his nephews, nieces or other relations. If he be poor, he sees no particular reason why he should strive to amass wealth, as riches may only serve to bring down upon him the ire of those who wish to fatten on his industry. If he offend, unintentionally and even innocently, some haughty despot in authority, a severe bastinado, or perhaps the loss of his head pays the forfeit.

"Thus property and even life being insecure, no inducement is held out to the people to march on the road of civilization. There exists no spirit of emulation amongst them, and they drag on their existence as nearly as possible in the same listless and apathetic manner in which their fathers have done before them. Add to this the religion they profess does not point out those duties of charity which give such a zest to the enjoyment of those who practise them, nor does it inculcate those principles of universal love and that desire to spread around them all the joy and happiness of which they may be capable which shine forth so beautifully in the Christian code. Thus the Turks are not solicitous about bettering the condition of their neighbours, nor do they trouble themselves for the sake of any prospective advantage which posterity might reap from their labours; but they come into the world, live as their fathers did, with as little trouble as possible, and sink into the grave without having performed any positive and visible service to their fellow men.

"The state of abject poverty in which so many of them live, the manner in which they dwell crowded together in so small a space, the insufficient and abominably filthy way in which many of them are dressed, and the generally poor and unwholesome nature of their food, all tend to engender disease and to preserve amongst them the germs of disease ready to break out again on the first favourable occasion.

"Unfortunate as it would apparently be for England in a political point of view were Russia to become the master of Constantinople, yet such a circumstance I for one would scarcely regret, believing that it would serve so far to break down the stubbornness in which the Turks preserve their faith in the Prophet, and to destroy those extraordinary notions which they have so long entertained, that on the whole the human race would be a very great gainer by such an event.

"The Turkish Empire is, however, evidently approaching dissolution. Within itself it contains the seeds of decay, as all despotisms do, and it is doubtful if all the influence of the European Powers combined with the exertions of the Turks themselves will long be able to support that edifice, once of such gigantic mould, but which now seems tottering to its base."

At Smyrna, the Barkers received him with unfailing kindness for the third time, and entertained him till November 10, when he sailed in the *Levant* for Athens.

The second visit to Athens was prolonged far beyond his intention by the difficulty of getting a passage to Italy, which he greatly desired to see. Not a single boat going to an Italian port offered for more than a month, and in the latter part of the time he became thoroughly miserable—"suffering from ennui, nothing to do, and completely tired of Athens." It was an illness, heralded by coughing and fainting fits, that brought on this disenchantment, for up to then he had been zestful enough, sightseeing diligently with King.

He made no entries dealing with the public affairs of Greece except a brief account of its brand-new monarch [1] who had just entered his capital. Bright saw King Otho, with his brother the King of Bavaria, at a ceremonial in church:

"[*December* 13.] I stood very near them. There was a platform raised, and over it a canopy surmounted by a crown; the canopy, etc. of crimson. On the platform were two chairs richly ornamented. The two kings came in one carriage and walked together into the church, and stood during the whole of the service or the *Te Deum* under the canopy. Louis of Bavaria appears about 55 to 60 yrs. old, with a withered countenance, whiskers and moustachios and hair grey. He had a blue sash on, and in military dress he is not very kingly in appearance. Otho is 21 years old, about 5 ft. 8 in. high, slender, but well made and stands well. He has some moustachios, but no whiskers; nose short and face rather compressed or flattened; on the whole rather pleasing—and he looked pleased. The people seemed very loyal."

The remaining entries made in Athens record the stages of his illness and the sensations he experienced. The treatment which followed on a consultation with "Dr. Roezer, the King's physician," was drastic. He was bled in the left arm "by a Greek barber;" his

---

[1] Otho of Bavaria, who arrived to take up his new kingdom while Bright was ill. This prince, true to the tenets of the school of despotic government in which he was brought up, soon tested the loyalty of the Greeks to the breaking-point of revolution. In 1862 he was finally driven out of the country.

chest was blistered; he drank hot water; he took forty grains of sulphate of quinine:

"The effect of this is curious. It causes a murmuring in the ears and a medley of every description of music. The triangle was most heard, perhaps, and the piano—the drum even; nay, almost every instrument appeared to bring its share to the grand concert which for the night and following day surprised and I may say amused me."

While continuing his efforts to "quit this country, of which I am more weary than ever," he "put to paper" some notes on "the condition of a man ill at a distance from home." It must not be forgotten that the distance in time of Athens from Rochdale seemed immense in the year 1835.

"[*12th.*] The room I occupied was about 5 yds. square and opened out of the dining-room of the hotel. This caused a great noise morning and evening during the breakfast and dinner hours. From this cause, also, my room swarmed with flies, and when I awoke on a morning I might count 150 flies, or more probably, on the top of my bed. During the fever I could not bear a fire, and the room was so damp that my cloak, which was on the bed, was almost wet, and the top coverlet also. In the room beneath lay the cook, or some poor creature, suffering from the fever, and his moanings added not a little to the unpleasantness of my situation. I had an Albanian servant, who waited pretty well upon me, and I cannot but feel grateful to J. King for his many kind offices; but, during the whole time, I was continually thinking of home and friends there, and many times rambled in imagination over every corner of our premises; and after my reveries was chagrined to find myself still in Athens. I often thought of Walter Scott's words speaking of woman—

> When care and anguish wring the brow,
> A ministering angel thou——

and would have given everything I possessed to have been in my own bed, nursed and attended by my excellent sister Priscilla.[1] I suffered intense agony of mind, surpassing much the pain of the disease, for I thought, 'Suppose I die in Greece? What will be the feelings of my poor father?' And then I remembered his words the morning I left home, 'Perhaps I shall never see thee again.' Sickness at all times is bad,

[1] Afterwards the wife of Duncan McLaren, M.P.

but 3,000 miles from home, in an almost inhospitable country, in a miserable inn, without the possibility of obtaining the necessary comforts, and unattended by one's friends,—then its horrors are aggravated, nay increased 1000 fold."

5

He had celebrated his twenty-fourth birthday in Athens on November 16. He spent Christmas Day at sea. The vessel in which he finally got away was a Greek sailing packet going to Malta, ill found, with no instruments of navigation and not even a good chart. He and King took their own provisions and their own beds, and they slept with five other men in "a very small chamber, about 7 yards by 4, which also serves for breakfast, dining and drawing-room." But the voyage thus undertaken, in spite of bad navigation, delays in calms, and physical discomfort in gales, seems to have been one of the best he ever had: he escaped sea-sickness.

The motion of a sailing vessel ("there is not that tremor which is so disagreeable from the working of the engines on a steamboat") failed to upset him—ample compensation even for the inconvenience of cabins in which one could not stand upright and a passage lasting ten days from the Piræus to Valetta. He ate plum pudding. He even made an apple dumpling: "J. Wilkin took the paste department and I cut the apples; however, it was not boiled enough by dinner time, and we ate it afterwards to our tea." He drank the light sweet wine of Tenos—that liquor in a butt of which the Duke of Clarence was drowned. He played écarté at night. He revelled in pork and eggs for breakfast. He listened with philosophical patience to the captain reading the Arabian Nights' tales in Greek to amuse himself and the crew while he waited for some passing ship to tell him where he was.

They ought to have been anchored at Malta on Christmas Day, "but from our capt.'s having no instruments on board, and bad charts, our calculations are wrong, and no land is visible this morning. We know not where we are, and are in fact lost. . . . The captain and men are capital sailors, but have neither instruments nor good charts." There had been a storm overnight, and their water had run short. But though he was very glad to hear the sound of the chain running through the hawse in Valetta Harbour on a brilliant moonlit night, the entries show that he had really passed a not unpleasant voyage.

They spent nearly three weeks in Malta, most of the time in the durance vile of quarantine, and Bright, taking cold, came again under the quinine regimen. In the two or three days of liberty allowed him, the most interesting visit he paid was to H.M.S. *Canopus*, a man-of-war of 84 guns, taken by Nelson from the French at Aboukir: "she is a splendid vessel and a crack ship of the squadron." On the whole he was thoroughly bored—too bored even to write up his diary. He records ten days in a few lines, in this fashion: "January 4, 5 and 6.— Passed in reading, chatting, gaping, and wishing our quarantine was over. Read Pindar's works and found them extremely witty and clever, but irreligious and gross."

But at last he was able to realize his fervent desire to see something of Italy. On January 14 a xebeck of 70 or 80 tons sailed from Valetta for Catania, and they secured a passage for five dollars by provisioning themselves. So, in a very small cabin, which "smelt horribly," and in the company of an American traveller from Kentucky, they said good-bye to Malta, and landed at Catania two days later.

The scenery of Italy, its aura of great history, the buried cities of Vesuvius, the remains of the grandeur that was Rome, made a vivid and lasting impression on him. He writes of them all with the enthusiasm of a young man whose imagination has been stirred and stimulated to the uttermost. But, as always, he keeps eyes wide for observation of the social and political state of the country, and talks candidly to his diary about it. Especially was he stirred to contempt by the plague of mendicancy and graft in a land where backsheesh would do everything and without it nothing could be done. On his landing at Catania:

"[*January* 16.] The papers of the ship, passports, bills of health, etc., in number about 20, were read by an officer who displayed more of the importance of officer than I have ever seen before. He stood erect as possible and read over the Italian with the air of a person of more consequence than exists in the Kingdom of Naples. Certainly he threw somewhat contemptuous glances upon the suppliant Sicilians, and very forcibly reminded me of Shakespeare's
'Man dress't in a little brief authority.'
He was evidently a man whom a fee would have reduced to submission and who would have licked the dust from the shoes of a superior."

Catania surprised and pleased him. He had not expected to see so fine a city. But "one great blank all who visit Catania must admit to exist,—the absence of female beauty. Indeed, few *young* women are to be seen, and those in general very *plain*." [1] He attended a funeral service for Bellini the composer, who had lately died of cholera in Genoa. From Catania, he went by road (in a barouche with three horses abreast) to Messina. This journey of 66 miles lasted from ten at night to four the next afternoon, an average of less than four miles an hour. The hours during which he rolled along the shore road, with Scylla and Charybdis in sight and Stromboli smoking in the background, made up for the discomfort of the jolting night ride during which sleep was impossible. The glorious scenery enthralled him. He had another touch of fever in Messina, and the warm baths prescribed by a Dr. Nimmo seem to have done him more good than all the cuppings and leechings of the Greek barbers. He reached Naples, via Palermo, by steamer.

The morning of the arrival in the Bay of Naples was wet and gloomy. Vesuvius hid his head in thick clouds, and "all around bore a melancholy aspect." Nevertheless, he had three interesting days. The Hotel de la Victoire gave him a bedroom for five calinos (or 1/8) a day, but charged him 2/8 a day for firewood, which was necessary but "very dear." From this head-quarters he drove to the chief points of beauty or interest in the district. He spares his diary any details of the great museum: "I neither attempt a description of the *chefs d'œuvre* to be seen here, nor even particularize them, not being a connoisseur in these matters. I must refer to the many books containing full accts. of these wonders." Nor does he enlarge much on the visit to Pompeii, which so filled his mind with speculation. He notes the evidences up to then disclosed of the life lived by the Roman leisured classes in the first century; but it is the disaster which overtook them that most stirs his imagination:

"In wandering through the streets of Pompeii, the traveller cannot but partake in some degree of the solemnity which pervades the ruins of this ill-fated city. The mind reverts to the moment when the convulsion of nature caused its destruction, and contemplates with a feeling of horror the dreadful situation of the unfortunate inhabitants. Mount Vesuvius, the cause of this awful catastrophe, still vomits forth flame and proclaims that he still possesses the power to overwhelm the presumptuous mortals who have dared to locate themselves on his demesne."

[1] He had an appreciation of feminine charm. At Messina a few days later, he notes: "Have been to the Gardens, which is a sort of promenade. Military music and much company. Ladies excessively plain."

While Bright was in Naples, Queen Christina died, shortly after giving birth to her son:

"[*31st.*] About 17 days ago was born the only son of the King of Naples [1] and great rejoicings took place in consequence. To-day at 12 o'clock precisely, the Queen died. All festivities are prohibited and the Carnival, it is supposed, will not be held."

Travelling from Naples by diligence, in the company of two Americans (Mr. Joseph Neide, "who was very intelligent and agreeable," and Mr. Metcalf), Bright and King entered Rome on February 3. They descended at the Hotel d'Allemagne, "where we are comfortable: our room cost 4 pauls (20*d.*) per day, breakfast 1/–, dinner 18*d.*—everything good."

In Rome, he became the perfect tourist. He saw everything that could be crammed into the few days of his stay, hiring a barouche for three dollars a day, and driving around indefatigably to antiquities, churches, galleries, and cemeteries. He was under such an urge to note the particulars of his sightseeing, and wrote on it at such length, that there was apparently no time to record those general impressions of the life of every day which had made so lively an actuality of his diary up to this point. St. Peter's smites him with awe: "All that I have read and heard of this church falls short of conveying an adequate idea of its splendour and beauty." He looks, "or rather runs" through the Vatican Museum. The Coliseum brings him back to Byron: "The largest monument of Róman grandeur . . . surpassed all I had read and imagined of it, and recalled forcibly to mind the lines of Byron—

> While stands the Coliseum, Rome shall stand.
> When falls the Coliseum, Rome shall fall."

His neat pages are a veritable itinerary of Rome. But in one entry he describes a spectacle which only those could see who were in Rome at this moment:

"[*February* 5.] We were admitted into the Palace of the mother of Napoleon who died a few days ago and who is now lying in state. In the centre of a large and handsome apartment was spread upon the

---

[1] Ferdinand II wedded Christina, daughter of Victor Emmanuel, four years before. She had not long been dead when he married Maria Theresa, daughter of the Archduke Charles of Austria, and entered upon the disastrous association with a despotism which ultimately won for him the execrated name of "King Bomba," and led to Gladstone's atrocities campaign in 1851.

floor a large piece of worked velvet, a figure of a crown, etc., at each corner. In the centre of this was an *elegant* coffin of mahogany, standing upon 6 nobs or feet, which raised it about 3 inches.

"The head of the corpse was a little raised by pillows of white satin. It was dressed in a habit with sleeves very wide, of black velvet, lined with white satin, cap and rather long scarf of white flowered silk, gloves white silk, and white satin shoes. On the breast a very beautiful silver cross with a figure of the Saviour. The countenance could not but astonish all who beheld it. It had almost the colour of health with the exception of a *slight* tinge of black on the lips and nostrils. The forehead and cheeks were but little wrinkled, and sleep rather than death seemed to have thrown his mantle over the venerable lady who lay before us.

"She must have been a remarkable woman, for even in death there was an appearance of great power and firmness about her. Her features were good, particularly the nose. A smile seemed to play upon her lips, but it was only in the somewhat high cheek bone that I fancied I could discover a resemblance to her son. She was about 88 yrs. of age, I believe,[1] tho' from the appearance of the corpse I should not have judged her more than 60 to 65. She is said to have left behind her an immense property."

There is an interest which he could not himself have foreseen in the note he makes upon a visit to the Protestant Cemetery near the pyramid of Caius Cestius:

"[*7th.*] The tombstones display taste and architectural beauty. On one modest slab of marble is this sorrowful inscription—

This grave contains all that was mortal of a young English poet, who on his death bed, in the bitterness of his heart at the *malicious power* of his enemies, desired these words to be engraven on his tombstone: 'Here lies one whose name was writ in water.' Feby. 24, 1831.[2]

Above the inscription is a sculpture of a broken harp. . . ."

[1] Letizia Buonaparte was born in 1750, and was therefore 86 at the time of her death. She had gone to live in Rome after the Battle of Waterloo. Bright thus had the last glimpse of a "majestic beauty" that had dazzled three generations of Europeans.

[2] He copied the date wrongly. It is 1821. Bright returned to this scene on his second visit to Rome in 1857: "Saw the simple stone over the grave of Shelley and the sad inscription over that of Keats." (Diary, Feb. 1, 1857.)

Bright may have been familiar with Hazlitt's scathing attack on the Blackwood gang for their treatment of Keats, and so diligent a student of Byron must have known by heart the eleventh canto of *Don Juan*. Not till after his second visit in 1857 did men learn that, as Mr. Symonds says, Keats had given for his epitaph "gently and without bitterness the words, partly taken from a phrase in Beaumont and Fletcher's *Philaster*, —'here lies one whose name was written in water.'" And then, while the lettered world discussed the question whether the inscription should be changed to fit the facts more closely and do better justice to the poet's memory, Bright was in the thick of politics.

Fitted in between Castor and Pollux and Nero's Golden House in his adventures is an account of how he took part in the Carnival. He was in the barouche with King driving from the Pincian Hill to the Corso:

"This is the first day of the Carnival and the Corso is fitted up for the horse races. From 2 to 5 it was a promenade for carriages and foot passengers and was greatly crowded. Plenty of soldiers were about to preserve order, and our carriage being very handsome, and our driver in livery, we joined the throng and drove slowly backwards and forwards in true Hyde Park style. The windows were almost all decorated with crimson cloths edged with gold, and with the beauty and the fashion of Rome, and the streets had an extremely gay and fairy-like appearance.

"There is a very curious custom here during Carnival. They make a sort of comfits of flour and sugar, I suppose, but soft, so that they almost fall to dust on striking against anything. These are taken to the windows in large quantities and are thrown by the ladies who view the promenade on those who are engaged in it. We were peppered with them continually in passing and looked more like millers than travelling gents. Many carriages also had them and threw them unsparingly on all who passed, and especially on those with particularly fine coats on. The dust, however, leaves the cloth easily and no injury is done. The ladies in open carriages have a fine wire shade which they hold before the face to prevent injury to the eyes, etc.

"We bought a paper of these comfits and of course revenged ourselves upon all those who showered them upon us.

"At 5 o'clock the gun was fired and the carriages left the Corso. Soon after, the centre of the long street was cleared and the race began. The horses were 5 or 6 in number, and dressed gaudily; but their splendour was like the splendour in which man often foolishly indulges, extremely painful or at least irksome, for attached to the trappings are pricks or sharp points which goad the animal as he runs and causes him to exert his utmost speed. They are started without riders and consequently without bridles, and gallop up the street as fast as possible, the crowds which line the Corso on both sides shouting and showering on the affrighted beasts comfits, etc., and thus enjoy the pleasure of a horse race! The horses galloped once the length of the street and the novelties of the day terminated."

Having exhausted as many of the sights of Rome as he could crowd into five days, he left what he twice curiously describes as "the so-called Eternal City," taking the courier for Florence. He and King had to pay 22½ dollars each for being driven 180 miles in 36 hours, which he considered "extremely high." But Florence was worth it. He did all the sights, reflected over the tombs of Michael Angelo, Galileo, Alfieri and Machiavelli, and quoted Byron to himself on the "four minds" from which, as from the Elements, all Creation might be furnished. He left the city with regret; it seemed to him "very desirable as a place of residence." At Leghorn he struck the last day of Carnival, bought two figures of Tasso and Dante at Micalis's shop, and sailed in a small steamer for Genoa.

In this abortive voyage occurred the wildest excitements of his tour. It came on to blow hard:

"The captain thought it prudent to return, and before seven o'clock we were again in the port of Leghorn and our worst apprehensions were realized. The port is not a good one. It is formed by a mole of no great length which affords but poor protection for the shipping. We let out three anchors, dragged them, and were drifted so near the shore just opposite the Health Office that we struck several times. On the right a Genoa schooner ran upon the rocks, and a small vessel kept here as a guardship ran foul of us twice. Our anchors became entangled, and we were apparently in imminent peril."

Eventually, they brought up in a comparatively safe part of the harbour, and got to bed at two in the morning. Another false start next day prolonged the stay in Leghorn and he spent the enforced leisure with Henry Petty, a business man of the place who had relations with his firm, and indulged in a little Byron worship. The house in which

Byron lived "was close to us—coloured pink, with green window frames and blinds, rather a nice looking villa. It occupies the best situation in a neighbourhood commanding a fine view. . . . At dinner Mr. Petty mentioned that a Captain Roberts wished to sell a meerschaum pipe which had belonged to Lord Byron. I sent for it, and bought it—but I am not sure that Mr. Petty did not make me a present of it." He spent two or three days at Genoa, calling there on Nicolas Moro, with whom the Brights had business. He records a dinner with Moro "in the real Italian style," and the fact that Mrs. Moro was the daughter of a general officer in Napoleon's army who lost his life in the retreat from Moscow.

Going on to Marseilles, he travelled thence to Paris by the *malle-poste*, taking 78 hours for the 600 miles. An interesting travel note is that, for the ascent of ten miles near St. Etienne, the vehicle was drawn by eighteen horses. Two days in Paris brought the long jaunt to an end, and he came home by Calais and Dover. This is the final entry: "My travel has occupied more than six months, and its cost was about £250."[1]

[1] Having incorporated the diary of his travel into the Memoir, Bright resumed the summarized story of his youth in Lancashire, and carried it down to his brief first marriage, the death of Mrs. Bright, and the beginning of the Corn Law campaign.

CHAPTER III

THE MEMOIR CONTINUED

FROM this time I remained much at home and engaged in my father's business as a cotton-spinner and manufacturer.

I have omitted to notice a matter of great importance in connexion with my political career—my first meeting with Mr. Cobden. I had invited him to attend a meeting on the Education Question in which he was then taking great interest. The meeting was held in the school-room of the Baptist Chapel in West Street.[1] I spoke at it, having care-fully written out what I had to say. I didn't "break down" but was in some fear of failure, and I suffered so much that I resolved never again to write and commit to memory another speech, a resolution to which I have adhered.

Mr. Cobden spent the night at my father's house, and from this visit began a friendship which continued unbroken so long as Mr. Cobden lived. He died on April 2, in the year 1865.

I took a lively interest in some questions which excited and in some degree disturbed our town, the most important being that of the im-position of Church Rates. The Vicar of this parish [2] came down from Kent, and was totally unacquainted with the people and with the opinions of this district. He fought for the supremacy of his Church: we resisted him and his party, and after great meetings and furious contests and costly lawsuits we put an end to Church Rate contests and to Church Rates in this parish. I took an active part in the discussion of the question, and once spoke to a very large meeting in the old Church Yard, my platform being one of the tombs standing near the church.

But a greater or a more pressing question soon came forward, into which I was drawn by an irresistible impulse. I refer to the question of the Corn Law, and its effect upon the condition and sufferings of our population.

In the year 1838, when in Manchester on my regular business, I one day met Mr. Prentice, of the *Manchester Times* newspaper. He

[1] Rochdale.　　　　[2] Rev. Dr. Molesworth.

52

JOHN BRIGHT
From the portrait by C. A. Du Val

asked me to attend a small meeting to be held that evening to form an association which, he said, they were determined should not be dissolved until the Corn Law was abolished. Unfortunately for me, I could not attend the meeting. There were, I think, only seven persons present, and six of them, if not indeed all of them, were Scotchmen.

On coming home, I told my father what Mr. Prentice had said. He replied that he had heard of repealing the Corn Law many times, but he had no faith in it: he could not see how it was possible to repeal it against the forces which supported it. The small Committee became an Anti-Corn Law Association, and then it became a League; and, eight years after the forming of Mr. Prentice's Committee, landowners and farmers, and monopolists and protectionist Lords and Commons were vanquished, and the cruel and odious Corn Law was repealed.

In this year other events occurred in which I was much interested. I was invited by John Fenwick of Newcastle, to visit him on the occasion of the meeting of the British Association, and spent several days in his very hospitable home. His daughter had married my friend Robert Schofield of Rochdale, and it was in this way the invitation came to me.

I was glad to go to Newcastle in the hope of seeing more of a girl I had seen some months before at the General Meeting of Ackworth School. Whilst at Ackworth, my dear sister Margaret[1] came to me to tell me she had seen a girl she wanted me to see, so much was she charmed with her. We went together and stood near her as she was engaged with a stall on which were displayed for sale small articles made by the girls at the school.

I was much struck by the sweet countenance I was brought to see. It had on it the best of beauty, the beauty of goodness. The sweet picture did not fade from my heart, and led to much in the future. In the autumn of 1837 I was at Newcastle with two of my sisters, and at the house of Edward Richardson we met for the evening the young lady I had seen at Ackworth, when my interest in her was increased so that I was glad to accept my friend John Fenwick's invitation in the month of May, 1838. During the week I had opportunities of seeing the eldest daughter of Jonathan and Rachael Priestman of Summerhill. Her parents were ministers, and the family in all respects to be admired. The result was that later in the autumn of 1838 I again visited Newcastle, with the consent of her parents, and made her an offer of marriage.

We were not married till the 27th of November, 1839. It was a day of winter and of snow. We came to our happy house by way of

[1] Afterwards the wife of Samuel Lucas, editor of *The Morning Star*.

Hexham, Carlisle, Patterdale, Ambleside, Lancaster and Whiterock. The house we came to is the one I now live in (1888). It was built for me by my father, but has been since enlarged. We gave it the name of "One Ash," partly from the ash tree which stood and yet stands near the front door, and partly in sympathy with or remembrance of the house of my ancestor, John Gratton, who lived at "Monyash," near Bakewell, in Derbyshire.

The year 1840 passed happily for us in our new circumstances, and on the 10th October our household was increased by the addition of a little girl, now, when I write this, the mother of six children, living with an excellent husband and family at Street in Somersetshire.[1]

Early in the next year the health of my dear wife began to fail. In the spring we went to Newcastle in the hope that native air might be of service, and there we consulted Dr. Headlam, a physician of much repute. He advised us to go south. We left Newcastle and went south as far as Leamington, where we consulted the famous Dr. Jephson. He was most kind and attentive, but the case was beyond his skill.

We remained in Leamington during the summer. We had a nice house, No. 20 Clarendon Square, the highest house in the row on the left-hand side going up from the town. We drove out almost daily in the neighbourhood of Leamington, and my precious wife was not unhappy as her strength very slowly declined. Our dear child was left with its grandparents at Newcastle. I was almost entirely with the dear, patient invalid during her stay at Leamington.

On the night of September 9, the end was evidently near. Hæmorrhage came on, after retiring for the night, and in the morning of the 10th the pure soul passed to its Maker, and I was left desolate.

My friend Cobden was in Leamington on a visit to some relations, and then took place the interview and the conversation to which I referred after many years on the uncovering of the statue erected in his honour in the Exchange at Bradford.[2] We then, in fact, made a

---

[1] Helen Priestman Bright, who became Mrs. W. S. Clark, of Street, Somerset.

[2] "At that time I was at Leamington," said Bright in this speech (July 25, 1877), "and I was, on the day when Mr. Cobden called upon me—for he happened to be there at the time on a visit to some relatives—I was in the depths of grief, I might almost say of despair, for the light and sunshine of my house had been extinguished. All that was left on earth of my young wife, except the memory of a sainted life and a too brief happiness, was lying still and cold in the chamber above us. Mr. Cobden called upon me as his friend, and addressed me, as you may suppose, with words of condolence. After a time he looked up and said, 'There are thousands of houses in England at this moment where wives, mothers and children are dying of hunger.

solemn compact that we would give ourselves up to the great work of repealing one of the most cruel laws ever passed by a Christian legislation, the law which made scarcity and famine when English harvests were not abundant.

I will not describe my home after my return from Leamington. The motherless child was with me. My sister Priscilla came to live with me, and her loving kindness to the child and to me cannot be described in any words I can write.

During the months I was at Leamington, I was much interested in the great and growing Corn Law Question. On one occasion I went to a great meeting at Bristol in company with Mr. Cobden and George Thompson, the eloquent opponent of Negro Slavery. I also wrote some articles condemning the Corn Law and showing its mischief and its wickedness in one of the Leamington newspapers.[1]

Now,' he said, 'when the first paroxysm of your grief is past, I would advise you to come with me and we will never rest till the Corn Law is repealed.' I accepted his invitation."

[1] The Memoir ends here.

CHAPTER IV

THE FIVE YEARS' WAR

I

THE memorable meeting of the Seven Men in Manchester which inaugurated in earnest the campaign for untaxed food was held on September 24, 1838, at the York Hotel. The Anti-Corn-Law League was therefore three years old when Bright began to fulfil his solemn compact with Cobden.

That, of course, was not the inception of the movement. Joseph Hume, Grote the historian, Molesworth the Colonial reformer, Roebuck and other Philosophical Radicals had formed an Anti-Corn-Law Association in London two years earlier. But though these eminent men understood never so well the science of Political Economy—and pursued with never so brilliant logic the great argument that like minds, from Adam Smith to Pitt, had endeavoured to apply to practical fiscal politics—they understood not at all the art of appealing to the imagination, the emotions and the altruism of the nation.[1] They could never have raised the towering wave of popular feeling which swept away the Corn Laws, emancipated the nation from the deep depression of mind and the fearful suffering of body into which agrarian Protection had plunged it, and brought in the great era of plenty and prosperity. That task was left for the practical men, the industrialists, the merchants, the workmen of the North who lived in the midst of the welter of misery created in the manufacturing towns by twenty years of food taxes. Nor could they ever have persuaded the farmers, as Cobden and Bright persuaded them, that the Corn Laws were as injurious to rural as to urban England.

The resurrection of Free Trade as a vital issue in English politics, after the long régime of high protection, high rents, scarcity, starvation

---

[1] "The free-traders," Lord Sydenham said with a pang, "have never been orators since Mr. Pitt's early days. We hammered away with facts and figures and some arguments; but we could not elevate the subject and excite the feelings of the people." (Morley's "Cobden," Chap. 6.)

and pauperism whose beginning had coincided with the outrageous Corn Law of 1815, dates from that meeting of the seven men in Manchester. The real weight behind the movement first made itself felt when Cobden, two months later, carried through the Manchester Chamber of Commerce a resolution in favour of repeal. What these men of business did—manufacturers, merchants, hard-thinking and far-sighted men—was to stiffen and point the spear of the political economists and give practical direction to the vague search of the tortured millions for justice and a tolerable life. They converted into real politics the passion of Ebenezer Elliott's "Corn Law Rhymes," and precipitated into action the irony of Perronet Thompson's "Corn Law Catechism." Their motives were misunderstood and misrepresented then as they are often travestied now. They were accused of advocating cheap food as a means to lower wages—falsely, for the League specifically based its appeal to the people of England on the theory that Free Trade would improve wages. They held that the liberation of trade from fiscal fetters would bring benefit to all classes. It did, and the benefit was greatest among the classes most depressed by protection. Fortunately Bright left in his diaries a considered statement of the case which for six years he argued with such apostolic fervour, and it contains the best possible refutation of the legend that the repeal of the Corn Laws was the demand of a rapacious clan of greedy middle-class capitalists for their own aggrandizement. This document will appear in its place. The core of it is that food taxation "affects various portions of the community in the inverse ratio of their power to endure it;" "this law-made famine is unequal, sparing the rich and crushing the poor."

Bright's plea, urged for five long years with all his humanitarian zeal and flaming eloquence, was essentially a plea against food taxes. True it involved the general argument that unimpeded trade was the interest of the whole nation. But the League aimed primarily at the release of the working mass of the people, then unenfranchised and politically helpless, from the tyranny of an artificial cost of living and an artificial scarcity of food. This cannot be made too clear if the League campaign is to be understood. The protection which Cobden, Bright and Fox, Villiers, Ashworth and Thompson set out to destroy was the protection of the landed interest at the expense of the nation. Many of the Leaguers were manufacturers, and their crusade, in its eventual results, destroyed with the same blow such protection as their manufactures still enjoyed. Admittedly it was not very great: in the year 1840 something over £20,000,000 was raised by import duties, and of this sum little more than £1,000,000 came from duties on imported manufactures. The fact was that Free Trade, except in agricultural produce, had made much progress long before the League was born. Huskisson's Budgets in 1824–25, and Poulett Thomson's who succeeded him, had greatly reduced the tariff on imported manufactures, thus picking up again the enlightened policy which Pitt was pursuing when the French War brought his fiscal reforms to an end. The Free Trade doctrine met with practical resistance only from the landed interest; but that great interest, even after the Reform Act of 1832, dominated Parliament.

It was not mainly in the cause of agricultural production or of the farmer's well-being that the overwhelming majority of landlords and their supporters in the House of Commons maintained the Corn Laws, but in the sacred cause of rent. War conditions had brought an enormous increment to the rent of land; in many parts of England it doubled in twenty years, and in Scotland more than doubled. The war, putting up the prices of food produce to unexampled heights, worked a revolution upwards and downwards. It was the fortune of the rich and the ruin of the poor. The landlords not only raised their rents, but took large areas of fresh land into arable cultivation. In the hundred years from 1760 to 1860 over seven million acres of common land were enclosed; the English peasant was wiped out. Bright thundered night after night against the needless miseries inflicted upon the artisans of the North by the Corn Laws; but the working of those laws was just as disastrous in the agricultural villages of the South. They had been prosperous enough in the eighteenth century. But now the landless labourers whose forbears had been sturdy peasants and commoners were living a degraded life on six or eight shillings a week in crowded cottages. In a Dorsetshire village the number of inhabitants per house averaged 36. In 1842, though more than 120,000 people emigrated, nearly one-tenth of the total population of the kingdom was living in the workhouses, or scraping an existence outside them on the pauper dole. To this pass the enclosure of land, the amalgamation of farms, and high protection had brought the common people.

"*Familles!*" cried Châteaubriand, when the Emperor sent his famous messages of reassurance to Paris after deserting his broken and retreating army, "*séchez vos larmes: Napoléon se porte bien.*" Sir John Sinclair, the founder of the Board of Agriculture, unconsciously parodied the fierce irony in a letter describing the transformation that had been wrought in the parish of Melrose: "Except in the case of the carrier and the miller, who rent a few acres, a small farm is nearly unknown.

58

The displacing of the old small tenants was at first viewed with deep regret, but the introduction of a better and more spirited style of agriculture has, in a limited period, raised the rental of the parish from £4,000 to nearly £20,000 a year." Disinherited Englishmen! dry your tears: Rent is doing well. If in Devon you are living on a mixture of barley meal and potatoes, and are, as the lecturers of the League report, "ready for pikes and pistols," calm yourselves. Do not listen to these agitators. Heed Sir James Graham describing the idyllic life you lead without knowing it—"the incense-breathing morn, the neat thatched cottage, the blooming garden, the cheerful village green." If you feel hungry, follow the advice of the Hereditary Earl Marshal of England—hot water with a pinch of curry-powder in it is good for the hunger. And is it not true, as a very reverend Dean remarks, that if you cannot get bread or even potatoes, there are generally swedes, turnips or mangel-wurzels to be had?

Such was the rural revolution above and below: the owners of land twice as prosperous; the common people of the country-side sinking deeper every year into wretchedness and beggary. Between these two layers of rural society were the farmers, and the forty years of War and Protection had wrought great and bewildering changes for them also. In the thirty years before the French wars the price of wheat had run between 34s. and 57s. Farming was then fairly prosperous, but the farmer, generally speaking, was a working man and no great gulf was fixed between him and his labourers in social customs and status. During the wars the price of wheat was never below 49s. and it rose as high as 126s.; and wheat can be taken as a rough index of the price of food-products in general. Willy-nilly the farmer became what a hundred years afterwards was called a "profiteer." True, his landlord put up his rent, and in the long run he was not much better off, but there was a time-lag between the rise of prices and the increase of rents. In 1804, in order to safeguard the higher prices which had been reached, a Corn Law was passed which provided for heavy rates of taxation on wheat imports when the home price fell below 63s. But it never did so fall. Between 1804 and 1815 its lowest price was 70s. and it soared to the figure already mentioned.

A nation exhausted by the war, whose poorer classes had been going steadily downhill for years, had reason to hope, after Leipzig, that the cessation of fighting and the re-opening of trade routes would put an end to scarcity and artificial dearness. But the landlords and the farmers, with the help of a willing Parliament, saw to it that the poor should not even now get bread at less than famine price, since bread at a world price would have reduced rents and profits. There was, it is true, a momentary gleam. Between Leipzig and Waterloo, wheat fell with a rush from 100s. to 65s. But Parliament hastened to push it up again and the gleam vanished. The infamous law of 1815 actually prohibited any importation of foreign corn until the price reached 80s. and of Colonial corn (there was very little of that) until it reached 67s. Thus were the rents of the landlords, the profits of the farmers, and the starvation of the poor secured at one stroke. In the preceding quarter of a century spasms of easy wealth-making had raised the farmer in the social scale, and his increasing poverty had depressed the workman. The sporting type of farmer who lived "the life of a gentleman" was the product of the war. He meant to keep his gains. The Corn Bill of 1815, perhaps the most cynically callous piece of economic legislation in the history of England, roused the wrath not only of the mass of people whom it directly attacked, but of every class which was not directly interested in this piece of agrarian brigandage. The City protested; every great town in the country remonstrated; many of them sent up petitions: Parliament took no notice. The workpeople rioted; they attacked the bread shops; they assembled in multitudes at Westminster. All in vain. The Bill passed by a two-thirds majority. "Peterloo" was fought on the field where the Free Trade Hall now stands; Ebenezer Elliott rhymed; Perronet Thompson catechized. Still nothing was done; the condition of England continued to degenerate; the chasm dividing "the two nations" widened. Between the Act of 1815 and Peel's budget of 1842, there was only one alteration in the Corn Law. In 1828 Parliament lifted the prohibition and substituted duties on a sliding scale: the tax was to be a shilling a quarter when wheat was at 73s. or over; but as the price fell the impost increased steeply. The net result of this change in the law was practically no change in the household budget. The agrarians sought to fix the price of wheat at about 63s. a quarter, and at that price the poor could not have bread. Taxation on meat ruled even higher; but it did not affect the poor, because they rarely ate meat. "Did you ever set eyes on a pennyworth of mutton?" asked Colonel Perronet Thompson, in his description of what he called *The Siege of Bolton*. "Come here and you shall see how rations are served out under the Landlord's state of siege. It might bait a rat-trap. Pennyworths of mutton and halfpenny-worths of bread cut off the loaf are what the shopkeepers of Bolton deal out to the inhabitants of their Jerusalem."

The depression of every interest in the land, save rent and corn-growing, had disastrous effects on trade. Export was at its worst in the period of highest protection. Though the population rapidly increased, in the first five years of the 'thirties exports were less than they had been fifteen years before; not till after Peel's first Free Trade Budget in 1842 did trade begin that immense expansion which transformed the country out of recognition in a quarter of a century. Twenty-five years later, Bright, in one of his Reform speeches in the House of Commons, defending himself against the denunciations of his opponents in Parliament and the Press, drew a picture of that transformation in one sentence:

If now, in all the great centres of our population—in Birmingham with its busy district—in Manchester with its encircling towns—in the population of the West Riding of Yorkshire—in Glasgow and amidst the vast industries of the West of Scotland—and in this great Babylon in which we are assembled—if we do not find ourselves surrounded by hungry and exasperated multitudes—if now more than at any time during the last hundred years it may be said, quoting the beautiful words of Mr. Sheridan, that

"Content sits basking on the cheek of Toil"—
if this House and if its statesmen glory in the change, have I not as much as any living man some claim to partake of the glory?

But in 1841 there was no content and no glory, only a carking misery and gloom. By preventing or restricting the import of foodstuffs we prevented or restricted the export of manufactures; more, we stimulated the industrial development of countries which would have bought our manufactures in exchange for their food. At the same time scarcity and dearness of food killed the home market for manufactured goods. When those people who could feed themselves at all had done so, however inadequately, they had no money left for any other purpose; the rest of them were paupers living on the rates. Cobden told the House of Commons that the annual expenditure of the rural labourer on manufactured goods, if boots were not reckoned in, did not exceed thirty shillings, and that he contributed to the revenue less than fifteen shillings a year.

2

This was the state of the country when Bright entered the fray in the autumn of 1841. Peel had just settled down to the work of that momentous Parliament, which in six years wrought the greatest revolution of the nineteenth century, when Cobden wrote to his friend (October 9) urging that something new was wanted to give novelty to the work of the League, and asking him to devote part of the winter to the task of bringing agitation to a head. Up to this time Bright's efforts against the Corn Laws had been confined to his own town of Rochdale. At the beginning of 1839 he convened an open-air meeting which three thousand working men attended, and asked them to declare that the Corn Laws crippled commerce and manufactures, raised up rival manufactories abroad, were injurious and oppressive to the great bulk of the population, and that the working classes were "grievously injured by this monopoly of the landed proprietors." The working men of Rochdale were quite prepared to agree with him that the Corn Law was injurious, but at that moment they put the Chartist cause before Repeal, and carried an amendment declaring that the Corn Law agitation was "made up to divert the minds of the people from the only remedy for all political grievances." It was a common attitude just then. The working men deeply suspected the motives of the manufacturers who were asking for Free Trade—unjustly for the most part, and especially so as far as Bright was concerned. He was as ardent a political reformer as any Chartist. But he had the satisfaction, soon after, of seeing the dangerous moment pass and suspicion vanish. In less than a year he had successfully started a Rochdale Anti-Corn Law Association with a large working-man membership, and two months later a petition for Repeal was signed by 9,700 people—"almost every adult male in the town."

The covenant with Cobden in 1841 had this result—that Bright's success in Rochdale was now repeated in every corner of the country. Cobden's biographer has finely said that the alliance between these two more than doubled the power either of them could have exerted without the other. How powerful it was the history of the League from that winter onwards manifests. The novelty Bright brought into the campaign was not only the strength of his native eloquence but a glowing passion, a spirit of prophecy, an almost religious exaltation. The repeal of the Corn Laws became to him a sacred mission. Only by the complete rout of selfishness entrenched behind these odious laws, he had convinced himself, could the misery of the common people be mitigated. There were a hundred economic reasons for storming the tariff wall; but the paramount reason was to bring bread to the table of the workman and his children. Before long he had become the most active and the most popular of League speakers.

That winter was followed by five years of incessant and prodigious labour. In the speech at Bradford thirty years after, already quoted, he said that during the whole five years "almost every working hour" was given up to the settlement of the question "whether it was good for a man to have half a loaf or a whole loaf." Before the spring of 1842 he had travelled far, up and down the country and across the Irish Sea, proclaiming the gospel of the whole loaf. His labours were not confined to speech-making. He wrote for the League's publication, *The Anti-Corn-Law Circular*, and for the newspapers; he collected statistics; he worked in every conceivable way at the task of making known to England the real causes of its seething pauperism, its idle mills, its empty dwellings and its crowded prisons. And in February he was among the hundreds of manufacturers who came up to London from the North as a League deputation to see Peel and to demand, in the interests of their workpeople and of their industry, the immediate repeal of the bread tax.

Peel, then meditating the first of his Free Trade Budgets, did not intend to include the Corn Tax in his measures of remission, and he refused to see the deputation. Whereupon London witnessed the astonishing spectacle of this crowd of manufacturers in top-hats and frock-coats walking as a "demonstration" arm-in-arm from the Strand through Whitehall to Palace Yard like any Chartist procession, struggling with the police at the entrance of the Court of Requests (where Parliament then sat while Barry's pile was building), crying out for "Total Repeal!" and "Cheap food!" meeting Peel as they went back through Parliament Street and greeting him with a chorus of "No Corn Law!" "Down with Monopoly!" "Give bread and labour!"

The origin of the Free Trade policy which has sustained the weight of the ever-growing fabric of British industry, commerce, shipping, and finance, for ninety years, is often overlooked or misunderstood. Industrial protection was not a characteristic tenet of the Tory Party when Bright set out campaigning for Free Trade; it was concerned chiefly about agricultural protection. Nor, as Disraeli pointed out, was Free Trade a Whig doctrine. The first and greatest step in the resumption of Pitt's policy was taken by a Tory Prime Minister with a Tory Cabinet and carried through a Tory House of Commons. The Budget which Peel had in incubation at the very moment when, from his carriage in Whitehall, he looked with a sombre eye on those middle-class demonstrators, was a Free Trade Budget. It has been truly described as the most momentous of the century.

The Report of the Committee on Import Duties (1840) was the rock on which Peel built. That great document became one of the major scriptures of the League because of the armoury of argument and statistics it contained. But in fact it had none of the characteristics of a propagandist Report. It was a cold and scientific analysis of the Protective tariff and its effects on manufacture, trade, wages, and living. The Committee found its facts in a long experience of protection, low and high, and drew its illustrations and conclusions from that experience without regard to their compatibility or otherwise with orthodox economic theory. It utterly condemned the tariff as it existed in 1840 —the huge conglomeration of duties which Sydney Smith's famous category satirized—erratic, illogical, jumbled together, as tariffs generally are in the scramble of individual interests to get protection. Duties were put on to produce both revenue and protection, but effective protection involved rates so high that they produced no revenue. The system punished the revenue, the home consumer and the export trade alike, for the benefit of the clamorous interests. Colonial preferences operated entirely at the expense of the consumers in these islands. A duty which kept out foreign goods taxed the home user of goods in that class by the whole difference between their protected price and the world price. This result was specially marked in the price of food: the Committee reported that the amount of indirect taxation paid by consumers of food was greater than the total of all the other taxes imposed by the Government. Duties so high as to be prohibitory injured production at home and restricted trade; they were injurious both to wages and to capital. Where protective duties were not so high as to be prohibitory, they acted in the same manner if in a lesser degree. The consumer paid a "tax," equivalent to the amount of the duty, on all protected goods, and the greater part of it went not to the revenue but to the interest protected: the actual revenue from duties levied in the interest of the protected manufacturers at that time was only half a million. One of the strong points of the Report with which the League made play was the effect of a protective tariff on wages. Foreign competition was necessarily most severe in the products of low wages; but in an exporting country like England other advantages might outweigh a disadvantage in the money cost of labour. Countries where wages were lowest did not of necessity manufacture most successfully—as is recognized to-day— and the working classes would be best served by an extension of commerce which would enlarge the field of labour. This important truth was triumphantly demonstrated within the next thirty years. The Committee, in effect, rejected Protection in practice, and recommended an immediate reform of the tariff which would retain import duties for revenue purposes on only a small number of articles of general consumption, and so permit the largest possible consumption of those articles and the largest possible yield to the State. The Committee prophesied —again with accuracy—that the result of this change of policy would be not a loss, but a considerable gain in revenue.

Peel's tariff proposals, prepared by Gladstone at the Board of Trade, put into force—though with one large reservation—the principles of the Report. Duties on 750 articles of importation were reduced. Raw materials and semi-manufactured goods came down to nominal figures; prohibitions were removed from fully manufactured goods, and protective duties greatly reduced. Peel claimed as his object the reduction of the cost of living, and it was a just claim. To make up the temporary loss of revenue, he put the income tax at sevenpence. In thus calling in direct taxation to redress the balance of reduced customs duties, he inaugurated a principle which has governed our fiscal system for nearly a century. It was indeed a revolutionary Budget.

Its merits were, however, obscured to the eyes of the Leaguers by its one great defect: it did not give Repeal. The Minister had a tactical reason for refusing Repeal—his leadership of a House in which the landed interest was supreme; but he also undoubtedly entertained at that time a conscientious scruple on the corn question—he hesitated to take a step which might make the nation dependent upon imports for its staple food. He therefore took a half measure, readjusting the sliding scale of the corn tax to maintain the price of wheat as nearly as possible at 56s. The actual amount of the duty with wheat at the price then prevailing would be 9s. As the duty under the old scale stood at 23s. the remission was considerable. Nevertheless, the protective effect of the scheme remained; bread could not fall to what Cobden called its "natural price," and the sugar duties were retained. The tariff which was to bring down the cost of living kept it at an artificial height in the two articles of greatest consumption, and therefore of greatest moment to the poorest people. The rents of the landlords of England and the profits of the planters of the West Indies were to be secured by the continued suffering of the artisans of the North, and the labourers of the South. The League consequently intensified rather than mitigated its campaign, acting in the spirit of the covenant between the two leaders: "We will never rest till the Corn Law is repealed."

Bright had, curiously enough, a juster appreciation of the meaning of Peel's Budget than Cobden, who was blinded by his anger at the retention of the Corn Tax and unreasonably suspicious of the income tax. Bright thought the scheme of the Budget "very beneficial." He criticized the income tax, not in principle, but because of the incidence of this particular measure which, he said, bore heavily on all industry except agrarian industry. The general exemption was £150; the farmers exemption £300; and the tax on agricultural incomes (calculated on rent) above £300 was halved. Bright advocated a property tax, which he said would be much fairer. Many of the principles he enunciated have since been applied in the form of estate duties and graduation. But to him these things were of minor concern compared with the all-important corn tax, and on this he instantly took his part in the task of setting the North in a blaze. Never were meetings so crowded and so angry, nor petitions so eagerly signed. The burning of Peel's effigy after it had been hanged on a gibbet was no part of the League's programme, but it became a ritual of the mob. The rage of the populace was fanned by its growing distress, which reached desperation point in 1842. The Queen's letter to the clergy ordering collections in church for the benefit of the starving served only to aggravate a people who knew that Parliament was denying to them the only remedy for starvation. The incident provoked an interesting letter from Cobden to Bright, suggesting that he should write on it in the *Circular*. The clergy, he said, almost to a man upheld the Corn Law and themselves had an interest in keeping up the price of bread. How futile to attempt to sustain the manufacturing population on charitable donations!—"the wages paid in the cotton trade amount to twenty millions a year. Reduce that amount even ten per cent.—and how can it be made up by charity?" Bright responded by developing the theme in the *Circular* of May 19.

But in the meantime an event of great significance had happened. At the end of February Cobden made his speech in the House against the Corn Law proposals in Peel's Budget. He accused the Government of legislating deliberately to keep up the price of food in the interests of the landlords. He destroyed the legend that cheap wages meant cheap labour, proving that England's comparatively high wage rate gave it the cheapest labour in the world. He denied that to depress the mass of the people could promote the prosperity of industry. "By deteriorating the population, of which they ought to be so proud," he declared, "they will run the risk of spoiling not merely the animal but the intellectual creature. It is not a potato-fed race that will ever lead the way in arts, arms, or commerce." The indictment stung. The country party put up Bousfield Ferrand (then member for Knaresborough) to reply with a *tu quoque*. Not for nothing was this ardent Young Englander known in later years as "Bully Ferrand." He pursued social reform with a ferocity worthy of a worse cause. He seemed unable to breathe any other air than violence. In later years, when Young England was no more and he might have been expected to mellow, it is recorded that Ferrand maintained his reputation for malignity by describing an eminently respectable Englishman, Sir Michael Seymour (who happened to be opposing him in an election at Devonport), as "a cowardly assassin" and his supporters as "liars" and "rascals." His talent for vituperation was now called in to turn the tables on the manufacturers, which he did first by a personal attack on Cobden, and then by a general onslaught on the whole tribe of industrialists. They were the true oppressors of the poor, not the corn taxers. They compelled their workmen to live in cottages which they owned and to pay unjustly high rents. They poisoned their workmen with "the vile rags and devil's dust which they used for the fraudulent adulteration of their cloth." If there were a scarcity of flour, that was because the manufacturers used it to make paste for dishonestly daubing the face of their calico! And so on.

Though there was a streak of truth in this—Bright acknowledged, in a letter about the incident to Cobden, that some employers did practise trucking and tyrannize in the matter of cottages and rents—Ferrand's gross farrago of malice and libel reflected the general ignorance of the country party about industrial life, and their bitter hatred of the industrialists. As Cobden said, a man could then be branded with no more decided stigma in the House of Commons than by calling him a mill-owner. But in the North, where the facts were known, Ferrand's outburst provoked a storm of resentment. It led Bright to do an unheard-of thing. On the 1st of March he attended the Exchange in Manchester and at one o'clock invited the members to go out on the pavement in Ducie Place to hold a meeting of protest. Scandalized officials tried to prevent him from making the appeal, but he got his meeting and was himself elected to the chair. He told the crowd that he had attended Change for the last two years and week by week had wondered what sort of men were those he met there, who crawled about grumbling at bad trade but dared not lift their hands against its cause. Then Henry Ashworth moved a petition to Parliament, Sir Thomas Potter seconded, and it was carried unanimously. "I spoke a few minutes," Bright wrote to Cobden; "Ferrand was denounced as a vile blackguard, the House warned of their doings. The whole passed off with great éclat, and everybody seemed pleased it was done."

But neither petitions, nor threats of wholesale passive resistance to the payment of taxes (suggested by O'Connell and toyed with by Cobden), or of the closing down of mills (considered by Bright as a possible means of persuasion) had any effect on Peel and the Government. The Budget passed and the new sliding scale of corn taxes came into operation. The League had a long road to travel yet. And it was a difficult road. In August, the workmen started their own movement of passive resistance in the pathetically ineffective strike known to history as the "great turn-out." They resisted the wrong people. The movement was, in fact, an ill-conceived spurt of Chartism—ill-designed because there were no funds to support it, and ill-timed because the manufacturers in a decaying market were utterly unable to pay the higher wages or give the shorter hours demanded. Though brief, the strike created some bad feeling. A few indiscreet employers itched for a fight. "I rebuked him," said Bright of one of these, and "defended the people. They ought to implore the Government to repeal the Corn Law." Perhaps the most notable result of the "turn-out" was that it prompted him to compose an address "to the Working Men of Rochdale" which not only had much to do with the peaceful ending of this particular folly, but also laid down in a few plain and vigorous paragraphs the principle that the liberation of trade from artificial restrictions was the common interest of employers and employees. This document is printed in full in the collection of Bright's letters edited by Mr. Leech.[1] In it he declared, with his usual acumen, that the principles of the Charter would one day be established. But they could not wait for that. "As intelligent men, you know you cannot raise wages by force . . . Your first step to entire freedom must be commercial freedom—freedom of industry. We must put an end to the partial famine which is destroying trade, the demand for your labour, your wages, your comforts and your independence . . . Every man who hastens by a single hour the abolition of the Corn Law shortens by so much the duration of your sufferings. Whilst the inhuman law exists, your wages must decline. When it is abolished, and not till then, they will rise. If every employer and workman in the Kingdom were to swear on their bended knees that wages should not fall, they would still assuredly fall if the Corn Law continues. No power on earth can maintain your wages at their present rate if the Corn Law be not repealed." He ended by saying that the doors of the Bright mills would be open whenever they wished to resume work. "I invite you to come,

[1] "The Public Letters of the Rt. Hon. John Bright, M.P." Collected and edited by H. J. Leech (1885).

and you shall be treated as I trust you have ever been—as I would ever wish you to treat me."

The men returned to work and Bright went back to the task of the League. Its Council had decided to raise the heroic fund of £50,000 that year, so that "literature" might be sent into the house of every elector in the kingdom and the band of lecturers and missionaries augmented. Despite the prevailing depression, the money had come in before the end of the session: industry was fighting for its life.

Bright spent the winter in that long pilgrimage away to the extreme North and into Scotland, with Cobden and Perronet Thompson, which excited *The Times* to speak of them as "capering mercenaries . . . frisking about the country." *The Times* no doubt knew better, and meant only to be offensive; for there was nothing mercenary about them. Cobden's absorption in the League's work brought him to financial disaster; the cost of the campaign to Bright was very heavy. But an incident which occurred a little later in the West of England shows how this irresponsible and unworthy accusation poisoned the air. At the same time it illustrates the dialectical method of the campaign. Bright, having addressed a great meeting in the Theatre Royal at Plymouth, went over the border to Devonport for another. Here the Tories had issued placards urging their supporters to "prevent the lecturer from boasting of his visit as a triumph"—an incitement which the nature of the proceedings rendered null. For, a local curate having challenged Bright to a debate, he accepted and a gladiatorial display of speech, reply, and counter-speech, lasting several hours so absorbed the crowd that the rowdies forgot to be disorderly. The Protectionist resolution moved by the curate had only a handful of supporters. Bright's amendment, moved in a speech described by a local reporter as "luminous and argumentative," was adopted with few dissentients. He told the crowd how pleased he was to travel to that far country to promote the repeal of the Corn Law. "Yes," shouted a voice, "and well paid for it!" "If I were paid for my services," said he, "it would not make me any the less regardful of the truth. If Mr. Thomas" (that was the curate's name) "ministers, he is remunerated by somebody. But the only compensation I have the honour of receiving is the joy of spreading true principles among my fellow subjects."

3

Bright entered Parliament in 1843. He himself was not eager to take this step. Business claims at Rochdale pressed him hard, and his relatives were opposed to his election as a break with the traditions of the Society of Friends. On the other hand, Cobden powerfully urged him forward.

His own sense of obligation to his less fortunate neighbours turned the scale. How strong this feeling was may be gauged by a letter in which he communed on the subject with his mother-in-law, Mrs. Priestman. It is the more deeply significant because he could never have supposed any eye but hers would read his words: "Conscious of the increasing hazard we run owing to the long continuance of monopolies, and beholding the appalling sufferings of multitudes of my fellow creatures, and satisfied that all benevolence and charity and the teaching of religion and of schools fall short of much of their full effect owing to the degraded and impoverished condition of the people, I should feel myself guilty—as possessing abundance and leaving others to hunger, nakedness and immorality, and deepest ignorance and crime—if I were to retire into domestic quiet and leave the struggle to be carried on entirely by others." The die was cast in April when a by-election took place in the City of Durham. He went down, was elected as Liberal candidate and in due course stood on the hustings to oppose Lord Dungannon, the Tory nominee.

Bright's personality and his frank, unaffected style of speech made him exceedingly popular with the multitude. But the multitude had no votes, and Lord Dungannon, who was in the field a week before him and had the backing of the Londonderry interest, polled 507 to his 405. After the election it transpired that Lord Dungannon possessed another advantage of which Bright knew nothing—the local custom of pricing votes at a sovereign apiece. Upon this discovery, at the instance of the League, a petition was filed. The evidence, taken before a committee of the House of Commons with Lord Ashley in the chair, showed that 300 electors had received the customary reward, and Lord Dungannon was unseated. Bright stood again at the consequent election in July, and this time defeated Mr. Purvis by 488 votes to 410. He won entirely on his advocacy of the repeal of the Corn Laws as the first interest of the working masses of the people, and the greatest need of British industry. "I am a working man as much as you," he said. ". . . I come before you as the friend of my own class and order; as one of the people; as one who would, on all occasions, be the firm defender of your rights, and the asserter of all those privileges to which you are justly entitled."

Rochdale rejoiced fervently over his victory. His own workers, demanding a holiday, celebrated it with processions and brazen music. The noise it made throughout the North and wherever the League was at work, rumbled into London, into Westminster, and even into Printing House Square, where *The Times* (certainly with no approval of a person like Bright) wrote of his return as a portent because in his candidature he had defied Whigs and Tories alike. *The Times* thus betrayed a keener sense of actuality than the *Chronicle*, which claimed the election as a Whig victory. At a League banquet at the "Crown and Anchor" the night after Bright had taken his seat, he himself declared that it was "not a party victory." It was, in fact, a League victory.

He made his maiden speech on August 7 during a debate on Import Duties. It was remarkable for a direct and prophetic address to Peel: "I should be glad to see the right honourable baronet not the Minister of the Queen merely, but the Minister of the people also. I should rejoice to see him disconnect himself from the party whose principles he declares to be unsound. I should be glad to see him bearing in mind the source from which he has sprung, the source of his power and wealth, as it is the source of much of the power and wealth and greatness of this Empire."

The curious incident of Peel's attack on Cobden in February, of Brougham's support of Peel, and of the castigation which Bright administered to Brougham, occurred before he entered Parliament. An allusion to it will be found in 1857, when Bright had composed his quarrel with Brougham and sought to visit him at Cannes. Its practical importance lay not in the circumstances of the dispute, but in the psychological repulsion and attraction between Peel and Bright which it revealed. Peel was the son of a cotton-spinner, as Bright reminded the Extraordinary Meeting of the League held at Manchester (February 23). If the Prime Minister had followed his father's trade, said Bright, he would have been a Leaguer. He ought to have been a Leaguer. He proclaimed Free Trade views. When he was asked why he did not enforce them, he replied that this was not the time. "When will be the time?" asked Bright. "Do you think Monopoly is about to become just, merciful and generous? Do you think that, having gorged themselves for a few years more on the spoils of your industry, they will be more likely to . . . give up freely that which they now refuse to you? I tell you that it is a hypocritical pretence to say that this is not the time. It is now the time: the hour is now striking." Thus early he clearly had Peel in view as the statesman who would repeal the Corn Laws.

But the hour did not strike for two years. It was delayed until the winter of 1845 by the fact that the Free Trade elements of Peel's Budget of 1842 combined with a run of good harvests to brighten the prospects of industry and to ease the woes of the people. But the League not only kept a steady course towards Repeal; it increased the pressure. The fund of £50,000 raised in 1842 was followed by a fund of £100,000 the next year.

After Durham, the League (which had already begun the monthly demonstrations at Covent Garden Opera House regularly addressed by Bright and W. J. Fox) tackled the formidable task of winning a by-election in the City of London. "Come up!" Bright wrote to Cobden, then at Manchester. "*We* must do it, if it be done. And Repeal is not far off when this election is won. No one dare afterwards contest a borough against the League. *Le jour viendra*. I have not been in bed for two nights, but am not much tired." Assailed in this spirit, the City of London surrendered. Pattison, the League candidate, defeating Baring by 6,535 votes to 6,334. City opinion began increasingly to be cast on the side of the League.

More important, the League carried the war into the country-side. It had already converted a few of the big Whig landlords; now it went out for the farmers. In the extraordinary rural campaign of 1843 and 1844, the combination of Cobden and Bright on the platform was even more effective than in the great town meetings. Cobden arguing and persuading, Bright hot-gospelling and raising an economic cause to the heights of a religious crusade, they swept through the country north and south, east and west, meeting with a little political or social opposition at first, but soon becoming invincible. The meetings often took the shape of tournaments between the League speakers and their opponents, and they lasted for hours. The labourers naturally hailed the League as a deliverer; but the labourers, like the miners in Durham, had no votes. Cobden and Bright triumphed by convincing the farmers that Protection had never benefited them and could not benefit them—that Protection meant high rents, and high prices for all they consumed or used, while the artificial raising of agricultural prices diminished the general prosperity, and in the end defeated itself by reducing consumption. The experience of many years of high Protection had put the farmers in a mood to listen to arguments. By the end of 1844 the League met with no opposition at all in the rural districts. "If a silly squire or a foolish farmer attempted any disturbance or interference," wrote Bright, "these round-frocked men (the labourers) were all around us in an instant, ready to defend us."

It was now that Bright wrote in his Diary, after a brief record of his goings and comings during 1843, the reasoned statement of his position to which reference was made above:

"Corn Law.

"Monopoly of the home market given to the proprietors of the British soil, under pretence of public good. Monopoly presupposes some advantage to those who possess it.

"It gives to them the possession of the market and excludes foreign grown corn in order that in a market insufficiently supplied they may obtain a higher price than their corn is really worth. This higher price can only be obtained by preventing the food market being as abundantly supplied as it would be if the regular laws of commerce were not interfered with. This higher price therefore exists and is procurable only from the existence of scarcity intentionally created by law.

"This increased value places the food out of reach of those whose means are most limited, whilst the more wealthy classes are still able to procure as much as they require. The pressure of scarcity comes then upon the poorest portion of the people.

"In a besieged city the rich and powerful can hold out longest— the poor and defenceless feel famine soonest.

"This law-made famine is unequal, sparing the rich and crushing the poor.

"Famine on board ship at sea would be equally borne by all. Admiral and cabin-boy would share the biscuits, but as the Corn Law scarcity is created for the especial benefit of one class, it is but likely that all the suffering should be averted from that class.

"The scarcity affects various portions of the community in the inverse ratio of their power to endure it. The labourers probably are the only class that feel it in a positive insufficiency of food, and of these the weakest and poorest, whose labour is least valuable and least skilled, bear the greatest intensity of the suffering. Thus Hand-loom Weavers and Farm Labourers are always heavy sufferers from scarcity.

"That portion of the population, a portion of whose food is thus withheld, or who are in consequence of the high prices of their usual food driven to articles of a lower quality, are evidently prevented from continuing or becoming consumers or purchasers of manufactured goods, clothing, furniture, hardware, earthenware, etc., and thus the demand for these articles declines so soon as a serious advance in the price of food takes place.

"Not only is the demand for manufactured goods cut off so far as this portion of the people are concerned, but a class, probably quite numerous, above them in the social scale find it as much as they can do to provide food enough of their usual quality, and are compelled greatly to restrict their purchases of articles of manufacture, and to discontinue the consumption of many of them, and thus also all persons engaged in manufacturing pursuits find their customers impoverished, and the demand for their labour partially or wholly destroyed."

Throughout his life whenever his Free Trade position was challenged, Bright returned the same answer. Abundance was the first and the greatest interest of the people. Even in bad times—it was his argument during the agricultural depression of 1879—people suffered far less than they did in the terrible years from 1839 to 1842. He met the "Fair Trade" agitation of the 'eighties in the same way. "To imagine that your suffering springs from hostile tariffs is absurd, because you have had great prosperity under the same tariffs," he told an advocate of reciprocity; "but to suppose your case will be improved by refusing to buy what you want from foreigners, to punish them for not buying freely from you, seems to me an idea and a scheme only worthy of the inmates of a lunatic asylum." "The true course for England is to open her ports as widely and completely as possible whatsoever may be the tariffs of other countries." "If you doubt what Free Trade has done for England, go back to your histories and read what was the condition of our working men and their families for the first forty years of this century, when everything was supposed to be protected, and compare it with what it is now." He had a solid economic foundation for his conviction, but the conviction itself was purely humane: protection injured the poorest and weakest part of society, and therefore, whatever else it wrought, it was evil.

It appeared likely when the year 1844 opened that Repeal could not come before the next General Election. The pressure upon the Government was somewhat relaxed by the better harvests which eased the cost of living and by the operation of Peel's tariff reform which had already stimulated trade. The League therefore betook itself in hard earnest to the winning of the election whenever it should come. The Reform Act of 1832 had left the big towns much under-represented and had kept in being a large number of small boroughs; the electoral system was still heavily weighted in the landed interest. Cobden now produced an ingenious scheme to secure a footing for the Free Traders in the counties. Every Free Trader who could raise the small amount of capital required was persuaded to buy up a "forty shilling freehold," which would give him a county vote. It was a piece of tactics which neatly countered the manufacture on the other side of "faggot votes" by the landlords, who, as Cobden said, made "brothers, sons, nephews and uncles of their tenant farmers qualify for the same holding" by swearing that they were partners in the farm.

Bright entered heartily into the scheme, and large numbers of voters were added to the register. "We shall make short work of some of the monopolist county seats at another election," he wrote. ". . . It is now the towns against the squires, and the towns will win." About £250,000 was said to have been invested in these freeholds. In the three counties of Lancashire, Cheshire and Yorkshire, five thousand "forty shilling freeholders" were put on the register, and the same process went on all over the country. Long afterwards he was accused of having indulged in the manufacture of faggot votes in order to win an election. His reply (addressed in 1879 to the *Birmingham Daily Post*) has an academic interest: "The votes . . . were obtained by the real possession of a real property. The faggot votes to which objection is made are created by a deed giving a rent-charge upon a property for which it is understood nothing is paid, and on which nothing is received; the whole thing being on parchment and no real ownership being created or intended." Apart from the "registration" movement, however, 1844 was a year of educational rather than of political progress for the Leaguers. In Parliament they did rather less well than before. In the happily improved condition of the country, the old apologue of the devil sick and the devil well might have been aptly applied to it. Bright's speech in support of Villiers's annual motion for Repeal was heard with less patience than the House would have displayed in a year of acute distress, and it was just at this time that he fell upon his notorious difference with Lord Ashley.

4

It is difficult to understand the opposition of a passionate humanitarian, as Bright was, to the admirable factory legislation advocated by Lord Ashley, without recreating the atmosphere of the time—an atmosphere of intense antagonism between the supporters of the policy of cheap and abundant food and the supporters of the Corn Laws. Lord Ashley proposed to limit by law the hours of labour in the factories, but left the agricultural industry alone. Bright prophesied and believed that a reduction of factory hours would mean a reduction of the wages earned. As a matter of history it did not; but before the Factories Acts of 1847 and 1850 were passed, Free Trade had been established and the Corn Laws repealed, so that the circumstances were completely changed. Bright always declared that without Repeal his prophecy would have been fulfilled; possibly he was right.

During the controversies with Lord Ashley in 1844, however, Bright saw in him the representative of a class living on an industry whose conditions were worse than those of the cotton factories, an industry in which the hours of labour were unlimited and the wages microscopic. Lord Ashley at that time, with the rest of his class, refused the repeal of the Corn Law which alone could give their labourers a decent existence. That was his offence. Bright's own firm were employing something over 500 workpeople, and paying wages ranging from 6s. 3d. for the youngest girl to 16s. for adult males. The rates compared favourably with the prevailing earnings of the day, and sensationally with the wages of the farm labourers. The firm also maintained a school for the children, an adult school, a reading-room and a news-room. Bright said, with humour and truth, that the country party "when they view from their distant eminence the state of the manufacturing districts, look through the right end of the telescope; what they see is thus brought near to them and greatly magnified. But when they are asked to look at the rural districts they reverse the telescope, and then everything is thrown to the greatest possible distance and is diminished as much as possible." His position was that while the protection of children by law against parents and employers who would work them improperly was just and necessary, the relations of adults with their employers should be left for settlement between them without State interference. He did not himself believe in long hours of labour. He was as emphatic as Lord Ashley in proclaiming that a ten hours day was quite long enough. "But," he told the House of Commons, "I differ on the point whether a reduction of time ought to be carried out by the Legislature or by a regulation between the masters and the operatives themselves." He stood firm on that principle, and held the position to the end. It was not an equivocal position, as his critics have continually suggested when fulminating against the Manchester School. "I still hold the opinion," he wrote in answer to a newspaper criticism forty years later, "that to limit by law the time during which adults may work is unwise and in many cases oppressive. . . . You may remind the writer that I sought to give the workman two loaves of bread when his party wished to give him only one."

This year Bright couched a lance at another dragon. If the Corn Laws were the enemies of abundance, so were the Game Laws, and he attacked them with equal vigour. He scored one of his earliest Parliamentary successes when he forced the Government to grant a committee of inquiry into these laws. Game preservation was in his view an unmitigated evil for the farmer, and involved the nation in social disturbance and severe loss; but his chief indictment against the Game Laws was that they increased scarcity. Looking back to the nightmare of 1839–42, he declared that in that period game destroyed "as large a quantity of the produce of the soil of England as the whole amount we imported from abroad." Preparing the bomb he was to explode on the Government at the beginning of 1845, he collected during the winter a great body of exact evidence. He worked up the statistics of farmers' losses; he got together a moving story of the poacher's underworld, its robbery and violence and the legal retaliations upon it which created infinite bitterness; he procured records of the actual destruction of food by game. The farmers began to see in him the most effective champion of one of their greatest grievances; in this matter they "swore by him." And when he put his case before the House of Commons he did it with a restrained realism and an absence of virulence which robbed the country party of all excuse for ignoring or denouncing him. No Ferrand was put up to slay him; instead Sir James Graham thanked him for his tone and temper, confessed that he had made out a case, and gave him his Committee.

The inquiry bore no fruit in legislation then, but it had two important results: it modified the hideous severity with which poachers were punished, and it induced in landlords a spirit of greater accommodation to injured farmers. What was immediately vital in this movement, however, was its effect upon the campaign against the Corn Laws. The farmers who "swore by" Bright because of his championship of their interests against the game-preservers, were the more inclined to listen to his advocacy of Free Trade.

But in truth by the spring of 1845 the battle of Free Trade was won. The League had converted the country. Peel's Budget of that year carried on the work of tariff extinction and reduction, and left no doubt of his ultimate acquiescence in the full doctrine. The success of the measures already taken made it certain. The revival of industry and commerce between 1842 and 1845 was not entirely but in large measure the result of Peel's first step towards Free Trade in the former year, and from this point onward he was the predestined instrument for the final conversion of Parliament.

5

"Trade continues good," wrote Bright to Margaret Priestman at the New Year, "and throughout the cotton district there is a manifest improvement in the condition and temper of all classes. We hope to make this perpetual." They founded the rosy hope on the conviction that Repeal was now not far off. Yet in fact, though Repeal was accomplished within a year, the very success of Peel's tentative tariff reforms would probably have delayed the establishment of the free market for food at least till another election had passed but for the fatal conjunction of a frightful outbreak of potato disease in Ireland and a disastrous harvest in England. That summer, and well into the second half of the year, the League thought even intenser efforts than any yet made would be needed to force the hand of the House of Commons. But then first came the dire news from Ireland, which in a potato-fed country meant famine. And next came the autumn rain, which meant famine in England also if England persisted in trying to feed itself on home-grown corn. The transformation was immediate, and by October Repeal seemed imminent. Peel and Graham agreed that the Corn Laws must be suspended, and admitted that once withdrawn they could never be re-imposed. In the last week of the month Bright told Margaret Priestman that the Corn Laws were "on their last legs." He expected that the ports would be opened by an Order in Council, "and if they are we shall make it difficult to close them again. On every hand there is expectation that we shall have repeal next session. Our fear is of a partial measure, a fixed duty or a lower scale; but I have some faith that Peel will do the thing completely when he next touches it." But the very finality of the step prevented Peel and Graham, Aberdeen and Herbert, who all saw it inevitable, from carrying their colleagues with them then. Accordingly in the last two months of the year, after the frequent Cabinet meetings of the first week of November had come to naught and left things as they were, the League sprang into new and still more volcanic activity. Bright, with Cobden, worked as he had never worked before, rushing north and south to address crowded meetings day after day—Manchester, Sheffield, Leeds, Wakefield, Bradford, on successive days of one week; then Gloucester, Stroud, Bath, Bristol, Nottingham, Derby, Stockport, with hardly a day's grace between. It was a labour of Hercules, but it was worth while. The swelling force of the campaign became resistless when Lord John Russell wrote (November 28) the celebrated Edinburgh letter abandoning his half-way house of a "moderate fixed duty," came down on the side of total repeal, and brought the Whig Party with him. "Lord John Russell's adhesion made the victory of the League certain," wrote Lord Morley. "Mr. Bright happened to be on the platform of a railway station in Yorkshire as Lord John Russell passed through on his way from the North to Osborne. He stepped into his carriage for a few moments. 'Your letter,' said Mr. Bright, 'has now made the total and immediate repeal of the Corn Law inevitable; nothing can save it.' The letter had in fact done no less than this." Peel called his Ministers together, and on December 4 *The Times* announced that Parliament would meet in January and that the Government would at once ask it to repeal the Corn Laws. The celebrated announcement was premature. Peel again failed to carry his Cabinet. The confused transactions of the first two weeks of December—the resignation of Peel, the failure of Russell to form a Ministry, the recall of Peel—dashed the hopes which had inspired Bright on the morning when at Stroud he read the statement of *The Times*; and the League drove on harder than ever. It packed Covent Garden Theatre with the biggest audience it had ever assembled in London, and Bright, in his best form, thrilled it with an analogy between this desperate conflict with the landed interests and the ancient struggle of their ancestors against the Crown. "If they refused to be the bondmen of a King, shall we be the born thralls of an aristocracy like ours?" A louder knell than this sounded in the ears of the Protectionists when the League (having already raised £100,000 the year before, and with £250,000 invested in forty shilling freeholds) at this eleventh hour inaugurated a new campaign fund of £250,000 (Manchester, December 23), £60,000 of which was subscribed at the first meeting. Bright regaled Miss Priestman with an account of "the most extraordinary meeting, probably, ever held in the Kingdom. It lasted from 11 to 3 o'clock on the market day. Exchange and dinner hour alike disregarded—crowded and earnest to a degree heretofore unequalled." Bright Bros. were one of twenty-five firms which subscribed a thousand pounds each. It was the last triumphant effort. Six months later (July 2) the League had done its work and was disbanded.

Peel came back to office at Christmas, at last with a Cabinet pledged to Repeal, and announced his policy on February 16. Bright described to his sister that famous occasion: "Peel delivered the best speech I ever heard in Parliament. It was a truly magnificent speech, sustained throughout, thoroughly with us, and offering even to pass the immediate (repeal) if the House are willing. Villiers, Gibson and myself cheered continually, and I never listened to any human being speaking in public, with so much delight." He put some of that feeling next day into the form of a spirited defence of Peel against the execration which his former allies now poured upon him, and especially of his conduct during the December crisis. Experience having shown the Minister that it was impossible to retain office and the Corn Laws at the same time, said Bright to the angry Protectionists, he resigned: "he was then no longer your Minister; he came back to office as the Minister of his Sovereign and of the people." Of Peel's speech on the 16th, he said, "Wherever there is a man who loves justice, and wherever there is a labourer whom you have trampled underfoot, that speech will bring joy to the heart of the one and hope to the breast of the other."

The internal convulsions which rent the Tory Party and for many years paralysed it into impotence are no part of Bright's story. The great fight was over, and he turned to other causes which brought him into stern conflict impartially with Whig and Tory. The League's victory—and no one denied that the League had won the victory, Peel least of any—was at once a consummation and a starting-point. Bright, seconding the resolution for the liquidation of the League a week after Repeal had passed the House of Lords, said it had taught the people the value of a great principle. "They have learned that there is in public opinion a power much greater than that residing in any particular form of government ... and ... that the way to freedom is henceforward not through violence and bloodshed." The deep purport of the lessons in democratic principle and political tactics learned in these five years is seen in every subsequent campaign of his life.

A single extract from his diary of the great Free Trade year has been preserved:

"[1846; 7 mo. 28].—Division on Sugar duties resolutions:—For, 265; Agt., 135; 130 majority.

"In the Lobby was alongside Sir R. Peel. Asked if he was recovered from his late accident, his foot having been cut by the breaking of a china basin.

"Sir R. inquired if I had been in Lancashire lately and what was doing. Said I had, and that the people were delighted with the results of the Session, and I wished personally to thank him for his great services to the cause of Free Trade.

"Sir R. said he had had no conception of the depth of feeling which had possessed the public mind on the question, especially in Scotland, where he thought every town and village almost were unanimous on the question. He remarked, how happy it was the question was settled, and what a condition we should have been in now when the blight in the potatoes was making so much progress. He hoped the use of Indian meal was extending and that suffering would be avoided.

"I told him it was greatly extending in Lancashire, at which he expressed his gratification, and said he felt great pleasure at the satisfaction evident among the working classes at what had been done. I told him I thought no Minister had ever retired from office more universally regretted. He added, 'or more execrated by the Monopolists,' and laughed with the consciousness of the victory which had been won."

Only one episode of the Corn Law period remains to be recorded. In September, 1845, Cobden wrote to tell Bright that he had resolved on retiring from politics in order to save his business from the disaster which threatened it owing to his long devotion to public affairs. Morley made classic Bright's wonderful letter in reply, and Mr. Trevelyan has dealt quite fully with the incident. Sufficient to relate that the correspondence reveals in a glowing light the spiritual brotherhood of the two men, and that the sequel—in which Bright and his friends in Manchester raised a fund to free Cobden's business from embarrassment, and save Cobden himself for the League—is creditable both to the public spirit and the private generosity of a memorable body of Englishmen.

CHAPTER V

A VICTORIAN LOVE STORY

I

FREE Trade won, Bright turned for a brief space to his private concerns before going forward to the battle of Irish freedom and electoral reform. The day after his talk with Peel, he wrote to Cobden:

"[*July* 29, 1846.] I confess that I am seeking the good opinion of a lady for whom I have long felt a high regard, and have some hope of being successful. . . . It is pleasant, after the Seven Years' War of the League, to look to domestic peace."

The lady whose good opinion he sought was Miss Elizabeth Leatham, of Heath, near Wakefield.

He was now thirty-five, a widower, a national celebrity, a vigorous intellect, a great orator, but naturally a little set and serious in his mental habits. On his thirty-fifth birthday he wrote: ". . . So half the time allotted by the Psalmist is over and the latter half has begun. This is a solemn consideration, and it startles me every birthday to think how the sands of life are flowing out and how little has been done in the years that are past." Nevertheless, the story of his second courtship and marriage is a beautiful idyll.

His one brief year of supreme happiness with Elizabeth Priestman and the tragedy of her death were six years away. His little Helen, the light of his life during all that time of mourning, was six years old. "One Ash" seemed lonely. Public duties and private business anxieties pressed hard on him. Then, in 1845,[1] he met Margaret Elizabeth

---

[1] On the eve of the triumph of the League (Nov. 29, 1845) he wrote to Margaret Priestman: "On 6th day morning, before leaving Wakefield, I called on W. H. Leatham at the bank. He is not fully converted, but he said his mother had been, by reading my speech or speeches. . . . She has given her son £5 to send to the League, so I thought I ought to walk up and thank her, which I did. I took dinner with them, that is with Margaret Leatham and her daughter."

Leatham, the daughter of William Leatham, then dead, a banker, of Wakefield. The firm, eminent in Yorkshire in the heyday of local banks, was Leatham, Tew & Co. Gurney Barclay, then at the head of Barclay's Bank, married Miss Leatham's sister. Two of her brothers subsequently became Members of Parliament—William Henry Leatham, who sat as a Yorkshire County Member, and Edward Aldam Leatham, who represented Huddersfield.

Miss Leatham was a charming girl of twenty-four, serious-minded but of a cheerful and open disposition—greatly attracted by the earnest and vivid man whose interest in her was so keen, but a little timid of his intensity. Her family, Quakers of the old school, at first displayed no enthusiasm whatever for the idea of an alliance. The now vanished prejudice among the landed and professional classes against the "taint of trade" was still active in an era when society was still purely aristocratic, and no tradesman could find a doorway into the halls of the governing classes. The private banker of that day, whether Conformist or Nonconformist, held himself on a different plane from that of the manufacturer and merchant. And Bright, notwithstanding his great popularity and his political eminence, was after all a Radical cotton-spinner from Rochdale. Furthermore, he never took any trouble to conceal himself under any pretensions whatever. He would not, even at Wakefield, tone down his democratic prepossessions, mitigate his deadly criticism of the aristocratic system, modify his opinions or subdue their expression. In a word, he would not be anything but John Bright. When, therefore, his acquaintance with Miss Leatham developed (as it soon did) first into admiration and then into ardent love, he had to cut his way to her through a forest of prejudice. The Leatham family's final capitulation was one of the finest of all the tributes to John Bright's quality.

The correspondence with Miss Leatham, which began soon after their early meetings, is the best authority for the life of Bright during the years following the repeal of the Corn Laws. He first wrote in July, 1846, and from that time onwards he sent her a letter almost every day he was away from her side, until her death thirty-two years afterwards. It is no exaggeration to say that the love he revealed to her in a walk near her home in the summer of 1846 strengthened and deepened with every year that passed.

2

No one can read without emotion, even eighty years after they were written, Bright's letters during the first twelve months of their acquaintance. They rise through all the gamut of the lover's fear and hope and rapture from the humility of the suitor to the triumph of the accepted. They leave an overwhelming sense of the exquisiteness of Bright's character, his sensibility and his spotless honour as well as the richness and strength of his intellect.

At first, Miss Leatham was uncertain of herself. She liked him. She admired him. The ardour of his temperament, his mastery, his candour, his achievements, were fascinating to the young woman living sheltered amid the quiet refinements of a wealthy Quaker home; but she found it all a little disturbing. For some months she withheld a definite promise. His plea to her is contained in a long series of urgent letters, reinforced by visits wherever and whenever he could contrive them.

"I daresay thou thinks me somewhat rugged as to the outward habits and manners," he said in the first letter after his declaration. "And I am sensible that Nature has not gifted me with the qualities of which many are possessed; but I have a heart to feel emotions far more tender than I can give utterance to, and I often long for that sympathy which is only possible in the union of heart and interests which I seek.

"At first I admired thee as a girl, shall I say, of frank and agreeable manner. Then as one entertaining noble and generous sentiments. Now I know thee to be pure in motive, benevolent and warm in heart, of cultivated mind and of refined affections; and do not blame me if I say that I love thee with a strength of sentiment which I had ceased to expect I might feel again.

"What can I say more? That I have not more to offer thee is in some degree my fault, but perhaps more my misfortune. If I were better as a man, more intelligent and informed and amiable, had higher position and greater wealth—all I am and have is for thee and offered to thee. Only in one thing can I suppose myself on a level with thee—in the reality of the love I feel; and, in the consciousness that I am favourably regarded by thee and respected, I shall be, so far as love and tenderness are concerned, all that I can promise. I have told thee all this many times when conversing with thee, and yet I repeat it as if it were new! . . ."

She pens a shy answer to the hurricane lover. He responds: "I am very grateful for thy note, short as it is, in acknowledgment of mine. Thou told me that caution was prominent in thy character, and I cannot deny it seeing that the first letter I am privileged to receive from thee gives proof of it. And yet I love that little note because it is thine. . . .

But I will have faith. . . . My dearest!—am I heaping up disappointment to myself, or only anticipating what I may know more of in days to come?" And again, at short intervals: "Our correspondence seems rather one-sided so far. Nevertheless, I do not complain. . . . I think of thee almost continually and often wonder art thou ever thinking of me—favourably, I mean, and with a prospect of decision in my favour. . . . Whilst I am admiring thy caution, I am hoping that it may be feeling somewhat satisfied, and that when I come down thou mayst be prepared to say rather more than heretofore about the future." "This short, hurried note is not worth sending, except that I wish to have the opportunity of again telling thee how tenderly I love thee, and it is sweet to me to write even if thou art not yet at liberty to respond."

His pleading grew more fervent as the weeks went on. His mother-in-law, Mrs. Priestman, thought re-marriage a proper thing and this a most suitable marriage, and lent him her influence. His sister Priscilla added hers. Gradually, the reserves of the Leatham household were broken down, and Miss Leatham yielded to his insistence and her own inclination. For nearly three months he had written to her almost daily, had enlisted Milton in his aid (and reinforced Milton with William Cullen Bryant). He had pictured for her the alterations he was making at "One Ash" in the hope that she would become its mistress. He had awakened her sympathy with his beloved little Helen. He had walked and ridden with her at Harrogate. There had been a suggestion of a business visit to America: he rejoiced that he had not gone, because "I have been far happier spending some days with thee and writing to thee, and reading thy kind notes. I cannot tell thee how often I have read them. . . ." Some friends at Rochdale got married and left: this diminution of his circle was an additional reason why she should come and enlarge it. In the fashion of lovers from the beginning of Time, he pressed Heaven and earth into the service of his cause.

The citadel began to show signs of distress in the early days of October. The note of triumph crept into his letters when he was permitted to pay a visit to Heath about that time—a note of certainty that he would return with the guerdon in his possession. "I feel delighted that I can hope within twenty-four hours from this to be with thee. . . . I seem always to tell thee the same things—of my love of thee and of the manner in which thou art constantly before me, and of the longing I have that thou shouldst accept me as thy dearest friend. . . ."

He spent a week at Wakefield. At the end of it they were engaged.

Miss Leatham surrendered during a walk on the 20th of October. His early letters had been inscribed to "My very dear friend, Margaret Elizabeth Leatham." That night he wrote to her exultantly, "My beloved Elizabeth!—What an eventful day is this to me and thee! Thy goodness to me filled my heart with joy." And on the next day, "Thou wast very kind yesterday, and thy tender confession compensated me for all the anxieties I have endured. When I left thee yesterday, thou looked tender and kind at me: doubt seemed all but if not entirely gone, and confidence had taken its place." As usual in his moments of high emotion, he flew to his Milton. "This afternoon I have been reading the fourth book of *Paradise Lost*. It is a wonderful work, and Milton was surely right when he said such works were only fitly done by inspiration of God and after devout and earnest prayer." Then the beloved little Helen must be brought into his paradise. "Helen . . . is very beautiful to-day, and sweet in temper as usual, and has said her reading lesson well and written in her little copy-book. I look at her even with increased interest now, and when I look at her I think of thee and of thy kindness to me and her." And again a few days after: "My dearest, I look forward to thy kind care of her with many grateful feelings towards thee. If it be permitted for those who are gone to know anything of what is done here, her sainted mother too will be grateful that a tender care is vouchsafed to her dear child."

His sister Priscilla told him he was too old for "a romantic attachment," and must conduct himself very soberly. "I think I have done so," he wrote to Miss Leatham. But while no frenzy of passion need be looked for in his letters, they burn with a hot and steady flame. "I feel very happy in the assurance of thy affection and often make resolutions in my own mind that I will strive to deserve it. How strange it seems that all my anxieties and wishes having reference to thee should come to this at last! Dost thou ever look over the past and trace the little incidents which have marked it and which to me seem like steps by which I have gradually gained the proud and happy position thou now permits me to occupy? My dearest Elizabeth!—after all thy three months' deliberation, thou now admits I was right at the first. I told thee I was not mistaken, and now we both agree and see matters in the same light. Many thanks to thee. Words are utterly incapable to express how grateful I am to thee. . . ."

"I write as if I were assured thy sentiments were just like mine, forgetting that thou art too young yet to be 'wildly in love,' and yet possibly I may be right in believing that thy heart is sensibly touched

HELEN PRIESTMAN BRIGHT

and that words of tenderness from me meet with a fitting response. . . . Dearest Elizabeth, forgive all this if it seems hardly matter-of-fact enough for a letter from me. If my heart feels such things towards thee, may I not utter them?"

He went to Ben Rhydding, near Ilkley, for a "cure"—some trouble in the throat. "Do not think many waters can quench my love for thee. . . . What a terrible thing is *etiquette* that thou cannot come here for a day or two, however much at leisure at home." "It is a most pleasant thing to think that thou art willing to be mine, and that often in the day thy heart turns to mine as mine turns to thine with a fond hope that each may contribute to the happiness of the other. I hope now thou hast almost or altogether got rid of thy doubts and fears, and that thou canst entirely believe that I love thee with all my heart." "The incredulous, when once convinced, are often the most firm in believing. Thou wert incredulous for weeks and months. Now, I trust, thou wilt atone for the past by present and future confidence."

If she is cautious, he is frankness itself. He will not have her under any false notions as to his character and habits and the probable course of their married life. "I think, dear, we have the consolations of all the soothsayers, young and old, almost. . . . I do not fear myself, except that sometimes I am not quite sure that I shall drop into the regularity and quiet of domestic and married life so completely as thou wilt wish me to do. Priscilla has allowed me, or I have taken, great liberty, and therefore I shall put in a plea for great indulgence and allowance on thy part—at least till I become again accustomed to the yoke. But thine will not be a severe yoke. Love makes even fetters pleasant, and, loving as we hope to love each other, I have a strong confidence we shall contribute to each other's happiness."

He would not, however, have been John Bright if his letters had consisted entirely of protestations of devotion. He wished his bride to be interested in the things that interested him. He told her of his intellectual as well as of his emotional exercises. He recommended to her his poets and explained to her his politics. She received what according to modern ideas would be a very liberal allowance of Milton; but as experience proved it was not a surfeit. "After tea" (at a family party) "it was proposed that we should have some reading, and I was employed to read *Paradise Regained*, which I read through in about two hours. It is a noble and most devout poem, and I think we all felt that the time had been well spent. It is wonderful how Milton maintains the simplicity and dignity of the Scripture account of the

Temptation of Christ, and how he impresses his reader with the truth and solemnity of what he writes. The more I know of this, my favourite author, the more I admire and love him; and some day I hope thou and I may enjoy to read him together in our own comfortable library. . . ." That dream was realized in due course. Some lines of Whittier appeared in the *Manchester Examiner*. "Don't omit to read the poetry in the *Examiner* to-day. I think it very beautiful. Whittier seems a true poet—poet and prophet both, and his muse is on the side of liberty and mercy."

"I wish thee," he wrote, "to be interested in the things that interest me, as I shall always like to know something of those in which thou art engaged." He had been telling her the trade news from America—a fine season and good crops—and his hopes that this would react favourably on Lancashire. "Perhaps thou art not accustomed to hear much about matters of business. I think them of great importance to ourselves and to the country, and therefore speak of them; and I have no sympathy with the school which asserts that such things do not come within the province of ladies. . . . This seems a letter of business and many details. Its chief object, however, is to say that I tenderly love thee and am always grateful to thee, and that I am for ever thy devoted friend, *John Bright*."

All his life, after he had become a national figure, he was pestered by applications for his portrait—and the portrait was a laborious performance in the days before easy photography. "To-day I have been kept at home by unexpected visitors—first a Mr. Black, an artist, who came over to make a sketch of my personal appearance for the purpose of making a lithographic portrait to be published by the editors of the *Manchester Times*. It is a sort of martyrdom, this sitting for portraits and being exposed for sale afterwards, and in this case I made a great sacrifice of my own inclination for fear the *Times* should say I refused to sit because I did not wish to give them any advantage over the *Examiner* —these portraits being a common method of adding to the sale of a newspaper." [1]

He was taking the waters at Ben Rhydding. "My baths are just as before. The bath man says I should like them better if I were worse in health; but, not being ill, I hardly know what good they can do. I hear that one of the bathing women (attendants on the ladies) is an

---

[1] Bright's intimate connexion with the *Manchester Examiner* extended over many years. He wrote for it constantly, both at this period and after its amalgamation with the *Manchester Times*.

'adorer' of me. She is a most enthusiastic Leaguer, and once went some miles to Keighley to hear me speak. She asks the bathing man if he does not consider it a great honour to attend me. He says he does not know, 'but, if it were Prince Halbert, he would bath him!' "

But, whatever material, grave or gay, he works into his letters to the beloved one, he comes back to the leitmotiv in every other page. These lines from the missive of Christmas Day will serve to sum them all up: "I love to think thy mind is pretty much made up, and that thou now feels as if thy future course were linked closely with mine. May I not think so? I am building my house with that hope. I am thinking of it daily, hourly. I am picturing my future plans with thee. I am living with them and for them, and already in my heart thou hast adopted my precious little girl. May I not, then, deem thee mine, and all that concerns thee or me concerns us both? What a precious thing is that mysterious sympathy which binds hearts together and makes them one! . . . I feel that I am a happier and a better man since I have cared for thee and since I have had ground of hope that thou wouldst care for me."

While Bright courted Miss Leatham, Manchester wooed him. His long political connexion with the City began at the end of 1846. The ardent Free Traders of Manchester, knowing for how much he had counted in their victory, were naturally eager for closer relations. Negotiations to secure his candidature at the next Parliamentary election opened in the summer. In August, when he went down to Durham for a dinner given in his honour by the Mayor and Corporation, they were in full swing. He himself looked upon membership for Manchester as an honour for a Lancashire man, and it was geographically a more convenient constituency for him than Durham. It would involve heavy labour, as he told Miss Leatham, but—"I love the manufacturing districts on many grounds and shall chiefly rejoice in being returned for Manchester because it may enable me better to defend the rights and interests and character of the population among whom I live."

Not all the Free Trade Whigs in that population, however, were enamoured of the idea that the sturdy Radical Bright should represent them. A scheme was hatched between the "United Tories and Rene- gade Whigs" for putting up an aristocratic Whig candidate (in the person of Lord Lincoln) who would at once give adherence to Free Trade and cut a more conventional figure in politics than the outspoken

Quaker cotton-spinner, upon whom tradition and party ties sat so lightly that it was never known what he would say next.

On this, a newspaper war broke out. The *Manchester Times*, backing Bright, said that to compare Lord Lincoln with him was "to compare a hillock with a mountain and Tom Thumb with Goliath." But the *Manchester Guardian* fought tooth and nail against Bright's nomination. It produced what he called "a most malicious and false article against me," charging him with having excluded Cobden from the representation of Manchester to gratify his own ambitious views. Having placarded the town with a denial of this untruth, and dealt with it in detail at a general meeting of his committee, he plunged with customary enthusiasm into the campaign.

"Yesterday," he wrote to Miss Leatham on December 1, "I was indoors, going through the volumes of Hansard's Parliamentary Debates to extract some particulars of Lord Lincoln's votes, to show what he has been and is; and this afternoon I have been preparing them for the *Examiner*." A requisition to Lord Lincoln obtained eleven or twelve hundred signatures, but "I think the opinion gains ground that Lincoln will not come forward."

On December 5, "in the midst of many and exciting occupations:" "The *Examiner* will tell thee what has been done. The *Guardian* admits this morning all the blunder I charged him with, and his tone is subdued, and evidently that of a losing man. The *Courier* writes still more so" (it is the old Tory paper), "and he speaks of his fear that Lord Lincoln's partial promise to another constituency may prevent his coming to Manchester,—thus preparing the way for the refusal they anticipate from him. However, my friends are very united and are working hard. . . . I met Garnett, the editor of the *Guardian*, yesterday. He was dining at the Club and I sat almost close to him. We had some conversation, and I told him what I thought of him. He was subdued and felt himself most awkwardly situated."

The Lincoln cave ignominiously collapsed. At the General Election of 1847, Bright and Milner Gibson were returned unopposed. But in the meantime, Bright conducted himself as though he were certain to have an arduous fight. In the course of a regular "ward campaign" in Manchester, he made ringing Radical speeches night after night. Gentle Miss Leatham is startled by their vehemence. He writes to her on this.

"I think it quite possible to avoid saying what it is not proper to say and yet to avoid flattery. The passages to which thou refers me" (obviously passages of Scripture) "evidently intend that opposition should be met in a Christian spirit. But this does not mean that words of strength and truth should be avoided for fear those of whom they are spoken should be offended. Whatever is said should be without malice and ill will, but firm and truthful denunciation of what is wrong cannot be condemned without involving the condemnation of all the Scripture writers and speakers. I am not accustomed to speak in public from passion or impulse, and few men bear so little ill will to others as I do. I am not unmindful of the necessity of caution, and *thy* warnings, above all others shall be remembered." And again, when he is preparing a reply to the "feebly vicious" writing of the *Guardian*, he tells her, "I shall not forget thy counsel about severity of language."

As Miss Leatham followed the Manchester controversies in the pages of the *Examiner*, she found its didactic fury as disturbing as the vigour of her lover's political oratory. "Thou quarrels with the *Examiner*, and perhaps with some reason. But thou hast not seen the writing of the opposite party! It may be some consolation for thee to know that none of the articles to which thou refers are mine, although I am not quite sure that I think of them quite as thou dost."

One of John Bright's most notable achievements was to prove that robust politics, Manchester Radicalism and romantic love were not incompatible. The completely successful process of interesting his bride in the principles that possessed him and the issues that absorbed him began before their marriage. He embodies in his love letters every now and then little essays on big themes.

"To-morrow you are going to hear Vincent. I am glad you do not mind the stories about his Chartist principles. . . .

"It delights me that thou art disposed to hear for thyself rather than to be guided by the insinuations which are always thrown out against men whose tendencies are towards democracy. Dr. Arnold says, 'Democracy may be fever, but Aristocracy is consumption.' The former, I fancy, we should prefer. . . .

"Didst thou see in any of the papers the account of the battue at Lord Salisbury's when Prince Albert, the Duke of Wellington, Lord John Russell and others were present? In little over two hours they killed 318 head of game, chiefly pheasants and rabbits. I wrote an article about it for the *Examiner* on Seventh Day evening, which, if inserted, thou wilt see next week. I think the Queen, as patron of the Society for the Prevention of Cruelty to Animals, should counsel her 'subject' husband against such barbarous slaughter of defenceless animals for amusement only. . . . The Prince (by courtesy, I presume) was allowed to kill 150 of them!"

". . . I trust to thy lenient judgment of my speeches and writings. Thou hast lived in a quiet 'genteel' world, and art unused to the strife of political life, and some things may startle thee which, after all, may not be wrong. And be always sure that I am anxious not to impair my own usefulness or to damage the great cause I now represent here by anything imprudent or wrong."

"[*April* 21.] I spoke last night on the Education scheme, and was tolerably satisfied with myself; but my views on this subject do not find much sympathy in an assembly so aristocratical as the House of Commons . . . The report on the Factory Bill has been received. The 3rd reading is not yet fixed, and muddling legislation threatens to involve the country in mischief if not in ruin. The inclination to interfere in everything by law is about the worst sign of the times.

"[*May* 6.] Thy note is rather hurriedly written, dearest, but I love it notwithstanding. I wish I could have more of thee; and yet hereafter I shall hope to see thy writing improve, and it only requires a very little care, and the observance of a very simple rule to make it all I could wish to see it." (The newspaper had been gossiping about their wedding.) "The note in your paper is only the result of the incessant craving for the news which newspapers must supply. The annoyance is that the law should require the notice to be read before the Board of Guardians; and this was done to insult dissenters and to make people still marry at church. But do not mind it, dearest. Our married life may make amends for some small troubles now: I hope and trust so.

"[11*th.*] (*After recording an engagement to meet next day 'Elihu Burritt, the learned blacksmith from America.'*) I send thee the *document* from our Monthly Meeting, and the certificate of the Registrar, both of which, along with thy Registrar's certificate, must, I believe, be handed in at your next M.M. in order to our being 'liberated.' . . . Thou wilt have heard, probably, that the notice in the Wakefield paper, or an announcement founded upon it, has appeared in nearly every paper in the Kingdom. Last night Lord Morpeth met me in the Writing Room and congratulated me on my prospects, and said 'he did not know a more estimable family.' That is a compliment from a lord which some people would value. I was sitting behind Lord John Russell last night, and he turned round and said, 'Well, Mr. Bright, I wish you joy.' I thanked him for his good wishes, and then we had some conversation on the state of the country and the Navigation laws.

"[*24th.*] (*Planning a honeymoon tour.*) I think, dearest, I have found out a very agreeable tour. From Wakefield to Worksop, through Doncaster and Tickhill, is 35 miles. Worksop is in the midst of some of the loveliest scenery in England, called the Dukeries, and if it have a good inn I think we may go there first, and, after seeing the parks of the dukes, go on to Chesterfield, Matlock, Buxton, and on to Wales as before intended.

"[*26th.*] I have bought thee a dressing case which I am sure will please thee. Also a small one for myself.

"[*June* 6.] Hast thou forgiven me for my rudeness yesterday, when I kissed thee in the presence of thy mother and cousin? I did not premeditate such an offence, but could not at the moment of my departure refrain from what I trust was but an innocent expression of my tenderness towards thee. . . . What a strange year I have passed since thou put thy arm in mine as we walked to the kitchen garden at Upton! First of all was my resolution to speak to thee of what my heart had long felt, which was daily gathering strength and purpose. Then there was the longing for some opportunity to tell thee what I thought and the dreamy expectation that something would turn up to help me. Then the accidental discovery at Addingham Meeting and the two evenings spent with thee at Bolton Bridge. Then the desperate resolve to ask thy dear mother's permission to come. Then the other visit, with the pleasant walk we took the following morning, with all its interesting explanations. Then the general Meeting at Ackworth with its almost agonies of suspense. Then a succession of visits at Heath and Harrogate, some of them pleasant and some very much the contrary, until the 20th of 10th month, when thy consent was given, and when I felt myself blessed and compensated for my fears and much anxiety . . .''

3

On June 10, he took her out of the "quiet, genteel world" of Heath into the family life which was soon to teem at "One Ash," and into the busy sphere of politics. No marriage has ever been more successful. No husband adored more steadily, no wife loved and admired and served more constantly. As their family increased, it became difficult and then impossible for Bright on his narrow means to keep a house going in London in addition to "One Ash." So that, after six years, he spent the session in London lodgings, and she remained at Rochdale, to which he sped at every available week-end or break in his parliamentary duties. But the outstanding evidence of his devotion is the fact that whenever he was absent from her during thirty-one years he wrote to her a letter every day and generally a long one.

Six weeks after his marriage (July 29, 1847) he became one of the members for Manchester. In the following year his sister Priscilla, freed now from the ties which had bound her to "One Ash," was married to his friend, Duncan McLaren of Edinburgh. McLaren did not belong to the Society of Friends, and the Society consequently excommunicated her. The rule against the marriage of Friends outside the Society was repugnant to Bright's sense of right and honour, and it led to the only notable entry in his diary for the year 1849:—

"[*April* 5, 1849.] To-day my dear sister Priscilla was disowned on the ground of her marriage contrary to the rules or practices of the Society. I protested against this course as unjust to her and injurious to the Society. But our Monthly Meeting seems to be unable to perceive any distinction in cases; flagrant immorality and the marriage of a member with a religious person not a member are visited with the same condemnation. The Society may well not extend. It is withering almost to nothing. Its glorious principles are made unsightly to the world. Its aspect is made repulsive. It keeps out multitudes by the imposition of tests and observances which can never be of real importance, and it excludes many from its fold who have done no moral wrong, and whose assumed error may have been highest virtue. The glory cannot but depart from a body which weighs principles and forms in the same balance. It does not, indeed, observe 'days and months and times and years,' but it has elevated 'peculiarities' into points of Christian observance, and has done that which is, to some extent, the making broad their phylacteries. Can the Society reform itself, or will it slowly sink?" [1]

[1] Mrs. McLaren eventually rejoined the Society.

CHAPTER VI

IRELAND IN THE HUNGRY 'FORTIES

I speak as a representative from a county which suffers extremely from the condition of Ireland. Lancashire is periodically overrun by the pauperism of Ireland; for a year past it has suffered most seriously from the pestilence imported from Ireland; and many of the evils which in times past have been attributed to the extension of manufactures in that county have arisen from the enormous immigration of a suffering and pauperized people driven for a sustenance from their own country. As a Lancashire representative I protest most solemnly against a system which drives the Irish population to seek work and wages in this country and in other countries, when both might be afforded them at home. Parliament is bound to remedy this state of things.

—John Bright, Dec. 13, 1847.

I

THE more or less continuous series of diaries begins with Bright's painstaking records of a visit he paid to Ireland in the autumn of 1849 in search of first-hand information about the effects of the Famine and the Rebellion.

His position in the Irish controversies which, from the days of O'Connell to those of De Valera, agitated British politics more fiercely than any other domestic question, has been coloured for recent generations by his difference with Gladstone in the crisis of the 'eighties. The separation made sombre the last two years of his life. But nobody had cause to be surprised or hurt by Bright's conduct in that crisis. He was a Unionist by absolute and lifelong conviction, and "Honour Bright" would not palter with his conscience—even if it meant that, when at last his sorrowful silence was forced by the dissolution of 1886, he had to deal so faithfully if ruthlessly with his old ally and chief and to come down with the hammer-blow that finally ruined Gladstone's slender chance of success at the polls and smashed the Liberal Party for twenty years.

When he told Chamberlain, after the rejection of the first Home Rule Bill, that he was against anything that took the shape or the name

95

of a Parliament in Dublin, he was merely reaffirming what he had said during the Kerry election fourteen years before,[1] and repeated more than once.

"To have two Legislative Assemblies in the United Kingdom would, in my opinion, be an intolerable mischief," he wrote to O'Donoghue on hearing that he had been represented in Ireland as an advocate of Home Rule. But his honourable, humane and enlightened views on Ireland, illuminated in eloquent and close-reasoned speeches from 1843 to the end—forty years during which he studied the problem of Irish government with infinite pains—separated him sharply from the sentiments and motives that in the main dictated English opposition to Home Rule.

In its proper place will fall his note on a talk with Lord Dalhousie before the General Election of 1885, in which he suggested a scheme of County Councils for Ireland, with a central body in Dublin dealing with "education, local taxation and control"—his last contribution to Irish statesmanship before Irish statesmanship disappeared in the hideous welter that began in 1886. Here it needs only to show the genesis of his Irish policy and the drastic thoroughness of the study on which he based it. The speech in the House of Commons quoted at the head of the chapter was made on the third reading of the Coercion Bill passed in 1847 to cope with an outburst of agrarian crime in Ireland which had deeply shocked the public mind. It was under the provisions of this measure that the revolts of '48 were suppressed and Smith O'Brien and other rebel leaders tried and convicted. Bright admitted the necessity for special powers and voted for the Bill. But he had previously presented to the House a petition against coercion signed by 20,000 Irish in Manchester, and he could not give a silent vote. In this impressive speech he warned England and the Government that, while force might be a necessary temporary expedient, force was no remedy,[2] that the Irish terror had its origin in the twin grievances of the Land and the Church. Until the feudal and ecclesiastical fetters were removed, there could be no diminution of poverty and pauperism in Ireland and no peace for England.

Bright knew more about Irish poverty and its consequences than most members of the House of Commons. Irish misery, bursting out of Ireland, festered in Lancashire. In his youth he had seen it, seeping wretchedness, from the windows of the house in Rochdale, about the

[1] Letter to O'Donoghue, January 20, 1872.
[2] He did not coin the famous phrase till 1880; but the argument was identical.

factory gates, in the slums of Manchester, along the docks of Liverpool. He came to the conclusion that "the great cause of Ireland's calamities is that Ireland is idle . . . and therefore she starves. Ireland starves and therefore she rebels." But Ireland's idleness was for the most part a forced idleness. Let the Irish come to England, or cross the sea to the United States or Canada, and they were about the hardest-working people in the world. When Lancashire manufacturers employed them they worked well, were trustworthy, quiet, "as well disposed to the law as the people of this country."

Long before the grievous year of '48, Bright had resolved the paradox in his clear, relentless mind. He told the electors of Durham in 1843 that Irish discontents were due to "an absentee aristocracy and an alien Church." In the four great speeches in Parliament which he devoted to Ireland between 1845 and the spring of 1849, he hammered home with heavy and persistent blows his demand for the two reforms which he perceived could alone bring to the country any measure of social peace and economic prosperity—the abandonment of the Protestant ascendancy and the establishment of the principle of tenant right. All other devices were ineffective palliatives. He would not vote for the Maynooth Grant because it was "hush-money" given to stall off the demand for religious equality. He consented to the grants to distressed areas only because it was "a question of life or money," but he declared that "the Poor Law as a means of regenerating Ireland is a delusion." The only cure was to "free the land." "I shall be told," he said, "that I am injuring aristocratic and territorial influence. What is that in Ireland worth to you now? . . . The people of Ulster say we shall weaken the Union. . . . There has been no honest attempt to make a union with the whole people of Ireland up to this time. We have had a union with Ulster, but . . . there never can be a union between the Government and the people whilst such a state of things exists as has for many years past prevailed in the South and West of Ireland."

He was stirred to the bottom of his soul by the sufferings of the Irish poor; by the hopeless disorder and needless penury of a fine people; by the thought of the half million of them who in two years perished miserably in workhouses, on the highways and in their hovels—"more, far more, than ever fell by the sword in any war this country ever waged;" by the embitterment of the thousands driven to America to be "the implacable enemies of England." His protests rose in a great crescendo, culminating in that famous apostrophe in 1849 [1] to the panegyrists of "our glorious constitution" who pointed to England steady as a rock while the thrones of Europe were being overturned. "It is true. . . . But take all the lives that have been lost in Europe amidst the convulsions that have occurred, take all the cessation of trade, the destruction of industry, all the crushing of hopes and hearts, and they will not compare for an instant with the agonies which have been endured by the population of Ireland under your glorious constitution."

It was characteristic of Bright that in his most impassioned moods he never lost touch with the solid ground of fact. Some few passages in this fine speech are almost incandescent. But in the main it is a prodigious recital of facts about Ireland, statistical comparisons of Irish with English conditions, citations of authorities on the legal and social aspects of the land question. Two or three months later, he had taken both his ardour and his facts across St. George's Channel, to inform the one and confirm the other. During a part of his stay he was accompanied by a Commissioner of the Board of Works.

The diary of this journey of inquiry—to which he appended a large number of notes on the evidence before the Devon Commission [2] and the reflections of his own mind on the land problem—provides a striking example of his passion for accurate information and diligence in digesting it. In Ireland he is not a sightseer. Absent the description of places and scenes, the historical notes, the pleasant observation on incidents of travel that make up his journals of continental tours. Lacking also any touch of romantic generalization. He is in a severely business-like mood. Bright saw Ireland in the melancholy deeps of misery that opened after the famine and the rebellion. He was intensely moved by visual realization of the reported horrors that had reinforced his arguments in Parliament; but the expression of that profound feeling was now relegated to his letters home—to his wife and to Cobden. To them he spoke of the silent cruelty of the territorial system, of the misery of roofless houses and lands laid waste, of the impromptu cemeteries where the teeming

[1] House of Commons, April 2, 1849; debate on the grant in aid to certain Irish Unions.

[2] The Report of the Devon Commission had shown that the improvements of land were made by the tenants and that progressive increases of rent had been practised so as to amount to systematic confiscation of these improvements. It attributed to the system much crime and disorder and declared that Parliament should interfere. Accordingly the same year (1845) Peel's Ministry introduced a Bill for protecting the tenant against the landlord. It was received with execration in a House where the landed interest was dominant, and the Government dropped it.

victims of starvation, fever and cholera lay "uncoffined and unknown." But to the notebooks which he kept as an armoury for his twenty years' campaign in the causes of Disestablishment and Land Reform he committed only the cold, grave, damning record of economic and sociological fact. He hardly troubled to complete a sentence, so pressing was the impulse to get it all down on paper at the end of the day's journeying

2

The very first entry presents in a few simple words, noted in talk with Sir R. Kane, a startling vision of that Irish hopelessness which tormented him:

"Industrial or farming work for paupers difficult, for anything must be better than condition and employment of peasantry, and labourers would flock to workhouse labour, and farm after farm would have to be taken. True difficulty of the Poor Law that people are so depressed [that] no relief can be given which will not draw men to it from ordinary labour and means of living."

To resolve the difficulty by giving this nation of farmers and peasants a reasonable interest in the land and a reasonable opportunity of making a living upon it was the purpose of this intensive study, and it became one of his chief preoccupations as a politician during the following years. His tour took him from Dublin through Wicklow south and west by Wexford, Cork, Kerry; then north through Limerick and Tipperary into Connaught, whence he returned to the capital.

It was an exhaustive journey, employed wholly in searching out people who could give him light on the economic problem of Ireland. In a month, from August 10 to September 8, he records interviews with over sixty persons to whom he applied for facts bearing on the two questions of the land and the establishment. He found all the evils of a feudal system exaggerated by absentee landlordism, by complicated land laws and customs. He found the farmers who possessed capital unable to buy their farms because of difficulties of transfer and title, in a state of insecurity as tenants, making no improvements because there was no guarantee of compensation, therefore farming ill and paying low wages. He found landlords everywhere refusing leases to Roman Catholics because a lease conferred a vote—the landlords themselves in London, Paris or Naples; the agent in Dublin; the sub-agent in the country, with "drivers" and sub-drivers on the estates, screwing out money by raising rents on improvements and evicting tenants who would not or could not pay. He found everywhere abject poverty, intense suffering, half-ruined hovels, crowded workhouses. Everywhere, that is, except on the few estates where leases were granted or the tenants were allowed to buy their farms. There, as at Kilmore, "small farms, extraordinary industry, all the land under tillage . . . cottages good and neat, land well cultivated." If tenants had security for improvements, he was told, "the land would become every man's savings bank, in which his gains would be deposited, safe for himself and advantageously for the country."

In Bright's memoranda made at the end of the tour can be seen the germ of the Tenants' Rights Bill which he afterwards drew up and promoted in Parliament, unfortunately without success. The triumph of his policy was delayed till he and Gladstone in alliance carried through the Land Act of 1880, when Parliament was less completely dominated by the landed interest. But his notes in 1849 contain every argument upon which the remedial legislation of the last half-century has been based:

"Are gentry, or farmers and peasantry most essential to Ireland? A question for Parliament worth discussing.

"In 1849 our Irish people flee to America from the oppression and misery inflicted by the proprietary class, as 200 years ago Englishmen fled from the tyranny of the Church. America is the great refuge for the suffering and oppressed.

" To press for the poor rates from the occupiers, whilst their position remains as it is, is to bring about their irretrievable ruin. They have no security; they give no employment; paupers increase by eviction process, and upon them comes the ever-increasing burden. The policy of the landlords renders it impossible for the tenant to give employment and absorb the surplus labour, and at the same time heaps upon him increasing rates.

"The landlords don't perceive that they are large sharers in everything which begets improvements and investments on the soil—better cultivation, more produce, more power to pay rent, and the security for it is the greater.

"All advance in the classes below them tends to their good without exertion on their part.

"Farmers have burdened the land with cottiers, and have taken enormous rents for hovels and patches of land; but this comes of the few proprietors and the general neglect of their property and duties.

"Some persons assert that with a long lease no compensation is necessary: that 21 or 31 yrs. or more enable a tenant to recover what he has expended; but this is to forget that the tenant has a right to the gain of his investment and to the investment or principal also.

"Would it not be as just to say that, the landlord having received a good rent for so many years, the land should then belong to the tenant as that, the tenant having made his farm answer by reason of his investment upon it, the sum invested should ultimately belong to the landlord?"

3

The following extracts from the journal of the tour will give an idea of the method of his inquiry. He has set out from Dublin into County Wicklow:

"[*August* 16, 1849.] Mr. Glascott, agent, Camolin Park, Mountmorris Estate. (Camolin park) 6,500 acres; £4,500 annual rent. 400 acres of planting; 60 or 80 acres of bog a stone's throw from house door. Late Lord Mountmorris received £16,000 a year, and never expended a shilling on improvements. Now people sent away to America or elsewhere, altho', if the estate were well cultivated, there is not population to cultivate it. 'Tenant Security Bill' would set all the tenants improving. If estate could be sold in portions, tenants or their friends would buy their own farms. Now farms cannot be bought: encumbrances and costs and insecurity of title prevent it.

"[*17th.*] Father Miller, priest or curate of Kilmore, went with us to see the people. Small farms; extraordinary industry; seaweed in great abundance—manure of great effect for one crop. All the land under tillage. People have leases. Some have bought their farms and are become comparatively rich. Called on an old man (Stafford) who bought his farm 15 years ago, had paid for it, and is now possessed of 3 or 4,000 £. About 50 acres statute. Spoke to him about long leases or ownership as compared with uncertain tenancy, and asked, would he have built that house if land was not his own? He looked a look of wonder, as if an answer was not necessary, and said, 'Give us security; give us that encouragement, and we'll bate the hunger out of Ireland.'

"The cottages are good and neat, the land well cultivated, the people doing well.

"When Hutchinson's property was offered for sale to the tenants, many of them became purchasers with their own or borrowed money, which they have since almost wholly paid off.

"Father Miller asked me about prices of corn and said if they keep near the present rate, with security to the tenantry, they could beat England in corn and would do well. He showed me good houses and farm buildings built by tenants under leases which have expired, and the buildings are now the property of the landlord, and the rent is raised 20/- per acre, or in many cases more than that, and new leases are refused.

"[*23rd.*] Cork to Skibbereen. At Skibbereen, into the market-place. The town rather busy and crowded, as it is the season for the turf being brought in for sale. Saw a young woman having a basket or skip of turf for sale. She asked 1½*d*. for it. We had it weighed: 62 lbs.—cutting, drying, carrying 8½ miles for 1½*d*., and a woman standing by said she would take 1*d*. for it. Potatoes 3*d*. per stone; herrings 6 for a penny.

"In the baker's house was a farmer: 5 acres, £12 a year. One-third has been remitted for the last two half years, but could be raised again at any time. Asked him if long leases or compensation for improvements, what then? Answer: 'Nothing could keep them from it [improvements]; they would work day and night at it.' He said if he had money he could turn out the best tenant in the district, for they had no leases and a higher offer would be taken and the tenant turned out.

"Ruined cottages in great numbers during the day in Skibbereen, and in almost all the journey. Women sitting or standing about their cabins with countenances of deepest dejection. In the workhouses, 665 boys and 578 girls under 15; infants, 108 under 2; 530 men, and 755 women. Women and girls look much better than men and boys in health; very many widows and orphans among them.

"Way to Bantry: land uncultivated, and undrained cottages in ruins. Aspect of country most cheerless, the people living in desolation.

"[*26th.*] To Tralee by Coach. Coachman: asked him why land along the road was not cultivated. 'How should it be if a man could not get a lease? Leases were not common.' Surgeon, a passenger, living at Tralee, said dispossession after improvements was of every-day occurrence; leases less frequent and of shorter terms than formerly. Farmers put money into Savings Banks and said if put into the land it was given to the landlord. Tenants quick to follow example of improvement. Scotch farmers had done good by example. Emigration great. Capital going away, for poor rate, county rate, and high rents, and no security drove it away. Money sent home by emigrants in large quantities. Bad dwellings morally and physically injurious to the farmers, and disease lingered about their dwellings. Dare not seem to be comfortable, or rent would be raised. (Turkish Aga robs all who seem to have anything.—J. B.)

"[27th.] Mr. Stokes, County Surveyor: Pass Tenant Improvement Bill, and it will empty the workhouses; it will absorb all the labour of the country. Wages, now averaging thro' Ireland 9d. per day, would rise speedily to 1/- per day. . . . Fair tenant compensation, and he would become an agent in the worst part of Tipperary with a feeling of the most perfect security.

"[29th, at *Longfield*.] Bianconi. Maxims: he never forgives the man who tells a lie, or who takes anything clandestinely or dishonestly. 'Gives his men, if they retire, their full wages 5/- to 7/- per week as pension, and now these pensions are not 5 % on his expenses, for they never retire unless wholly unable to work, as their perquisites or fees are so much more than the wages. Governs his men not so much by surveillance as by moral principles.' Bianconi, Longfield: 1,000 acres.

"Longfield: bullet-proof windows and doors; yard with high walls; large doors, bullet-proof. Lord Hawarden's agent riding with armed men going before, inside fences, to protect him.

"Mr. Mulvany going with a proprietor thro' his demesne; proprietor armed to the teeth in open day.

"Scully was shot whilst fishing in his own grounds. Let Conacre at £14 per acre; received half money and half bills. Crop failed. People asked him to take the crops for the bills. He would not; would have all his legal rights—and was shot. When Major Mahon was shot, the people employed by Board of Works said, 'God be praised;' bonfires were lighted as a signal, and general satisfaction was felt.

"[30th.] To Scariff by shore of Loch Derg. Land almost wholly wasted. Houses unroofed. Mr. Purdon ruined; his cattle sold off. Young man standing on roadside surveying his former dwelling and land: his expressions of bitterness. 'Why till the land for the landlord? He may work the land for himself,' etc., etc.

"Miserable cabin in a quarry: a woman, boy and little girl; the ruins of their house just below. Scariff Workhouse: no agricultural employment; breaking stones. Saw Inspector and Vice; Guardians. Their account deplorable; almost every proprietor deeply embarrassed; their rates unpaid. The Protestant rector, Mr. Brady; also Mr. Drew and others. Rents asked still high; land waste in large tracts; the gentry never visit workhouse.

"[*September* 1.] Tuam. To Cathedral (Catholic). Called on Archbishop; not at home; left card. Father Ryan called upon me. With him to workhouse. Hundreds of applicants at door. Women spinning wool and flax, but no useful employment for the men.

"Archbishop has a plain house, such as a man with £600 a year would live in in England. Opposite is the palace and large demesne of the Protestant Bishop. Archbishop, £700 a year (lately only £300); Bishop £5,000 or £6,000.

"Evictions incessant. People hunted off the land. Proprietors, many ruined. Thro' the market at Tuam; potatoes good; people in better spirits.

"Houses and demesnes guarded. No stranger allowed to enter for fear of distress. They graze their cattle on Sundays, because on that day no distraint can be made. Some of these gentlemen still live as gentlemen and keep cars, horses, etc. Gentlemen evade the rate in every possible way—produce old leases, and litigate thro' all forms of law.

"[*3rd.*] Maam. Fair for cattle. Women selling socks, 2*d.* to 4*d.* per pair.

"[*4th.*] From Letterfrack to Leenane and Westport. Called at Thos. Eastwood's. He in good spirits. Says the people are what the tyranny and neglect of the proprietors have made them. They are full of suspicion, and require time to gain confidence and belief in anyone's good intention towards them. Graham, his and J. Ellis's landlord, is giving leases for ever; has secured his rental by it—gets now 8 to 10 p.c. on his outlay for the property, bought it for £15,000 about 6 yrs. ago; has refused £20,000 for it just lately. Is the only man who has a good tenantry in that district.

"The Clifden Union now occupies Bunowen Castle (Mr. O'Neile's) as an auxiliary workhouse; thus the paupers feed in the halls of the once rich and proud: a great moral lesson.

"Met a ruddy-faced gent. on horseback; servant or keeper on another horse carrying a gun; further behind 3 boys or young men with 3 couple of dogs. Asked who the gent. was. 'The Lord Bishop of Tuam.' What is his name? 'Mr. Plunkett.' Are you sure it is the Bishop? 'We are, sir.' Are those his dogs? 'They are, sir.'

Here was the Church Militant enjoying himself over the scenes of desolation. Did he think of the cause of the misery which had spread over the district?

"Met a gentleman who is enthusiastic about converting the 'Romanists.' Evidently not well informed on Irish matters, but credulous and crammed.

"It is a common thing to say Popery is the cause of the no progress of Ireland. Query: Which class has most neglected its duty in Ireland? Have not the landed proprietors, and are they not mostly *Protestant*? If Protestantism has not saved the proprietors, why say that Popery has ruined the peasants?

"[*5th.*] By car to Castlebar, with Mr. Mulvany and Barry. Saw drainage works, extensive and useful; whole valleys reclaimed and growing crops; hitherto under water at every tide. On the road, evidence of evictions. Whole villages of houses unroofed. In one village 5 houses thrown down on Monday week, the 20th of 8th month. Five families homeless; their rents paid to middleman; his lease thrown up, and head landlord (Sir Roger Palmer) ejected them. Eight children in one family, 6 in another; husbands, gone to England to the harvest, had written to tell them their answer. They could not eat their breakfast when they heard the news. A few rafters reared against the wall with sods over it and straw for a temporary hovel.

"A little further on, a boy lying by the roadside, thin to a skeleton; arms and legs those of a mummy. Said he was ill of the hunger. Appeared scarcely able to move.

"[*7th, Dublin.*] At the Imperial Hotel, saw Wm. Dargan, the railway contractor, a man of ability and merit. Has paid £5,000 per week for labour in Ireland for 5 years past. His opinion of the Irish: 'They only want the discipline of steady employment; they will give as good return for wages in labour as any people in the world.' 'They have had no good example, no instruction in industry, and no security for their industry.' He is greatly in favour of a Tenant Security Bill.

"Called on Count Straletski at Reynolds's Hotel. Count Straletski: 'If the Devil himself had exercised all his ingenuity to invent a scheme which should destroy the country, he could not have contrived anything more effectual than the principles and practices upon which landed property has been held and managed in Ireland.' Is greatly in favour of tenant compensation; it would stimulate labour; would absorb the surplus labour now idle in the workhouses. The landlords are evicting on the theory that the population is their ruin. Folly. The land without the population is nothing.

"Dined at Thos. Hutton's, Elm Park. A nice party: Lord Chancellor Brady, Judge Perrin, W. M. Donnell, of the National Schools Commission, Mr. Ball, of the Poor Law Commission, son of Judge Ball, Mr. Curran, son of the celebrated Curran, etc. I sat next to Judge Perrin, a pleasant and most sensible man. Against Capital Punishment: 'Judges should not be consulted on these points, for if Judges' opinions had been acted upon, sheep stealers would have been hanged still.' Is very liberal in his politics. Thinks Sydney Smith's sarcasm on Lord Jno. Russell absurd, except that he might and would attempt, but always failed at an obstacle. Thinks Clarendon ambitious; playing off parties with a view to Premiership. Has a high opinion of Lord Grey. Thinks and hopes Peel may do something more for us. Thinks Graham most able, but that his smile and simper and manner of condescension to be guarded against. Thinks that constant smile implies or begets callousness of heart and hypocrisy.

"Judge Perrin said the practice of raising rent on improvements, or of ejecting tenants, was almost universal in Ireland, the north excepted. He said the northern Tenant Right is of modern growth, for he scarcely heard of it when he went into that circuit as a lawyer. Said greater security was necessary, either by inducements to give leases, or by compensation; but was afraid of increased causes of litigation, which is one of the curses of the country. (But why so? Because the laws are for one party only.)

"At dinner this evening at Sir Robert Kane's: agreed to form a committee for forwarding changes in the laws on land and to prepare a Bill to give security to tenants for improvements in buildings, draining, and fencing. This Committee to correspond with me."

There is one allusion in his Diary for 1850 to this question. In June he saw Lord John Russell about it:—

"Conversation with Lord J. Russell on Irish Tenant Question. Lord John admitted the extreme hazard of leaving the question unsettled. He said the South of Ireland might be kept quiet; they would succumb as they had always done; but the people in the North were a more sturdy race, and, if they united with the South, then the question would assume another shape that would be difficult to meet. He was evidently anxious on the question, but, not understanding it, he seems hardly to know how to deal with it. I mentioned my having drawn a short Bill and wishing to show it to him, and he expressed a desire to see it."

Lord John and the Whigs took the extreme hazard. Nothing was done till Bright and Gladstone became partners in the great Liberal policy for Ireland nearly twenty years after.

CHAPTER VII

THE STRUGGLE WITH PALMERSTON

I

ALTHOUGH at the turn of the century Bright, in the full vigour of early middle-age, had become a shining figure in the nation, his noblest speeches were yet unborn and his finest work still to do. In the great campaign for Free Trade he spoke continuously, ardently, with ingenuity, force and freedom; but the conditions of that busy, hurried survey of three kingdoms and his sense of the urgency of a single question made for argumentative agility rather than for philosophic weight. The year 1850 marked the beginning of the harvest he had tilled in long brooding over the moral philosophy of politics, the possibility of the democratic government of a State on the basis of Christian ethics, the question of peace and war, the foundations of human freedom, the relation of nationality to political morality, the conditions of citizenship, the limits of toleration.

Bright never made a successful Minister. One chief reason why has been suggested—that he had no genius for detail and no industry in routine. There are, however, conspicuous examples of politicians, more impatient of detail and less tolerant of routine than he, who have succeeded in the highest offices of State. The likelier reason, as it will probably seem to readers of his Diaries, is that he referred every question of policy or of political conduct to first principles. "He is to be feared who fears the gods." To Bright more than to most mortals, Conscience was a god whom in the last resort he could not disobey. A conscience trained in the quiet of the Quaker spirit and nourished by the Inner Light was a greater force than ambition, fame, popularity or applause. It guided his conduct in fair weather and foul. To it he referred the decision of every crisis of his life. It gave him his authority with his fellow-countrymen and his importance in Parliament. To it he owed the singular impressiveness, the truly heroic magnitude, which he attained in the fierce contest with Palmerston and all that for which Palmerston stood. It was into this prolonged encounter that he marched in the year 1850, after a seven years' apprenticeship to the House of Commons.

During those seven years he had felt his way in the House with speeches on Free Trade and Ireland, which by their content no less than by their manner, had marked him out as a formidable Parliamentarian. But it was in the inevitable conflict between the unbending Quaker and the unbending War Minister that he showed how perfectly he had taken the measure of English politics and of his own strength. The drama opened with the Don Pacifico controversy, one of Palmerston's early assertions of his dictatorship of British foreign policy. The curtain did not fall till Palmerston himself lay dead.

But the year 1850 witnessed also the opening of a minor and a curiously interesting phase of Bright's career. His personal acquaintance with Disraeli, which ripened into so odd a friendship, began this January. At least, Disraeli now made his first appearance in the Diaries, though in the previous year they had paid each other considerable attention in speeches on the agricultural question:

"[*January* 4, 1850.] Dined at Bellamy's with Disraeli, strange fellow! Admits Protection gone. Did all he could to prevent squires and farmers making fools of themselves in the recess. When they came to *do* something on the opening of Parliament they were forced to take his proposition as an amendment, asserting only agricultural distress, and asking for relief for local burdens."

The association so born continued with a kind of half-earnest, half-amused liking on both sides for more than twenty years and ended only when Bright, in the Cabinet crisis of 1868, thinking Disraeli had made an unworthy use of the Queen's name, poured wrath upon his head in words which were never forgiven.[1]

The source of the magnetism that drew together these two personalities from alien and utterly incompatible worlds of tradition, custom, thought and purpose, is elusive. They sometimes found themselves in agreement on a point of detail or tactics—as in the campaign of Reform—but on no ground of principle had they a thing in common. Mr. Buckle finds the secret in the fact that "each sprang from a small and despised religious community, the one being a Jew, the other a Quaker, each had won his way to a front rank in the House by force

[1] See page 323.

of character and power of oratory; each looked at the political facts before him from his individual standpoint, and not by the aid of party spectacles, and each was strongly opposed to the domination of the Whigs. . . . There was, moreover, a democratic fibre in Disraeli as well as in Bright; though of course there was also in Disraeli an aristocratic fibre, which was wholly wanting in Bright, and in Bright a middle-class feeling which Disraeli certainly did not share."[1] The reader will doubtless place this interesting speculation in the light thrown upon their relations by Bright's own records.

They came together again in the summer. Palmerston's dictatorship was put to the issue in June; he won the first round after his greatest display of parliamentary skill and the finest oration of his life. The episode began with a motion of censure, carried by Lord Stanley in the House of Lords, upon the Government's undue interference in the affairs of Greece. No censure too condign could have been passed upon the mobilization of a British fleet and the provocation of what might easily have been a European war in order to force the Greek Government to pay the preposterous claims of a fraudulent Portuguese Jew. But Lord John Russell declined to be forced out of office by a vote of the House of Lords, and the strong position of the critics of the Don Pacifico folly was astutely flanked in the House of Commons by a motion of general confidence in the foreign policy of the Ministry, moved by Roebuck. The debate lasted four days, and was distinguished, apart from Palmerston's great apologia (with its high-flown peroration of "*Civis Romanus sum!*"), by first-class speeches from Gladstone, Peel, Graham, Cobden and Molesworth against him and Cockburn for him. This early conjunction of the Peelites and the Radicals on a non-economic question was noteworthy.

Disraeli rose late and said little except to declare his agreement with Lord Stanley. But before the debate came on he had explained his position to Bright, whose notes on the crisis follow.

"[*June* 21.] Conversation with Disraeli. He is annoyed at this crisis; wished the *Industrial* question to be settled finally before anything of this kind had come up to the vote (against Palmerston), and is certain that Peel and his party will oppose the Government.

"[*22nd.*] Met Cobden and Molesworth; discussed state of affairs, and decided that we should vote against the Government on the Foreign Policy debate, to come on on Monday next. We all felt we should

[1] "Life of Disraeli," Vol. III, p. 241.

degrade ourselves by supporting what we wholly disapproved of, and that the question was too grave to allow of our being neutral. The result may be of great importance, but we are not responsible for these difficulties: to vote with the Government would be inconsistent with our past opinions and policy and would destroy our self-respect and our influence for any good for the future. There is great commotion among the Whigs, and our friends of the Radical ranks at first looked at the dirty work they are to do with wry faces, but are gradually coming round to a stout defence of what they know is wrong but have not the courage to resist.

"[25th.] The event of the night was Lord Palmerston's speech. He rose at a quarter to 10 and closed at 25 minutes past 2, speaking four hours and forty minutes. It was a remarkable speech, most able, saying everything that can be said for his policy, but proving conclusively how dangerous that policy is—meddling everywhere, advising, controlling, encouraging, menacing, as he pleases, in every country not of first-class power in Europe. This speech and the debate in general only make it more imperative that this mischievous system should be checked.

"[28th.] Cobden spoke well and judiciously. I could not get in without putting him out, so did not speak at all. Peel made a most useful and excellent speech; no party feeling in it, and no wish to inflict damage on the Government, but an honest and simple avowal of his real opinions on the question before us.[1] Division at four in the morning, 310 to 264, majority 46 for the Government.

"[29th.] In the evening dined with Mr. Willcox, M.P., in Dorset Square. Mr. Cockburn, M.P., there, and somewhat insolent to Cobden, telling him he was no reformer, and that he ought to be turned out of the Reform Club,[2] because he would not vote to keep in a Liberal Government! What a strange notion of the duty of a member of Parliament some persons have! Mr. Cockburn has been in a fright all the week for fear if the Government went out he should miss his

---

[1] In a public allusion after Peel's death to these, his last words addressed to Parliament, Bright spoke of "that most beautiful, that most solemn speech." "Diplomacy," said Peel, "is a costly engine for maintaining peace, a remarkable instrument used by civilized nations for preventing war. Unless it be used to appease the angry passions of individual man, and check the feelings which arise out of national resentment, it is an instrument not only costly but mischievous."

[2] Bright was elected a member of the Reform Club on August 9, 1843. His proposer was Lord Marcus Hill, his seconder Charles Villiers. He used it constantly, almost daily when in London, for forty-five years.

appointment as Solicitor-General which he is expecting on the first vacancy.[1]

"This evening Sir Robert Peel was thrown from his horse on Constitution Hill. The accident it is feared will prove serious.

"[*July* 3.] Startled this morning by hearing that Sir R. Peel had died last night at 10 minutes past 11. This event has shocked me very much. On reading the particulars in the *Daily News*, I could not refrain from tears; I felt as if I had lost a dear friend, so great has been my admiration for the recent career of this great states-man. . . .

"[4th.] This week has been remarkable for the loss sustained by the death of Sir Robert Peel, and probably on no former occasion has there been expressed so universal a sorrow on the death of any public man. Every family seems to feel the sorrow as its own. The last ten years of his life have certainly been devoted to the true interests of his country, and with extraordinary results. His labours and sacrifices on the Corn Law question have endeared him to the nation. I heard his last speech (against Palmerston's foreign policy) on the day before the fatal accident occurred: it was a great speech, in its principles, in its temper and moderation, in its tone altogether. Had he known what the morrow would bring forth, he would not have needed to omit or add a word. Would that his dying words might sink into the hearts of statesmen and people.

"[5th.] My recent vote against the foreign policy of the Government has been much condemned in Manchester by men who ought to know better.[2] They seem to wear their principles but loosely and expect me to do the same. They are deluded by the notion that Palmerston is Liberal at home and abroad, and by fears that *Protection* can be restored: the first is untrue, or at least is wholly unproven, and

---

[1] The vacancy occurred in July and Cockburn, filling it, took the first step on his road to the Lord Chief Justice's seat.

[2] Two days earlier, he had written, in reply to Mr. John Heywood, of Manchester, defending his vote. The question at issue, he said, was: "Shall the Foreign Minister of this country be permitted to interfere in the affairs of other countries in cases where the direct interests of this country do not require it? Shall he advise, and warn, and meddle in matters which concern only the domestic and internal affairs of other countries?" Such a policy led to irritation, to quarrels, and might even lead to war. "I would not, for a moment, sit for Manchester, or for any other constituency, if it was to be understood that I am to forget my own character and long-held principles, and what I believe to be the true interests of the country, to abandon all these, and vote as the necessities of *party* may require, at the crack of the treasury whip."

the latter is simply childish. I cannot and will not be in Parliament a mere joint of a Whig tail."

There was one question of the year in which Bright found himself entirely at one with the Ministry—the grant of constitutional Government to Australia. Lord John Russell introduced the Bill in February. It designed to carry out Sir William Molesworth's conception of the Colonial system, and would have anticipated the Commonwealth Act by fifty years but for the action of the House of Lords which struck out the clause providing for a Federal Assembly. Of the Bill in its original form Bright highly approved. "Colonial policy explained by Lord John Russell in a long speech," he wrote. "Very important. Colonies at the Cape and in Australia to have Legislative Chambers, and to have a liberal self-government. Great agreement in the House on the subject. Marvellous absence of prejudice when the objects are ten thousand miles away. Should like to move that the Bill be extended to Great Britain."

No long time passed, however, before Lord John fell out of his good graces again. The No Popery crusade loomed up.

2

Most men examine their consciences and review their careers as they approach that dividing line between youth and age which is the fortieth year of their lives. Bright was especially prone to self-examination. Though he lived the life of a man of action and was never morbidly introspective, he found it profoundly interesting to range up the ideal John Bright alongside the real John Bright, compare them, and reprove the material simulacrum for its failure to rival the visionary original. He whose ruthless candour never faltered in public was always ruthlessly candid to himself in private. So it was this winter of 1850–51, when he passed his thirty-ninth birthday and became a Man of Forty.

He spent the winter chiefly at "One Ash," studying hard the technical details of the Indian cotton question, preparing speeches to make at Manchester, engineering the Indian mission of Mackay,[1]

[1] Bright had moved in the House of Commons for a Royal Commission to inquire into the obstacles which prevented the increased growth of cotton in India. The Government refused it. He went down to Manchester, and organized a fund of £2,000 under the auspices of the Chamber of Commerce, and Mr. Alexander Mackay, the author of a notable book on America, "The Western World," was sent out as a Commissioner of Inquiry. Unfortunately Mr. Mackay died in the East; but his reports were collected and published under the title of "Western India."

collecting funds to pay his salary and expenses, writing articles on the subject for the *Manchester Examiner*. But these things were subsidiary to protracted discussions on the business of Bright Bros., then suffering from trade depression, and to the activities of those "evenings at home" which he loved above all things. His Diary teems with allusions to talks and walks with "dear Elizabeth" and of the things they read together. Mrs. Bright, alarmed by the prevalence of smallpox, had persuaded the servants to be vaccinated by setting the example herself. She became ill. His prescription for her solace was to read poetry to her over the November fireside:

"[*November* 13.] To meeting. Dear Elizabeth not out, suffering from inflamed arm, the result of vaccination. . . . Read *Midsummer Night's Dream* to her. . . .

"[14*th.*] At home. Read *Excursion* to dear Elizabeth."

She was a young wife of three years' standing with the beginnings of a family. The picture of the Tribune of the People and his spouse in their modest house taking their simple pleasure in Shakespeare and Wordsworth has a placid charm: it provides at once a background for the vivid life he lived in public and an explanation of his four-squareness to all the winds of fortune. A day or two later he takes stock of his achievements and shortcomings:

"[16*th.*] My birthday. I am now entering my 40th year. How serious this seems, if it be true that 'a man is either a fool or a physician at 40.' It is worth considering what progress I have made in wisdom and conduct, and in those things which ought to be the main objects of our pursuits.

"I have learned a good many things doubtless, and my experience, I hope, may be useful to me if I am permitted to live much longer. But the past 20 years or more show many more matters of regret than of satisfaction. I have not been industrious enough. I have not sufficiently cultivated my mind, and still less attended to my heart. There are some things in which I have been too easy, as in matters of business and property. I have given all my time to the public.

"The last nine years exclusively have been given to public affairs. They have not, I trust, been uselessly spent, although, as for myself, they have left me with impaired circumstances and with prospects far less cheerful than I once looked forward to. I must try to be more prudent as regards myself and my family, without neglecting such things as may be required and which concern the public.

"The past year has been one of great anxiety in business, and I have seen my means gradually wasting without the power to prevent it. It has also had its heavy trial in the death of my very precious sister; [1] but, so far as my own home is concerned, it has been a year of great comfort. My dearest Elizabeth and the darling children have been treasures of great and increasing value, and, in reviewing the whole year and its troubles, this is no small blessing to be thankful for. Evening: I read the *Merchant of Venice* to dear Elizabeth.

"[19*th*.] Finished an article on the 'Pope, the Priests and the Panic.'

"[21*st*.] This evening read Dr. Wiseman's 'appeal' on the outcry against his appointment as Catholic Archbishop of Westminster. It is a remarkable production, most ably written, and is a complete reply to the insane bigotry by which he has been and is assailed. His remarks on Lord J. Russell's letter and Lord Truro's speech at the Mansion House dinner will not be soon forgotten. His vindication of the creation of a Catholic hierarchy in this country, and his defence against the violence of the State Clergy are masterly and unanswerable.

"My house is dull to-night—wife and children at Heath. How comfortless the world is without sympathy."

Before Christmas he had paid short visits to Birmingham and to London. Both Bright and Cobden (and especially Cobden) took a keen interest in what was called the Freehold Land Movement, the precursor of the building societies and schemes of State-aided house purchase which have since transformed so large a part of England. The Freehold Land Society of Birmingham had large estates where the working-men could by thrift obtain houses on a system of deferred payment. A conference of the societies was held on November 26 and 27, at which both Bright and Cobden spoke. But the chief object of the visit was a Peace meeting held in the Town Hall, where Bright addressed an audience of 5,000 people for an hour, "and, I believe, satisfied the audience more than myself." Cobden begged him to be there, "if for no other purpose, to let the fools and knaves who are raising this Guy Fawkes outcry, know that there are people in the country

[1] Esther, who had married Mr. (afterwards Sir James) Vaughan, the Bow Street magistrate.

who are thinking of something more important than the Queen's spiritual supremacy."

Going on to London for a Conference of Friends at Devonshire House "on the vexed question of tithes," he spoke there (much in the same sense as in the House of Commons a year before) "in favour of payment of tithes as a fixed property tax fairly due, although badly applied by the State." He remarks sadly that in these meetings of Friends "facts and arguments often have small weight: what has been done in times past on the 'feelings' of certain members is too much the rule for the bulk of them." He visited the rising buildings of the Great Exhibition in Hyde Park, and met Paxton who explained the works to him. And before returning north he went to console his brother-in-law, Vaughan, in Gloucester Terrace: "Much interested in seeing dear Esther's sweet baby last evening and to-day. What a sad blank has been made in this house since I was here less than four months ago!"

Back in Rochdale he encountered once more the question which had impassioned him and embittered his spirit when, eighteen months before, the Society of Friends disowned his sister because of her marriage to Duncan McLaren:

"[*December 5.*] Monthly Meeting. Present Hannah Rhodes and Elizabeth Pearson, from United States; the former spoke with feeling and effect.

"Elizabeth Midgley acknowledged as a Minister to-day. I spoke in favour of a postponement, but against the opinion of the meeting. I think the step is premature and not the best for E.M. or the Meeting.

"For the first time our Monthly Meeting has retained in membership a Friend who has married a person not a member. One of Charles Parry's daughters (Sophia) has been married at the Registrar's Office to a young man (Robt. Blayder, of Warrington) who is not a Member, though he has attended meetings. After much discussion it was determined not to disown her. Strange that this should be thought a great concession! But it is so, for our rules have been unwise in this particular, and with us have been rigidly enforced.

"Evening: Writing letters. Children delicious this evening. What a delight they are to us!

"[*17th.*] With Bazley and H. Ashworth into Manchester. At 12 o'clock to the Town Hall, on the invitation of the Mayor, to meet Abbot Lawrence, the American Minister, now on a visit to A. Henry's. I spoke briefly, next after the Bishop, and alluded to the Pilgrim Fathers, and the political and religious freedom of America. The meeting passed off very well, and Lawrence was pleased."

The year ended quietly, Bright at home reading Hallam to his wife, writing about India, listening charmed to the conversation of Edward Miall who came to visit him, deeply engaged in the details of establishing the carpet-weaving business which Bright Bros. were now adding to cotton-spinning and manufacturing, and indulging in only one burst of controversy when, at a meeting of the Mechanics' Institute, he "spoke (as chairman) chiefly against newspaper taxes."

3

The No Popery campaign, which Bright, despite his robust Protestantism, viewed with supreme scorn, came to a head in the first half of 1851, when Lord John Russell replied to the Papal Pastoral establishing a new Roman hierarchy in England by introducing a Bill forbidding the use of episcopal or territorial titles without the authority of Parliament. The chief event of the session to Bright personally was the unanswerable speech in which he riddled Lord John Russell's case. He took infinite pains with this declaration of his faith in tolerance; the preparation of his facts and arguments occupied him many days. In the background of these labours, and of two family tragedies, moves the kaleidoscope of political crisis (abortive resignation of "Lord Johnnie," abortive attempt of Stanley to form a Government, reappearance of "the old faces in the old places"), and behind that again the gorgeous diorama of the Great Exhibition.

Business cares pressed heavily on him at the beginning of the year and up to the opening of the session in February. The only diversion of this period at "One Ash" was a visit of two Friends from Providence, New Jersey, John and Elizabeth Meader, with whom he conversed "on the New England education, and on Catholicism in America and its delusions." [1] He found their company "very pleasant." On February 4, he arrived in London, staying for a time with the bereaved Vaughan in Gloucester Terrace, and was soon in the ruck of the No Popery squabble.

"[*February* 6.] J. B. Smith came in at tea, with a China paper giving curious accounts of missionary doings at Loo Choo and in China

[1] Bright made large use of the Massachusetts system in the current controversies about religious education in State-aided schools.

—as bad as the 'papal aggression.' From 10 to ½ past 12 preparing notes for a speech on papal question, but find the subject too large for a speech of moderate length.

"[*7th.*] To the House. Lord Jno. Russell brought forward the 'papal aggression.' His speech very good if delivered some 300 years ago, but bad as regards the presént case and his proposed measure against the Catholics. As usual a great deal of clap-trap in it. I spoke during the evening to a good House, most attentive. My object was to show the total failure of the past attempts to repress Catholicism by legislation, and the uselessness of the Established Church.[1]

"[*13th.*] To the House, calling at Fendall's Hotel to meet Association for the repeal of the taxes on knowledge. . . . Debate on agricultural distress. . . . Several Irishmen, naturally indignant at the course taken by the Govt. on the 'papal aggression' in re-enact- ing a new penal law, voted against them. Lord John's speech was feeble, and Disraeli in his reply too much of a buffoon for his position.

"[*14th.*] To the House. 'Papal aggression' again. F. Peel made an admirable speech against any new legislation on Catholic question. Gibson also made a good speech on the same side. Division: only 63 against introduction of the Bill. Brotherton behaved badly— attacking Gibson and myself as not representing our constituents and in order to justify his own slavish submission to the Whigs.

"[*15th.*] By train at 10 to Manchester. Mr. Roberts in the same carriage and we played at chess during the journey. Home at ½ past 6, all well, and evening most pleasant.

"[*17th.*] To a meeting of members, called by Mr. Hume, to consider the necessity of making some representation to Lord J. Russell on the subject of Reform. About 30 members present. Agreed to call a larger meeting for Thursday at 2 o'clock.

---

[1] The Government's measure was intituled "The Ecclesiastical Titles Bill.' Bright told the House that the cry of No Popery had not been raised by the Dissenters. They "stood aloof from the roar." It was raised by the Churchmen. The measure was a sham, an attempt to bolster up the ascendancy of the Church Establishment. Lord John Russell said the Church of England was the most tolerant on earth. The most tolerant Church on earth every year entered a Friends' meeting house in London and stripped it of its furniture to pay Church rates! In reply to the suggestion that England showed "symptoms of returning to Rome," he asked where the symptoms were? Lord John had supplied the answer in the Durham Letter: he had "discovered that that great institution, which was supposed to be a bulwark of Protestantism, turns out to be a huge manufactory of a national or home-made Popery."

"[*20th.*] Called in upon Cobden. . . . Meeting of members, about 50 present. Some difference of opinion. Mere Whigs and worse, like Sir E. N. Buxton, resolute not to stir.

"At length a Declaratory Resolution was agreed to, drawn up by Cobden. Only two hands held up against, it was signed during the day by about 50 members. It stated the opinion of those who signed it in favour of reform and urged the Govt. to move on.

"House at 4. Locke King brought on his motion for extending £10 franchise to the counties. Lord J. Russell replied, and admitted almost everything, and declared his willingness to extend the franchise, and his intention to open the next session with a Bill for a further reform in Parliament. So the meeting of members—and the present necessities of the Govt.—have had this good result. Cobden made a good speech, and we divided with 100 for and 52 against the Motion, thus defeating the Govt. by a large majority.

"To the Reform Club, and wrote a long article on the 'Position of the Ministry' for the *Examiner and Times*. It is believed the Govt. is about to be overthrown. The defection of the Irish members owing to the new 'penal law,' and the unpopularity of the Budget, are the immediate causes of their difficulties. It is said the Tories are to oppose the renewal of the Income Tax, and, if so, the defeat of the Govt. appears certain, as the Metropolitan and some other members from our side are expected also to oppose it.

"[*24th.*] To Reform Club. Much gossip and many rumours on ministerial crisis.

"To House. Lord John Russell made a statement of his reasons for resigning: majority of only 24 on Disraeli's motion, and beaten on Locke King's motion. Not candid in this, as the 'Papal Bill' and the Budget had much to do with it. House adjourned to Friday to allow Lord John to 'reconstruct' a Cabinet if possible. It is rumoured that Sir Jas. Graham will not join the new combination.

"Reform Club. Wrote an article for the *Examiner and Times*. Rumour that Lord John has failed to reconstruct, and that Lord Stanley was again making the attempt.

"[*27th.*] Wrote an article for the *Examiner*, 'Who Wrecked the Ship?'

"To Club to dine. Stanley has failed to form a Govt. at which of course the Whigs rejoice. Wrote a letter to the *Manchester Guardian* contradicting his lies and slander. Sent a copy of it to the *Examiner*. Also wrote article on the crisis for the *Examiner*. Home by ½ past 12.

"[*March* 1.] By 10 train to Manchester. Found much interest excited by the attacks of the *Guardian*, and my reply.

"[4*th.*] There are rumours of fresh assaults in the *Guardian* of to-morrow. It will not surprise me if another batch of lies are brought out. The news to-day is that the Govt. is restored without change, for want of successors—the old faces in the old places, and if the old policy, then certainly before long a like result.

"[5*th.*] To Newcastle with dear Helen; met her and dear Elizabeth at Normanton.

"[6*th.*] My bro. in law, Albert Leatham, and Rachel Pease married this morning at Darlington. Everything went off satisfactorily. About 40 to dinner, and a large party in the evening. The bride a sweet girl, and a favourite with all who know her.

"[9*th, at Rochdale.*] To Meeting twice. Dear Elizabeth only there in the morning. A sweet quiet day at home. Our darling children, so lovely and so loved. Our home seems almost all we can wish for. The evening spent most pleasantly, till my departure for Normanton by train at 8 o'clock. Reached Normanton at ½ past 10. The mistress of the house collects autographs and wished for mine. She had not the Queen's, but had the Queen of Song's—Jenny Lind and Made. Sontag (Countess Rossi).

"[10*th.*] By train at 7 to Ambergate and Matlock. To Leigh Green to see Dr. Gillum, an eccentric old man (82), who proposes to make me his executor, and to leave his property for public objects. Found him very deaf, and not very clear as to what he intended. I advised him to leave his property to his relations, and that no man should do otherwise without strong reasons. He is living with Mr. Wass, whose wife is a distant relation of Dr. Gillum. They want him to remember them, as is natural, and would be glad if I would advise the old gentleman in their favour.

"[14*th.*] House. 'Papal Bill' 2nd reading. The speech of the evening was by Roundell Palmer, M.P. for Plymouth.[1] It was admirably logical and conclusive, and one of the very best speeches I have ever heard in Parlt. It would seem impossible for the Bill to survive such a demolition of its character.

"Conversation with Ellice on state of things with Govt. He said, 'John, if he were driven out, would leave the place very uncomfortable for those who drove him out.'

[1] Roundell Palmer, the first Lord Selborne, had been elected at Plymouth at the General Election of 1847.

"Palmerston refused the Foreign Office passport to the Greek, Palanidi, for whom I applied, as being contrary to regulations.

"Amusing conversation with Disraeli in the dining-room. He spoke of the duty of 'destroying the red-tapists,' and urged that if the Whigs went out we should prevent their 'leading the Opposition,' which was our only chance of doing away with their sham party, etc.

"Long conversation with Sir C. Wood, in the room behind the Speaker, on his Budget. Found him disposed to do the best he could, but not courageous enough. I pressed on him the advertisement duty as one he might repeal without much loss.

"[15th.] With Cobden into his house till near 1 o'clock. Conversation on Manchester Education scheme, on the position of the Whigs, and their 'Papal Bill,' on the West Riding and his chances of return, and whether the Stockport people would have their old representative or not. I offered, if an arrangement could be made, to retire from Manchester to Rochdale, to allow him to come in for Manchester, but he would not hear of it, tho' I would do it with pleasure on his behalf, for whom my respect and admiration increase the longer I know him.

"On coming home found a letter from Chas. Walker on the Rochdale representation.

"[16th.] Spent 2 hours nearly in making notes for speech on Papal Bill.

"[18th.] Our dear boy's birthday. How much of pleasure we have had in the first 3 years of his life! May he become, as he grows older, more and more endeared to us by his kindness and goodness!

"[20th.] House. Could not get to speak, as too many claimants for the 'Speaker's eye.' Only rose once, when Sir Jas. Graham rose and was called. His speech was magnificent, in matter, in manner and in language. It produced an extraordinary sensation in the House, and will doubtless do the same in the country.

"[21st.] To the House. Intended to speak but was not called Thomas [1] under the Gallery.

"[22nd.] To Manchester and home. Found my Father better Dear Priscilla had arrived, owing to Father's illness.[2]

"[23rd.] To Meeting in the morning. Spent some time with my father. He is much shaken, but I think will rally from this attack.

[1] Thomas Bright, his brother, who devoted himself to the management of the business as long as he lived.
[2] His father had been ailing for some months.

"[24*th.*]   At home.   A sweet walk with dearest Elizabeth. . . .

"[25*th.*]   To London—a pleasant journey.   Bought Pope's poems and read the *Dunciad* on the way.   To the House.   Debate on the Popery Bill, but could not get an opportunity to speak.   Division at 3 o'clock: 434—95.   Gladstone made a great speech, and the Govt. cut a sorry figure.   To bed at 5 o'clock.

"[27*th.*]   Wrote an article on the expected Budget for the *Examiner and Times*.

"[29*th.*]   To Reform Club, and met Mr. Brown, a native African, resident at Whydah on the west coast of Africa.   T. Bazley [1] came in, and we discussed the question of cotton growing in Africa, and agreed to furnish him with some agricultural implements that he may encourage a beginning of cotton cultivation in Africa.

"To 17, Edwards St., Portman Sq. to see the exhibition of Electro Biology, which was not very successful, only one young man becoming really susceptible of the mesmeric influence.

"[30*th.*]   To House.   Army Estimates.   Sir Chas. Wood.   Had a talk about his Budget and the dangers of the Income Tax.   Asked me who wrote the article in the *Manchester Examiner* on the Budget? Thought it a very fair article, and did not complain of it—only that it was much like the conversation he had with me some days ago.

"[*April* 2.]   To Moffat's to dinner; a large party.   An evening foolishly spent chiefly thro' the folly of Osborne, who prefers jokes and ridicule and nonsense to any useful and agreeable conversation. Revd. Lord Saye and Sele of the party, and I rode with him in his carriage as far as the end of Park Lane.   He seems a liberal and kind man.

"[10*th.*]   Wrote a letter to Mr. Chadwick declining to become a candidate for Rochdale.

"[11*th.*]   Disraeli's motion on relief to Agriculture.   I spoke for ¾ hour; division close.   Only 13 majority for Govt. [2]   Walked up to Glos'ter Terrace and to bed at ¼ to 4.

---

[1] President of the Manchester Chamber of Commerce; later Sir Thomas Bazley, M.P.

[2] Disraeli's motion was to the effect that, in any relief to be granted by the omission or reduction of taxation, due regard should be paid to the distressed condition of the owners and occupiers of land in the United Kingdom.   Bright sliced through the pretences of the debate.   If the motion were carried, he declared, it would but serve to delude the occupying farmers "into the belief that the thing which was really intended as a measure to cement a party in Parliament is intended to do something for their benefit."   He said some prophetic things.   "Mr. Disraeli knows perfectly

"[*14th.*] With Cobden to Exhibition, along with Jas. Mellor and Miss Mellor. Great progress being made for the opening, but much still to be done."

The Easter Recess passed amid domestic delights at "One Ash." Mrs. Leatham was there from Wakefield. The only fly in the amber was the increasing weakness of his father. Politics intruded on this scene but once, when a meeting of his constituents in Manchester demanded a carefully prepared speech. Cobden's doubts about the West Riding had come to nothing (he was re-elected unopposed next year) and Bright stuck to Manchester. The big meeting in the Free Trade Hall heard three hours of political exposition from him and Gibson, carried a vote of confidence and support, and everything went off "most satisfactorily." Having examined the register of electors for the borough of Rochdale, and "found the Liberal Party greatly increased in strength during the last ten years," he was back in London at the end of April, attended the opening of the Exhibition on May Day, and the same evening encountered another tragedy in the Vaughan family.

"[*May* 1.] Exhibition opened. I was present at it. The pageant was striking, and the building [and] the products of industry. Thousands present. The Queen and Prince, and their children, the general good humour prevailing all conspired to make the day one not likely to be forgotten. The Court dresses looked absurd, and Cobden was the only man of the Commissioners who wore a plain evening dress.

"Everything went off admirably. The Prince of Wales struck me as a boy of delicate health, rather timid and thoughtful in expression,

well that so long as the hon. gentlemen opposite will have this question of Protection as the main part of their policy, their leaders are destined to sit on the shady side of the House." He denied that the landowners were suffering from any distress: no class passed so successfully through every commercial hurricane and disaster. The farmers were suffering from depressed prices. But "this distress is not a rare malady with the occupiers of land." It was attempted to attribute all the woes of the farmers to Free Trade. He showed that violent appeals for the relief of the farmers from distress had been made in Parliament from 1815 onwards. There is a strangely modern note in his conclusion: "If you talk here for ever of agricultural distress, you will still find that there is no remedy which it is in the power of Parliament to give. The only possible chance for the farmers is in the exercise of those virtues and those talents by which the rest of their countrymen thrive. And if they exercise their own energies, and cultivate the quality of self-reliance, I am convinced that this country, with the finest roads, with the best markets, and with a favourable climate, will be found to triumph not only in her manufactures but also in her agriculture."

his sister, a frank, pleasant looking and apparently healthy child, seemed to enjoy the scene.[1]

"I remained in the building from 11 to 5 o'clock, and, with Chas. May, examined many interesting objects.

"House. Between 8 and 9 o'clock I learned from J. B. Smith that Vaughan's poor baby was dead. I hastened up to Glos'ter Terrace and found Mrs. Vaughan in great trouble. Vaughan himself in bed, with his doctor attending him. The baby had been well as usual till 5 o'clock, when she suffered from a fit from which she did not recover. In 10 or 15 minutes she was gone, almost unconsciously to those around her. She will be a great loss to her poor and stricken father, who suffers deeply.

"[*2nd.*] This morning saw Vaughan in bed, more tranquil, but very ill in his head.

"Went to the undertakers and took steps to have a slight sketch of the dear child made. Wrote to Newcastle, to Thomas, Jacob[2] and to dear Elizabeth.

"[*3rd.*] Remained in town owing to the grief in Glos'ter Terrace. Jacob and Margaret came up last night, and called this morning.

"[*5th.*] To Kensal Green with the poor little child. Buried her in her dear mother's grave. Jacob and Margaret and myself only there. It was a sad scene. In the evening I went down by night mail to Heath, arriving at 5 in the morning, and returned with dear Elizabeth by the train on the same morning."

This was one of Mrs. Bright's comparatively rare excursions to London. She stayed ten days, and went several times to the Exhibition with her husband. During this stay, he made the great speech on the Papal Bill which had been so long in gestation, but she did not hear it, being then at Leyton.[3] He had spent Sunday, May 11, with her there, left her with her relatives for a day or two, and late the next evening came his opportunity to deal with Lord John. The only reference to it in his diary is the following sentence:—

"[*12th.*] I returned to town, dear Elizabeth staying till Fourth Day. House: I spoke on Papal Bill for an hour or more from 11 to 12 o'clock."

[1] The future King Edward and the future German Empress.
[2] His brother, afterwards M.P. for Manchester.
[3] At her sister's, Mrs. Gurney Barclay.

The speech thus curtly dismissed, though not of unusual length, was one of Bright's major performances in the House of Commons. Loaded with fact, powerfully argued, it contained many memorable passages. He spoke with the certainty of intense conviction. Nobody in England was a more ardent anti-Romanist than he on the religious plane, but, with the surety of a prophet, he saw the infinite mischief of this particular State persecution of a religious minority. He admitted that the language of the Papal Bill was offensive,—"such language," he said, "as might have been used by Hildebrand, and very like what is used in our own legal documents . . . such as I despise and loathe." But it was rather a form than a substance, and offered no justification for the proposed legislation. He blew to atoms the contention that the appointment of Roman Catholic Bishops in England was an invasion of the prerogative of the Crown: "The Queen has not the power of making Roman Catholic Bishops, and therefore the making of them by the only Power on earth that has authority to make them is no invasion of the prerogative of the Crown." "I am no friend," said he, "to the Bishops of any Church. But my individual opinion has nothing whatever to do with legislation on this question. I am not so presumptuous as to say to another church that Bishops are not necessary for that Church; and if Bishops are necessary for the Anglican Church, who can say they are not necessary for the Church of Rome?"

He made his strongest points almost in the language of a seer, especially in allusion to the woe that was being piled up in Ireland. "It is not a question of Protestantism. It is a question of politics. . . . Who is injured by the Bill? The noble lord does not touch the Pope. . . . The true sufferers will be the wearer of the crown and the millions of subjects professing the Catholic religion. . . ."

"The noble lord," he said, towards the end, "has quoted Queen Elizabeth and the great men of the Commonwealth as though it were necessary now to adopt the principles which prevailed almost universally two hundred years ago. Does the noble lord forget that we stand on the shoulders of our forefathers and can see further? . . . This House is not the place for religious questions. But, reflecting on the deep mysteries of religion, on my own doubts and frailties, on the shortness of the present time, and on the awful and unknown future—I ask, what am I that I should judge another in religious things and condemn him to exclusion and persecution?"

"[19th.] To Rochdale at ¼ past 9. Called on my father; found him up, but sadly shattered—old and thin, and evidently a changed man. He was kind and pretty cheerful, but it made me sad to see him apparently so verging on his end.

"[*24th.*]   To Eastbourne Terrace, and spent an hour with Thomas and Caroline, who had just arrived.   Thos. in good spirits at the progress of the carpet trade, and the improved prospects of the cotton trade.

"In the Exhibition, met Sir J. Graham, who was enthusiastic, spoke strongly against Papal Bill, and said he should reserve himself for 3rd reading, and then again speak against the Bill itself.

"Met also Duke of Newcastle, who, as usual, was very friendly. I hinted to him that their party should throw themselves more on the people, and outbid the Whigs on Parliamentary Reform, and express themselves during the Recess.

"Met Rungor Bapojee, the Vakeel of the late Rajah of Sattara. He complained of the treatment of the Rajah's family.

"Immediately afterwards met Lord Broughton, and spoke to him on the subject, and he said he thought they ought to be treated liberally. I urged that generosity would make more friends than cruelty.

"Met also Chas. Dickens, and was introduced to him by Paxton. It was in the little room where J. Whitworth was exhibiting his machine for measuring the millionth part of an inch.   Dickens's face scarcely indicates the possession of the powers of mind he has displayed, tho' it is intelligent in expression, and pleasant to look upon.

"[*25th.*]   Called on Cobden; took a stroll with him in Kensington Gardens.   The day very pleasant, the gardens most delightful. . . . During this week attended a few sittings of the Yearly Meeting.   Dissatisfied as usual at the determination of the leading 'Friends' to resist any changes, or any fair consideration of the state of the 'Society.'

"[*June* 4.]   To Mrs. Gibson's to a crowded party.   Curious medley: Count Thomar, the ejected Portuguese Minister, Mazzini, Louis Blanc, etc.

"[*7th.*]   Home with all my family   Pleasant to be at 'One Ash' again.

"[*10th.*]   To Manchester.   To Carr's, coachmakers, to hire open phaeton for dear Elizabeth.

"[*11th.*]   To Meeting this morning.   Very few friends there. My father and Jas. Midgley both seriously ill.   The upper row [1] seems almost gone.

---

[1] Where the "Ministers" sat, facing the Meeting.

" Cousin Saml. Bancroft[1] and his daughter Elizabeth, and Aunt Wood, and Jacob up to tea. A pleasant evening. Our American cousins very agreeable and intelligent.

"[*16th.*] With Vaughan to sculptor's (Manning) to see the figure for dear Esther's tomb.[2]

"[*17th.*] Cobden's motion for reduction of armaments. Palmerston slippery as usual; Brotherton & Co. believing as usual—they have faith even as a little child! Home late, and to bed at 3 o'clock.

"[*18th.*] Dined with Ewart in Cambridge Square. Dr. and Mrs. Chambers there. The doctor thinks heavy taxes a blessing to a country. I asked him if he thought *footpads* stimulated industry, as he said taxes did? He said, no, they were irregular—the steady pressure of taxes was the best! His wife more sensible, and an amiable and good person I should think."

4

The No Popery Bill passed the House of Commons on June 27, went through the House of Lords without amendment, and received the Royal Assent on August 1. Nothing more was heard of it till its repeal in 1871. Nobody took the slightest notice of it. The Roman prelates used their titles. The Common Informer failed to inform. The Act was dead at its birth.

Bright's diaries are missing from this point until December, 1852, when he records at length a very curious conversation with Disraeli. In the meantime Palmerston had fallen, dismissed from the Ministry by Lord John Russell for his indiscreet applause of Louis Napoleon's *coup d'état*; the Prime Minister in turn had been defeated on the Militia Bill on a motion by Palmerston—his "tit for tat on John Russell;" Lord Derby had formed his first Government with Disraeli as Chancellor of the Exchequer; and in the General Election, which returned a Parliament not very different from the last, Bright and Gibson were re-elected for Manchester with a large majority. While the Whigs squeezed out the dregs of their authority in 1851, Bright stumped the country for Reform and the Ballot (he had a good deal to do with the production of the timid little Bill by which Lord John Russell sought to prove that he was not really "Finality John"); and when the Tories

---

[1] Mr. Samuel Bancroft, of Wilmington, Delaware, U.S.A.

[2] Vaughan had taken a trip to Belgium after the collapse caused by his little baby's death, and returned in better health.

came in he challenged them again and again to declare themselves on Protection.

Of Disraeli's Budget (December 3, 1852) which doubled Sir Charles Wood's house tax in order to halve the duties on malt, and applied an income tax for the first time in Ireland in the form of a levy on funded property and salaries, Gladstone declared that it juggled with taxation without any attempt at improvement or reform. It was doomed from its inception. The discussion upon it, fierce and long, had been in progress many days when Bright sat down late on the night of the 15th to record one of the most fantastic proposals of coalition ever born, the phantom child of Disraeli's musings upon the sad lot of a Chancellor in a tight corner:

"[*December* 15, 1852.] The debate on Mr. Disraeli's Budget is now exciting great attention. . . . He proposes to take off half the Malt Tax; this is the chief proposition of his Budget and that on which his fate will turn.

"This evening about nine o'clock I received a note whilst at the Reform Club from the Chancellor of the Exchequer (Disraeli) asking me to call at Grosvenor Gate to see him; this was rather in consequence of a conversation I had with him yesterday in the Lobby of the House.

"I waited upon him soon after 10 o'clock, found him near the top of the house, in his morning gown, surrounded by books, pictures, mirrors, etc. I told him I felt in a difficult situation, seeing how entirely opposed we had been in political life. He said he would speak without reserve, as he thought that, however opposed, there had been a good deal of free conversation and he thought even some sympathy between us. He then entered on the desperate condition of their affairs, and the almost certainty of their defeat on the following night, spoke of that *infernal question*, the question of Protection; said his difficulty had been his and their promises to the country party and farmers, local burdens, and now Malt Tax. He said he only touched Malt Tax because could not touch tea duties [1] as proposed without touching malt—was forced to try something for the farmers and to venture on malt; he had not supposed the opposition would be so great. If he could get a vote, a majority of *one* only, his honour would be saved and he would give up House Tax and Malt, and remodel his scheme.

"He spoke of what he was proposing to do in reforming departments,

[1] There was a proposal to reduce the duty on tea, gradually over a period of six years, from 2s. 2½d. to 1s.

of Lord Chandos's business talents in reforming Irish offices and saving money at the Horse Guards, that he intended a thorough examination by a Commission into management of dockyards, etc., and would save a very large sum. Speaking of expenditure he mentioned those *damned defences*, and said he had cut and slashed them to bring the estimates for them to a more moderate sum. He entered into an examination of all our taxes and stated his views with regard to future changes and remissions.

"He spoke of his party, how well they had followed him, how faithfully they were prepared to support him. There was no jealousy—Cabinet friendly and disposed to act liberally—and he thought his party 'having stood so much already' would stand a good deal more if necessary. He then adverted to his wish to get rid of the old stagers and old 'red-tapists' and said he could not see why we, that is Cobden, myself and Gibson—our section—should not some day be with him in a Cabinet; not within 24 hours, but before long: it was quite possible and not difficult.

"I laughed at this as impossible and partly at the serious face he maintained as he explained his views. I objected that, putting aside the immorality of such changes, the constituencies would not permit it.

" 'Oh,' he said, 'a man of genius and power may do anything with a large constituency; I think I could represent Manchester, and be a very popular member.'

"I assured him he was greatly mistaken in supposing the Manchester people would be trifled with, and I asked, 'How is it possible for you and us to work together?'

"He said we much mistook them. I said they must change their name and repudiate all their antecedents before we could ever act with them. He said there was scarcely one member of their Cabinet who would not at once retire to make room for any gentleman who would be likely to give them strength.

"He spoke of the new Administration, admitting that his defeat was certain, asked if I thought Cobden and myself were included in it, and said: 'If you are included in it, or are likely to be, if you see your own game in what is going to be done, then may God help you forward, my dear Bright, and no man will be more delighted than I shall be to witness your success.'

"He said no man knew what he had struggled against and overcome; he had been a Minister and was now about to be beaten. He had always felt the insecurity of their position, and had not removed to Downing Street on that account. He would not keep office or try to cling to it if they could not have *power*, and it was clear they had not the numbers with them to enable them to go on, and it was doubtful if they could live till Easter if they now escaped.

"I was with him from 10 to half-past 11 o'clock, and the above is a sketch of the conversation that took place.

"This remarkable man is ambitious, most able, and without pre-judices. He conceives it right to strive for a great career with such principles as are in vogue in his age and country—says the politics and principles to suit England must be of the 'English type,' but having obtained power, would use it to found a great reputation on great services rendered to the country.

"He seems unable to comprehend the morality of our political course, and on this ground was probably induced to seek the interview with me.

"[*16th*.] The debate closed this evening. Disraeli rose at 10 and spoke till near 1 o'clock. He fought for his life, and never man fought more desperately or with more skill and power. This speech was his greatest speech; he was in earnest; argument, satire, sarcasm, invective, all were abundant and of the first class. His peroration was short, to the point, and forcible; but the 'numbers,' as he said to me yesterday, were against him. Gladstone made a great speech in reply, only part of which I heard.[1]

"The division gave 305 to 286. Government beaten and House adjourned to Monday.

"[*18th*.] This morning I walked through the Park to the Club; met Sir James Graham, passing through St. James's Place. I told him he knew our course—a good Government, acting honestly and doing well, would have our support; we should not depart from our independent line of action. He said: 'I don't approve of that. I think your position in the House and the country, your popularity, the large party you influence, and your great public services, which I would be the first to recognize, all entitle you to a share in the Government,

---

[1] Gladstone noted in his diary (Dec. 18): "I was on tenterhooks, except when his superlative acting and brilliant oratory from time to time absorbed me and made me quite forget that I had to follow him. His speech as a whole was grand; I think the most powerful I ever heard from him. At the same time it was disgraced by shameless personalities and otherwise; I had therefore to begin by attacking him for these. . . . I am told he is much stung by what I said. I am very sorry it fell to me to say it. God knows I have no wish to give him pain; and really with my deep sense of his gifts I would only pray they might be well used."

and I shall think no Government properly constituted in which you have not a part. I think it a most unsound principle that men who so greatly influence opinion should not bear a portion of the responsibilities of the executive Government; now that is my opinion.'

"[*22nd.*] Hayter came to me with message from Lord John Russell to Cobden and me, apologizing in some sort for our being left out. If offered anything it should be in the Cabinet, but the difficulties insuperable now; high opinion of me—honest, consistent, etc., and hoped we should comprehend the difficulties without supposing him unmindful of our claims,—all which, of course, I fully understand. I told him what we want is not office for ourselves but for men and principles such as we value, that our future course would be like our past, clear and resolute, not factious, but pursuing our own objects, etc. Saw Villiers, evidently surprised and not well pleased with things rumoured. I advised him to leave the Whigs and go with us; we were the party, and had the policy and principles, and our time would come.

"[*January* 3, 1853.] At home. Elizabeth on horseback to Healey, I walking alongside.

"[*4th.*] To Manchester. Wilson proposes a meeting, before Parliament meets, of influential men of the district to express our view of public affairs.

"Newspapers contain reports of election of new Government.[1] Lord John Russell and Sir Jas. Graham attempt arguments against the Ballot: both speak foolishly, and as if they thought their hearers fools—or as men do, driven by necessity to folly instead of argument, when argument fails them.

"[*7th.*] To Manchester to the dinner given to Mr. Ingersoll, the American Minister. The Mayor in the Chair; about 130 persons present. Mr. Ingersoll's speech not very clear—loose and ill connected —with a good wholesome spirit throughout it. I spoke late, near 11 o'clock, unsatisfactorily to myself: the matter not well suited to the time, and the time too short for the matter. What a folly to spend

[1] Lord Aberdeen's "Ministry of All the Talents," which was destined in another year to involve the country in the Crimean War, had been completed on December 31, and Parliament had adjourned to February 10. The Ministry's talent was its undoing. Greville wrote prophetically (Dec. 24): "In the present Cabinet are five or six first-rate men of equal or nearly equal pretensions, none of them likely to acknowledge the superiority or defer to the opinions of any other, and every one of these five or six considering himself abler and more important than their Premier." Sir William Molesworth provided the Cabinet with its small leaven of Radicalism.

so much of the evening in songs and glees and music, as if sensible men cared for these when met on an occasion like this! We are still but emerging very slowly from barbarism.

"Home by luggage train, and arrived at 2 o'clock in the morning.

"[11*th*.] Manchester. Long conversation with Wilson about proposed meeting before Parliament meets. Cobden dissents, but we think him wrong.[1]

"Hear my speech displeased some of the snobs at the dinner the other day. Anything, however absurd, may be said in favour of Lords and privilege; anything here is considered 'extreme.' Our friends are much pleased with it, and I don't particularly wish to please those who can't be ranked under that title.

"[13*th*.] Rochdale Station. Met Mr. Crosland and brought him up to tea. Stayed the night. He has a curious mind, sincere but with crotchets. He is a vegetarian, and in that I suspect he is very rational.

"[14*th*.] Annoyed this morning by Dearden's refusal to consent to the transfer of the Common to the Town's authorities; churlish act done in a churlish manner.

"Wrote letter to Cobden to advise a meeting in Manchester before Parliament meets.

"Mr. Mitchell from Montreal at the office. Learnt from him that Ballot has recently been established in the Municipal Elections in Canada. Formerly riot and intimidation, now tranquil as possible. The question is growing there, and it is expected it will before long be applied to Parliamentary elections also. Legislative Council in Canada is nominated and a Bill to make it elective is proposed. Thus Englishmen are everywhere more rational than in their own country.

"[15*th*.] To Manchester. A Mr. Catterall of Preston called on me, wishing me to interfere to get him an appointment as Judge of County Court—rather an odd request to a stranger, and one I am not likely to serve him in, for members not devoted to 'party' are not distributors of patronage.

"Wilson described an interview with Cardwell, the new President of the Board of Trade yesterday. He thinks Cardwell timid, without force and originality, which is also my opinion of him.

"[17*th*.] Home. Clear frosty day, very pleasant. Elihu Burritt and John Petrie came to tea. I walked down with them to the Public

[1] Cobden was never so impassioned as Bright in the cause of electoral reform. It was almost the only bone of contention between them.

Hall to a meeting which E. Burritt addressed for an hour on his favourite topic, 'the ocean penny postage.' His facts were convincing and his language beautiful and impressive. I spoke briefly in seconding a petition to Parliament. The meeting was a very satisfactory one.

"[18th.] To Manchester. Discussed proposed meeting with Wilson and others; generally in favour of it.

"In the evening received a letter from Cobden, in which he positively declines to attend it if held, on the ground that our motives would be misunderstood or misrepresented. He goes to the Peace Conference, because there is a party doing something or attempting something, and wishes a movement for the Ballot, but is tired of speech-making leading to nothing, etc.

"I think him entirely wrong, and acting as if he were disposed to 'abdicate' as a political leader. A meeting would give him a good opportunity of advancing his views.

"I am greatly annoyed at this difficulty, for it tends to show that Cobden is rather shrinking from maintaining the fight in which he has been so long engaged.

"[23rd.] Spoke to Chas. Parry on the subject of his daughter's marriage, and urged him not to be annoyed unreasonably that she had married out of the Society. Such things must be in so small a body, and might be often for the best. The control of parents was not intended to be absolute.

"[24th.] A nice letter from my precious Helen to-day from Bristol. Her letters show she is growing out of a child, and threatens to become a woman.

"[25th.] To Manchester—arrangements for the meeting next week. . . . To Whitworth's [1] in Chorlton St. Admirable establishment for machine making, chiefly tools. Examined his machine for measuring the standard yard, by which he can measure to the millionth part of an inch.

"[26th.] This morning I have received a copy of Cobden's pamphlet '1793 and 1853,' and have read it through with intense pleasure. It is written with excellent tact and temper, is clear in its historical narrative, sound in its principles, and calculated to produce a powerful and very useful effect on public opinion.[2] It should be

[1] Afterwards Sir Joseph Whitworth, the eminent engineer and inventor.
[2] Cobden's brilliant attempt to stem the invasion panic of 1853. "If it did not work a great national conversion, at any rate it did not fall dead. Opinion decided against him for the hour, but that the question should have been regarded as an

published at a very cheap rate, and sent as a peace messenger into every house in the Kingdom.

"[27th.] To Manchester this morning, along with my father-in-law, to the Peace Conference at the Corn Exchange. Well attended; Geo. Wilson in the Chair. I spoke on 'Arbitration in place of War'—without preparation, but so as to please the friends of peace present.

"Dined at the Palatine Hotel, a company of about 25. Before dinner a subscription was begun for the promotion of peace principles and information. Sturge, Thomasson, Hadfield and Geo. Bradshaw each put down £500—others £200 and £100. The plan is to raise a fund of £10,000 and to employ lecturers to teach the people.

"Home evening; making notes for speech to-morrow evening at Free Trade Hall Meeting.

"[28th.] I went to Manchester after dinner, and to the Free Trade Hall peace meeting at 7 o'clock. A magnificent meeting; Geo. Wilson in the Chair. Speakers: Jno. Burnett of Camberwell, Milner Gibson, Cobden and myself. I spoke for an hour and felt exhausted by the effort. Was not very well satisfied, but my friends evidently were, so suppose my speech was not without effect.

"With Wilson and Gibson to the Clarence Hotel till ½ past 1. Coffee and conversation as to political future. Gibson thinks the old Whigs who are excluded from the Government are not content, and look to some better understanding with us; they now begin to discover that *our* views are those of the *ancient Whig party* (which is quite true) on the questions of Reform and Military expenditure.

"[30th, at Wakefield.] Dr. Irvine of Leeds, homœopathic physician, came over to see Mother. Speaking of their medicines he mentioned one of them, 'lachesis' I think, which is obtained from a poisonous snake in Sumatra. Dr. Hering, now of Philadelphia, obtained it, and he supposes a few drops of the poison from one snake had supplied Europe. He said it was a very valuable medicine. I think this story is more difficult to believe than anything else I have heard in connexion with the new science.[1]

"[31st.] *The Times* to-day has about 16 columns on Peace question:

open one was the first preliminary condition of the world coming round to his view." (Morley's "Cobden," Chapter 23.) "Bright came up to me to-day when we met, and exclaimed, 'What a glorious pamphlet you have written!'" (Cobden to his wife, Jan. 27.)

[1] See page 139.

report of our meetings, Cobden's pamphlet, and a 'leader.' So the question is being well discussed.

"[*February* 1.] *The Times* to-day has a long article on my speech at the Free Trade Hall. It is something to make so powerful an organ of opinion debate questions with us. By and by *The Times* will write for us—that is, when public opinion goes with us.

"[*3rd.*] To Manchester at 3 o'clock. At six to the Town Hall: a very good meeting [1]; 350 present, active and influential men. Speeches: Gibson very good; then Brotherton, Jas. Heywood, Hy. Ashworth and myself.

"I spoke on the Ballot, exhibiting mode of voting in Massachusetts, U.S.A., and the explanation produced a good effect. Jas. Heywood moved a resolution requesting the Lancashire Liberal Members to consider themselves a Committee to aid in procuring for Lancashire its share of representation in a new Reform Bill.

"[*4th.*] After dinner to Oldham, with Chas. Walker, to attend meeting in honour of W. J. Fox, M.P.[2] An interesting meeting, but most painfully crowded. A poetical address, written by J. C. Prince, was read by a young woman, whose reading was tolerably effective, tho' her pronunciation was very faulty. The address was written in a richly bound album in which were recorded the names of 1,646 women who had subscribed to a purse of £120, also presented, along with a beautiful signet ring, to Mr. Fox. Altogether it was a very gratifying proof of the kind feeling existing between the Oldham people and their representative. Fox answered in a very elegant and eloquent speech. I spoke after him, but not well, or so satisfactorily as I could have wished.

"[*8th.*] Manchester. Called on Edmd. Potter who wished to see me on the Soap Duties as affecting the printers as well as the poor. I advised him to get up a deputation to the Chancellor of the Exchequer.[3]"

5

Parliament assembled on February 10 for the session of 1853. The war crisis began three months later, but at the opening of the recess, Bright still believed in the probability of a peaceful settlement.

---

[1] The meeting Cobden declined to attend.

[2] Fox, the Unitarian Minister who became (as Bright told his son) "the orator" of the League.

[3] The deputation duly arrived in Downing Street on the 22nd, and was introduced to Gladstone by Cobden and Bright, who notes: "Mr. Gladstone very patient, taking notes of every point."

The drums beat loudly while Westminster was silent, and roused him to a great effort at the Peace Meeting in October at Edinburgh. But in the earlier part of the year his mind was absorbed by the questions of India and Reform. He left home for London on February 9.

"[10th.] Startled at the news of an insurrection in Italy, and that Mazzini had left England for the scene of action. Greatly fear we may hear of his falling into the hands of the Austrians, from whom he will receive no mercy.[1]

"To the House with Gibson. Took our seats on the front bench below the 'gangway.'

"Lord Jno. Russell explained the measures to be introduced by the Government. 'Reform' to be postponed till next session! No more *men* to be proposed for Army or Navy, which is a proof of the false character of the alarms recently spread about the dangers of invasion, etc.

"[14th.] Reform Club, and met Paxton, who gave me a glowing account of the Crystal Palace now building at Sydenham; the like of it the world has never yet seen.

"[16th.] This morning concluded to take a house, No. 4, Hyde Park St., £220 to July 1, '53. Expensive, but a capital situation.

"[23rd.] Reform Club, where I found a message by telegraph from Heath, giving a worse account of dear Elizabeth [2]: 'Patient worse, come—no immediate danger.' This alarmed me. I returned a message that I would leave London at 5. Vapour bath, and off at 5 o'clock, Great Northern Line. Old Lord Salisbury in the carriage down to Hatfield. As we were starting, he said to a youth travelling with him and sitting opposite him, 'We have got Mr. Bright on the train with us, I am told.' I said nothing, and so we travelled on in silence. From Hitchin to Wakefield I was alone in the carriage; the night frosty and very clear, the journey cold. At Wakefield at 11 o'clock, and at Heath at ½ past 11. Greatly pleased to have a better account of my poor wife on my arrival: unfavourable symptoms of the morning had disappeared.

"[24th.] At Heath. Mr. Bennett, surgeon of Wakefield, up,

---

[1] Bright's apprehensions came to nothing. Mazzini had taken a good share in the arrangement of the outbreak at Milan, and contrived to keep out of the hands of the Austrians. In due course he was back in London, striving for Italian unity and preaching Italian liberty in his paper, *Pensiero ed Azione*.

[2] Mrs. Bright, who was staying at her mother's, had been taken ill two days before.

and Dr. Ramsbotham, homœopathic physician, of Huddersfield, here also. Bennett rather awkward at seeming to act with an 'irregular' medical man! Dear Elizabeth improving nicely. I am engaged in writing letters half the day.

"[*25th.*] Dear Elizabeth better to-day. Her accident supposed to be owing to a start of her horse about 6 weeks ago. . . .

"[*28th.*] Left Heath from Oakenshaw at 11 o'clock; Euston Station at ½ past 5, having been detained a little at Harrow Station, owing to a slight accident to the engine. Borrowed another engine from a luggage train.

"[*March* 2.] Dined with Sir Wm. Molesworth. Party consisted of Lord Aberdeen, Sidney Herbert, F. Peel, B. Osborne, Chichester Fortescue, Lord and Lady Beaumont, Lord and Lady Lyttelton, Lord and Lady Wodehouse, Lady Mary Wood, Sir W. and Lady Molesworth and myself.

"Lord Aberdeen, a quiet, sensible man, not likely to go wrong, judicious and liberal, and sincere. At ½ past 10 other company began to arrive and about 11 I escaped. Lord Wodehouse well disposed, but not 'heavy weight.'

"Home and discussed the unprotestant character of English Protestantism with Vaughan till 1 o'clock.[1]

"[*4th.*] Met in the smoking-room the American Secretary of Legation. Conversation on Slavery. He, being a slave owner from South Carolina, thought the 'institution' a blessing to both races, etc.!

"[*6th.*] To Stoke Newington to spend evening with Sam [2] and Margt. Chas. Gilpin came in: talk about Kossuth, and his being watched by detective police, etc. Walked about 4 miles homewards, and then a cab—the night wet and unpleasant.

"[*7th.*] Message from Mr. Horsman.[3] Called upon him at 4

---

[1] This late conclave, doubtless, à propos of the stir created by some charges of persecution at Florence which had aroused an anti-Catholic clamour. Bright makes note of a speech in the House on this subject by Frederick Lucas, who "showed that English toleration means Protestant toleration and religious liberty to those that agree with us."

[2] His youngest brother.

[3] Edward Horsman, chiefly famous for the roughness of his tongue, was a member of Parliament for forty years. A Palmerstonian Liberal, he distinguished himself by opposing every step the Party took towards reform. He provoked Bright to one of his immortal phrases. Bright thought Lowe's hostility to the Reform Bill of 1866 due to Horsman's influence, and it was Horsman of whom he said that "he has retired into what may be called his political Cave of Adullam, and he has

o'clock; subject, the Huddersfield election. Asked me if Manchester would start a candidate against Sir Jno. Ramsden in case he came out, should the petition against Stansfeld succeed.[1] He supposed hostility to Geo. Loch, from his interference at Manchester. I could give him no answer, but that I thought there was a party in Huddersfield which would not like Sir J. Ramsden to sit for that boro', as he had so much property in it, and that they would like someone of more radical and dissenting politics.

"[8*th*.] Conversation . . . with Rothschild on Jew Bill. The Baron told me a curious thing of Lady Peel—that during her husband's lifetime she was often excited almost to insanity, and that her husband only could quiet her. His looking into the room where she was had the immediate effect of subduing the disturbance of mind under which she at times laboured.

"The present Sir Robert Peel seems to partake of this misfortune, for he is reported to become very much excited at times, and to damage the furniture, and do foolish things in his passion.

"[11*th*.] House. Spoke an hour and asked a question on the intentions of Govt. with regard to the future govt. of India.[2] Answered rather snappishly by Lord Jno. Russell. Several Members spoke, and all, except Sir R. Inglis, disapproved of the intention of the Govt. to continue the present govt. of India without more extensive inquiry.

"A discussion in the Lords on the same subject. Afterwards the Jew Bill: 2nd reading. Divided, and carried by majority of 51.

"[14*th*.] Suffering to-day from cold in the left ear; very inconvenient; rather deaf from it.

"[15*th*.] Went with Vaughan to see Dr. Chapman, homœopathist, in Grosvenor St. He gave me pulsatilla, and I gave him a guinea.

"[16*th*.] To see Mr. Toynbee, the aurist, 18, Savile Row. He examined my ears; tube inflamed and swollen in left ear. Prescribed for me.

called about him everyone that was in distress and everyone that was discontented." But he had succeeded only in hooking Lowe. "This party of two," said Bright, "reminds me of the Scotch terrier, which was so covered with hair that you could not tell which was the head and which was the tail of it."

1 Stansfeld was unseated.

2 Bright was working up to the first of his greatest speeches on India, delivered in the House in June. (See p. 145.) His thoughts centred intensely on this problem. A week later he addressed a commercial meeting in Manchester on Indian affairs and complained that neither its resolutions nor its petition to Parliament were "earnest enough."

"Drove round to leave cards on Lady Granville, Bruton St., Lady Molesworth, Eaton Place, and Lady Mary Wood, Chesham Place. Invitations from these quarters give small pleasure and some inconvenience to a man whose time is occupied, and whose mode of life does not fit him for the 'gaieties of the great.'

"[*18th.*] To Carlton Gardens to deputation to Lord Palmerston. A host of 'Medicals' there. Speeches and great protestations of regard for the public good. Macaulay there. Asked him if he agreed with the intended 'Medical Bill.' He said he did not. They proposed to take power to reject or expel a man for immorality—as for instance, for writing an indecent book—and then after expulsion, if he performed a surgical operation, it would be a penal offence! I objected also to their taking power to expel those guilty of 'irregular practice,' under which I presume 'homœopathy' would be included.

"To Mr. Toynbee in Savile Row. Paid him 2 guineas for two visits. My ear much better.

"House. Canada Clergy Reserves Bill. Spoke after midnight with evident effect, against omitting the 3rd Clause in the Bill, by which clause is abolished the guarantee given in 1840 to secure £9,280 per ann. to the English and Scotch Establishments in Canada.[1] Lord Jno. Russell yields the clause to the clamour of the bishops and Mr. Gladstone, doubtless. I advised Lord John to be bolder and to lay hold of questions with a larger grasp, etc. In the cloak-room or cloisters, met Lord John on leaving the House. He said to me, 'Mr. Bright, when you get a man with the grasp you speak of, the whole thing will go to pieces.' I said I thought more might be done than is done. Adverting to what had passed a week before on the India question, I said I thought he was unnecessarily angry in his speech, as I had offered to say not a word if it would be more convenient to him. He said 'he only expected me to speak a few minutes, and I had spoken an hour.' I told him we were always very civil off the stage, but in the House I thought he picked more quarrels with me than with anybody else. To which, laughing, he replied, 'I think it is so; yes, I think it is so.'

"Walked with him thro' Westminster Hall, speaking on India, and advising him not to go wrong by hasty legislation, but he did not say anything decisive.

[1] The Clergy Reserves Bill, introduced by Mr. Frederick Peel, Under-Secretary for the Colonies, aimed at giving Canada the control of its own relations with the Churches. The Conservative Party, backed by some of the bishops, opposed it violently but without avail.

"[19*th*.] To King's Cross Station—Cardwell, Monckton-Milnes, etc. (part of Railway Committee) witnessing experimental trial of mode of communication between guard and engine driver on train.

"[24*th*.] Went over to Gloucester Terrace to prepare to remove my luggage and books to Hyde Park St. Walked in the Park with dear Elizabeth; shopping, and seeking where to hire a good brougham and horse.

"[25*th*.] Conversation with Sir W. Molesworth in hall of Reform Club. . . . Spoke of India. Explained to him my views of what should be done, his opinion coinciding, as he assured me. He said he should convey my ideas on the subject to his colleagues. I told him we considered him the guarantee for the liberality of the Govt. and hoped he might be able to go on with the Cabinet.

"[30*th*.] Walked with E. in Kensington Gardens. Called on Cobden, who remarked in conversation that in this country there was scarcely open a great career for an honest politician. To rise in this political system a man must become a part of it—as hollow as itself, and willing to employ any instrument of fact or argument that may serve him for the moment.

"[*April* 9.] Read April number of 'Bleak House.'

"[13*th*.] Dined with J. B. Smith to meet Mr. Trescott, American Secretary of Legation. Dr. Gray, of the British Museum, there. He spoke of the panic of the 10th of April, 1848, when the Chartist insurrection was threatened; of the defence of the Museum, 200 tons of stones being placed on the roof to hurl on the heads of the people; provisions for a siege of 3 days, all eaten up by 12 o'clock the first day; the Museum built admirably for defence without intending it, stairs cut down to prevent people getting into the medal-room, etc.

"[14*th*.] R. Schofield wished me to see a new invention in the application of Indian rubber. Went with him to Leicester Square. The article is mixed with coal-tar and other substances, and is convertible apparently into almost everything that can be thought of. A Mr. Goodyear,[1] an American, is the patentee. Proposed to form a Company to work the patents.

"Spoke to Lord Palmerston about a youth named Tyrrell, now under

[1] Bright met Mr. Goodyear the next day and discussed with him the different uses of his device. Goodyear's method of vulcanizing rubber was one of the most fruitful of all the American inventions in that age of teeming inventive ingenuity in the United States.

sentence of death at Liverpool. Urged that it was a case for commutation of sentence.

"House. 'Taxes on Knowledge' discussed on Milner Gibson's motion. His speech admirable and the debate good. Majority against the Govt. Resolution to repeal Advertisement Duty carried.

"Our men frightened when they heard that Disraeli was going to vote with us!—afraid to carry their object, fearing to hurt a Govt. which refuses them this trifle!

"[15*th.*] Had some talk with Wood [1] on the vote of the preceding night and the position of the Govt. and our section, and told him plainly that a large party could not be kept together without some respect being shown to every influential section of it. We wished the Press to be free from taxes, and no consideration of convenience to a Govt. would prevent our insisting upon it.

"House. Jew Bill, 3rd reading. I spoke during the debate: compared Inglis with Rothschild, both deriving their morals from the Mosaic Law. Asked where the remedy if the Lords persist in rejecting the Bill? [2] Would the Ministers resign? And recommended the abolition of all Parliamentary oaths.

"[17*th.*] House at 4 o'clock. Gladstone's Budget.[3] Spoke 5 hours: clear and able statement, bold scheme of changes in finance and taxes; tea, soap, legacy duty, stamps, assessed taxes, etc.; a shabby proposition about Advertisement Duty which we shall try to improve. If the panic of the autumn and winter had not absorbed about a million, how much more might have been done! But John Bull is a fool, and his Press is dishonest.

"[19*th.*] Home Office on behalf of Tyrrell, now under sentence of death at Liverpool. Learned that his life would be spared.

"[22*nd.*] To Reform Club, and with Gibson to see Gladstone on Advertisement Duty and Newspaper Stamp. Cobden, Ewart, Smith, Hadfield, Shelley, Williams, Wilkinson also there. Long conversation, and hope we have done some good. Gladstone's pro-

[1] Sir Charles Wood, then Secretary for India.

[2] The House of Lords did throw out the Bill. Bright's remark is an interesting anticipation of his attitude towards Bradlaugh. See p. 508 *et seq.*

[3] The first of Gladstone's thirteen Budgets and the most distinguished in that it put an end to a long period of confused financial expedients, dealt boldly with the problem of Income Tax, removed nearly 140 existing duties and reduced nearly 150 others. The Newspaper Advertisement Duty, which Gladstone proposed to reduce from eighteenpence to sixpence, was wiped out altogether by a vote in the House of Commons.

position is to reduce Advertisement Duty from 1/6 to 6d., and to take off stamp on supplements containing only advertisements. Altogether a bad proposition, and founded on great ignorance of the question. We puzzled him a good deal I think, and hope for some gain from the interview.

"Jos. Sturge and E. Burritt came down about Ocean Penny Postage.

"Conversation with Mr. Lowe on Indian affairs, and he seems very liberal, and to see through the hollowness of state-craft in this country.

"[24th.] To Meeting twice to-day. Saml. Gurney there in the morning, and we brought him to Upper Grosvenor St. where he is staying. It is always pleasant to meet him, for he is a man of a noble spirit, kind and generous beyond most men.

"[28th.] Conversation with Lord J. Russell on taxes on the Press. Explained to him the heavy taxes on paper, stamp and advertisements, which he admitted were very heavy. He did not see why 'news' was not an article to be taxed, but it should be a small tax! How puerile for a leading statesman! News is information, facts, knowledge, the very life of intelligence, and this the leading Whig statesman of our day considers a fitting object for taxation! It were as well to make all children who go to school pay a tax to the Govt. for liberty to do so, or that every workman hiring a book from a library should pay a tax upon it to the Exchequer! 'Woe to a country when its Princes are children.' What, then, is in store for a country when its foremost statesmen think intelligence a fit subject for taxation?

"[29th.] House. Short discussion with Palmerston about charges against Kossuth. Palmerston out of temper, knowing that he is in a scrape. Budget debate very dull, and again adjourned.

"Conversation with Disraeli in the dining-room. He urged that our tactics were wrong in supporting this Budget,[1] that this Govt. was secured in power by it, that really there are now no questions to separate town and country, that a new Govt. would have invited Lord Grey to join it, as well as the 'Manchester party,' and that we were wrong in consenting to be outside, letting men who had all along opposed us carry our measures. He spoke of the kindness and affection of his friends to himself; spoke in very high terms of Lord Stanley, and said that, even if office were unattainable, his position was one of great interest: he liked the House of Commons very much.

[1] Three days later Disraeli attacked the Budget in a speech which Bright says was "well reasoned and good under the circumstances. But generally the Budget not assailable. Division gave a large majority for the Government."

"[*May* 3.] Irish Land Bills Committee. Palmerston evidently against any honest legislation for tenantry, which I explained to Lord J. Russell during the evening, and warned him against the course his colleague is taking.

"[5*th.*] House. Questions to Govt. as to the employment of spies to watch Kossuth. I denounced *The Times* for its base slanders upon Kossuth.

"Late in the evening there was a 'scene.' Mr. Duffy charged the Govt. with practising corruption on Irish Members: words 'taken down.' Duffy refused to retract. Consideration adjourned, and he to attend in his place at 4 on Friday.

Home with Smith, Walmsley and Mr. Heywood of Bolton.

"[6*th.*] House. The 'Duffy' scene renewed, but soon disposed of. Irish row for some time.[1] Character of the House not gaining by these exhibitions. This does not refer to Duffy, but to others in the debate which followed.

"Engaged with Serjeant Shee in considering clauses of Tenants' Compensation Bill. Walked up to Charing Cross with F. Lucas.

"[10*th.*] House. Bill to inspect Nunneries carried by first reading against Govt. Bigotry had the majority.

"[14*th.*] With E. to see Albert Smith's 'Ascent of Mont Blanc,' which is an amusing and interesting exhibition.

"[18*th.*] To Devonshire House, Yearly Meeting.[2] Very pleasant to see so many friends again. Lindley Murray from United States. Reflections having been made on his conduct when in England some years ago, he expressed his sorrow and humiliation that his conduct and conversation had not been consistent with the character of a minister of Christ. On a review of what had occurred, he had felt sincere regret. He trusted his friends would forgive him as they hoped that God for

---

[1] The Irish had voted against Disraeli's Budget in December and turned out the Derby Government. According to Gavan Duffy, there were negotiations with the Cabinet for Irish support on condition of the adoption of the Tenant Right Bill which Serjeant Shee had in hand and had been read a second time. It is suggested that Disraeli consented to the bargain, but that Dublin Castle and the Irish landlords prevailed. When the Aberdeen Government was formed, three minor posts were given to Irish Catholics—Monsell (afterwards Lord Emly), John Sadleir (who committed suicide to avoid penal servitude), and Keogh (who became a judge). These appointments were said by Duffy, F. Lucas and their friends to involve the abandonment of pledges for the sake of places. Duffy declared that he had seen corruption practised on some of his colleagues which recalled the days of Walpole and Pelham.

[2] Of the Society of Friends.

Christ's sake had forgiven them.   It was an impressive scene.   There were tears in many eyes—in mine among the rest. . . .

"To Vaughan's to dinner. . . .   'Table moving' talked about and tried after dinner.   Successful, apparently, on one trial, but not on a second attempt.   Four persons sat round a small table with their hands upon it and each person touching his neighbour's hand right and left. After 12 or 15 minutes, the table began to move and went round rapidly, so much so that it was difficult to keep up with it.   I don't know whether this is a delusion or not, but it seemed real, and the actors denied any trick, and I think they are to be believed.[1]

"[19th.]   Dined with Moffatt.   Superb dinner as usual.   Cobden, Villiers and Gibson there, with others,—so pleasant evening. Returned to House, having missed several divisions.   It is wrong to dine out when the House is sitting.

"[24th.]   Much amused to-night by receiving a note of invitation to dinner for E. and myself from Lord Shaftesbury to meet Mrs. Stowe.[2] Having previously an engagement to dine with Frank Crossley for the same evening, and again to attend the Birmingham meeting, I cannot dine with my ancient opponent, the calumniator of the Factory population.   In truth I don't wish to fraternize with him, for I think him in many things a mischievous character, and I am not inclined to 'lionize' anybody, altho' for Mrs. Stowe I have great admiration.

"[25th.]   Read this evening a pamphlet on Church Rates by Lord Stanley, well written, and very liberal in spirit, indicating a large freedom from prejudices and bigotry.   I suspect some of his friends will begin to doubt his orthodoxy in 'Conservatism.'

"[28th.]   Fenton's Hotel to dine with W. Brown; party of 30 or more.   Mr. Van Buren, ex-President of United States, there; many Americans.   The ex-President a pleasant sensible man, more English than American in appearance.

"[30th.]   Molesworth called me out behind the Speaker's Chair to speak about the Turkish difficulties—evidently serious.[3]   Molesworth against intervention, and wished to know what the public were thinking of it.   *Daily News* for war, and urging Govt. to oppose or attack Russia.   I was earnest against it, saying that Turkey could not

---

[1] A fortnight later, away from the experts in a family party at Newington House, Edinburgh, the home of his brother-in-law, Duncan McLaren: "We tried table-turning, but did not succeed."

[2] Harriet Beecher Stowe.

[3] The first hint in the Diaries of the onset of the War Crisis.

be maintained, and that a war would inevitably hand Constantinople over to the Russians. I suggested the strangeness of the calamity if Molesworth should be found a member of a War Govt. Cobden also saw him, and urged the same views, and told him he would leave twenty Cabinets rather than be involved by them in a war of intervention. Disraeli asked the Govt. if orders had been sent to Admiral Dundas to proceed with the English Fleet from Malta to the Dardanelles? Lord Jno. Russell declined to give any answer.

"[31st.] House. Questions on India. Contrary to all rumour and expectation, the Govt. announced their intention to bring forward their India Bill on Friday. Debate on Irish Church going on. Lord John spoke most illiberally on the subject, which forced me to reply. Considered to be effective by my friends, judging from the cheering. I shall have small chance of amity with Lord John: he is weak and inconsistent.

"[*June* 2.] Home early. Sat up till ½ past 1 preparing extracts for speech to-morrow if required.

"[3rd.] Preparing notes for speech on India question. One o'clock, Irish Tenant Right Committee, till near four o'clock: some progress made.

"House. Sir Chas. Wood spoke from ½ past 5 to ½ past 10 in defending Indian Govt. and explaining his proposed measure. It was the least interesting speech on a great subject I have ever heard from a Minister. The House became thin, and most people were very weary and sleepy. The proposition itself is a miserable expedient, pretending to do something, but really leaving matters much as they are.

"When the Minister sat down, I rose and spoke from ½ past 10 to ½ past 12, answering many of his statements, and attacking his plan of amending the Court of Directors. The House quiet and interested. I never spoke with more ease and satisfaction. So many compliments and congratulations when I sat down as to force me to ask myself whether I was not more pleased at my own success than at having done something for good govt. in India. Debate adjourned. The issue of this question depends mainly on the course taken by Lord Derby and his friends.[1]

[1] The speech of June 3 was the first of the five great speeches on India which Bright made in Parliament between 1853 and 1861. He and Cobden led the campaign against the scandals and errors of the irresponsible government of India which the Mutiny brought to an end in dire calamity. For months he had been informing

"[4th.] Indian Reform Meeting. Mr. Ferguson from Calcutta there, and to come to see me to-morrow. My speech has evidently given great satisfaction to our Indian Reformers.

"Lord John's speech on Irish Church has given new offence to the Catholics, and Monsell, Keogh and Sadleir have resigned their offices in consequence. There is a rumour that Lord Aberdeen disavows the expressions and opinions of Lord John, and that the resignations may possibly be recalled. What a source of national ill is this 'howling' Protestantism, and what a decrepit statesman is Lord Jno. Russell to lend himself to the miserable cry!

"[5th.] Evening, I went over to Cobden's; a nice quiet party. Kossuth looking well and interesting as ever. He thanked me very warmly for my defence of him in the House of Commons from the attacks of *The Times*.

"Senator Douglas from Illinois, United States, there—a little, dark, but firm-built and intelligent-looking person, called in his own country 'the little giant.' Evidently a man of superior mental power, distinct and logical in his style of speaking. He was in the House of Commons on the recent Irish Church debate, heard my speech, and expressed his surprise that such sentiments were fairly listened to and considered in this country: thought them more like the sentiments prevalent in their Congress.

"From Cobden's to Grosvenor Gate, and called on Disraeli, on the India question. Found him amusing as usual and perfectly frank. Discussed condition of the Govt. and of the Tory Party. He thought

his own mind and endeavouring to inform the mind of the country on India. The subject was hardly a day out of his thoughts and his reading was almost confined to it. He had taken part in forming an Indian Reform Association. In May he spoke on India to a meeting at Bristol; on June 1 he addressed 2,000 people at Birmingham. Wood's proposals, which he now denounced, amounted mainly to a feeble shuffle of offices in India, leaving untouched most of the evils of dual control and perpetuating the worst features of the East India Company's régime. Its sole virtue was that it introduced the competitive system into the Civil Service. Bright's sentences rang like a prophetic knell: "Should the people of India be goaded by our treatment into insurrection, we must reconquer the country or be driven ignominiously out of it. I will not be a party to a state of things which might lead to the writing of a narrative like this on the history of our relations with that empire. . . . Let us act so at this juncture that it may be said of us hereafter that, whatever crimes England originally committed in conquering India, she at least made the best of her position by governing the country as wisely as possible, and left the records and traces of a humane and liberal sway." "I am very anxious to see a much wider employment of the most intelligent and able men amongst the native population."

Lord Derby not disposed to office again. On the India Bill, proposed to decide before second reading. Possibly Lord Stanley would move some resolutions adverse to going on, or to some part of the scheme. He told me a curious story of Mr. Lowe, of the Board of Control, and Mr. Delane of *The Times*. A friend of Disraeli's, taking up some papers from the table of the House, took up by mistake a note which proved to be written by Delane to Lowe, asking him to write an article attacking Graham and Co. for being disposed to allow the 'great criminal' to escape—meaning Augustus Stafford, who has been in trouble about the Dockyard appointments.[1] It is odd and not very creditable that Mr. Lowe, a member of the Govt., should employ himself in writing against his superiors in office.

"[10*th*.] Cobden, Smith and Walmsley called, and we went on to the Bank of England. Joined Van Buren and his son and Hume; went thro' the Bank. Saw an Australian 'nugget' weighing about 130 lbs.—gold and quartz—worth £5,000 or £6,000. Gold value one million in flat bars, etc. With the same party to Lloyd's Insurance rooms and coffee room, news room, etc.

Six years married to-day. How time flies!

"[11*th*.] With dear E. and H. to Sydenham to see the Crystal Palace. A wonderful project; the situation charming; the building magnificent; the grounds promising to be most attractive.

"Mr. and Mrs. Gilpin, from United States, here to spend the evening; he a relative of dear E. Was Attorney-General of the United States. Very intelligent man, and have much enjoyed his company.

"[14*th*.] Long talk with Sir James [Graham] on Newspaper Stamps and Gladstone's scheme with regard to them. Urged upon him the propriety of conceding something to those who support the Govt. and our great dissatisfaction with the course taken on this subject. He repudiated all wish to tax the Press. Asked what we wished to have done, and was disposed to consider the question again.

"House: Berkeley's motion for the Ballot. I spoke after 12 o'clock for nearly an hour; too long at such an hour, but even then compelled to compress, and on the whole not well satisfied, tho' many

---

[1] Augustus Stafford, one of the "Young England" Party, Secretary of the Admiralty. This was not his last trouble about the dockyards. It was alleged, in connexion with a petition that unseated two members for Devonport in 1865, that Stafford had stood at the dockyard gates as the workmen came out during the election and that he had entertained the officials and leading men to dinner. Disraeli then proposed the complete disfranchisement of dockyard boroughs, but the clause to that effect was knocked out of the Reform Bill.

spoke well of the speech. Division 172 to 232. The question seems making some progress.

"[18*th*.] By 10 train to Manchester. Home by 6 o'clock. Shocked this evening by a fatal accident to Absalom Mason, one of our wagoners, run over by his wagon, on his way home from Manchester. Left a wife and 7 children. How sudden this event, and how awful! but how continually we forget the uncertainty of life!

"[22*nd*.] Ill with toothache, a bad finger, and generally out of spirits.

"[25*th*.] At home preparing for speech on 2nd reading of India Bill. Troubled all day with pain in the face. Teeth or tic, not sure which—but very unpleasant.

"[26*th*.] At home all day, suffering a good deal from my teeth. In such condition employment is almost impossible, and idleness is distressing. G. Moffatt called during the afternoon; pleasant chat with him. He thinks the Whigs consider the 'Manchester School' to have rendered Govt. by their party no longer possible.

"[27*th*.] Morning, preparing for speech on India Bill. . . . House at 6 o'clock. Spoke from 10 to $\frac{1}{4}$ to 12; full House. Sensible effect of my attacks on East India directors. Hogg rose, evidently excited. His reply weak, and himself 'showing symptoms of distress.' [1]

"[*July* 1.] House. Advertisement Duty. Govt. had a majority in one division, and we beat them afterwards in two divisions, rejecting the proposition to continue a 6*d*. Advertisement Duty. I spoke, and compared American *New York Tribune*, and its price, with our newspapers. No answer made or possible to our speeches. Cobden spoke well and earnestly.

"[4*th*.] Spoke to Geo. Fitzwilliam about the Petition from Electors of Peterborough complaining of the undue influence of his father, Lord Fitzwilliam, in the elections of that city. Conversation with him about speaking in the House. I wondered such as he did not work and take a position in the House. Referred him to Duke of Newcastle, Sidney Herbert, Lord Stanley as industrious and useful members of the aristocracy. Why nobody among the Whig party? Why not he? Told him if I were Lord Fitzwilliam's son I would soon be Prime Minister, would give something of mine to the policy of the country. He said he could not speak—had great difficulty at elections. 'His

---

[1] On the 30th, the second reading of the Bill was carried by a large majority. Bright notes the acute division among the Tories, only 110 of whom voted for Lord Stanley's amendment. "Lord Derby's friends" had not lived up to their opportunity.

tongue seemed to cleave to the roof of his mouth.' He was very nervous; and it was no use trying, etc. He seems without force, and I suspect he is somewhat dissipated, tho' naturally amiable and quick of disposition. Walked up to St. James's St. with Lord Robert Grosvenor. Conversation on Newspaper Stamp question, in which he agrees with me. On Education question: directed him to a recent return I moved for, showing increase of children at school in this country.

"This evening, W. Brown introduced me to Govr. Brown, of U.S., just returned from St. Petersburg, where he has been Minister for 3 years. Had an interview on Thursday week with the Emperor Nicholas, who expressed his disbelief in war and his anxiety for peace, did not think actual hostilities would come out of the present disagreements between Russia and Turkey, etc.

"[7th.] Rumours of war, and of dissensions in the Cabinet, that Lord Aberdeen has resigned, overcome by Palmerston's intrigues, etc. Probably no truth in rumours, only it is difficult to see how Aberdeen and Palmerston can act together on any foreign policy.

"[9th.] News to-day considered more warlike, but I cannot believe in war arising out of present differences. Home early, and a pleasant saunter in the Park with dear Elizabeth. Our dear Boy 'A' has been in bed for two days, ill, but is apparently recovering. His complaint is a 'rash' very much like measles, just now very prevalent. Prince Albert is suffering from them, and the Queen's eldest boy has had them.

"The weather has been very warm for a few days, and harvest prospects are improved, both here and on the Continent. A week hence we hope to be down at home—a tempting thought after the turmoil and unrest of a three months' stay in London. But my 'London Season' may last, and will probably last, six weeks longer! What a clumsy machine our House of Commons is! The English people get on really without much Govt., or they would not tolerate such a complex and wretched instrument of legislation as now exists in this country.

"There have been great rumours of divisions in the Cabinet on the Russian-Turkish question, and probably with some foundation; but they have somewhat died away again, and it is supposed Lord Aberdeen and the Peace party have the majority in the Cabinet, and that Palmerston is not all powerful there. If this is so, it is fortunate for this country and the world.

"[14th.] Preparing matter for India Bill discussion, on employment of natives and uniting the two departments in England under one roof.

"Nothing yet settled about Advertisement Duty. I have given some members of the Govt. to understand that we shall consider their refusal of our wishes as a proof of their desire to repudiate us, and as a declaration of war. And so it will be—and so we shall treat it.

"[15th.] Slave Trade Treaties Committee. Examined Captn. Hamilton, who has been engaged in the Slave Trade Suppression service. His evidence shows the whole thing to have been a failure and a blunder. House at 6 o'clock. India Bill: some clauses passed. Attempt to get rid of the directors' oath, almost all on our side of the House for it, Govt. excepted. They, voting with the Tories, continued the oath.

"[18th.] Mr. Ellerby, from St. Petersburg, called. Conversation on Russian affairs. Character of the Czar's sons: oldest amiable and mild, the second reckless and ambitious. Probabilities of civil war when the present Emperor dies. Rigid censorship of newspapers.

"[20th.] House of Commons. In the majority against the repeal of the Attorneys' Certificate Duty. Mr. Gladstone announced his intention to entirely repeal Advertisement Duty, so our labour has not been in vain. This is an important step towards a free Press.

"[29th.] To Manchester and London (from Rochdale). Euston Square at ½ past 4. No cabs at work in London. Station Yard an amusing sight—butchers' carts, greengrocers' carts, and carts of all kinds almost, got together to take away passengers and luggage. The streets are much more quiet than usual. The absence of cabs reduces every day almost to the quietude of Sundays. Skinner St.[1] and by river to House. India Bill: moved my clause which was lost by 100 to 72.[2]

"[30th.] This morning the cab-insurrection is at an end, which is a relief to persons who live so far westward as I do just now.

"[31st.] Vaughan called for me, and with him and Judge Haliburton of Nova Scotia (Sam Slick). Went to Beckenham, Kent, to W. A. Wilkinson's (M.P. for Lambeth), chiefly to see Oliver Cromwell's head, which it is believed he possesses. From the facts known with regard to it, it is highly probable that it really is Cromwell's head. The pike is still in it on which it was affixed over Westminster Hall.

"[August 8.] To Corbyn & Sons. Concluded bargain for a barouche: if bought, 127½ gns., or hired, 35 gns. per ann., and may be

---

[1] The London office of his firm.

[2] Bright moved a clause to sell India House and bring the two departments of the Indian Government at home under one roof.

bought within two years, deducting sum or sums paid for hire and adding interest of money. Corbyns to repair, except in case of accidents, and to paint once in 5 years. Concluded to take on job or hire for the present.

"[10*th*.] Thro' the Park with Cobden. With him afterwards to dine at Fenton's Hotel with Mr. Brown, M.P. Among those present was Mr. Slidell, American Senator, who appeared to be a sensible man with more of the Englishman than American in his manners.[1]

"[12*th*.] So I have concluded this long Session, during which I have undergone much labour, and, I would hope, not wholly without result, tho' the Indian Bill has sorely disappointed me. The English Parlt. is a clumsy machine to work: it is a wonder that anything good comes out of it."

6

The first month of the Recess passed in family reunion at Rochdale. Mr. and Mrs. McLaren were among the visitors, but they left before the new carriage arrived home to be admired, and the new chestnut horse which he bought at Myers's stable in Manchester for £55. The subscription of £25,000 for building the new Free Trade Hall, an enterprise that deeply interested Bright, was completed during these weeks. Among his pleasanter distractions he counted visits from Whitworth (who had been to the New York Exhibition as a Commissioner, and brought back a report on American manufactures and labour-saving machinery) and from Robert Leech, who called to talk about the monetary difficulties he foresaw in America; going out on fine nights to see the comet; haunting the *Examiner* office to talk newspaper "shop." In September he took Helen to Newcastle to the Priestmans', and accompanied his father-in-law to Tynemouth and Cullercoats, "to get information as to the size, weight and price of fishing nets, with a view to decide if a machine for making nets by power would be likely to answer. Much pleased with the industry and civility of the fishermen. About 35 boats in the village, using ten or twelve nets in each boat." He pursued the question of nets with the makers (Preston and Rae) in Newcastle, and talked it over afterwards with Whitworth in Manchester.

---

[1] Mr. Slidell was one of the two Confederate agents, Mason and Slidell, who entered the pages of international history in 1861, when they were forcibly taken off the British steamer *Trent* by Captain Wilkes of the Federal ship *San Jacinto*, at the serious risk of war between England and America.

He now contemplated for himself a little tour in France: the purchase and study of "Markham's History of France," which he records, was a characteristic preliminary. On September 16, having convoyed his daughter back to school at Brighton, he crossed from Folkestone to Boulogne. His jaunt led him, after two days' sightseeing in the capital, to Rouen and Havre, by boat to Caen and diligence to Cherbourg and Granville. Thence he drove through the heart of Brittany by Rennes to Nantes, returning up the Loire to Angers and Tours. He made a diversion by train to Bordeaux for a single day, then turned back to the Loire for more castles (Amboise and Blois) and so home, by Paris and Calais. This was fairly constant locomotion. He did the journey in twenty days, and gave himself no time to write more than a mere itinerary. The solitary comment in his diary on a thing seen was made at Tours: "Service in the Cathedral: a gorgeous idolatry."

In October he attended a conference of the Peace Society in Edinburgh [1] with Cobden, and returned to take his family for a holiday to Blackpool. Its happiness was disturbed by the news of his brother Gratton's illness abroad.

"[*October* 30.] A note from my Brother Sam saying that they had learned by telegraph that our poor Brother Gratton was lying at Boulogne at the point of death, and that Jacob was gone off instantly to Boulogne. Our last letter from Gratton was from Venice, and spoke of his having been ill, but that he was better. Now we hear of his being at Boulogne, returning doubtless in consequence of increasing illness. Poor fellow. I would fain hope he may yet be spared.

"Another letter from Henry Fowler informing us of the sudden death of Robert Barclay on 6th day morning. All this sad news has much distressed us. Three years ago, during our trip of a few days to the Lakes, dear Esther was in her last illness and we only knew of it

---

[1] Bright's Edinburgh speech is admirable reading to this day. He had at his finger-tips every diplomatic detail of the Eastern Question, and vigorously chastised the policies that were leading up to the Crimean War; but the more permanent and at the same time the most striking part of the address was its analysis of the economic and moral consequences of war and the dangers of large armaments. His plain category of historical fact and his broad generalization of humane principle are the perfect commentary on Tennyson's ill-mannered explosion of jingoism and bad temper in the foolish lines of *Maud*:

This broad-brimm'd hawker of holy things,
Whose ear is cramm'd with his cotton, and rings
Even in dreams to the chink of his pence . . .

just before we heard of her death. Now dear Gratton is ill, perhaps dead, and away from home, and we hear of it while enjoying this peaceful scene.

"[31*st*.] No further news to-day. It must be Bologna in Italy where Gratton is lying ill.

"[*November* 6.] A very quiet day at Blackpool, the sea unusually calm. A few more people here to spend the day. A sweet evening with our precious children. A melancholy feeling over everything, as we have yet no intelligence from poor Gratton. I much fear we shall only hear that he has sunk under the malady, and that Jacob even arrived in Bologna too late to see him alive.

"[*9th*.] This afternoon received letters from Thomas and Sam conveying the sad intelligence that our poor Brother Gratton was indeed taken from us. A telegraphic message from Bologna from Jacob was received yesterday which terminates the suspense in which we have been for nearly a fortnight past. This is to me a very melancholy event, and the circumstances attending it add much to the severity of the blow. We know almost no particulars and wait Jacob's return with anxiety. Poor Gratton—so early gone—so far away from us and amid strangers!

"[*December* 3.] To Manchester, League rooms, to decide on Free Trade Prize Essay. Wilson, Paulton, Hy. Ashworth there. The award is in favour of motto 'Be just and fear not,' [1] written by Mr. Dunckley,[2] Baptist Minister in Salford. He has already gained a prize for his essay 'The Glory and the Shame of Britain.'

"[*6th*.] To Manchester, League rooms. Mr. Dunckley came, and was informed that his essay had been awarded the first prize. He is a young man with a good head and a lively spirit, and will be an acquisition to our district.

"[*16th*.] At home. Read 'Vivian Grey,' Disraeli's first novel. Clever. His hero's principles seem to have been those of the writer in his political life.[3]

---

[1] This was Bright's own motto.

[2] Afterwards editor of the *Manchester Examiner*. He wrote over the pseudonym of "Verax."

[3] Bright did not read largely in fiction. His daughter Mary (Mrs. Curry) writing of his illness and convalescence in 1870, said it was then that he first became acquainted with many of the best novels, which she read to him. He had the good Victorian's joy in Scott and Dickens, but poetry and history were his favourite reading. He notes having read this winter, in addition to all the essays sent in for the Free Trade Competition and his Markham, a pamphlet on Greece and the Greeks, Madame

"[17*th*.] To Manchester, League rooms, to inspect plans of the new Free Trade Hall.

"Yesterday, heard from Cobden with a note from Villiers to say that Palmerston has left the Aberdeen Govt. *The Times* confirmed the statement. Opposition to any Reform Bill is the pretence, and, tho' he hates reform heartily enough, his secession is but a blow long meditated, I suspect, to destroy the Ministry for the chance of coming in as Premier himself. This event is important, because Palmerston is a dangerous fellow, a mere adventurer and impostor, but clever and altogether unscrupulous, and precisely suited to take the lead of the scattered forces of the Tory party. I am glad he has taken this step. He is unmasked at length, and I hope the Tories will now get their own.

"[20*th*.] To Manchester, and to London by the 12 train.

"[22*nd*.] Reform Club. Saw Jno. Dickenson on India Reform matters. Long chat with Villiers on prospects of the Ministers. He, seeing everything as usual thro' a rather gloomy medium, believed the Govt. could not stand a week after Parlt. met if Palmerston joined the Opposition. The Reform Bill intended, he thought, would be a measure of importance.

"Met Lord Ernest Bruce in the Haymarket. Discovered from his conversation that an effort was making to get Palmerston back again, and intrigues afloat to force a modification or withdrawal of the promised Reform Bill.

"[27*th*.] To Manchester. Determined to adopt Mr. Walters's plans for the Free Trade Hall, the votes being 10 to 4 in his favour."

de Staël, the poem, *Discovery*, of his brother-in-law Edward Leatham (afterwards M.P. for Huddersfield), Byron's *Sardanapalus* (to Mrs. Bright), and Locke's "Reasonableness of Christianity."

CHAPTER VIII

THE ANGEL OF DEATH

I

FOR Bright the terrible year of 1854, shadowed by the tragedy in the Crimea, opened in profound and prophetic gloom. His New Year sky was overcast by private as well as by public griefs, and especially by the death of his brother Gratton, whose fatal illness Jacob Bright, when he returned, attributed to a fever caught while bathing at Venice.

Such Arctic weather as that of January, 1854, is rare in England. "So much winter is strange to this generation," Bright said. On the way from Manchester to Rochdale one night, his train was snowed up. He had to sleep at Middleton, and next day to walk seven miles home. "Hard work," he wrote. "Snow very deep; carts and wagons, full and empty, left in the road. Saw a cow being dug out of a drift in which she had been buried during the night. How she lived thro' it is strange. The whole traffic of this district has been suspended since yesterday about noon, many mills not working for want of coal. Our mills stopped at ½ past 4 last evening to give the people a chance of getting home, but about 60 or more of them slept in the mill rather than encounter the danger of attempting to go to their own homes. They were furnished with a good supper in the schoolroom and were not unhappy at their singular position. We have had no London papers since the day before yesterday, and no London mail or letters to-day. Such a storm of snow has not been known for very many years."

The month passed at "One Ash" quietly, amid family gatherings subdued by sorrow. The only interludes were visits to Manchester and Sheffield to make speeches on some public occasions. Into the first he was persuaded against his will by Cobden, who had got up a meeting on a local education question. "I have some hesitation about it, but do not like to shrink from any good work in which he is engaged." So he spent an evening making notes for a speech, and went next day to Manchester: "Education meeting in the Mechanics' Institution. Spoke for an hour, showing that the arguments of the voluntaries are untenable, but giving them high credit for their efforts and labours."

Then there was a Reform banquet at Sheffield. Cobden, Lord Goderich and Bright spoke,—Cobden "not so well as usual, the subject of Reform being not so familiar to him as economical questions." The diners of the 'fifties were greedier of oratory than their modern successors ("My speech an hour and a quarter"); but Bright was not altogether without bowels of compassion for his listeners. "How difficult it is to speak briefly!" he confides to himself. "It seems to become more difficult. Am certain it does not arise from love of it— rather, I suspect, from full acquaintance with the subjects discussed and anxiety to state the case so fully as to convince. . . . Cobden and I went to Edward Smith's—and talked till two in the morning."

The little cloud no larger than a man's hand now floated well above the horizon. But in January it was still possible to reason on "the Eastern question." Milner Gibson, Cobden and Bright addressed a meeting on the 24th at the Albion Hotel in Manchester and propounded their peace views to an approving audience: "An excellent meeting. Gibson spoke well; Cobden's speech admirable. Much said on the Eastern question, and difficult for anyone to come after them; but I got through satisfactorily. We were strong for peace and non-intervention, and the meeting responded to our facts and arguments." A few months afterwards, for reciting the same facts and using the same arguments, Bright was burned in effigy.

The diaries of the war period contain a full record of the Parliamentary situation from day to day, and they clearly display his own reactions to the War spirit. But they show us nothing whatever of the reactions of the War spirit to John Bright. His soul broods continually on the folly of the nation and agonizes over its growing sufferings; what passes in the outer world, the contumely of the mob, the fickleness of former friends, leaves him apparently indifferent. He makes no personal complaint that the people of England turn away from their idol. He can, and does, encounter Palmerston in debate and leave him without a rag of logic or humanity to clothe him in political decency; but of the studied personal insolence of the man whom Disraeli called "the patrician bully of the Treasury bench," hardly a word. He dwells alone with his own strong conscience and waits. There are few more splendid spectacles of moral courage in all the pageant of political history than that of Bright and Cobden with their backs to the wall braving a hostile and malicious world during the first year of the war, knowing it for a crime, and daring to testify to their knowledge in the teeth of public hatred and private obloquy.

All other topics in his journals are subordinate to this; but Bright interested himself in a varied collection of public and semi-public questions in the course of the year. He wrote a good deal for the *Manchester Examiner*, discussed schemes for acquiring a weekly paper (*Diogenes*) in London, and for starting a daily paper in Manchester; spoke on Church Rates; pressed for the ballot at elections; advocated decimal coinage; campaigned against capital punishment; and pursued with all his old vigour the one remnant now left of the "taxes on knowledge," the stamp duty on newspapers.

He left for London on January 30, to enter upon a Parliamentary session destined to be at once one of the most sorrowful and one of the most triumphant of his political life. His daughter Helen was with him, on her way back to school at Brighton. He saw her off at London Bridge Station, "in good spirits." Within a week he was breasting the full tide of the fierce controversy which overbore every other interest for two years.

"[*January* 31.] House opened to-day. Popular excitement disappointed as usual. Opposition not serious. Much doubt, evidently as to foreign policy (Eastern question) and unwillingness to quarrel with Govt. Lord Jno. Russell made defence of Prince Albert against charges recently brought against him.[1] His speech very good, and explanations considered satisfactory.

"[*February* 3.] Called on Mr. Buchanan, the American Minister, on the subject of wearing 'Court dress' and his absence from House of Lords at the opening of the session. Found him a fine old man, tall, grave and sensible, very friendly and frank in conversation. He told me he had been connected with the Democratic party all his life and intended to maintain his consistency in all things. 'Gold lace and embroidery' he utterly rejected. It had been suggested that he should appear in a dress like Washington's, but that was antiquated and odd, and 'it would be affectation to appear in the dress of the Father of his Country.' He had thought of blue coat (common dress coat) and the 'American Button,' but somebody from Sir Edwd. Cust, Master of Ceremonies, proposed a single-breasted coat, stand-up collar, and

[1] That he was a pro-Russian and had conspired with Lord Aberdeen to promote the policy of the Emperor Nicholas.

the 'American Button,' to which possibly he might consent, but had not decided. He said nothing wrong had been done or said to him —on the contrary, every respect and kindness was manifested by the Govt.[1]

"We spoke of cool treatment of distinguished Americans here: Van Buren here last year and not invited to Court. Senator Douglas, here then, left letters and cards upon high personages (officials); some or many not even returned, and no attention paid him. Going to France— received by Emperor and Empress; to Russia—kindly welcomed by Nicholas. These things make impressions, and Van Buren and Douglas, too, as he knew, felt it, and the contrast could not pass unobserved. I proposed to mention the 'Court dress' question in the House to have some explanation. Mr. Buchanan thought it better not, unless Lord John Russell agreed to it, and would say what was proper in a few words. So agreed that I should see Lord John. I did so when the House met: 'He had written to Lord Clarendon about it.' I urged that the steamer of to-morrow ought to take out his explanation. He said, 'There will be another boat, I suppose.' 'Yes,' I replied, 'when it is too late. Some reckless portion of the American Press will make mischief if possible, and your explanation will come when the harm is done.' Finding him cold and indisposed to say anything, I desisted, and made no remark on the subject in the House, tho' I think something should have been said. Mr. Buchanan said he should write a private note to his Govt. explaining the whole thing to prevent misapprehension.

"What a miserable wretched thing a Court must be, if so much depends on its chief officers and visitors putting on a dress fit only for a buffoon!

"[6th.] Lord John's speech on change of oaths on taking a seat in the House.[2] A good speech. Change very good if oaths not to be

---

[1] Similar questions arose in 1929 in connexion with the dress worn by General Dawes at Court.

[2] The question had been active ever since 1847, when Baron Rothschild, elected for the City of London, claimed his seat, but could not take the oath of allegiance in the prescribed form—"on the true faith of a Christian." The House of Commons carried a resolution for the amendment of the form (Lord Ashley the chief opponent, Gladstone, Disraeli and Lord George Bentinck the curiously associated supporters of Lord John Russell's motion); but not for another ten years were the disabilities of the Jews removed. An Oaths Bill was carried by the Commons in 1849 and rejected by the Lords; the same fate attended the Bill of 1851, and that of 1853. In the Bill of 1854, now mentioned by Bright, Russell proposed to substitute a simple oath of allegiance for all the clumsy forms then in existence.

abolished altogether, which would be the wisest course. Lord John intimated that if Lords reject Bill, it might be necessary to reconsider the resolution which prevented Rothschild from taking his seat, and to propose to admit a member who was willing to take the oath in such manner as is binding on his conscience. This is the true solution of the question, and should have been done years ago.

"[*8th.*] This morning to my new quarters, 4, Bennett St., St. James's. Vapour bath. Dined with Lord Granville: small but very pleasant party—Lord and Lady Granville, Lord Glenelg, Lady Ailesbury, Cornewall and Lady Theresa Lewis, Bishop of Oxford, another gentleman whose name I did not catch. Dinner very nice and moderate and the company free and cheerful and pleasant.

"Conversation with Lords Aberdeen and Granville on Eastern question. Both as strong for peace as I am, but thinking the country violent for war. I blamed the Govt. having committed themselves to intervention, and not having extricated themselves when the Turk began the war against their advice. Both evidently felt that an error had been committed. Aberdeen said 'the independence and integrity of Turkey' was a phrase which had no meaning, could not be. Peace might have been made half a dozen times over if Turk more reasonable and not under the influence of fanatical party acting in the belief that, having England and France to back them, it was a grand opportunity for them to fight Russia. Aberdeen thought Russia did not want more territory but sought *influence* and was really for peace if escape could be made for her. He told the Queen that loyalty was found with the Radicals at Manchester, alluding to my speech at the recent meeting there, rather than with the Tories and the Tory Press! I asked if he could learn anything further very soon. He said, 'No, not for some time,' and then, turning to Lord Granville, he said, 'You know how I should bet upon it,' to which Granville replied, 'Yes, and Palmerston thinks still we shall have peace.'

"I told them that men in high office did wrong in letting public go wrong without fully explaining a question and putting them right, and advocated the freedom of the Press from penny stamp as means of liberating the Press from Pall Mall cliques.

"The Bishop of Oxford very clever, and pleasant, and disposed to be civil to me. What a distance separates his position and perhaps his views from mine! This is written immediately on my return to my lodgings.

"[*9th.*] Cobden called; going out of town to Midhurst. Discussed my conversation with Lord Aberdeen, and his meeting on the 'Taxes on Knowledge.'

"[10*th*.] Called on E. Satterthwaite [1] and ordered him to sell Crystal Palace shares—a considerable loss, but fear to lose more if war break out.

"House: Bill to suppress Bribery at elections—a vain attempt without Ballot.

"[13*th*.] Lord John's Reform Bill. Tame speech. Disfranchisement good, and also the extension of county franchise. Distribution of seats very bad—nearly all to the counties and not in proportion to their present representation or population or property.

"A new scheme of representing minorities, detestable on every ground: would half-disfranchise Manchester and other large boroughs to which three members are given—that is, one additional member. Majority would choose two members and minority one, so that the result of Manchester would be one vote instead of two for Liberal measures.

"What a miserably small man Lord John is! Nothing broad, nothing simple in his policy! [2]

"[15*th*.] War again believed in to-day. I am distressed and disgusted beyond description at the folly of Govt. and people. I met Lord Shaftesbury this morning. Talked over Russian question; told him they had restored the Pope to his throne, and now they were going to fight for Mahomet! What next?

"[17*th*.] House: Eastern question, but did not stay to hear the debate. So oppressed with a sense of the mischief gathering around us, and of the folly of the Govt. and country that I would gladly escape the subject, especially as the debate had no definite purpose.

[1] His broker.

[2] Of this Laodicean project, Bright remarked in his big speech at Birmingham four years later "the least said the better." It was too strong for the Whigs, too feeble for the Radicals, and pleased nobody. The device of securing "minority representation" by giving electors in three-membered constituencies only two votes was tried afterwards, but abandoned in the Reform Act of 1884. Lord John Russell proposed some "fancy franchises"—e.g., representation of public bodies (including the Inns of Court!). Bright's downright mind scorned all attempts to dilute the plain principle of election by majorities. His speech on Lord Grey's proposals in 1865 denounced the special representation of universities, professions and trades. "Look with the greatest possible suspicion upon any of these fancy propositions of Reform. . . . If any man comes before you with a complex and involved scheme which is difficult to understand . . . he does not offer you solid coin with the impress of the British Constitution upon it, but he offers you flash notes. . . ."

Home (Bennett St.) and read thro' the first volume of Sparke's life of Washington.

"[18*th*.] Shares and funds much depressed. War considered imminent.

"Dined with Thos. and Caroline and Miss Moore at 32 Norfolk St.; afterwards with them to see and hear Mr. Woodin, of the 'Carpet Bag.' His performance clever in many things, but I find none of these things afford me much pleasure or amusement. I never had much enjoyment from exhibitions of this kind, or from theatrical performances, and, as I grow older, they become positively wearisome.

"To call on Cobden: found him deep in the Eastern Blue Books, preparing for a speech on Monday evening. He had been into the City, and had sought and obtained useful information on Russian and Turkish question, as to trade, progress and sentiments of population, etc.

"Coming home down Bond St., met Lord Granville and a gentleman I did not know. Lord Granville called out. I stopped, and we had a chat about affairs. 'Had he any consolation?' He 'feared he had not, but would not give up a hope of peace so long as no blow was struck.' Asked me what I thought of Lord Grey's speech the other night. He thought it admirable and closely reasoned, and he feared that six months hence it would be found a formidable text-book against them. He should not have liked to have undertaken to answer it. I spoke of the rising of the Greeks, which he thought likely. Then what a position to be in!—to be fighting for the Turk to maintain his despotism over the Christian majority in Turkey in Europe! To which he answered, 'I suppose Lord Stratford must bully the Turks as hard as he can into granting privileges to the Christians.' [1] I told him I thought they had brought the country into a horrible mess, and that, were I a Minister, I would resign before I would share such responsibility. At which both he and his friend laughed, for resignation on such grounds is, I suppose, thought to be foolish and showing a disposition too squeamish for a statesman.

"[21*st*.] Meeting of members called by Hume to consider Reform Bill. From 40 to 50 present; Hume in the Chair. He spoke entirely for the Bill and the Govt. I took a different course, criticizing the Bill throughout, repudiating the redistribution of seats to the counties, and the project of representing the minority, and declaring that nothing should induce me to support the Bill in that shape.

"This opinion, as to minorities, shared in by everybody present

[1] Lord Stratford de Redcliffe, Ambassador at Constantinople.

apparently, except by Mr. Fox and Cobbett from Oldham. Hume objected to put a resolution to that effect—would have everybody support 2nd reading; but finally agreed he should state to Lord John Russell the opinion of the meeting, and that we should meet again on the Minority question next Friday.

"[*22nd.*] Talk with Ellice and Parkes at the Club, from which I gather that the Govt. is in a desperate mess with the coming war, and their position with their Reform Bill far from pleasant. But for the necessities of the war, I think they could not keep in office long.

"Note to Lord Jno. Russell declining invitation to dinner for the 25th. It is awkward to dine with Ministers when one differs so entirely from them, so it is fortunate I am going down home at the end of this week, and thus I can easily give a reason for not accepting the invitation.[1]

"[*26th, at Rochdale.*] To Meeting in the morning. A sweet quiet day with dear Elizabeth and the darling children.

"Yesterday Oswald Baynes sent us a nice chestnut horse, just a match for 'Rhyl,' good character and handsome, apparently exactly what we have been looking for: price £33; eight years old. We propose to call him 'Chester,' where he was purchased.

"[*March* 1.] This morning at ½ past 1 o'clock our family increased by the arrival of a little girl. Everything going on quite favourably. The children amazed and delighted at seeing their new little sister.

"[*4th.*] Dear Elizabeth and the baby going on very favourably. The last few days, since the birth of the little girl, have been more than commonly happy with us.

"[*9th.*] Slept little last night, thinking of the recent dinner to Sir C. Napier at the Reform Club and the discreditable speeches made at it. Excited and not well.[2]

"House: intending to say something on the speeches at the Napier

---

[1] See page 270.

[2] Sir Charles Napier, who had been given command of the Baltic Fleet, was entertained to dinner at the Reform Club by the Liberal Party on March 7, with Palmerston in the chair, and Sir Wm. Molesworth and Sir James Graham among the leading performers. Graham, First Lord of the Admiralty, made a statement gross even among the jingoistic vapourings of which the speeches chiefly consisted: "My gallant friend says when he goes to the Baltic he will declare war; I as First Lord of the Admiralty give him free consent to do so." This was three weeks before the declaration of war.

dinner, but Graham did not come in till public business had begun. He afterwards explained his absence satisfactorily, and asked me to put off my question or remarks till Monday, as he was going down to Portsmouth to-morrow. He told me he had given orders to liberate Mr. Clerk, a Coast-guard's man who was on board a man-of-war but had conscientious objections to going to the war, as he had had for some time past to his situation in the Coast-guard.

"[13th.] House at 4 o'clock. Spoke in condemnation of the dinner to Sir Chas. Napier at the Reform Club: blamed Palmerston, Graham and Molesworth for attending it, and denounced the reckless levity manifested on the subject of war by the Ministers of a civilized and Christian nation. Palmerston very insolent in his reply; called me the honourable and 'reverend' Member, was called to order by Cobden, and made a most lame and ineffective speech, as was admitted by all his friends in the House. Molesworth very angry and very bitter,—owed no allegiance to me, admitted I was 'an able man' but 'full of illiberal and narrow-minded prejudices.' The three Ministers evidently in a desperate mess, and made worse of their wretched attempts to get out of it.

"[15th.] To E. Satterthwaite's and made a purchase of Consols at 91⅛, owing to report of fresh propositions from Prussia in favour of peace, to which Russia is supposed to be willing to agree. . . .

"Reform Club, reading over debates on Russian and Turkish question in 1791. Fox and Burke and Whitbread strong against England supporting Turks against Russia.

"Yesterday had a talk with Disraeli in the Library. He insists that war is the result of the Coalition. Any Govt. with a united policy, under one head, would have preserved the peace. Spoke of his shilling edition of his novels. He said he had sold more than 300,000 copies in less than a year—that 400,000 copies would give him a profit equal to his salary as Chancellor of the Exchequer!

"Up till half-past 3, writing a long letter to Lord Aberdeen on behalf of peace, urging the acceptance of new propositions said to have been offered thro' Prussia on behalf of Russia, reminding him of his heavy responsibilities, and pointing out that it would be more glorious to fall in the endeavour to preserve peace than to reign thro' the calamities of war.

"I have written this letter under a pressure of anxiety I could not withstand. It may do no good, but the smallest effort, tho' unsuccessful, should not be neglected.

"[17th.] Drove up to Argyle House and left my letter to Lord Aberdeen.[1]

"[21st.] Among my letters, one from Lord Aberdeen, very friendly, and expressing the 'deep impression' my letter had made on his mind, inviting me to call upon him on the Sunday. Wrote to him to explain why I had not sooner received his note,[2] and received a reply asking me to call upon him to-morrow.

"There is much frankness and simplicity in the language and correspondence of the Prime Minister.

"To Skinner St. Business dull. The coming war deranges trade, and deters every one from contracting engagements. Funds and shares declining almost daily.

"House: discussion on Income Tax, in which I take little interest. Am unwilling to vote for any increase of taxation to defray military expenses.

"Evening with George Wilson in the smoking-room. Home, and read private correspondence between Emperor of Russia and our Govt. on Turkish difficulties. Amusing enough, showing anxiety of Emperor to act along with England in his designs on Turkey. Lord John Russell's dispatch admirably written and good in tone.

"[22nd.] To Argyle House to see Lord Aberdeen. Expressed his fear that hostilities with Russia were now unavoidable; his great sorrow at this result. When offered the Premiership, was sensible of his deficiencies and unfitness for the position; accepted it reluctantly, as it was wholly unexpected by him. Consoled himself with thought that at least he could preserve peace, and yet step by step we had approached the verge of war. Deeply regretted that the propositions, on the supposed receipt of which I had written my letter to him, had not been made. Assured me that the slightest opening would be seized by him to prevent war, or to conclude peace. Would avail himself of any proposal for mediation and for peace, '*even if he stood alone.*' He expressed himself as much obliged to me for my letter, and would receive with the utmost willingness and pleasure anything I could say that might promote or enable him to promote peace. His grief was such

---

[1] Bright told Lord Aberdeen that, in one sense, he had more interest in preserving peace than any other man in the kingdom. The Administration would be known in our annals not as the Russell or the Palmerston but as the Aberdeen Administration, and upon him as Prime Minister would "rest the blame or the praise which this generation and which posterity and impartial history will award to the policy which is now to be pursued."

[2] He had been home for the week-end.

that at times he felt as if every drop of blood that would be shed would rest upon his head. He repudiated the ideas of those who insisted on schemes of humiliation of Russia by depriving her of the Crimea, and expressed his belief that Turkey, or the Turks as a Govt. at Constantinople, could not survive the war. Said the Emperor of the French had behaved very honourably, and had so far been even more pacific if possible than his own Govt., but now perhaps might be more disposed for war. Thought with me that the publication of the secret correspondence might incense him more against Russia. Did not believe that Austria had any arrangement with Russia, but went with England and France 'in the cause,' altho' not willing to join in the war; that the neutrality of Austria and Prussia would be directed to insist upon negotiations at the first opportunity.

"Spoke of the newspaper Press. I pointed out how much it is in the hands of individuals and cliques, referred to the *Morning Post*, Palmerston's paper, and its abuse of Lord Aberdeen, and urged that the repeal of the Stamp was the only mode of improving the character of the English Press.

"He inquired as to carriage of Russian produce in English vessels; said Govt. would have nothing to do with privateers, and intimated they would interfere as little as possible with commerce carried on in neutral ships. He spoke of French alliance—so far very honourable; but some doubts as to the harmony when French and English troops were side by side, altho' the Admirals had agreed perfectly. Did not wish English troops to come into contact with Greek insurgents. Admitted that the Consular statements as to internal condition of Turkey were much worse even than appeared in Blue Books, as the worst parts were necessarily omitted to avoid damaging the case of the Turks.

"The conversation lasted more than half an hour. He was very free, and apparently very sincere, thanked me for my letter, and assured me again how much he should strive to avert war, or to make peace at the earliest possible period. The answer of the Emperor of Russia was not yet come. Could only expect a refusal: *possibly* it might be in such a shape as to delay an immediate commencement of hostilities, tho' not to be anticipated as probable. Believed the Emperor had not desired war, but was now irritated, and, tho' a clever man, still might be ungovernable after the disappointments he had met with, and the provocation naturally arising from all that has occurred.

"I left Lord Aberdeen with the belief that he is sincerely anxious to avert the horrible calamity impending over Europe, but I suspect he is not sufficiently master of his own Cabinet, and has been dragged by his colleagues into a course which is entirely opposed to his own convictions. I will hope that if any chance of peace arises he will have the firmness to seize it at all hazards to his own tenure of office, which, indeed, I fancy he does not value highly.[1]

"[*23rd.*] Home early and writing letters till near 2 o'clock. Amused to-day by a most familiar nod from Molesworth, who, after his angry remarks the other night, does not seem inclined to quarrel. It is politic not to make enemies in the House, so Ministers think, I suppose.

"[*24th.*] Conversation with Mr. Walter of *The Times* on the war. Urged him to seize any chance of preserving or making peace. Remarked upon *The Times* being browbeaten into a support of the war. He said when the country would go for war, it was not worth while to oppose it—hurting themselves and doing no good. Walked up with Cobden. Continued fall in funds and all shares from alarm of war and drain of gold: money becoming dearer. Such is a portion of the penalty we pay for our foolish and wicked determination to meddle in the Russian and Turkish quarrel.

"[*25th.*] Call from young man wanting some employment. Lost character for honesty, and an outcast seeking pity and help. Told him to call again. Will see if anything can be done for him. Emigration and a change of name almost his only chance. Society is very cruel in these cases, and I would not help it to trample on the fallen.

"[*29th.*] Up till 3 o'clock reading over Blue Book on Turkish question. *Declaration of War* in the papers this morning: a sad result of 12 months' negotiations.

"[*30th.*] Home early, reading Blue Books on Eastern affairs, and considering matter for a speech to-morrow night on the address in favour of War with Russia."

2

The speech on Lord John Russell's motion for an Address in reply to the Queen's War Message was the first of the great Crimean orations by which Bright earned the wonder and admiration of the House of Commons and the execration of a populace that had adored him. He stated the grounds of his opposition to the war in a perfectly built argument, calm in style, highly documented—the solid platform from which

[1] The verdict of history on "the British Aristides" has singularly confirmed Bright's view of Lord Aberdeen.

he afterwards soared to unprecedented heights of oratory: "I have no special sympathy with Russia, and I refuse to discuss or decide this question on grounds of sympathy with Russia or with Turkey; I consider it simply as it affects the duties and interests of my own country. . . . Alliances are dangerous things. . . . I would not advise alliances with any nation, but I would cultivate friendship with all nations. . . . The past events of our history have taught me that the intervention of this country in European wars is not only unnecessary but calamitous."

"[*31st.*] Preparing for Speech. House at 4 o'clock. Lord John moved address in answer to war message; not much responded to. After him Mr. Layard attacked the Govt., showing their differences and their bad management of Foreign policy.

"I spoke next more than an hour and a half, well listened to, and with effect on many members judging from their warm congratulations when I sat down,—Roundell Palmer, Lord Harry Vane and a dozen others speaking to me in most complimentary terms. From this and other evidence I am satisfied there are many calm thinking men in the House who condemn the war but feel it difficult to oppose it. Palmerston spoke later in the evening—flippant and superficial as usual in his attack on me. Time will show who is right in this war policy. Rothschild, speaking to Gibson to-night, said a country with 800 millions of debt should have considered much and seriously before it involved itself in another war.

"Pressure in money market increasing. Met Mr. Evans of Manchester who is seeking to borrow £15,000 for a rich Irish contractor (Dougan) and offering 10 *per cent.* for the loan for a year! How must other contractors be? One of them lately (Peto) told me they, that is himself and partners, held contracts for 17 millions sterling!

"Met Mr. Hincks to-day at Reform Club—he is Prime Minister of Canada. Also introduced to Lord Elgin in the Lobby,—late the Governor of Canada Asked after my brother Jacob, whom he had met in Canada. He looks like a very sensible man, well qualified, as he has proved himself to be, for the high office he has held.

"[*April* 6.] House. Home before midnight. Finished reading Disraeli's 'Sybil'—remarkable book in every way.

"[*8th.*] Home early, and up till after one o'clock writing out my speech on War question for publication in a pamphlet by the Peace Committee.

"[*9th.*] An amusing incident to-day in coming up St. James's at one o'clock. Lord Elcho, Mr. Rutherford the Scotch Judge, and Lord Brougham standing together. As I came up, Brougham offered his hand to me in the most polite manner, was glad to see me, and entered into most friendly chat as if we had been meeting and talking every day for years. Some ten years ago we had a correspondence not of an amicable character, and since then have had no communication of any kind. The quarrel arose out of an article reflecting on him in the *Anti-Corn Law Circular,* and which he imputed erroneously to me. Speaking of the war, he seemed to take a less unfavourable view of affairs than I am able to do. He is a wonderful man for his years— and seems almost as young and active as at any time for 20 years past.[1]

"[11*th.*] House. Lord John Russell explained why abandonment of Reform Bill was decided on. Towards the end of his speech, adverting to suspicions of his friends that he was not sincere, he became much affected, and at length was in tears, and unable to speak. The House cheered, of course, to give him time; but he scarcely recovered himself. It was quite a scene, and, after it, it was impossible to say anything harsh of the matter. I spoke, expressed my belief in his sincerity, but showed that the Bill was not calculated to excite any feeling in the towns, as they gained nothing by the Bill. Hoped for something better in happier times.[2]

"Rumours that Prussia is going with Russia. Panic in the Funds, and great fluctuations. War disturbs everything. It has destroyed the session, and will greatly injure, if not disgrace the country. Lord John admitted that the Govt. must have resigned but for the necessities of the war.

"[12*th.*] By 9 o/c. train to Chester and Wrexham. Lord Alfred Paget in the same carriage. During the journey spoke of the 'scene' in the House the preceding evening, and of Lord John's fit of crying as he announced the abandonment of the Reform Bill. Lord A. said he was 'almost choked with emotion as he saw the distress in which Lord John evidently was.' As he told me this, I observed tears trickling from his eyes, showing that his sympathy was not mere transient feeling. During a stage or more I was with Sir Jno. Young and his wife (he is Irish Secretary), a fair and liberal man, and generally popular in his office. His wife an interesting person. At Wrexham conveyance

---

1 See page 214.

2 The country had, in fact, been indifferent to the question of Reform at the General Election of 1852, had witnessed with equanimity the postponement of a Bill in 1853, and was now absorbed in the War.

for me to Brymbo Hall. Arrived soon after 4. Met with a hearty welcome from W. H. and C. Darby.

"The party consisted of J. B. Gough,[1] the American Temperance orator and his wife, Jno. Littleboy and his wife from Liverpool, etc.

"Evening to Wrexham Temperance meeting. I was prevailed upon to be Chairman. Gough's speech very effective and well recd.

"[*13th*.] Walked over to see Richd. Rawlins and his paper mill; then rode on to the Rhudy Taboy Mine. Dined there; then to Bwlch Winn Mine. Then to see some curious large stones on the adjacent moor, and then home to Brymbo Hall.

"Evening to Wrexham Temperance meeting, very much crowded. Smith Harrison of Liverpool in the chair. Gough's speech admirable and most effective.

"[*14th*.] This morning a long excursion on foot to 'Nant y Neath,' a romantic glen. Dined at the head of it. Scrambled up and down rocks and clambered up watercourses thro' a most romantic pass. Then walked back, well tired, having had a delightful excursion.

"Evening. Tea party at the Hall, of the chief workmen of the company. I spoke for half an hour on War and Reform Bill, Gough on his great subject most amusingly and instructively, others with judicious observations. A little singing, and the evening was passed very pleasantly.

"[*18th*.] To Manchester. Discussion in the train there and back on the War—people befooled by Govt. and Press.

"Our carpet trade grievously injured by War raising price of tow (flax). Arranging to-day to use cotton instead of tow. Difference in cost from £12,000 to £15,000 a year on the quantity in use, and probably more.

"[*26th*.] Day of Humiliation and Prayer on account of war with Russia. It is wonderful what an amount of hypocrisy or of ignorance there is in this proceeding.

"The Govt. secures the co-operation of the State Church, and thus attempts to obtain the concurrence and sympathy of the 'religious public' to their wicked policy. Humiliation is indeed admirably suited to the

---

[1] J. B. Gough, of whom Dr. Lyman Abbott said that his history was the history of the Temperance Movement in America, was of English birth, the son of a sergeant in the line, and was born in Kent. He had a stormy career, with more than one lapse from sobriety. During a later visit to England he brought and won a libel action against Dr. Lees of the United Kingdom Alliance, who had overstepped the mark in accusations against his character and conduct.

occasion, for what feeling is more appropriate when we engage in the slaughter of our fellow-men,—for no definite object, for no object in which we have any real interest,—from whom we have recd. no injury, nor indeed so much as an insult? Prayer for success seems much like a gang of burglars seeking the Divine blessing upon their guilty enterprises.

"The public sentiment is demoralized and Christianity is impeded, and its character tarnished by impieties of this kind.

"[29th.] To Hart & Co., Broad St. Buildgs., to inquire about new discovery of 'vegetable wool' by a Belgian. Saw many articles made from it. Appointed to meet the inventor on Wednesday next.

"Dined with Mr. Dickenson at 39, Upper Brook St. A pleasant party: Dr. Mayo and his wife, Mr. Yarrell, a naturalist of some note; Mr. Brown, great botanist, somewhat like the late Wm. Forster in appearance; Mr. Delane, Editor of *The Times*, who must always be a man of importance so long as *The Times* retains its present position. A good deal of conversation with him on the war. His opinion as to its non-necessity and its impossibility for the ostensible object of it, agrees precisely with my own. His theory that the war will last 6 or 7 years, that England and France will assume Govt. of Turkey during that time, and finally put on the throne of Constantinople some European prince. Mine rather that the war will not last so long, but that the difficulties of the case will force all parties to an earlier settlement, Constantinople to be a free city, with provinces an independent state under some protection from the Great Powers.

"[*May* 1.] Left House early. To Reform Club. Saw Mr. Clarke there, who told me of a very insulting dispatch from Lord Clarendon to the Brazilian Govt., very annoying to the Brazilian Minister here. Also that he suspects some negotiation is going on with France to put Count Montemolin on the throne of Spain in place of the unhappy and dissolute woman now reigning in Madrid.[1]

"[4th.] House: Cardwell's Railways Bill. Spoke a few words in favour of delay.

"Talk with Disraeli in the dining-room. He thought it time to declare for a 'peace' policy. I condemned his having sanctioned the war, but he said it could not be helped. He thought Gladstone's finance measures very bad, which is the general opinion. Spoke against Palmerston, whom he described as a bully, a successful bully—the most popular Minister, but without any following either in or out of Parliament.

[1] Isabella II.

The way to Parliamentary success was 'to be feared;' till a man would damage or overthrow a Govt. he had no chance of being one of the governors, etc.

"[5th.] Preparing notes for speech against the war if opportunity should offer.

"[6th.] Read Bowyer's 'Public Law' and Fox's speeches.

"[7th.] Hy. Ashworth called, and I went with him to Westminster Meeting. Eli and Sybil Jones there; meeting very solemn and their addresses and sermons impressive. His 'Let the wicked forsake his way, and the unrighteous man his thoughts' etc. very logical and beautiful. She poetical as usual, and winning in her sermon; but more striking in her prayer, which began with, 'O Thou! before whom the angels bow, and the Archangels veil their faces and adore.' I spoke to them afterwards; found them preparing to leave for the States about the 20th inst. I regret their departure, having been much drawn towards them during their visit to this country. I know no ministers I have ever heard with equal pleasure and profit—profit, I fear, however, only of a fleeting character, for in this terrible confusion in which I live, a confusion apparently inseparable from a political career, impressions of good are soon obliterated, and indifference and sometimes worse than indifference succeeds. I do think God has spoken thro' these good people, and directly to me, however I may fail to hear or to obey. How transcendently is their position for time and for eternity above all that the most brilliant successes of public life can give!

"[8th.] Gladstone's Budget of taxes for war: doubled Income Tax,[1] Malt Tax increased one-half, Sugar and Spirits increased, altogether raised about ten millions! So much for the beginning of a most needless war!

"[11th.] Westerton's.[2] Bought Miss Bremer's 'Homes in the New World'; it looks like a charming book. Disraeli spoke highly of it to me the other day.

"[12th.] House. Scotch Education Bill. Came away early, and did not vote. Govt. were beaten upon it, and their Bill rejected. Such is the end of all the measures of this composite Govt., or of most of them. The war only saves them—they live on the necessity created by their most wicked act!

"[16th.] House. Gibson speaking on Newspaper Stamp Law. He spoke well. I spoke on the debate and evidently with great effect,

---

[1] The rate of Income Tax was raised from 7d. to 1s. 2d.
[2] The bookseller, in Piccadilly.

exhibiting *The Times, Melbourne Argus, New York Tribune, Potteries Free Press*, and *West Sussex Advertiser* to the House, showing the unfairness of the stamp, and its effect in destroying a cheap and local Press. The House seemed entirely convinced—so much so, that Palmerston was obliged to withdraw motion for 'previous question' moved by Attorney-General, and to Gibson's resolution—which we consider a great triumph for our cause.

"[18*th*.] With J. B. Smith to House. Nunneries Bill withdrawn. Spoke briefly against attempts to legislate against Churches and Sects. With Cobden to 23, Lowndes Square, to dine with Mr. Locke, M.P. A quiet family dinner; afterwards Lord and Lady Granville's evening party; rather crowded. Home at 12 o'clock and sat up foolishly till 3 o'clock reading 'Coningsby.'

"[19*th*.] Headache all day; sitting up too late last night. House. Spoke a night or two ago to Sir C. Wood on behalf of Tyabjee, from Bombay, wishing to be introduced to the Queen. He refused. Found him only 'an overgrown shopkeeper' in Bombay. 'Not the sort of person' to be introduced; could only introduce people from India of equal rank, etc., as people introduced at home, etc. I urged the policy of treating Indian native merchants with some notice. All this nothing in the eyes of the President of the Board of Control.

"[30*th*.] To Westbourne Terrace to dine with J. B. Smith, M.P. Met there Honble. Mr. Leaver, of Boston, a leading man of that city, and of the Whig party there.

"Walked down with Cobden. Met Lord Alfred Paget in Berkeley Square, who complained of my damaging speech last night against the Govt. His sympathies are so entirely with Lord Jno. Russell, that he feels acutely when anyone on our side says a word against him.[1]

"[31*st*.] My American relatives, Jno. Bancroft and his wife and sister, and dear Margaret called. Went with them thro' the Houses of Parliament and for a few minutes into Westminster Abbey. Then up the river to Battersea and Chelsea and back. In the evening to Jas. Bell's, Devonshire Place, to meet a number of Friends and friends of peace: much conversation but nothing important done.

"[*June* 1.] After dinner at the House, a conversation with Disraeli

[1] On the withdrawal of the "Disfranchisement Bills," there had been a debate on the 28th with some acerbities between Lord John and Disraeli. Bright in a short speech had declared that the Government "existed only on the war," had brought great evils on the country, and were undermining the Parliamentary system by keeping office when unable to carry any of their measures.

on affairs—he wishing a reconstruction of parties, conceiving the idea that some on our side might join him. Explained his theory of government in this country: our chance of continuing a first-rate country depends on maintenance of free aristocratic institutions. As a republic, must be far inferior to America. Is for changes and reforms consistent with this idea. Church question will settle itself by the growth of population not belonging to it.

"[8th.] To Manchester [1] and on to London by the 12 o'clock train. A sad accident with dear Elizabeth's favourite horse 'Rhyl.' Driving into Manchester, he came down and cut his knee most severely. He is ruined, and I have been melancholy all day, knowing the disappointment it will be to dear Elizabeth; he is such a favourite with her, so handsome, and of so sweet a temper.

"[9th.] Changes in the Govt. Strutt retires; Lord Granville succeeds him to Duchy of Lancaster, to give Lord John Russell Presidency of Council. Sir Geo. Grey to Colonial Office in place of the Duke of Newcastle, who becomes Minister of War—a new office, of unfortunate omen, I think.[2] Govt. not improved by accession of Sir Geo. Grey. He is in reality a Tory and of the 'professing religion' caste, which is worst of all—subjects him to Church and Bishops.

"[12th.] To Mr. Rahn, American dentist, 1, North Audley St., whose skill is I suspect superior to that of our dentists.[3] In Berkeley Square met Lord Granville. Chat about the changes in the Govt. He said people insisted upon it that he ought to have a grievance, but he had not. Wished to strengthen the Govt. by taking in Sir Geo. Grey. I spoke of disagreement of Govt. and that they were not a Liberal Govt. He said the real Tory in the Govt. was Lord Palmerston: many of his colleagues were very Liberal.

"Immediately afterwards met Lord Carlisle. He is recently from Constantinople. Asked him the state of things there. He replied by a gesture that it was too bad to be described.

"[13th.] Heard in the House from good authority that much dissension exists in the Cabinet. Molesworth not satisfied at not going to the Colonial Office, etc. Palmerston too, it is said, intriguing with

---

[1] He had spent the last few days at "One Ash."

[2] Hitherto the Secretary of State for the Colonies had also been Secretary for War.

[3] Mr. Rahn afterwards did a good deal of dentistry for Bright, who frequently had trouble with his teeth. He acquired a liking for Mr. Rahn, and was greatly distressed by his illness and death from paralysis.

Tory party, object being to make him Prime Minister in case Aberdeen Govt. is overthrown, which I suspect cannot be long delayed. The Coalition this year is a failure and everybody feels and admits it to be so.

"[14th.] Brighton Station at ½ past 5 and met darling Helen; brought her to Bennett St. where she stayed the night. Cobden went with us to see Friend's Diorama of Canada and the Niagara Falls—a beautiful picture and worth seeing. Later I went up to Gloucester Terrace to Vaughan's party, stayed an hour, and came away with McLaren. To bed at 1 o'clock. My precious child sleeping in my dressing-room—how sweet and how innocent! What a charm in that last word, and how little we can claim it as we go on in life!

"[15th.] To the Euston Station with dear Helen. Sent her down by the 10 train. Her little visit has been very pleasant. . . .

"House: presented a petition from two labourers complaining of being sent to prison and treated as felons for non-payment of Church Rate of 1/9. So much for our Established Church in the year 1854.

"[17th.] Reform Club: bath, dinner, a game at billiards with Collier, M.P.[1] Home: read a little of spirit manifestations in a book left for me by E. T. Wakefield. Can't understand it, and can't believe it—tho' too much evidence to justify an absolute denial of the phenomena.

"[18th.] House. Church Rate Bill, 2nd reading. Spoke in the debate; complimented on speech. Lord John's reply wretched and discreditable, a Tory speech. Not a cheer from our side; Tories cheered, his friends disgusted. Division 182 for Bill; 209 against. Reform Club to dinner. Home and prepared speech to oppose Irish *Regium Donum*.

"To be right in a debate is the source of great power. Lord John could not make a fight: his case desperate. I could pity him, but for his inconsistency and dishonesty: it is time the Dissenters found him out.

"[July 4.] To Mr. Rahn's—but could not attend to me to-day. Saw a sweet little girl of 9 yrs. old, a daughter of the Earl of Dunraven, whose mouth and teeth have been most successfully treated, a remarkable deformity of the teeth being in process of perfect cure.

"Reform Club: discussion on points of the war, with some men very valorous whilst fighting is at a distance, and who seem incapable of taking any fair view of the conduct of the Emperor of Russia.

"[6th.] House at 6. Spoke for an hour against Irish *Regium*

[1] Sir R. P. Collier, the first Lord Monkswell.

Donum: division 149 to 62, votes prevailing against facts and arguments.[1]

"[17*th*.] In Downing St., meeting of 'Supporters' (?) of the Govt., called by circular from Lord Jno. Russell. 150 members or more there.[2] Apologetic speech from Lord John; remarks by Vernon Smith, Horsman, Hume, myself and others—not flattering to Govt., showing dissensions existing and displeasure with the Administration. Graham looking 'pious,' that is, hypocritical. Palmerston also a curious study during discussion.

"[18*th*.] This morning received a short note from dear Margaret from Waterford with the afflicting intelligence of the death of my dear mother-in-law,[3] during her journey in Ireland on a religious visit, after an illness of six weeks. This is a sad stroke to my dear relatives and to me. She was a woman of singular intelligence and virtues and piety, and her removal from among us will make a void which can never be filled up. She was a Christian in life and in death, and leaves a bright example for the guidance and encouragement of all who knew her. Her kindness to me during the 16 years I have known her has been that of a mother, and I would mourn her as 'one that mourneth for his mother.'

---

[1] Bright looked backwards in this speech to the Maynooth Grant debates and repeated with force the argument he had then used and was to use again in the controversies of 1868 and 1869—that the *Regium Donum* was a pill to cure earthquakes, and that the only true solution of the Irish Church question was disestablishment.

[2] Lord John had some cause for the grief which induced him to summon this famous meeting. The Government throughout the session had failed to command the support of Parliament on any major matter except the war. Lord John was obliged to withdraw his Reform Bill; his Jew Bill was defeated; and in this summer his Oxford Reform Bill (or rather Gladstone's) was transmogrified. Because in its original form this Bill failed to remove any of the grievances of the Dissenters, Bright called it a "pusillanimous and tinkering affair." He said Dissenters were always expected to manifest too much of the inestimable qualities spoken of in the Epistle to the Corinthians: "To hope all things, to believe all things, and to endure all things." The House of Commons accomplished a notable exhibition of independence, freed the Nonconformists from theological tests at matriculation, and admitted them to the B.A. degree. They did not receive the complete franchise of Oxford till seventeen years after.

[3] Rachel Priestman played a great part in the life of Bright. After the death of his own mother she did, in fact, fill the void in his heart. She was buried at Jesmond Cemetery on the 26th. Bright attended: "Father leaning on the arm of his daughter Margaret; Anna Maria spoke at the grave. Mr. Tanner prayed. The meeting solemn. E. Tregelles, May Lloyd and Mr. Pease spoke. . . . The day closed with solemnity and quiet."

"Evening, dined with Monckton Milnes. A pleasant party: Duke of Newcastle, Lord John Russell, Bishop of Oxford,[1] Mr. Crawford, M.P. for Ayr, Mr. Sickles, of American Embassy, Genl. Thomas of U.S., Mr. Brunel,[2] engineer, and others.

"Amused at sitting next to the Bishop, who is a clever and amusing person. He spoke of Lord John as a 'little gamecock,' not a 'great' gamecock. He lamented the Church had been so long represented by Sir R. Inglis in the House of Commons: 'People thought the life of the Church was that death.' He thought Cobden favourable to Church; evidently liked Cobden's simplicity and earnestness. Discussion at table on opening letters by Secretary of State. Conversation with Duke of Newcastle on Newspaper Stamp; urged him to help repeal of Stamp. Wilson Patten at the dinner,—always cheerful, amiable and intelligent. Walked down with Mr. Brunel—intelligent and lively.

"Glorious summer day, promising well for harvest. How good is the good Giver midst the follies and crimes of the nation!

"[29th.] With J. Dickenson to King's Langley, Hertfordshire. Met there Dr. Mayo, Mr. Dasent, of *The Times*, and his wife, etc.

"[30th.] Enjoyment of the fields, the growing crops, the sun, the glorious summer.

"[*August* 3.] With Helen to the Crystal Palace. The day very wet, and the charming grounds therefore scarcely visible. The interior wonderful, but not sufficiently furnished with objects of interest. Returned to London Bridge Station, and sent Helen off to Brighton along with three of her school-fellows returning to school.

"[5th.] Met Lord Granville. Talk with him about Rochdale magistrates, and on the war. He is much for peace; did not believe Emperor of Russia ever intended war. We have played the 'game of brag' so often (Palmerston has, he said) that he thought the same thing was to be done again. He should think it criminal to carry on the war beyond its object: success no justification for continuing it unnecessarily.

"[9th.] Preparing for leaving town to-morrow.

"A miserable session—much labour and no result; politics gloomy, Europe overrun by war or despotism, and England no wiser than in the last generation.

"I have withstood the war clamour and am in a small minority

---

1 Wilberforce.

2 Brunel was at the height of his fame. He was employed this year in the designing of a floating gun-carriage for the attack on Cronstadt, and the next on a work more after Bright's heart—the hospital buildings on the shore of the Dardanelles.

apparently, but hope sometimes for better times. My position in the House, not worse but better, notwithstanding my opposition to policy of Govt. and House. If permitted to come to another session, hope for a better hearing for, or more concurrence in, what I believe to be sound principles. Have met with many marks of respect and good feeling from men of all parties in the House, and have much reason to be content with what has taken place there so far as I am personally concerned.[1]

"[15th.] Shocked yesterday to learn the sudden death of Lord Jocelyn from cholera.[2] I met him in St. James's St. this day week: conversation about Indian finance statement. I noticed a more than usual paleness on his countenance. This was on the 8th, and he was seized and died on the 11th or 12th.

"[October 3.] To Manchester. On my return found Mr. H. D. Gilpin from Philadelphia. He stayed with us till the 5th and then went on to Hemsworth. Much interesting conversation with him as to his travels in Europe and on American affairs.

"[November 3.] Dined with Mr. Buchanan, the American Minister, in Harley St. A fine old man, lively, full of anecdote. He had just received intelligence that the French Govt. had retracted their foolish prohibition to Mr. Soule, Minister to Spain, to enter France, thus avoiding a serious dispute with the States.

"[4th.] By 10 train to Rhyl. In The Times to-day a long letter against the war, written by me in answer to a letter from Absalom

---

[1] The Parliamentary vacation lasted till December 12. Bright was in Lancashire most of the time, varying the round of business and public affairs with a short family holiday in North Wales. Business was a severe anxiety. The carpet factory needed more capital to cope with American trade and the necessary long credits, and this was provided by the Brights, Ricardo and Cooke in equal portions. War conditions greatly disturbed all trade. The war itself passed into a gloomy crisis during these months. The fatal misunderstanding and errors before Sebastopol had plunged the army into a pit of disease and needless suffering in a winter campaign for which no preparations had been made. The country had heard of the Alma (Sept. 20), Balaklava (Oct. 25), Inkerman (Nov. 5). The Light Brigade had been sacrificed. The awful storm of Nov. 14 had begun the tale of disaster and torture which was to make the next few months among the blackest in English history.

[2] The visitation of Asiatic cholera this summer caused great anxiety. It had originated in a great outbreak in the East in 1850, which reached Europe in 1853, fell with terrific force on the armies in the Crimea, and ultimately ravaged both North and South America. In England it was not so destructive as the epidemic of 1848–49, which killed over 50,000 people. It was followed by energetic measures of sanitation.

Watkin, inviting me to 'Patriotic Fund' Meeting at Manchester. My letter will not be popular, but it is true, and I do not expect to see it answered. The country is drunk just now, and will hear nothing against its passion. The time may come when the truth will be admitted, but too late to stop the horrible evil of this wicked war. Failing trade, and taxes, and possible disasters during the war, may recall men to their senses.[1]

"[16th.] *My Birthday*; 43 years old. Time Flies![2]

"[17th.] Cobden and I walked out after the sportsmen, Walmsley, Mallaby and Kindersley shooting. Left Locksley Park at noon, and to Rhyl.

"[30th.] With dear Elizabeth and Albert and Baby to Hemsworth.[3]

"[*December* 1.] Dinner party there. J. Holdsworth and his wife and son, and Miss Booth and Edwd. and Mary Jane Leatham there.

[1] The famous "letter to Mr. Absalom Watkin, of Manchester," which appeared on the eve of the Battle of Inkerman, was an epoch-marking point in the War controversy. Bright and Absalom Watkin (the father of Sir Edward Watkin) were old friends. They had worked together in the League, and Watkin had proposed Bright's candidature for Manchester at the Liberal Party meeting in November, 1846, and seconded his nomination on the hustings at the General Election of 1847. And though they fell to poles asunder about the War, happily the difference did not impair their friendship: a year later Watkin was proposing Bright's health at a dinner party and saying (very truthfully) that they were "both pugnacious and both sincere." Mr. A. E. Watkin, in his edition of his great-grandfather's "Journal" (Fisher Unwin, 1920), prints together Bright's letter and Watkin's reply. This conjunction shows how Bright's expectation that his indictment of the diplomatic origins of the war could not be answered was fulfilled. Watkin hardly attempted an answer except by way of a general denunciation of the Tsar as an insolent and unprincipled aggressor. Both the argument of the moment and the logic of events justify Bright. His letter was, in fact, a documented review—of the war-seeking policy pursued by Lord Stratford de Redcliffe at Constantinople, the reckless exploitation by the war party at home of the so-called "massacre of Sinope" when the Russians did to the Turkish fleet what we had done to the Danish fleet at Copenhagen, the determination of the Government to fight Russia though the Russian Government had accepted the British terms of peace (in the Vienna Note), and to ally themselves with Turkey, though Turkey had rejected the British terms and gone to war against British advice. It was a prophetic utterance as well as an historic statement. Its words shadowed forth the days of the Bulgarian and Armenian atrocities: "We are building up our Eastern policy on a false foundation—namely, on the perpetual maintenance of the most immoral and filthy of all despotisms over one of the fairest portions of the earth which it has desolated, and over a population it has degraded but has not been able to destroy."

[2] He was at Locksley Park with Cobden, on a visit to Mr. Mallaby.

[3] Hemsworth Hall, the house of his brother-in-law, W. H. Leatham.

178

Stupid discussion about the War. I almost lost my temper to hear men outside a lunatic asylum talk such helpless rubbish.

"[5*th*.] To Manchester. Home, and to Bible Meeting. Hugh Stowell there, attacking Emperor of Russia and the Pope as usual. I complained of this, showed that the Emperor subscribed to Bible Society by remitting duties on Bibles, and that abusing the Catholic religion was not the way to convert them, and not proper for a Bible Meeting.

"[6*th*.] W. Littlewood and H. Dunckley up here. Asked me to be a President of a society with a religious test—'Young Men's Christian Association.' I declined, disliking tests of this nature.

"[12*th*.] House. Debate unimportant and somewhat flat.[1] Three o'clock in the morning, met with Disraeli in St. James's St., and walked up to Grosvenor Gate with him. His view of the war unfavourable, and particularly of the Crimean expedition.

"[14*th*.] Wrote to S. P. Robinson about meeting at Manchester to condemn my letter on the war. The simpletons! How little they know their own interests!

"[18*th*.] To Manchester. Public meeting called to declare against my 'letter' and sentiments on the war. The Town Hall crowded. Mayor in the Chair. Nobody could be heard. 'Show of hands' taken five times, and Mayor unable to decide; finally dissolved meeting. Afterwards to League Rooms; crowded. Spoke at some length, pleasantly to myself, and well received by all present. Dr. Halley, a leading Minister of the Independents, also spoke effectively.

"Whole object of the public meeting to damage me. Scheme totally failed. War party have rather lost than gained by it. My friends greatly pleased with the result.

"By 5 o'clock train to London.

"[19*th*.] House. Foreign Enlistment Bill read a second time; majority 39 for it.

"[20*th*.] House. Foreign Enlistment Bill again debated. Helen up from Brighton—to Aunt Lucas's."

3

On December 21 the House of Commons listened to one of the two most electrifying speeches ever made in their Chamber, both by John Bright. He spoke after midnight, in the third reading debate on the Foreign Enlistment Bill. As he developed the grave indictment which melted away into a simple and earnest appeal to the honour and humanity

[1] Parliament reassembled on this day.

of the House, Ministers fastened glassy eyes upon him; the crowded Chamber was hushed into a paralysed silence; men were deeply distressed. He rarely rose nearer to sublimity than in the simple passages describing the loss of Colonel Boyle, the member for Frome, culminating in the words, "The stormy Euxine is his grave; his wife is a widow, his children fatherless . . .;" and of Colonel Blair: "Who is there that does not recollect his frank, amiable and manly countenance? . . . Well, but the place that knew them shall know them no more for ever."

His closing sentences fell like hammer-strokes: "I am not, nor did I ever pretend to be, a statesman; and that character is so tainted and equivocal in our day that I am not sure that a pure and honourable ambition would aspire to it. I have not enjoyed for thirty years, like these noble lords, the honours and emoluments of office. I have not set my sails to every passing breeze. I am a plain and simple citizen, sent here by one of the foremost constituencies of the Empire, representing feebly, perhaps, but honestly, I dare aver, the opinions of very many and the true interests of all those who have sent me here. Let it not be said that I am alone in my condemnation of this war, and of this incapable and guilty Administration.

"And even if I were alone, if mine were a solitary voice, raised amid the din of arms and the clamours of a venal Press, I should have the consolation I have to-night—and which I trust will be mine to the last moment of my existence—the priceless consolation that no word of mine has tended to promote the squandering of my country's treasure or the spilling of one single drop of my country's blood."

This declaration was the climax of a discourse of sincere and sustained fervour. But the orator's passion was softened down to a solemn intonation of eloquence in harmony with the solemnity of that dark winter. The House sat spell-bound, then cheered, then fell silent again. There were some calls for Gladstone, who sat on the Treasury Bench motionless and afflicted. No one wished to speak A division was taken and the House adjourned.

This speech can hardly be read without a tremor even now, three-quarters of a century after its noble, wellnigh faultless periods fell on the ears of the House of Commons. It gets a scant notice in the diary:

"[21*st*.] House. 3rd reading. Admirable speech from Cobden, calm, well reasoned as usual. Lord John Russell misrepresented him late in the evening, and I replied after midnight. Everybody said it was a great success, the House much excited, cheering; and compliments and congratulations in profusion. Govt. did not reply, because my case unanswerable, I verily believe."

He went home for Christmas, took walks in the wood near "One Ash" with his wife, tramped the frost-bound roads admiring "winter in all its charms," and read Churchill's poems while the house slept at night.

4

The "incapable and guilty administration" fell at the beginning of the session of 1855. The mismanagement of the Crimean campaign and the atrocious sufferings of the army led to Roebuck's motion for a Committee of Inquiry into the conduct of the War. Gladstone called the proposal unconstitutional because it transferred responsibility from the advisers of the Crown to a Parliamentary Committee. But neither the House nor the country was in a mood to bother about constitutional niceties. Bulwer-Lytton's epigrammatic saying more nearly reflected the general feeling: "Dismiss your Government and save your Army!"

The Ministry of All the Talents was actually brought down by the talent of them all that thought itself superior to the rest—Lord John Russell's. He seized on Roebuck's motion as a motive for the act of sabotage—said that, as he could not resist it, he must resign. Lord John's course was incomprehensible both by the constitutionalist who cherished the doctrine of Cabinet responsibility, and by the common man who had the ordinary notions of honour in public affairs. Roebuck's motion was carried by a majority of 157, and Lord Aberdeen went out.

The intrigues and manœuvres which took Palmerston to the height of his ambition—to be Prime Minister of the British Kingdom at war —find daily reflection in Bright's notebooks. In the New Year he went to Brussels on a business visit, and, after the usual address to his constituents in Manchester, settled on January 22 in new London lodgings at 9, Little Ryder Street, St. James's, which he found "very comfortable and much to my taste."

"[*January* 25.] Club. Learned that Lord J. Russell had resigned. House at 4. Resignation of Lord J. Russell announced by Hayter and adjournment till to-morrow moved. Lord John could not or would not resist Roebuck's notice for Committee to inquire into mismanagement of the War. This is the reason given, but notoriously there are other reasons. Rumours that all the Govt. will go out and not unlikely.

"Weather very cold and unpleasant—the streets indescribably dirty.

"[26th.] House. Explanations from Lord J. Russell: unsatisfactory. His resignation based on unwillingness to oppose Roebuck's motion for Committee into mismanagement of the War, yet would not vote or speak for the motion! Evidently he has deserted his colleagues in their hour of peril, after urging them to and joining them in all the acts which have ended so disastrously for the army and the country. There is much cowardice or treachery in this course.

"Debate on Roebuck's motion languid, and the House in confusion as to the division.

"Spoke to Mr. Ellice, long a great friend of Lord John's. He said, 'Do you think anybody will act with him after this?' evidently disapproving of his course.

"Spoke to Mr. Gordon, Lord Aberdeen's son. He said Palmerston was to be Minister of War. Aberdeen had required a distinct understanding as to the proposed peace. Palmerston was willing to put in writing that he was willing to make peace on the terms offered, without requiring the capture or surrender or demolition of Sebastopol!

"It is expected Govt. will be beaten, and will then resign. But, beaten or not, I think it impossible for them to go on.

"[27th.] Club. Much gossip. People generally condemning Lord John Russell's resignation. Great animosity against Peelites and Aberdeen. Hayter tells me that the Duke of Newcastle has resigned, and that the Govt. must fall (probable new Premier, Lord Lansdowne) and that Lord Grey will take office, and not impossibly may be Prime Minister!

"[28th.] Saw Villiers. Learned from him the great probability that Ministers would resign on Tuesday next, and that Palmerston would be Premier and go to the House of Lords, Lord Grey probably to War Department, and Lord J. Russell to lead in the Commons! An arrangement not very likely to last—a mere shuffling of the cards, and not promising a change of policy, unless Lord Grey stands by his former opposition to the War.

"[29th.] House. Debate on Roebuck's motion against Govt. Bulwer and Gladstone good speeches, particularly Gladstone's. Disraeli and Palmerston inferior. Majority of 157 against Govt. I abstained from voting: impossible to support Govt. after what I had said of their policy, and yet unwilling to support what appeared something like a conspiracy against Lord Aberdeen.

"The Govt. of course will now resign. It is a just retribution overtaking them for their 'incapable and guilty' conduct in involving the country in a needless war. The aspect of affairs is very dark, politically and commercially.

"After 3 o'clock when I went to bed.

"[*30th.*] Great confusion in all camps. Everyone puzzled as to the new Govt. The Lords Palmerston, Russell, Grey, Derby and Aberdeen heard from everybody in conversation, but nobody knowing anything, tho' everybody constantly inquiring.

"House: adjournment till Thursday, when explanations will be made. Lord Aberdeen gone to Windsor, and not yet returned. It is expected Lord Lansdowne will be sent for by the Queen to give his advice. The simplest solution of the difficulty would seem to be that Lord Derby and his friends should come, but this would be thought by many a grave disaster: a war with a Tory Govt. may be worse than a war with a 'Liberal' Govt. I doubt it extremely.

"Walked up with Smith to see Cobden: long chat with him on public affairs. His contempt of Lord Jno. Russell's course strongly manifested.

"Weather very winterly—snow and hard frost, streets covered with ice, and walking difficult if not dangerous.

"[*31st.*] A day of gossip as yesterday. Reported that Lord Derby has been recommended to the Queen by Lord Aberdeen, which seems to have thwarted the views of the Whigs.

"[*February* 1.] Called at 10, Eaton Place West, to see Mr. Blackett, ill from a paralytic seizure. Saw him in bed, not so ill as I supposed. He seemed greatly pleased that I had called upon him, poor fellow. I hope he may recover soon, for, as a young Member of the House, he is an acquisition.

"House: nothing doing, and nothing known except that Lord Derby has failed to make a Govt. Nobody out of his party disposed to join him.[1]

[1] Disraeli was furiously disappointed when he beheld, in Lord Morley's words, "a golden chance of bringing a consolidated party into the possession of real power flung away." Lord Malmesbury describes him "in a state of disgust beyond all control; he told me he had spoken his mind to Lord Derby and told him some very disagreeable truths." Lord Morley's lucid account of the crisis ("Gladstone," Book IV, Chapter 6) relates it from the inside of both the Aberdeen and the Palmerston Cabinets; Bright is on the fringe.

"Duke of Newcastle made a speech to defend himself from Lord Jno. Russell. The latter comes very badly out of the matter by which he has overthrown the Govt.

"[2nd.] House. Genl. Evans there to receive the thanks of Parlt. Speaker addressed him in language and in a manner that could not be surpassed. He returned thanks, but with bad taste, adverted to the recent speech of Lord John Russell in moving thanks to the Army, complaining that his Division (the 2nd) had been omitted to be mentioned as it should have been. The effect was painful. Everybody felt it, and Lord Palmerston, in moving that the Speaker's Address and Evans's reply should be entered on the Journals of the House, moved that 'so much of the reply' as conveyed the thanks and gratitude of Genl. Evans should be so entered, thus marking for exclusion such parts of it as commented on Lord John Russell's alleged omissions. A somewhat interesting ceremony was thus marred, and the impression was unpleasant.[1]

"[14th.] Nearly a fortnight at home owing to break-up and reconstruction of Govt. Palmerston Prime Minister! What a hoax! The aged charlatan has at length attained the great object of his long and unscrupulous ambition. He (Palmerston) is believed in by a shallow portion of the public, and he has had the advantage of a 'cry' from a portion of the Press, but it passes my comprehension how the country is to be saved from its disasters and disgrace by a man who is over 70 years of age, partly deaf and blind, and who has never been known to do anything on which a solid reputation could be built, and whose colleagues are, with one exception, the very men under whose Govt. everything has been mismanaged!

"A very pleasant fortnight at home. The weather most severe— frost and snow, and winter more than common. Indoors, things very cheerful—home and wife and children comfortable and happy. To-morrow expect to return to town as the House opens the following day.

"[16th.] House. Palmerston's first night, and a failure. His speech not well received and his promises with regard to Army, etc., reforms not clear and satisfactory. The reply of Disraeli clever and telling. The House bewildered and disorganized. Long conversation

---

[1] Sir De Lacy Evans, M.P. for Westminster, commanded the 2nd Division at the Battle of the Alma. He fell under severe criticism afterwards when it became known that he had advised Sir Edmund Lyons that the troops should be withdrawn from the Crimea.

with Sidney Herbert. Asked him if peace was probable? He thought there were hopes of a settlement; that Lord John would hardly go to Vienna if he did not believe he could make peace; he was a difficult man to manage; people did not know when they had him; too much under influence of men much less capable than himself, as Col. R. and J. A. S., etc.; he showed off best at the Table of the House, etc. Spoke about the causes of the War. He said the Vienna Note was a bad business, and the Turk should have been made to take it, etc.

"Walked up with Cobden and Pilkington. Night fearfully cold. Great fire across the river, and sky magnificently illuminated.

"[17th.] Colonial Office with Mr. Roebuck and Mr. Little from Newfoundland; also presented memorials from Gibraltar complaining of Sir R. Gardiner, the Governor.

"Talk about affairs. Mr. Herbert said the whole thing, Crimean expedition, war, and Parliamentary crisis was a 'damnable mess,' that they (Peelites) should not be in office, but that Lord Derby should have come in; that they had been urged to join him, but impossible—no man's reputation could stand such rough handling as would be undergone by jumping from one side of the House to the other in that way. He did not know if Louis Napoleon would go to the Crimea, but had better not. 'He will never get any credit in the Crimea.' [1]

"[18th.] With Vaughan . . . along the Serpentine: scores of thousands of people on the ice; wonderful turn-out of people. . . . Layard in my room at midnight, and long talk on public affairs. His feeling one of great despondency.

"A few days ago, heard that a Mr. Morrison of London had left me by will a house and 27 acres of land at Frimley, County of Surrey. He was for *peace*, and left land also to Cobden, and legacies to some others. This is curious. [2]

"[19th.] House: Army Estimates. A good speech from Mr. Layard on mismanagement of war. Feeble reply from Palmerston. He is rapidly sinking in the estimation of the House, and the country must soon find out that he is a bubble and a sham.

"[20th.] This morning is the funeral of Eliz. Gurney, wife of Saml. Gurney. A very kind and good woman is gone. A numerous

[1] The plan of the French Emperor for going to the Crimea and finishing off the siege of Sebastopol himself happily came to nothing through his jealousy and fear of Prince Napoleon, the hated cousin who would have been appointed Regent of France during his absence.

[2] See page 191 (Feb. 28).

family and a large circle of relatives and friends will deeply mourn her loss.

"House. Rumours of further confusion. Talk with Disraeli. Thought one or two speeches weekly like the one I made before Christmas would break up the Govt. in a month. I said I wanted *peace*, not to break up Govt.; but if they would not make peace, then I would make war upon them. He returned to an old topic, on my saying I thought they (Derby party) would come in soon: he could not see why I should not join Lord Derby's Cabinet! I smiled, and said I could never lift up my head after such an act—it would destroy me, etc. He thought Palmerston done: 'you may see the breed, but the action and power are gone,' etc.

"Saw Villiers. Learned the great chance that Gladstone and Herbert would break with Palmerston, that Palmerston would fight on till removed by a vote of the House, and would fill up his Govt. as he best could. I advised Villiers to get the Colonial Office, even tho' they might not last long; it would help his position for the future. He spoke of somebody for the under-offices—Secy. of Board of Control in particular. Would Otway or Danby Seymour take it? He had recommended his Bro. Clarendon and Sir C. Wood to offer *me* something! I smiled at him and said, 'Do you think I could be clerk to Sir C. Wood?'

"Mr. Gordon came to me and wished me to call on his father, Lord Aberdeen, and I engaged to do so to-morrow.

"Cobden showed me a note written by Mr. Delane of *The Times* to Mr. Caird, in which he said: 'Cobden and Bright would be our Ministers now but for their principle of "peace at all price," against which I have done all I can to warn them.' Such is the utter confusion into which the war and the faction of Lord John Russell has thrown the Govt. There is great anxiety apparent everywhere, and the war abroad and the Govt. at home seem equally unmanageable.

"[21*st*.] Cabinet again in disorder. Gladstone, Graham and S. Herbert have resigned at the Cabinet this morning, and other 'Peelites' are expected to go out with them. They are supposed to object to Roebuck's Committee, but I suspect they feel Palmerston's lead to be a failure, and they escape from a Govt. which cannot go on. Palmerston will try hard to hold on. If he takes in the old Whigs excluded when the Aberdeen Govt. was formed, he will be no better off than before, for their incapacity is proved and notorious, and a Govt. of new men can hardly stand a trial. In fact, with his leadership, I believe any Govt. will make blunders and fail, and confidence in them is impossible. A Derby Govt. is the natural result of these difficulties, and yet that could only live by the forbearance of its opponents.

"Exeter Hall: crowded meeting on the 'Taxes on Knowledge.' Speakers, Dr. Watts, Apsley Pellatt, M.P., Cobden, self and Geo. Dawson of Birmingham. Gibson in the Chair and spoke well. Meeting enthusiastic, and all went off well.

"Layard in my room, concocting an experimental Cabinet for Palmerston!

"[22nd.] Heard this morning of the death on the evening of the 20th of our old friend Mr. Hume, M.P., a tried friend of the people and of freedom. His loss will not easily be repaired.

"Called upon Lord Aberdeen: an hour's conversation with him. Spoke of the resignation of Graham, Gladstone and Herbert; regretted it and did not approve of it. He had recommended them to take their seats on the bench behind us, and to act along with the 'Manchester School.' Thought Gladstone was destined for more than he had yet done, and hoped that now he 'would take a new start' in a liberal and useful public career. A new constituency would be well for him. Had hoped the 'Papal aggression' question would have separated him from Oxford, but it had not.

"When they joined the Palmerston Govt., Palmerston had given him (Aberdeen) specific assurances in favour of peace, and he now thought peace very probable from Lord John's mission to Vienna. Alluded to the alliance with France as a difficulty, but hoped Louis Napoleon would be induced to go with English Govt. for peace, notwithstanding position of affairs in the Crimea. Spoke of Lord Stratford de Redcliffe in strong terms: his temper, passion, and obstinacy; appeared to be willing to sacrifice everything to his personal hostility to Russia, etc.

"Spoke of Lord John: had hoped to have his (Aberdeen's) place, and, from his joining his Govt., had intrigued against it, his wife and the persons influencing him instigating him to attempt to regain the Premiership. Was sorry the whole of their correspondence had not been published, as it would have given a fairer view of their difference on the subject of the Duke of Newcastle. That his Cabinet had been harmonious during the two years, with the exception of the restlessness of Lord Jno. Russell. 'He had but one thing on his conscience'—he now knew 'what was meant by being *dragged* into a war;' but it had come on step by step. He hoped peace would now be made. He had told Palmerston that he could make peace on terms, for which, if he [1] had made peace, the people would have been for 'cutting off his head;' and he thought Lord John's and Palmerston's recent speeches showed they felt their responsibility, and were anxious to make peace.

"Spoke of Gladstone's exculpation of Lord John's conduct in breaking up the late Cabinet, and said it was extravagant and absurd, and he had told him so—that is when Gladstone had said that the man must be contemptible who charged Lord John with cowardice or treachery in running away from his colleagues. Asked me to call on him when I felt disposed, and spoke in a very friendly tone of his son's intimacy with Cobden and myself in the House of Commons.

"House. Palmerston announced the resignation of his three colleagues, and that explanations would be given in the House to-morrow.

"Spoke to Admiral Dundas in the Lobby. He told me that he and the French Admiral, Hamelin, were from the first wholly against the expedition to the Crimea. With regard to the Sebastopol business, 'he dared not say what he thought would come of it.' [2]

"A Greek gentleman, a merchant, lodging here, came into my room, and we had a long and interesting conversation on the war and the condition of Turkey and Greece. He had just returned from Dresden where he had been to see Prince Woronzow with regard to merchandise seized by Russian troops in Asia, and by some accident not delivered up to his agent. The Prince deplored the war and the infatuation of the English people, 'so serious a people as the English.' Said that Mr. Cobden and Mr. Bright had alone told the truth, and nobody had answered them. The Emperor could not make further concessions than he had made, but was anxious for peace. The Russian people all united with him on the war, and in defence of their country. My Greek visitor came in that he might thank me for the justice I had done to his countrymen.

"[23rd.] House, to hear explanations as to the secession of Graham, Gladstone, and S. Herbert from the Ministry. Graham's speech masterly against Committee of Inquiry into the state of the Army before Sebastopol, etc., and showing that his opposition to that Committee, to which Palmerston had consented, was the cause of his retire-

---

[1] Aberdeen.

[2] Dundas, in command of the Fleet in the Black Sea, had been recalled and superseded by Sir Edmund Lyons. He was violently attacked for not assaulting Sebastopol by sea. Lyons, however, proved equally wedded to the classic naval theory that wooden ships should not contend with stone fortresses.

ment. He sat in my usual place on the second bench below the gangway, Ministerial side, and nearest to the Ministerial benches.[1]

"I spoke next (the House very full, and every gallery place full) for about ½ an hour, for peace, arguing that, terms being offered and accepted, why carry on the war? Why not an armistice? That Palmerston and Lord J. Russell were mostly responsible for the war, and could most easily extricate us from it. That while negotiations were going on, and peace possible, I would not oppose Palmerston, and appealed to him to crown his long life by aiding the restoration of peace. I was overloaded with compliments. Sir C. Wood said to me, 'portions of your speech were more eloquent than anything I ever heard before in my life.' Jas. Wortley, Recorder of London, said, 'I must thank you for your speech. My wife was in the gallery, and you have made her cry, if you think that a compliment.' And other expressions of admiration and approval from great numbers.

"I have thought about this very much—how much there is of food for vanity and self-love, and how a foolish pride may be created and fostered by it. I have felt its influence, for it is something rare that one from so humble a beginning, born and reared in an almost singular retirement, of a Sect by many ridiculed and despised, without real trained education, and without wealth, and without political influence of any kind, should be permitted with any effect, and with any acceptance, to speak to an assembly so critical, often so hostile to my views, and so powerful in everything affecting the interests not of England only but of the world. I would wish to avoid vanity, and to be rather grateful that I am permitted and enabled to speak in such an assembly on behalf of peace, and of political morality, and to feel how solemn is the responsibility of such a position."

5

The "Angel of Death" speech, perfect in form, the loftiest and simplest expression of compassion and the most earnest appeal to humanity that the House of Commons had ever heard, is hackneyed by the reiterated quotation of one sentence. Nevertheless it has the immortality which belongs to sincerity clothed in beauty.

The diary shows that Bright did not expect it to make a sensation. A gleam of hope for peace had suddenly appeared. Palmerston sent

[1] "After considering various *sites*, we determined to ask the 'Manchester School' to yield us, at any rate for to-morrow, the old place devoted to ex-ministers." (Gladstone's diary, Feb. 22.)

Lord John to the Peace Conference at Vienna. Not that Palmerston meant business: he was quite determined to make no peace until at least Sebastopol had fallen. But Lord John himself wished to accept the Austrian proposal for compromise on the sole remaining one of the "Four Points" in dispute—the question of naval power in the Black Sea. Acceptance would have brought the war to an end. Palmerston refused. At this moment, however, the merest hint of a possibility of peace was enough for Bright. He concentrated all his powers on an appeal to Palmerston to take this chance of finishing the carnage and the woe. That was the origin of the Angel of Death speech.

The famous figure had come to him as he lay awake that morning, "thinking of my speech and all the calamities which the war had brought about. . . . I did not think anything more about it except that it was true, and I was surprised at the effect which it produced on the House of Commons." Disraeli told him, "Bright, I would give all I ever had to have made that speech you made just now." "Well," said Bright, "you might have made it if you had been honest."

The passages which most thrilled the House and the nation came towards the end: "I . . . notice that an uneasy feeling exists as to the news which may arrive by the very next mail from the East. I do not suppose that your troops are to be beaten in actual conflict with the foe, or that they will be driven into the sea; but I am certain that many homes in England in which there now exists a fond hope that the distant one may return—many such homes may be rendered desolate when the next mail shall arrive. The Angel of Death has been abroad throughout the land; you may almost hear the beating of his wings. There is no one, as when the first-born were slain of old, to sprinkle with blood the lintel and the two side-posts of our doors, that he may spare and pass on; he takes his victims from the castle of the noble, the mansion of the wealthy and the cottage of the poor and lowly, and it is on behalf of all these classes that I make this solemn appeal."

He turned to Palmerston and entreated him to take advantage of Vienna to end the war. "By adopting that course he would have the satisfaction of reflecting that, having obtained the object of his laudable ambition—having become the foremost subject of the Crown, the director of, it may be, the destinies of his country, and the presiding genius in her councils—he had achieved a still higher and nobler ambition: that he had returned the sword to the scabbard—that at his word torrents of blood had ceased to flow—that he had restored tranquillity to Europe and saved this country from the indescribable calamities of war."

Bright's accents and words continued to echo through the corridors of Parliament and the homes of a now chastened country for many days.

"[*February* 24.] Gibson and Layard in my room. Layard was offered office of Under-Secretary of War, but to-day Palmerston tells him he cannot appoint him, but offers him Under-Secretaryship of the Colonies, which Layard has refused.

"[*25th.*] Danby Seymour called. Palmerston proposed to him to be Secretary of the Board of Control, but this morning cannot give it to him, which disappoints Seymour. Sir Erskine Perry called. Long conversation with them. Perry compliments me; says he does not 'flatter' me; wishes me when the war is over to lead the independent party in the House. Everybody expects me to be in the (not this) Cabinet. Great changes coming: Whig party worn out; no office, even highest, to which I may not aspire, etc. I spoke of my Sect and principles as great obstacles to any official career, which he and Seymour would not admit. I suspect they know little of the influence of the oligarchy which has ruled this country since 1688. My taking a Cabinet office would be deemed little less than a revolution, if I maintained any decent consistency. Besides, is it not as useful to teach the truth to the people from an independent and unofficial position? Time will show.

"[*27th.*] House. Under the gallery spoke to Dr. McHale, Catholic Archbishop of Tuam, an intelligent and gentlemanly person: he is on his way back from Rome. Also to Dr. Guthrie, a distinguished Minister of the Free Church of Scotland, a most able and laborious and benevolent man. He was excited about my late speech. He had read it 'with boundless admiration.' The figure in which the Angel of Death is represented to be so near that we can hear 'the beating of his wings,' he thought one of the finest flights of oratory he was acquainted with. Its effect upon him was 'perfectly electrical,' and he wished me to send him a copy of the speech if it be reprinted.

"[*28th.*] To Staines by railway, and then drove over to Bagshot, to see the land and house left me by Mr. Morrison. The land is uncultivated and growing for the most part fir or pine trees and furze; the house small but comfortable.

"Called upon Mr. Andrews, the tenant, who is a solicitor, and requested him to have a valuation of the property, and to ascertain if it could be sold, and at what price. Mr. Morrison was 84 years old and died only a few weeks ago.

"[*March* 2.] House: *Death of Emperor of Russia announced.*[1]

"[*3rd.*] By 10 train to Manchester. . . . Rochdale Station, my dear wife waiting for me in the carriage. Children and herself all well. A happy evening.

"The death of the Emperor of Russia is confirmed, an event of importance, tho' whether favourable to peace or not is not certain. The obstacle to peace, in my opinion, is in Paris, and not in St. Petersburg. Death is the great leveller: one moment, Emperor and Autocrat of all the Russias, wielding almost absolute power over 60 millions of men, and contending with three Empires in arms against him; the next moment a lifeless corpse, unable to lift a finger, or to articulate a word! It is a strange proof of the ferocity and barbarism and hardness of feeling engendered by war that the announcement of the death of Nicholas was recd. with loud cheers, it is said, in Drury Lane Theatre, at some assembly in Nottingham, and at a concert in Liverpool! A tribe of red Indians could not have manifested a feeling more truly indecent, or more opposed to all moral and Christian sentiment!

"[*8th.*] Call from a person calling himself Mr. Stratford, begging; son of Earl of Aldborough, etc. Refused to give him anything without references. As he was going away, an officer of the Mendicity Society came in and took him off to Marlboro' St. Police Station as a well-known impostor. What a curious phase of human and London life must be that of an impostor of this kind! How much of the character is due to misfortune, and how much to crime and guilt?

"House. Long discussion on quarrel between Admiral Napier and Sir James Graham, in which Graham figured to a disadvantage. Gibson made an excellent speech in favour of the Admiral's case.[2]

"[*10th.*] Dined with Mr. Buchanan, the American Minister, 56, Harley St.—a party of 18 or 20. A particularly pleasant evening, excepting only some regret that Jno. McGregor, M.P. for Glasgow, made himself laughed at.

"Mr. Buchanan told me he had recently dined with the Queen— had a long conversation with her. Her regard for Lord Aberdeen

---

1 The Tsar Nicholas died from the effects of a chill caught at a military review.

2 Sir Charles Napier, who had been given "leave" by Graham at the famous dinner at the Reform Club to "declare war," quite rightly refused to carry out the Admiralty's instructions to attack Cronstadt. He returned to England at the end of 1854, and in February, 1855, was elected M.P. for Southwark. He retained the seat till his death in 1860.

quite remarkable. He (Buchanan) thought him the best of all the official people he had met in England.

"[16*th.*] Dined with Ernest Bunsen, Regent's Park. Prince Nicholas of Nassau the only visitor (except myself)—an intelligent and agreeable young man.

"[20*th.*] House: discussion on motion to open British Museum and National Gallery on Sunday afternoon, for which I voted.

"[22*nd.*] With deputation from Manchester to Lord Palmerston to present memorial in favour of peace. Well received, and our object not displeasing to the Minister.

"[23*rd.*] With large deputation to Sir Geo. Grey on Factory question. Speakers rather angry and very firm. Not much result I fear.

"[25*th.*] Read Jefferson's 'Life.'[1]

"[26*th.*] Newspaper Stamp; 2nd reading carried by majority of 54. Admirable speech from Sir E. Bulwer-Lytton. Disraeli very dishonest, voting with the Opposition notwithstanding his well-known opinions.

"Some rumours that Russia is unwilling to make concessions in the Black Sea.

"[*April* 3.] To the Crystal Palace in the afternoon. Met Lord Canning there. Talk about the Conference at Vienna. He thought 'peace not off the cards,' and if Nesselrode went to Vienna, 'we might back peace.' Evidently puzzled with the war, and the way to get out of it.

"This morning Mr. Wilson of Brook St. came to see dear Helen and examined her with reference to the state of her chest and lungs. His report not assuring: tendency to disease and great care advised. This, tho' what I knew before, made me very sad. She is a darling child, and I could ill bear to see her fade, and I not able to render her any help.[2]

---

[1] The great part played by Bright in the maintenance of friendly relations with America during the Civil War gives interest to the direction of his mind thus early towards American affairs. It is not possible to identify the "Life" here mentioned. The most recent Jefferson biography of any importance was George Tucker's, published at Philadelphia in 1837. During 1853–4, nine volumes of Jefferson's "Writings, Correspondence, etc." had been published in New York.

[2] The death of her mother in consumption made him very apprehensive. Helen Bright, however, married Mr. William Clark, of Street, Somerset, and had 6 children, all of whom are living. She died, aged 86, in 1927. Her husband had died in 1925 at the same age.

"[5*th.*] To Manchester: meeting in the Town Hall on the war. Spoke an hour both against the war and the management of it, and showed the worthlessness of the conditions of peace on a par with the pretences for and objects of the war. A good meeting and crowded.[1]

"[11*th, at Rochdale.*] To Meeting. Afterwards to visit the Stores of the Co-operative Society of 'Equitable Pioneers' in Toad Lane.[2] Interested in their success and the extent of their business.[3]

"[16*th.*] West End crowded: Louis Napoleon passing thro' to Windsor.[4] Vapour bath. House: saw Villiers; learned from him the desperate difficulties of the Govt.

"Disraeli told me if peace now not made, he should go against the war, whatever might be the course other men might take; but he seemed to think peace would be made.

"[17*th.*] Many calls on me this morning: Mitchell Henry, McEnteer, and A. H. Dymond on case of Baranelli, under sentence of death. His insanity appears proved.

"[18*th.*] Saw Villiers. Lord John is not returning at once from Vienna. From what Villiers says, I gather that Lord John is determined on peace if it be possible, and that peace may come out of the desperate difficulties of the Allies.

"To Thurloe Square (45) to dine with Mr. Dickenson, Junr., —a pleasant party: Mr. Dasent of *The Times*, F. H. Robinson, Professor Powell from Oxford, and their wives, etc. Mrs. Powell said to me, 'Oh, Mr. Bright, I can't tell you how much we have been delighted with all you have said against the war,' etc.

"Coming home, called in at the 'Cosmopolitan' Club, 30, Charles St., Berkeley Square, of which, without application on my part and without my knowledge, I had been elected a member. Found a large room, used often as a studio—pictures finished and unfinished on the walls. Present: R. M. Milnes, Lord Stanley, Layard, Mr. Harcourt,

---

[1] A different story from that of the Manchester meeting of the previous year.

[2] "Toad"—a curtailment of "T'owd Lane," *anglice* "The Old Lane."

[3] The Equitable Pioneers Society originated the Co-operative movement in this country. It was established in 1844.

[4] Louis Napoléon made an astonishing impression on Queen Victoria in this visit. He flattered her Majesty with an astuteness which overcame her native dislike for adventurers and upsetters of thrones. She gave him the Garter, and the war-drunk mob made of him a popular hero. In August the Queen paid him a return visit at St. Cloud. The French, having no enthusiasm either for the war or for the British alliance, omitted to make of her a popular heroine.

Mr. Ferguson, Higgins (the 'Jacob Omnium' of *The Times*) and a few others whom I scarcely knew and whose names I do not now recollect. Conversation from 10 till 1—twice a week. Tea, coffee, etc. An intelligent party and worth spending an evening with. The rule of admission is not very well defined. 'A man must have done something' to be entitled to be elected. He must have made himself something of a 'notable' in some circle, large or small.[1]

"[*19th.*] Cobden and Layard in my room discussing the war. Streets crowded with people to see Louis Napoleon. Banquet at Guildhall. Rumours of a battle at Balaklava and defeat of the Russians.[2]

"[*20th.*] House: Budget. Enormous expenditure: 86 millions; loan 16 millions; new taxes $5\frac{1}{4}$ millions; tea, coffee and sugar taxes increased. Backwards in everything during the war. The nation mad or blind.[3]

"[*27th.*] Called on Lord Aberdeen. A long conversation with him on the war and chances of peace. He evidently much conscious of the misfortune of the war. 'He was the greatest culprit among those to be blamed,' etc. He knew people were not to be forgiven 'on the ground of good intentions.' 'Many reasons why he had not resigned[4]'; the Queen thought 'he might preserve peace,' or failing that, 'might soonest restore peace,' etc.

"[*May* 2.] Called at Cosmopolitan Club coming home.

[1] Monckton Milnes (Lord Houghton) was the "father" of the Cosmopolitan, and, as Mr. Frederick Harrison said, "a kind of perpetual president." Sir Algernon West gave an account of the Club in the *Cornhill*, June, 1903. It was for many years a favourite resort of artists, writers, travellers, eminent soldiers and lawyers, especially on Sunday evenings. Matthew Higgins made a notable figure in the London of that day. He was of West Indian descent, and remarkably tall. It is said that he and Thackeray, also a big man, went together to the Egyptian Hall, where a giant was to be seen at a shilling admission fee, and the doorkeeper refused to accept their shillings on the ground that the show did not take money from professionals. Bright wrote to his wife in February: "I walked into Piccadilly with 'Jacob Omnium,' the *great* man thou saw get out of the train at Bletchley. I fancy he has been a good deal in tropical climates, which perhaps may account for the luxuriance of his growth."

[2] There had, however, been no serious fighting since the unsuccessful attack on the Malakoff on February 24.

[3] Sir George Cornewall Lewis in his first Budget had to meet a deficit of 27 millions. He borrowed 16 millions, put the Income-Tax up from 1*s*. 2*d*. to 1*s*. 4*d*., and added to indirect taxes—thus taxing every class in the nation. It was a fair Budget under the conditions, and was not seriously opposed.

[4] I.e., before the outbreak of war.

Thackeray there and others. War and difficulties of Govt. and country chief topic.

"Gladstone at the House said the negotiations were 'all alive' still. Rumours of the state of things in the Crimea unfavourable.

"[7th.] Prospects of peace more remote to-day. French Foreign Minister resigned,[1] and it is supposed Louis Napoleon resolved on war.

"[9th.] House. Marriage with Deceased Wife's Sister; second reading carried by only 8 majority. Bill can hardly pass.

"[11th.] House. Newspaper Stamp Bill passed the Commons. Our labours on this question have had a great result, and earlier than we at one time expected. Milner Gibson's conduct of the question has been admirable, and Cobden and I have given him throughout our hearty assistance.

"[16th.] House: Church Rates, 2nd reading, carried 217 to 189. Palmerston made a foolish speech and excited hostility against him on our side. He should lead the Tories, not the Liberals.

"[17th.] J. Whitworth, civil engineer, called about 'standards of length.' Showed me his improvements in rifle and cannon: melancholy to think that the greatest ingenuity of the country is now employed on instruments of destruction!

"[21st.] House. Gibson's motion postponed—a curious story. On reaching the Lobby of the House, I met Sir Jas. Graham. He said Gordon (Lord Aberdeen's son) wished to see me. I found him in the Division Lobby. He said his father (Lord Aberdeen) was anxious that the motion should not come on for a few days at least; Herbert and Cardwell had a difficulty in voting with us; Herbert had arranged a question for Palmerston, and the answer was to justify Gladstone in asking Gibson to put off his motion. He thought a postponement wise, as negotiations were still going on, and hoped when it did come on, that Herbert and Cardwell would vote with us, etc. I replied that I would consent to what his father recommended, because I had faith in his honest intentions for peace; but I had doubts of the advice of some of his friends, remembering how they had served us on the 'just

---

[1] M. Drouyn de Llhuys, the Emperor's best Minister, was forced into resignation by Napoleon's determination to go on with a war which the French nation hated and might have been ended by the adoption of the Austrian proposals. Lord John Russell, who held the same views, also resigned, but withdrew his resignation on an appeal from Palmerston. Drouyn de Llhuys was succeeded by Walewski, neither honest nor able.

wise and beneficial' question when Villiers moved the Free Trade resolution against Lord Derby's Govt.

"Herbert put the question. Palmerston replied. Gladstone asked Gibson to postpone, and Gibson was compelled to consent. The fact is that the Peelites were either alarmed at the position they had taken with us, or did not like to seem to act under our leadership.[1]

"[*June* 3.] Preparing notes for speech on the war. The subject too great, and much puzzled how to compress it, and what to say.

"[*5th.*] House. Sir Jas. Graham, earnest speech for peace. Cobden opened the debate in his best style: close reasoning, apt illustrations, statesmanlike views, and solemn warnings—produced a great effect evidently.

"Mr. Brown introduced me to Mr. Fillmore, ex-President of the United States. He and Mr. Van Buren, also ex-President, both under the gallery this evening—a remarkable event.

"What must they think of the follies of this country and its Govt.!

"[*6th.*] Cobden's lodgings. Long and interesting conversation on our position, and that of the country. He gave me very judicious hints as to my speech in the present debate. It is a great advantage to have a man of such honesty and sagacity to consult with and to discuss with upon all public questions.

"[*7th.*] House. Spoke on war debate one hour and 50 minutes (9.40 to 11.30). Attacked the Ministers severely, and urged the folly and criminality of the war. My friends content, and many congratulations from them.[2]

[1] Milner Gibson had tabled a motion of censure on the Government for failing to secure peace by means of the Vienna Conferences. Disraeli moved a vote of censure two days later on different grounds—the ambiguous language and uncertain conduct of the Government and their slackness in carrying on the war. Gladstone took this opportunity of ranging himself definitely with the peace party, and was followed by Roundell Palmer and Lord Stanley. The motion failed: Disraeli was in a minority of a hundred.

[2] Disraeli's motion lost, an amendment by Sir F. Baring became substantive, and was debated together with an amendment by Lowe. The debate closed on June 8, when Lowe was negatived and Baring carried without a division his resolution for the prosecution of the war. Bright's speech was a closely prepared indictment of the Government and a slashing attack on Palmerston and Russell. Russell did not long survive the exposure of the inconsistency of his present bellicose attitude with his acceptance of peace terms at Vienna. He was forced into resignation in July. Palmerston, said Bright, was "a man who has experience, but who with experience has not gained wisdom, a man who has age, but who, with age, has not the gravity of age." Disraeli said the same thing in other tones in *The Press*: "A

"Before speaking, whilst taking some tea in the smoking-room and considering my speech, Mr. Gordon came to me. We spoke about Lord J. Russell's conduct to Lord Aberdeen—of his object in going about the country in the autumn of 1854 to rouse the war spirit, as if to enable him to put himself in a position of advantage in opposition to his chief, etc. I hear the Court have had an interview with Lord Aberdeen. Queen and Prince angry at the course taken by the Peel section, and remonstrated with him upon it. He defended the policy of those who wished to put an end to the war, as the most conservative, and referred to the course I had taken upon it, and to what opinions I had expressed as to the possible effect of the war on the institutions of the country; also that I was not one on whom the Court should look with suspicion, that I was not hostile to the monarchy, but might rather be trusted as an honest friend, standing by sound principles as the true conservatism, etc.

"This must have been an amusing conversation—in which I am recommended to the Court by a Conservative statesman as one on whom they may rely as a friend!

"Rather excited with speaking, and slept very little during the night.

"[*8th.*] Debate concluded without division. The argument and the oratory much on the side of the peace party. And yet the war will go on—such is the horrible difficulty in which vicious or feeble statesmen have involved the country.

"[*15th.*] Board of Trade on Liverpool Town dues. A long chat with the Duke of Newcastle in Cockspur St. He is going to the East on a tour of information. Evidently uneasy about the war and the discredit which attaches to public men. Spoke of Lord Jno. Russell: said he had fallen very much in his estimation during the two years he had sat with him in the Cabinet. He seemed to have no policy, changed often; no force of mind on questions of magnitude; was not much except when speaking at the Table of the House. Sir Geo. Grey, on the contrary, had risen in his estimation, etc.

"[*20th.*] Called in on the 'Cosmopolitan.' Introduced to Mr. Elwin, editor of the *Quarterly Review*,[1] a mild and pleasant and intelli-

comic premier" with a wallet of "small pleasantries of an excruciating kind;" "a gay old Tory of the older school, disguising himself as a Liberal and hoaxing the Reform Club." Bright's speech contained two prophetic passages—one dealing with the rising might and wealth of the United States, and another welcoming the Peelites to his side.

[1] The Rev. Whitwell Elwin, rector of Booton, began his connexion with the *Q.R.* by deputizing for Lockhart, and succeeded him on his death in 1854.

gent man apparently. It is amusing that such men should wish to be introduced to me.

"[*22nd.*] Mr. Ionides, the Greek Consul, called: talk on the war, Russians, Greeks, and Allies.

"This morning's news from the Crimea unfavourable. 'Malakoff' Tower and 'Redan' attacked, the former by the French, and the latter by the English, and unsuccessfully. Much loss of life. Again mourning in families to gratify ministerial ambition and national arrogance.

"[*23rd.*] Dined with Lord Goderich at 1, Carlton Gardens. A pleasant small party: Roebuck, Harcourt, Lord and Lady Hobart, etc. Long chat with Lady Hobart, a charming and good person evidently. Explained to me a scheme for a home or shelter for young women employed as milliners, etc. Her husband is against the war, and wrote an excellent letter to *The Times* some time ago on the subject. She can't quite comprehend the whole question of War or Peace—that is, the abstract principle. I have engaged to send her a copy of Dymond's 'Essays.' Mr. Higgins came in, and I walked with him up into Piccadilly, talking over affairs, which are very gloomy.

"Home, and read Sebastopol Committee Report [1] till near 2 o'clock —and then to bed.

"[*27th.*] Called at Cosmopolitan Club. Talk with Lord Stanley. Had been to Oldham, laying first stone of a Literary Institution. Was proud of Lancashire; thought we did not enough understand each other in that county. Interests the same now. 'You don't want to be governed by your operatives any more than we by our labourers.' Mr. Fairburn had told him that, taking Manchester Exchange as one centre and St. Paul's as the other, Manchester and 30 miles round it has more population than St. Paul's and 30 miles round it. A wonderful fact: 'evident that county has not its share of influence, and he could not oppose Parliamentary reform from that feeling,' etc.

"Drury Lane Theatre. Meeting of the 'Administrative Reform Society' held this evening: Chas. Dickens made an excellent speech— so I hear from those present.

"[*30th.*] Mr. Stafford, M.P.,[2] called, and went with him to call

[1] The report was presented on June 18. Roebuck had been appointed chairman of the committee he demanded, but little of his draft report was left in the final document, for which Lord Seymour (afterwards Duke of Somerset) was chiefly responsible. The Report involved soldiers, sailors, transport officers and diplomatists in one great condemnation, but lavished its severest strictures upon the Aberdeen Government for its lack of foresight.

[2] See page 147.

upon Lady Alice Peel, the wife of General Peel. She is the daughter, I believe, of the Marquis of Ailsa. Stafford told me she is very 'Russian' —that is, opposed to the war—and she wished me to call upon her. So we went to lunch, and had a pleasant visit and conversation. Lady Alice is much against the war. She said she thought all the foreign diplomatists in London, France and Sardinia excepted, were against the English policy, and that the French people are altogether against the war. She doubts the long duration of the present rule in France.

"She wished me to come again on the 11th of the coming month, to meet Mr. Bernstorff and the Oxholmes—I fancy Swedish and Danish diplomatists, etc., which I engaged to do.

"By 5 train to Godalming. W. R. Grey in the same carriage. An open phaeton and one *excellent* horse took me to Dunford, near Midhurst, where Cobden lives, and where I received a hearty welcome.

"[*July* 1.] A glorious day. A nice house, and a pleasant family. A charming prospect from the windows and the lawn. On the left a high bank on the side of a hill, covered with the freshest and most thriving trees. On the right, more distant, the downs, being hills of considerable elevation marking a clear and striking outline against the blue sky. Between these, a rich and lovely scene covered with waving grass and growing crops of grain.

"In the afternoon Cobden and I mounted his ponies and made an excursion to the top of the downs, coming back by Lavington House, a residence of the Bishop of Oxford. We had a charming ride: the scene from the downs extensive and rich, the villages cheerful, the little churches picturesque, the whole calm and retired as if great cities had no existence.

"[*2nd.*] Conversation with Members on state of affairs, much gloom evidently prevailing. The death of Lord Raglan,[1] known here on the 30th ult. (the day before yesterday), has produced a sad effect. Spoke to C. P. Villiers on French affairs. He said that railroads and imports were to be additionally taxed, and that direct taxes also were to be increased; that a loan of 30 millions was to be raised, and more men to be called out. Will France bear it, and at a time when bread is dear and trade is not good? May not the next startling event in Europe be an explosion in France?

"[*16th.*] Lord Jno. Russell resigned office on the 13th. Explana-

---

[1] The Commander-in-Chief in the Crimea died of cholera ten days after the tragic and sanguinary failure of the attack on the Redan, which, against his own judgment, he had undertaken to oblige the French.

tions this evening, and not satisfactory. He was in favour of Austrian project of peace, but, as the Cabinet refused to concur, he kept his office. My colleague Gibson brought all this out by questions in the House, and, a cry being raised against Lord John, he was forced to resign.

"[17th.] Roebuck's motion of censure to follow up the Sebastopol Committee's Report. The debate not very good.[1]

"[19th.] Adjourned debate on Roebuck's motion. I spoke and attacked Palmerston with force—and some success.

"[26th.] To lunch at 3 o'clock with Lady Alice Peel . . . Count Bernstorff, the Prussian Minister and his lady; Count Vitzthum, Saxon Minister; Disraeli and Mrs. Disraeli; some attachés of the Prussian Embassy here and in Paris, etc., thus French chiefly spoken— rather troublesome for me, as I get on well only with my own language. Conversation with one of Lady Peel's daughters on public morality and military profession, and promised to send her a copy of Dymond's 'Essays.'[2]

"[27th.] Cobden, Jas. Bell and H. Richard called on project of a penny daily paper in London.

"[August 3.] House: debate on Vienna Conferences. Laing made a good practical speech; Gladstone a speech of the highest class, proving his superiority over all other men in the House. His case against the Govt. going on with the war irresistible, and felt to be so.[3] Cobden made a descent on Molesworth for his treachery to his old friends and principles. The new Colonial Secretary looked foolish under the chastisement he received.

"[7th.] House. Indian Budget. Spoke for an hour and a half on Indian finance and general question of Indian affairs. Small House,

[1] Roebuck's motion was a censure on the Aberdeen Government, which no longer existed; but if carried it would have made inevitable the resignation of Palmerston and half his Cabinet. It was shelved by the device of "the previous question."

[2] Count Vitzthum records some of the talk of Disraeli, who sat next to him at this party: "I have always thought Gladstone, Bright and myself the three most energetic men in the House. I have watched Gladstone very carefully, and am convinced that his strength of will is inflexible. Bright is sometimes blunt, but his eloquence is most powerful. He has not the subtleness of Cobden, but he has far more energy, and his talents are more practically applied. . . ." (Vitzthum, Vol. 1, Chapter 6.)

[3] This speech, made in the last Crimean debate of the session, is one of the two which Lord Morley describes as "of extraordinary power of every kind. His position was perfectly tenable, and he defended it with unsurpassed force." The session of 1855 marks the beginning of the attraction between Bright and Gladstone, which led to alliance and ultimately to the foundation of the modern Liberal Party.

but attentive, and we slew Hogg and Mangles, East India Directors, on the question of torture in Madras.

"The House accepted two resolutions of mine which I think will be useful.

"[9th.] By 10 train to Manchester and home. What a relief to be free of this lamentable session! War is the grave of all good, whether in administration or legislation, and it throws power into the hands of the most worthless of the class of statesmen. Hence a session with no result, and a Palmerston in the place of Prime Minister.

"[10th.] Home.

"[15th.] News of successful bombardment of Sveaborg recd. to-day; but I can't see how this will secure Turkey or affect question of preponderance in the Black Sea!

"[16th.] To Manchester. . . . New Brown Street and League rooms, with Wilson, Rawson and Ireland, making calculations as to chances of success for a penny daily paper in London. Opinion that 30,000 circulation would cover cost, and any larger number leave a profit.

"[20th.] Manchester. Met Joseph Sturge and Geo. Wilson about penny daily paper in London.[1]

"[September 7.] To Dartford, Kent, to see Mr. Applegarth about machine for penny daily paper. Came up from Greenhithe by boat.

"[8th.] Saw Mr. Haly on the paper business.

"[10th.] To London. News of the assault on Sebastopol—partial success. Later in the day—evacuation of south side of Sebastopol announced. The question now: what next?"

---

[1] The rest of the month was occupied by a visit with Mrs. Bright and his son Albert to the Priestmans at Newcastle and a tour in the Lake District.

CHAPTER IX
AN INTERLUDE ABROAD

I

AS his correspondence with Cobden testifies, Bright watched with undiminished vigilance during the early autumn of 1855 the sequelæ of the fall of Sebastopol, and continued to press for the immediate Peace which Napoleon now wanted and Palmerston feared. But the scene began to dim for him as the year advanced. He found himself drifting outside the political ring, losing touch with the negotiations that issued in the establishment of *The Morning Star*, becoming oblivious to all the interests which had filled his life for twenty years. When Peace came in the spring, he was a sick man indifferent to everything but the passing hour and his immediate surroundings.

No one in England had been more racked by the misery of the war. He had lain for two years under the immanent sense of a solemn duty —at all costs to testify against it, to endure insult and ignominy, to perform the labours of a slave with mind and tongue and pen, to press every ounce of his strength into the service of Peace. It broke him up. By January he was a nervous wreck. His last acts before the darkness came down were two appeals for appeasement—the first a letter to Sir George Grey urging that he and the moderate men in the Cabinet should stand for Peace at once on moderate terms; the second a Peace speech to his constituents in Manchester. This is a Memorandum which he made when beginning to recover from his illness nearly a year after:

"About the middle, or near the 20th, of the 1st mo. 1856, I found myself suffering from an attack of giddiness in the head, which deprived me almost entirely of the power of mental labour. An important meeting was fixed for the 28th in Manchester, at which my colleague, Gibson, and myself were to meet a large number of our constituents, and I greatly feared that I should be quite unable to attend it. I consulted my medical adviser Mr. Holland, and he recommended me to 'take freely of nux vomica,' a medicine of the homœopathic system. I did so, and was able to attend the meeting, and spoke for nearly two hours, with as much force and result as when in my usual health.

"At the close of the meeting, it was remarked that I was flushed in the face, and suffering from the excitement of the effort. It is now, when I write this, nearly 10 months since that meeting and that speech, and from that evening to this, I have not recovered my health or strength so as to permit me again to speak in public, or to undertake any public labour.

"A few days after the opening of the session, I went to London, in the hope that a change of air and scene would relieve me, but I was unable to attend Parlt. and returned home. Again I went to London, but was still unable to attend the House, and after consulting Dr. Kidd, of 60, Moorgate St., I again returned home.

"On the 4th of 3rd mo. I went to Ben Rhydding, nr. Otley, Yorkshire, to the hydropathic establishment, conducted by Dr. McLeod, and remained there 8 weeks, till the 30th of 4th mo. The first fortnight I was much worse. The giddiness had left me very much before going there, and now came on a distressing pressure on the top of head and on the forehead. From this I very slowly recovered, at the same time finding the brain so excitable that a few minutes' conversation or a little reading, or the writing of a short note, gave me a feeling of discomfort and distress. I suspect that my stay at Ben Rhydding was altogether a mistake. The water treatment may or may not have been injurious to me, but the large company there was certainly most unsuitable for me.

"Left Ben Rhydding for home, April 30, and remained at home for a fortnight. Then on the 15th of 5th mo., I left home for Scotland, having my Bro^r. Jacob with me for a week or 10 days. I visited Inverary; then to Dalmally, on Loch Awe, where I was joined by my Bro^r. Thos. and his wife and my dear daughter Helen. We went on to Oban, and to Invergarry and Tyndrum. Here I was left with dear Helen, and we spent about a fortnight in Mr. Ellice's lodge at Ardochy, on Loch Garry, till driven away by the rain.

"We proceeded to Drumnadrochit and Inverness, into Sutherlandshire to Lairg, Golspie, Thurso, John O'Groat's, and Wick, (and) to Inveran on the river Shin, where my friend Thos. Thomasson, of Bolton, was salmon fishing. There we stayed a fortnight, in great enjoyment, and with great benefit to my health. Then to Inverness,

Nairn, Forres, Elgin, Aberdeen, Perth, Edinbro', Newcastle and home on the 31st of 7th mo., after an absence of 11 weeks.

"I was greatly better from this journey, and 3 weeks afterwards (8/21) I went again to Scotland to join H. Ashworth and T. Thomasson, at their shooting quarters at Morven Lodge nr. Ballater, and remained there till the 10th of 9th mo., except that I paid a visit of 3 days to Advie on the Spey, where P. Arrowsmith, of Bolton, and Robt. Munn, of Bacup, had quarters.

"On the 7th of 9th mo., I lunched at Birk Hall with Sir Jas. Clark (M.D. to the Queen). He was very kind in advising me as to my state of health.

"September 10th to Aberdeen; 11th to Haddo House to visit Lord Aberdeen, and remained there a week. Then to Callander to spend two days with my dear Sister Priscilla, at the farm of Bochaske, where she was staying for a time. Home on the 25th, having stayed two days at Heath. This journey was of no apparent benefit to me, as I saw too many people—and talked too much."

At this point the Memorandum, apparently written about the middle of November, merges into the Diary which he then resumed. October had been spent with his family at Llandudno, and during this month he "sensibly improved." He was then persuaded by Dr. Kidd and Sir James Clark, backed by the earnest wishes of his friends, to go abroad. John Church Backhouse, of Darlington, had been ordered to Algeria for the winter, and Bright agreed to accompany him. So he spent his forty-fifth birthday on the steamer *Henri Quatre*, crossing from Marseilles to Algiers—and spent it miserably enough: the years that had passed since he was last in the Mediterranean had not in the least modified his relations with the sea. Arrived in Algiers, he and Backhouse went shares with another invalid, a Yorkshireman named Shepherd, in the tenancy of a house at Akha, the *Maison Chauve*—so called not because of any special nakedness of its own: it was the property of a Monsieur Chauve.

His stay of just over a month in North Africa provided him with many new experiences, and a new line of study: the impact of French commercial civilization upon an old Mohammedan culture. There were new colours for his eye, and above all warmth and fine air and the distraction of novel scenes within easy reach. The sojourn did him good. But, in his state of health, he found the separation from his family irksome. He gets excited about the expectation of letters from home; when they fail to arrive the most brilliant African sky grows dark. "The steamer not in, which is disappointing." Next day: "No steamer in yet, and again disappointed of letters." And then: "The steamer in—happily . . . letters . . . welcome and refreshing . . . the details of our darling children always delightful to me." One day he had seven letters from various members of his family: "the day therefore one of great interest and much pleasure." His daughter Helen was to meet him in France in the New Year, and towards the end of his stay that was his one preoccupation; "the expectation of seeing dear Helen so soon makes my heart light and my journeying a pleasure."

He was an invalid recovering, and therefore a little whimsical. But, as the record of this six months' travel grows, it is easy to see his mental vigour coming back, his universal curiosity reviving.[1] Before long his passion for new knowledge and the intensification of old knowledge blazes as brightly as ever. In the intervals of sightseeing, he is reading Lyell's "Elements of Geology." He mentions it first just after his arrival in Algiers in November: "Am now able to read with more pleasure than for nine months past. What a blessing this is I cannot describe." He leaves it on the 30th December at Nîmes: "Finished reading Lyell's 'Geology' to-day: a very interesting book from which I have learned something."

But there are lighter tasks than Lyell. He engages an old French Protestant minister in Algiers, M. André, to give him lessons in French. The pastor comes to the *Maison Chauve* in the morning and administers the dose; in the evening, Bright does his exercises in translation. He makes progress. He is keen enough to walk into the city to buy a French Grammar and a copy of Ponsard's comedy, *La Bourse*. He goes to the French Protestant chapel on Sundays, and finds the sermons "more easy to follow,"—can even make précis of them for his journal. And when he is about to leave Algiers,—"Paid off M. André, 40 francs —in all 60 francs for French whilst here; 16 lessons at three francs—and the rest because M. André is poor and has been ill-used."

Then there was drawing. Some strange urge set him trying a prentice hand on the pencil at the age of forty-five. The topic bursts into his diary unheralded and unexplained. "I sought out Mr. Vacherot,

---

[1] Ill-conditioned gossip spread absurd rumours about Bright's illness. They gave occasion for one of his famous quips, when he told a meeting at Bradford (Jan. 17, 1859): "One Scotch Lord told a great audience that I have been afflicted by a visitation of Providence, and that I am suffering from a disease of the brain. His friends can tell whether that is a complaint with which he is ever likely to be afflicted."

an artist, to give me some lessons in drawing, and agreed with him to come out and see me to-morrow. . . . Mr. Vacherot came, and we walked up the hill and sat down in a field to sketch. But I am a sad bungler, knowing nothing of the art and fearing almost to put the pencil to the paper. Perhaps I may gather courage and knowledge by and by." He perseveres. "A small attempt to sketch this morning. I am childish at it. Attempted a sketch of a house below the garden, and did not wholly fail; but failed in trying to copy a square pillar with a flower-pot on top of it." He gets rather tired "by the attention necessary to learn anything," and is sorely discouraged by his results; but he has already begun to see things with the eye of the practising artist. In one of the narrow old streets he observes an Italian and his monkey, "a most obedient and amusing animal," with a crowd of spectators, Moors, Jews, and negresses, "timid women peeping out of small windows and half-opened doors, anxious to see but fearful of being seen;" and his comment on it is, "A correct picture of the scene would be valuable." On a visit to Bou Jarna, seeing the small vaulted chapels or tombs of those persons "of superior character or piety," the Marabouts, amid palms and cactus, Backhouse and another visitor took photographs; but, "I made a slight sketch of two of them."

Mr. Vacherot's tuition cost him fifty francs. There is no evidence that he pursued the study of drawing after he left Algeria.

2

In reading the extracts from his diary which follow, we must have in mind a sick man coming gradually back to health, very sympathetic with the other sick people around him, living with Backhouse and Shepherd, both suffering from chest trouble, in a country house outside Algiers, receiving there other English people seeking health and pleasure in the air and sunshine, e.g., a family named Mayer, Mr. Bell, the consul, Mr. Elmore, the vice-consul,—doing his best to entertain them all with his talk, which was easy, and with readings aloud of a Lancashire dialect book, the "Felly fro' Rochda'," which he made amusing, and all the time flinging his thoughts across sea and land to Lancashire and his own folk.

"[*December* 2.] Looked into a Mahomedan school—tidy and comfortable; about 50 boys sitting on a raised platform surrounding a good-looking black man, and moving their bodies forwards and backwards towards the master, repeating passages from the *Koran*, being taught evidently on the Lancasterian principle. Looked in upon a scribe, a fine-looking black man with a spotless white turban, sitting at his table with paper and ink before him. His inkstand had 5 or 6 small inkwells in it, containing ink of different colours with which he writes (copies) books in various colours, giving beauty to the manuscript. It is a sort of illumination, and very pretty. The Mahomedan school above mentioned, was very different from a Jewish school into which we ventured the day before: the whole place, and the passage to it, were filled with nasty smells, and the children had a sickly and neglected appearance.

"[3rd.] Sought out a Moorish bath but found men can only bathe from 6 in the evening to 12 at noon. From noon to 6 in the evening the bath is appropriated to women. Walked thro' the old streets for an hour—interesting, as before; but there is evidently much poverty and much degradation among the native classes. . . .

". . . Walked home and met Mr. Elmore going up to dine with us. . . . He speaks Arabic, and has great advantages in obtaining information. He thinks favourably of the success of the French in colonizing and improving the country, observes their attempts to enclose the neighbouring territories between them and the sea, and believes they will some day, if not interfered with by England, have the whole southern sea-board of the Mediterranean—which I think quite probable, and I don't see that England would suffer from such an event. Mr. Elmore is surprised at the supineness of the English Govt. on the subject, and, looking at their policy and assertions as to the 'balance of power,' it is rather odd they don't regard as important what is being done in Northern Africa.

"[14th.] Met Mr. Mahony, American Consul. . . . He mentioned the effects of sea bathing here. It excites so much that he could neither sleep, nor write, nor do anything. Others have experienced the same thing. Therefore sea bathing is not practised here.

"[19th.] Strolled to the Great Mosque: saw the Cadi sitting in his Court. The persons coming in on business kneel down and kiss his hand, and then squat down on the floor to state their case, having left their shoes at the door. The Cadi or Cadis (for there seem several, tho' one chief) well dressed, intelligent looking gentlemen—turbans of spotless whiteness.

"[20th.] After dinner I went in to town, and with the Mayers to Mr. Brown's, a French gentleman here of English descent, and with them to see a Moorish party or ball. The house was crowded, the lower floor of the court with guests and musicians. The music consisted of drums and something very like the bagpipe, and was very monotonous. After that singing, equally monotonous, but low and rather plaintive.

"There was no dancing whilst I stayed, and it was said the police were opposed to it. The Moorish women who dance are not of the best character, or they would not venture to break in upon the customs and laws of their religion. We saw no Moorish women, but the ladies of our party were admitted to see them upstairs. There were many Jewesses there, richly dressed but not striking in appearance as regards personal beauty. Great order and decorum prevailed, and we were treated with great politeness.

"[*22nd.*] Took a Moorish bath, rue de l'État Major. Not so hot as I expected. Half a dozen negresses washing the linen of the establishment in the room where the bathers undress and dress. Called on Mr. Vacherot and paid him 50 francs for his lessons in drawing. Took a boat in the harbour and went on board the *Metidja*, the steamer for to-morrow. I don't like her very well: *screw*, like the *Henri Quatre*, and I suspect will roll about fearfully unless the weather is very fine. Just now there is a prospect of fine weather, so am disposed to go in her rather than wait 4 days longer for the *Thabor*, a paddle-boat, which I should prefer."

The boat was slow; the coal was bad; the *Metidja's* best was a tiresome eight knots. But on the whole the weather was fine, and Bright did not get sea-sick. Also, in happy contrast with his experience in the Mediterranean twenty-two years before, he managed to spend part of Christmas Day ashore. So that this may be reckoned among his more prosperous voyages. He found rain in Marseilles, and dirty streets, and the city looking on the festival of Noel "very much like an English Sunday." Two days later, however, he was at Nîmes, in a pleasant and familiar atmosphere. In the rue Plotine lived Mlle Benezet, who kept what was called the Friends' School, and to this retreat he made his way the day after his arrival.

"[*December* 28.] Found there Robt. Howland, son of the late Geo. Howland of New Bedford, U.S., who is here with his mother who is on a religious visit, Jno. Yeardley from England, S. Bass from Brighton, and two daughters (Sarah and Felicia, I think) of the late Emmanuel Cooper. They had 'Meeting' in the schoolroom, and I stayed with them. About 25 girls were there, who are boarders and come from the district. Jno. Yeardley spoke in English and Mlle Benezet interpreted for him, and he parleyed very briefly in French.

"[*29th.*] This morning Eliza Gurney and R. and C. Alsop came here on their way to the train for Valence. I was able to give E. G. some account of J. C. B.,[1] who is, by marriage, her son-in-law; she told me she had visited the Empress of Russia in Nice, and that the Empress asked 'if a distinguished Englishman (!), Mr. Bright, was in the neighbourhood, as she had seen or heard that he was travelling in France or Italy?' E. G. replied that she did not know that he was in that part of Europe or in the neighbourhood. The Empress said 'he was a friend of theirs, or friendly to them, and had been just to them and to Russia;' and I think E. G. said that she wished to see him.

"E. G. much urged me to call upon the Empress in Nice, but I told her I always avoided 'great people' unless I had some special object which obliged me to see them. She then asked me to convey a book which she had promised to send to the Empress, and which was already made up, and addressed to her. I undertook to have it forwarded to her, tho' I did not promise to deliver it in person. She said the Empress appeared about 65 years old, thin and delicate in health, but a person of much dignity; that she spoke of her husband, the Emperor Nicholas, as one of the noblest men that have ever lived. She appeared as if she had recently borne much grief.

"[*30th.*] Sent off home a letter written last night. To-day dear Helen is to leave home to join me here. How pleasant to have her sweet company in my journey! I hope to have her by the end of the week.

"Walking out this morning, I met with Mr. Perrot, an antiquarian, who has a small collection of curiosities, and who has written on the monuments of Nismes and of France, as well as on the mummies of Egypt. He has a new idea on the Egyptian mythology—new, at least, to me. He insists upon it that the Egyptians worshipped only one God, and that the animals they are supposed to have worshipped were only the representatives of qualities or virtues, of which some were reckoned as intercessors with the Deity. He has a mummy in an elaborately decorated coffin or sarcophagus, and he gave me a most interesting description of the decorations upon it, from which he certainly appeared to make out a good case in favour of the Egyptian worship. His reading of the hieroglyphics seemed reasonable, and his explanations have done

[1] Backhouse.

something to meet the difficulty I have always had in believing that the Egyptians, so learned and so capable, could possibly have a worship so degrading as that which history has attributed to them."

3

Big things were happening at home while Bright leisurely wandered over Europe during the first half of 1857, gathering strength for the exertions of the great decade which was to include the Indian Mutiny, the American Civil War, and the new Reform agitation. He was "out of politics" still. But with returning health there came a re-orientation of his mind. A fast-growing interest in the critical affairs of the hour reveals itself no less in the diaries than in his letters.

He began to stir when Palmerston flung the nation into an unwarranted war with China as a sequel to the seizure of the *Arrow*. Cobden leading them, the Radicals in Parliament combined with the Peelites, Disraeli's Tories and Lord John Russell to defeat the Government. Palmerston dissolved. The loss of Bright's seat at Manchester in the Jingo general election that followed did but prepare the way in his absence for that new phase of his political life which began with the unopposed election at Birmingham later in the year. But for the time it seemed dire disaster. Milner Gibson was involved with him in the *débâcle*. Cobden had heroically tried at the same time to fight Bright's election for him at Manchester and solicit a new constituency at Huddersfield himself. He too went down. Fox and Miall were thrown out. The election, indeed, dealt a staggering blow to the "Manchester men." As Bright wrote to Cobden from Venice, it was a "sudden break-up of the School of which we have been the chief professors."

He could watch these things from afar with a more detached and speculative eye and in a more philosophic spirit than if he had been in the thick of the struggle; but he watched them, as his tour drew to a close, with a reviving fervour for the causes of peace and democracy which events were challenging with relentless persistence. When he heard the Manchester result, he wrote to his wife: "Thy wish is accomplished, and I am free without having run away from my post! . . . Honest men are not in demand just now. Shams are more needed for the foolish notions which are abroad. Perhaps wiser times may come." And to his diary he confided: "Private life is infinitely preferable to public honours if unaccompanied by a consciousness of independence and rectitude of conduct." But he wrote to Cobden, with his usual prescience: "Ten years hence those who live so long may see a complete change in the public mind on the questions on which the public mind has recently been so active and so much mistaken." Ten years later almost to the day, the heyday of the new Liberal Party had begun. Bright had carried through a triumphant campaign for the household suffrage. He was Gladstone's most valuable henchman. He had reached a peak of popularity in the country which it is given to few statesmen to attain.

But in this spring of 1857, meandering, musing, recuperating, he allowed neither news from England nor the several political encounters which happened to him in his travels to detract from the exquisite pleasure he took in the company of his daughter and the delight of playing cicerone to her. Helen Bright was then a girl of seventeen on her first tour. She had already become his favourite companion, and their common rapture in things seen is reflected in his notes on the adventures she shared with him. He revelled in showing and interpreting to her the wonders of the ancient world, the lakes of Italy, the mountains of Switzerland. When she fell ill with measles in Rome, he agonized over her and nursed her with tender diligence. When she recovered he displayed almost a lover's joy.

Helen was escorted to Lyons by her uncle, Thomas Bright, and her father met her there on January 2. They went joyfully together through the Riviera to Genoa and to Rome, where they remained two months (January 25 to March 25). Together they took lessons in Italian: "I am not very sanguine of success; but my darling Helen will, I think, make progress." There is an attractive picture of father and daughter in their apartments at the Hôtel de Russie, with their heads bent over Dona Boschi's Italian Grammar, "learning the verbs *avere* and *essere* and writing the first exercises . . . a most pleasant evening." He took her to St. Peter's, where she found the service, in spite of the presence of the Pope and the cardinals, "rather tedious than pleasing." She did the round of the antiquities. She enjoyed Carnival immensely. For himself Bright was glad when Carnival ended, but "Helen has had a time of extreme enjoyment,—and the amusement has served to dissipate me a little, which, I think, is not without its use."

It was towards the end of their stay, on March 13, that she developed what seemed like a feverish cold, but turned out to be measles—a disease then rampant in Rome. Bright deplored the absence from the city of Dr. Franco, a homœopath; but he called in a Mr. Mackern who practised on the same principles, and was "very kind in his attentions. Pulsatilla—two drops every three hours." Five days in bed and the necessary time for convalescence delayed their departure for Florence, and when they did get off the girl was still very weak: "She has rested her head for many hours on my shoulder. I have been very anxious about her." But she recovered at Florence, and had only one slight set-back during their long itinerary of Northern Italy. She explored with him its cathedrals and picture galleries and palaces in Bologna, Ferrara, Padua, Venice, travelling by post-chaise, rail and gondola. She saw a comedy in the open air at Verona. She watched him fishing in Lake Como and Lake Maggiore. She crossed the Alps with him to Geneva, and they fetched up on May 21 at Lyons again.

In the evening of that great day, "we walked to the Paris and Lyons railway station and met the train from Paris a little before ten o'clock. Dear Elizabeth arrived by it after a journey of 316 miles from Paris. Our six months' separation is at an end."

Now Palmerston might rage. The ungrateful voters of Manchester might desert. The School might collapse. The political heavens might fall. But the Bright family was reunited and all was well. The happiness of the reunion shines through the pages of his diary as clearly in the ellipses as in the entries—which, from this time forward, become more scanty. They toured Switzerland by Geneva, Chamonix, Neuchâtel, Lausanne, Berne, Thun, Grindelwald and Bâle. They passed into Germany early in June, coming home by Mannheim and Cologne and Brussels. Their last set excursion was to Waterloo: "The day fine, the excursion pleasant; but now more than ever one is led to ask what the battle was fought for? Surely not to keep the Bourbons on the throne of France?"

Some extracts from his notes on matters of public or quasi-public interest follow.

"[*January* 6, 1857.] Left Aix at 8 this morning . . . stopped at St. Maximin . . . The Hôtel de France kept by a man who would probably take to the road if it were as safe as his present plan of robbing travellers. For a small lunch his charge at least double that of any good and honest hotel-keeper for a similar provision. Our courier violent, but without much effect.

"[*8th.*] Left Frejus at ½ past 9 for Cannes where we arrived at 2 o'clock by the pass of L'Estrelle. We walked for more than an hour along the fine road over the mountains; the scenery very beautiful, and in some parts approaching the grand. Hôtel du Nord here—not very good.

"On inquiry, found that Lord Brougham [1] was in England, so was disappointed at not being able to see him. We walked out to his house and spent half an hour with Mr. Woolfield, who is staying there.

"[11*th, at Nice.*] With Mr. Ellice to dine with Lord Ashburton. Ourselves and Lord A. Conversation pleasant—on the penny newspapers and the Press in general, etc.

"After dinner into the drawing-room to Lady Ashburton: conversation almost entirely political. The lady ridiculed Ellice's Whiggism, did not trust Disraeli, lamented Peel. She and her husband strong against Palmerston and his foreign policy. Discussed Peel's sons— Sir Robt.'s foolish speech on his Russian journey, and Frederick's unpopularity. I defended Frederick, as did Lady A. Discussed Lord Stanley, and again Lady A. was on my side in defending him. Ellice thought him an enigma—not equal in his powers.

"Lord Dufferin and his mother, Lady Dufferin, came in: the lady in favour of the Whigs. The evening passed pleasantly.

"[12*th.*] Called upon Mr. Ellice and found there the Baron de Meyendorff, the chief of the suite of the Empress of Russia. He is an intelligent and moderate man. He spoke in sorrow of the war, and especially of the deeds of the English Fleet on the coast of Finland: they were not of this age and were wholly unexpected. The French were not implicated in them, and the feeling against England was very strong in consequence. To think of them made him miserable. Half his library consisted of English books; he spent much of his leisure in reading them, and he had hoped to find England such as she was described in English books, but he had been grievously disappointed.

"He thought England and Russia might preserve the peace of the world, etc. His conversation that of an enlightened and amiable man.

"With Mr. Ellice and Helen to call upon Lady Ashburton; Lady Ely there, a very pleasing person. The ex-Duke of Parma there— not a striking example of royalty or of Duke-ry. Afterwards, a very

---

1 Brougham, then 78, had ceased to attend the Committee of the Privy Council, but still went to London to hear appeals in the House of Lords. In the strange episode of 1843 (when Peel accused Cobden of "menacing" him because he had said he held the Prime Minister "individually responsible" for the position of the country) Brougham had burst into the controversy and charged the League with stirring up the people to violence and even to assassination. (Peel's private secretary had been shot by a madman.) Bright came to Cobden's rescue in a correspondence with Brougham, and, like Ben Jonson's honest rustic, cudgelled him thriftily. But they had since tuned their flutes. Brougham's olive branch was the present to Bright of a complete set of his Works.

pleasant drive with Mr. Ellice: his narrative of the rise of the Denison and the Baring fortunes interesting and amusing.

"A note from Baron de Meyendorff, to say that the Empress wished to see me, and fixing 8 o'clock this evening.

"Being too late to go, wrote him to say I would delay my departure for Genoa, if another hour could be fixed for to-morrow.

"[13th.] This morning recd. a note from Baron de Meyendorff fixing 1 o'clock for the interview with the Empress. Helen went with me. Being the Russian New Year's Day, there were assembled a good many officers and others of the Russian suite. Whilst they were being presented to the Empress, I was below with the Baron. His conversation pleased me much. He said, 'It is all very well for Mr. Ellice to say we should try to be friendly with England. I admit it, and wish it. It is easily said, and easy for him to say it; but it is not so easily done. Look at your Press! Can there be friendship or a solid peace with such continual calumnies and lies as appear daily in your Press? Look at this speech of Sir R. Peel—and defended and praised in the *Morning Post*, the organ of your Prime Minister!'

"He said that an English lady here had been requested by the Queen of England to inquire kindly on her behalf after the health of the Empress, and that Lord Clarendon had written to a lady here wishing her to say to her that he condemned the proceedings of the English Press, but that the Govt. had no power to control it, and that any attempt to check or influence it would only make it worse. I told him I thought Clarendon might be sincere in that, but that Palmerston was not, and that Clarendon unfortunately allowed himself to become the tool of Palmerston.

"He spoke of the horrors of the war. He had expected, if anything wrong and contrary to the customs of modern warfare were done, it would rather be done by the French than the English; but the result showed how much he had been mistaken. The English Fleet in the Gulf of Bothnia, and the conduct of the troops at Kertch, seemed to have left a soreness and a regret which he could not conceal.

"He said he had lost a son, who was killed on the last day of the siege at the storming of Sebastopol—and his eyes filled with tears, and he for an instant turned away to hide his emotion.

"We walked upstairs, and thro' a large room, in which the members of the family were at breakfast, among them the Grand Duchess Hélène and the Grand Duke Michael: into another room in which was the Empress alone, taking tea.

"The Baron introduced me, and I introduced Helen, when she

215

said, 'Take a chair,—and how old is she?' We were seated almost close to her when she said:

" 'I have wished to see you, and am glad you are come, for I have observed all you have said, and I think you speak like a man who speaks from his conscience, and what you say is true.'

"I said I had opposed the war in the interest of England and of truth, as well as in that of Russia, for I thought war as bad for England as for Russia. She said:

" 'Yes, certainly. What can England gain by the war? It has cost *us* much,' referring as it seemed to me particularly to her family.

"She asked why I came to Nice and where I was going. All of which I explained to her. She asked if I knew Mrs. Gurney, whose visit she liked very much; if we were Quakers, as she was one; if the Quakers lived in villages or towns of their own, as settlements; if all the members preached, and if I preached?

"I explained to her that the Friends were against war, and reminded her of Jos. Sturge's visit to St. Petersburg, and mentioned his recent visit to Finland. She said any aid of the kind proposed to the poor people in Finland who had suffered from the English Fleet could do little for them.

"When we rose to depart the Empress rose, and said, extending her hand, 'I must shake hands with you,' and then, turning to Helen, she said, 'And your daughter—a pretty girl;' and then drawing her to her, she kissed her with a motherly affection on both cheeks and on her forehead.

"She then said to me, 'And are you ill now?' I said I was greatly better, but my head would not bear very much reading or talking or mental labour. She said to Helen, 'And are you alone with Papa and with no Mama? Your talking will not make him ill, it will be a repose to him.' She walked half across the room, and we bowed and took our leave.

"During the conversation the Grand Duke Michael came in, and the Baron introduced him to me, or me to him. He seized my hand like a fellow-countryman; speaking good English, said he was very glad to meet me, and was polite and free.

"On going out, he was at the door, and shook hands again with me and with Helen, with a cordiality showing that the feeling created by the conduct of England and the English Press did not extend to us.

"As we passed the table where the rest of the family were at breakfast, they rose and bowed politely to us. I returned the civility, and we left the room.

"As we descended the stairs to the carriage, the Baron de Meyendorff said, 'Is it not a good thing that these great people in their hearts continue still to be human? She is so good and so kind that I love her as my mother,' and his voice faltered with the strength of his emotion.

"There was no stiffness, no coldness, and no ceremony; and therefore there was no difficulty. The Empress looks very old. She is very fair in complexion, *very*, *very* thin, with a quick eye and with a kind expression. She is above the middle size in height, and her manner is dignified and easy. She is evidently very delicate, and I should think her life a very precarious one. She speaks English with considerable fluency.

"The weather has been unpleasant to-day, wet and cold; so we concluded not to leave Nice till to-morrow. We dined with Sam [1] and Selina, and the evening was spent most pleasantly with them.

"Lord Dufferin wrote to me to-day to offer me the use of an 'excellent little nag' if I was staying here, which is very kind of him. Indeed people everywhere who know me seem only too kind to me.

"[*20th, at Genoa.*] Dined with Mr. Brown, the consul, his wife and son and daughters. Mr. Hardwicke, London police magistrate, and his Swedish wife there. Mr. Brown clever, sensible, and talked to me almost more than my head would bear. Lord Jno. Russell's visit to Turin was spoken of. The leading people there, who met him at dinner at Sir J. Hudson's, were grievously disappointed with him—'with his manner and his matter.' This is not to be wondered at. 'Lord Malmesbury greatly pleased' the same critic, which I thought rather a severe condemnation of Lord John.

"Mrs. Brown spoke of Cobden's visit to them in 1847. She was prejudiced against him—did not like anybody connected with cotton, etc.; but was soon much pleased with him, and with his conversation, and his information on all subjects. Thought Mrs. Cobden a charming little woman, etc.

"[*24th, at Leghorn.*] Visited the Jews' Synagogue, which is very large, and remarkable for its marble interior; also a splendid reservoir and filtering reservoir for water to supply the city. It is 20 feet deep, but so clear that an inscription at the bottom can be easily read. The water filters thro' beds of pebbles as it passes into the main reservoir.

"Helen remarked that she would rather see it than any number of statues,—and I am not sure she is far wrong, for it is really a very beautiful thing to see, and it gives health and pleasure and life to the

[1] His brother, who was staying at Nice.

people of Leghorn; and doubtless there is much that is a fashion in the *excessive* admiration which is bestowed on works of art.

"[*26th, in Rome.*] Met Forbes McKenzie (late M.P.) in the street. He said the telegraph announces that Graham and Gladstone have joined Palmerston's Cabinet. Doubtful, I think, but not impossible after the changes I have seen. Last night I dreamt I was at the opening of the session, and heard Roebuck speak. My old labours sometimes seem to haunt me, and I am very sad at being excluded from the field where so much is to be done or attempted."

4

"It is a year to-day since my last speech in Manchester" (wrote Bright in Rome on January 28). "I was ill then, and should not have undertaken the labour which the meeting in the Corn Exchange threw upon me. I dare not, however, regret what was done. It was the pouring forth, if I may so speak, of what was in my heart, and of what filled my very soul at the time, and, if it prove the last speech, and I am no more able to tell the truth to my countrymen from the platform, I will not regret the effort then made, terrible as is the price it has cost me. I have worked *in earnest* in the political field, and if any meaner motive has ever stimulated or guided me, if ambition, or any love of display or of popularity has at any time led me on, of which I am little conscious, I think I can honestly say that a love of what I have believed to be the truth, a strong desire for the good and true greatness of my country, and an unchangeable hostility to the selfishness and fraud which distinguish the Government of the English oligarchy, have been the mainsprings of my public and political conduct. I have not sought that which is to be gained by submission to the ruling parties, and I have endeavoured to act uninfluenced by the clamour or the momentary and impulsive applause of the people. I look with gloomy forebodings on the consequences which may, and which probably must, result from the follies and the crimes into which ignorance and passion so frequently lead or impel my countrymen.

"I write this surrounded by the ruins of the once mistress of the world, and from her history, and indeed from all history, I learn that loud boasting, great wealth, great power, extended dominion, successive conquests, mighty fleets and armies, are not immovable foundations of national greatness. I would rather rely on an educated and moral people, and on a system of Government, free at home, and scrupulously moral and just in its dealings with every other Government and people.

"[*29th.*] From the *Manchester Examiner* I learn that *this evening* the Annual Meeting in the Free Trade Hall is being held, and I am so many hundreds of miles away. I have been very melancholy this evening, for I find my poor enfeebled head less strong than I supposed it to be, tho' so greatly stronger than it was some months ago.

"[*30th.*] We called upon Mr. Mackern, who is Dr. Kidd's brother-in-law. He is travelling for relaxation. We spoke of the hostility of the Romans to the French troops, and even of the Roman troops to them. No association: French have their own cafés, etc. Of the general discontent prevailing, which seems to be universal; of the disorder in the Papal finances; of the keenness and cleverness of the Cardinal Antonelli; of the nothingness of the Pope except as a puppet; of the menaces against the priests in case of another revolution, uttered and believed in by quiet persons who cannot be accused of enthusiasm, or hot-headedness, or of much political feeling.

"[*February* 3.] I went to Piale's to see the papers. The news room is closed on fête days by order of the police, and is not allowed to be open after 9 at night on any other day. The Roman system is one of repression and fear, and I speak to no one on the subject who does not express his contempt for it, and his hope that it may speedily come to an end.

"[*5th.*] Spent an hour in Piale's news room in the evening. Read an article in the *Post* on the death of Princess Lieven, insulting to her memory and not creditable to the writer—doubtless instigated and ordered by Palmerston, long the enemy of this celebrated Russian lady. I had, and still have, a letter of introduction to her from Lady Alice Peel, which now I must return to the writer of it. Read also a good article in the *Nord* of Brussels from the *Morning Star*. I hope its good opinion of Mr. Gladstone may be sustained by events. One statesman with intelligence and a conscience may do something to save the State.

"[*6th.*] At 12 to the Vatican Museum. Spent nearly 3 hours there in seeing the magnificent collection of antique statuary, unequalled I suppose in the world. I am not able to feel the enthusiasm which some men feel or affect for the 'crack' pieces of sculpture, if one may use a familiar or almost slang word. The Laocoön and the Apollo failed to give me the pleasure I derived from two statues in the Braccio Nuovo of the same gallery—the 'Minerva Medica' and the 'Modesty' which is placed exactly opposite to it. There is something of repose and dignity in these figures, and of sweetness in the countenance of the 'Modesty,' which is rarely or never found in the undraped figures on which so much praise is expended. As an effort of artistic skill, exhibiting a knowledge of anatomy, and a scientific acquaintance with form, a nude statue may have much in it worthy of admiration, and it may excite wonder at the skill of the artist; but it cannot, to me at least, communicate the pleasure which, judging from what is written on the subject, others seem to partake of so largely.

"Our notions of beauty are associated with a draped form, and with a countenance full of benignant and intellectual expression, and I suspect, if the truth were acknowledged, a figure like the 'Modesty' or the 'Minerva' communicates generally more of what is pleasing to the mind than any of the more famous nude figures which are to be seen in the Italian galleries. The only exceptions probably are to be found, if found at all, among 'scientific' artists, who regard what is accurately scientific as the chief beauty. Among the nude figures, the 'Pugilist' of Canova appears to me of remarkable power and beauty as a work of art, and should entitle the great modern sculptor to take his place alongside the most famous of the great ancients.

"[*8th.*] In the afternoon to the Church of St. Carlo, in the Corso. A priest, a Russian I suppose, was preaching in the Russian language to a large congregation.

"After he had finished, an Englishman, Dr. Manning, not long ago of the English State Church, preached in English: his text 'And there was a marriage in Cana of Galilee, and *Mary the Mother of Jesus was there.*' He referred to the various periods of festivity and solemnity in the Church—Advent, Christmas, Epiphany; and said there had always been a Divine Teacher since the Ascension of Christ. That Teacher was the Church. Spoke·of the Deification of Saints, and of one superior to them all, the 'Mother of God.' The Mother of Jesus was the Mother of God, not of the Godhead. Jesus had called us all His Brethren. We were thus allied in kindred to His Mother. He reverenced her and regarded her above all next after God His Father, and, after God and Christ, we ought to love and reverence her. Not to believe her infinite or eternal, but as the Mother of Jesus; and that, thro' her, blessings are showered upon us—for that nothing that she asks of her Divine Son is denied to her. We are to worship her,— that is, to regard her with love and reverence, with the feeling with which we regard goodness and greatness, and sanctity and majesty. Objected that little is said of it in the New Testament: we must look to the spirit rather than to the letter. One word or one phrase of Scripture is enough, and that which he had quoted, 'And the Mother of Jesus was there,' was enough.

"In all the ancient schisms from Rome, as the Greek, and the Coptic, the reverence for Mary had been retained, and therefore Socinianism had never infected them; for, wherever Mary was held in high esteem, there the doctrine of the Incarnation of God was never denied, whilst in Germany and Switzerland, in France, England, whatever had left the Church of Rome, having no regard for the Mother of Jesus, had also abandoned to a large extent a belief in the Incarnation of the Divinity. He would not say as the apostle said 'Anathema Maranatha,' for we were not to judge; but he would say he should think little of his love to Christ and to God that was not accompanied by a love to Mary the Mother of Jesus.

"He more than once made use of the term 'rigour of argument,' and professed to reject metaphor; and yet jumped to conclusions in a manner amusing enough if the subject had been one of less gravity. He concluded by exhorting all to worship (in his sense) and to defend the worship of the Mother of God. When the courts of Heaven were more full, when the purified were gathered to the Kingdom, when those in white were before the Throne, on that high day none need be ashamed of having upheld the practice which he had then urged upon his audience; for, as at the marriage feast of Cana in Galilee, so at that great marriage feast, 'the Mother of Jesus would be there.'

"There was a very large congregation, and, of course, largely composed of English visitors and residents. The sermon occupied 55 minutes. The preacher is moderately tall with an expression of intelligence rather than of force, and with a countenance indicating sincerity, earnestness, reverence and goodness. His manner was good, his gestures elegant and natural, his voice clear and impressive and pleasing; and his language was choice and eloquent, tho' moderate, and without any touch of passion.

"If I could have shut my eyes or ears, or mind, to the *matter* of the sermon, I should have spent an hour of enjoyment such as I could not easily forget; but I was reminded of a smart saying, I believe of Mr. Hutt, M.P., on the subject of the present Lord Ravensworth's oratory, when he spoke in the House of Commons as Mr. Liddell. Mr. Hutt is reported to have said, 'That man is a very good speaker if you don't listen to what he says.' So of Mr. Manning's sermon—admirable if you don't regard in the least what he has said.

"Met an Englishman or Irishman, I think the latter, coming out of the church who said he believed everything the preacher said!

"[*15th.*] A drive out on the Appian Way; then sauntered round the 'stern round tower of other days,' and entered it to see the interior of this ancient and renowned tomb—its desolateness showing how worthless are all the contrivances for giving immortality to that which is only mortal. . . .

"Afternoon to St. Carlo, and heard Dr. Manning again on the same subject as last week. Beautiful in language; more earnest and anxious in expression than before: but, if possible, more shocking in the fearful maltreatment of the New Testament and in assertion of doctrines and practices which, to me, seem condemned alike by the letter and the spirit of the inspired volume.

"[*17th.*] In the evening we dined with Sir Jno. Login and his party at the Hôtel de Londres. Col. Caldwell and his wife were there, Sir Jno. and Lady Login, Mr. Leslie Melville, and the Maharajah of Lahore. Discussed Indian affairs at some length, the Maharajah saying that he agreed with me, and that he had heard no one speak so much to his mind on Indian affairs before. He seems intelligent and amiable, but not of *much force* either of mind or body.

"[*20th.*] Whilst at dinner had a call from a Mr. Edmond Waters, an Englishman and a 'pervert,' as Protestants call the newly converted to Rome. He seems determined to make an acquaintance with me, and is wonderfully civil: invites me to take tea with them at his house to meet a Mr. de Vere and somebody else—one of the Wilberforces, I think. These are zealous missionaries for the Papal superstition, and their whole soul seems thrown into the cause of their new love. What a marvel that any man coming to Rome should not be cured of any sympathy for the Pope and the gigantic imposture of which he is the nominal head!

"In the evening to the Hôtel de Londres to Sir J. Login's—met there Mr. and Mrs. Forbes. He is a Church of England Minister, and officiates in the American Mission or Embassy Chapel on 1st day afternoon. A very pleasant and a good man I take him to be!

"Went with Sir J. Login's party to see what is called a Masque Ball, but what is really rather a sort of evening promenade, where many women and some men wear masks. But it is a dull affair on the whole, and, looking down upon it, I thought it looked very much like a great meeting dispersing. The men had their hats on, and black hats and black coats, seen from above, are anything rather than picturesque.

"[*25th.*] Was accosted in the Piazza di Spagna by Mr. Eddison, of Nottingham, whom I knew some years ago, but did not recognize. He arrived in Rome a week ago, and had been a fellow-passenger from Marseilles in our old boat the *Calabrese*, with Mrs. Stowe, the author of 'Uncle Tom' and 'Dred.' She is at 110, Via Frattina, where I think I must call upon her.

"[*March* 3.] Called on Mrs. Stowe, but she was not in, so we were disappointed.

"[*5th.*] News recd. by telegraph that Palmerston and his crew had been beaten on Cobden's motion on the China outrages by a majority of 16. This rejoiced me greatly for many reasons: that it will serve as a check to the monstrous insolence and guilt of English agents abroad, who so readily have recourse to violence on the smallest pretext; that it will probably overthrow the most unscrupulous and profligate Minister the country has had in my time; that it will be a blow to the secret gang who manage *The Times* newspaper in the interests of Palmerston; that it shows there is yet a moral sense in England. And I am especially delighted that the blow has been struck by my own greatest political friend, and in accordance with the policy we of the 'Manchester School' have ever professed and defended.

"[*6th.*] Read Cobden's speech on the China outrage: simple, clear, logical conclusion, severe and unanswerable. The only drawback to the delight with which I have read it is that I was not there to hear it, and to support it, if not with a speech, with my vote.

"[*7th.*] J. Kershaw called in the evening, owing to the news that Palmerston is to dissolve Parliament. He urged me to write at once to Manchester and to become a candidate on the ground that my health is so far improved. I must decide to-morrow.

"[*8th.*] Afternoon, wrote to Geo. Wilson, enclosing an address to the Electors of Manchester.

"[*10th.*] Went with Mr. Waters to call on Mr. Cass, the American Minister, at the Braschi Palace. In the evening we went to 110, Via Frattina, to take tea with Mrs. Stowe and Mrs. Perkins. Booth Eddison and his son, from Nottingham, and an American gentleman were there. After some general conversation we entered upon the great American slavery question and discussed it with freedom, particularly as to the late presidential election; the *Kansas* question, the means of enabling slaves to escape, etc.

"I endeavoured to show that the election of Buchanan instead of Fremont was an advantage at this moment to the liberty cause in which, after some discussion, I think Mrs. Stowe was not indisposed to agree, tho' the result of the election was evidently a great disappointment to her.

"This lady has evidently quick perception, much feeling, softness of voice and manner; and, after having read her admirable books, she does not disappoint me. The evening to me was a very pleasant one.

"[12th.] Called on the Kershaws; discussed Dr. Vaughan and the late war, which rather excited me. Helen dined with them; and I dined with Mr. Cass, American Minister, at the Braschi Palace. The party consisted of about 24: three princes, Massino, Santa Croce, and a name I don't know how to write; 'Monsignors' Talbot and Bedini, I think; the Brazilian Minister, and one or two others of the diplomatic craft; a few Italians, French and English. The dinner was in the first style. In the drawing-room cigars were handed round, and no ladies were there. All the company left at about ½ past 9, except myself, and I remained talking with Mr. Cass till near 11 o'clock. The account I heard of affairs here, as well politically as socially and morally, is extremely unfavourable.

"I asked 'Monsignor' Talbot how many students for the priest-hood from the United Kingdom there were here. He said in the Irish College and the Propaganda each about 50, Scotch 16, English 30; and in different other places or institutions more than 60—altogether more than 200—and they remain on an average about 4 years.

"[16th.] Mr. O'Connell called to ask me to go to the reception to-night at the Austrian Embassy on the occasion of making a new Cardinal! I did not, however, accept his invitation, altho' it was kindly meant.

"[19th.] Artists' Club news room. Read in *The Times* an extract from the *Manchester Guardian* that Sir Jno. Potter and 'Bob' Lowe are to be the opposition candidates in Manchester. This news does not alarm me, although of the result I can foretell nothing. Ignorance, passion and credulity are great weapons for my opponents, and they may prevail, tho' I shall not believe it till I see it. If they do succeed, it will only show that consistency to principle and fidelity of service are not sufficient to secure the confidence of the electors of Manchester. If I had bent the knee to power, and if I had sought and accepted (and *if I had sought, I might have had*) some office in the Govt., these crawling fellows that now combine against me would, I suppose, have been equally disposed to crawl to me. It is a melancholy thing to observe how slow a people are to discover their true friends. A member of the aristocracy, or anyone willing to act with the aristocracy and *for them*, is accepted by the people as if he were the friend of the people. A man may, I fear, in England, make his Parliamentary career subservient to the ruling class, and to his own personal interests, and be more certain of the approval of large and influential sections of his countrymen, than by any amount of disinterested devotion to their true interests. But if they are ignorant of the measures necessary for the public welfare, how can they be expected to distinguish the men most disposed to serve them faithfully?

"[21st.] Manchester news. Meeting of the opposition: Nield, O. Heywood and Pender all trotted out as anxious to ascertain 'if Manchester has been suitably and truly represented during the past ten years!' Nield and Co. have not, that is certain; and yet I suppose these uncomfortable members of the constituency would not have crept from their holes if they did not calculate on so much dissatisfaction as would enable them to win. They have always deceived themselves before, and perhaps they may be no wiser now. Time will show.

"[29th, at Florence.] Read *Galignani*: Manchester meeting. *Times* article—unjust to Cobden and too laudatory of me. Why I know not.

"[30th.] This evening received by telegraph the news of the result of the Manchester election.[1] It is fitting that, having discarded their faithful representatives, the electors of Manchester should humiliate themselves by returning men wholly incapable of doing them any good or of sustaining the character of their representation in any way.

"Sir J. Potter is known chiefly as a vain man who ate and dined his way to a knighthood thro' the mayoralty of Manchester. In 1846 he made a voluntary promise to me that he would be no party to any opposition to me, which promise he broke, inasmuch as he was one of those who brought down Lord Lincoln to oppose me and has since been associated with my strongest opponents. But vanity and a small ambition are too much even for personal honour and for truth. His colleague, Aspinall Turner, is a man of energy in business, is supposed to be rich, is apparently purse-proud, pompous, and vulgar. He was so much a toady of the East India Co. or an enemy to me, that when in 1851 I moved for a commission to go to India to inquire into the obstacles to the growth of cotton in that country, he sent up a resolution of the Directors of the Commercial Association to the East India

[1] Sir John Potter, 8,368; Jas. Aspinall Turner, 7,854; T. Milner Gibson, 5,588; John Bright, 5,458.

Directors to say that no inquiry was necessary, and this resolution was read against me in the House of Commons, I think on or about June 18, 1851. He is not, therefore, a very fitting representative for a city depending on the prosperity of the cotton trade. If I were disposed to be vindictive, I should feel amply avenged on the constituency when I see the men they have delighted to honour. I have done my duty by them, and am free. They prefer men who will serve the aristocratic faction which uses the Liberal Party for its own purposes. It is necessary, therefore, that they should discard Gibson and me, for we cannot serve it, and private life is infinitely preferable to public honours if unaccompanied by a consciousness of independence and of rectitude of conduct.

"[*April* 6.] To Lord Normanby's for a call: a charming villa, views hardly to be surpassed. Should like to hear Lord Normanby's details of the *coup d'état* in Paris, and of Palmerston's complicity in it. Some day all the details will be known, but perhaps not in our time.

"[*7th.*] Bought a small picture, Gaspar Poussin, 150 francesconi, and, along with Capt. Harvey, of Cowden, Eden Bridge, Kent, a 'Salvator Rosa' for 500 francesconi. The latter we are to sell in England.

"[*10th, at Bologna.*] Called at the Hôtel del Pellegrino, at which my poor Bro^r. Gratton died. Saw the room—how sad! With dear Helen to the Cemetery. Engaged the mason to repair the simple monument over his grave. Wept tears of bitter sorrow over the tomb.

"[*22nd, at Venice.*] To see the celebrated 'Last Supper' of Leonardo da Vinci. Drawing noble, the countenance of the principal figure having more of strength and gravity, combined with gentleness and sorrow, than I have seen in any other attempt to portray the character of Christ. Again to the Cathedral: interior most impressive; outside a glittering toy, costly but not satisfactory.[1]

"[*26th, at Turin.*] Called upon Count Cavour, and had a long conversation with him. He is about my age and firmly built, but scarcely so tall as I am, I think. A large head, fair complexion, an eye expressing mildness and firmness, a mouth very pleasing, but showing strength; has the appearance of an intelligent English gentleman farmer rather than of a *fine* and subtle Italian. I was greatly pleased with him—with his frankness and his fairness in speaking on any question

[1] At Lausanne, May 29: "To see the Cathedral: interesting from its simplicity, after the overdone decorations of the Romish churches."

that was discussed. I warned him against the professions of the English Government (Palmerston) as to Italian freedom. Sir C. Shaw was present during our conversation.

"[*May* 10, *at Arona.*] The Duke and Duchess of Manchester: spent some time with them before they left; subject, politics and primogeniture! On which last the lady did not agree with me—tho' one would not willingly differ from one so attractive.

"[*14th.*] To Villeneuve, where we took the steamer, and, after a pleasant sail over the whole length of the lake, we reached Geneva before 6 o'clock. The Grand Duchess Olga, sister of the present Emperor of Russia, and her husband, the Crown Prince, I think, of Würtemberg, were on the boat. She is a beautiful woman, in figure and in face. He is rather a coarse-looking man, and had the appearance of an English agricultural and sporting gentleman."

5

Two episodes of this tour throw a pleasant light on the character of Bright. The first is the episode of the Bust.

Bright's reactions to works of art were quite individual. He was one of those observers of famous things who like what they like, are not in the least affected by fashion, and hate affectation. Admiring a "Holy Family" by Andrea del Sarto, he would say so; but if he thought the representation of Eve in a fresco by Sodoma at Siena without exception the most pleasing figure he had ever seen, he would say that too. This is the sort of thing he would record in his notebook for his own satisfaction (he had been looking at the statue of Moses by Michael Angelo, in the Church of S. Pietro in Vinculo): "It is magnificent as a statue, but not as a *Moses.*" His comments on the Laocoön and on sculpture of the nude have already been quoted. He found a hurried round of a gallery very unsatisfactory: "it is wearying to the eyes and to the body and irritating to the mind." But works of art fascinated him, and when he could see them at ease his observations on what he saw disclosed a fine natural taste. A Murillo seemed to cast a spell on him wherever he encountered it. Before he left Rome he ordered copies of some pictures to be made for him. The two he mentions are Guido's "David," and a Murillo "Madonna and Child." He sought out artists and sculptors in their studios—Gibson the sculptor and Williams the painter both received more than one visit, and both heard Bright sigh, alas! that he was not a rich man who could take away the things he would like to possess.

Among the studios into which he found his way was that of Engels, the sculptor of a statue of "Faith" which Manchester was presently to see at its Exhibition of Art Treasures.   How it arose does not appear, but the question came up at the first visit whether Engels should do a bust of John Bright.   His charge for a bust in marble was fifty guineas. Bright went away and thought about it.   A week later he was there again, and learned that the cost of the model and cast, without the marble, would be thirty guineas, "which seems to me high—at least, it is more than I expected.   However, as he said in explanation, the model is the work of the artist and the marble that of the workman chiefly."

Bright's frugal objections to paying the gigantic sum of thirty guineas for a bust of himself having been overcome, he arranged to give sittings—on terms: if the bust did not succeed, he was at liberty to reject it.   The sittings were many, extending over a month.   But, as it approached completion, the bust did not please him.   He called in Gibson who suggested alterations.   The alterations were made.   Still the result failed to satisfy him, and mournfully he told his diary, "There seems to be something in my face which defies the art of painter and sculptor alike, for hitherto nobody has succeeded in making a decent portrait of me."   In this instance, however, Engels conquered the intractable at last, for an artist friend of his called at the studio, and, observing the bust, exclaimed that he had seen that gentleman at the Café Grec on Saturday evening.   Bright was astonished.   He had been in the café for but a few minutes and only on that one evening.   But the incident seemed to assure him that Engels had achieved a good likeness, and, as everybody else approved, he made payment and the bank was instructed to forward the bust "by way of Leghorn to W. Bright, Liverpool." Upon which the subject disappeared from the diary.[1]

The second episode discovers Bright in the only capacity of sportsman he ever assumed.   It began with the purchase of fishing tackle at Milan for use on Lake Como and Lake Maggiore.   With his usual particularity, he set down the cost of all the gear he bought—"not bad, considering where I got it."   His rod cost him 10 francs, his reel 10, small line 3, long line and frame 10, flies 7, minnows 12,—and he added a spare top, casting lines and gut, which brought the total bill to 55

---

[1] Sitting to sculptors became a bore to him.   In 1860, he notes (Jan. 31): "Mr. Boryczenski called and wished to alter the bust he made for me six months ago. He is to come here to do it."   (Feb. 1): "Boryczenski here: worked nearly two hours with me.   A great nuisance, this bust-making and likeness-taking.   Hope I have nearly seen the last of it."

francs. A fly fisherman was surely hardly ever equipped so cheaply! But it is sad to relate that after preparation so exciting he flogged the lakes in vain, for his aggregate catch so far as he records it amounted to one fish—and he did not get that one with the fly.

Bright had become a fisherman the year before in Scotland on the advice of Dr. McLeod, of Ben Rhydding, and this adventure on the lakes was part of his apprenticeship to the gentle art. Later on he was to reap better harvests, and fishing became his chief recreation and solace during the latter part of his life. It would, however, be excessive to describe him as a keen fisherman, for, though he took a fair number of trout, and had the pleasure many times of playing and landing a salmon, it was never in him to be an ardent sportsman. The lakeside and the river attracted him, the mild exercise and distraction from affairs did him good; the catch was the last thing that mattered. He himself said, a few years before his death, that the hours he spent on the river bank enabled him to recover the health he had lost "in long nights in the House of Commons and in the fierce political conflicts of the time."

Until the intervention of Dr. McLeod, he seemed to have done no fishing of any sort since as a boy he haunted the streams of the Pennine Hills; so that the Milan outfit went into the boat on Lake Maggiore with a novice at the butt. Also the weather was cold—of that type when, according to the adage, "the fishes do bite the least." Nothing reached the creel as the result of two hours' work on Maggiore. No better fortune attended him at Lugano. Then at Como, he had the fisherman's usual adventure. He baptized a "particularly attractive" glass minnow: "Caught one fish, and then something large, probably a pike, carried away my bait. . . ." His last reference to the subject on this journey is at Bellagio, where he caught views of unsurpassed loveliness, but no fish: "Spent four or five hours on the lake, but the trout and pike kept aloof."

By no means the least engaging trait of Bright's simple straight-forward character revealed in these records of his travels, is the almost accusing tally he keeps against himself of personal expenditure. Whether he is buying a picture, or sitting for a portrait, or engaging rooms in an hotel, or changing his courier, or fitting himself out as a fisherman, he sets down the cost with the invariable air of wondering whether John Bright ought to be spending so much on his own enjoyments and satisfactions. Arrived at the Hôtel de la Russie in Rome, he states the terms: "A salon and two bedrooms, and a courier's room, for 15 francs a day; breakfast and dinner and fire and lights will come to 35 francs per day, or nearly ten guineas a week, which is dear, but cannot be helped, I suppose." In a few weeks, however—he had found a way of helping it by going into rooms at 248, Via di San Romualdo, "at 45 scudi the month, which is about half that which I am paying in this hotel."

The party returned to England on June 15, and within a month a rejuvenated John Bright was in the thick of the political fight again. At the end of the year he added this summary note to his diary:

"*In July*: Scotland, Helmsdale, to fish with Thomasson and Geo. Crosfield; little water and little fish.

"Visited Sir Jno. Login and the Maharajah Duleep Singh at Castle Menzies; dined with them at Taymouth Castle with Lord Breadalbane. Went a nice picnic party up Glen Lyon, and was hurried away to Edinbro' to meet Mr. Sturge on the occasion of the death of poor Muntz and a vacancy in the representation of Birmingham.

"They promised to return me without opposition, and, perhaps foolishly, I consented to sit if elected.

"I went to Tamworth to meet a deputation from my committee and wrote a letter to the electors, and was finally elected without opposition.

"In October went to Llandudno with my family—remained there 7 weeks.

"Came up to London and spent two days with W. S. Lindsay at Shepperton-on-Thames, with Cobden. At Christmas spent a few days with Cobden at Midhurst—Helen with me."

CHAPTER X
MEMBER FOR BIRMINGHAM

I

BETWEEN his return from the Continent in the summer of 1857 and the opening of the Parliamentary session of 1859, Bright fell out of the habit of regular entries in his diaries. In the lassitude left by his long illness, events of deep interest to him and of the first importance to the world passed with little or no notice. When he did begin again the daily record of his movements and reflections he prefaced it with the words, "Too idle to keep up my notes since last session."

This was unjustly severe upon himself. Only bodily weakness could have kept Bright silent in those momentous days; and the fact is that he made no speech, either in Parliament or in the country, until the end of October, when he addressed for the first time the Birmingham constituents who had elected him a year before.

The hiatus, unfortunately, leaves us without note of any kind on the Indian Mutiny period. His deep study of the Indian problem and his overpowering interest in it would have given a singular value to his comments and judgments. But he made only one public allusion to the Mutiny while the tragedy worked itself out during all those agonizing months from Cawnpore to the fall of Delhi. It was contained in his telegram to the Birmingham Election Committee, replying to a question about his attitude towards the military measures then in force:

> The success of the Indian Revolt would lead to anarchy in India, and I conceive it that it is mercy to India to suppress it. I should insist on an improved Government for India for the future.

How he did so insist, and with what vision he laid down the lines of practicable reform in India can be seen in the four great speeches he delivered during the next two years.

His election for Birmingham signalled the opening of a new epoch in Bright's political life no less laborious and no less fruitful than the

231

two well-defined phases that had gone before. It was the epoch of Reform. It witnessed the creation of the modern Liberal Party, in which the coming together of Gladstone and Bright was unquestionably the dominant factor. He could have found in all England no more appropriate platform from which to proclaim his doctrine of Reform than the teeming City of Birmingham, then represented in the House of Commons by only two members. Nor could the ardent democrats of Birmingham have discovered among the politicians of England a member more after their own hearts than Bright. They displayed their affinity for him, indeed, by returning him without fail at every election for thirty years thereafter. With Birmingham as his fulcrum, he began his third long stretch of Titanic labour—in the causes of electoral equality, Indian progress, Irish appeasement and American unity.

Birmingham did more than to provide him with a platform: it gave him lifelong friends like Chamberlain and Dale, George Dixon, Joseph and Charles Sturge, J. S. Wright and Thomas Lloyd. Having resolved to repair the damage to the country done by the electors of Manchester when they threw Bright out of Parliament, the stalwarts of Birmingham decided to do the thing handsomely. On the death of Mr. Muntz they induced Duncan McLaren to hunt his brother-in-law out of his Highland retreat, ascertained his orthodoxy on the Mutiny, got him down as far as Tamworth to consult, offered to pay all his election expenses, and, when he gave his consent, had the satisfaction of seeing the Conservative candidate retire immediately from the field.

He took his seat for Birmingham on January 9, 1858, "amid friendly cheering on both sides of the House, and much friendly greeting from my old acquaintances." The next day he called on Lord Aberdeen: "found him feeble in health, though cheerful; seems very anxious as to irritating questions between France and England."

"[*January* 15, 1858.] Walked more than eight miles to-day. House: India Bill.[1]

[1] Palmerston's Bill for transferring the government of India to the Crown under a President and Council. Baring proposed an amendment in the interests of the East India Company, which was defeated (Feb. 18) by 318 to 173. The days of the East India Company were manifestly numbered; but it obtained a short reprieve by the unexpected convulsion which swallowed up Palmerston's Government a few days later. Ridicule killed Lord Ellenborough's halting compromise of a Bill, introduced in the early days of the succeeding Derby Government. Disraeli threw the remains out of the House and agreed to proceed with a Bill based on resolutions.

"Speaking with Sir J. Graham, referred to his domestic trouble, the loss of his wife. He said such things drew us from so eager a pursuit of fame or of business, showed how much all is vanity. 'How little is Fame worth striving for!' he said. 'Look at Peel—sympathy and feeling on his death, and now little thought of; even the Duke of Wellington, dead and buried—a nine-days' wonder, and the world passes on.'

"I said I thought Peel injured himself by the two books he had left behind him on Catholic Emancipation and Corn Law repeal. He said he thought they had injured him, but he was unfortunately too sensitive, and Disraeli found this out and attacked him accordingly, without hating Peel, but as a way to his own elevation.

"[16th.] Across the Park to Gibson's, talking over the proposed resolution against the 'Conspiracy Bill.' [1] Lord Jno. Russell came in, for the same object. He approved Gibson's proposition, as did Sir J. Graham who had been with him earlier in the morning.

[*Note made in* 1859.] "Too idle to keep up my notes since last session. I was in Scotland at the end of last session (1858) on the Shin with Thomasson and Crosfield, and to the West of Sutherland alone. Fishing not good; weather wet, and too much water in the rivers. In the autumn I was at Llandudno with my family.

He drew up the resolutions himself, and Lord Stanley took charge of the measure which, becoming law in August, finally put an end to Company rule in India. The other chief measure of the period of Bright's silence was the "Jew Bill" which settled the angry controversy of the preceding ten years and enabled Baron Rothschild, who had been returned by the City of London at every election during the decade, at last to take his seat.

[1] The Conspiracy Bill was brought in by Palmerston as the result of the agitation in France over the Orsini conspiracy, which was said to have been "hatched" in England: the bombs used by Orsini and his Carbonari were, it seemed, manufactured in Birmingham. The Bill made conspiracy to murder a felony; previously, in England and Scotland, it had been, like other conspiracy, a misdemeanour. It was a reasonable change; but a proposal to alter English law at the dictation of a passionate France, expressing itself with excessive violence, aroused the wrath of the country to such a point that an amendment drawn up by Lord John Russell, moved by Milner Gibson (now member for Ashton-under-Lyne), and seconded, without a speech, by Bright, was carried against Palmerston by a majority of 19. Gibson and Bright were the tellers against the Government in this division. Palmerston resigned, to make way for the Government of Lord Derby and Disraeli, which lasted little more than a year. The amendment was an ingenious piece of Parliamentary tactics, which unhorsed the Government without condemning the principle of the Bill. Palmerston's collapse on this minor question so soon after his triumph at the polls in 1857 provides striking illustration of the instability of parties in the decade which followed the Crimean War.

"[*October* 27 *and* 29.] Attended meeting and dinner at Birmingham. Speeches. Reporters more numerous than at any meeting ever held before in the country. Telegraph and special trains—as if some very important person here to utter words of great import!

"Afterwards attended great meeting in the Free Trade Hall, Manchester, along with Mr. Gibson; tickets 5/–, and 3,500 persons present.

"Afterwards attended great meetings in Edinbro' and Glasgow on Reform question.

"Afterwards at Bradford, and explained my plan of distribution of seats for my proposed Reform Bill."

2

The speech at Birmingham on October 27 was doubly memorable—in the personal and in the political sense. It was Bright's first big speech for nearly three years, and the country manifested a curious excitement about it. *The Times* had a special train to convey the report back to London. The Town Hall held five thousand people packed together, as Dr. Dale said, to hear a fierce assault on the fabric of privilege. But Bright's first few sentences hypnotized those thousands not into a fury of wrath against privilege, but into a mood of awed and breathless silence as he spoke of his recent experiences. How he had been reduced to the weakness of a little child. How he had been unable to read or write or converse for more than a few minutes at a time "without distress and without peril." How, "from that condition, by degrees so fine as to be imperceptible even to myself, I have been restored to the comparative health in which you now behold me. In remembrance of all this," he asked quietly, "is it wrong in me to acknowledge here, in the presence of you all, with reverent and grateful heart, the signal favour which has been extended to me by the Great Supreme?"

The storms of political passion, said Dr. Dale, were for a moment stilled: "We suddenly found ourselves in the presence of the Eternal, and some of us, perhaps, rebuked ourselves in the words of the patriarch, 'Surely, the Lord is in this place and I knew it not.' "

The political importance of the speech lay in the fact that it was the first of the series of thirteen great orations on Reform which Bright made between 1858 and the passing of the Reform Bill nine years later. In it he outlined the scheme of the Bill which he prepared and circulated among statesmen and politicians in the following session. This was, with immaterial differences, the scheme Disraeli passed into law in 1867, when Lord Cranborne (afterwards the famous Marquess of

Salisbury) scornfully said that if to adopt the principles of Mr. Bright were a Conservative triumph, the Conservative Party had never won so signal a triumph. In 1858, however, there was no great demand for reform among politicians, though Bright's working-class audiences at Birmingham, Manchester and elsewhere were enthusiastic enough. It is worthy of note that Bright, while declaring his perfect constitutionalism and his desire to be quite practical, indicated that he was theoretically in favour of manhood suffrage. "Personally I have not the smallest objection to the widest possible suffrage that the ingenuity of man can devise." But he did not think manhood suffrage a practicable proposal for a Reform Bill in 1858.

This subject continued to absorb his mind at the opening of 1859. The Manchester speech, another made in London, and one at Rochdale (on January 28) were reprinted together as a pamphlet. His son Leonard [1] was born on February 24. At the end of the month he went to London.

"[*March* 1.] Called on Jas. Clay, M.P., in Montagu Square (No. 25) to discuss my Reform Bill. Left him a copy of it. Called on Lord Aberdeen. Found him looking shattered and old, but not sensibly worse than last year. He is very anxious about the chances of continental war. Thinks badly of Louis Napoleon: no truth or faith in him. Lord Cowley: mission to Vienna [2] is French, not English. Louis Napoleon proposed it to him, and he came to England to give it the appearance of an English mission. He had written instructions or conditions to which probably Austria may agree; but, if war is intended, other grounds will be found for it.

"Speaking of Gladstone's mission to the Ionian Islands he, Lord Aberdeen, told him he wondered Bulwer-Lytton had not asked him to black his boots for him, and advised him strongly not to go, as did other friends of his. But his Homeric fancies prevailed, and he went—must be damaged by it. When he went was less than ever disposed to join Lord Derby, and thinks he cannot be more so when he returns. [3]

"The Derby Reform Bill brought out last night is an insult to the

[1] He died at an early age, and was buried in the graveyard of St. Tudno on the Great Ormes Head, Llandudno. See page 282.

[2] On the Italian question.

[3] Lord Derby had offered Gladstone either the Board of Control or the Colonial Office on the retirement of Lord Ellenborough in the previous May. The invitation was supported by Disraeli. Gladstone refused. The curious correspondence is given in Morley's "Gladstone" (Book IV, Chapter 9).

country, and cannot pass. It will help Reform and ruin the Government.

"[4th.] Called upon Lord J. Russell. Long conversation on Reform. Before going to the meeting fixed for Birmingham wished to see what the Whigs were disposed to do in case of a change of Government.

"Found him not disposed to anything positive: the ballot still a difficulty, not so much on its own account, as on the ground of his personal consistency. His views on the franchise on the whole moderate and liberal.

"Sir Jas. Graham came in. I think he is less fastidious than Lord John. I explained my views clearly, and left Lord John a copy of my Bill. I told him the old Whig course would end in the disruption of the party and another resignation within the year, and that without a new policy it was useless to take the Government.

"[21st.] Govt. Reform Bill: 2nd reading moved. Lord Jno. Russell moved an amendment in a judicious speech. Lord Stanley defended Bill, but with difficulty; evidently not with his convictions.

"Conversation with Sir E. Bulwer-Lytton during the debate: 'his sympathy with advanced Liberals; their Bill opened out important principles for future adoption—for the first time abandoned *property* as a qualification for voters, giving the franchise to supposed intelligence when not connected with property, etc.'

"Also with Lord Stanley. Told him we made great allowance for him, as his father was First Minister. He said 'he had his work given him and he had done it,' and with an expressive look which showed how little he had liked the work. He asked my opinion of a £6 uniform franchise for boros. and counties. I thought it probably the best franchise that could be adopted for the country. He said I should be surprised if he told me of one person who was disposed to such an arrangement; for himself he could go with it willingly. Agreed that distribution is most difficult question to determine and to pass thro' Parlt.

"Horsman made a great speech all wrong—cheered lustily by Government party. He has been 23 years in Parliament and nobody knows what he is for, which is a sufficient proof, I think, that his course has not been very direct.

"I presented a petition from Birmingham signed by more than 40,000 persons. A petition from Manchester had 53,000 names to it.

"[22nd.] Spoke to Sir C. Wood. Found him treating the Reform demand with contempt: nobody wants Reform, etc. I warned him against the mistake he and his friends are committing. Chas. Villiers also assured him he was wrong.

"Came up with Mr. Stuart (Dorsetshire). He spoke yesterday against Government Bill, tho' intending to vote for it. Disraeli 'cut' him for his rebellion, which Stuart thought shabby and foolish, tho' in no degree a misfortune to himself.

"It is said Lord Jno. Russell is beset with the old Whig crew, who are alarmed lest he should stand out for popular reform. Verily these men are blind, and some rude shock only will open their eyes!"

3

Two days after the talk with Sir Charles Wood, Bright launched at Disraeli's "Fancy Franchise" Bill a shaft of ridicule which inflicted a mortal wound. The debate lasted seven days. On April 1, the Government found itself in a minority of 39 when the House divided on Lord John's amendment. Lord Derby at once announced a dissolution, and the Parliament of 1857 came to an end on April 23.

The Italian and French armies were then facing each other in Northern Italy. Though a warlike statesman in search of a pretext might have found stronger reasons for a military alliance with Napoleon against Austria than had existed for the alliance against Russia, happily this country kept out of the quarrel. Lord Derby, while the elections were in progress, issued a proclamation of British neutrality, which was accepted by the Opposition without demur. Derby won thirty seats; but parties in the new House were very evenly divided, and he could not command a majority. On the other hand, the Liberals had found a sort of unity, and celebrated it at the meeting in Willis's Rooms mentioned in the diary on June 6.

The Derby Government did not survive the debate on the Address. The curious episode of the Queen's attempt to secure a Granville Government delayed the inevitable for a few days, but by June 12 Palmerston leaped into the saddle for the second time. His Ministry was formed between the two battles of the Franco-Austrian War: Magenta on the 4th, Solferino on the 24th. Bright resumes his notes amidst the manœuvres of the Cabinet makers.

"[*June* 3.] Yesterday morning met Lord John by appointment at Milner Gibson's, 49, Wilton Crescent.

"He was very frank and explicit in his conversation with us. The 'situation' still embarrassed. Lord Palmerston and he quite agreed on foreign policy—absolute neutrality, and no Austrian sympathies. Thought war with France only was possible, and only possible with existing Government. Knew that French Government felt this Government was unfriendly to it, and there was a danger of growing coolness.

"On Reform: some of his friends urged the £6 rating in preference to £6 rental franchise. I opposed this strongly; told him he would be suspected of betraying the cause or of weakly giving it up. I would not go across the street for £6 *rating*: the Tories proposed that (many of them) and why turn out a Government if to gain nothing by it? I would not stir in the matter if the £6 rental now to be departed from. He said he should adhere to the £6 rental.

"Palmerston and he had no difference on these questions. As to precedence, nothing had been said between them. I told him that, were I in his position, I would not sit on the same bench in the House of Commons with Lord Palmerston Prime Minister; but that if Palmerston were in the House of Lords, and he leader of the Commons, then he might consent to Palmerston being nominally first. He did not know if Palmerston would go to the Peers, but thought Lady P. was rather in favour of it. He said he should not take office under Palmerston both being in the Commons.

"He said they were both convinced that it was desirable to extend the basis of the Govt. and to take in men who had the confidence of the independent section of the Party. It was understood that an amendment would be moved on the Address, and that a meeting of the Party would be held on Monday, and he wished Gibson's name to be appended to the circular calling it along with his own and Palmerston.

"The interview was on the whole satisfactory and there was great freedom in the discussion.

"Walked into St. James's St. with Gibson to call on Mr. Seward, Senator from the United States, who had left his card on me at the Club; but he was not in.

"Club: gossip in abundance. Mr. Ellice showed me letters from Paris on the war and the state of affairs.

"*Star* office. Wrote a short article on the '*situation*.'

"[4*th*.] Spent an hour with Mr. Lowes Dickenson in Langham Place sitting for a portrait to be published by Mr. Fairless, of Newcastle-on-Tyne.

"Called on Lord Aberdeen. Long chat, chiefly on the war and the Govt. position. He is evidently strongly anti-French; said in former times English statesmen would at once have joined the war against France to prevent her gaining successes and too much power in Europe, but things are changed, and it may be for the better. He thought this Govt. was really neutral in intention, and that tho' the sympathies of the Court were with Prussia and Germany, yet they wished Germany and Prussia to remain neutral.

"As to home affairs, he thought no arrangement had been made between Russell and Palmerston, and that people said the fate of the Govt. was in *my* hands, for without union nothing could even be attempted. It was not certain that either of them would be sent for by the Queen, for 'she cordially hated them both,' and perhaps liked Lord John less than Palmerston. Gladstone, so long hostile to Palmerston, was full of Italian sentimentality and would now serve under him. Sir Jas. Graham, he believed, had *finally* concluded not to take office again. He thought Lord John did not intend anything unfair or contrary to what is honourable, but that he was capricious, and rendered himself liable to be misunderstood.

"He remarked on the difficulties of the proposed meeting of the Liberal Party on Monday next, and said that answers and explanations given to a party *now*, such as would have been given 50 years ago, would not or might not succeed in satisfying it; but he thought much depended on the meeting.

"[*5th.*] Much conversation with Gibson as to the 'situation,'—policy and personnel of the next Government; that at least 2 of our Radical or independent section should be in the Government; that I knew they would ask him, but that they are most anxious to avoid asking me. They fear me, and some of their *oligarch* friends and families would consider my joining a Government as little less than the beginning of a revolution. They ask me continually 'when Cobden is expected home from America' and evidently wish to ask Gibson and him, to avoid asking me.[1] Blind fools!—they think Cobden more easy to manage and less dangerous to them than I am. I don't think anything will induce him to join them, nor do I see how I could, with my convictions or scruples on many questions.

"It is pleasant to watch this gang of aristocratic conspirators brought into trouble. We have spoiled their game thoroughly. Whether we

---

[1] Cobden, who had been out of Parliament for two years, was elected for Rochdale during his absence in the United States. He arrived in the Mersey on the 29th to find a letter from Palmerston offering him the Presidency of the Board of Trade, and another from Lord John urging him to accept it. Cobden refused.

can break it up is not yet certain; but I think the people, insulted, betrayed and plundered, will get something out of the present confusion. We have the key in our hands, and nobody will pass into office by us without paying toll to the people and to freedom.

"[6*th*.] Meeting at Willis's Rooms, King St., St. James's. About 270 members present. Palmerston spoke; then Lord John Russell. Then calls for me, and I spoke; afterwards, other members. The best report of the meeting will be found in the *Morning Star* of June 7, '59.

"[7*th*.] House: debate. Disraeli, a long and very clever speech; otherwise a dull night. Palmerston's speech at the end not good.

"[9*th*.] House: debate.[1] I spoke from 6 to $\frac{1}{2}$ past 7. Full House, most attentive, and the speech thoroughly well received. My argument that their 'neutrality' consisted in preparations for war, and their promises of Reform could not be relied on; that if there was a difference of principles and policy between the two sides of the House, and if the contests at the elections were serious, then it was essential that a change of Government should take place that the majority might rule.

"[10*th*.] Debate: Gibson spoke well, and as usual logically and to the case. Division at 2 o'clock, morning of the 11th: For Government 310; Against 323.

"[11*th*.] Lord Derby resigned. Nothing further known.

"[12*th*.] To Westminster Meeting. Thunderstorm at 2 o'clock.

"On Wednesday, 8th June, met Lord Stanley near Temple Bar, and walked with him to the far end of King William St., City. Talked of India, War, home affairs, and his anxiety for peace real. He said, 'If you become a Minister, you will discover that there are high people whose wishes are not like yours and mine, and it is not easy to withstand them,' alluding doubtless to the tendencies of the Court.

"He urged me to accept office if offered to me, on the ground that the more peace men in the Government, the more peace was likely to be kept.

"With regard to this question of taking office, I am in a great dilemma. It may not be offered, but if it be offered, I am, or shall be, sorely puzzled. On consultation with some of my friends, and with my bro^r.-in-law, Duncan McLaren, one of the most capable, and judicious, and honest men I know, I incline to this conclusion:

"That if the Whigs are willing only to have Gibson and Cobden

[1] On the Address.

with them, or any two of us, we should insist on three being admitted, as only a moderate representation of the 'independent party.' That if they refuse this, then we should refuse to enter, unless Cobden or I should be unwilling to enter on any terms, and then two, if willing, might go in. That one only, say Gibson, should not go in alone, and that it is better to bide our time, and to form opinion outside, than to enter a Government without satisfactory conditions. It is certain that this question of a new Government is a very difficult one for the 'families'—first between the rival old leaders, and then between them and us. A few days, however, must clear up some of the fog which now obscures everything. I do not think I can ever consent to hold any office in the Government of this country.

"[13th.] Called on Lowes Dickenson to finish portrait. Club to write letters, etc.

"Evening called on Gibson. Lord John Russell had been there, and was then with Lord Palmerston. Lord John proposed certain names for offices—wished Gibson to be Secretary of State for the Colonies, and that Mr. Cobden should have Presidency of the Board of Trade offered him on his return from the U.S., he being expected home by the end of this week. Lord John had spoken of me. Neither he nor Palmerston had any objection to my joining them. Lord John would have wished it. Possibly some timid people might think it going a little too far, and they might be startled with such a proposition. The 'Court' were rather favourable than otherwise to our section of politicians. Gibson understood that if Cobden declined the Board of Trade, it would be offered to me.

"All this conversation has relieved me greatly. I could not have taken office if directly offered, and I infinitely prefer Gibson and Cobden to go in, if, indeed, Cobden will accept it, which I think is not likely. We have succeeded in breaking down the exclusiveness of the family party, and this is something. I am still free, and, since the conversation with Gibson, I have felt as if relieved from a great difficulty. If asked directly, I must have refused; and then any observation in future about the exclusiveness of the Whigs would have been answered by the remark that I had been asked and had refused.

"In truth, I do not see how I could join Palmerston for whom I have felt so much contempt, and against whom I have spoken so freely, and in whom I can have no confidence; and I suspect I should be miserable in a Court dress, and in official fetters. Better teach the people something good for the future than resign oneself to work institutions already in existence. Few men can do the former; the latter is but a matter of routine.

"[14th.] Called on Gibson this morning. Lord John had seen him. Spoke of our section, and thought, as they were breaking new ground, it would be better to do it handsomely and to offer office to Gibson, Cobden and me. I suspect, however, there are insuperable difficulties in the way of such a course. The old place-men will surrender nothing, and with them in the Government there is no room for new men.

"Dined with Hargreaves at the Club. Gibson came in, and I walked with him to Hyde Park Corner. His interview with Palmerston: difficulty about Colonies—could not have more than 4 Secretaries of State in House of Commons; would offer him an office of 'efficiency and responsibility.' Evidently, the chief offices are to be given to the old place-men, and the crumbs to the representatives of Independent Liberals—that is, if they will take them.

"I advise Gibson rather to decline and let us retain our freedom and our power. Standing aloof, we can secure a full recognition of a free Cabinet by and by. Cobden is said not to be coming before the end of the month, which makes the position still more puzzling.

"To the *Star* office, and wrote a severe leader on the Whig place-men and the three Baronets who are so clamorous for office.

"[15th.] Club. Received a letter from Lord John Russell, explaining the part he had taken in the forming of the new Government. Seats in the Cabinet would be offered to Gibson and Cobden. Palmerston would not offer me office, not on account of my views on Reform, but owing to my opinion or sayings with regard to institutions 'which are considered essential by a majority of Englishmen.' [1]

"This is amusing, and I suppose the excuse will serve its purpose. Palmerston would not have raised himself in my opinion by offering me office, and I could not have accepted it or anything else at his hands. . . .

[1] In the course of the interview with Palmerston when he refused the offer of the Board of Trade, Cobden was asked to mention the name of anyone "excepting Bright, Gibson and yourself" who could be brought into the Cabinet as the representative of the Radicals. "I urged that Bright had been unfairly judged and that his speeches at Birmingham, etc., were not of a kind to exclude him from the offer of a seat, and I remarked that he had very carefully avoided personalities in those speeches. 'It is not personalities that are complained of; a public man,' said he, 'is right in attacking persons. But it is his attacks on *classes* that have given offence to powerful bodies, who can make their resentment felt.' " (Cobden to Mr. Sale, July 4, quoted by Morley, "Life of Cobden," Chapter 28.)

"Came with Gibson to *Star* office—he is very anxious that Cobden should join the Government and feels that he cannot leave Lord John Russell without giving him cause of offence. He indicates that 'they,' the Cabinet makers, have something in view for me, but he is not at liberty to say further about it, but it is not a Cabinet office. All of which is absurd, for surely they don't dream of purchasing my silence on the questions on which I have been accustomed to speak and act freely before the public? He thought the article in the *Star* of to-day had been of use in somewhat disturbing the jobbers in political places.

[*Note made at the end of the year.*] "In the autumn went to Llandudno for a month: weather not favourable—great storms, in one of which the *Royal Charter* was lost; 450 persons perished. I went to the scene of the wreck a fortnight afterwards.

"[*December 3.*] My dear Aunt Margaret Wood died, *as the good die.* We are all very sorry to lose her, our oldest and best friend."

4

Having recorded these passages, Bright dropped his diary again, and did not pick it up until the beginning of the session of 1860. In the meantime two things of vital consequence to the Liberal Party and to the country had happened. The wanton scare of a French invasion had begun, and Cobden had negotiated the Commercial Treaty with Napoleon. The only representative of the Radicals in Palmerston's Government was Milner Gibson, who took the place designed for Cobden at the Board of Trade. Bright had been almost alone in his approval of Cobden's refusal of office, and had predicted that a few months would reveal its wisdom—as in fact they did; for within less than half a year Cobden was writing to Russell in earnest protest against the militarism of the Government, and Gladstone, at the Exchequer, was wrought up to a fierce intensity of moral struggle between his office and his convictions.

It is now common ground that the patriotism and statesmanship of three men, Gladstone, Cobden and Bright, did more than anything else to check the mad jingo dance in which Palmerston beckoned on a panic-stricken country to war with France. Their chief instrument was the Commercial Treaty. Of this idea, Lord Morley wrote ("Gladstone," Book V, Chap. 2), "Bright had opened it, Chevalier had followed it up, Persigny agreed, Cobden made an opportunity, Gladstone seized it."

The danger of war had been as imminent as it can only be when a nation is frightened. Palmerston contrived to frighten England thoroughly. There was a Navy scare: Napoleon had almost as many ships as we possessed. An Army scare: we had no military forces to resist the French invasion invited by our weakness. The one good thing that came out of the welter of folly and deception was the Volunteer movement. The nation's pro-Italian sympathies and its traditional anti-French animosities made it an easy morsel for the fire-eater in Downing Street, for the Treaty of Villafranca was regarded as a betrayal by Napoleon of the Italian cause. Admiration of Cavour and detestation of our late Crimean Ally combined to put the people in the right mood of bellicosity; and though at this moment Napoleon needed and desired nothing so much as a secure peace with England, we might well have found ourselves at war with France, and the rising edifice of British prosperity laid in irredeemable ruin, but for the great idea propounded by Bright and put into execution by Cobden's voluntary mission in Paris.

An early entry in the diary for 1860 tells the story. Bright had gone to London for the session on January 23, lodging at 33, Green Street, Park Lane, conveniently near Milner Gibson, who lived at No. 3, Hyde Park Place, opposite Marble Arch.

"[*January* 25, 1860.] To Downing St. to see Mr. Gladstone, Chancellor of the Exchequer, by appointment. Conversation on Commercial Treaty with France, the Budget, and the Paper Duty. He is miserable at the reckless expenditure got up by the tax-eating and War party. His language very strong, for he feels it deeply.

"Speaking of the Treaty, he said he was more obliged to Cobden than he could express in words—he had done it all—and that no other man could have done it. He considered it a grand success, and its results could hardly be too much thought of, etc.

"Sir Jas. Graham came in: is strong for repeal of Paper Duty. Gladstone asked him and me to dine with him on Saturday, to which we consented.

"Up to my sister Margaret's in the evening to a party. Met there a Mr. Morris, who is a dwarf of 29 years old, 3 ft. 8 ins. high—just like a boy of 7 or 8 years old, intelligent and well formed. He paints nicely, and earns his living by the sale of small pictures. He is delighted that he is independent by his own exertions.

"The Commercial Treaty with France signed yesterday by Cobden on behalf of this Government—a wonderful event, and may have great and blessed results. It has come about curiously. Near the end of last session, I made a speech on expenditure and taxation and urged free trade with France, recommended reduction of wine duties, etc., as the best means of putting an end to the chances of war. When this speech reached Paris, M. Chevalier, the eminent French economist, wrote to Cobden expressing his high approval of it, and his opinion that something might be done, wishing that Cobden and I should see M. Persigny, the French Ambassador, who would be very favourable to a better Trade policy between France and England. Cobden saw him, but I did not. Mrs. Cobden and her children being in Paris, Cobden was to spend the autumn there, and, with the aid of M. Chevalier, he succeeded in inducing the Emperor to consider the question of the French Tariff. And by his judgment, patience, intelligence and tact [he] has brought about a Treaty invaluable, as I hope and believe, to both countries and to Europe.

"It is a crowning reputation for him, and will compensate for many anxieties he has suffered of late. Lords and diplomatists, spending £15,000 a year, have been in Paris for half a century past, and have done nothing. Cobden, a simple citizen, unpaid, unofficial—but earnest and disinterested—has done all. If our statesmen were such as he, what would England not become! I rejoice in his success as if some great blessing had happened to myself. Such events are compensations for the disappointments and wearisome labours of public life.

"[26th.] To *Star* office and House. Spoke briefly on the Wakefield bribery case, recommending suspension of writs for Wakefield and Gloucester for a period of 10 years as a punishment for their corruption.

"[27th.] Herbert Spencer, author of 'Social Statics,' called this morning. He is writing an article on 'Reform and its Perils' for the *Westminster Review*. His theory is that Reform is only dangerous from the erroneous social and economical theories of the working men. He had been told that I lost my seat for Manchester owing to my opposition to the Factory Bill—which is absurd.

"[28th.] Dined with Mr. Gladstone in Downing St. Mrs. Gladstone there, Sir J. Graham, Bulwer Lytton, Dr. Phillimore, Mr. Scott, architect of Foreign Office plans, Mr. Wortley, and Mr. Herbert of Kerry.

"Mr. Herbert thought a French landing in Bantry Bay would be welcomed by Irish people in the south generally, so ill is the feeling against England.

"Sir J. Graham earnest about China difficulties.[1] Urged Gladstone not to let China be discussed till his Budget was brought in; thought Government could not be defended on China and ought to have withdrawn Mr. Bruce. I pressed the same views. Gladstone, evidently most miserable upon it, said 'all our policy with China was vile and vicious to the last degree;' no remedy except by entire change of policy 'over the way'—that is, at the Foreign Office. He said to me, 'Go and see Lord John Russell about it.'

"[*February* 1.] To Foreign Office: long conversation with Lord John Russell,—Reform, China, and Budget. Urged on him to give 40/— freehold franchise to Scotland. He said some persons, not Tories, were not in favour of it. I said, Panmure and Moncrief, and the Parliament House (Edinbro') Whig party probably were not, but they were in the place of the Tories of 30 years ago—dispensers of all the patronage of Scotland—and so exclusive that I thought he himself would be too liberal for them. He smiled and said he thought that was very much the case.

"On the China question, I urged the necessity of sending out some other man to control or supersede Bruce, who, to his original unfitness, now added that of having been irritated and beaten and humbled by the Chinese Pei-ho disaster, and would be less likely than ever to conclude any satisfactory negotiation. Lord John disposed rather to adopt Bruce's groundless suspicions against the Chinese; did not wish to snub or humiliate Bruce; thought the nation would have complained if the Fleet had left the Pei-ho without an attempt to go up the river, and that Lord Malmesbury's instructions went far to justify Bruce.

"I told him the Government might be damaged, if not destroyed on this question,—that he and Gladstone and Gibson were especially involved in it, after the course they had taken in 1857, and that an address to the Crown to supersede Bruce might be carried if judiciously proposed. I complained, too, of the partnership with France in Chinese affairs. They had no trade there, and our interests and theirs were

[1] Mr. Frederick Bruce, the first British Minister to Peking, by his indiscretion in insisting upon going to the Chinese capital by the River Pei-ho instead of by the land route, as the Chinese wished, brought on another Chinese War. While Mr. Ward, the American Minister, was content to go by land, Mr. Bruce attempted to force the passage of the Pei-ho ("the road of honour") with a small naval squadron under Admiral Hope. The passage was resisted, there were heavy casualties among the British and among the French who accompanied them, Hope was wounded, and the expedition went back ignominiously to Shanghai. The sequel was the war of 1860 and the capture of the Taku forts.

not the same. He admitted this to be a great difficulty. French wanted military renown, which was not our object in China. , I urged him strongly to send out another man to China, and warned him against the fatal blunders they were committing.

"Lord John asked my opinion on the Paper Duty. I recommended its repeal, as a great relief to industry and a great act of justice to an important trade. As a matter of policy, too, I urged that it would gain for the Government the general support of the Press for their financial scheme.

"[2nd.] With Hargreaves to the City to see a loom working designs by means of magnetism instead of the Jacquard machine. The invention is by Mr. Borrelli, of Turin, and is one of a beautiful, and I think, most valuable character. . . .

"House: Motion to refer Civil Service Expenditure to Select Committee. I spoke for it, and the motion was carried against the Government. I shall be sorry if it weakens them now when they are disposed to do some good, but I hope it will strengthen them in the direction of economy. I am the more anxious, because it was generally admitted and said that my speech carried the majority against them.

"[5th.] Home: read poems by Mr. Stigand, a volume sent me by the author. *Samson and Delilah* is fine and remarkable, when so little was left after Milton on the same subject.

"[10th.] Gladstone's financial statement: a great speech on a great theme, well received on our side of the House.[1]

"[20th.] Budget and Treaty. Disraeli wished to change course of proceeding to embarrass the Government, but was beaten by a majority of 63.

"[23rd.] Debate again. I spoke in favour of the Budget and Treaty. Not much satisfied, but my friends were more so. I had not enough thought over the parts of my speech, but hope I put some points clearly. Quoted a line from Beaumont and Fletcher in the last sentence, which I thought good:

'Bright as the breaking East, as midday glorious.'

Read also a passage from Disraeli's novel of 'Coningsby' in favour of a commercial treaty with France, which caused great amusement.

"[24th.] Debate: Gladstone's speech admirable, sound, and liberal,

[1] The great Budget, complement of the Commercial Treaty, in which Gladstone took the customs duties off 371 articles and abolished the excise duties on the manufacture of paper, the "taxes on knowledge."

and moral. How infinitely he excels the ordinary race of statesman! Disraeli laboured and in difficulty—his task an impossible one.

"Division 2 o'clock—339 to 223, 116 majority, which settles general question of Budget and Treaty. Walked up home with Gibson to 33, Green St., Park Lane, at 3 in the morning.

"[25th.] Evening to dinner with Hargreaves. Met Mr. and Mrs. Bigelow, New York. He is a partner with the poet Bryant in the *New York Evening Post*, and is a pleasant and intelligent man.

"[28th.] Dined with Vaughan in Gloucester Terrace. Missed a debate on the proposed annexation of Savoy to France. Wished to have spoken 10 minutes, to have said something sensible on a topic so foolishly treated by most men who are talking about it.

"[*March* 1.] Reform Bills: £10 and £6; rental suffrage; not unsatisfactory. Change of members miserably insufficient; no small boroughs extinguished. Main questions of Reform left unsettled.[1]

"Discussion on removal of duties on import of silks. I spoke shortly in favour of free trade in silks. Ayrton made a dishonest speech for Protection—old fallacies and old charges against us.

"[5th.] Called on Count Persigny, French Ambassador, at Albert Gate. An hour's conversation on question of annexation of Savoy to France. On Press laws in France, of which he said he was the author. They were necessary when factions and parties were contending for the Crown. When dynastic questions gone, then constitutional freedom would reappear in France. The Count is an intelligent and agreeable person and is well disposed to England.

"House: discussion on Savoy. I spoke briefly, condemning the war projects of the opposition.[2]

[1] Lord John Russell's fond but abortive attempt at a grandiose celebration of the anniversary of his Reform Bill of 1832. He introduced (on the exact date) a set of timorous proposals which the Opposition held up by Parliamentary "tactics" till April. Then the Lords appointed a Committee of Inquiry to ascertain whether the Bill would not add more voters than the 200,000 estimated by the Government. Lord John seized the pretext to withdraw the Bill.

[2] Cavour's deal with Napoleon, involving the cession of Nice and Savoy to France in return for concessions elsewhere, infuriated not only Garibaldi but the English people. They ignored even if they realized the fact that Nice and Savoy were both more French than Italian; they ridiculed Napoleon's contention that an Italian power commanding the passes of the Alps would be dangerous to France; they looked upon their whilom ally as a selfish and dishonest schemer who had sold Italy. The sudden blaze of wrath threatened to ruin all the good that had been done by the Commercial Treaty. Lord John Russell fed the fire with an intemperate speech. Bright's appeal to the country through Parliament was that it should look after its

"[12*th*.] House at 8 o'clock: Paper Duty, 2nd reading carried by 245 to 192; good result. Walked to Green St. with Gibson; home by 3 o'clock. Late nights frequent, but something is being done, which compensates.

"[13*th*.] Mr. Boryczenski, sculptor. The bust has arrived: does not appear to me superior to the first.

"[18*th*.] This is my boy Albert's 12th birthday. Every year brings him nearer the period of greater anxiety to his parents, and of greater responsibility to himself.

"[19*th*.] Reform Bill, 2nd reading. Spoke for an hour—part on details of the Bill.

"[22*nd*.] Reform Bill debate continued: Opposition speakers seem to make me their chief text. Walked up home after 12 o'clock, very much tired, having been at the House since 1 o'clock, 11 hours. From 2 to 3 on Committee, Bible Printing Patent: chairman's resolutions carried against renewal of the patent and in favour of perfect freedom of printing Bibles.

"[25*th*.] Dined with Hargreaves. Mr. Bigelow from New York there."

5

With a few other unimportant entries the diary of 1860 ends. In finance and fiscal questions, the great preoccupation of the session, Bright found himself supporting Gladstone and criticizing Palmerston at every point. A momentous issue now united the two Liberal statesmen of the future more closely than ever before. The House of Lords threw out Gladstone's measure for the repeal of the Paper Duty, and thus raised the vital constitutional question which, after slumbering again for half a century, was finally settled by the Parliament Act of 1910. The Commons were bound to resist and did resist the assertion of a right in the Peers to interfere with taxation. But their leader, Palmerston, had one foot in the enemy's camp. He had, indeed, basely betrayed Gladstone in the notorious letter to the Queen expressing the

own affairs. He never tired of protesting against Palmerston's besetting vice of meddling in every European question that arose. "Perish Savoy!" he now cried. "I say, perish Savoy—though Savoy, I believe, will not perish and will not suffer—rather than that we, the representatives of the people of England, should involve the Government of this country with the people and Government of France in a matter in which we have really no interest whatever." This was described as an "un-English" speech; but it helped common sense to prevail. We did, on this occasion, look after our own affairs.

opinion that if the Lords rejected the repeal of the Paper Duty they would "perform a good public service," and there was some talk of Gladstone's resignation, or alternatively of a Radical revolt which would turn out the Government.

Bright told Walpole (who presided over the Committee appointed to draw up the evasive resolutions Palmerston proposed to the House) that if Coke and Selden, Glanville and Pym, and such defenders of the rights of the Commons, could come back, they would "spit on the Committee of Privileges." Gladstone chimed in, "Yes, and roll it in the mud and the House of Commons with it!" But Bright thought that to destroy the Government and place the Opposition in power just then might "bring us into many perils," and that it would be well to let the matter go over to the following session. He acted in concert with Gladstone in the preparation of an ingenious plan for spiking the guns of the Peers. By the device of gathering all the financial measures of the following year into one Bill, Gladstone deprived the Upper House of all power to tamper with taxation unless it was ready to dare the Commons by rejecting the whole Budget. The House of Lords wisely forbore to give that fatal hostage to Fortune until 1909, when, at the invitation of Lord Milner, it "damned the consequences" and brought upon itself the retribution of the Parliament Act.

Bright was also with Gladstone in his protest against the ten million pounds scheme of fortifications at Portsmouth, Plymouth, Chatham and Cork. The results of that most gratuitous of all squanderings of public money still stand. They are known to this day in their localities as "Palmerston's Folly"—a curious historic justification of Gladstone and Bright.

There followed the wordy warfare between Palmerston and Napoleon about the cession of Savoy. The Prime Minister made a series of speeches which it might be possible to understand if he had meant to declare war on France in order to force the retrocession of Savoy, but otherwise seem mere bluster and braggadocio. Their chief effect was to embarrass Cobden, then in Paris settling the details of the tariff under the Commercial Treaty.

In November, Bright crossed the Channel to pay Cobden a visit, and with him saw the Emperor. Cobden's diary (Morley's "Cobden," Chap. 31) supplies the picture of this meeting which Bright's records lack. He says that the Emperor "expressed to Mr. Bright his high sense of the course he had taken in always trying to preserve a good understanding between the two countries. . . . He laughed at the report that he was preparing some boats for the invasion of England, when it turned out that they were intended to carry coals from the interior to Brest. . . . In the course of the conversation he mentioned as a secret that he had bought the *Chronicle*, London newspaper, and he offered to put it into Bright's and my hands to be under our control. I parried this proposal by saying that such arrangements could never be kept secret, and I rather surprised him by saying that I had heard some months since of his having bought that newspaper."

Bright, according to Lord Morley, did not recollect that the Emperor said he had "bought" the *Chronicle*, but that he had secured an influence in it or over it. The political object of this interview, the abolition of the passport system between England and France, was achieved.

CHAPTER XI

THE FRIEND OF THE NORTH

I

NOT even his self-immolating conduct during the Crimean War outshines the courage and sagacity of Bright's campaign for the American cause in England in the four tragic years of 1861–1864.

True, his was not a solitary voice. Other men of eminence, and of the greatest eminence—the Prince Consort, the Duke of Argyll and Lord Stanley, for example—stood out high above the ruck of folly, prejudice and envy in which English statesmanship grovelled so abjectly while the Republic fought for its life. But Bright's was the clearest, the most distinguished, and finally the most regarded of all the voices that, from the onset of the crisis to the end, never wavered in support of Lincoln and the Union. The brilliant course of his advocacy can be followed in his speeches and in the letters to Sumner. It explains why Bright, who never set foot in America, was of all Englishmen in the 'sixties the most admired and revered by the American people.

He faced unflinchingly the animosity of ignorance and the contempt of aristocratic presumption even in such eruptions of national passion as the quarrel over the affair of the *Trent*. But still more remarkable than this heroic temerity were his calm temper and unerring foresight. In a long lifetime Bright gave the world many evidences of political wisdom, but never more immediately and decisively than now did he tear out the core of a question. Stripping the North *v.* South controversy of all its camouflage of fiscal grievance and constitutional conundrum, he disclosed to the nation its fundamental issue—Freedom or Slavery. By forcing the question of emancipation uppermost in the public mind he performed a signal service to his country and to humanity, for to this question England could give in the long run but one answer. It was the conclusive counterstroke against those powerful social and political elements in English life which, jealous of the advancing wealth and power of America, desired nothing so much as its dismemberment.

Bright might fairly claim to have foreseen long ago not only the struggle in America, but its consequences in England. In 1850, when he moved in Parliament for a Royal Commission on Cotton-growing in India, he had said these words:—

Whilst the production of cotton in the United States results from slave labour, whether we approve of any particular method of abolishing slavery in any country or not, we are all convinced that it will be impossible in any country, and most of all in America, to keep between two and three millions of the population permanently in a state of bondage. By whatever means that system is to be abolished, whether by insurrection—which I should deplore—or by some great measure of justice from the Government, one thing is certain, that the production of cotton must be interfered with for a considerable time after such an event has taken place; and it may happen that the greatest measure of freedom that has ever been conceded may be a measure the consequences of which will inflict mischief upon the greatest industrial pursuit that engages the labour of the operative population of this country.

No long time after the first shot in the war was fired from Morris Island came tragic proof of his perspicacity. The desperation of the struggle in America and the cotton famine in Lancashire in the end brought home to the majority of the British people the clarity of his judgment before they had been persuaded of the justice of his views.

In the beginning of the session of 1861, before the American crisis had developed, his mind was running mainly on Reform and Economy. The Government's treatment of Reform intensified his suspicion and dislike of Palmerston's régime. Lord John Russell, on February 5, made a speech which pricked him deeply. He "threw over the Reform question in a speech of offensive tone and language. I replied, and spoke on the general question. Had great difficulty in restraining my indignation at his conduct. I shall keep no terms with this Government for the future. It is base, as was the former Government of Lord Palmerston. How long Mr. Gladstone and Mr. Gibson will go through the mire with them I know not."

Lord John's offence was not confined to Reform. Three days later Bright notes a "conversation with Sir J. Graham. He condemned Lord John's hectoring dispatches to foreign governments, especially to France; thought our relations with France alarming, looking at the tone of these dispatches. Thought Budget difficult: question of direct or indirect taxation would be fought; did not see how Gladstone could go back from Peel's policy to his own." [1]

[1] Lord John Russell went to the House of Lords in the following July as Earl Russell of Kingston. Sir James Graham died in October, having sat 31 years in the House of Commons—successively as a Whig, a Peelite, a Conservative and a Liberal. He was a successful First Lord of the Admiralty, and on the floor of the House a formidable debater.

Nevertheless, Gladstone carried his Budget without real difficulty. He reduced the Income Tax from tenpence to ninepence and abolished the Paper Duty. The Opposition had resisted the extinction of the "tax on knowledge" as fiercely as in the previous year, and, when the Bill reached the House of Lords, the Duke of Rutland, prince of last-ditchers, still wanted to "damn the consequences." Lord Derby's wiser counsels prevailed and the Bill passed—a notable victory for Gladstone, in that he secured Budgets thenceforth from interference by the Peers, and for Bright, who had hammered away so persistently at the last irritating obstruction that lay in the way of a cheap Press.

Meanwhile the American sky darkened. The early successes of the South stiffened the backs of the English reactionaries. They were not confined to one party. If the Tory aristocracy contributed several supporters to the cause led by Bright, the Liberal Party lent Palmerston, Russell, Gladstone, Roebuck and others to the partisans of Secession. Even Cobden was unsound at first,—strangely misled by the irrelevant fact that the Secession states were theoretically Free Traders whereas the Union was Protectionist. Lord Morley records a breakfast party (Motley, the historian, Cobden and Bright present) when Cobden attacked Motley, amid Bright's protests, for something he had written in favour of the North. Thus, the first man Bright had to convert to the view that the moral issue of the struggle overweighed every other was his own staunch friend and ally. Cobden had been brought to reason before the time came for his next speech to his Rochdale constituents, and was soon writing to Sumner in the same strain as Bright himself.

Bright's own demonstration to America of his friendship, his clear understanding, and his determination to carry the mass of the English people with him began in letters addressed to Sumner immediately after the battle of Bull Run. In the winter came one of the two great tests to which Englishmen were submitted by the war, the affair of the *Trent* —the stopping by the Federal Navy of a British ship and the forcible arrest on board of the Confederate agents, Mr. Mason and Mr. Slidell. The Government handled that crisis on the whole with eminently good feeling and tact, save for one lapse by Lord John Russell. Bright never had an instant's doubt how it should be handled. His Rochdale speech, a week after the news arrived, was the first clear call to sanity amid the thunders of *The Times* and the ravings of politicians of the baser sort—"all up in arms," as he said, "every sword leaping from its scabbard, and every man looking about for his pistols and blunderbusses."

He told his hearers that the conduct pursued ("and I have no doubt the same is pursued by a certain class in America") was much more the conduct of savages than of Christian and civilized men. He appealed to reason, to the sense in both nations of infinitely greater issues than the *Trent*; and he appealed successfully. The American Government gave up Messrs. Mason and Slidell, and the crisis, with its real menace of war, passed away.

England had cause for fervent gratitude to Bright, who sounded thus early the note of warning wisdom. The beam of light he then shot into the future of the American Continent even now seems almost a magical revelation. He said:

> Whether the Union will be restored or not, or the South achieve an unhonoured independence or not, I know not and I predict not. But this I think I know—that in a few years, a very few years, the twenty millions of Freemen in the North will be thirty millions or even fifty millions, a population equal to or exceeding that of this Kingdom. When that time comes I pray that it may not be said amongst them that in the darkest hour of their country's trials, England, the land of their fathers, looked on with icy coldness and saw unmoved the perils and calamities of her children.

To Sumner the same note of prudence and moderation: "If you are resolved to succeed against the South, have no war with England; make every concession that can be made; don't even hesitate to tell the world that you will even concede what two years ago no Power would have asked of you rather than give another nation a pretence for assisting in the breaking up of your country."

Motley wrote to Bright to thank him for the Rochdale speech, its breadth and accuracy of view and its thorough grasp of the subject: "Thank God our noble mother-tongue is not entirely given over to revilings and denunciations of those who speak it beyond the sea. And I honour you more than I can tell for your courage in thus standing up, in the midst of the tempest of unreasoning wrath now sweeping over England, to defend not an unpopular but apparently a hated cause."

The speech made a deep impression everywhere. Cobden wrote: "Your admirable address cannot fail to do good. But it is a mad world we live in! Here am I in the midst of extracts from Hansard, etc., to show up the folly or worse of the men who have been putting us to millions of expense to protect us from a *coup de main* from France, and now we see the same people willing to rush into war with America and leave us exposed to this crafty and dangerous neighbour! Might we not be justified in turning hermits, letting our beards grow, and returning to our caves?" Cobden, however, was never so apostolic as Bright in the cause of the North. At this time he doubted the possibility of victory and thought that if the Federal Government did not raise the blockade of the Southern ports there would be intervention before a year was out. "I don't believe the North and South can ever lie in the same bed again," he wrote to Paulton. ". . . But our friend Bright will not hear anything against the claims of the North. I admire his pluck, for when he goes with a side it is always to win. I tell him that it is possible to wish well to a cause without being sure that it will be successful." Time and fact brought him round to the view which Bright, on his Pisgah height, had seen from the beginning.

The Rochdale speech was made on December 4. In January Bright was at Birmingham for an address at the Chamber of Commerce dinner, and in February we find him seeking new lodgings in London for the opening of the Parliamentary Session.

"[*February* 6, 1862.] Fixed at No. 4, Hanover St., Hanover Square, house of Mr. Bowater, tailor. Nice rooms: sitting-room, bedroom and dressing-room. £3 per week to April 1, and £4 per week after that date so long as I keep them towards end of Session.

"House at 5 o'clock. [Queen's] Speech as usual containing nothing. Debate more favourable to United States than I expected: this refers chiefly to Disraeli's speech.[1]

"[9*th*.] Westminster Meeting. To Paulton's to tea. Long talk with him and Cobden on America, and on Cobden's book on the Panics of the last twenty years.[2]

"[10*th*.] Called on Sir Geo. Grey, Home Office, with memorials for release of two prisoners. Spoke to him on behalf of Jno. Nichol,

[1] "When I consider," said Disraeli, "the great difficulties which the statesmen of North America have to encounter, when I consider what I may call the awful emergency which they have been summoned suddenly to meet, and which, without giving any opinion upon the causes of these transactions, I would venture to say they have met manfully and courageously, I think it becomes England, in dealing with the Government of the United States, to extend to all which they say at least a generous interpretation, and to their acts a liberal construction." Disraeli, however, was no more percipient than the majority of politicians and "educated people." He prophesied in the following year that the America which survived, "after the waters have subsided," would be an America "of armies, of diplomacy, of rival States and manœuvring Cabinets, of frequent turbulence, and probably of frequent wars."

[2] "The Three Panics." Lord Morley calls this pamphlet "a strenuous and humiliating narrative of the incoherent alarms of invasion which had seized successive governments in 1848, in 1853, and in 1862."

who is a candidate for Chair of English Literature at Glasgow; also on subject of Wakefield Bribery prosecutions.

"[11*th*.] Called on Mr. Adams, U.S. Minister, at 5, Mansfield Street.[1] Found him in good spirits as to the prospects in the States. He thinks 3 months will do much to point the future of the great contest. He thanked me most heartily for my speech on American affairs.

"[14*th*.] Cyrus Field, from the U.S., called.[2] He is interested in the Atlantic Telegraph scheme. Conversation on American affairs. Is in good spirits at prospects of Washington Government.

"[17*th*.] To breakfast with Paulton to Cleveland Square. Cobden there in bed with a cold. He wished me to speak on the vote of money for the troops sent to Canada, and to give his notice to-morrow on International Maritime Law. House: spoke on the Vote,—not as I wished to do. Suffering from cold and swollen face. I was not at ease and not well prepared. Still, I entered my protest against exhibition of force and menaces in the late dispute with the U.S. Government. Palmerston replied civilly, and well from his point of view: he believes in force and in force only.

"[21*st*.] S. Lucas called; also Mr. Thurlow Weed, from the U.S., Cyrus Field, of the Atlantic Telegraph, and Mr. Lampson, an American long resident in London. Talk on America and much on their Tariff. Mr. Weed is an old man, rather heavy and quiet in appearance, but giving evidence of strength and thought. He

---

[1] Charles Francis Adams, the son of one President of the United States and the grandson of another, succeeded Dallas as Ambassador in London on the accession of the Lincoln Government. He arrived in London on the eve of the British Proclamation of Neutrality (May 13, 1861). Bright complained with some reason that the issue of the Proclamation which acknowledged the South as a belligerent Power was not delayed until Adams could be informed of it in friendly communication. Adams remained at the Embassy till 1868. He possessed and used great ability in successive crises during the war. He died in 1886.

[2] Cyrus West Field, the New Englander, who became a constant correspondent and friend of Bright, had made a fortune as a paper manufacturer at the age of 34, and retired from business. In association with Peter Cooper and others he formed in 1854 the New York, Newfoundland and London Telegraph Company, which laid a cable to Ireland. This failed. In 1858 another cable was put down, over which messages were sent for a fortnight before it also broke down. The schemes now under discussion brought about the first successful cable connexion, laid by the *Great Eastern* in 1866. Field received much honour and the thanks of Congress. A more dubious contribution of his to human happiness was the construction of the Elevated Railway in New York City.

wishes to call again, and I shall value his information and judgment much.[1]

"[*March* 3.]   At home for more than a week, and return to London more than ever disliking the Parliamentary life and its sacrifices.

"[*4th.*]   Call from Mr. Robilliard, who believes it is his duty to call the attention of Christians to the inconsistency of War and the killing of men with the requirements of Christianity.   House: Saw Sir George Grey about Wakefield prosecutions, which are, I believe, to be abandoned.[2]

"[*6th.*]   Writing letters and reading American papers.   News exciting and favourable to North: capture of Fort Donelson, etc.

"[*7th.*]   House: American blockade discussed.   W. E. Forster's speech good,[3] and his facts quite destructive of case against blockade. Solicitor-General (Roundell Palmer) made an admirable speech,— language, facts and sentiments good.   South gained nothing by the discussion.

"[*8th.*]   Breakfasted at Fenton's Hotel at 10 o'clock with Cyrus Field, of Atlantic Telegraph.   Met there Mr. Adams, Thurlow Weed, Mr. Lampson; also Sir Rowland Hill, W. E. Forster, A. Kinnaird, Pender of Manchester.   Called on Mr. Ellice, M.P., in Arlington Street.   Long chat on America.   He is full of fears for the future.

"[*10th.*]   House: dull enough, as usual.   Bar of Lords: heard Lord Russell on the Blockade.   Hoped North would agree to separation from South—a monstrous proposition from an 'impartial' spectator, and one which he ought not to have made.   American news favourable, though not very important.

"[*11th.*]   House: discussion on Maritime Law; interesting— feeling of House with us.   Adjourned to Monday next.   Palmerston made a positive and foolish declaration against it.

"[*12th.*]   To Mr. Thomas's studio, Alpha Road, to see statue of Joseph Sturge to be erected in Birmingham.   Good as a likeness, but not classic-looking in costume of one of our Sect.   House: Marriage Bill thrown out.   Another proof of insolence of political Church in

---

[1] Thurlow Weed had for many years been one of the leaders of the Whigs, political ancestors of the Republican Party in the United States.   He was among the early patrons and employers of Horace Greeley, who edited for him and his associates the campaign paper, *The Jeffersonian*, started at Albany in 1838 in connexion with the Presidential Election of 1840.

[2] As, in fact, they were shortly afterwards.

[3] Forster was sound on the American question throughout, displaying great courage and all his characteristic tenacity.

this country. Dined at W. E. Forster's. Stansfeld, M.P., and Mr. Bunsen there; also Mr. Townsend of the *Spectator*, formerly editor of the *Friend of India*. Townsend clever and liberal, but does not appear to see politics from any strictly economical or moral point of view.[1] Stansfeld walked home with me, and we talked till near one o'clock. He said he could not speak well except with and under a strong conviction that what he was saying was true and that he ought to say it.

"[*13th.*] Dined with Sir J. Login, 5, Lancaster Gate. A pleasant party: the Maharajah Duleep Singh there, also Princess Gouramma, daughter of the late Rajah of Coorg, and now married to Lady Login's brother. She is a small, delicate-looking person, and not much dark or Indian in appearance and complexion.

"[*16th.*] Evening, called on Paulton. Talk with Cobden on debate of to-morrow on Maritime Law.

"[*17th.*] Notes for speech on Maritime Law. Home Office with Memorial from Birmingham in favour of a convict, Farghan, under sentence. House: debate on Maritime Law. Cobden to have opened it, but so unwell and hoarse as to be unable to speak. Lindsay took his place. I was very sorry Cobden could not speak. He would have treated the whole question with a breadth and a force that would have done great good; his state of health is not satisfactory and gives me much uneasiness. I spoke later in the evening. House very attentive. Had great freedom of thought and expression, and had only to curb myself from saying too much, and from the temptation to sarcasm or ridicule when referring to the position of Palmerston on this question.[2] My brother Thomas under the Gallery. He came up with me and stayed an hour or more.

"[*25th.*] To Manchester (from Rochdale) and by ¼ past 4 train to London. New carriages, lighted with gas, and making the journey in 5¼ hours exactly.

"[*27th.*] To *Star* office with J. B. Smith to see what news from the U.S., every item of which is greedily looked for. Mr. Seward,

[1] Meredith Townsend shared with Hutton the honour of bringing the *Spectator* to the position of authority it attained in the latter part of the nineteenth century.

[2] Bright had a Peace man's interest in the question now known as the Freedom of the Seas, and had studied it deeply. He held firmly to the principles which had been asserted by the United States between 1812 and 1860 as to the right of search of neutral shipping. He did not fail, of course, to point out that if the action of the Lincoln Government in the *Trent* affair was inconsistent with those principles, the claims we now made as neutrals were irreconcilable with our traditional views as belligerents.

American Secretary of State, has sent me a handsomely bound volume of his dispatches.

"[*28th.*] House. Education Minutes dispute compromised. A weak Government can only do evil: good is forbidden by power of Opposition.[1] Evening, read a good pamphlet from Boston on the growth of cotton by free labour.

"[*29th.*] Wrote letters to States, one to Mr. Bancroft, historian of U.S.A.

"[*31st.*] House: discussion on land fortifications expenditure, and their uselessness with iron-plated ships. I spoke briefly, urging Government to suspend further expenditure. Letter from Rawson this morning stating that arrangement was made for securing a 'sett' or piece of land near Dolgelly to work a gold mine, to extract gold from a quartz lode. Readwin to have half; Rawson, Bradford, Buckley, Walters and I to have other half.

"[*April* 1.] S. Lucas[2] called: proposal for *Star* Company to conduct *Dial* weekly. To 28, New Finchley Road, evening party at Revd. Newman Hall's. A pleasant party. Mr. Cremer, American, there with invention to stop railway trains suddenly. Much talk on American affairs, and, after most of the company had gone, on English politics.

"[*7th.*] House: Disraeli made a strong speech against Gladstone on his Finance.[3] Gladstone's reply good and moderate in tone. Gladstone asked me to come to breakfast with him on Thursday morning sometime after the Easter Recess: he gives Thursday mornings to seeing his friends at breakfast.[4] Propose to go home to-morrow morning."

[1] On the Code of 1862, introduced by Lowe, incorporating "payment by results," withdrawing subsidies from Training Colleges, and limiting the effective curriculum to the Three Rs. "No serious and well informed student of education, judging freely and without bias," said Matthew Arnold, "will approve the Revised Code."

[2] Bright's brother-in-law, who had married his sister Margaret. He edited *The Morning Star* until his death.

[3] Disraeli that night coined an epigram and an epithet which have passed into English currency. "Expenditure depends upon policy," he said. And, suggesting that an agreement should be made with France on the proportionate strength of the two navies, he condemned "bloated armaments." As was well said, Cobden might have made the speech. Gladstone proposed no remissions of taxation in 1862: he pointed out that the increased trade with France due to the Commercial Treaty was offset by the decreased trade with America due to the closing of the cotton ports by blockade.

[4] The regular Downing Street "breakfast party," which Gladstone established, became an important part of the machinery of government during the War administration of Mr. Lloyd George.

Bright makes no record in his diaries of one episode of these early days of April. On March 6 the Chamber of Commerce of the State of New York had passed and forwarded to him a resolution of gratitude for his advocacy of the "principles of constitutional liberty and international justice for which the American people were contending." On April 4, having gone with John Hodgkin to see Mr. Adams and had an hour's talk with him on the temper of the people of the two countries, he sat down to write his acknowledgment of the resolution. He told the Chamber of Commerce that the sentiments he had expressed were those of the great majority of his countrymen. "I believe," said he, "there is no other country in which men have been so free and prosperous as in yours, and that there is no other political constitution now in existence in the preservation of which the human race is so deeply interested as in that under which you live. This is true beyond all doubt, when applied to the Free States of your Union; I trust the time is not distant when it will be true all over your vast territory from the St. Lawrence to the Gulf of Mexico."

2

For Bright's great part in the preservation of peace between England and America in the latter half of 1862, the only records are the Sumner letters and his speeches. During these months the Cotton Famine was at its worst. If, nearly twenty years before, the steps he had advised towards an increased cultivation of cotton in India had been taken, the blockade of the Confederate ports would not have involved the manufacturers and workpeople of Lancashire in the woes of that appalling time. It was no consolation to Bright to know this. He threw himself with equal eagerness into Lord Derby's great movement for relief, and into the task of salving Anglo-American friendship from the wreckage of the *Alabama* blunder.

The trouble created by Lord John Russell's supine folly, in allowing the *Alabama* to sail from Birkenhead and become a Southern privateer in the teeth of all the protestations of Mr. Adams, was in full blast when another bombshell burst. This time it was thrown by Gladstone, of all men. The notorious Newcastle speech was the worst mistake of his career. Bright's prompt action and the fortunate accident that about the same time Lincoln took the crucial measure of his policy, proclaiming the freedom of all slaves on American soil, combined to nullify the effect of Gladstone's blunder. Bright had leaped at once to a realization of the danger. He passed condign censure upon the fatal epigram—that Jefferson Davis and his friends "had made an army, were making a navy, and had made, what was more than either, a Nation." He wrote to Sumner: "A vile speech . . . full of insulting pity for the North and of praise and support for the South. He is unstable as water in some things; he is for union and freedom in Italy, and for disunion and bondage in America. A handful of Italians in prison in Naples without formal trial shocked his soul so much that he wrote a pamphlet and has made many speeches upon it, but he has no word of sympathy or of hope for the four millions of bondsmen of the South!"

Happily for both countries, Lincoln's Proclamation, issued in October, reached England when the excitement caused by the *Alabama* and the Newcastle speech was at its height. Lincoln now formally and clearly placed the issue of the war where Bright had placed it from the first—upon the question of Free State versus Slave State. There was a mighty and immediate swing of public feeling in England to the side of the North. The fashionable world still clung to its sympathy for the Planter Republic and did not go over till the North had won.[1] But the middle classes and the working people had no more hesitations when once the lumber of State Rights, liberty of Secession, and all the rest of it had been brushed aside and the war stood revealed in its true character as a war of liberation. It prevented the various plans of intervention that were being hawked about behind the scenes from coming into daylight. It strengthened the hands of Bright and his followers.

His joy in the new policy, reflected in his correspondence, inspired the great oration of December 18 at Birmingham. He had gone down with Scholefield to address their constituents, determined to put the American question before them as fully as an hour's highly documented exposition could do it, and especially that they should understand the cotton situation. He did, in fact, analyse that part of the subject in much detail. But Scholefield, who spoke before him, had exhibited a somewhat detached view of the great struggle in the West—what Bright called a "political" view—and it tempted him to a great effort to review the war in its moral aspects. A rapid but masterly account of the causes and the progress of the upheaval, and of the development of British opinion about it from the *Trent* to the *Alabama*, merged into an impassioned justification of the Union, and ended in a peroration of fervid eloquence.

[1] Lord Hartington attended a ball in New York wearing the Confederate colours.

I blame men who are eager to admit into the family of nations a State which offers itself to us, based upon a principle, I will undertake to say, more odious and more blasphemous than was ever heretofore dreamed of in Christian or Pagan, in civilized or in savage times. The leaders of this revolt propose this monstrous thing—that, over a territory forty times as large as England, the blight and curse of slavery shall be for ever perpetuated.

I cannot believe for my part that such a fate will befall that fair land, stricken though it now is with the ravages of war. I cannot believe that civilization, in its journey with the sun, will sink into endless night in order to gratify the ambition of the leaders of this revolt, who seek to

> "Wade through slaughter to a throne
> And shut the gates of mercy on mankind."

I have another and a far brighter vision before my gaze. It may be but a vision. But I will cherish it. I see one vast confederation stretching from the frozen North in unbroken line to the glowing South, and from the wild billows of the Atlantic, westward to the calmer waters of the Pacific main,—and I see one people and one language, and one law, and one faith, and, over all that wide continent, the home of freedom, and a refuge for the oppressed of every race and of every clime.[1]

He was able to write to Cyrus Field in the following February: "Opinion here has greatly changed. In almost every town great meetings are being held to pass resolutions in favour of the North and the advocates of the South are pretty much put down."

The diary was resumed with his journey to London for the session of 1863, when he lodged again at Hanover Street.

"[*February* 5, 1863.] Called at U.S. Legation, 5, Portland Place. Saw Henry Adams and the secretaries, Moran and Wilson. Took down particulars of bark *Maury*, stopped in New York Harbour by U.S. Government on charge of being vessel of war for Russia during our Russian War in 1855. Strong contrast between this case and that of the *Alabama*, now cruising against U.S. ships.

"[8*th.*] Evening by Underground Railway to Paddington. To William Hargreaves' in Craven Hill Gardens.[2]

"[9*th.*] Called on Mr. Adams, U.S. Minister: a long conversation

---

[1] When someone suggested to Bright in after years that this was the finest of all his perorations, he did not disagree. His son Philip read it over to him some two years before his death. He smiled when the closing words were reached, and said, with gentle irony, "Except the Chinese."

[2] Powers to construct an underground railway from Edgware Road to King's Cross had been obtained in 1853. This was the first piece of intra-urban railway in London. Lord Aberconway, Bright's nephew, is now the Chairman of the Metropolitan Railway. Bright often stayed with Mr. Hargreaves at his house, "Sendholme," near Woking.

with him. Spoke of the *Alabama* steamer. He thought it best not to have the case brought before Parliament at present. Correspondence between him and Foreign Office not yet closed on building ships for Southern conspiracy. Till after one o'clock reading Lyell's new work on 'Antiquity of Man,' which I find deeply interesting.

"[14*th*.] Home till 18th. My dear good father-in-law died on the 13th, closing a long and virtuous life by a tranquil death.[1] (18th) To Newcastle. (19th) Funeral. Quiet party, not large. Meeting solemn. John Ford spoke beautifully. 'In thy presence is fullness of joy; at thy right hand are pleasures for evermore.' In the evening a few friends at Benwell Grange. John Pease, Charles Brown and others spoke.

"[20*th*.] To Newcastle. Called on Geo. Mennell and Chas. Bragg. In the evening left by 11 train for York, leaving dear Helen with her aunts. It was exciting and painful to leave a circle so much loved and now so changed; but it seemed a translation rather than a death that had made the change.

"[21*st*.] From York home.

"[23*rd*.] Went with Gurney B[arclay] to Liverpool. Visited the *George Griswold* from New York, the 'relief ship,' and saw the *Achilles,* from Philadelphia, coming into dock.[2]

"[28*th*.] To Mr. Phillip, Kensington, to have my face painted into a picture for the Speaker. Picture good as a picture, and likeness remarkably good, but absurd at the same time. Cabinet men on each side. Palmerston speaking. Cobden and I up behind Ministers, as if supporters, which we are not. On the table, French Commercial Treaty lying open, as if glory of Palmerston's Government, when Cobden and I know he did all he dared to make the Treaty miscarry. The Speaker compliments us by asking us to appear among the chief men

1 Jonathan Priestman, the father of Bright's first wife.

2 America profoundly admired the demeanour of the Lancashire population in the cotton crisis. It was dignified, orderly, understanding beyond all praise. Though Lancashire suffered horribly by the Union's blockade of the Confederate ports, which starved it of raw material, the people never faltered in their support of the Northern cause. England and the British Empire came to their rescue with the great relief fund organized by Lord Derby. Then a proposal was made in America that help should be sent from there. Bright, with unerring psychological insight, urged upon Sumner to send not money but something that could be seen: "If a few cargoes of flour could come, say 50,000 barrels, as a gift from persons in your Northern States to the Lancashire working men, it would have a prodigious effect in your favour here. Our working class is with you, and against the South, but such a token of your goodwill would cover with confusion all who talk against you." The suggestion was adopted and the prediction realized.

in the House, and we submit to please him, because we greatly respect him; else we should not appear among those who are supposed to be supporters of Palmerston."

3

Bright spoke at the meeting held in Rochdale to express the people's thanks to the merchants of New York for their assistance. In March he presided over a great meeting of the Trade Unionists of London at St. James's Hall, convened to support the principles of human freedom for which the North was fighting. In June he took the chair at a meeting of the Union and Emancipation Society to hear an address from M. D. Conway, a Virginian.

On the last day of that month, still absorbed in the American question, he administered to Roebuck, the Radical member for Sheffield, a castigation perhaps as devastating as one man had ever given to another in the House of Commons. Roebuck had proposed a motion for the recognition of the Southern Confederacy as a Sovereign State. He delivered himself into the hands of Bright by supporting his case with a personal message from the Emperor Napoleon, who more openly desired the dismemberment of the United States than even the most ardent Southern adherent in England, being then involved in the Mexican adventure whose only chance of success was division and hostility in the neighbouring Republic.

Bright leaped upon Roebuck. He reminded the House that five years before, when the Queen visited Napoleon at Cherbourg and Roebuck was present, he had expressed the horror he felt, "when I saw his perjured lips touch that hallowed cheek;" and that still more recently Roebuck had declared that he had "nothing but animosity and bad faith to expect from the French Emperor." A man who had held these opinions of Napoleon, and now invited the country to join hands with him in an adventure more disastrous than Mexico, was fair game. Bright flayed him alive and threw the debris contemptuously away before he went on, in an effort of high and sustained eloquence, to persuade the House of the folly and the peril of toying with recognition.

Gladstone, still strangely blind to the issues and ignoring the facts, did another disservice to the cause of Anglo-American unity by predicting again the failure of the North. But Bright's speech left nothing to be said. It killed Roebuck as a politician, and it put a term to the manœuvres for the political recognition of the Confederacy. Roebuck's motion was shelved by adjournment. Within a few days Gettysburg was fought and the turning-point of the war had come. Lairds' went on building iron "rams" at Birkenhead, which were intended to form the nascent Southern Navy of Gladstone's dreams. But this time the Government made no mistake. They forbade the departure of the ships from the Mersey, and thereafter the Confederate party in England dwindled alike in numbers and in vociferousness. The transient dream of European intervention was lit up again for a moment by the suggestion that Louis Napoleon might try to liquidate his Mexican adventure in some agreement or alliance with the Confederacy; but Gettysburg and Vicksburg happened, Grant sprang into the picture, the North dominated the Mississippi Valley, and the dream faded never to be revived.

One other event of the year may find place here. An English subject, Alfred Rubery, "aided and comforted" the Confederates by engaging in a plot to seize a ship in San Francisco Harbour and take her out as a Southern privateer. He was arrested, convicted, sentenced to ten years' imprisonment and a fine of ten thousand dollars. Bright appealed for a show of clemency to the misguided young adventurer. He was only twenty, and the son of respectable parents. The Court in California which tried him, while conscious of great public indignation, declared that the people would be satisfied if he were pardoned "at the request of Mr. Bright, who is a true friend of their country." [1] Lincoln knew how to make a fine gesture. He issued the pardon, which, after reciting the facts, proceeded:

Now therefore be it known that I, Abraham Lincoln, President of the United States of America, these and divers other considerations me thereunto moving, and especially as a mark of the esteem held by the United States of America for the high character and steady friendship of the said John Bright, do hereby grant a pardon to the said Alfred Rubery, the same to begin and take effect on the twentieth day of January, 1864, on condition that he leave the country within thirty days from and after that date.

As entries in the diary show, the Rubery Case came into an English Court of Law in 1864. [2] In connexion with that proceeding, Bright wrote a letter narrating the facts about his intervention.

"It was," he said, "Mr. Rubery's brother, Mr. John Rubery, of Birmingham, who applied to me and asked me to endeavour to procure

[1] In the Yosemite Valley, the Californians placed on two giant redwoods tablets bearing the names of Cobden and Bright. " I hope you were pleased with the compliment paid us in California," Cobden wrote (Oct. 16). "There is a poetical sublimity about the idea of associating our names with a tree 300 feet high and 60 feet in girth. Verily it is a monument not built with men's hands."

[2] See page 278.

his liberation. . . . Mr. Rubery was arrested at San Francisco on the charge of being concerned in fitting out a vessel called the *Chapman* for the purpose of privateering under the flag of the Confederate States. When he was arrested and imprisoned, I wrote to a friend of mine in America with a view to obtain a lenient consideration of his case. The President, very properly, declined to interfere with the matter while it was in the course of law. Rubery was tried and convicted with some of his associates. He was not sentenced to death: the Government of the United States, so far as I know, has never yet inflicted that punishment for treason; but he was sentenced to ten years' imprisonment and a fine of 10,000 dollars.

"When I saw the report of his conviction, I again wrote to my friend in Washington, and he brought the case before the President; and I am informed, in a letter dated the 15th of December (1863), that the President has pardoned Rubery, and that the pardon will be issued as soon as the papers can be prepared. . . .

"Mrs. Rubery, the mother of the misguided young man, is a widow lady well known and much esteemed in Birmingham, and I need not tell you that it has given me much pleasure to have been able, in part, to relieve her great anxiety as to the fate of her son."

"[*February* 4, 1864.] House: Debate on Address. Tone of House not warlike. Mr. Goschen, M.P. for City, seconded Address. Spoke well: one sentence aimed at me and cheered by Opposition. This Oxford 'young man of great promise' has, I suppose, already found out the way to please the Aristocratic Order. It shows a disposition which does not promise honesty or generosity in his Liberalism. The future will prove what he is.

"There was no great sympathy expressed for the Danes, as many members spoke rather for Germany.[1]

"[*6th.*] In the evening up to Gordon St., to Maggie's.[2] Evans[3] came in: talk on America chiefly; he thinks the war will be over during this year. Walked home, read Massinger, and to bed. Have brought

---

[1] The Schleswig-Holstein question had come to a head in January with the Austro-Prussian ultimatum to Denmark. Wrangel had occupied Schleswig on February 1. The proceedings were in violation of the Treaty of London, but, though Palmerston and Russell would have gone to war even without allies, the majority of the Ministers and the Court also were opposed to a war policy.

[2] His sister, Mrs. Lucas.

[3] Father of Sir Francis Evans, M.P. for Southampton, and chairman of the Union-Castle Steamship Company.

up my volumes of the old dramatists. Their writings, with many beauties, are too gross to be read either with pleasure or profit, and I shall exchange them for works more suitable for my library.

"[7*th.*] My brother-in-law, James Vaughan,[1] has just been appointed Police Magistrate at Bow Street, £1,200 a year. I did not apply for the office for him, not wishing to ask for anything from the Government for any relation of mine; but he stands well in his profession, and the appointment is generally approved of.

"[8*th.*] House at 4. Spoke shortly on the Townley case, defending Sir George Grey and condemning capital punishment. Walked up at midnight with Lord Stanley, talking on Patent Laws. Read New Orleans rule of General Butler, and to bed at two o'clock.

"[9*th.*] M. D. Conway, American, [called]. Wrote some autographs for New York Bazaar.

"[11*th.*] Home early. Reading Life of General Butler, U.S. Taking of New Orleans; bombardment of forts; and destruction of 'Secesh' Fleet.[2]

"[12*th.*] House: discussion on U.S. seizure of ships running blockade. Attorney-General and Lord Palmerston spoke in language very different from that used last year. As the U.S. Government shows signs of strength and of coming success, so our· Government becomes more civil. Their conduct is guided by some other principle than that of honour and magnanimity.

"Walked up with Disraeli. He thinks we shall not have war on the Denmark question, but that Louis Napoleon is looking for some occasion to 'rectify' the French frontier on a portion of the Rhine.[3]

[1] Afterwards Sir James Vaughan: he died in 1906 at the age of 92.

[2] Admiral Farragut (famous for the distaste for iron ships which led him to declare that he would never go to hell in a tea-kettle) had in April, 1862, after brilliant operations in the Mississippi delta region, reduced New Orleans. General Benjamin Franklin Butler, formerly a successful lawyer, was placed in command of the city. He acquired unenviable celebrity by the order, so generally misunderstood and reprobated abroad, that women insulting Federal soldiers in the street should be treated as women of the town. Lord Palmerston in the House of Commons described it as "infamous." Jefferson Davis outlawed Butler. The only thing that can be said in favour of the edict is that it was never once enforced. This was not Butler's only disservice to the Union. He seized a sum of 800,000 dollars deposited with the Dutch Consul in New Orleans. This indiscretion brought about his removal from the command.

[3] Disraeli had recently written to Sir George Sinclair: "An English Government that, in its wisdom, goes to war with Germany, must make France the mistress of Europe."

"[13th.] Thomas Yeatman, American and Southerner, called. Said South were discovering that all their Slavery policy was wrong. Much discussion as to mode of dealing with Slavery, and as to filling up their army with black troops, going on at Richmond; difficulties great.

"[15th.] Called on Mr. Gibson at Board of Trade. Saw him and Lord Granville. Both said that probabilities of peace were increasing. 'Things look· rather better.' House: Mrs. Barlow, wife of General Barlow, of U.S. Army, called and saw me in the Lobby; took her to the Ladies' Gallery. A clever, interesting woman, full of life, informed on political questions. She hoped I would 'think her polite, as she had not asked for my autograph!'

"[16th.] To breakfast with W. E. Forster, 35, Pall Mall. Met Mr. Evarts from New York. Conversation on America. Mr. Evarts a good representative of his country. Club: call from Mr. Marshall, New York merchant, with an introductory note from Chas. Sumner; a fine old man, earnest and loyal to his country.

"[18th.] Call from Cyrus Field, of the Atlantic Telegraph; to breakfast with him to-morrow morning at Palace Hotel, Buckingham Gate. Call from Fredk. Edge, correspondent of the *Star* in the U.S. They are both confident the great war will end in its main features during this year.

"House: Conversation with Mr. Gladstone. Wished to speak to me on the questions on which he had spoken or written to Mr. Cobden— about some attempt to reduce French armaments, and about the possibility of reducing expenditure here. Cobden would undertake nothing as to French armaments. Mr. Gladstone thought Income Tax was injurious in promoting extravagance: money so easily raised by it. Not difficult to get rid of Income Tax if disposition to economy encouraged. Thought House more friendly to economy than it had been since Russian War, which broke down all [the] disposition to moderate expenditure cultivated since 1828 or since Reform Bill. He asked me to think this point over. He would not advise indirect taxes, but thought more might be raised by House Tax and taxes on bequests, etc.

"[19th.] To Palace Hotel, Buckingham Gate, to breakfast with Cyrus Field. Also there, Judge Winter, of Georgia, and Selea Martin, once a slave in Georgia, now a minister of a chapel near London! Judge Winter believes the South is nearly exhausted, and cannot carry on the war much longer.

"Home Office with deputation on Sewage of Birmingham.

"House: debate on establishment of assizes at Leeds or Wakefield. Division in favour of Leeds. Edward Leatham [1] made a good and amusing speech for Wakefield.

"[*March* 1.] To Lambeth Baths: meeting to open 'Working Men's Industrial Exhibition.' Lord Shaftesbury in the chair. I spoke for 20 minutes without preparation, but was kindly received and endeavoured to say something useful.

"[*3rd.*] Mr. Barrett, from U.S., just from Italy [called]. He thinks Italy on the eve of war with Austria or of revolution in her Southern provinces.

"Received this morning invitation from Lord Russell to dinner for the 12th. Since his abandonment of cause of Reform, have not had any intercourse with him, and since his acceptance of a peerage have not even seen him except once or twice in the House of Lords. Another engagement for the 12th to dine with Mr. Everest will prevent my dining with him.

"Called on Mr. Adams, U.S. Minister. Found him uneasy at the irritation caused by Confederate privateers fitted out in England. Lord Russell worried by 'Secesh' Peers and Commoners, and almost afraid to do right.

"[*4.th*] Wrote to Governors of the States of Rhode Island. Michigan and Wisconsin, U.S., to ask for information as to the abolition of Capital Punishment in those states, in anticipation of coming debate on that question in the House of Commons.

"House: debate on infringement of our neutrality by Richmond rebel Government, interesting, and on the whole satisfactory.

"[*5th.*] Edwards's Hotel, to breakfast with Mr. Evarts. Only himself and his son there beside myself. Conversation of much interest on American affairs.

"[*7th.*] To the City, 160, Gresham House, to see an American invention for knitting; inventor, Mr. Dalton, an Englishman born, but American from his youth. A beautiful invention and promising much success. He wants £4,000 for it for this country.

"House: Government Annuities Bill. Gladstone's speech in favour of Government entering Life Insurance business; a doubtful scheme, I think.

"[*8th.*] Dalton, American inventor, called; also Mr. Evans, with samples of knitting he brought from States.

[1] Bright's brother-in-law, his wife's youngest brother, was Member for Huddersfield.

"House: Education debate. Cobden there for the first time this session. He is stouter and looks well, but I am not satisfied with the state of his health. Mr. Gladstone asked him and me to call to-morrow on him to have some talk on taxes and matters appertaining to his office.

"[9*th*.] Wrote autographs for New York Fancy Fair, and took them to Mrs. Adams. She spoke of Mr. Stanley,[1] son of Lord Stanley of Alderley, his earnestness about America and his zeal for the North. His talk rapid and earnest; 'would talk my hair off my head.' Knows every minute detail of U.S. affairs: 'knows more than Mr. Adams a pile' (i.e., a heap, or great quantity, more than Mr. Adams) of details of geography, etc. Mr. Adams wishes this Government to remain in. It is working fairly now with America. He hopes and believes that Mr. Lincoln will be re-elected.

"Called by appointment on Mr. Gladstone, 11, Carlton House Terrace. Cobden should have been there, but dared not come out on so cold and wintry a day. Gladstone's conversation for nearly an hour very interesting—on Reform, Income Tax, and reduction of expenditure. Thinks Government and House treated people badly on Reform, and believes the question must come up again soon. Conscious, evidently, how Palmerston had thrown over the question: it should be a vital question with any Government dealing with it. Thought Income Tax might be got rid of and a portion of it got back by extended 'death duties' (legacy and succession duties). Hopes more economical times are coming.

"[10*th*.] Cyrus Field called: left me an interesting letter from Mr. Chase, Finance Minister, U.S. J. Dalton, inventor of knitting machine, called and brought me his specification.

"To Home Office with Memorial on behalf of Hall in Warwick Gaol.

"[11*th*.] Saw Sir Geo. Grey on Hall's case at Warwick. Urged that he was bound to consider the opinions of the population among whom the crime was committed. His decision so far is adverse, and I telegraphed to Mr. Morgan, Birmingham, as I left the House near midnight.

"[12*th*.] Called on Mr. Scholefield,[2] and went to Home Office to see Sir Geo. Grey on the case of the convict Hall at Warwick. Could make no impression on him. Public opinion goes for nothing with him. He displayed the strength of a weak man, which is obstinacy. He

[1] Edward Lyulph Stanley, M.P. for Oldham and afterwards Lord Sheffield.
[2] His colleague in the representation of Birmingham.

told me last night that he had consulted Lord Westbury, Chancellor, and from him I should not expect anything beyond a legal view of the case. Deputation greatly disappointed. Called on Lord Henry Lennox, 50, Portland Place, on same case. He had written to me upon it. He was not in.

"[13th.] Papers from Mr. Morgan on the case of Hall to be sent to Sir Geo. Grey.

"Dined with Mr. Adams, U.S. Minister. At home, before going to Mr. Adams's, found a letter from Sir Geo. Grey saying he had reprieved the convict Hall at Warwick: great relief to me, for his fate has been a burden on my mind for some days.

"House: Roebuck made a disgraceful attack on the American Government. I spoke briefly in reply and in condemnation of his conduct.

"Conversation with Gladstone behind Speaker's chair on his Budget. His conversation with Cobden on Friday on Income Tax, etc., had pleased him. He told me, speaking of duty on Fire Insurance, that the exemption of farming stock from the duty was 'a most iniquitous exemption,' but he thought no power could now abolish it.

"Talk with Milner Gibson: Ministers for peace, and danger of war much less than it had been.

"[15th.] S. Lucas called. *Standard* enlarged, which may force *Star* to enlarge at an expense of £3,000 a year, which is unfortunate.

"Dined at the Palace Hotel with Cyrus W. Field and directors and friends of the Atlantic Telegraph. An interesting evening: a great undertaking, and earnest men are engaged in it.

"[16th.] Dined with J. B. Smith.[1] Met there Bishop Colenso: parsonic looking. No conversation with him, but not impressed with him—perhaps prejudiced against him. Sir John Bowring there also. Did not speak to him. His China War crime against his ancient professions fills me with disgust."

The next entry in the diary refers to an incident, famous in its day, which more than sixty years after may need a brief elucidation. Mazzini, the prophet of Italian unity, who was commonly under sentence of death in connexion with his political campaigns, at this time lived mostly in London, where he edited the Italian revolutionary paper, *Penziere ed Actione*. One of his most constant English friends was James Stansfeld, then Member for Halifax, who had recently taken his

[1] Member for Stockport, Chairman of the Anti-Corn Law League.

place on the Treasury Bench as Civil Lord of the Admiralty. He was
to have a long political life, to become one of the most respected of
Liberal statesmen, and to succeed Mr. Chamberlain at the Local Government Board when the Home Rule split occurred. In 1864, however,
he was the youngest member of the Government, with his reputation
to make. A bomb burst beneath him. A paper with the words,
"Mr. Flowers, 35, Thurloe Square," was found in the possession of a
certain Greco, on trial in France charged with conspiracy to murder
Louis Napoleon. The address in Thurloe Square was Stansfeld's,
and Mr. Flowers (or alternatively Signor Fiori) was a pseudonym of
Mazzini. The Italian leader's letters were thus addressed to him for
his safety and convenience, with the consent of his friend. No evidence
was produced that Greco had ever corresponded with Mazzini; Mazzini
denied any knowledge of the conspiracy—and Stansfeld knew nothing
about either the plotters in France or the contents of Mazzini's letters.
But the discovery was made the occasion of a violent onslaught in the
House of Commons upon the hapless Civil Lord. Disraeli charged
him in his most highfalutin strain with being a medium of correspondence "between the assassins of Europe." Feeling ran very high.
The Government, to its credit, would not throw Stansfeld to the wolves,
and it stood in danger of defeat. In these circumstances Bright came
to the rescue as the diary modestly relates. But for his speech Stansfeld
might have been destroyed and the Ministry overset. Stansfeld was
keenly conscious of the service Bright had done for "the last appointed
and youngest member of the Government," and wrote to him a letter
of fervent thanks.

"[*17th.*] House: Unpleasant discussion between Mr. Gladstone
and Mr. Sheridan, M.P. for Dudley, in which the former was not
successful. Later in the evening, an attack made on Mr. Stansfeld,
M.P. for Halifax and Junior Lord of the Admiralty, in connexion with
his intimacy with Mr. Mazzini, the Italian patriot and 'conspirator.'
Opposition very savage and excited. Disraeli's speech very bad in
tone and manner. I spoke after him, referring to his 'simulated horror,'
and the ungenerous conduct of his party towards Stansfeld. What I
said seemed to have a great effect in lessening the furious excitement
which prevailed. Division believed doubtful, but a majority of 10 in
favour of the Government was the result. Several members, and some
of the Government, told me that my speech turned the passion of the
House, and saved the division and the Government.

"The night very squally, and not creditable to the House or satisfactory to the Government.

"[*April* 8.] House: came away early and took a vapour bath and home for a quiet evening. Read 'Cudjo's Cave,' a story of secession in Tennessee—exciting and well written.[1]

"[*11th.*] Down to the Board of Trade about ½ past 2 and stayed there till 7 to see the Garibaldi procession. Mr. Malet of the Board of Trade and W. T. M. Torrens were with me. The people, numbers without number, made a grand display. I have seen nothing equal to it before. . . . Walked up with J. Wilson Patten, M.P. for North Lancashire. He came to me to express his opinion of my speech on the Stansfeld-Mazzini affair, and spoke in most complimentary terms of it. He is just the sort of member to whom my appeal was made, and the House is often prevented from doing foolishly and passionately by the presence of men of like moderation and character. To bed at 2 o'clock.

"[*13th.*] House: County Franchise Bill defeated by majority of 27. Palmerston made a speech for the Tories rather than for his own side. Evening, to University College, to preside over special meeting of the Debating Society. Spoke for ½ an hour, chiefly on the use of oratory in advancing political reforms and freedom. Debate interesting on Public Schools."

---

[1] Bright was so interested in this book that he finished it at a second sitting next evening, and immediately lent it to his niece, Kate Lucas (afterwards Mrs. J. P. Thomasson). It became the favourite book of the Bright children. Mr. Herbert Putnam, the Librarian of Congress at Washington, has kindly given me some account of the forgotten work that stirred up such excitement in the family. "Cudjo's Cave," by J. T. Trowbridge, is an anti-slavery novel, first published at Jackwood, and afterwards (in 1864) at Boston by J. E. Tilton and Co. It became highly popular. In his own autobiography, published in 1903, the author confesses that he was entirely ignorant of the topography and dialect of the country in which he laid the scene of the story—Eastern Tennessee. Though it seceded, there were many Unionists in that State. The tale relates, through the adventures of the hero, Penn Hapgood, a young Quaker school-teacher, the persecution of the partisans of the North by their Confederate neighbours. Its chief figure is Pomp, a big runaway slave, who hides in a cave in the woods already inhabited by another black fugitive, Cudjo. The cave becomes the cache of all the Abolitionists of the district and eventually the regional storm-centre of the war. This novel with a purpose seems to have stood well above the common level of earnest dullness by reason of the author's skill in handling adventure and depicting character.

4

The most spectacular event of that spring in London was the reception of General Garibaldi. He appeared under the ægis of the House of Sutherland, received the Freedom of the City, addressed a crowd of 20,000 at the Crystal Palace, and was lionized far beyond his heart's content. Bright, having seen the procession in Whitehall, met Garibaldi two days later at Stafford House, and again on the 19th. The confused story of the Patriot's sudden departure from England three weeks after his landing, to which Bright refers, has often been told, and the oftener it is told the more obscure it becomes. There is no doubt that in many quarters the adulation of Garibaldi gave great offence. The ostensible reason for the abrupt ending of his visit was that he could not stand the strain of the thirty provincial demonstrations arranged in his honour, and that if he could not accept all the invitations he would accept none. It failed to convince many people, among them Bright. Garibaldi himself, indeed, insisted on making one provincial visit—to Cornwall to see his old friend and comrade-in-arms, Colonel John Peard, known to fame as "Garibaldi's Englishman." The Duke and Duchess of Sutherland accordingly took him down to Penquite before he sailed in the duke's yacht for Caprera.

"[*April* 13.] To Stafford House: reception in honour of General Garibaldi. A large company. Going upstairs from the hall, met Lord Derby coming down. At the top of the staircase, met Lord Russell. In the company, saw nearly all the Ministers—Duke of Argyll, Lord Granville, Palmerston, Gladstone, Cardwell, Villiers and Gibson. Duke of Argyll introduced me to Garibaldi. He was walking along the balcony overlooking the hall, leaning on the arm of the Duchess of Sutherland. I shook hands with him. He said, 'I am very glad to know you.' I said, 'We are glad to see you here, but I am afraid the kindness of your friends will be too much for you.' He said, 'And it is all so new to me.' Soon after he left the company, as he retires early.

"From the balcony I saw him limping down the staircase into and across the hall, leaning on the arm of the graceful Duchess of Sutherland. Her face is intelligent and very charming; his rather weather-beaten, but indicating a most kind and generous heart.

"The house is very grand—hall, staircase and reception rooms, on a magnificent scale, exceeding that of any other house I have been in in this country. Duke and Duchess of Argyll were very civil to me. She is of the good breed of the Howards, and so far as my experience goes they are all kind and good people.

"I had a long talk with Mr. Gladstone—among other topics upon Ireland and the Irish Church. He thought, when the Liberal Party is restored to life, that question would come up for settlement, and he should regard it as one of the great purposes of the Party, altho' it would necessarily separate him from the University of Oxford.

"It was a singular spectacle to see the most renowned living soldier of Democracy cared for as by a loving daughter by a lady who is Countess and Duchess, at the head of the aristocracy of England. Lord Stanley said to me a day or two ago, 'I wonder if it ever occurs to the Duke [of Sutherland] that if Garibaldi had his way, there would be no Dukes of Sutherland?'

"It is Garibaldi's magnanimous disinterestedness which gains him universal sympathy, tho' I suspect some of his aristocratic 'friends' here rather patronize him to keep him from alliances of a democratic character.

"[15th.] House. Left early to go to dine with Cyrus W. Field and a large party, 50 at least, at the Palace Hotel. Mr. Adams, U.S. Minister, there. I sat between him and Mr. Evarts of New York. Speeches during the evening. I spoke on the jealousy of America felt in England.

"[16th.] Evening at J. C. Hall's at a séance of the 'Spiritualists.' Mr. Home, the great medium, there.[1] Manifestations as usual, except one thing new to me. Small bell taken from hands of two of the party and transferred across the circle, and laid on the lap of another, a lady, Mrs. Hanna, sitting next to me. Curious and not explained: all hands on the table at the time.

"[18th.] House: 'Bob' Lowe's explanation and defence on leaving office. Adverse vote a week or two ago drove him out. He has been hardly treated, but, as he has never shown mercy to others, he has received none. It is thought his Chief, Palmerston, has not supported him, and that there is now a sore that will not soon be healed. The Government were beaten later on in the evening on a clause in the Penal Servitude Bill, the Opposition being for more severity with convicts. It is time the Government resigned. Its weakness is deplorable, if its strength were to be desired. A story in the House that Garibaldi is going away on Friday.

[1] D. D. Home had come to London from America in 1855.

"[*19th.*] Met Cobden at Mr. Seely's,[1] 26, Princes Gate, and saw Garibaldi and his sons; also Mr. Saffi, one of the triumvirate which governed Rome in its short life in 1849.

"Garibaldi said to me, 'I am of your principles, for, if I am a soldier, I am a soldier of peace.'

"There is a singular kindness and gentleness and dreamy enthusiasm in his face and in his eye, and a charming simplicity about him. He is going away. It is said, and doubtless truly, that the Government wants him out of the country. They fear he may excite political feeling in the provinces; or his presence here be annoying to the French or Austrians; or the Queen is irritated at the manner in which he has been received. Perhaps there is truth in each of these stories. His going thus suddenly will give great dissatisfaction to the country, and may have an effect on the Administration.

"[*27th.*] Call from W. Roberts, Great Easton, Rockingham, a lawyer of 22 years' standing: understands more or less 15 languages, ancient and modern, yet in difficulty, and wishes help to get some promotion in his profession. Wish I could do something for him, for he is ill qualified to struggle in the world.

"[*May* 3.] House: Capital Punishment. I spoke at some length and with evident effect on the House.[2] Discussion very good. Mr. Denman and Lord Henry Lennox made good speeches. The question has advanced greatly, and has never before received so much attention in the House.

"[*6th.*] Interesting conversation with Lord Stanley in the smoking-room. Lord Derby unwilling to come in unless prospect of sustaining his Government by majority in Parliament. Did not think this Government would go to war for Denmark. Emperor not disposed for war, and rather favoured Denmark united with Sweden and Norway. Spoke of Ireland, on which Lord Stanley made use of phrase, 'that infernal Irish Church,' but did not see how it could be dealt with, and thought no change short of extinction would be of any use.

[1] The father of General John Seely, M.P., afterwards Secretary for War.
[2] Mr. Ewart had tabled a motion for the Abolition of the Punishment of Death. Bright, who at every opportunity urged that the capital sentence should be abandoned, spoke with great moderation and reasonableness. He quoted the experience of states in which the death penalty had been forbidden, and asked, "Is this nation worse than other nations? Cannot the lenient laws practised with perfect safety in many other nations of the world be practised in this nation and at the same time leave us perfectly secure—at least as much so as we are at present? I say we may wash vengeance and blood from our code without difficulty and without danger."

"America: I condemned the tone of Lord Derby in speaking of the seizure of the 'rams' at Birkenhead, in which Lord Stanley did not differ with me.

"Rumours of Lord Palmerston's more severe illness. Walked up with Mr. Gibson, who was with Palmerston during the day and thought him better. Gibson uneasy about the Danish question, but Cabinet not for war, the most warlike among them only wished to protect Copenhagen from bombardment.

"[8*th*.] Dined with Mr. Adams, U.S. Minister, in Upper Portland Place. Met Mr. Dayton, U.S. Minister to France, there; an intelligent and gentlemanly man, but not in good health.

"[9*th*.] Jno. Dickenson and S. Lucas called; also Jno. Rubery, from Birmingham, with his brother, Alfred Rubery, who was pardoned by the President of the U.S. at my request. Long conversation on the action for libel against the *Birmingham Daily Post* which Alfred Rubery has commenced.[1]

"House till midnight. Met Mr. Eaton, of Madison College, New York State. Most grateful to me for my friendship for his country.

"[11*th*.] Baines's motion for £6 franchise. Gladstone spoke admirably on the question of suffrage. His speech caused great sensation, and is considered as marking out his line in the future."

Gladstone and Bright had much in common, both in their political ideals and in their personal traits; but it was the question of Reform that in the early days exerted the strongest influence upon their co-operation as Liberal leaders. To say that this declaration of the Chancellor of the Exchequer caused a great sensation is to put the case mildly. If Gladstone had suddenly proclaimed himself an Atheist and a Jacobin there could hardly have been more fuss. Yet he did but assert a

---

[1] Sir Charles Hyde has kindly supplied me with the particulars of this action. It arose out of an article in the *Post* on January 5, entitled, "Mr. John Bright and a Birmingham Pirate." Alfred Rubery alleged that the article imputed to him a misappropriation of money from his brother. Bright's letter (already quoted, p. 266) was written to correct what he thought to be exaggerations in the article. The *Post* promptly expressed its regret that it had been misinformed, but Rubery persisted in his action for libel. It came before Mr. Justice Mellor on June 25, when the *Post* denied that the article made the suggested imputation, repudiated any malice or negligence, and brought five guineas into court. After a consultation between counsel, it was announced that a settlement had been reached for forty shillings. Mr. Justice Mellor said it did not appear to him, from a perusal of the article, that there was any such imputation as had been alleged.

commonplace of democracy. After showing that less than one-fiftieth of the working-men of the country were enfranchised, he went on: "I call upon the adversary to show cause, and I venture to say that every man who is not presumably incapacitated by some consideration of personal unfitness or of political danger is morally entitled to come within the pale of the Constitution."

Palmerston, at home with the gout, was paralysed with astonishment. Disraeli said Gladstone had "revived the doctrine of Tom Paine." He himself told a correspondent that he had unwarily set the Thames on fire; "but I have great hopes that the Thames will, on reflection, perceive that he had no business or title to catch the flame and will revert to his ordinary temperature accordingly."

When this Parliamentary excitement had died down, Bright turned aside from politics for a few days to visit his friend Thorold Rogers at Oxford. There was something not exactly wistful, but a little wondering, touched with a faint regret, in John Bright's reaction to Oxford. He loved it very much. It honoured him in later years as it alone can honour great men of all sorts. But Oxford had not been kind to men of Bright's origins and religious temper, and there was bound to be a certain reserve in his admiration. However, with congenial souls like Thorold Rogers and Goldwin Smith he was perfectly happy. Goldwin Smith, then Regius Professor of Modern History, has left a pleasant allusion to this visit in his Reminiscences. "When the commercial battle between the new England of the North and the old England of the South was over," he wrote, "he [Bright] softened very much towards old institutions, as old institutions did towards him. As he sat on my lawn at Oxford one summer afternoon, when the music of bells was floating from the ancient city, I overheard him say, 'It would be pleasant to be eighteen and to be coming here.'" There was, at this time, a powerful link between Bright and Goldwin Smith. The don shared with the politician the affection and gratitude of the American people. He had been a brilliant advocate of the Union and of Abolition, and his pamphlet of 1863 ("Does the Bible sanction American Slavery?") had persuaded towards the Northern side a large and influential class in England. Not long after Bright's visit, he went on his lecturing tour in the United States, and four years afterwards he had finally abandoned England and Oxford for America and Cornell University.

"[*May* 14.] To Oxford. Mr. J. E. Thorold Rogers met me at the station and I remained at his house till the 16th. Walked in some of the college gardens till dinner. At dinner, Professor Smith and his clever sister, Miss Smith, and Professor Blackie, of Edinbro'.

"[15th.] Professor Goldwin Smith to breakfast. Greatly pleased with him; calm, thoughtful, conscientious, and profoundly instructed he seems to me. It is a pleasure to listen to him.

"Visited gardens and colleges and dined in the 'Common Hall' at University with Goldwin Smith; dessert after it in the 'Common Room.'

"To Sir B. Brodie's to tea,—a pleasant party.

"[16th.] Breakfast at Oriel College, invited by Mr. Neate, M.P. Off by train at 11. My little visit to Oxford has been an unmixed pleasure to me. Everything was beautiful—the buildings, the gardens, the weather, the season; and the society was most cultivated and liberal. Mr. Rogers very kind. He is a very able and laborious man.

"[28th.] Crossing Pall Mall, opposite Reform Club, met Bishop of Oxford,[1] who shook hands with me whilst we ran some risk of injury from carriages passing. I said, 'Don't let us be run over.' He said, 'It would be curious if we should die together.' I said, 'Perhaps we should not find ourselves so far apart hereafter as we do here.' He smiled and we passed on.

"[June 1.] Called with H. Ashworth at St. James's Hotel on Mrs. Duncan, an American lady. Not a very pleasant visit: boasting of her loyalty to her country, but loud in her abuse of Mr. Lincoln and all connected with his Government. I told her such language was offensive to me from an Englishman, and I did not wish to hear it from an American. A clever and good-looking woman, but not a good specimen of the American lady.

"Dined with P. A. Taylor, M.P. Mr. Conway, U.S., there. Declaimed against Mr. Lincoln, and urged that English friends of the North should say nothing in his favour, etc. I disputed some of his positions, and thought it would be impertinent in me or in any Englishman to say anything in public on the subject.

"[12th.] Dined with Mr. Adams. Met there Mr. or Colonel Aspinall, son of Mr. Aspinall who was here last year. Mr. Trevelyan, son of Sir Charles Trevelyan, also there. After dinner, Miss Cushman, the American actress, came in: a woman of much sense and force of character.

"Mr. Morell, School Inspector, called; also Dr. Masson about his grievance with the Belfast Presbyterians. My time is sorely

[1] Wilberforce.

occupied with these and similar cases in which I can generally do nothing.[1]

"House: left early to meet Bevan Braithwaite [2] and Levi Coffin (U.S.) at my lodgings at 7 o'clock. L.C. is a quiet 'back country' Friend, who has devoted himself to the assistance of the fugitive slaves. Not less than 3,300 of them have passed through his hands during the last 30 years. He has had 17 of them in his house at once, and in one case a poor negro died in his house after having been nursed for 9 weeks during his sickness.

"L.C. comes here to try to interest us in the condition of the Freedmen, and I hope he may succeed. Unfortunately, he does not speak well and his object might be more powerfully advocated.

"[18th.] Mr. Wing, solicitor, called. Wishes me to give evidence in trial, Rubery *v.* Feeney, of the *Birmingham Daily Post*.

"[20th.] News of the destruction of the *Alabama* corsair arrived.[3] 35, Bedford Square, at 7 p.m., to a meeting with Levi Coffin, of Indiana, U.S., on subject of raising funds to help freed negroes in U.S. A good meeting, and something will be done, I hope.

"[*July* 2.] House. Disraeli led off the debate,[4] and Gladstone followed. The case against the Government strong, but not put in its strongest light. Gladstone felt his case weak, but perhaps made the best of it. General Peel's speech remarkable for its decided non-intervention sentiments. The Government will suffer in the debate as they deserve to suffer.

"[5th.] To Fry's in Baker St., to sit for a photograph. This rage for portraits is troublesome. House. Cobden opened the debate

---

[1] The diary is freely sprinkled with notes of "calls" made on Bright by all sorts and conditions of men and women suffering from real hardship or imaginary grievance.

[2] Bevan Braithwaite, a barrister, was the most eminent "Minister" of the Society of Friends. Bright had a great regard for him.

[3] By the Federal steamer *Kearsage*, off Cherbourg.

[4] The debate on Disraeli's motion of censure on the Government for "failing to uphold the integrity and independence of Denmark," lowering the just influence of England in the councils of Europe, and thereby diminishing the securities of peace. The Conference of London had failed and Bismarck's policy was triumphant. Palmerston and Russell were notoriously restrained by the majority of the Cabinet from intervention against Germany. Disraeli himself, in fact, did not approve of intervention. The House of Commons and the country wanted neither war with Germany nor the displacement of Palmerston. The sham fight ended with the acceptance of an amendment by Kinglake avoiding the direct issue of Disraeli's motion by declaring merely against interference between Germany and Denmark.

in a very able and useful speech. It is evident that our years of preaching on Foreign Policy and non-intervention have not been without effect. Horsman made a great speech, tho' much of it was wrong. Home late: bed at 2 o'clock.

"[6*th*.] I could not sleep much last night or this morning, the brain running on the debate and a speech. I may speak before the debate ends.

"Dined with Mr. Seely. Mr. Mazzini there, much older looking than when I met him last, many years ago, but the same intelligent, thoughtful and kind expression of countenance. Grant Duff, M.P., and E. Watkin, M.P.,[1] there. Walked home with Watkin, and conversation on America.

"[7*th*.] Made some notes on question under debate in the House. Consultation with Cobden, and concluded not to speak. It is impossible to speak for the Government, and to speak against them and vote with them is difficult to explain. Excitement in the House, and much difference of opinion as to coming division.

"[8*th*.] Debate not very good, but great excitement as the division approached. Government majority 18,—313 to 295. Tho' the vote is for the Government the censure of the House is very generally expressed. To bed after 3 o'clock."

5

The letters to Sumner continued while the tide of war turned and flowed towards the Federal victory. Bright watched with anxious hope the campaign for Lincoln's re-election; he looked on as all the world looked, breathless, at the fierce and uncertain struggle before Richmond between Grant and Lee; he listened with ear to ground for the rumble of Sherman's march.

Into this world of suspense fell a grievous domestic tragedy—the death in November of his third boy, Leonard, then five and a half years old. The child was a favourite of all the family, a delightful little fellow, highly intelligent, somewhat like his father in features. The loss, which almost broke the hearts of Bright and his wife, came suddenly. The child had contracted scarlet fever during a visit to Llandudno, where the family spent a month's holiday every summer

---

[1] Son of Absalom Watkin to whom Bright addressed his famous letter on the Crimean War (see page 178). Edward Watkin (1819–1901), chairman of the Manchester and Sheffield, the South-Eastern and the Metropolitan Railways, was the earliest advocate of the Channel Tunnel, a scheme which had Bright's full approval and support.

school vacation. He died in a few days. The blow was the bitterer because he had seemed to make perfect recovery from a serious illness in the spring of that year.

Bright and his wife stood one November afternoon ("very lonely," as he wrote in a beautiful letter to his elder children at school) looking down into a little grave in the windswept churchyard of St. Tudno on the Great Ormes Head. "The wildness and desolation of the place were relieved by the calmness and mildness of the day. . . . I found it impossible to stay longer in Llandudno, everything reminded me of our loss in such a way that my heart seemed ready to burst as I walked through its now quiet streets. . . . And thus we left our darling Leonard in his loneliness and peace. . . ." The words on his grave are: "And there shall be one fold and one Shepherd."

He now approached a year which brought two of the sharpest joys and sorrows of his life—the triumph of the American cause and the death of Cobden.

"[*February* 11, 1865.] To Johnson's, Euston Road, to order a marble tablet or headstone for the little grave on the Ormes Head. . . . As I went, and as I returned, my eyes filled with tears as I thought of that most precious child so suddenly taken from us. It is a consolation to be able to believe that 'there shall be one fold and one Shepherd.' Home early. Came up in a cab with J. Parkes, and read Life of Sir John Eliot till near midnight.

"[13*th.*] Went up with Milner Gibson, to dine with him. Mr. Lefevre, M.P.[1] for Reading, also came up. A pleasant evening of conversation and political discussion. Walking home with Lefevre, he asked if I thought he should take the office of Secretary to the Poor Law Board if it was offered him? I said what could be said for and against, and left him to decide. The day most winterly, frost keen and snow still in the streets.

"[15*th.*] Received a deputation of good men, Baptist ministers, asking me to present a Petition to the House on our ecclesiastical establishments. They wished also for a Committee of Inquiry into them. I objected to this on the ground of its uselessness, and indeed that it could not be obtained, saying that the State Church can only come to an end by explosion from within or from political and democratic changes in our representation and Government.

"[17*th.*] Not very well this morning, and troubled with trifling

[1] Afterwards Lord Eversley.

matters—invitations and duties ahead, and the wish to go home for a few days. I seem to become less able to determine what is best on matters of no great moment.

"[20th.] Lunched with Mr. Speaker. Met there Mr. Adams, U.S. Minister, Lord Taunton, and W. E. Forster, M.P., and his wife. In the evening met General Barlow, U.S. Army, under the Gallery.

"[March 2.] At the House, wrote a note to Mr. Gladstone to decline his offer to place me on the Railway Commission about to be appointed. I cannot afford to give more time and labour to the public.

"[5th.] A most pleasant walk with Cobden.[1] Found him pretty well in health, but looking older. Intelligent and agreeable as ever. Spent the day with him. Much talk on America and Canada and politics generally.

"Read correspondence with Mr. Gladstone, who offered him Chairmanship of the Board of Audit, with £2,000 a year, which he declined without hesitation, condemning expenditure and waste of the Government. Read letters also from Duke of Argyll chiefly on Canadian affairs.

"[11th.] To breakfast with Lord Hy. Lennox at 13, Albert Terrace, Albert Gate. Met there Mr. Ayrton, M.P., Pope Hennessy, M.P., Mr. Earle, Mr. Cole and Mr. Burch. A small house, quite a cottage, but probably as much as the younger son of a Duke can afford to have. Gossip: among other things that Duchess of Montrose and many others 'in Society' were losing money in the 'Secesh' Loan. To Rolls Court: met Roebuck, M.P., there to present a Memorial to Sir Jno. Romilly, the Master of the Rolls, from Attorneys' Clerks. Romilly gave each of us a good pamphlet, just out, in favour of the Ballot. To Radley's Hotel, to meeting with delegates from Trades Unions on question of Reform.

"[13th.] House: Debate on defences of Canada, and spoke at some length.[2] Not much satisfied with myself, but hope what I said

---

[1] At Midhurst.

[2] The debate arose on the Report of Colonel Jervois on the Defences of Canada. Bright put all his energy into the fight against proposals to fortify the country. In nothing during all the American controversies was his wisdom more signally manifested. Canada was not for war; England was not for war; America was not for war. Whence, then, was war to come? If there were war, Canada could not be defended. But there would be no war. "I believe," he declared in an inspiration of prophecy, "that these two great commonwealths will march abreast, the parents and guardians of freedom and justice, wheresoever their language shall be spoken and their power shall extend." A week later he returned to the attack. If war ever occurred, its

will tend to good. The debate will be useful both here and in the States. To bed at 2 o'clock.

"[*17th.*] Called at 135, Regent Street, and saw a patent American churn. The butter made in 4½ minutes. The invention simple but most effective.

"Found card of invitation to dinner from Lord Russell. Have not spoken to him for about 5 years, since his ill conduct on the Reform question.

"[*21st.*] Invitation to dinner from Lord Russell—declined it: likely to be away next week.

"[*22nd.*] Called on Mr. Cobden, 23, Suffolk Street. Found him in bed—ill since coming to town.

"[*25th.*] With Elizabeth to Bristol and Clifton.[1] Before leaving town, called on Cobden but did not see him. He is very ill, and I am very anxious about him. Bath Hotel, Clifton. Spent the evening with McLaren and P[riscilla].

"[*April* 1.] Called 23, Suffolk Street to inquire about my poor friend Cobden. Did not see him, but the account of him gave me great alarm.

"Dined with W. Jackson, M.P., and left immediately after dinner for Suffolk St. Remained there with Geo. Moffat, M.P., till after midnight. Did not see my sick friend. Mr. Fisher and Dr. Roberts proposed that I should see him, but I feared to excite him, and refused to go up unless he wished it. Mr. Fisher told him I was in the house. He turned to Dr. Roberts and said, 'Doctor, I am in your hands, and perhaps in those of Death. Ought I to run the risk of any excitement?' Dr. Roberts thought not, and thus I missed the chance of seeing him again when he could have known me. I went home, calling with Moffat at the St. James's Restaurant to get some 'invalid turtle' for him, which Moffat took to Suffolk St. whilst I sent a telegram to Mr. Sale of Manchester. I was very sad. At 8 o'clock next morning, being Sunday,

"[*2nd.*] I heard the bell ring, and sprang up to dress, conscious of the ill-tidings that were coming. A note from young Mr. Fisher asked me to come down, as my poor friend was worse and sinking.

---

cause would arise not in Canada but in England. "There is no more prospect of war between Canada and the United States alone than between the Empire of France and the Isle of Man."

[1] During a four days' stay at Bristol, he attended the Friends' Meetings at Bristol and Sidcot, and visited the Commercial Rooms, where he was well received.

I was with him soon after 8 o'clock. I found him insensible and dying. Mr. Fisher, his son (who is to marry Mr. Cobden's eldest daughter), Dr. Roberts, Geo. Moffat, who came after me, Mrs. Cobden, and her daughter Ellen (Nelly) were in and about the room. There was a stertorous breathing which gradually became shorter. There was no apparent pain. Not a limb stirred. He lay breathing out his precious life, and for 3¼ hours I watched my greatest friend of more than 20 years as his life ebbed away. At ¼ past 11 o'clock the breathing ceased. There was a moment of suspense: a pallor spread over the face, and the manly and gentle spirit of one of the noblest of men passed away to the rewards which surely wait upon a life passed in works of good to mankind, a life of unselfish benevolence, and of unspotted honour.

"And what a scene as the spirit passed! The wife on one side, the daughter on the other—kissing the pale face as it grew every moment more pale, with plaintive exclamations, 'Darling, my own darling!' and 'Oh, Papa, why do you go away?' It was a scene never to be forgotten. His hands were still warm, and the warmth of life was still on his forehead after life had fled. We stood, and looked, and wept with almost breaking hearts, and then came away with a burden of grief hard to bear. I pressed his hand for the last time, and kissed his forehead, and left him with a sense of the loss I have suffered.

"To the Reform Club with Moffat, and wrote letters to H. Ashworth, T. Thomasson; and home.

"To Gordon St. Found McLaren and dear Priscilla there. We all wept as tho' one of the dearest of our circle had been taken.

"Mr. Gorrie, a writer in the *Star*, came. W. Evans came in also. We talked over the life of our friend, that Mr. Gorrie might write a memoir for the *Star*. Late at night Evans and I went to the *Star* office and heard a portion of it read.

"[*3rd*.] House. Great sorrow manifested on all sides. Palmerston and Disraeli spoke in fitting language of the loss the House has sustained. I wish his eulogy could have been spoken by men more in harmony with his own great and good character. I thought the House expected something from me. I was bowed down with grief. My eyes were filled with tears. I stood up trembling, and with my heart bursting and my head on fire. I pressed my forehead with my right hand to steady my brain. I said, 'It may be expected that I should say something on this sad event, but I feel that I cannot speak. Every mark of sympathy shown by the House is most grateful to my heart, but the time since I was present when the manliest and gentlest spirit which ever tenanted and animated a human form took its flight is so short that I must leave to a calmer moment what I may have to say to my countrymen on the lesson which is to be learned from the life and character of my friend. He has been my friend and as my brother for more than 20 years, and I did now know how much I loved him till I found that I had lost him.'

"I sat down sobbing with grief, and trembling with excitement and passionate sorrow. There were many Members present whose eyes were filled with tears. Such a time has probably never been known before in the House of Commons.

"In the evening called in Gordon St.

"[4th.] To Suffolk St. Found the poor girls in grief and excitement; Nelly almost delirious. I took her out for 4 hours. We called in Gordon St., where dear Maggy comforted her. Then on to Craven Hill Gardens and called on W. Hargreaves. Stayed there an hour or more. Then walked with her in Hyde Park. Then called at a shop in Piccadilly and bought her a sweet nosegay,—a red rose, a white rose, and some lilies of the valley, which she longed for to place on the bosom of her father. I took her to Suffolk St. and went with her into the chamber, and saw her place it over the heart which had loved her so tenderly. At ½ past 6, saw the sad family off for the Waterloo Station. In the evening went up to Paulton's in Cleveland Square. J. B. Smith there, and T. Thomasson and his son. Much talk about our loss.

"[5th.] Home at 11. Found a letter from Lord Kinnaird with an apology for an unkind remark he made upon me some years ago at Dundee (?) and which has caused estrangement between us. He wishes all to be forgotten before we meet at the funeral of my lost friend. I must write to thank him for his letter. He is a good man.

"[6th.] T. Thomasson called. With him to Pulteney Hotel, Albemarle St., and left a letter for Lord Kinnaird. Called with him on Mr. Bazley and talked over our lost friend's affairs.

"By 3.50 train to Midhurst—at Dunford about 7. Mrs. C. calm and bearing up well; the children also, except Nelly, whose sufferings have been extreme. I seemed to have more influence with her than any of her family, and I tried to soothe her. In the house were Mrs. Ashburner and Mrs. Letherby, friends of Mrs. C.

"[7th.] This morning I spent a long time, probably near 2 hours, in the library, where the coffin was, with the children; Nelly could scarcely leave it. Jane [1] was there with me, and said she often read

[1] Now Mrs. T. Fisher Unwin.

the 'Sermon on the Mount' to her father: 'he always said it was so very beautiful.'

"I saw little at the church, for I could not look up into the faces of so many I knew. The church is new and very nice; everything around it seems arranged to please the eye. The landscape is very charming, and the sunshine seemed to fight against the sorrow in our hearts. There were many hundreds of persons present. I was one of the pall-bearers, Mr. Gladstone and I walking foremost, Mr. Villiers and Mr. Gibson next, and others following. When the coffin was being placed in the vault, I could hold out no longer, and my anguish found some vent in passionate sobs and tears. I think I am becoming weaker that I am thus affected. Generally men seem to become harder and less given to tears as they grow older. In me, it is not so. It may be that this event, almost unconsciously to myself, brings me nearer to my own end, and points to the time when I must follow the path which all must tread.

"I remained at Dunford for the day. Mr. Thomasson was there and his son John [1]; also Professor Rogers of Oxford. In the evening I found poor Nelly walking alone in the field above the house: she 'could just see Lavington Church' from that high ground. I took her home, and tried to comfort her young but almost broken heart.

"I saw Mrs. C. in the evening. She was calm and very kind; hoped I would help her and advise her at any time, and come down to see them.

"[8th.] I have passed a terrible week. The whole seems a troubled dream. The friend of 25 years is gone, and I can no more ask counsel of him or give him help. We have striven together for freedom and justice, and have done something for both that cannot be undone. Henceforth, if any henceforth is permitted to me, I must work alone; but I feel as if I could do little more, for, as I looked into that vault at Lavington, it seemed to me that half my public life was buried there. But I will thank God that I have had such a friend, and that I have been permitted to be the friend of such a man."

6

The first care of his friends after Cobden's death was the welfare of his widow and family. In the week following the funeral, Thomasson, Rawson and Bright called a meeting of a few intimates at Manchester to consider a suggestion that had occurred to Bright. They learned

[1] Mr. John Thomasson married Bright's niece, Kate Lucas.

7. This morning I spent a long time, probably near 2 hours in the library, where the coffin was, with the children - Really could scarcely leave it - Jane was there with me, & said she often read the "Sermon on the Mount" to her Father - he always said it was "so very beautiful."

I saw little at the Church, for I could not look up into the faces of the many I knew - the Church is new & very nice - everything around it seems arranged to please the eye - the landscape is very charming - & the sunshine seemed to fight against the sorrow in our hearts - there were many hundreds of persons present - I was one of the pall-bearers. Mr Gladstone & I walking foremost: Mr Villiers & Mr Gilson next. & others following.

When the coffin was being placed in the vault, I too could hold out no longer, & my anguish found some vent in passionate sobs & tears. I think I am becoming weaker that I am thus affected. Generally men seem to become harder & less given to tears as they grow older. In me, it is not so. It-

PAGES FROM DIARY, APRIL 7, 1865

that Cobden's trustees could command about £20,000, and that the property left would be about £15,000. Bright proposed that a fund of £20,000 should be raised to add to the other capital resources and make the future of the family secure. This plan was adopted, together with a resolution to refrain from applying for any Government aid or Parliamentary vote. There were present (in addition to the three named), Hadfield; John Platt, of Oldham, the great machine-maker; Robert Platt, of Stalybridge; Joseph Leese; John Slagg; and Sir James Watts. These stalwarts raised £6,000 in the room among them to give the fund a start.

Almost immediately another blow fell on Bright. His brother-in-law, Samuel Lucas, who had admirably conducted the *Morning Star* since its beginning, died on the morning of the 16th after a short illness. "How soon," Bright exclaims, "this loss and shock succeed the other, and how unstable everything seems!" Lucas was buried in Highgate Cemetery on the sunny morning of the 21st, and Bright turned to the sorrowful business of finding a successor for him at the *Star*.

In the meantime news had come of the defeat of Lee and the capture of Richmond; and the by-election at Rochdale consequent on Cobden's death had been won by Bright's friend, Thomas Bayley Potter (Potter, 646; Brett, 496). It was a hotly fought affair. The town was "very excited all the week: much fighting and drinking—as usual under our system of elections."

"[*April* 22.] Called on Mr. Beales, Stone Buildings, Lincoln's Inn, on future management of the *Star* paper, he being one of the directors of it. Called at the *Star* office to ask them to insert lines on Mr. Cobden by Hon. Mrs. Norton.[1] Called on Paulton in Cleveland Square to see Mrs. Cobden, to remove an unfavourable impression as to the subscription now being raised for her children.

"[*23rd*.] News received of the surrender of Lee and his army to General Grant. This may be taken to be the end of the great and wicked rebellion. Slavery has measured itself with Freedom, and Slavery has perished in the struggle. How often have I longed and prayed for this result, and how much have I suffered from anxiety while it has been slowly working out, I only know! This great triumph of the Republic is the event of our age, and future ages will confess it, for they will be better able than this is to estimate the gain to freedom and humanity which will spring from it. I have had an almost unfaltering

[1] The reputed model of Meredith's "Diana of the Crossways."

faith from the beginning, and I now rejoice more than I can tell that the cause of personal freedom and free government has triumphed. The friends of freedom everywhere should thank God and take courage. They may believe that the world is not forsaken by Him who made and rules it.

"[29*th.*] Home. While at Dolgelly on the 27th heard of the shocking tragedy in Washington, the murder of President Lincoln. For an hour or near it, I felt stunned and ill. It is a terrible event, but it will not affect the issue of the great struggle, tho' it may change some of its details. I will not write an eulogy on the character of President Lincoln. There will be many to do that now he is dead. I have spoken of him when living, both in my speech at Rochdale in the winter of 1863/64 and in the letter to Horace Greeley written before the Presidential Election in the autumn of 1864. In him I have observed a singular resolution honestly to do his duty, a great courage, shown in the fact that in his speeches and writings no word of passion or of panic, or of ill-will, has ever escaped him; a great gentleness of temper and nobleness of soul proved by the absence of irritation and menace under circumstances of the most desperate provocation, and a pity and mercifulness to his enemies which seemed drawn as from the very fount of Christian charity and love. His *simplicity* for a time did much to hide his *greatness*, but all good men everywhere will mourn for him, and history will place him high among the best and noblest of men.

"I have had no direct communication with the late President, but my letters to Chas. Sumner as well as those from Cobden were frequently read by him, and he sent me, thro' Mr. Sumner, in his own handwriting, a draft resolution which he suggested as likely to be useful if adopted at public meetings held in this country in favour of the North. It referred to the question of Slavery, and the impossibility of our recognizing a new State based on the foundation of human bondage.[1]

"[30*th.*] At home quietly. What a terrible month has passed

[1] Lincoln sometimes read Bright's letters aloud in the meetings of the Cabinet at Washington. The resolution to which Bright referred was drafted by Lincoln as follows: "Whereas while heretofore States and Nations have tolerated slavery, recently for the first time in the world an attempt has been made to construct a new nation upon the basis of and with the fundamental object to maintain, enlarge and perpetuate human slavery; therefore/Resolved, that no such embryo State should ever be recognized by or admitted into the family of Christian and civilized nations; and that all Christian and civilized men everywhere should, by all lawful means, resist to the utmost such recognition or admission."

over us! I feel as if I cannot yet comprehend the changes which it has seen!"

The "great and wicked rebellion" being at an end, Bright joined characteristically but discreetly in the appeal for clemency to the rebels. He records having written (on May 16), "a long letter to Mr. Sumner against execution of rebels and traitors," and there was never any doubt where he stood in the controversies between President Lincoln and the Senate. After a spell with rod and line on the Spey, and some reunions with his wife and boys in London (two of his sons were then at Grove House School, Tottenham), he got back at the end of May to work in the House of Commons. There were some discussions with Gladstone on a proposed pension to Mrs. Cobden, which she declined, and many negotiations about the future of the *Morning Star*.

"[*June* 6.] To Rochester and by boat to visit the *Great Eastern*, the 'big ship.' Dear Helen and W. S. Clark with me. Spent 3 hours on the monster ship; saw the 'cable' for the Atlantic Telegraph. Lunched with Captain Anderson, who was most kind to us. We met on the vessel W. H. Russell, once and often *The Times* correspondent. He goes out with the *Great Eastern*. The day very hot.

"[7*th.*] From 12 to 3 sitting for portrait to Mr. Fagnani.[1] Evening: dined at the Alexandra Hotel with Mr. Morton and other Americans, among them Mr. Adams; all very kind to me.

"[13*th.*] *Star* office: Board meeting. Appointed Mr. Dymond business manager and Mr. McCarthy editor, the former 8 guineas weekly, and the latter £500 a year, with 5 p.c. on profits to be divided between them. House. *Star* office, and spoke to McCarthy about the editorship. He pleased and content.[2] Mr. Paget, M.P., Nottingham, spoke to me at the House. He and the Speaker had advanced £1,000 each to assist Mr. Cobden in payment of calls on the Illinois shares, Mr. C. never knowing of the act of the Speaker.[3] Both sums

[1] The portrait by Fagnani occupied much of Bright's time during the summer. The sittings bored him sadly.

[2] Justin McCarthy was then 35. The editorship of the *Star*, which he held till 1868, gave his first responsible position in London to one of the most sparkling of the great galaxy of able journalists Ireland sent to England during the nineteenth century. Bright and his friends did not know that they were nurturing with a salary of £500 a year the talent of the future Historian of Our Times and the leader of the Irish Party in its stormiest days.

[3] Mr. Evelyn Denison (afterwards Lord Ossington) was elected Speaker in 1857 and succeeded by Mr. Brand in 1872.

have been cancelled to Mr. Thomasson, and Mr. Paget wished me to know of the Speaker's kindness, and that I might some time mention it to Mrs. Cobden. This kindness and this delicacy in the mode of doing it have pleased me much.

"[14th.] Dined with Mr. Everest, Cleveland Square. Met Dr. Gray, British Museum, and Professor Frankland. Their ignorance of U.S. affairs astounding, and Dr. Gray's prejudice discreditable to him.

"[16th.] To various studios, to select artist for Reform Club bust of Cobden. Three only are possible—Mr. Noble's, Marshall Wood's, and Mr. Burnard's.[1]

"[18th.] Dined with Mr. Tite, M.P., in Lowndes Square. Saw there 2 pictures for which he has just given 4,000 guineas! One by David Roberts (interior of cathedral at Vienna), the other a sea or harbour piece by Stansfield.

"[28th.] Saw Mr. Brown about new Atlantic Telegraph, but cannot undertake to join any public company.

"[29th.] Read my brother Jacob's address to the electors of Manchester.

"[30th.] With Lord Stanley to National Portrait Gallery in Great George Street, and then to Hanover Street to see Fagnani's portrait of Mr. Cobden, which he liked very much, and thought the Gallery must have it."

[1] Noble's bust was eventually commissioned by the Club. N. N. Burnard had, however, modelled one which was much admired. Bright went with Fagnani to see it a few days after.

CHAPTER XII
THE TRIUMPH OF REFORM

I

IN the month of July, 1865, the Parliament of 1859 was dissolved and a new one elected with an increased Whig and Liberal majority of 50. Palmerston thus found himself at the head of a Government ostensibly stronger than before. But only ostensibly. Events soon uncovered its weakness.

The elections, fought in the main on Reform, had powerfully reinforced the Radical wing of the party. Bright loomed larger than ever in the hopes of the "masses" and the fears of the "classes." Then in October the death of Palmerston took the heaviest brake off the wheel of Reform. It did not immediately come full circle. But, with Russell as Prime Minister and Gladstone leading the House of Commons, the way slowly opened out for advance to the final struggles and the crowning achievements of Bright's career. They came within the next three years. The householder was enfranchised. Ireland was emancipated from the trammels of the State Church.

Bright's journals of the eighteen months from June, 1865, are missing, if even he kept journals in the midst of the heroic and continuous labours, first of a heated Parliamentary session and then of the great campaign in the country which was the prelude to the Reform Act of 1867. It was the period of the "Cave of Adullam" speech, and the defeat of Gladstone's modest Reform scheme (after he had resoundingly "passed the Rubicon, broken the bridge and burned the boats") by the Adullamites in combination with the Opposition; of the resignation of Russell and the accession of Lord Derby's third Ministry, still in a minority; of the riots in Hyde Park and the vast demonstrations addressed by Bright in many cities; of his memorable visit to Ireland and the speech in the Rotunda at Dublin; and finally of the adoption by a Liberal House of Commons of a more radical measure at the bidding of Disraeli than it had refused to Gladstone twelve months before.

Through all these months of ceaseless activities and wild excitements, Bright became more emphatically than ever the Tribune of the People and the bugbear of the upper classes. When he took up the diary again on the first day of the session of 1867, the world was awaiting the imminent revelation of the Derby Government's intentions about Reform.

"[*February* 5, 1867.] House, 4 o'clock. Tory Government 'all in a row' on the Treasury Bench. The Party puzzled at its position on Reform question. Gladstone spoke with dignity and discretion; Disraeli excited and nervous. Monday next will disclose schemes of the Tory leaders on Reform.

"This morning ordered a coat below stairs,[1] and had a curious conversation with Mr. Price, Mr. Bowater's foreman. Mr. Price is a believer in some sort of divination or astrology, and studies the 'crystals.' He said to me: 'This is the last time the Queen will open Parliament, she will die about next February. Lord Russell and Lord Derby will go about December. Lord Derby will have a terrible illness. The Prince of Wales will be in great trouble about some woman about the month of June.' I looked surprised, and said, 'Do you believe all this?'

"He said, 'Oh yes, I have seen it all. I foretold the loss of the *London* and many other things. It will all come as you will see.'

"He then proposed that I should see his 'crystals,' and mentioned several persons who had seen strange things in them. Perhaps I shall see them some day, for it is curious to ascertain why such things should be believed.

"Heard this evening that my old and dear friend W. Hargreaves is very seriously ill.

"[*6th.*] Albert called this morning: pleasant talk about his college studies.[2]

"[*7th.*] Mr. Brown, of Canada, called to talk over the 'Confederation scheme.' To the City to see Mr. Morley[3] on subscription for Mr. Beales. A noble fellow is Morley. To 'East London Railway' office for some information as to whether our money will be thrown away.

[1] It will be remembered that he lodged above Mr. Bowater's tailor's shop in Hanover Street.

[2] There are many references in the diaries to his meetings with his sons. John Albert Bright became M.P. for Central Birmingham at the death of his father, and later M.P. for Oldham.

[3] Samuel Morley, the famous M.P. for Bristol, father of Arnold Morley and Charles Morley. Mr. Edmund Beales was president of the Reform League.

Back by train from Cannon St. to Charing Cross—a grand improvement for the traffic from the City to the West End. Evening at home. Albert came in for 2 hours very pleasantly. I enjoy his visits very much.

"To *Star* office: talk about Jamaica prosecutions with Mr. Gorrie and Chesson.[1] Received note warning me of plot to assassinate me on Tuesday next! My letters contain many that are curious, and some that are insulting and offensive.

"[9*th*.] Mr. Howe, of Nova Scotia, called: long talk on 'Confederation scheme.' Mr. Howe against it for his Colony.

"[11*th*.] With deputation of Reform League to see Mr. Gladstone to present an address to him. Evening: House. Disraeli's speech on his Reform Resolutions.[2] Speech very bad in every respect; much unfavourable comment, and nothing satisfactory as to Reform.

"[12*th*.] Dr. Tupper, Prime Minister of Nova Scotia, called. An hour's talk on 'Confederation scheme.' He is in favour of it. Mr. Wilkinson, American inventor of printing machine, called.

"To Mr. Burnard, to see his model of my bust for Mr. Seely; considered good.[3]

"House: nothing new: general opinion much against Government resolutions on Reform. A meeting of the Liberal Party intended for next week to determine course when resolutions moved on the 25th.

"[21*st*.] T. A. Readwin called, and I signed the transfer of all my shares in the Carn Dochan Gold Mine, in which we have lost a large sum and gained some experience.

"[25*th*.] House. Disraeli explained Tory Reform, a wretched proposition. I spoke against it. The whole discussion greatly injurious to the Administration.

"[26*th*.] Meeting of Liberal members at Mr. Gladstone's house: very large, and Party more united than for a year past. I spoke briefly,

[1] The prosecution of Governor Eyre and his subordinates for atrocities committed after the suppression of disturbances in Jamaica.

[2] The Resolutions, a feeble feeler by Disraeli, appeared to be designed to discover how little Reform the House would stand. Divisions in the Cabinet accounted for their manifest futility.

[3] Neville Northy Burnard, the self-taught artist, son of a stonemason at Altarnon in the wild Cornish moors, was in 1867 at the height of his fame and prosperity as a sculptor. He had made portrait busts of Gladstone, Cobden, Thackeray, Mrs. Beecher Stowe and J. B. Smith, and he had carved the statue of Ebenezer Elliot placed in the Market Square of Sheffield. Later in the year he did for Bright a model of Cobden's right hand. Not long after this, Burnard took to drink, deserted his art, became a tramp, and was lost to the view of London. He died in Redruth Workhouse, and had a pauper's funeral in Camborne churchyard.

urging more active policy against the Government and its sham Reform measures.

"House: Disraeli withdrew 'Resolutions.' I spoke, urging the proceeding with the Franchise Bill by itself.

"[27*th*.] House: voted for Bill to allow Lord-Lieutenant and Lord Chancellor of Ireland to be of the Roman Catholic Church.

"Evening, dined with J. B. Smith, and had an interesting conversation with Alderman Salomans, M.P., on condition and prospects of the Jewish persuasion—much modified of late years, and hostility to Christianity much diminished.

"[28*th*.] House: Canada 'Confederation Bill.' Spoke briefly on the haste with which the Bill is being pushed forward, and on the folly of forming a Senate by appointment of life members.[1]

"[*March* 1.] House: position very curious. Tory Party in chaos. Cabinet divided. Party divided, its members speaking openly of the anarchy that prevails.

"Conversation with Disraeli in the Lobby. Asked him what was to be done, and could he do it? He said he 'would do it if he could; was doing all he could.' I said, 'You ought to have taken me into your counsels.' He said, 'I offered you that in 1852, you remember.' I said, 'Yes, but I do not mean officially.' He said, 'The Whigs have only betrayed you: I told you they would do nothing for you.' I replied, 'I want nothing. I am satisfied with my position, and office would be intolerable to me.' He said, 'Well, I have had enough of it. I have had 30 years, and 20 years as leader of a party. I am sick of it, and if I can get this thing done, then I shall (or can) go away.'

"I told him of a conversation with three of his party in the smoking-room—how far they were willing to go, and that, at the pace they were moving, I should soon have to hold them back. He thought they were fair specimens of a considerable section of the party. I advised him to advance his offers so far in regard to the suffrage that he would not be

[1] This Bill, introduced by Lord Carnarvon in the House of Lords, was a legacy from the Liberal Government. The objections of Nova Scotia, which had been exercising Bright, were overcome. British Columbia, as well as Newfoundland and Prince Edward Island, stood out, but all the provinces save Newfoundland came into the Confederation later. Bright, like many other men of his time, thought the ultimate destiny of Canada might be union with the United States, and he objected to the guarantee of three millions for railway development which was part of the scheme. But he concluded by expressing the desire that the Canadian people should do whatever they thought best for their own interests, and his ardent wish for their greatness and welfare.

driven to accept defeat on every proposition—that £5 rating franchise, or household suffrage, would save him in the boroughs, and that £10 or £12 would do for the counties.

"He said he did not care much for the counties: the Working Class Question was the real question, and that was the thing that demanded to be settled. He had once proposed a £10 franchise for the counties. He said, 'You will attack me whatever I propose.' I said, 'No, I will not; I will do all I can fairly to help a Bill through, if you will do the right thing. I am against faction, and if our leaders do as you did last year I shall openly denounce them.' I told him that people said he and I always fought with gloves on, but sometimes I had been tempted to take them off. He said, 'there had always been something of sympathy between us,' which I suppose is true—tho' our course and aims have seemed so different.

"I spoke to him about passing only a 'Franchise Bill' as the only thing possible for the session—and urged it strongly upon him to give up the 'Distribution of Seats' portion of the measure, should we ever reach it. He made no reply, but the argument on that point may affect his opinion, and I hope may induce further consideration of it.

"As we were talking, Mr. Brand,[1] the Opposition 'Whip,' went by, and Disraeli said, 'He will think it is a Coalition'—that he and I should be seen in conversation at such a crisis as this.

"At parting, he pressed my hand with an apparent earnestness of feeling, saying, 'Well, whatever happens, you and I will always be friends.'

"Disraeli has been possessed by a devouring ambition—not to preach and act the truth, but to distinguish himself. 'We come here for fame!' he said to me many years ago. And he has distinguished himself, but on a low field, and with no results which can be looked back upon with satisfaction.

"[*2nd.*] Dined with Mr. Bunsen, Abbey Lodge. After dinner, Hepworth Dixon came in: talk on America. Said President's 'confidential adviser' was the notorious Mr. Wikoff, once employed to write up Palmerston in European journals. He told me I was the most popular man in the United States!

"[*3rd.*] Westminster Meeting: J. H. Douglas, from U.S., there. A striking sermon from him, parts of it very fine and very touching. I was moved by his fervour. There is a mingling of intellect and devotion which is remarkable in him.

[1] Mr. H. W. B. Brand, afterwards Speaker of the House of Commons, elevated to the Peerage as Viscount Hampden.

"Derby Government in a crisis. General Peel, Lords Cranborne and Carnarvon resigned: object to Reform as urged by Disraeli. Excitement in political circles. I seem to feel it less than others, but am deeply concerned in the evident progress the Reform question is making.

"[4th.] House: Ministerial crisis. Three Secretaries of State resigned: places easily filled up, and Government will attempt to go on. Derby and Disraeli intend to propose and carry a Reform Bill. Great interest excited: wonderful conversions to Household Suffrage on every side. I begin to be an authority with the Tory Party! What next?

"[5th.] Dined with P. A. Taylor at Aubrey House, Notting Hill; met there, with others, Professor Fawcett, M.P., and Miss Cobbe.[1] Conversation on Women's Franchise, which I do not much favour. Miss Cobbe a very intelligent woman, with good sympathies.

"News of Fenian rising in Ireland—how disgraceful to the Imperial Government!

"[8th.] House: spoke briefly in discussion as to whether the Volunteers could be called out to suppress riots and internal tumult. The law is clearly against it, but the Government gives no decided opinion. Much gossip but no news as to future of Government or their promised Bill.

"[12th.] Heard this morning of the death on the 10th of my old friend and neighbour, Henry King,[2] after a long illness. He has led an innocent and, up to his powers, a useful life—and has been a kind and generous man.

"This morning I have sent a Memorandum on the Reform question to Mr. Disraeli to point out what seems to me to be the duty of the Government in the present crisis.[3]

"[18th.] House. Reform Bill a failure; the debate much against the Government. I did not speak: not well, and head not clear.

---

[1] Frances Power Cobbe.

[2] The father of the companion of his youth in the tour of the Near East.

[3] Mr. Trevelyan prints this Memorandum in full ("Life of John Bright," pp. 381–2). The chief points in Bright's suggestions were: household suffrage *sans phrase* in the boroughs ("the oldest and wisest basis"); failing that, a rental franchise of £6 or a rating franchise of £5; for the counties a £10 or £12 occupation franchise; for London a lodger franchise. "A Bill framed as above sketched would pass without difficulty. . . . These suggestions are made with an honest purpose—to assist in the settlement of a great question—and with no hostile feeling to the existing administration." They did, in fact, provide the distinctive features of the Bill which Disraeli ultimately passed.

"[19*th*.] Called on Mr. Gladstone to discuss course to be taken on Government Bill. He strong in condemnation of Bill, and wishful to oppose the 2nd reading. There were 25 or 30 of the Tory Party at least who would oppose Bill. I agree with him as to the proper course, but doubt if our side will take it. Much jealousy; some fear of dissolution, however absurd this may be, and much ignorance of Parliamentary tactics.

"House: saw Mr. Walpole on Factories Bill, and on case of a wretched man (Wager) under sentence of death at Derby.

"[20*th*.] Called on Lord Russell: talk about Reform and the position of affairs in the House. He looks old and is slightly deaf, but not feeble.

"House: in majority against Church Rates.

"Dined with Lord and Lady Hobart. Found there Duke and Duchess of Argyll, Lord Strangford, Dean Stanley and his wife, Mr. Browning, the poet, and Mr. Auberon Herbert. After dinner others came in: the evening very pleasant.

"[21*st*.] Home Office with deputation to Mr. Walpole, to obtain respite for convict at Derby.

"Meeting at Mr. Gladstone's (Liberal Party). Agreed not to oppose 2nd reading of Government Bill owing to differences of opinion in the party.

"I consented to the policy adopted, tho' expressing my entire dissent from it.

"Evening, to Lord Russell's for an hour or more. Only their own family there, with Arthur Russell, and a lady visitor. Pleasant evening: Lord Russell cheerful and disposed to anecdote.

"[22*nd*.] Sentence on Wager at Derby is commuted. Sent the news by telegraph to his father at Hassop, Derbyshire.

"[26*th*.] Reform debate: excellent speech from Sir Roundell Palmer. I spoke at length, and to the satisfaction of our friends. Disraeli followed, amusing but not statesmanlike: disposed to surrender much. The critical time will come on motion to go into Committee."

2

After many hesitations, the Opposition allowed the Bill a second reading without a division. Disraeli had adopted the principle of Household Suffrage, but spoilt the simplicity of the plan with illiberal reservations and restrictions (excluding the compound householders and all lodgers) and with "fancy franchises" for education and wealth.

The task of the Radicals in Committee was to shear away all these excrescences, and they performed it with exemplary success.

"[*March* 28.] In Regent St. met Mr. Gladstone and Sir W. Heathcote. Shortly after, Mr. Gladstone overtook us and told me he had come out to call upon me. I said I was going to call upon him, and would call in half an hour, which I did. Long conversation on course to be taken on the Reform Bill. He purposed to move resolutions (on motion that 'the Speaker do leave the Chair') to fix the franchise in boroughs which the House would agree to. Thought £5 rating the point which would meet the views of a large majority of the House, to which I assented as probably the best thing that could be carried, and as much better than Bill of the Government as it stands, or as the House will accept it.

"Spoke of Disraeli and his severance from his party, and of his personal character and qualities, and said, 'I do not despair of meeting you some day at Hughenden Manor'—Disraeli's house in Buckinghamshire.

"A meeting of the Party to be called this day week, when resolutions to be submitted to them.

"House: voted against Flogging in the Army. Came up home feeling that I had taken cold, and suffering from soreness of the chest.

"[29*th*.] Not well this morning. Have a cold. Mr. Rogers, from Oxford, called. Long talk on the exclusion from Parliament of 'persons in holy orders.' He told me that on the repeal of the Corn Law, Disraeli wrote to Sir Robert Peel offering to go with him in all his political objects, to which Peel wrote a contemptuous answer.

"[30*th*.] Dined with Vaughan. Met there the Dean of Cork; intelligent and liberal. Conversation on Ireland and Irish Church, and afterwards on Mr. Trench, 'revivalist,' and 'assurance of faith.'

"[31*st*.] Slept badly, coughing much—from too much talking last night, probably. . . . Read *Paradise Regained* this morning with renewed and increasing pleasure.

"[*April* 2.] Mr. Gladstone called to discuss proposed resolution before going into Committee,—an 'Instruction' to the Committee. His activity and acuteness and earnestness are remarkable.

"[5*th*.] Meeting at Mr. Gladstone's: satisfactory. Agreed on 'Instruction' to be moved on going into Committee on Reform Bill.

"[6*th*.] Miss Heptinstall called: wished me to sit for half an hour that she might correct a small bust she is making of me. I could not well refuse her, as she may be making something by it.

"[7th.] Notes for speech on Bill. Late in the evening, called on Mr. Gladstone on the subject of expected conflict in the House to-morrow.

"[8th.] Called on W. E. Forster, M.P., 80, Eccleston Square, and discussed with him our position on the Reform question.

"House: expected debate abandoned. Some malcontents on our side met this afternoon; conspired to defeat measures of Mr. Gladstone; urged him to withdraw 'Instruction' to the Committee, to which he consented. They have done their utmost to humiliate him and the Liberal Party.[1] The Bill went into Committee; and Disraeli in great spirits at the failure of the effort which was to have been made against him.

"The corruption of the House is something extraordinary. Men fear a dissolution and will descend to any meanness to escape it. They are destroying the unity and power of the Liberal Party, and are making its leader an object of commiseration.[2] They are more willing to express want of confidence in Mr. Gladstone than in Disraeli!

"Great panic in the City to-day from talk and fear of War between France and Germany,[3] and between England and Spain.

"[9th.] Call from W. E. Forster on Reform Bill. From Brigham Young, Junr., and Mr. Richards, from Salt Lake. The former is the son of the Mormon chief—a plain, quiet, and sensible person. Mr. Richards an intelligent and well informed man. They called on me, as one well known in the States, and to converse about their position in America, and because they were trying to do good, and to find a home for multitudes of poor people from every country who were disposed to settle among them.[4] Whilst they were here, Mr. Dudley, U.S. Consul at Liverpool, called.

[1] This was the "Tea Room Party." It refused to vote for the restrictive part of the Instruction (to amend the law of rating by relieving small occupiers from liability to rates, and so fix a minimum qualification for household suffrage) which kept out what Bright in an unfortunate moment had called the "residuum"—"a small class" which would be better unfranchised "because they have no independence whatever. . . . There is no class so much interested in having that small class excluded as the intelligent working men."

[2] The internal acrimonies and animosities of the Liberal Party were notorious. Lord Halifax (the Sir Charles Wood of Palmerston's Government) said he had "never seen anything like it."

[3] On the Luxemburg question.

[4] The Mormon Community had just settled down to steady progress under Federal authority after the conflicts of the 'fifties. Brigham Young, junior, Bright's visitor, subsequently seceded from the Church with a large number of other anti-polygamists.

"[10*th*.] Much discussion going on as to Mr. Gladstone's amendments on Reform Bill. Mr. Gladstone spoke to me in the Lobby. He is evidently much annoyed at the distraction in the Party, and thought I was ill used by some of our Radical members, whose course is certainly neither wise nor generous.

"[11*th*.] House: debate on Amendment to the Reform Bill. A good deal of excitement, the question being critical. The Amendment is one rejecting the 'personal payment of rates' as purposed by the Government, and establishing equality among all classes of voters.

"Walked up with Sir Roundell Palmer. He is the very first in the first rank of lawyers in this country, and will probably soon be Lord Chancellor.[1]

"[13*th*.] Division last night: majority 21 for Government. I spoke in the debate. We are destroyed by deserters from our Party, some honest and misled, some far from honest.[2]

"[22*nd*.] To Birmingham: dear Elizabeth with me. Great meeting in the Town Hall; spoke an hour and a half; voice unusually good.[3] Queen's Hotel for the night. Mary Priestman there also.[4]

"[*May* 2.] Debate on 'residence' clause in Reform Bill: two years or one year. Government defeated by large majority. Conversation

[1] Roundell Palmer was offered the Woolsack in 1868, when Gladstone took office. He declined the office because of his objections to the Irish Church proposals. In 1872, however, on Lord Hatherley's retirement, he took the Great Seal and became Earl of Selborne.

[2] The division was on an amendment by Gladstone to remove the obligation of the personal payment of rates as an essential qualification for the franchise and to give the vote to the householder whether he paid the rate direct or through the landlord. Figures:—For the amendment, 289; against, 310. Twenty Liberals had abstained and 43 had voted with the Government. Gladstone thought seriously of retiring from the leadership of the Party in consequence of this blow to his authority. Disraeli, who was in great form, made in this debate his adroit use of an exquisite irony of Erasmus. Retorting upon Mr. Beresford Hope, one of his followers who had said he should vote against the "Asian Mystery," he said: "When he talks about an Asian Mystery, I will tell him that there are Batavian graces in all that he says, which I notice with satisfaction and which charm me."

[3] This speech included his often-quoted tribute to Gladstone: "Who equals him in earnestness? Who equals him in eloquence? Who equals him in courage and fidelity to his convictions? If these gentlemen who say they will not follow him have anyone who is equal, let them show him. If they can point out any statesman who can add dignity and grandeur to the stature of Mr. Gladstone, let them produce him!"

[4] Bright's sister-in-law.

with Mr. Gladstone. He is in good spirits, and does not abandon the contest with the Government.[1] Conversation with Mr. Walpole on Hyde Park Meeting and Reform League. He is always kind and moderate.[2]

"[3rd.] House: Presented Petition from Mr. Congreve, and others of his 'Comtist' views, in favour of mercy to Fenian convicts. Some foolish members interrupted me, and were put down by the Speaker. Spoke on Hyde Park Meeting with much ease and freedom. Debate on same subject. Government weak and foolish, daring neither to consent nor to oppose.

"[4th.] Called on Burnard, the sculptor, and paid him £10, being the balance I owed him for the completion of the marble hand of my lost friend. It is from the cast taken of the right hand immediately after death.

"[5th.] To Brunswick Hotel, Jermyn St., to meet Mr. Senator Sherman, of Ohio, and Mr. Kasson, of Iowa, with Mr. Dudley, U.S. Consul at Liverpool. Good specimens of American public men. Mr. Sherman's eye and manner denote a superior man, qualified to advise his countrymen.[3]

"The conversation turned first on our Reform question, and then on U.S. finance and tariff.

"[6th.] House: Reform Bill Committee; not much progress made. Government fresh tricks to induce Liberals to support them. (Temperature to-day 84 degrees.)

[1] Gladstone had recovered from the shock of the "Tea Room" movement, and on the resumption of the debate after the Easter Recess the reformers were in better heart. Mr. Ayrton's amendment to reduce the residence period for qualification to one year, to which Bright alludes, was carried by 81 votes, and the Government gave way.

[2] The sequel to the disturbances of the previous year. The Reform League had announced a Hyde Park meeting, and Walpole issued a warning to the public not to attend. It was, however, held (by Lord Derby's instructions) without interference. Colonel Dickson addressed two hundred thousand people in the Park as "My friends and fellow-trespassers." The trespassers did no damage whatever. Walpole resigned the Home Office: a sorry result of the mismanaged episode.

[3] Senator John Sherman (brother of General Sherman, the hero of the famous march to the sea), one of the most eminent statesmen and financiers of the nineteenth century. At the time of his visit to Bright he was a member of the Senate Committee on Finance, and shortly after became its chairman. His influence carried the Legal Tender Act and the substitution of a National for a State banking system. Sherman, active in politics to the very end of the century, was McKinley's first Secretary of State. Age and the pressure of the office during the Spanish war compelled him to resign in 1898 after one year of office. He died in 1900.

"Great meeting in Hyde Park perfectly peaceful; Government in discredit and humiliated by their foolish conduct on this question.

"[*7th.*] Called on Mr. Gladstone on proposition to move Clause to admit occupiers of 'clear yearly value' of £5 to franchise in boroughs where compounding for rates is in practice.

"[*8th.*] Mr. Oliphant called. Long conversation on his change of views and life, and on Mr. Harris, American Spiritualist. Very curious and interesting.[1]

"Evening dined with Lord Russell; pleasant conversation with Lord Dufferin on Irish affairs.

"[*9th.*] House: Reform Bill, Mr. Hibbert's amendment. Spoke against inequality and injustice of the Bill. Majority 66 against us, so many men on our side deserting their party and their principles. Home very late, and much disturbed at the course taken by so many of my friends.

"[*10th.*] J. B. Smith spoke to me about his vote the previous evening. I asked him not to talk about it. I would give him my opinion of it, and say no more: 'It was the most entirely wrong and the most disgraceful vote which had been given by any Liberal member within my Parliamentary recollection.'

"He said how satisfied he was with it. I answered, 'Then we may say no more about it.'

"Called at the *Star* office. Home early: read newspapers, and closed with Milton, who seems to take me for the time above the troubles of this world and the meanness of common men.

"[*11th.*] Call from Mr. Evans; his friendly talk and intention quite pleasant amid the disappointments now pressing upon me. To Mr. Gladstone's with a numerous deputation from the North, to present addresses, etc. Speeches good, and so also Mr. Gladstone's reply. I spoke shortly before the conclusion of the meeting.

"Evening: dined with Duke of Argyll. A very pleasant party: Dr. Blackie, of Edinbro'; Dr. McCosh, of Belfast; W. V. Harcourt, Lord and Lady Amberley, and some others there. The family very pleasant.

---

[1] The brilliant and witty Laurence Oliphant had been elected for Stirling Burghs in 1865. About this time he fell under the influence of Thomas Lake Harris, the head of the Spiritualist community at Brocton, Lake Erie. Within a few months he had thrown up Parliamentary life and joined Harris at Brocton, submitting to him as a spiritual guide and living the material life of a farm labourer. He remained under this queer domination more or less until 1881. Bright was invariably curious about the doctrines and claims of Spiritualists.

Duchess evidently a charming and good woman. Harcourt said, 'She is a kind of angel, so good and pure.'

"Walked home with Harcourt. Speaking of Mr. Lowe, he said Lowe told him that Disraeli told him last year that if he came into office, he pledged himself as a man of honour that he would not consent to any reduction of the Borough franchise. His treachery in this makes Lowe very vicious against him.

"[12th.] Met Thomas Johnson, of Manchester, who went with me to Westminster Meeting. He told me he had bought Turner's picture called 'Modern Italy' yesterday for a friend of his in Lancashire for 3,300 guineas!

"To dinner with Laurence Oliphant, M.P., near Clarence Gate. Met five young men from Japan, students here, and passed a most pleasant evening with them. They are robust, and very intelligent, scarcely so tall as Englishmen, but strong in build, and with heads of more than average breadth and power. They have the 'eastern' eyes, rather high cheek-bones, and are slightly dark complexioned, tho' one of them is lighter than many Englishmen, and the hands of one of them are quite as white as is common here. Two of them have been in America with Mr. Oliphant, and they gave me an account of a curious change which came over them there. They seem to have had no religion before, except that one said he prayed to the spirits of their dead Mikados, but his faith in them had faded away during his stay in England. They thought Christianity was one of the superstitions of the world, useful perhaps in England, but no more true than other superstitions. Whilst in America they saw Mr. Harris, a remarkable man, a Spiritualist of the Swedenborg School. He preached to them and to a few of his friends in a private room. They were strangely moved: one of them shed tears from the effect produced upon him. He sat between them, grasping the hand of each of them. The one who had not cried felt his right arm tremble, and for many weeks it was affected by a nervous trembling which he could not explain.

"When away from Mr. Harris, on a visit to Canada, they could think of nothing but him, and what he had said to them. They call him not Mr. Harris, but 'Faithful,' and seem to regard him as their deliverer from their ancient state of ignorance and darkness. They now pray to God, read the Bible, and feel themselves drawn near to Christ,—have, as they believe, a constant sense of what is right or wrong for them to do. They are what, in the language of the high Spiritualist school, is called 'open,' and are in a sense 'mediumistic' and are affected strongly by the 'states' or 'conditions' of those about them. In a Roman Catholic Church in New York, they were strangely affected by the superstitious practices they saw, and were so disturbed by them, that they were obliged to leave the place. One of their party is just gone back to Japan, under an urgent impression that it was his duty to go.

"I asked if they would be likely to meet with difficulty or persecution in Japan. They thought not, but they were ready to die, if need be, for their new faith and for Christ.

"Before dinner they sat in silence for two or three minutes, after the manner of 'Friends,' and with a most devout aspect: this is their usual custom. Two of them explained all this to me with great modesty and seriousness, and told me how much happier they had been since their acquaintance with Mr. Harris.

"Their countenances, as they related all this to me, were most intelligent and pleasing, and one of them had a look of goodness and beauty that was most striking.

"This theory of theirs, and of Mr. Harris, is founded on a belief that it is possible for Christ, in His spirit, to take possession of the soul, and to become almost physically incorporate with man. They feel some change in their 'breathing,' as if He filled their lungs, and they have at times a certain fluttering or trembling of the heart, as if their whole system were touched by the influence of His presence in them.

"We talked of 'Friends' and their views, and I explained them briefly, referring to the idea of the 'inner light,' and of the direct communion between the spirit and the human soul.

"These young gentlemen are gentlemen in manner, and in conduct and thought, and would bear themselves becomingly in any English society. Mr. Harris's idea is that the Japanese are a very sensitive and 'receptive' race, and that they may probably receive the new religion with ease and fervour. Mr. Oliphant says they are a charming people, and their country and its climate not surpassed by any other in the world.[1]

"We spent a most interesting and pleasant evening, not without instruction I hope, altho' it was not easy to comprehend the true nature of the change these young strangers have undergone.

"I walked home in the cool night air, and read Milton's War in Heaven in *Paradise Lost* before going to bed.

"[13th.] Received a very kind and interesting letter from my dear Helen this morning.[2] She condoles with me on the defection of my

[1] Oliphant had been appointed First Secretary of Legation in Japan in 1861.
[2] His daughter, Mrs. W. S. Clark, of Street, Somerset.

friends in the House, and asks me if I should be pleased at the prospect of having a little grandchild?

"[*15th.*] Professor Rushton, Cork College, called, to ask me as to studies and qualities and training requisite to form an Orator! An earnest man, anxious to render himself more capable of teaching.

"Evening: St. James's Hall, great meeting on Reform. Samuel Morley in the chair. W. V. Harcourt spoke: heard him for the first time.

"[*28th.*] Norton Edwards called to model bust of me, for Staffordshire Parian Bust. To Devonshire House meeting: spoke on the abolition of slavery in Brazil.

"House: Reform Bill. Spoke against restrictions on franchise granted in the Bill, and showed that the Bill adopted the precise franchise I recommended in 1858/59.[1]

"[*29th.*] Evening, dined with Mr. Gladstone. Large party: Bishop of Oxford, Lords Granville, Spencer, Cowper, Dean Stanley and some ladies present.

"More company after dinner, among them Lady Stanley of Alderley, Lord and Lady Airlie—her train troublesomely long. It is strange that women of sense should run into extremes of fashion. Mr. Gladstone's drawing-room has many pictures and proofs of the taste and refinement of its owner. Spoke to Auberon Herbert about his change from the Tory to the Liberal Party. He found he could no longer honestly become the candidate of a Conservative Party in a constituency. He is Lord Carnarvon's brother, and takes a different view of politics from his brother. The Bishop pleasant and talkative. He thought the dealing with the Irish Church could only be *to destroy* it: there was no middle course. He asked me as to my preparation of speeches, as to notes, illustrations, quotations and 'perorations,' etc. Spoke of Brougham's writing out his best passages.

"Mrs. Gladstone a pleasant kindly woman. The children take more of her than of Mr. G. and will not be likely to have the wonderful intellect of their father.

"[*June 2.*] To Westminster Meeting. Eli and Sybil Jones from

[1] Lord Cranborne said the Bill in its final shape, after countless transformations, was "the result of the adoption of the principles of Bright at the dictation of Gladstone." Bright's scheme of household and lodger franchise in the boroughs and a £10 franchise in the counties was expounded in his speech to his constituents at Birmingham in October, 1858, and incorporated in the Bill which he drafted for the following session.

U.S. there. *She* spoke beautifully. She is as full of beauty and poetry and goodness as ever, and her address was most touching. *He*, solid and practical and very earnest. The meeting a memorable one.

"Evening, dined with Mr. Adams, U.S. Minister; small and pleasant party. Mr. Kasson, from Iowa, there. He is arranging postal treaty with our Government and is an intelligent and agreeable man.

"[4th.] Call from Dr. Payne, coloured Bishop, from Wilberforce College, U.S., with letter from Theodore Solist, once tutor at Heath.[1]

"Call from Mr. Peabody, on proposed visit to him at Castle Connell on the Shannon. Agreed to go there on Saturday next, nothing unforeseen preventing. A fine looking old man, and happy in the review of his great generosity in the bestowal of his great wealth.

"[17th.] House: Reform Bill. Division *against* additional members to largest cities. Many so-called Liberals opposed us, to their great discredit.

"Walked up thro' the Park at midnight with Mr. Gladstone. Spoke of the reckless and unwise character of the House. Since Russian War, he thought the tone of the House greatly changed for the worse. In Sir Robert Peel's time a more just and even liberal spirit prevailed.

"[18th.] Mr. Chesson called about proposed breakfast to Wm. Lloyd Garrison, the noble American Abolitionist. House at 2 o'clock. Debate on Union of Durham University with London University to return Member to Parliament. Spoke against Union. Government defeated and proposition rejected.

"[19th.] House: Lord Amberley's Sunday Lectures Bill; spoke briefly upon it. Evening: University College Soirée: large and pleasant company. Spoke to several of the professors—Hirst, Foster, Williamson, etc. Saw Seeley, reputed author of 'Ecce Homo,' a book which has made some sensation lately.[2]

"House: 'Voting Papers' Clause discussed and rejected. I spoke last in the debate—my voice good.[3]

[1] His wife's home near Wakefield.

[2] "Ecce Homo" had been published in 1866, anonymously. Seeley owned his authorship not long after.

[3] The "Voting Papers" clause, which the House rejected by a majority of 38, anticipated the conditions of the modern provision for absent voters, but without any stipulation for the ballot. Bright's admirable speech was a powerful argument for the ballot. He pointed out that the system proposed would lend itself to dangerous fraud. "Either let us have the open voting which we have, and which we all understand, and which we have had from time immemorial, so that we understand the good

"[*23rd.*] Evening to Mr. Hughes (Tom Brown) to *cold* Sunday dinner: a very pleasant evening. Colonel Bonamy and Auberon Herbert there. Hughes and Herbert walked home with me, and conversation here till ½ past 12 on politics, laws of primogeniture, and condition of people.

"[*29th.*] Breakfast, St. James's Hall, to Wm. Lloyd Garrison, American Abolitionist. A remarkable meeting: 300 to 400 present, beside many hundreds in galleries. The Duke of Argyll, Lord Russell, and many other influential persons present.[1]

"[*July* 1.] House: spoke on clause to give additional Member to Liverpool, Manchester, Birmingham and Leeds, to which Government and House agreed.[2]

"[*2nd.*] Dined with Lord Houghton, 16, Upper Brook St : Lord Halifax, Mr. Gladstone, Julian Fane, Mr. Ritson, Frederick Harrison, Mr. Winthrop, U.S., Mr. Monteith. Heat of weather destroyed my pleasure during the evening.

"[*4th.*] Mr. Coningsby called to ask me to indorse Mr. Whiteing, 'costermonger,' as a candidate for a seat in Parliament under the new Bill. Long conversation with him on politics and on 'working class' notions and feelings.

"[*5th.*] Breakfasted with Sir H. Holland. Talk on instinct or reason of dogs from watching a Scotch terrier: intelligent and amusing.

"Goldwin Smith called. Conversation on doubts as to New Testament history: his doubts as to miracles,—but none as to the spirituality and truth of Christianity.

and evil of it, or let us go to that more excellent way of polling by the ballot. At least do not let us make a change the results of which would in my opinion lead to very great danger in the corrupt exercise of the franchise."

[1] Bright presided over this famous meeting and spoke at his best. He had the history of the Abolitionist movement at his finger-tips, was well read in Lloyd Garrison's great career, and knew the labours of all "the heroic band who have made America the perpetual home of freedom." He did homage to the generosity of the conquerors in the war: "An ancient and renowned poet has said—

'Unholy is the voice
Of loud thanksgiving over slaughtered men.'

It becomes us not to rejoice but to be humbled that a chastisement so terrible should have fallen on any of our race; but we may be thankful for this—that this chastisement was at least not sent in vain. The great triumph in the field was not all; there came after it another great triumph—a triumph over passion, and there came up before the world the spectacle not of armies and military commanders, but of the magnanimity and mercy of a powerful and victorious nation."

[2] The four great cities had to be content with the meagre representation of three members each until the Redistribution Act of 1885.

"[15*th*.] House: 3rd reading of Reform Bill. Spoke briefly. Amusing recriminations between Lowe and Disraeli, and a severe speech from Lord Cranborne against Disraeli. Bill passed with cheers from our side."

3

The Bill in its final form was highly satisfactory to the Reformers. They got household franchise in the towns, lodger votes, one year qualification; copyhold franchise was reduced to £5; occupation franchise in the counties to £12; the "fancy franchises" were dropped, and so were the property franchise and the dual vote, and the compound householder. Gladstone and Bright had won all along the line. Lord Cranborne's remark has been already quoted; he added that Disraeli's policy was "a political betrayal which had no parallel in our annals." Disraeli had, in Lord Derby's words, "dished the Whigs;" Lord Derby himself spoke of the scheme as "a leap in the dark." If the prophets of woe who made the House of Lords ring with their cries in 1867 could revisit the glimpses of the moon in 1930 they would wish to re-say their speeches, and a resuscitated Carlyle would re-write "Shooting Niagara"— or burn it. The Bill passed through the Lords without substantial amendment. The one alteration adopted, on the suggestion of Lord Russell and proposed by Lord Cairns, was the provision relating to the three-membered cities referred to on pages 312 and 332.

"[*July* 16.] Attended the funeral of my poor friend and colleague Wm. Scholefield,[1] in the cemetery at Kensal Green. He died very suddenly on the 9th inst. His courtesy and kindness to me since I was first elected for Birmingham have been remarkable. He was a kind and honourable man, and I feel his loss much.

"[18*th*.] To Birmingham: dined at Mr. Rylands' with a few of our leading friends. Meeting in the Town Hall crowded beyond all comfort. My speech intended to keep constituency right in coming election consequent on the death of Mr. Scholefield.

"[19*th*.] No House this evening owing to Grand Ball to the Sultan at the India Office. I have declined invitations to glorify the Sultan, for I am opposed to the traditional policy of the Foreign Office which binds up English interests with maintenance of the Ottoman Empire.

"[22*nd*.] Call from Mr. Motley, U.S. Minister at Vienna. Also

[1] M.P. for Birmingham.

from Mrs. Scott, of Birmingham, whose son is under sentence of death at Warwick. I have very little hope of his life being saved.

"Good news of Birmingham Election: Mr. Dixon elected by a great majority over Sampson Lloyd.[1]

"[24*th*.] A call from Mr. Jules Schvarez, from Hungary, with a letter from Kossuth: a young man devoted to education and science. House: 3rd reading of 'Church Rate Abolition Bill.' To Mr. Burnard, sculptor, and sat for an hour to finish bust for Mr. Seely.

"Long conversation during the afternoon with Mr. Gladstone in the Lobby on future course. Ballot, Ireland, and Education question. Found him earnest, especially on Ireland, liberal on Education, and open to discuss the Ballot. He thinks the Irish question the most urgent.

"[25*th*.] Home Office to see Mr. Hardy on case of Scott, under sentence of death at Warwick. Presented Memorial to him.

"House: introduced Mr. Dixon, who took his seat. Mr. Stansfeld, who is Mr. Dixon's brother-in-law, walked up to the House with us.

"[27*th*.] To Shepperton, to see W. S. Lindsay: Mr. Caird with me, an old friend of Lindsay's. Found him well in health, apparently, but unable to walk from paralysis. His house and grounds beautiful.

"[28*th*.] At Shepperton. Lindsay read me some letters written by my lamented friend Mr. Cobden, one referring to my illness in 1856.[2]

"The day lovely. Caird and I walked over the farm, and in the afternoon we sat with Lindsay under his grand elm trees on the bank of the Thames, which here runs thro' his estate. We came back to London by the 4.40 train.

"I dined with Mr. Adams this evening. Met there Chancellor Zebrisky, an American lawyer, and his daughter, and Mr. Raymond, of the *New York Times* newspaper; also Mr. and Mrs. Kuhn, the daughter and son-in-law of Mr. Adams.

"Discussed Free Trade and 'reconstruction' late in the evening.

"[29*th*.] Called on Lord Russell to urge him not to support the 'cumulative' vote, or any interference with existing mode of voting for as

[1] George Dixon was a brother-in-law of James Stansfeld. Mr. Sampson Lloyd eventually won a seat at Plymouth in 1874.

[2] Cobden wrote to more than one friend during Bright's illness in 1856. Morley's "Life" quotes a letter to Joseph Parkes: "Perhaps there never were two men who lived in such transparent intimacy of mind as Bright and myself . . . Bright's loss, if permanent, is a public calamity. If you could take the opinion of the whole House, he would be pronounced by a large majority to combine more earnestness, courage, honesty and eloquence than any other man."

many candidates as there are members to be elected. He is confused in his notions on this subject, and has been reading a pamphlet by Jas. G. Marshall of Leeds, a curious source of guidance for a statesman! [1]

"Dined at 32, Upper Brook St. at Mr. Hamilton's, M.P. for Salisbury. Met there the Bishop of Oxford. The Bishop assailed Lord Russell with great severity, and has evidently a great contempt for him. Lord Russell is not a Churchman in the sense of the Bishop, and may not expect much mercy from him. House: discussion on Bill to prohibit meetings in the London parks. I spoke against the Bill."

Bright suspended his diary during the summer and autumn.

The Government had dealt wisely with the abortive Fenian plot at Chester and with the Irish risings in the spring. There were no hangings. The disappearance into penal servitude of Burke, the last of the Dublin prisoners, marked the ignominious end of the Fenian movement in Ireland.

Less wisdom was shown in the treatment of the three men convicted at Manchester in connexion with the shooting of Sergeant Brett. That they deserved to be hanged cannot be doubted. They were all young men engaged in a desperate political conspiracy, and knew that they carried their lives in their hands. But that it was unwise to hang them is equally beyond dispute. The Irish race all over the world canonized them as the "Manchester Martyrs." If Mr. Gathorne-Hardy, the Home Secretary, had yielded to the forcible arguments of expediency pressed upon him and sent them into the long obscurity of penal servitude, they would soon have been forgotten. As it was, the "Manchester Martyrs" added just one more ingredient to the hell-broth of Anglo-Irish relations. Bright's mind was full of this tragedy when he took up his diary in November.

"[*November* 21.] Home Office: talk with Mr. Hardy in favour of Fenian convicts at Manchester, without avail, I fear. Tories know little mercy; terror is their only specific.

"[*24th.*] The hanging of the 3 men at Manchester has caused some

[1] Lowe had moved in the House of Commons in favour of cumulative voting, i.e., allowing a voter in a two- or three-membered constituency to give all his votes for one candidate. Both Disraeli and Bright opposed it, but it was proposed again in the House of Lords, and again rejected. The Peers did, however, force into the Bill a clause to which Bright (joined in this instance by both Gladstone and Disraeli) objected just as strongly. Voters in three-membered constituencies were given only two votes—a clumsy device for securing "minority representation."

excitement. I scarcely slept on Friday night. My mind seemed constantly with the doomed men.

"The Marchioness of Queensberry's letter to them is beautiful: my eyes filled with tears as I read it.

"[26*th*.] Manchester Election. My brother Jacob returned by a large majority. The unjust verdict of 10 years ago is now reversed.

"House: dull debate on Abyssinian Expedition. Leaders of both sides involved in the blunders committed on this matter.

"[29*th*.] My brother Jacob introduced to the House by Mr. Bazley and me; he was kindly received by our friends.

"[30*th*.] An hour and a half with Mr. Gladstone this morning on future politics: on Ireland in particular. He is willing wholly to suppress State Church in Ireland, but with a wish it had not been necessary. Conversation very free and interesting. Lord Russell's activity not very useful to the party, I suspect, in the judgment of some of his old colleagues."

CHAPTER XIII

THE IRISH CHURCH

I

SOON after the Parliament met in 1868 for what proved to be its last session, Lord Derby, then in very ill health, resigned, and Disraeli entered upon his first brief and stormy year as Prime Minister. He was even more effectively in a minority than Lord Derby, for the Irish question, forcing itself into the forefront of English politics after twenty years of neglect, began to knit the Liberal Party together. Bright had a glimpse of the coming harvest of a lifetime of hard labour. Unhappily, it proved hardly more than a glimpse.

"[*March* 9, 1868.] To Town for the session.

"Since the House opened Lord Derby has resigned and Benjamin Disraeli reigns in his stead! A great triumph of intellect and courage and patience and unscrupulousness, employed in the service of a party full of prejudices and selfishness and wanting in brains. The Tories have hired Disraeli, and he has his reward from them.

"Called on Lord Russell: talk on Irish Church. He is willing to support any good settlement, and at least one which is not good.

"[10*th*.] House: Irish debate. Maguire opened; Lord Mayo for Government,—speech of 3 hours and 20 minutes—wearisome speech, manner and matter equally poor. Government plan not likely to suit Ireland or England.[1]

"Walked up thro' the Park with Mr. Gladstone. He is strong on

---

[1] Lord Mayo, Chief Secretary for Ireland, proposed to establish a Catholic University, with a Royal Charter and a grant from Parliament. No party then wanted the scheme. In the end Lord Mayo dropped it. But it gave Bright the cue for one of the happiest of his apologues. The plan, he said (March 14) reminded him "of an anecdote which is related by Addison. He said there was a man in his county—I don't know whether it was Buckinghamshire or not: he was not a Cabinet Minister; he was only a mountebank—but this man set up a stall, and to the country people he offered to sell pills that were very good against the earthquake. . . ."

Irish Church, and is for some resolution or Bill on it, to meet Government proposals if bad.

"[11*th*.] House: Church Rate Bill passed thro' Committee. It is the Bill I recommended to the House several years ago. It withdraws all power of compelling payment and substitutes for it the voluntary system.

"Evening: occupied in making notes for speech on Irish question.

"[12*th*.] To Mr. Gladstone's at 12 o'clock at his request. Met there Lord Granville, Mr. Cardwell, Mr. C. Fortescue, with Mr. Brand and Mr. Glyn, to discuss course on Irish question. Agreed that a *specific* motion should be brought forward after present debate is over, in such form as to pledge the House to the abolition of the Irish Church. I was thus admitted to a sort of 'Opposition Cabinet Meeting,' and feel myself somewhat embarrassed at the prospect of responsibilities which I do not wish to undertake.

"[13*th*.] House: spoke in the Irish debate from 9.40 to 11 o'clock with great freedom of thought and speech; most successful in its temporary effect on the House, and much cheered. Our friends greatly satisfied.[1]

"[14*th*.] Last night and to-day almost overwhelmed with compliments on my speech, but hope my head is not turned or weakened by so much praise. Lord Dufferin wrote me a very kind note—thinks the speech will do 'incalculable good' in Ireland.

"Evening: dined with W. V. Harcourt ('Historicus' of *The Times*). A pleasant party: Lord and Lady Hobart, Mrs. Lloyd Lindsay, daughter of the Crœsus Lord Overstone, Julian Fane from the Paris Embassy and his wife, and others. After dinner, Lord and Lady Cranborne came in. He very pleasant and thoughtful, evidently in a great puzzle about present position of affairs; his distrust and dislike of Disraeli not concealed.

"[16*th*.] General Prim, now refugee from Spain, called. Conver-

---

[1] Bright in this speech repeated the arguments he had used twenty years before —that the woes of Ireland were mainly due to "an absentee proprietary and an alien Church." He pressed hard for land purchase instead of the loans for tenants' improvements which the Government proposed. Then he proceeded, with close reasoning and a lofty but sober eloquence, to put the case for Irish Disestablishment. He declared that the question could be settled only by mutual and reasonable concession: "I say, if it ever does come to be dealt with by a great and powerful Minister, let it be dealt with in a great and generous spirit. I would counsel to all men moderation and justice. It is as necessary to Protestants as to Catholics and Nonconformists that they should endeavour to get rid of passion in discussing this question. . . ."

sation on Spanish affairs. The nation Liberal; the Court most hostile to freedom. Queen shockingly immoral, and all the prestige and honour of the royal family gone. Expects a revolution before long.[1]

"House: Irish debate. Gladstone spoke for 2 hours, 10 to 12 o'clock, and Disraeli followed till ½ past 1. Gladstone good and firm on Irish Church. Disraeli ambiguous and his manner laboured, giving the idea that he was the worse for the brandy and water he drank before he rose and during his speech.

"I think the Liberal Party could not stand such a 'leader' as he is.

"[19*th*.] Mr. Rogers, from Oxford, called, proposed to me to edit two volumes of my speeches, and to arrange with Mr. Macmillan to publish them, to which I agreed, and am to send him volumes of Hansard, *The League* newspaper, etc., from which he will select them. This relieves me of a considerable labour; Mr. Rogers is an able man and can get thro' a good deal of work.[2]

"To 11, Carlton House Terrace, to Mr. Gladstone's. Met there the Duke of Argyll, Lord Granville, Mr. C. Fortescue, Mr. Cardwell, Mr. Brand and Mr. Glyn—to consider 'resolution' on Irish Church of which Mr. Gladstone is to give notice in the House. After 2 hours' consultation, a resolution was drawn up and agreed to.

"[20*th*.] Mr. Howe and deputation from Nova Scotia called. They came to protest against their forced union with Canada, and the question is likely to give some trouble.

"I was the only Member in the House who protested against this forced union last session, and urged that it should be delayed till the opinions of the people of the Colony could be ascertained at their approaching General Election. My advice was not taken.

"House: Mr. Gladstone gave notice that on Monday he would produce his resolutions.

"Lord Mayo has agreed to liberate a Mr. O'Sullivan, who has been in prison for a year or more on suspicion of Fenianism, on the strange condition that he is not to go back to the County of Limerick to his family before the 1st of August. His case has been brought before me thro' our manager, Samuel Tweedale, of Rochdale, who is acquainted with him.

"[21*st*.] Mrs. O'Sullivan, cousin to the supposed Fenian, called, and I told her what Lord Mayo had agreed to do.

[1] The Revolution occurred exactly six months later, when Serrano and Prim returned to Spain, rallied the Liberals, and overthrew the dynasty.
[2] Professor Thorold Rogers.

"[*23rd.*] With my brother-in-law, Edwd. A. Leatham, to introduce him to the House on his election for Huddersfield.

"Mr. Gladstone gave his resolutions to the House.[1] They seem to meet with favour with the Liberal Party.

"[*26th.*] Breakfast with Mr. Miller, 55, Lancaster Gate. A large party: Dr. Guthrie, of Edinbro', Dr. Halley, Dr. Newman Hall, Dr. Gladstone and others. Conversation on Irish Church and my plan, which was rather favourably criticized. Some explanations from me removed some objections.

"Dr. Guthrie, Mr. Allen, Dr. Halley, Newman Hall, Mr. Mattheson and Dr. Gladstone are favourable specimens of ministerial order.

"Flogging in the Army abolished in time of peace by vote of the House. I am sorry that I was not present at the division.

"[*28th.*] Mr. E. C. Delavan, of New York, called—a fine looking man 76 yrs. of age. Father of temperance reformation in America: has devoted 40 yrs. and his fortune to the cause. Mr. Baker, of Manchester, 'Alliance' Secretary, came with him.

"Evening: dined at Willis's Rooms with 200 M.P.s to present a testimonial, value near £2,000, to Mr. Brand, M.P., for many years the 'Whip' of the Liberal Party. The 'Whip' is the organizer and manager of the Party, gives notices to its members, and gives them information, and assists generally to get majorities in the House. Mr. Brand has made himself popular with the Party. Mr. Gladstone was in the Chair. The dinner was good (the cost £2 2/– each person) and the whole affair was well managed.

"[*29th.*] Evening: dined with Milner Gibson, Layard, Hy. Reeve, Editor of *Edinburgh Review*, Fleming, of Poor Law Board, Mrs. Ford, etc.[2]

[1] The first of the three resolutions declared that the Church of Ireland should cease to exist as a State establishment; the other two were consequential. (See page 318.)

[2] Henry Reeve, the much-travelled journalist whose knowledge gave *The Times* its peculiar authority in foreign affairs between the Revolutions of 1848 and the close of the Crimean War, was a Norwich man, educated at the Grammar School under Edward Valpy, the dominie who trained the young ideas of James Martineau, the Rajah Brooke, Sir Archdale Wilson and George Borrow. He had fallen into the editorship of the *Edinburgh* almost by accident. Cornewall Lewis had relinquished it to enter the Cabinet in 1855, and Longman asked Reeve to look after the April number. He edited every number thereafter for forty years—till his death in 1895.

Sir H. A. Layard, the excavator of Nineveh, had been in and out of Parliament since 1852. Gladstone made him Chief Commissioner of Works in his 1868 Government, but in 1869 he retired from politics into diplomacy. As Ambassador at Con-

"[*30th.*] House: Gladstone moved resolutions on Irish Church. Speech good in every respect. Lord Stanley followed. Speech altogether weak, and badly spoken, or rather *read*, for he speaks from a written speech. A bad night for the Government.[1]

"[*31st.*] House: an effective speech from Hardy, but a 'no-surrender' speech—absolutely in favour of Irish Church. I spoke from 11 to 12 o'clock and closed the debate. Our people cheered greatly when I rose, and I hope what I said is likely to be useful, appealing to the better nature of my audience and not to 'party.'[2]

"[*April* 1.] With T. B. Potter to 'Cobden Club,' most unwillingly, for I do not see the use of the Club, and I feel too sad at the loss I have sustained to enable me to enjoy evenings of gossip and almost of frivolity in connexion with any institution bearing his name.[3]

"[*3rd.*] Division this morning at 2 o'clock—majority of 61 against Government.[4]

"[*20th.*] House: Mr. Gladstone absent—strange enough. Intended to have spoken on position of Government, but was prevailed upon not to speak in his absence. This was a mistake, I think, and I regret not having acted on my own feelings in the matter.

stantinople in 1878, he sent the notorious dispatch about a Russian war move on the Turkish capital which threw Gladstone and Bright so closely together in their resistance to the wave of "Jingoism."

Mrs. Ford was the widow of Richard Ford, the author of the famous Handbook to Spain and one of the mainstays of the *Quarterly*. She was Sir William Molesworth's sister, and one of the most delicately charming and perhaps the shyest of all the great Victorian ladies. She had, however, the Cornish zest for affairs. Mrs. Ford lived well into the twentieth century, and died at 95 in the year 1910.

[1] The three resolutions condemned the Irish Church as an Establishment while suggesting safeguards for vested interests; declared that it was inexpedient to exercise public ecclesiastical patronage in Ireland; and prayed the Queen to put at the disposal of Parliament so much of that patronage as was hers.

[2] A second eloquent appeal for reasonable concessions to Irish opinion. Centuries of force had produced anarchy: we should take shame to ourselves, get rid of antiquated prejudices, cease to fear hobgoblins, and accomplish a great act of reconciliation and atonement.

[3] The Cobden Club has, to say the least of it, completely lived down what seemed to be its nascent reputation for frivolity.

[4] Lord Stanley's amendment to Gladstone's resolutions, which, if carried, would have left the question for the consideration of the next Parliament. Disraeli, who in 1844 had summed up the Irish situation in the words, "a starving population, an absentee aristocracy, and an alien Church," now depicted Gladstone as a Guy Fawkes acting as agent for Ritualists and Papists. But the division was the writing on the wall which predicted the coming General Election and the Act of 1869.

"[21*st*.] Dined at Club: long and interesting conversation with Mr. E. J. Trelawny, the friend of Byron and Shelley.[1] Mr. Mill spoke in favour of the gallows in the House. I was not present or must have answered him, and have been too ill to attempt to speak. It is deplorable that the gallows should find a friend in Jno. Stuart Mill, and many will be shocked at his view upon this question.[2]

"[22*nd*.] To meeting in Mr. Spurgeon's 'Tabernacle' on Irish question. I was Chairman. The speakers were Mason Jones and Fawcett, M.P.

"The building large and admirably adapted for great meeting: crowded in every part.

"I spoke for half an hour, heard in every part without difficulty.

"[25*th*.] Dined with Chichester Fortescue and Lady Waldegrave. A large party: among them the Comte de Paris and his wife, Mr. Speaker and his wife, next to whom I sat at dinner, with Mrs. W. E. Forster on the other side. After dinner I had a long conversation with the Comte de Paris on English and French affairs. He is a great friend of America and reveres the memory of President Lincoln. Speaking of France, he said it was a great trouble to be kept out of their native country. As to the future, he thought all was uncertain. Between them and the Republicans there was no great difference. Universal suffrage was a settled fact, and the only question was whether an hereditary or elective head of the State.

"I told him I thought all the world admitted the dignity with which all the family of the King Louis Philippe had conducted themselves since the reverse of their House. I was introduced to the Countess, who is pleasing looking, and has an expression of *goodness* which is very attractive.

"Conversation with Lord Clarendon. Angry at the course of the Government. Thinks Disraeli is poisoning the mind of the Queen on Irish Church question.[3] Her seclusion unfortunate, as it shuts her out from the truth and from good counsel. Mr. Gladstone came in. Spoke strongly on the retention of office by the Government after such a great defeat, and regarded Irish question as much more serious than they could

[1] "Shelley's Cornishman," E. J. Trelawny, author of "The Adventures of a Younger Son," was then 76 years of age. After he was 80, Millais painted a portrait of him in "The North-West Passage." "I am sound, wind and limb," he was writing about this time; "my faculties are all perfect, sight, hearing and feeling; bathe in the sea, ride and walk, etc."

[2] Mill, though opposed to the abolition of capital punishment, had joined in the appeal against the hanging of the Manchester Fenians.

See page 323.

be induced to regard it. News to-day that Prince Alfred (Duke of Edinbro') has been shot in Australia—seriously, but not fatally injured.[1]

"[27th.] House: Irish Church resolutions in Committee; dull debate. Walked up here with my brother Jacob at 12 o'clock. It is very pleasant to have him in the House, where he is respected by all who know him.

"[28th.] Dr. Tupper from Nova Scotia called for 2 hours. Long talk on difficulties between Nova Scotia and Canadian Confederation, which he thinks I can help to remove. A great blunder has been made, and it is not easy to remedy it. Perhaps moderation may do it.

"[29th.] House: rumours of dissolution if Government driven to extremity.

"[30th.] Mr. Howe, Nova Scotia, called. Long talk on affairs of Colony.

"House: Irish Church resolutions, debate and division—330 to 265. House adjourned till Monday. Some sort of crisis—whether resignation, or dissolution, or attempting to go on stumbling thro' the session, is not yet known. Gladstone's speech very good. The debate on the whole has been dull.

"[May 1.] Mr. Rogers called about a portrait for the edition of the speeches. I thought it an indication of personal vanity to have a portrait, but he thought it useful, and Mr. Macmillan has offered Mr. Rogers £250 for editing the volumes, and for the right of publishing them.

"To Devonshire House: meeting of Members to consider Boundary Bill of Government. Much objection to it.

"To Mr. Gladstone's at 2 o'clock. Met there Lords Russell and Clarendon, Sir Geo. Grey and Mr. Cardwell, Lord Hartington, Mr. Brand and Mr. Glyn. Long talk about the probable course of Government and course of Liberal Party. Nothing settled: to meet again when anything further is known.

"Weary and uncomfortable from want of sleep. At the Club in the evening, much gossip, as usual when there is a Ministerial crisis.

"[2nd.] Club: Mr. Wales and Mr. Toncey to look over Club house—members of Union League Club in New York.

[1] The young Duke of Edinburgh, the Queen's second son, was a keen naval officer. In command of H.M.S. *Galatea*, he had left Plymouth in January, 1867, for a voyage round the world, and was now on his second visit to Sydney. At a public picnic at Clonfert, in aid of the Sailors' Home, an Irishman named O'Farrell shot him in the back with a revolver. Happily the wound was not dangerous. He recovered, resumed command of his ship within a month, and arrived at Spithead on June 26.

"Evening: dined at Royal Academy dinner. A great company, about 170. President of the Academy, Sir F. Grant, in the chair; on his right Prince of Wales, Duke of Cambridge; Duke Saxe-Weimar, Prince Teck; on his left Duke d'Aumale and Prince Christian; Archbishops, Bishops and Lords and Dukes in abundance.

"Speeches poor. Prince, however, spoke nicely and moderately. After dinner tea and coffee in next room. Prince spoke to me about his recent trip to Ireland, which has pleased him greatly. I told him there must be legislation as well as civilities, but that I thought his visit had been very wise. He said he believed the presence of the Princess had increased the good feeling of the people, and I answered that her going was most judicious.

"Referring to the speaking after dinner, he said he wished me to have spoken, and felt more nervous than usual when he saw that I was there. I said I thought his speech would give general satisfaction, and especially in that part where he referred to the attack upon his brother in Australia. I expressed my disbelief in the act being that of a conspiracy in this country, to which he assented, saying that whilst in Ireland he was closely surrounded by all sorts of men, and he might have been easily assailed if any such conspiracy had existed. He was very affable, and there is a kindness in his manner which is pleasing.

"The Duke of Cambridge spoke to me also of the Irish visit, and with evident satisfaction. He said the Irish had some reason to think that they had been 'cold-shouldered' as compared with England and Scotland. I urged upon him that there must be legislation as well as courtesies. He seemed to know nothing about the Ministerial crisis in which we now are, and asked me if I knew anything. I told him that Lord Melbourne's advice to the Queen in her young days should be always her guide: she should keep herself in accord with the majority of the House of Commons, and that all that is good in our system is safer in the hands of a man of high honour and noble sentiments than in those of a clever adventurer.

"The Bishop of Oxford remained late, and we looked at some pictures together, Professor Huxley being also with us. I asked the Bishop why he wore a *violet* coloured coat. He said it was proper for his position and order, and added, 'It means I suppose that Bishops should be *inviolate*'—at which we laughed. I walked to the Club with Professor Huxley after a pleasant evening.

"[4*th.*] To Mr. Gladstone's at 2; met there Duke of Argyll, Lord Granville, Cardwell and Glyn. Discussion as to probable course of

Government and our course in case of no resignation. To go directly on with Irish Church resolutions. I was struck with an observation by Mr. Gladstone, showing his sense of the responsibility upon him. 'He wished they (the Government) could go out without anybody being required to go in.'

"House: rumours contradicting each other; belief in resignation story almost general, but wholly mistaken. Disraeli's speech very good for his purpose, calm, well considered, ingenious, and well spoken, but pompous and fawning when speaking of his interview with the Queen. He had advised the Queen to dissolve Parliament or accept their resignations, but in such a way as to prevent her doing either, and therefore he would go on, looking to a dissolution when the new constituencies would be registered, perhaps in November next. Mr. Gladstone followed, declaring that he would go on with his resolutions on the Irish Church.

"I spoke later, condemning the Government and pointing out that its course would delay all dealing with the Irish Church till the session of 1870. Some weak or base men on our side are glad of any excuse to avoid dissolution and to keep the Government in for various selfish purposes, and therefore the course taken by the Government will be agreeable to them. Walked up from the House with Ralph Earle, an intelligent man, once Disraeli's private secretary, now unfriendly to him.

"[5*th*.] House: debate on explanations, very humiliating to Government. Disraeli's dissimulation and untruthfulness manifest. Coming home at midnight, met Mr. Gladstone in Regent St. Quadrant. Some chat with him on position of Government. We stood under a lamp in a passage out of the street whilst he read me a suggested resolution on the unconstitutional course of the Minister in holding over the House a menace of dissolution if an adverse vote on the Irish Church Bill founded on the resolutions now being urged by Mr. Gladstone thro' the House. The day has been cold as winter with a piercing east wind.

"[6*th*.] Mr. Baker Green, Counsel for Barrett, convicted of firing the barrel in the Clerkenwell explosion, called to arrange for visit to Home Secretary to present memorial of facts sustaining the alibi in the recent trial.[1]

"[7*th*.] To Mr. Gladstone's. Duke of Argyll, Lord Granville,

[1] The Fenian outrage which blew up part of the wall of Clerkenwell Prison (Dec. 13, 1867) killed six people living in houses near by. Five men and a woman were put on trial, Michael Barrett alone being convicted. The attempt after the conviction to prove an alibi failed, and he was executed.

Cardwell, Lowe and Glyn there. Consultation as to further steps in the House on Irish Church resolutions. Strange to meet Lowe in consultation with Gladstone after what occurred two years ago on the Reform question.

"House: a night of stormy debate. I attacked Disraeli with great severity at the close of the discussion—compelled to do it by his insolence. The House rang with the cheers of our party. His reply showed how hard I had hit him; but the punishment was just, and I spoke the truth as I believed it. There was extraordinary excitement throughout the House."

2

It was in the speech described in the last entry that Bright accused Disraeli of "talking at large in a manner at once pompous and servile" of his interviews with the Queen, and told him that any man who put the Sovereign in the forefront of a struggle like this was guilty of "a very high crime and a great misdemeanour against his Sovereign and his country." The attack fired Disraeli to an incandescent rage and ended their tolerant and whimsically friendly relations of twenty years. Gladstone's resolutions passed through Committee at the end of the debate.

"[*May* 11.] Ralph Earle, M.P., called. He thinks Disraeli is preparing for dissolution; his party cannot stand much more humiliation. Auberon Herbert called; asked me to dine this evening with his sister, Lady Portsmouth, at Batt's Hotel, Dover St.

"To Batt's Hotel to dine with Lady Portsmouth and her brother, Mr. Herbert; Frederick Harrison, Mr. Roundell and Geo. Trevelyan, M.P., there. A very pleasant party, and conversation till midnight. Lady Portsmouth a nice person, sensible and gentle, with all good instincts. She asked me to go down to Hampshire to visit them sometimes during the session.

"[*13th.*] House: Oxford Tests Bill. Beautiful speech from Coleridge.[1] No division, but there is a great majority in favour of the Bill.

"To dine at Orleans House, Twickenham, with Duke and Duchess

---

[1] John Duke Coleridge had been returned for Exeter in 1865. Gladstone made him Solicitor-General in 1868, and subsequently Attorney-General; and he conducted the prosecution of the Tichborne claimant. In 1880 he became Lord Chief Justice of England. His talents as a speaker earned for him the sobriquet of "Silver-tongued Coleridge."

d'Aumale. Mr. Villiers went and returned with me. Large party, about 24, to dinner, English and French. Of the former,—Lord and Lady Kimberley, Lord and Lady de Grey, Lord and Lady Dartry, Fortescue and Lady Waldegrave, Chas. P. Villiers, Mr. Bagehot of the *Economist*. M. Say and his wife, son of Horace Say, the French economist, whom I visited near Paris many years ago, Mr. Langel and his wife, and two French countesses, etc.

"It was a grand dinner: silver plate or plates, and everything in great beauty; the dinner less heavy than an English dinner; wines very choice, I was told, and of special vintages.

"I sat between Madame Say and Mrs. Langel. We remained in the dining-room a little after the ladies—half-way between the French and English customs—the Duke d'Aumale saying that he thought the ladies rather preferred that to the French custom. After returning to the drawing-room, we examined the pictures, especially some recently purchased—one by Ruysdael and some by Decamps, beautiful and costly pictures. The little Duchess (she is very little) walked round and explained to me some of the pictures, pointing out their peculiar points of interest and beauty.

"I had a pleasant talk with M. Say about his father, who is not now living, and about France and the Emperor, of whom it is reported that Persigny said lately, 'I can get at his intelligence or intellect, and not at his will,' meaning that the Emperor has become less firm and strong, and less able to decide anything submitted to him. M. Say thinks Mr. Rouher very good on economic questions, but bad on general politics, and that he will not long retain his place.

"The party broke up at 11 o'clock, the Duke offering Mr. Villiers and me a fine cigar as we left.

"The evening was spent most pleasantly. The dining-room was built in Queen Anne's time, and the house is large and abounding in means of comfort and in decoration and proofs of the wealth and good taste of its owners.

"[14*th*.] Mr. Beales and Prince Zartorisky (Pole) to talk over prospects of Poland. The Prince an amiable man; but his views as to the future of his country are very different from mine.

"[15*th*.] Mr. O'Sullivan called to explain the hardships he has suffered as a prisoner under suspension of Habeas Corpus in Ireland.[1]

"Deputation from Presbyterians in Ireland to make better terms on

[1] The Derby Government had in January suspended the Habeas Corpus Act in Ireland until March 1, 1869.

Regium Donum in case of disestablishment of Irish Church. Montgomery (Moderator), Mack, and Rogers—the last a very unsatisfactory specimen of a Christian Minister, fierce against Catholics, and full of greed for public money for his own sect. I rebuked their miserable subservience to the Tory and Church party.

"Mr. Howe and Mr. Annand from Nova Scotia, asking me to present their Petition to the House. Mr. Rogers to discuss my speeches for his volumes.

"House: presented Petitions from Nova Scotia against union with Canada, and gave notice to call attention of the House to them.

"[16th.] Mr. W. H. O'Sullivan called on his case: cruelty and insult to him whilst in prison at Limerick.

"[17th.] News arrived last night that the Senate of the United States had not convicted President Johnson on the 11th Article, which is supposed to be equal to a general acquittal.[1]

"Evening, dined with Mr. Fite, M.P.—not a dinner party. Saw some of his old and scarce books—Bibles, Miltons and Shakespeares—scarce and valuable. He is rich, and indulges in these treasures and in good pictures. He is always kind to me, and I like the evenings spent at his house.

"[20th.] House: Libel Bill. Voted against making things said in speeches equal as libel to things written and published.

"Evening: dined with Mr. and Mrs. Glyn in Berkeley Square. Mr. and Mrs. and Miss Gladstone there, Lord Kimberley, Edward Ellice and his new wife, Mr. Whitbread and his wife, and Arthur Otway. Sat between Mr. Ellice and Lady Kimberley—both very pleasant. Lady Kimberley told me much of her experience as wife of Lord-Lieutenant of Ireland, of the sham and rottenness of the Viceregal institution, of its costliness and uselessness, of her husband having at the 'Drawing Rooms' to kiss some hundreds of ladies presented to him, and of the curious people who were sometimes seen at the Viceregal balls, etc.

[1] Andrew Johnson, then Vice-President, succeeded to the Presidency of the United States on the assassination of Lincoln. The next three years passed in a series of bitter disputes with Congress, the President demanding severer conditions for the return of the Secession States than Congress was prepared to impose. He appealed to the country, but the electors supported Congress by great majorities. Finally Johnson attempted to remove Secretary of State Stanton against the will of the Senate, and he was then impeached. The necessary two-thirds majority for conviction could not be obtained, the voting being for "Guilty" 35; for "Not Guilty" 19. Johnson was succeeded in the Presidency by Ulysses Grant in 1869.

"Lord Abercorn, now Lord-Lieutenant, is said to carry his mock dignity to such a height that his wife is obliged to make a low bow to him if she leaves the room—and that he exacts such manifestations of deference from all his family! I called her ex-Queen of Ireland. She is a lively, pleasant, little woman, and too natural for a 'sham dignity.' Walked up home with A. Otway. He thought it would not be easy to find suitable men for a new Cabinet. I am already half-appointed 'Secretary of State for India'! My friends little know how little I wish for office, or how insuperable are the difficulties in the way of my accepting it, if offered to me!

"[25th.] Mr. Baker Green and Mr. Lewis, counsel and attorney for the Fenian convict, Barrett, called. Gave them a letter to Mr. Hardy at the Home Office. The case very painful to me. The doubts existing should prevent the execution, but I fear will not influence the Home Secretary.

"[26th.] To Irish Office, with deputation to Lord Mayo to procure release of a boy of 18, convicted of treason-felony in Ireland, son of Mr. O'Sullivan of Kilmalloch.

"[28th.] Called on Lady Amberley. On her sofa, but no appearance of illness. Conversation about her visit to America. An engraving of Lucretia Mott in her room. Has called her baby 'Rachel Lucretia.'

"House: spoke against minority clause for Glasgow in Scotch Bill. Was angry, and might have spoken more effectively if more cool and calm.

"[June 3.] To Liverpool: great meeting with Welshmen in the Amphitheatre. W. Vernon Harcourt there. My speech difficult for me; voice not good, and my head not strong.[1] Spent the night at S. G. Rathbone's, 5 miles out of Liverpool, a pleasant place.

"[4th.] Breakfast in the Philharmonic Hall: 600 to breakfast; galleries crowded with ladies. Harcourt spoke well. My speech more satisfactory than on the preceding night.

[1] A meeting of the Welsh National Reform Association, formed "to rouse the Welsh people from the political apathy which had hitherto characterized them." Bright urged that the great qualities of the Welsh and their remarkable powers of religious organization should be applied also in the political field. He appealed to them to unite with all men who loved freedom, whether in England or in Ireland. His speech, in spite of his own fears, made a deep impression. The Welsh liked his style, and it has been said by competent people (including Mr. Lloyd George) that Bright's visit to Liverpool on this mission "did more than any other one event to make Wales active in the Liberal cause." (G. M. Trevelyan, "Life of John Bright.")

"[5th.] House: Irish Church Suspensory Bill passed through Committee.

"[6th.] Evening, with C. P. Villiers to York House, Twickenham, to dine with the Comte de Paris. A large party, several French gentlemen among them. M. Remusat, formerly Minister of Louis Philippe, present; also Mr. Fortescue and Lady Waldegrave, Mr. and Mrs. Cardwell, Villiers, Kinnaird, Mr. and Mrs. Reeve, Mr. Dicey, Langel, Miss Weston, etc. Sat next to Comtesse de Paris, a lady of charming manners and countenance, complexion and expression of great purity.

"The Count, intelligent and agreeable, explained his pictures, among them some of Ary Scheffer,—one, a sketch of the old Queen Amelia, of great interest.

"Kinnaird came back with Villiers and me: pleasant talk on Irish Church question, and on Roundell Palmer's difficulty in regard to it. He cannot get over his Church scruples, and therefore cannot vote with us, and will probably sacrifice for a time his chance or certainty of being Lord Chancellor in the next Administration. I have scruples which may prevent my joining a Government, and I can sympathize with him, and honour his adherence to his convictions.

"[7th.] Westminster Meeting: a striking sermon from Bevan Braithwaite on the danger of attempting 'to live a life of duplicity, or a double life,'—on having convictions and not living up to them. The meeting very solemn; myself much moved by the impressive discourse.

"Met Dr. Manning, Catholic Archbishop of Westminster, at my door. He came in and we talked for an hour—on Irish Church and on his Church, and on 'Friends'' views on 'interior religion' and communion with the Holy Spirit; all of which was of the essence of their Church and religion, but they added more and outward helps, etc. He thought, but for Reformation and Puritanism, that such a man as George Fox might have remained in their Church! He denied that the Catholic policy in different nations was determined by 'wire-pullers' at Rome, and had the firmest belief in the ultimate supremacy of their Church, to whose principles all people and all princes must be subject. He proposed to send me a book on the 'interior life,' and, for aught I know to the contrary, may have some hope of bringing me over to his views!

"He is a pleasant man to talk to—ingenious and serious, and is doubtless very honest and conscientious.[1]

"[16th.] W. Endicott, Junr., from Boston, here. Long conversa-

[1] The last previous reference to Manning in the Diaries was on the 8th February, 1857, when he heard him preach in Rome. (See page 220.)

tion on American affairs. He is well versed in financial and commercial matters, and thoroughly in favour of Free Trade.

"House: Spoke for an hour in moving resolutions on Petition from Nova Scotia; discussion useful, tho' the division against me.[1] Home late. Bed 3 o'clock.

"[17*th*.] I feel relieved now when the Nova Scotia debate is over. My work for the session seems wellnigh done, and I long for the country and for home. The session has been arduous and wearying, but evidently every day is breaking up old parties and old prejudices, and I have had my share in the great changes which are in progress.

"[18*th*.] This day 38 years ago—my dear mother was taken from us. One of the best of mothers and of women!

"[20*th*.] J. M. Duvault Blochet, from Sautenay, Côte d'Or, France, called: a fine old man, long a friend of dear Cobden and of me. He is a grower of wine—the largest in France of Burgundy wines. His reverence for Cobden wonderful. Said this morning, 'From his grave grow the hopes of his country;' and, 'When I think of him it always makes me a better man.' He insists on sending me a case of wines, tho' I told him I did not keep wine in my house, altho' I do occasionally take a little myself.

"[24*th*.] All morning with callers, Americans and others, Parker Godwin, *New York Evening Post*, one of them; Mr. Chafin, New York, and also Mr. O'Connell, legal writer, many years in London, poor and wanting help.

"[26*th*.] Mr. Rogers called. He undertook to examine for me Mr. O'Connell's 'Institutes of Jurisprudence—English and American,' to ascertain if they are worth publication.

"With Mr. Caird down to Shepperton to see our friend W. S. Lindsay. Found him very cheerful and busy. He has written a novel or story, 'Ashore and Afloat,' framed chiefly out of events of his own life, now in the press. A pleasant evening: dined with him and his wife and son.

"[27*th*.] H. Barker from Alexandria called on subject of proposal to hand over Europeans to Egyptian Courts and abolish Consular powers of judicature in Egypt. Merchants of course opposed to this.[2]

"Sir H. Holland called; asked me to breakfast with him on Wednesday morning next to meet Mr. Longfellow from U.S. Gossip with Sir Henry: he told me he had attended six Prime Ministers in his professional career. Thought some of our statesmen were not much supported by

[1] See page 296. [2] See page 35 *et seq.*

their wives, but I forbear to put down the cases to which he specially referred.

"[*28th.*] Called on Mrs. Cobden to ask her about a volume of Mr. Cobden's speeches which I wished to have published.[1]

"[*30th.*] To Palace Hotel to breakfast with Cyrus W. Field: M. Lesseps, of the Suez Canal, there; du Bierstadt, the great painter; Mr. Craven, engineer, from New York, etc.

"[*July* 1.] Breakfast with Sir H. Holland. Met Mr. Longfellow, American poet, and his daughter. Very pleasant time. Longfellow's countenance and eye charming; quiet strength and intelligence and goodness. Spoke of Dante. Spoke most kindly of J. G. Whittier, 'always ripening.'

"Edward Dicey called: talk about editorship of *The Star* newspaper.

"House: voted in favour of Mr. Coleridge's Bill to abolish University Tests.

"Evening: dinner to Cyrus W. Field, promoter of the Atlantic telegraph. Duke of Argyll in the Chair. I spoke, but my voice not very good. Lord Stratford de Redcliffe [2] sat near me and spoke to me, saying that a speech I made some years ago had given him great pain, but that he had not borne ill will against me; that he had always been for peace, and had been willing to surrender everything but principle. I told him I often heard these sentiments from platforms, but diplomatists and statesmen in action did not adhere to such professions of regard for peace. He spoke much too long for the audience, and became angry and rebuked them in a manner rather excited.

"The banquet must have been very pleasing to my friend Cyrus W. Field.

"[*2nd.*] Mr. Denison, Governor of Ohio, and late in the Cabinet of President Lincoln, called. Much talk on U.S. affairs, and on Mr. Chase and his longing for the Presidency.

"To Langham Hotel to see Mr. Bierstadt's pictures. Scene in the Rocky Mountains and a view of the Yosemite Valley, pictures of extraordinary merit in my opinion, and far superior to anything in the English Academy Exhibition."

During the heat of summer Bright, in a mood of weariness, absented himself from Parliament, and therefore did not witness the passing of the

[1] Cobden's speeches were published in two volumes, edited by Bright and Thorold Rogers, in 1870.
[2] See page 161 *et seq.*

Suspensory Bill by the House of Commons and its rejection by the Lords. He spent some time with the family at Rochdale and paid the promised visit to Peabody in Ireland. He notes briefly his goings and comings between July and the Proclamation which dissolved Parliament in November:

"Went to Ireland on a visit to Mr. Peabody at Castleconnell on the Shannon. Spent more than a week with him pleasantly. Weather intensely hot; river low; fishing very bad.

"A public breakfast given to me at Limerick. Speech on Irish Church question—well received.[1]

"Mr. Peabody is a remarkable man. He is 74 years old, large and has been powerful of frame. Has made an enormous fortune, which he is giving for good objects—chiefly for Education in America and for useful purposes in London. He has had almost no schooling, and has not read books, but has had much experience, and is deeply versed in questions of commerce and banking. He is a man of strong will, and can decide questions for himself. He has been very kind to me, and my visit to him has been very pleasant.[2]

[1] Bright told the people at Limerick that he was willing and anxious if possible to supplement the "fraudful" Act of Union by deeds of generosity and justice which should really unite the Three Kingdoms. He would undo the territorial and ecclesiastical arrangements of the last two or three hundred years—but "without inflicting on any living man the smallest act of injustice."

[2] George Peabody died the next year (Nov. 14, 1869) in London. He was one of the most lavish but also one of the most sagacious philanthropists of the century. Danvers in Massachusetts, where he was born in 1795, is now called Peabody. His ancestors had been farmers in Hertfordshire in the seventeenth century. Leaving the district school at 11, he became apprentice in a grocery store, and successively assistant to his brother in Danvers and to his uncle, who had a dry-goods store in Georgetown, D.C. After the War of 1812, in which he served as a volunteer, he entered into partnership with Elisha Riggs, who provided the capital for a dry-goods business while Peabody did the travelling through New York, Pennsylvania, Maryland and Virginia. The business proved enormously successful. When Riggs died in 1830, it was one of the biggest in the world. By 1837 Peabody had created a great concern of merchandise and finance in the City of London, and came out of the American business. But he remained profoundly interested in American welfare and gave vast sums to promote it—£200,000 for a scientific institution in Baltimore, £52,000 for education in Danvers, and many endowments to Harvard University. The greatest of all his benefactions, however, was £350,000 for working-class dwellings in London, which sum his will increased to half a million. The fund is still administered by the Peabody Trust. The Queen offered him a baronetcy, which he declined. Congress had given him a special vote of thanks in the year before Bright's visit to him in Ireland.

"Spent two days with Marcus Goodbody at Clara, King's County, on my way to Dublin.

"At the end of September, I left home with dear Elizabeth for 3 weeks. Visited darling Helen at Street, went on to Exeter, Plymouth, Falmouth, and the Land's End. We spent two days at Pengerrick with Robt. Fox and his two daughters [1]—a charming house and most pleasant family. On our return we spent three days at Torquay, chiefly with our friend Susan Midgley.

"After this, a week at Birmingham, preparing for the Election; then a week on a visit to Edinbro', to receive the 'freedom of the City,' and spoke at a great meeting there. Called for one night at Benwell House, Newcastle, to see my brother-in-law, Hadwen Priestman."

3

The summary dismissal, with the merest mention, of an event like the presentation of the Freedom of Edinburgh is characteristic of Bright's attitude towards his personal triumphs. It marked with an official seal, however superfluous, the fact that he had become far more than a first-class Parliamentarian and a popular politician: he had reached the rank of a national leader. The address from the City of Edinburgh described him as an Orator and a Statesman. His reply, no less than the matter-of-fact entry in his journal, emphasizes at once the simple sincerity of Bright's character and the secret of the universal respect which now began to envelop him. Oratory? He had fixed in his mind a phrase of his beloved Milton,—"Yet true eloquence I find to be none but the serious and hearty love of truth." Statesmanship? He repeated what he had said in the House of Commons many years before: "I have seen so much intrigue and ambition, so much selfishness and inconsistency in the character of many so-called statesmen, that I have always been anxious to disclaim the title. I have been content to describe myself as a simple citizen, who honestly examines such questions as affect the public weal and honestly offers his counsels to his countrymen."

After Edinburgh, Birmingham again. He made several election speeches, and remarks that one on Education "gave great satisfaction to my friends." The nomination took place on his birthday, Nov. 16:

[1] The Fox family was and still is highly esteemed among the small community of Friends in Cornwall for its eminence both in citizenship and in learning. Robert Were Fox, of Pengerrick, was a Fellow of the Royal Society, the inventor of the dipping needle, and a constant contributor to the scientific periodicals.

"Polling next day: three Liberals carried by a great majority, notwithstanding the odious Minority Clause.

"General Election: great majority for Liberal Party."

The "odious minority clause" of this allusion was the provision inserted in the Franchise Bill during its passage through the House of Lords, at the instance of Lord Cairns, that minorities should be represented in three-membered constituencies—of which Birmingham was one. Under this crude arrangement the voter had only two votes instead of three, and therefore a highly organized minority could return one of the members—if it were big enough. Birmingham was so pronouncedly Liberal that it could, by dividing its Liberal votes skilfully, make sure that the minority had no representation at all. Bright was a frank "majoritaire," and could never understand Lubbock and Courtney and their Proportional Representation scheme when the time came for him to listen to them. The three-membered constituencies, and therefore the whole of this machinery, disappeared in the Redistribution Act of 1885.

The Liberal Party, Bright now one of its acknowledged leaders, swept the country. Gladstone had a majority of 112 members in the new House and a plurality of more than half a million of the two and a half million votes cast. Disraeli resigned. Bright resumed his diary in December.

"Telegram (at home) to go up to see Mr. Gladstone. Long interview. He wished me to join his Government. I objected strongly, and would not consent or give a favourable answer, and left him at midnight. Did not sleep that night: miserable at the thought of entering office; and yet his urgent entreaty seemed to make refusal impossible. He 'thought he had a claim upon me which I could not reject.' Saw him again next morning (Saturday) and consented to accept the office of President of the Board of Trade. He offered me that of Secretary of State for India. Refused on grounds stated in my speech on re-election at Birmingham. Same evening went home puzzled and burdened with my new responsibilities.

"[*December* 9.] With the new Ministers to Windsor to accept office and to be 'sworn in'—in my case to be 'affirmed in.' The Queen was very considerate and kind to me; proposed, thro' Mr. Helps, Clerk of Council, to dispense with many of the ceremonies I disliked. So I was not required to kneel on kissing the Queen's hand, on taking the affirmation of a Privy Councillor, or on taking office.

"Introduced to Crown Princess of Prussia, who was most polite and friendly, and to Princess Louise.

"Re-election at Birmingham.

"[30*th*.] To Osborne with Lord and Lady Granville to dine with the Queen.

"Reached Osborne after 5 o'clock. Shown into a comfortable bedroom—4 wax candles burning on the chimney-piece. A servant came up to say H.M. invited me to dinner; he would come at ½ past 8 to conduct me to the dining-room. After dressing, down to Lord Granville's room. Dressing requires pantaloons—black silk stockings and polished leather shoes with buckles. At ½ past 8 we went to the dining-room, or rather to an adjoining drawing-room. Only six of us there: Lord and Lady Granville, General Grey and his wife, Lady Clifden and myself.

"In a few minutes the Queen came in, along with the Princess Louise and Prince Arthur. She bowed to the company, shook hands with and I think kissed Lady Granville, turned round and walked to the dining-room—all following without any special order. Dinner was at a round table. The Queen took her seat with the Prince on her right hand and the Princess on her left; next the Prince was Lady Granville; then myself; then Mrs. Grey, General Grey, Lady Clifden, and Lord Granville next the Princess. The dinner was elegant and quiet—nothing profuse or in excess. Five or six servants in ordinary black dress, and one tall well-looking man in some military costume.

"The Queen began the conversation by some remark to Lord Granville (it is usual for those present to wait till the Queen opens the conversation). It then went on much as at other dinners, except more quietly, as under a slight restraint. Some remark was made as to one of the pictures on the wall. Mrs. Grey mentioned which of the Queen's children were in it, when the Queen corrected her. I said I admired the portraits of children in their own homes, only regretting that they so soon grew out of the pictures and could hardly be recognized in them. The Queen answered, she thought the likeness might generally be traced. I said Nature gave great beauty to children of the poor as of the rich— in Wales I thought them especially pretty, and in Scotland, where they seemed to live in the open air.

"I quoted a saying of my brother Thomas who 'wondered, considering how beautiful the children are, where all the queer-looking old fellows come from.' This caused some merriment in which the Queen joined quite heartily. There was conversation about the little sea voyage and the weather, etc.

"Dinner lasted about an hour and a quarter, when the Queen rose. All rose with her and stood near the table or about the room. She takes this opportunity of talking to her guests. First she went to Lord Granville and spoke with him for a few minutes. Then she came on and spoke to me.

"I told her I wished to thank her for the kindness she had shown to me at Windsor in proposing to dispense with any portion of the ceremony which I did not like. She said she was 'always anxious to regard both the conscience and the feelings of others.' She knew something of the Friends: 'Mr. Allen (Wm. Allen) was one of them, and he was a great friend of my father's.' Some remark was made about Mr. Peabody: it arose from something about Ireland, and my having been there on a visit to him. She remarked what a very rich man he must be, and how great his gifts. I said he had told me how he valued the portrait she had given him, that he made a sort of shrine for it, and that it was a thing of great interest in America. I thought nothing in his life had given him more pleasure than her gift of the miniature, and that he had said to me, 'The Americans are as fond of your Queen as the English are.' To which she replied, 'Yes, the American people have also been kind to me.'

"She then passed on to the ladies, and the Princess came towards me and talked pleasantly. She said her sister, the Crown Princess of Prussia, had left a message for me: she was sorry they had been forced to go to Berlin before I came to Osborne, but a great State or Church ceremony required them to be home by New Year's Day. I said, tho' she had left her native country I thought when I saw her at Windsor she looked very happy, and I hoped she kept up her interest in England. She said there was no doubt of that. She was quite happy; and, as to her interest in England, she took a great interest in a Society at Rochdale called 'the Pioneers,' and read about it, and was glad of its success. This is the Co-operative Society of Rochdale. I gave the Princess some information about it.

"Then there was some chat about the dogs in the room, one of which had been much at sea with her brother, the Duke of Edinburgh, but was much happier on shore.

"The Queen then left the room, the Princess with her, the Prince kissing his mother's hand as he said good-bye to her.

"We then went to a drawing-room at some distance, the Prince with us, and spent an hour or more with the Household and a small party, among whom was Sir Edwin Landseer, the great painter. At 11 o'clock the company separated and went to their own rooms.

"The Queen looked a little nervous and shy, as she does often with strangers—her face rather red. She had suffered from headache during the day.

"[31st.] Next morning at breakfast at ½ past 9, I found the Prince, Colonel Maude, Lord Alfred Paget, and one other gentleman in shooting costume, going out for the day. After breakfast, I strolled about the garden with Lord Granville, the Queen having expressed a wish that I would stay till ½ *past* 1 and that she would see me after her drive. Lunch was before one o'clock, before which Lady Clifden brought me the Princess's album asking me to write something in it. I wrote the lines which I found in one of Whittier's prose Essays, quoted by him, I think, from an American, Dr. Holmes: [1]

> To things immortal time can do no wrong,
> And that which never is to die, for ever must be young.

"Mr. Duckworth, governor or tutor to Prince Leopold, asked me to write something for him, and I wrote:

> Yes, child of suffering, thou mayst well be sure,
> He who ordained the Sabbath, loved the Poor.

This, I think, is from Cowley, tho' I do not remember where I met with it.

"Soon after *one* o'clock a servant came for me, and I followed to an elegant room where I waited for the Queen. She came in immediately by another door, bowing to me, as I to her. I drew a chair from the table, and she sat down, I standing by the fire. She said she wished to say how much she had been touched by the kind manner in which I had spoken of her on more than one occasion: that I had said 'kind words which she could not forget.'

"I thanked her for this, and said what had happened on the occasion referred to was an unhappy accident: that I only said what I had always felt and said in private, and that the people were just and sympathized with what I had said. She replied that 'some people pretended they did not care for sympathy and could do without it.' She thought there was great good in sympathy, and 'that it was often a great alleviation in sorrow, and sorrow comes to persons of all classes.' [2]

[1] The lines are, however, from one of Cowley's Pindaric odes, *To Mr. Hobbes*.
[2] A speaker at the Reform meeting in St. James's Hall the year before had attacked the Queen in a graceless way for failing to come out of her palace and interest herself

"Something was said about my dear friend Mr. Cobden. She regretted she had not known him, but the Prince had a high regard for him. She asked after his family.

"Then something was said of the lovely prospect from the window. I said I had seen below an engraving of the old Osborne House, and it seemed a large house. 'No,' she said, 'it was not a large house, but we were very comfortable in it whilst this was building,' and this was said with a tone which indicated that she was dwelling for the moment upon days passed for ever.

"She spoke of Lord Granville 'who has always been a great friend of ours,' and of his wife, '30 years younger than himself.' Then of the Duke of Argyll, and of the Duchess, 'so charming a woman, as her mother was,' and of the recent marriage of the Duke's daughter to Lord Percy. Some reference was made to the political changes of late years, and I said I thought both the condition and the temper of the people were greatly improved since her accession to the Throne.

"I said Mr. Duckworth had spoken hopefully of the health of Prince Leopold. She said he was much better, but they had often great anxiety about him: two months ago they were very anxious. His constitution seemed feeble, and he had a singular tendency to bleed if bruised or cut even slightly.

"The attendant knocked at the door and said it was *half-past one*, when it was necessary to go to the boat. The Queen rose, bowed very graciously. I bowed; she went out at one door, and I at the other; and in the passage I found Sir E. Landseer, and, the carriage being at the door, we came away and up to Town together.

"The Queen looked much better than last evening. She was rather pale, but pleasant and cheerful, and there was a kindness in her eye and in the tones of her voice. She is smaller in height than I supposed, and rather stout, but there is grace in her movements.

"The Princess is a good size and good-looking, and 'looking good,' which is the best kind of good-looking. She is evidently intelligent and

in the demonstration in Hyde Park. Bright, who spoke after, condemned this allusion to the Queen and another remark about "her supposed absorption in her late husband to the exclusion of sympathy with the people." He said he was not accustomed to stand up in defence of the possessors of crowns, but this speech caused in him a sensation of wonder and pain. Many persons had done the Queen, "in her desolate and widowed position," a great injustice. "A woman—be she the Queen of a great realm, or the wife of one of your labouring men—who can keep alive in her heart a great sorrow for the lost object of her life and affection is not at all likely to be wanting in a great and generous sympathy with you."

cultivated. Landseer thinks highly of her character and her abilities. She draws well, and has made a marble bust of her mother of considerable merit.

"Prince Arthur is a nice-looking boy of 17 or 18, free and pleasant in his manner.

"A pleasant journey up to London with the great painter: his conversation and anecdotes interesting.

"I have written all this because my children wish me to do it: the details connected with Royalties have a great interest to most persons. I am not a 'courtier,' but I can respect an Ancient Monarchy, and can admire and even reverence a Monarch whom monarchy has not spoiled; and I have always felt a true sympathy with the Queen in her deep sorrow."

CHAPTER XIV

IN AND OUT OF OFFICE

I

FOR the few months of his tenure of the Board of Trade, Bright was a prophet in chains. Even if he did not make a fundamental mistake in taking office (and it can be argued, from one point of view, that he performed a public service of some importance), the acceptance of the burden at this point in his life was a personal tragedy. He already dwelt perilously on the brink of another breakdown: in a year he was over the edge.

But the personal point of view counted little with Bright. Gladstone's urgent insistence had roused his remorseless sense of duty. Together they had created the new Liberal Party. It was about to go into action for the first time. To have stayed outside the Ministry would have been to fly the field on the eve of battle. Ireland, Education, Army Purchase, the Ballot, University Tests lay ahead. He believed he could forward these causes better from outside the Ministry than within. Yet the major policies among them were his very own: in the popular mind his name was firmly joined to them: a Liberal Cabinet to put them into practice with Bright standing aloof would have been misunderstood by the newly enfranchised masses. No man in the country, perhaps not even Gladstone, commanded their confidence in the same way. For them his presence guaranteed, as nothing else could, the stability of the new Government, its emancipation from Whig monopoly, and its devotion to democratic and progressive principles. Bright was the deeply-needed hall-mark of Liberalism on a Cabinet which included Lowe as Chancellor of the Exchequer. In his admiration for Gladstone and his gratitude for the practical driving force Gladstone gave to Liberal ideals, and in his concern for the success of the new Government, Bright made the greatest sacrifice of his life.

"I abhor the very idea of joining the Administration," he told his sister. He was *already in office*, he added; "and who will take my place if I relinquish it?" A searching question. No prophet, expositor and

338

leader of the van of independent Liberal thought arose for many years to fill the "office" Bright gave up. None since has ever filled it quite as he did.

His abhorrence overcome, the Tribune vanished for a little space behind the walls of Whitehall, sat down at a desk in the Board of Trade, and kept his chair in the Cabinet room. But his temperament was intolerant of the routine details of administration. None knew it better than he. "You must do most of the work," he told Mr. Shaw Lefevre, who was Secretary; only important questions were to be brought before him. The one large matter dealt with at the Board in 1869 was the renewal of Cobden's Commercial Treaty with France, which he maintained against the academic objections raised in the name of Free Trade by Lowe. In the Cabinet, apart from the Irish Church Bill, his chosen game would have been Education. If the first Nonconformist who ever sat at that table in Downing Street had been able to make his mark upon Forster's measure, how differently the history of public education might have read! But before the Bill was drafted he was too ill to take an active interest in public affairs.

The incommodity of his situation and the on-coming of his illness are reflected in the diaries for 1869. After the account of his visit to Osborne there is no entry until February 27, when he sets down a few words about his early Cabinet experiences. From that point a blank till May, a bald record of movements till July, and then silence.

"[*February* 27, 1869.] I have been up in Town for about a month, and have been so much occupied as to be unable to go down home, even for a day: letters, calls, deputations, office papers, Cabinet Councils and the House. For several days 4 or 5 hours engaged on the Irish Church Bill, which is now finished and ready for the House. Mr. Gladstone's activity wonderful, and his knowledge extraordinary. He has had difficulty in removing Irish Bishops from the House of Lords, but no other of the Cabinet felt the same difficulty.

"The discussions are very free and general, and all is fairly heard and considered.

"One meeting was devoted to the Queen's Speech. I proposed a paragraph on the corruption and tumult at elections, and recommending inquiry. It was agreed to without any opposition. I hope it may lead to the Ballot and the suppression of the 'nominations' and 'hustings.'

"I find myself in hard work which must be attended to from day to day. My friends are all content with my having joined the Government. But I am not yet sure it was a right step. I hope it may turn out to have been so.[1]

"Have dined to-day with Mr. Speaker, with the Ministers and officials in the House: a pleasant party. The great 'dress' question has given me some annoyance; but a new regulation, which the newspapers say has been made to relieve me, has removed my objection to 'Court' or 'full dress.' Plain dress of black velvet is now allowed—coat like my old 'Friends' coat,' with trousers of the same material, no embroidery or lace or 'effulgent trumpery.' For the Court, 'breeches' instead of 'trousers.'[2] Some day, I suppose, these Court suits will no longer be deemed essential.

"[*April* 28.] Dined with Mr. Gladstone and met there Mr. [William] Morris, the poet and author of *Earthly Paradise*.

"[*May* 9.] The American question gives much uneasiness. The rejection of the 'Claims Convention' by the Senate is a great misfortune, and Charles Sumner's speech, so hostile and vindictive, has caused me much pain and disappointment.

"Cyrus Field called this morning to talk over the American dispute with us; he is unhappy about it.

"Called on Lord Clarendon to discuss the same question with him, and advised him to change his Minister at Washington. Mr. Thornton does not seem to me to comprehend American affairs.

"Called on Reverdy Johnson, the U.S. Minister. Am sorry for the failure of his efforts at negotiation. He means well, but has been indiscreet, and hence much of the anger against us in his country.[3]

"At 6 o'clock to Mr. Gladstone's, to a special meeting of the Cabinet to discuss the Bill for the removal from his office of the Mayor of Cork,

---

[1] He wrote to a correspondent who congratulated him on his first acceptance of a Ministry: "I have done it with extreme reluctance, but the pressure put upon me was more than I could withstand."

[2] Bright's Court suit now reposes in the Art Gallery at Rochdale among other personal relics.

[3] The *Alabama* claims were to have been settled by negotiation in a Mixed Commission. If the Commission failed, resort to arbitration of the head of some friendly State was proposed. Lord Clarendon, in fact, concluded a Treaty with Mr. Reverdy Johnson, who had succeeded Adams as Ambassador, for the submission of all the Anglo-American differences to arbitration. The Senate rejected the Treaty; General Grant, who became President in 1869, recalled Reverdy Johnson; Sumner declared in the Senate that the idea of arbitration was not compatible with the honour of America, and put forward claims variously estimated at between 400 and 1,600 millions. The crisis was protracted and bitter, and settlement was delayed till the autumn of 1872. Reverdy Johnson's "indiscretion" was a joking suggestion in a speech to the Colonial Society that Canada might be transferred to the Stars and Stripes.

whose resignation has been announced. If confirmed, it may relieve us from some difficulty.

"Cyrus Field and Reverdy Johnson tell me I shall have to go to America to settle our serious dispute. I hope not. Such an undertaking would oppress me sorely.[1]

"[31*st*.] House: 3rd reading of Irish Church Bill. Home by 3 o'clock. Up from Club with Wm. Cowper, M.P. Surprised to hear his remarks on the subject of Church Establishments: he thought the time for them and for the need of them was passing away.[2]

"[*June* 2.] Dined with the Chancellor of the Exchequer 'in honour of the Queen's birthday!' Afterwards to a great party at the Foreign Office. Met there Mr. Motley, U.S. Minister, just arrived, with General Badeau, his Secy. of Legation. Walked up with them to Manrigg's Hotel.

"[5*th*.] Cabinet Council. Afterwards called on Charles Tennant, 2, Richmond Terrace, author of the 'People's Blue Book' and other works. A cultivated and good man I think, but of curious opinions— Radical in some points, but in favour of Irish Church. Saw 3 daughters, one of them seriously ill. One, Dora, is one of my great admirers: quite a girl, perhaps 12 or 13 years of age. She has written me a letter, evidently from the fullness of her young heart, thanking me for calling upon them, and hopes she may see me again.[3]

"[6*th*.] Reading J. S. Mill on 'Subjection of Women:' interesting and well written, but in parts extravagant and absurd. Also 'The Bible —the Charter of the People,' showing how the wisdom of Moses and the precepts of Christ are in favour of the mass of the people. Many interesting things in it.

"[*July* 9.] To Windsor: Council. Sir W. Tite knighted."

[1] Bright never visited America, though America would have acclaimed him as it has acclaimed few Englishmen except Lord Bryce. There was a singular resemblance between Bright and Bryce in their understanding of America and their sympathy with the American outlook. In 1879 Bright received an official invitation from the President to visit him at the White House, but declined it. The next year he wrote that he would have gone if he had been "some years younger. . . . As age comes on, the youthful longing for travel lessens and disappears. . . . Lonely as I now am at home I should feel much more lonely abroad."

[2] Afterwards Mr. Cowper-Temple and Lord Mount-Temple; the author of the "Cowper-Temple" clause in the Education Bill.

[3] Charles Tennant, M.P. for St. Albans. The little daughter who admired John Bright became an eminent artist and married H. M. Stanley, the explorer, who was, in this year of 1869, commissioned by James Gordon Bennett to search Africa for Livingstone.

2

He made few speeches this year, either in or out of Parliament. One letter written for publication (June 9) caused more stir than any spoken word. In it he gave the House of Lords a prophetic warning. Their lordships were humming and ha-ing over the Irish Church Bill. He told them they were "not very wise." People would ask, he said, what was the good of a Constitution which gave a majority of 100 in one House for a given policy and a majority of 100 in another House against it. He urged them to bring themselves "on a line with the opinions and necessities of our day. In harmony with the nation they may go on a long time, but throwing themselves athwart its course they may meet with accidents not pleasing for them to think of." Fifteen years afterwards, in the conflict on the Franchise Bill, he adumbrated the policy eventually carried out in the Parliament Act. This time the Lords took warning and brought themselves, albeit unwillingly enough, into line with the opinions and necessities of the day.

While the Irish Land Bill was taking shape, he presented a Minute to the Cabinet in favour of land purchase in preference to Gladstone's plan of tenant right; but was quite willing to support the Prime Minister's scheme (since a complete measure of purchase found inadequate support from Ministers), regarding it as at least an effort to "allay much of the disquiet which has prevailed" in Ireland. He thought, however, that a Land Bill would be quite enough work for the session of 1870, and pleaded with the Cabinet to postpone the Education Bill till 1871 on the ground that "it is not easy to drive six omnibuses abreast through Temple Bar." The difficulties of 1870 proved how sound this judgment was.

But before Gladstone had begun to consummate his Irish policy and Forster to pile up the legacy of trouble in Education which clogged the steps of the Liberal Party for so many years, Bright had left the scene. "Forgive this poor little note, which I have written with much difficulty," he said to Gladstone (Feb. 8, 1870). "I have distinct warnings of an attack like that from which I suffered 14 years ago, and I dare not disregard them. I am quite unable to work and must leave London for a time."

Now, for many months, he was more gravely ill than in 1856. Three days after the letter to Gladstone he went to rest at the Queen's Hotel, Norwood; in March he changed to Brighton; then, on April 8, after a consultation with the doctors in London, to Llandudno—in an invalid carriage which the railway authorities insisted on attaching to the train, saying, "You deserve something extra;" though, Bright remarks, "I would have preferred a common compartment." He stayed at Llandudno till October, weak as a child, scarcely able to walk without help, oppressed by mental fatigue as well, though his tired brain remained perfectly clear. His wife and his daughter Mary [1] nursed him back to health.

He could read and write very little, but he liked being read to: Miss Bright read to him in these months many novels for which he had never before had time. The things he read for himself in the early days of his illness were *The Life and Death of Jason* (he had a taste for Morris's poetry) and a book by Ward Beecher on New England.[2] In fine weather he rode slowly over the sands and hills on a Welsh pony. He made the acquaintance of an old bed-ridden woman in a cottage in the hills, and paid regular visits, taking dainties for her and bones for her dog. The dog, "Robin," became his fast friend, and has many notices in his diary: Bright was an inveterate dog-lover.

So he returned by degrees to convalescence and an interest in the larger world. While Parliament seethed with the excitements of an historic session and Europe looked on at Nemesis measuring out his fate to Louis Napoleon, a few scanty and disjointed notes went down in the little book.

"[*June* 10, 1870.] Our wedding day, 23 years ago! Heard of the death of Charles Dickens.

"[*28th*.] Letter from Mr. Gladstone on death of Lord Clarendon.[3]

"[*August* 2.] Letter from Mr. Gladstone on policy for defence of Belgium—somewhat disturbed by it.[4]

[1] Afterwards Mrs. Richard F. Curry.

[2] The book was probably "Norwood: A Tale of Village Life in New England," published in 1867. Henry Ward Beecher had paid a visit to England during the height of the Civil War crisis, and delivered a series of addresses in London and the great cities in support of the cause of the Union.

[3] Lord Clarendon, "the last of the Whigs," died on June 27, aged 71, and was succeeded at the Foreign Office by Lord Granville. He "was half amused, half shocked to find himself sitting cheek by jowl with John Bright," says Mr. Herbert Paul, describing the formation of Gladstone's first Cabinet. ("History of Modern England," Vol. III, p. 155.)

[4] At the outbreak of the Franco-Prussian War, Gladstone disagreed with Lord Derby on the interpretation of the Treaty of Belgian Neutrality. Lord Derby urged that the guarantee of the Powers was "joint and several;" Gladstone that it was only "joint," and that there was no obligation on a single Power to act without the others. The British Government then proposed that each belligerent should undertake to

"[*3rd.*] Wrote to Mr. Gladstone resigning my office and seat in the Cabinet. I feel more quiet and less burdened now it is done. Did not sleep well last night: the subject disturbed me to some extent.

"[*5th.*] Letter from Mr. Gladstone troubled me, tho' very kind and considerate. Wrote to Mr. Gladstone suspending letter of resignation.

"[*8th.*] News of battle: defeat of French.[1]

"[*September* 3.] News of Emperor's surrender—if true.[2] Head weak this afternoon—too much exciting news of late for me.

"[*6th.*] French news: Republic again.[3]

"[*10th.*] Took bones for our favourite dog 'Robin.' Went in to see Mrs. Hughes—5 years in bed with rheumatism, but cheerful and happy. Quite a lesson to see her.

"[*11th.*] Wrote to Mr. Gladstone on mediation.[4]

"[*14th.*] Call from Lydia Howard, the child actress: interesting and amusing. She is only 6 years old. Gave her a rose, which pleased her.

"[*October* 15.] Received letter from W. E. Forster from Balmoral, informing me of the engagement of Princess Louise.

"[*16th.*] Wrote to W. E. Forster and Duchess of Argyll.

"[*November* 16.] Winter.[5] Ground covered with snow. My birthday, 59: how fast the years are running out!

protect Belgium against the other, and a Treaty to this effect was signed on August 10. But the Government also obtained a vote of two millions for increasing the Army and Navy, a proceeding admirably calculated to "disturb" Bright. Gladstone told him (Aug. 4) that it would not be right, "even if it were safe, to announce that we would in any case stand by with folded arms and see actions done which would amount to a total extinction of public right in Europe." Bright deplored any proceeding which might result in the application of force some day or other. Gladstone wrote again (Aug. 4): "It will be a great addition to the domestic portion of the griefs of this most unhappy war if it is to be the cause of a severance between you and the present Administration. To this I know you would justly reply that the claims of conviction are paramount. I hope, however, that the moment has not quite arrived." It was delayed for a few sorrowful months.

[1] The French defeats at Worth and Forbach occurred on the 6th.

[2] Sedan, September 2.

[3] The Third Republic was proclaimed in Paris on September 4.

[4] Thiers came at once to London, beginning a tour of the capitals of Europe seeking intervention in order to end the War. Few voices were raised in England for mediation. Bulwer's was one. He declared that the world was "on the verge of horrors at the mere thought of which Christianity and Civilization shuddered." Bright could not make his voice heard. The War took its course.

[5] The family had returned to Rochdale on October 27.

"[*17th.*] Wrote to Mr. Gladstone resigning office, and another letter on Russian question warning him against war.[1]

"[*18th.*] Letter from Mr. Gladstone, and wrote to him explaining letter of yesterday.[2]

"[*December* 20.] Resignation in papers to-day.

"[*29th.*] My old and dear friend George Wilson died this morning. A kind and noble spirit is gone from among us." [3]

3

A gracious letter from the Queen about his resignation reached him on New Year's Day.[4] Having answered it, he turned aside from public affairs and fought his illness at Rochdale until May. He was still slowly recovering strength, but suffered a good deal from small ailments and was a little cast down by domestic misfortunes—the death of Mrs. Leatham, his mother-in-law, at Heath (Jan. 7), and a troublesome indisposition of his daughter Mary. Bright, always curious about the claims of the mesmerists, called in two or three doctors who practised mesmerism in the hope that they might be able to do something to cure her insomnia. The results were apparently indifferent: Llandudno air ultimately did what mesmerism could not do. In May, he went off to Scotland, where he fished and made leisurely sightseeing tours till September

While in the Highlands Bright received through Lord Granville an invitation from the Queen to stay at Balmoral, but prayed to be excused; and for months his records consist of weather notes, a fisherman's tally of grilse and trout, and such laconisms as "River rising, but fish will not rise;" "Rain, no fishing;" "Grand view towards Skye from hill at Strome." As he said in one of his letters, "I really do not care much about the fishing. I get the exercise and am content, and if I get no fish I have not killed any creature living in these highland waters, which

---

[1] Gortschakoff had seized the opportunity offered by the disruption of France, one of the signatories of the Treaty of Paris, to declare the abrogation of the clauses providing for the neutrality of the Black Sea. The Government handled the crisis firmly, refusing to admit that one party to a Treaty could set aside any of its terms without the consent of the others. The controversy, which at times looked alarming, was peacefully settled at a Conference of the Signatory Powers in London (March 13, 1871).

[2] Several letters passed between them during the following month, Gladstone protesting, Bright insisting.

[3] George Wilson was the chairman of the Council of the Anti-Corn Law League, and had been associated with Bright from his earliest days in politics.

[4] This letter, with others, is in the Rochdale Art Gallery.

ought to be reckoned in the whole question." Occasionally he met celebrities on the same errand as himself: "Russell of *The Scotsman* on the boat; clever, well informed, but not highly scrupulous;" "Mr. James Procter, of Clifton, called; introduced his 'admirable wife;' she evidently not the weaker vessel." He read in the evenings, mainly in the Bible and Milton; but (Aug. 19)—"Read *Othello*; grand but horrid. Turned with infinite pleasure to Milton's *Samson*, where there is nothing to offend. Were Shakespeare so free as Milton from what is gross, how much greater a treasure he would be to the world!"

In September he varied the fishing with an excursion in Mrs. Bright's company through the Border country. They visited Abbotsford. "Mr. Hope Scott asked us into his house. Introduced to his daughter, the great-granddaughter of Sir W. Scott. An intelligent and good expression on her face, but not robust." At Peebles, "some interest excited by our visit; many friendly greetings in the street." At Inverleithan, "on our return, the street crowded to see us."

He spent most of October with the family at Llandudno, and there politics began to beckon to him again. Letters came from Gladstone and Granville on the subject of the French Treaty. He answered them. Gladstone wanted him to go up to London for a conclave. He wrote instead. But the old interests pressed in fast and hard upon him as soon as he had got back some measure of strength. He studies Gladstone's momentous speech at Greenwich.[1] Within another fortnight, the Prime Minister's eagerness to have him in counsel has persuaded him to spend two days at Hawarden.

"[*November* 13, 1871.] Willie [2] went home. Margaret to Liverpool. I with them to Queen's Ferry Station, and then to Hawarden Castle, to visit Mr. Gladstone.

"Walk in the Park with Mrs. Gladstone. Called in to see her Orphanage; 10 little boys in it brought down from London. Another orphanage of hers had scarlet fever and did not visit it.

"Jno. Murray, Publisher, and Mr. Hayward came from London.

[1] Momentous not so much in content as in circumstance. He made it (Oct. 28) on Blackheath Common to a crowd of 20,000, chiefly infuriated dockyardsmen and their friends up in arms against the discharges at Woolwich. Gladstone showed that though his Government had reduced the numbers by less than 1,500, his predecessors had got rid of 4,000. The occasion was remarkable as the first on which Gladstone, then 62 years of age, met and conquered by argument and eloquence, strength of voice and charm of personality, a huge and hostile crowd in the open air.

[2] His second son, William Leatham Bright, afterwards M.P. for Stoke-on-Trent.

Sir Stephen Glynne, Sir Geo. Prevost, and W. H. Gladstone, M.P., and his sister Mary there.

"[14*th*.] Long talk with Mr. Gladstone on public affairs. Confidential and interesting—Queen, Prince, republican nations, Army reform, Departments of Government, expenditure, foreign policy and prospects of the administration, etc.

"After lunch, long walk in Park, and in the rain. Mr. Gladstone, Sir Stephen, Sir Geo. Prevost, Mr. Murray, Hayward and myself walked about 4 miles. Very pleasant tho' wet.

"Evening: again with Mr. G. in private room or library till 11 o'clock. Urged me to enter Government again. Chancellor of Duchy, little work. House not pressing on me; in Cabinet he wanted me most. Long and very serious discussion. Objections urged by me chiefly on ground of health. Answer not required just now, but when Parliament meets.

"Lord Dufferin will retire from 'Duchy' and is intending to write 'History of Ireland.'

"[15*th*.] Further talk this morning on same subject till near 12 o'clock, when I left for Queen's Ferry Station. A pleasant visit. This morning Mrs. Gladstone read chapter in Timothy, and prayers, 10 servants and myself her audience. Others had been to church early, apparently the practice of the family."

Gladstone's diary records two conversations with Bright on the 13th, and five hours' talk on the 14th, "which kept me awake till four. A most rare event; but my brain assumes in the evening a feminine susceptibility, though, strange to say, it will stand a debate in the H. of C." In a letter to Lord Granville he said Bright was at Hawarden for forty-eight hours, of which more than a fourth were passed in conversation on public affairs: "We pretty well boxed the political compass." He was convinced that Bright's heart was still with the Government, and that his health, though requiring great care, would be equal to the moderate demands they would make on him. Bright had not at once rejected the proposal; Gladstone begged him not to refuse without taking the opinion of a first-rate London physician. "Altogether my experience of him was extremely pleasant, and he was popular beyond measure in the house, where the guests were one or two ladies and four gentlemen, Sir G. Prevost, a High Church (but most excellent) archdeacon, John Murray, the Tory publisher, and Hayward—whom to describe it needs not. One and all were charmed with Bright.

347

In his character the mellowing process has continued to advance, and whatever he may have been thirty years ago, he is now a gentle and tender being. . . . I will add but one word. He was deeply impressed with the royalty question." Lord Morley quotes this letter very fully. ("Gladstone," Book VI, Chap. 8.) The passage on "the royalty question" is a reference to Gladstone's very genuine if not well-founded apprehensions about the results on public feeling of the Queen's continued seclusion ten years after the death of the Prince Consort, and to his attempts to persuade Her Majesty to conquer her dislike of appearing in public.

"[*November* 16.] My birthday—60. How life wears away!

"[*28th*.] Letter to Mr. Gladstone—Education, etc.[1]

"[*December* 2.] Letter from Mr. Gladstone.

"[*3rd*.] Wrote to Mr. Gladstone—Education Bill and expenditure.

"[*6th*.] Wrote to Mr. Gladstone why I cannot decide till opening of the session.

"[*8th*.] £68.2.9 cheque from Mr. Macmillan for cheap edition of my speeches. Letter from Mr. Gladstone.

"[*9th*.] Prince of Wales—critical condition; supposed hopeless."[2]

4

Not for several months did Bright return to the House of Commons. At home during the early part of 1872, he busied himself with family affairs, walked and drove in the country round Rochdale, played billiards with his brother and his local friends at Green Bank, watched the thrushes and the blackbirds building in the holly bushes of his garden, and let the great world roll by.

His principal political visitor was Dr. Dale, of Birmingham, then riding on the flood-tide of his wrath against Forster's Education Act;

1 In this letter he declared his view of the Education Act. He did not know how the error of preserving and extending indefinitely the system of denominational schools was to be repaired; but if not repaired it would breed continual turmoil and might break up the Government and destroy the Party for a time. The Dissenters felt that "somebody in London is working the Machine for the Church." Bright said on another occasion that the Act was "the worst passed by a Liberal Parliament since 1832."

2 The Prince of Wales (King Edward VII) nearly died of typhoid fever. His recovery in January brought about a demonstration of popular rejoicing which marked the end of the anti-monarchical feeling whose growth had given the Prime Minister so much anxiety.

and Dale also was his principal correspondent. After the great conference of eight hundred indignant Nonconformist Churches at Manchester, which Dale attended, it was Bright who transmitted his protests to Gladstone. But except for a brief visit to London in April and a few casual hours in the House, he thought little of politics all that spring and summer.

He reached Town on April 8, had a two hours' talk with Gladstone on the next day, and lunched with the family in Downing Street. On the 11th he went down to the House. "Spoke to the Speaker, and to many old friends who received me very kindly." He had an interview with Lord Granville on the Treaty with the United States, and then London saw him no more for a long time. The main objects of his visit had been quite unconnected with politics; they were to buy a barouche and to visit his daughter Mary. The barouche bought ("complete with break 147 gs." from Corben and Sons), and the visit to Brighton accomplished, he went off to Scotland in May. Mrs. Bright joined him there in June. In July he returned to "One Ash" to receive his admirers from the Potteries who came to make him a gift which he prized very highly.

"[*July* 11.] Deputation from Potteries to present cabinet: Mr. Pidduck and others, 9 or 10 in number; all very kind. My little speech in reply was more easy to me than I expected, tho' I was nervous and timid at first. The party had a lunch-dinner with us. (Here also W. T. Shawcross, our Mayor, R. T. Heape, Geo. L. Ashworth and Oliver Ormerod; also my brother Thos., Caroline and Frank.) The cabinet is very beautiful, and looks more so every time I examine it.[1]

"[*25th.*] Telegram from Mr. Gladstone on my letter advising against prosecution of bishop and priests in Ireland, based on Keogh's judgment, asking me to come up to see him.[2]

"[*26th.*] To London by 11 train. Dined at Mr. Glyn's, 12, Carlton House Terrace. Mr. and Mrs. Gladstone there; also Mr. Melly, Mr. Paget, and Irish lawyer,—Wallis, I think. Long talk with G., partly on my letter, but more on my joining his Government.

[1] The cabinet may now be seen in the Rochdale Art Gallery.

[2] The famous and most intemperate nine hours' harangue of Mr. Justice Keogh in the Irish Court of Common Pleas, setting aside the election of Captain Nolan for Galway. The Catholic Archbishop of Tuam, two Catholic Bishops and a number of priests were "reported" to the House as having been guilty of intimidation.

Kind and most generous towards me, but the conversation disturbed me. Places me in difficulty from which I thought I had escaped 6 months ago.

"[27th.] Very hot day. Called on G. at 1 o'clock. An hour's talk on old subject and Irish question. Could not be mixed up with the fatal policy of prosecuting Irish bishops and priests, and should speak against it in the House if I had the opportunity and was able to do it. He threw all on the law and the Attorney-General, but his Government will be held to be responsible.

"[30th.] Wrote from Mt. Ephraim Hotel, Tunbridge Wells, to Mr. Gladstone declining Duchy of Lancaster."

Bright, having rid himself for a while of the vexatious problem of office in the Government, went North again in August, and was there till October, with one break of a few days at Tunbridge Wells and a visit to the Clarks at Street and the Priestmans at Bristol. While at Bristol, he "called at Cote Bank on Thomas Pease and saw his fine family—or a portion of it. We saw ten children; in all he has fifteen!" At the end of September he went to the Duke of Argyll at Inverary Castle.

"[September 30.] Posted to Dalmally, and on to Inverary. In castle grounds, horse shied, kicked, and broke carriage pole; no further injury. Walked on to the house, and was kindly received. Duke and Duchess, Lord Lorne and Princess Louise, Archibald and Walter, and young girls (4), Mr. Bradford, American artist.

"[October 1.] Morning: drive with Duke and Mr. Bradford. Afternoon, with Duke, and took up Princess who was walking to meet her husband.

"[2nd.] Walk with Duke to his gardens. After lunch D. and D. brought me 8 miles on my way to Dalmally; then in fly the rest of the way.

"A nice and good family, very kind to me. I said to Lord Lorne, on parting with him, 'You ought to be very happy,' and he said, 'And so I am.' The Princess simple and good; seems most pleasant and happy as a daughter of the house.[1]

"[16th.] By 10.25 to Kinross. Drive round Loch Leven. Visited Michael Bruce's house and his grave, and the grave of his friend Arnott at Portmeak; saw David Arnott there. Robt. Patterson, of

[1] See page 369.

Kinverswood, went with me. The day fine—sunshine as I stood by the young poet's grave and as I drove round the beautiful loch." [1]

Leaving Inverary, Bright passed a day or two with T. B. Potter at Pitnacree and went on to Loch Leven. On his way home, he halted at York.

"[*October* 26, *at York.*] To Walmgate Bar and my old school, now hardly discoverable in the changes of 50 years.

"[*November* 1, *at Rochdale.*] Voted at Ward Election this morning: my first vote by ballot.

"[*13th.*] Charles Sumner came for the night. Long and pleasant talk with him.

"[*14th.*] C. Sumner left us for Liverpool to sail in the *Baltic* steamer at 3 this afternoon. Wrote Duchess of Argyll with copy of Christmas Hymn, 'This morn of victory,' and sent copy of Barclay's 'Apology' to the Duke." [2]

During the winter at "One Ash," he effected a jail-delivery of his library, and presented 140 volumes of "Hansard" and many volumes of State Papers to the Rochdale Free Library. His one adventure was a visit to Lord Houghton at Fryston Hall, in Yorkshire. The house party included Sir W. M. Sterling, John Murray, the publisher, Sir B. Simeon, and Lord Anson. He passed the time talking Scottish politics with Sterling "till near three in the morning," and walking in the grounds with Murray. Then, having had a quiet six weeks at home in the New Year, he went to London to resume his place in the House.

"Much kindness shown me by members," he wrote when he returned on the first evening to the lodging he had taken at 26, Dover Street. Though his mind was not yet made up on the question of rejoining the Government, he found himself at once brought into consultation with

---

[1] Michael Bruce (1746–1767), son of a weaver, died of consumption at the age of 21. *Lochleven* is the best of his poems with the possible exception of the *Elegy written in Spring*, his swan-song:

"Led by pale ghosts, I enter death's dark gate
And bid the realms of life and light adieu."

[2] Robert Barclay (1648–1690), the eminent Scottish Quaker, author of "An Apology for the True Christian Divinity," and the chief exponent of the doctrine of the Inner Light. He was several times imprisoned during the seventeenth century persecutions of the Friends.

Gladstone on the Irish University Bill, the Education Act crisis (the Liberal Party was in the throes of the disruption over Section 25) and the besetting topic of public economy. In the brief interval before Gladstone's abortive resignation on the defeat of the University Bill (March 11) he sat to Lowes Dickenson for his portrait in the picture of the Gladstone Cabinet—a likeness which was, by the way, much to Mrs. Bright's taste. He made irregular attendances upon the House for the next three months.

"[*March* 1.] National Portrait Gallery. House. Debate and division: majority 3 against Government. Not home till near 4 o'clock.

"[*12th.*] Called on Mr. Gladstone. Lord Granville and Glyn there. Talk as to course to be taken. Resignation seems most probable. Mr. Gladstone left us to go to the Queen.

"[*13th.*] House. Mr. Gladstone announced the resignation of the Government. I went with him after adjournment of the House to his private room. His opinion that Disraeli would form a Government. Mr. Glyn thought he would not.[1]

"[*27th.*] Telegrams unfavourable about our poor brother. Sam, and this afternoon heard of his death, which took place at 12 o'clock to-day.[2] Was with dear Priscilla during afternoon and evening. A sad time for all of us.

"[*April* 1.] Westminster Palace Hotel: deputation from Birmingham on Education Bill. W. E. Forster. Talk with him upon it.

"Called on Mr. Gladstone. Long confidential conversation on affairs: Budget, prospects of Government. He still looks to my joining them if occasion offers.

"[*2nd.*] House. Forster: long discussion with him on 25th Clause of Education Bill."[3]

---

[1] Mr. Glyn was right. Disraeli would neither take office in the existing House nor advise a dissolution. He bided his time. Gladstone therefore remained in office till the débâcle of 1874.

[2] Samuel Bright died at Geneva. He was buried some months later at Rochdale (see page 353). John Bright's own death occurred on the anniversary of this day in 1889.

[3] Section 25 was that which enabled the School Boards to pay the fees for poor parents of children in denominational schools. The objection was to the colourable excuse this gave to Boards with sectarian majorities for subsidizing Church Schools. Bright's views against this and the other features of the Act which offended his principles as a Nonconformist were vigorously expressed in correspondence with Gladstone later in the year, and in his speech at Birmingham in October.

5

At the end of May, he set out with Mrs. Bright on a little tour in the West of England. Collecting the Clarks at Street, they went in a party to Dunster, to see the castle of the Luttrells, and on to Porlock and Lynton. The brief entries in his diary suggest much quiet enjoyment of the "Devonshire Alps"—walks in the Valley of Rocks, the coast drive to Ilfracombe, climbs to the top of the Capstone—and of his stay in the "clean and lively town" of Barnstaple. His only previous excursion to these parts was thirty-two years before, in the height of the Corn Law campaign: he recalled a meeting of the League which he had then addressed at Barnstaple. The Clarks went back to Street; the Brights penetrated farther west by Bideford and Westward Ho and Clovelly, returning to London through Salisbury. They stopped a night there, called on old Mr. Fawcett, and visited Stonehenge. From London he saw Mrs. Bright off to Rochdale and himself resumed the social and political round.

The Shah of Persia was the lion of the season. Bright, on account of the death of his brother Samuel, took no part in the festivities that marked that famous royal visit. On the other social distraction of the time, the Tichborne Trial, he made occasional memoranda. But his chief personal concern during the summer of 1873 was the pressure which Gladstone exerted upon him to return to the Ministry now that his health had been restored.

"[*June* 14.] Called on Mr. Gladstone on Irish farm purchase. Talk on the position of the Government and on the future. Called on Lord Granville at his large new house, 18, Carlton House Terrace.

"[18*th*.] House. Dined with Sir J. D. Coleridge, Attorney-General, 1, Sussex Place. His venerable father there, and Dr. Temple, Bishop of Exeter, and Millais the artist, etc. Great crowd to see the arrival of the Shah of Persia.

"[19*th*.] To breakfast with Mr. Gladstone. Bishop Moriarty, Dean Stanley, Mr. Martineau, Lord Lytton, Sir A. Gordon, Mr. Motley, Mr. Street, Dr. Smith, Sir S. Glynne, etc.

"[24*th*.] Did not dine with Lord Granville to meet the Persian Shah. The sad ceremony at home made it unsuitable.[1] Sorry that I am not with them.

[1] The funeral of his brother, Samuel Bright.

"[28*th.*] Wrote Persian Minister excusing myself from presentation to the Shah as I was going out of town. To Brighton.

"[*July* 1.] Westminster Palace Hotel, meeting of Nonconformists, etc., on Education Bill. Spoke to allay the prevailing passion, but without much effect, I fear.

"[3*rd.*] Queen's Bench—Tichborne Trial. Lunched with the judges, Cockburn, Mellor and Lush. The Czarevitch also there with Lord Kenmore. . . . House. Met Archbishop of Canterbury at Westminster Hall door. Both very ill since we met before. His greeting cordial and kind.

"[4*th.*] Langham Hotel, to see Bradford's pictures, U.S. artist. Very beautiful scenes in the Arctic regions.

"[14*th.*] Lunched with Mr. and Mrs. Gladstone. Prince and Princess of Wales and Russian Princess there. Duke of Cambridge. Afterwards many came. The Prince improved. The Princesses very simple and pleasant.

"[31*st, at Rochdale.*] Visit to cemetery to see the grave of my poor brother Sam. A quiet spot and near the graves of many known to me in their lives, our neighbours and townsfolk. Mr. Thomasson came to dinner. He brought me three volumes of MS. memoranda of Mr. Cobden during his negotiation of the Commercial Treaty with France.

"[*August* 3.] To Meeting twice. Letters from Mr. Gladstone and Lord Wolverton asking me to go up to London. Gave me much anxiety. Replied: Going up to-morrow."

The Ministry which Disraeli had dubbed in the previous year a "range of exhausted volcanoes" had fallen on evil days. The defeat of the Irish University Bill and the abortive attempt at resignation in March had been followed by the irregularities at the General Post Office in which Lowe, as Chancellor of the Exchequer, was involved. A shuffle and a reinforcement of the Government became necessary. Gladstone turned to Bright. The letter that reached "One Ash" that Sunday morning was what would now be called "an S O S"— "Changes in men there must be, and some without delay. A lingering and discreditable death, after the life we have lived, is not an ending to which we ought to submit without effort; and as an essential part of the best effort that can be made, I am most desirous to communicate with you here. I rely on your kindness to come up. . . ."

"[*August* 4.] London by 11 train. To Lord Wolverton, 12, Carlton House Terrace. In to see Mr. Gladstone. Long explanation. . . . Proposed changes. Urged me to take Duchy of Lancaster. Vital to his plans, etc. Dined at No. 12. Wolverton and Lady W., and Bruce [1] and myself. Talk with Bruce on proposition to him to take peerage and Presidency of Council to make room for Lowe at Home Office. Later on Goschen came in, and talked till one o'clock. He friendly to Lowe.

"[5th.] Saw Mr. G. again. Bruce accepts the offer to him, which surprised me. . . . Dined with Lord F. Cavendish and Lady. Mr. and Mrs. Gladstone there. More talk on Cabinet arrangements, etc.

"[6th.] Consented to Duchy conditionally, now or in October. Saw Childers at Reform Club to discuss office of Duchy. J. S. Wright to Birmingham, to tell them what was doing. Home by 2.45 train."

He was shocked during this visit to "One Ash" to learn of the death of his old friend G. L. Ashworth, whose funeral he attended. There were negotiations for his re-election for Birmingham on accepting office, about which Mr. Chamberlain and Dr. Dale went down to Manchester to see him. He dined with them at the Queen's Hotel, and had "much talk on the Education Bill and the Government." Then, after a visit to Hull with Mrs. Bright, and a call at Pontefract to stand with her by the grave of her father and mother, he went to Hawarden for a political conference with his chief.

"[September 13.] To Hawarden Castle, Mr. Gladstone's. Lord Wolverton, Lord and Lady Granville, and James Wortley there. In

---

[1] Mr. Bruce was created Lord Aberdare, and left the office of Home Secretary to become President of the Council, in succession to Lord Ripon, who retired. Childers also left the Ministry, and Bright took his place at the Duchy of Lancaster. Lowe became Home Secretary, and Gladstone himself at the urgent instance of his colleagues added the duties of Chancellor of the Exchequer to those of First Lord of the Treasury. This arrangement gave rise to the nice case of the Greenwich Election, which exercised the lawyers so profoundly. The question was whether Gladstone had accepted an "office of profit" which legally involved the vacation of his seat at Greenwich, or whether he was absolved by the Act of 1867, which provided that a member did not vacate his seat by accepting an office "in lieu of and in immediate succession to" another office. Bright, as was to be expected, took the line of common sense: the questions raised would be dealt with fairly by the House of Commons when it met, and, till then, as the Speaker had not issued a writ for Greenwich, Gladstone should assume that he was justified in holding his seat. In this he was supported by the eminent judgment of Lord Halifax. The Gordian knot was cut by the dissolution of Parliament.

the park to see the fall of the fine beech tree. Mr. Gladstone and his three sons working hard with their axes.

"[14th.] To church. Service 'high.' Three parsons: Rector, Stephen Gladstone, his cousin, Mr. Lyttelton, and Chamberlain. Mr. Gladstone most devout in singing, etc. To me much of the service seemed only fitting for a very ignorant people.

"[15th.] To Mr. Roberts's farm: walked back three miles with Lord Wolverton."

Gladstone's own journal again throws a little more light on the occasion. "Our politicians arrived," he wrote on the 13th. "Conversations with Bright, with Wolverton and with Granville, and with all three till long past twelve, when I prayed to leave off for the sake of the brain." Next day he recorded his attendance at church, morning and evening,—"a stiff task for an exhausted brain. But I cannot desist from a sacred task." There were more conversations that night. On the third day: "Spent the forenoon in conclave till two, after a preliminary conversation with Bright. Spent the evening also in conclave. We have covered a good deal of ground." And on the last day, before Bright left to see his son Philip at Pensarn, "Final conversation with Granville, with Wolverton and with Bright, who went last."

Bright had agreed to rejoin the Ministry, in spite of his personal distaste for office, out of sheer loyalty to Gladstone. He knew himself unfitted for administrative work; he was dubious about the Education policy of the Government and other things; and he had no illusions as to the state of opinion in the country, though he did not foresee the extent of the coming disaster. So that he went away to Scotland on a fishing expedition at the end of the month with no joyful anticipations of the immediate future. While trying over Kinnaird Water, without much fortune, he received "a letter from Lord Granville to go on Monday (to Balmoral). Cabinet meeting next week—disgusting!"

"[September 29.] By Pitlochry and Spittal of Glenshee to Balmoral. Met Lord Granville in the road, and with him to Garr Valt Falls. The Queen passed us driving towards Braemar. She did not dine with us—suffering from headache. Prince Leopold dined with us— Granville, Childers, Collins (tutor to the Prince), Lady Waterpark, Miss Phipps. After dinner, billiard room: played one game with Prince.

"[*30th.*] After breakfast, Council to prorogue Parliament. Then 'kissed hands' and received seals of Duchy of Lancaster. Queen most kindly: conversed freely on my health, the Education Question, Ashantee War, Miss Gladstone's marriage,[1] fine air and beauty of district, and her regret at not being able to dine with us yesterday. Left Balmoral at 12 o'clock, with Lord Granville and Childers in open carriage to Blairgowrie."

He arrived in London on October 2. On the same day, Sir Garnet Wolseley landed at Cape Coast Castle, and the Ashantee War, which ended in the capture and burning of Coomassie may be said to have begun. This was one of the saddest preoccupations of Bright during his brief and troubled term of office at the Duchy of Lancaster. He had talked of it with the Queen at Balmoral. He found it the subject of his first Cabinet Council, and for the next three months he laboured, with all his old passion for peaceful solutions, first to prevent the invasion of Ashantee, then, when that was hopeless, to get a settlement before the advance to Coomassie, and all the time to mitigate the war. He felt out of his element in a Cabinet engaged in warlike operations, and, though there was no occasion for great endeavours like those of twenty years before, he struggled hard against the pricks—was even driven to contemplate resignation.

"[*October* 3.] Cabinet Council, 3 o'clock. Ashantee troubles; long discussion; no result. . . .

"[*4th.*] Home Office with Lord Aberdare (Bruce) to discuss working men's questions. Cabinet 12 to 5. Ashantee policy to be pacific: no invasion of Ashantee, and no assault on Coomassie. Dispatch more moderate agreed to.

"[*5th.*] To Wanstead Meeting. Mary Rogers, from U.S., came to dine at Woodford. Afternoon, wrote address to constituents.

"[*21st.*] To Birmingham, to C. Sturge's.

"[*22nd.*] Bingley Hall. Great meeting."

This was the first meeting he had addressed since his illness began in 1870. Though he was destined to remain a great figure in the

---

[1] The Queen had been greatly interested in the engagement of Gladstone's eldest daughter, Agnes, the news of which he had communicated to her at Balmoral in August. She congratulated the bride-to-be in what he called "a most charming letter" to her father.

State, commanding ever-increasing reverence in Birmingham for another decade or more, it sounded like a swan-song. "The history of the last forty years of this country," he said to his constituents, "is mainly a history of the conquests of freedom. It will be a great volume that tells the story; and your name and mine, if I mistake not, will be found in some of its pages. For me the final chapter is now writing. It may be already written. But for you, this great constituency, you have a perpetual youth, and a perpetual future. I pray Heaven that in the years to come, when my voice is hushed, you may be granted strength and moderation and wisdom to influence the councils of your country by righteous means for none other than noble and righteous ends." He dealt at some length with the Education Act, describing it as theoretically unsound and practically mischievous. As was his custom in Birmingham, he lunched next day with the Artists' Club, saw Mr. Jaffray of the *Daily Post*, and dined with Mr. George Dickson. After a short vacation in North Wales, he got back to London in November to share the last turbid days of Gladstone's great Ministry, perplexed by the difficulties in West Africa, the clash of sectarian warfare over the Education Act, and the personal incompatibilities that invariably come uppermost in the old age of any Government. Amid these disquietments he passed his sixty-second birthday.

"[*November* 29.] Dined with Mr. Gladstone. Mr. and Mrs. Greeley there.

"[21*st*.] Cabinet: Ashantee. Tried to get limit to war,—not to invade Ashantee. Could not succeed. Hope I have somewhat moderated tone of instructions. Not well to-day. Wish I could clearly see it my duty to resign on Ashantee business, so as finally to quit office and public life. Dined at Club. Long chat with F. Pennington [1] on Woman's Rights.

"[24*th*.] Called on Dr. Andrew Clark [2] in Cavendish Square to consult him. An hour with him: complete examination. Will write out a Rule for me to live by. Diet suggestions.

"[27*th*.] Wedding Day, 1839. Sad memories. . . . Mr. Childers called: question of his joining bank in City.

"[28*th*.] Dr. Clark called with his Rules. Good, but hard to be kept in London.

[1] M.P. for Stockport.
[2] Afterwards Sir Andrew Clark. The eminent physician and trusted friend of Gladstone.

"[*December* 2.] Evening, Mark Twain's lecture on Sandwich Islands: amusing, but flimsy.

"[*3rd.*] Holman Hunt's picture, 'Shadow of Death.' Subject not pleasing to me, but the 'head' good, and the Virgin is a beautiful part of the picture."

The duties of the Duchy office were not onerous. He was able to escape to Rochdale and spend five weeks at his home before attending the obsequies of the first Government of which he had been a member.

6

A day or two after his submission to Gladstone's entreaties in the previous August, Bright received from Hawarden a letter of peculiar interest. It shows that the leader of the Liberal Party, seeking a confidant in the crisis of its fortunes, turned first among all his colleagues to Bright.

Gladstone was looking for some constructive project which might pull his followers together, and keep them together in view of the appeal to the country which must come before long. The great financier's thoughts naturally ran to finance. He now (on August 14) unfolded to Bright the ideas which he afterwards worked out in the letter to Granville on the eve of dissolution. Beginning "My dear Bright," and suggesting that they should "bid farewell to *Misters*," he expressed his hope that the reconstruction of the Cabinet and a bold measure of finance might restore the Government and consolidate the Party. His mind had been working towards the abolition of the Income Tax and the Sugar Duties, "with partial compensation from Spirit and Death Duties." He now wrote of a plan of financial reform as the "positive" force that might carry them onward. Such a force could not be found in a revision of the Education Act, or in local taxation, or in the suffrage. "We now have before us a clean stage for the consideration of measures in the autumn. We must, I think, have a good bill of fare or none. If we differ on the things to be done, this may end us in a way at least not dishonourable. If we agree on a good plan, it must come to good, whether we succeed or fail with it. Such are my crude reflections, and such my outlook for the future. Let me say again how sensible I am of the kindness, friendship and public spirit with which you have acted in the whole of this matter."

When almost exactly five months later Bright left home for London

(January 17), he found the Prime Minister's hopes laid in irretrievable ruin. To make possible the operation on which he had set his heart, a total reduction of three-quarters of a million in the Navy and Army estimates was needed (such was the scale of national finance in the 'seventies), but neither Cardwell at the War Office nor Goschen at the Admiralty would contribute a stiver. From that moment dissolution was unavoidable. The portents of the by-elections foreshadowed the rout of the Liberal Party which Disraeli duly consummated.

Bright had hurried to Downing Street on his arrival in town on the 17th and found Gladstone and Granville in mortuary conference. On the 18th, he notes, "Called on Mr. Gladstone for an hour; further talk on subjects of yesterday's conversation." "This day," Gladstone enters in his diary, "I thought of dissolution. Told Bright of it. In evening at dinner told Granville and Wolverton. All seemed to approve. My first thought of it was as an escape from a difficulty. I soon saw on reflection that it was the best thing in itself."

"[*January* 19.] To Mr. Gladstone's. He in bed with cold. Granville, Cardwell and Goschen there: a long talk on expenditure. Cabinet: Gladstone not present.

"[22*nd.*] Called on Childers, 17, Princes Gardens. Athenæum Club. Mr. Gladstone's. Dissolution probable. Lord Granville there. Read Mr. Gladstone's address.[1]

"[23*rd.*] Cabinet 12 o'clock. Dissolution fixed. Mr. Gladstone's address considered. Banquet at Lord Granville's in honour of the wedding of Duke of Edinburgh."[2]

The dissolution was announced on the 26th, and the General Election began at once. Astute observers of the political skies saw that the Government was foredoomed. But even Disraeli did not realize how powerfully the wind of fortune favoured him. He was alarmed by Gladstone's pamphlet. He called it "a prolix narrative," but he

[1] "A long address for an unnamed constituency—almost a pamphlet—setting out the case of the Government in an immediate appeal to the country." (Gladstone's diary, Jan. 20.) It propounded a scheme to reduce local taxation and repeal the Income Tax.

[2] The Duke of Edinburgh married on January 23, 1874, the Grand Duchess Marie Alexandrovna only daughter of the Tsar Alexander II. He succeeded to the Duchy of Saxe-Coburg Gotha. The dowager Queen Marie of Rumania is his daughter.

thought its freshness and boldness would revive Gladstone's authority and carry the elections.[1] Discontent with the Government and the divisions in the Liberal Party, however, had hurried the situation beyond the control even of the Gladstonian magic.

Bright went to Birmingham on the 30th to be re-elected unopposed: he and Dixon addressed their big meeting in the Town Hall on New Year's Eve. Bright's only allusion to it in his diary is: "Nervous—but did not break down." But while the Tribune of the People retained his august place in Birmingham unchallenged, in other towns the Liberal candidates went down like ninepins. Manchester, voting on February 7, turned out Jacob Bright. Gladstone scraped in second on the poll at Greenwich. The party lost 32 seats in the boroughs and 13 in the counties of England, and gave ground in Scotland and Wales, while Ireland displayed so little gratitude for the Irish Church and Land Acts that it sent back hardly more than a dozen supporters of Gladstone. The two main causes of the disaster were the acrimony aroused by the working of the Education Act (as Gladstone said, Roman Catholics voted against the Government because they were not denominational and Nonconformists because they were) and the hostility of the licensed trade. Bright told Gladstone that in Lancashire the publicans and the Roman Catholics had joined together, one for *delirium tremens* and the other for religious education!

The figures meant resignation—either peaceful suicide before the meeting of Parliament or violent death immediately after. Gladstone, the constitutional purist, would have gone on and met Parliament, on the ground that it was for the House of Commons to dismiss a Government and not for the electors at the polls. His colleagues persuaded him that immediate resignation was the better course.

"[*January* 16.] By 6.45 train via Sheffield to London. Call on Mr. Gladstone. Evening, dined with him. All the Cabinet present. Discussion till midnight. Resignation to-morrow. Release of Mellody, one of the Manchester Fenians, agreed: Mr. G. and Chancellor for it, myself of course, and some others; but many against it. Home very weary.

"[17*th*.] Duchy office: cleared off some work. Call on Mr. Theed, sculptor, to see statue of C. Villiers—very good—for Manchester Town Hall.

"[21*st*.] Windsor with Cabinet, to resign seals of office. Glad-

[1] Morley: "Life of Gladstone."

361

stone not with us. Afterwards to Reading, and on to Bridgwater, and posted to Street."

This instant escape to Street and the society of his daughter Helen, without even a look back to London after he had shaken off the toils at Windsor, is symptomatic of Bright's posture before politics in this period. His long illness and enforced absence from the arena dulled his appetite for fighting. Forty years of arduous work had produced a sense of fatigue which he could not throw off, and the gradual disappearance of contemporaries and friends oppressed him. He turned with relief to his domestic concerns, lived much at "One Ash," and varied its peaceful round with fishing expeditions. In March he was in Scotland, making his head-quarters at Invergarry with his friend Thomasson, revelling in scenery and gentle exercise, and occasionally rewarded by a ten- or twelve-pound salmon on favourable days.

After three months' relaxation, he reached London in the middle of April, and took his seat on the Front Opposition bench. The sensation of "greater freedom and less responsibility" was enhanced by the esteem in which the House held this particular exhausted volcano. "Not unpleasant," he pencilled in his diary at the end of the first day in the House. He attended the consultations of ex-Ministers on the position of the Liberal Party, but did not take his Parliamentary duties laboriously. Between April and his departure for Scotland in July, the most absorbing of his personal experiences was a frequent visit to Brighton to see his invalid daughter Mary, and his most notable social engagement the wedding breakfast of Miss Edith Smith, the daughter of his old friend J. B. Smith, M.P. for Stockport. "Good wishes for so fair and good a bride," he writes.[1]

He had a month with rod and gaff in Scotland in July and August. While fishing on the Naver and Loch Meadie, he records a visit to "a little school of ten scholars. Teacher a boy of 16; nice lad. Gave Mr. McHoy, the minister, 20/- to furnish them with new reading books." This, the minutest of Bright's many and constant private benefactions, is mentioned only for its quaint interest. His diaries contain ever-recurring notes (as a mere matter of account) of moneys paid out in what were for him considerable sums to persons and to

[1] Miss Smith married Mr. Edwin Lawrence, afterwards Sir Edwin Durning-Lawrence, who, twenty years later, sat as Unionist Member for the Truro-Helston Division of Cornwall, and became famous as an out-and-out "Baconian." Lady Durning-Lawrence died in 1929.

causes. This was the only way in which a prudent right hand revealed the deeds of a generous left; and the revelation was even then only partial, for the objects of his care are generally distinguished only by unidentifiable names or initials.

Fishing with varying fortune, making one diversion to visit Wick and the northern coast, and another to do some sea-angling at Lochinvar (he records one 12-lb. cod), he remained in Scotland till August 6. The next month he was at Brighton again, and while there went to Midhurst to visit Cobden's grave and call on Mrs. Cobden. Then began a tour of the South Coast and Wales (with an interlude at Street, his invariable Mecca), working round to Rochdale by way of the Welsh shore and Chester. In October he was back on the river, thrashing the Tay, and in the later months of the year alternated between Lancashire, London, and Brighton. An "old-fashioned" Christmas, the North frozen hard after severe snowfalls, was passed at "One Ash," with the usual family gatherings there and at his brother Thomas's house.[1]

[1] This house stands on the site of "Green Bank," where Bright was born. It is now a school.

CHAPTER XV

THE NEW IMPERIALISM

I

BRIGHT began to recover strength and confidence in 1875 and to take a more continuous and vigorous part in public affairs. It was the year of Gladstone's retirement from the leadership of the Liberal Party and the selection of Lord Hartington to fill his place. Bright found himself among many colleagues who deplored Gladstone's decision and doubted a future which placed even a man so generally loved and trusted as Lord Hartington at the head of the team while it still included the real leader. He wrote to Gladstone in January:

> If I could have foreseen either the result of the election of last year or of your retirement from the conduct of the Party, I should certainly have withdrawn from Parliament, where now I seem to have quite as little of a duty or of a mission as you have. The Front Opposition Bench is full of discord, and when you are not there full of jealousy, and I find myself without any particular attraction to any particular part of the House. However, I will not complain. Some door of escape may open for me, and I can become a spectator as you are proposing to be.

One of the chief reasons why Bright regretted the step Gladstone had taken was the promise it held out of personal separation from the warrior-comrade of the biggest fights of his later life. "I have had so much pleasure in your friendship, and have gained so much from it, that I would fain hope it need not cease now, when our association will necessarily be less frequent than it has been of late years."

His mood of disillusionment and disappointment reflected the feeling of the Liberal Party in the country. But Gladstone was, for the time, set upon his own emancipation; both Bright and the country had to accept it with what grace they could muster. Bright, indeed, took the chair at the Reform Club meeting of the Party which elected Lord Hartington, and remained loyal to him when the quidnuncs were busy spreading the noise of dissension. He had supported the claims of the aristocrat Hartington against those of the democrat Forster when the two names were under discussion, being unable to forgive Forster for what he regarded as the betrayal of the Nonconformists in the Education Act; and he continued to support Hartington's leadership during the thankless but honourable five years of its duration.

In the session which followed the Reform Club meeting, Bright resumed his practice of speaking in the House on questions which roused his sense of Liberty in danger or stirred his moral indignation. He took a leading part in the debates on the Tichborne Trial, and made one notable speech on the Burials Bill.

"Burials Bill: spoke just before division." So laconically he writes of the speech on April 21 which made historic what would otherwise have been a mere parliamentary hardy annual. The discussion and defeat of the Burials Bill, which sought to give Nonconformists the ordinary rights of human decency in the national churchyards, came round as regularly once a year as the Army Annual Act. It usually provoked a display of intolerance and cynicism the more discreditable to clerically-minded laymen because the hierarchy of the Church was, for the most part, more humane than the Parliament. On this night, Bright raised the banal proceedings on to the loftiest plane by the sheer beauty and sincerity of his speech, which acutely touched the touchable part of his audience and made a great impression in the country. His description of a Quaker funeral, simple and solemn as its theme, was deeply moving. He had the satisfaction of being a member of the Government which, in 1880, swept away for ever the scandal of the old Burial Laws.

He took a conspicuous part in the Tichborne controversies in the House of Commons. Parliament would never have been troubled with them at all but for one special manifestation of that invariably amazing psychological spectacle, the mass of the English people in pursuit of a popular hero. The Tichborne claimant was a charlatan; but a wonder-seeking public is always prepared to clap a halo on the biggest scoundrel if only his story be sufficiently incredible. "This tale," said a witty Frenchman, "is absurd: the best proof in the world of its truth." The popular belief in the Wapping butcher's fables was so strong at Stoke-on-Trent that it returned to Parliament with the then enormous majority of 2,000 the lawyer who had conducted Orton's defence—Dr. Edward Vaughan Kenealy. Kenealy was an able but excitable and ill-balanced man, and he had gone to extreme lengths for his client in the protracted trial of the case. But he was hardly entreated by the posturing Lord Chief Justice, Cockburn, and worse by the jury which gratuitously expressed its superfluous opinion about his conduct of the defence, and worse still by the Benchers of his Inn who disbarred him. The election at Stoke was an excessive expression not only of the fatuous belief in Orton, but also of the sober and proper condemnation which many serious people had already bestowed on the treatment of Kenealy.

Bright's calm eye had watched all this with a judicial gaze. He had attended some sessions of the trial.[1] He had lunched with the judges. He had read the evidence carefully. Convinced that Orton was an impostor and his story a lie from beginning to end, he said so in the House of Commons. He rebutted with equal force the accusations Kenealy brought against the court. But when Kenealy was elected to Parliament, and nobody could be found to sponsor him on his introduction to the Speaker, Bright offered to conduct him up the floor of the House. Kenealy preferred in the circumstances to introduce himself, which he did—adding a fresh spice of eccentricity to his reputation by hanging his umbrella on the Speaker's mace during the ceremony.

Bright said a few words on his case that evening: it was the first time he had spoken in the House for five years. One of the two chief Tichborne discussions which enlivened the session thereafter was raised on a motion of Privilege by Kenealy, who complained that, before his election, Mr. Evelyn Ashley, Member for Poole, had made the gross charge against him of putting into the box a witness whom he already knew to be perjured. Bright spoke that night before a distinguished "gallery," including the Prince of Wales, Prince Christian and ex-King Amadeus. But his greater efforts were reserved for the debates on the petition for the release of the Claimant (which had been presented on behalf of 200,000 pro-Ortonists), and on Kenealy's motion for a Royal Commission of Inquiry, which came up on April 23. His well-arranged information and lucid argument contributed largely to the result of what he aptly calls a "singular" division, in which the motion found only one supporter. The singular person who had a whole lobby to himself was Major O'Gorman, the Member for Waterford.

Later on there was some idea of restoring Kenealy's status as a barrister, the condition being that he should cease publication of the

---

[1] Bright's parrot learned to say, "Would you be surprised to hear . . .?" a formula in constant use in the Tichborne cross-examinations. "On one occasion," writes Mr. Philip Bright, "she said, 'Would you be surprised to hear that God is fond of Polly?' Who taught her this we never knew."

journal he had started immediately after the trial, *The Englishman*, in which he effected the hebdomadal discharge of his wrath. Bright undertook to try to persuade him into reasonable courses, and held conversations with him behind the Speaker's chair, to the great curiosity of the multitude not in the know. It was fruitless. Kenealy would not be managed. He started a variety of political hares during the rest of the Parliament, none of which would run, and at the election of 1880, Stoke dropped him as emphatically as it had picked him up. A fortnight after the declaration of the poll he died of heart failure.

The year had begun for Bright with the visit of custom to his constituents.

"[*January* 25.] To Birmingham. Dear Elizabeth with me. To C. Sturge's. Great meeting Bingley Hall. Got through my speech pretty well, and felt a great relief.

"[*26th.*] Breakfast party at C. Sturge's. Dear Elizabeth went home with Willie this morning. Evening to dine and stay at Mr. Chamberlain's. Very pleasant party. Long talk with Chamberlain till near one o'clock.[1]

"[*27th.*] To Arts Club. Evening to dine with G. Dixon. Large party. Talk with Dr. Wilkinson on School Board question.

"[*28th.*] Called on Mr. Gordon and Mr. Middlemore and H. Sturge. Evening, soirée at Town Hall, and spoke.

"[*February* 3.] Reform Club: meeting of Party. Myself in chair. Agreed to Lord Hartington as leader in place of Mr. Gladstone. Before meeting, I called on Lord Granville.

"[*18th.*] House. Dr. Kenealy sworn. I said a few words on his case—the first time for 5 years!

"[*23rd.*] By 9 train to Birmingham. Lunch with Sir Josiah Mason on beginning his College of Science. Spoke shortly. Admired his venerable and tranquil countenance. Returned by 6 train. A very pleasant day.[2]

[1] Mr. Chamberlain was at this time Mayor of Birmingham and in the heyday of his immense civic activity—deep in those great schemes of municipal services and slum clearances which inaugurated the modern prosperity of Birmingham and gave him his unequalled celebrity and authority as a municipal reformer. It was not till the following year that, on the resignation of Mr. Dixon, he joined Bright in Parliament.

[2] Sir Josiah Mason, the distinguished pioneer of the steel-pen industry, was one of Birmingham's greatest benefactors in the nineteenth century. He endowed the Scientific College, whose inauguration Bright attended, with property valued at

"[*24th.*] Copies of C. Sumner's letters given to Hamilton A. Hill, to be sent to Mr. Pierce, Boston.[1] Dined with Mr. Speaker, with members of late Government.

"[*March* 1.] Engaged lodgings at 132, Piccadilly: £10 per week, including everything but food.

"[*4th.*] House: Kenealy and Ashley. Spoke a few words.

"[*April* 7.] House: Women's Suffrage Bill; voted against.

"[*9th.*] To Lord Granville's to discuss the Natal Question and Lord Carnarvon's policy at the Cape in regard to the Zulu Chief, Langalibalele.[2] Home early, and reading, as last night. Finished Churchill's very remarkable book.[3]

"[*13th.*] House. Spoke on Privilege.

"[*15th.*] House. Debate on petition against Chief Justice and colleagues in Tichborne Trial. I spoke at some length in the debate.

"[*16th.*] House. Again spoke shortly on Kenealy. Home late, after midnight.

"[*21st.*] Called on J. B. Smith to inquire after Mrs. Smith: very ill. House: Burials Bill. Spoke just before division.[4] Evening, dined with Edmund Potter. Mr. Beard there, and Miss Cobbe.

"[*22nd.*] Note from Mr. Lawrence to say that Mrs. Smith died at 8.30 last evening. Sad blow for her husband and daughter.

"[*23rd.*] Dear Mary and Lillie came up from Brighton at 3.20. Mary to 132, Piccadilly: Lillie to Uncle Edward's, 46, Eaton Square. It is a happiness to me to have the dear invalid child here. House: Dr. Kenealy on Tichborne case. I spoke 11.30 to 12 o'clock. Had been urged to speak by several of my friends, and speech well received. Division singular: 434 to 1.

about £100,000, and its first building, erected at a cost of £40,999, was in Edmund Street, near the Town Hall. Sir Josiah had already created an orphanage at Erdington with an endowment of a quarter of a million.

[1] E. L. Pierce of Milton, near Boston, Mass., author of "The Life of Charles Sumner," was a close friend of Bright.

[2] It was in 1875 that Lord Carnarvon, as Secretary of State for the Colonies, moved by the success of the Canadian Federation Scheme, in which he had been concerned, propounded a plan of federation for the South African Colonies, and sent out J. A. Froude to inquire and expound. Froude's journey to the Cape produced gorgeous literary fruit in the first fifty pages of "Oceana;" politically, nothing but Dead Sea apples. Carnarvon and Froude were thirty years before their time.

[3] On Consumption. Bright had a tragic interest in the progress of medical science in the treatment of phthisis.

[4] See page 365.

"[26th.] With dear Mary (in her bath chair) round the Serpentine. A lovely morning and a most pleasant walk.

"[28th.] To Birmingham by 12 train. Lady passenger would confide to me some of her troubles—domestic; her husband's ill-treatment. Going to Birmingham to consult Mr. Millward, her lawyer. Did not ask her name; from Limerick, and had lived in Birmingham with her husband. Chamber of Commerce dinner in honour of Mr. Chevalier. Spoke, but not quite as I should like to have done. To Charles Sturge's for the night.

"[29th.] To lunch with Lord Granville. Bessborough, Sydney, C. Villiers, Spencer-Lyttleton, Miss Pitt there: a pleasant time. House: to introduce Marquis Tavistock, just elected for Bedfordshire. S. Whitbread and I walked up the House with him. The Duke asked me to be one of those who introduced him. Seems a pleasant young man, and Whitbread says he has plenty of brains. I told him I hoped he would sustain the reputation of his house. Tired and not very well. Went early for a quiet evening with my dear child.

"[May 1.] Called on Dr. A. Clark and asked him to come and see dear Mary. Reform Club. Home early evening: read Chili Commission evidence in Tichborne Case; most conclusive.

"[2nd.] Dr. A. Clark came at 2.30. Careful examination of my dear child. His report favourable on the whole. Will write it out, with directions for her management of herself.

"[12th.] Round the Serpentine with dear Mary. The day very fine and warm. . . . Evening, to dine at Argyll Lodge with Duke and Duchess of Argyll: Lord Lorne and Princess Louise, Lord F. Cavendish, Ned Leveson-Gower, Lord Granville's brother, and three of the Duke's children,—Victoria, Frances and another. I sat next the Princess. She is looking very well, and was very cheerful and pleasant in her conversation. The Duke told me she was a charming person in the family.[1]

"[13th.] Athenæum Club to dinner. Long chat with Sir Bartle Frere there on India. He referred to my speech on Indian affairs in 1858 and suggested I should elaborate it and not abandon the subject. He seems a good man, and has a great interest in India, and is far from

[1] Queen Victoria's fourth daughter, Princess Louise, was the only one of her children to marry a subject—the Marquis of Lorne, eldest son of the Duke of Argyll. The marriage, popular as a love romance in high quarters always is, took place in 1871. Lord Lorne sat in the 1874 Parliament for Argyllshire, and resigned his seat in 1878 on his appointment as Governor-General of Canada. See page 350.

content with our present policy, which he considers dangerous. He wishes intelligent natives to be more associated with Englishmen in all departments of the government of the Indian Empire. House: Adulteration of Food and Drugs Bill: I think a foolish measure.

"[21*st*.] Lunched with Quentin Hogg, 5, Richmond Terrace, to meet Mr. Moody, the American evangelist. Found him a sincere and capable man, much in earnest.

"[*June* 17.] House: spoke briefly on Commission to inquire into corruption at Norwich. Conversation with Dr. Kenealy about his expulsion from the Bar, and his wish to be restored.

"[18*th*.] Buckingham Palace Hotel, to lunch with Cyrus W. Field and party; Carl Schurz there, and other Americans.

"[19*th*.] To breakfast with Russell Gurney, M.P. Mr. Schurz there, Stafford Northcote, and others. Dinner with Mr. Goschen, M.P., to meet Mr. McKenzie, Prime Minister of Canada: a sensible and homely Scotchman.

"[20*th*.] Dined with J. S. Morgan, the American banker, 13, Princes Gate. Present: Dr. Potter of New York, Mr. and Mrs. Webster—she the daughter of Mr. Fish, Secretary of State.

"[22*nd*.] To breakfast with G. O. Trevelyan. Sir D. Wedderburn and Mr. Sidgwick there. Talk on spiritualism. The last is engaged in its investigation. House, evening, to dine with Geo. Smalley, *New York Tribune*. Carl Schurz, McCallogh, Morgan, and A. Arnold there; also Sir W. Harcourt.

"[25*th*.] To Richmond, and called on Lord Russell at Pembroke Lodge. Found him feeble and not able to walk much, and occasionally a little excited when speaking, but cheerful and clear in his mind. He seemed quite pleased to see me. Said, 'I have read your speeches with great pleasure,' and I answered, 'And I have read your book[1] with much interest,' to which he replied, 'And so we compliment each other!'— laughing as he said it. I told him the Palestine Explorers had discovered the 'City and Cave of Adullam,' referring to what he had said in his book on Mr. Lowe and others whom I had described some years ago as like the Adullam refugees of Scripture. This amused him much.

"Theo. Martin ('Life of Prince Consort') and his wife called; Duchess of Cleveland, dowager, also took tea with Lady Russell, and a young daughter and came back to London. Lord Carlingford in the same carriage. House for a time on Opium question.

[1] "Recollections and Suggestions," the composition of which had occupied Lord Russell's leisure since his retirement in 1866.

"[29th.] Called on Mr. Hawkins, Q.C.,[1] 12, Cleveland Row, on Tichborne case and falsehoods spread among the people, with plan for exploding them. To the Temple to see Mr. Hall, but could not find him; he was one of the counsel sent out to Chili. House. Home by 7 o'clock, reading Chief Justice's 'summing-up' in Tichborne—as interesting as any novel.

"[30th.] To dinner with Lord Coleridge. Large party, 22 in all: Archbishop of Canterbury, Bishop of Ely, Dean of St. Paul's, Lady Derby, Lowe, Goschen, Lord Hannen and their wives. Miss Coleridge, intelligent and good. Our talk at dinner: religion, silence in worship, and somewhat on poetry. A pleasant chat with Lady Derby —sensible and affable.

"[July 1.] House: Education votes. Met Mr. Chamberlain, Mayor of Birmingham. Long talk with him on Birmingham affairs.

"[6th.] Call from Joseph Arch of the Agricultural Labourers' Union—a sensible, and I think, an honest man.[2] Long talk on Union and the condition of farm labourers, and the question of giving them votes. He wished me to present a petition from them with 60,000 signatures, which I have promised to do. Athenæum Club to dinner: met Mr. Stoughton, dissenting minister, lately admitted to the Club.

"[7th.] Twenty-four years this day since my dear father died. House: presented a petition from 60,000 members and friends of Agricultural Labourers' Union in favour of Household Franchise in counties.

"[10th.] Called on Mr. Noble, the sculptor, in Bruton St. He is making a bust of me for Thos. Taylor, of Wigan. Sat an hour for him.

"[11th.] Call from Mr. Ward, from Nashville, Tennessee, U.S. He has a large school, 300 girls, of whom 100 in his house. He is spending his vacation in a journey to Europe with 5 young ladies, his pupils; a party of 10 or 11 in all. Interesting talk on Education. He spoke highly of the Jubilee Singers. Mentioned the growing good feeling between North and South. He had held slaves, inherited from his father.

[1] Afterwards Baron Brampton. Hawkins, who conducted the Tichborne prosecution, was raised to the Bench in the year following this entry.

[2] Joseph Arch, an agricultural labourer and the son of an agricultural labourer, was then in middle life, having been born in 1826. Ten years later, the County Franchise Act which Gladstone carried gave him the opportunity of standing as a candidate for Parliament, and his fellow-labourers in N.W. Norfolk returned him to Westminster. He failed in 1886, but was re-elected in 1892 and 1895. He earned the admiration and respect of all parties.

"[12*th.*] To Mr. Noble's in Bruton St. for more than an hour. He proposed to send me a small copy of a bust of Faraday, the great chemist, of whom he spoke in terms of admiration and affection. On one occasion Faraday, hearing the sculptor's chisels rattling in his hand, looked serious and said, 'The sound reminds me of the anvil: my father was a smith.'

"House till near midnight, when, weary, I paired with Lord Helmsley and came away.

"[13*th.*] To Marshall Wood, Osnaburgh St., Regent's Park. He is making a bust of me for the Union League Club in New York. I found, to my annoyance, that some friends of mine have commissioned him to make a statue of me for the Manchester Town Hall. I do not care for statues, and I have no wish to appear in marble in the Manchester Town Hall. He wishes me to assist him in his work, which I am little inclined to do. I think my friends might have paid some regard to my known aversion to statues. There have been only a few men worthy of statues, and to the memory of those so worthy, statues are not needed.

"Athenæum Club to dine. Met Mr. or Sir F. Halliday, once Govr. of Bengal, now of the Indian Council; also Sir B. Frere, who is going out to India with the Prince of Wales. The Queen was not in favour of the visit to India, tho' she had consented. He wished the Princess could go—not absolutely impossible, thought the scheme might be very good or very bad. To which I replied, 'Then, if danger of "bad," I would let well alone, and give up the scheme.' Frere thought the Prince sensible of the importance of his visit, and would make it useful so far as he could. Hoped his kindness to those about him and courtesy to the natives high and low might have a good effect, and perhaps make it the rule to treat them with a just consideration.

"Evening: dined with Chas. Howard, M.P., Palace Green, Kensington. He is brother of Lord Carlisle. Long in the House, always very friendly with me. A nice party: his son George and his wife, daughter of Lord Stanley of Alderley, their lovely little children; Trevelyan and his wife; Col. Ponsonby, the Queen's Secy., and his wife; Sir W. Lawson; Mr. and Mrs. Mundella. Interesting talk at dinner with Mrs. Howard on religious belief in connexion with the visit of Moody and Sankey and their revival services.

"I suspect her views, like those of her poor sister, Lady Amberley, have been influenced by Jno. Stuart Mill and his writings. Lyulph

Stanley and his wife, daughter of Lothian Bell, of Newcastle, were there: she sensible and pleasant.

"[*14th.*] Walked up to Marshall Wood's studio, 17, Osnaburgh St., and sat for bust. With him to Mayall's, to be photographed to assist him in his modelling. Athenæum Club to dinner, and then to the Treasury. Long talk with Mr. Stephenson, Solicitor of the Treasury, on Tichborne trial. Saw casts of feet of convict Orton. Stephenson sends me up volume of 'Summing up,' and of Coleridge's speech in first trial.

"The day soaking wet from 11 in the morning; myself weary and not well. Must leave town. At this season I seem to suffer tho' I am not doing much work of any kind.

"[*15th.*] Rain yesterday and thro' the night, and this morning continued rain; have rarely seen the streets so full of water, in every hole or depression. Damage to hay and harvest must be serious.

"To Victoria Station, to meet my dear girls coming from Brighton, and brought them to my lodgings.

"House: debate on expenses of Prince of Wales's journey to India, and spoke in favour of proposal of the Govt. My observations well recd. and much cheered by both sides of the House. Much of the discussion not satisfactory, and I thought it might be useful to say something friendly of the Prince, and to show how his visit to India might be useful.

"[*16th.*] House for a short time: talk with Mr. Gladstone about Judges and excessive cost of our judicial system. Home to tea with my dear girls.

"[*17th.*] To Euston Station with dear Lillie, on her way home, with her pug dog 'Cudjo'[1] . . . dear Mary remaining at the Boltons (Mrs. McLaren's) till I come back for her. Pleasant evening with my dear invalid girl, telling her of some incidents of my first marriage, of my acquaintance with the family of Helen's dear mother, of their virtues and hers; of our journey from Newcastle, of her illness, our residence at Leamington, of her death; details of her lovely character, and of the bringing up of her dear child Helen.

"[*August* 15, *at York.*] To Meeting. Remarkable sermon from J. S. Rowntree—his first appearance in the gallery since his great affliction, the death of his wife from a sad carriage accident about 2 months ago. He spoke from the words 'Art thou he that should come, or do we look for another?' Had the faith of the Baptist wavered

[1] So called after the character in "Cudjo's Cave": see page 274.

in his solitude and in prison? The mysterious events of our lives stagger faith, but we must accept the reply of Jesus to John's disciples— 'Go and tell John', etc. The sermon beautiful in expression and most impressive. Evening at Sarah Rowntree's and very pleasant.

"[16*th*.] Visit to James Backhouse's wonderful garden and grounds. Called on his aunts, at the house where Lindley Murray wrote his Grammar, and where he died. Called at Mount School and at the boys' school, Bootham—both nice schools.

"Also visited the 'Retreat' and saw my dear old Cousin Eleanor Whitehead, in her 91st year. Quite a picture of gentleness and goodness. She was in bed, looking quite happy and pleased at our visit, tho' at first she scarcely knew us.

"[*September* 4, *at Rochdale*.] Mr. W. Claflin (ex-Governor of State of Massachusetts) came and dined with us. He brought letters from J. G. Whittier and Mr. Kinsley, of Boston. He seems a sensible and pleasant man."

At the end of September he went to Scotland to fish for a fortnight, returning to the Lake District and paying a visit to Mr. W. Rathbone at Bassenfels.

"[*October* 16.] Left Bassenfels at 12 o'clock for Penrith and home soon after 6 o'clock. My visit very pleasant. The ladies, three Mrs. Rathbones—the venerable mother, 85 yrs. old, and the wives of her two sons (they are sisters), sensible and nice women. The children very agreeable. One sweet girl, Eleanor,[1] 3 yrs. of age, was a choice picture to look upon. Long discussion with the two brothers on the Drink or Licence question. They are for free trade in drink, limited only by the pressure of an increased taxation, and I incline to think they are right; but the question is very difficult.[2]

"[*November* 19.] To Carlisle and Brayton, to Sir Wilfrid Lawson's. Sir Harcourt Johnstone there, for discussion on Drink Question."

[1] Miss Eleanor P. Rathbone, now Member of Parliament for the Northern Universities.

[2] Mr. Gladstone had expressed opinions in favour of "free trade" in liquor. Mr. Bruce's Act of 1872, which was the first effective effort to regulate the sale of drink in towns, had provoked from Magee, the Bishop of Peterborough, his classic dictum that he would "rather have England free than England sober."

2

The "Drink Question," always a Riddle of the Sphinx for the Liberal Party, violently agitated it just then. The "Trade," using its whole weight at the General Election, had notably helped to bump Liberal candidates out of the scales. Bright well knew the handicap that was clapped on reformers immediately any suggestion arose of tackling the licensing laws. He spoke gravely of it in his addresses at Birmingham this winter.

But though he and Sir Wilfrid Lawson became great friends, Lawson never converted him to his principle of the local veto by plebiscite, then embodied in what was called the Permissive Bill. Bright disliked the licensing system administered by magistrates; but he distrusted even more a system which would put licensing questions to periodical tests in localities by "a fluctuating public opinion."

"I am in favour of municipal control," he had written to a correspondent two years before: that was, the control "of the ratepayers through the local Parliament which they elect. . . . The Town Council represents the town, and to its wisdom I would entrust the power to grant or refuse licences, subject, it may be, to such limits as Parliament may properly determine."

He never went back on that position. It was part of his general conception of local government, in which the authority, dignity and autonomy of the Town and City Councils had a foremost place. He did not live to see the Liberal Party under the guidance of his friend Harcourt come to grief over a "Permissive Bill."

The Birmingham speeches dealt with the Church, the county franchise, and thel and question. The reader will find in the diaries of 1876 and 1877 only a faint echo of the feverish excitement engendered by events in the Balkans. As often when a great issue loomed up, Bright crammed his thought and labour on the subject into preparation for his speeches. None could doubt where his sympathy lay in a conflict between the Turk and the humane sentiment of Europe; but his non-interventionist principles now placed him half-way between Disraeli, the pro-Turk, and Gladstone proclaiming the "bag and baggage" policy.

This moderating position happened to be precisely Lord Derby's. Disraeli's Foreign Secretary ensued peace as earnestly as Bright himself. On July 14, 1876, he received a deputation, headed by Bright, which came to urge upon the Government a strict neutrality in the dispute between Russia and Turkey. His satisfaction at finding the Foreign Minister as pacific as himself is expressed in the short note which is one of the few allusions Bright makes to the Eastern question. He put into his campaign for peace an energy scarcely less constant than Beaconsfield's dour striving for intervention on behalf of Turkey or less palpitating than Gladstone's passionate effort to bring England on the side of Russia; but it scarcely ruffles the surface of the diaries.

"[*February* 11, 1876.] Call from Rupert Potter with photos of Millais, H. James and myself, for me to sign as autograph.

"Dined with Mr. Gladstone. His son and bride there—she, like her family connexions, the Duchess of Argyll, etc., very nice but delicate-looking. Also there, Chas. Howard, Mr. Morier, from Munich, and Lord Rosebery, whom I met for the first time. Intelligent and liberal; my impression of him very favourable.

"[*18th.*] Call from Mr. Russell, of the *Liverpool Daily Post.* . . . House. Home early: read papers on 'Slavery Circulars.'[1]

"This morning heard result of Election at Manchester. My brother Jacob is returned by majority of 1,785. The election has excited great interest.

"[*23rd.*] R. N. Philips called: talk on Manchester election. Deeply regretted mistake made by his brother Mark in 1857, when he opposed Milner Gibson and me.[2] A fine, generous spirit in Robt. Philips. Dined with Mr. Speaker. Home with Tom Hughes in his carriage.

"[*24th.*] Breakfast with Sir W. Lawson. Walk in Park with Edmund Potter. Buckingham Palace at 3, to the Court: crowd, gold lace, many colours; brilliant. Many of my political acquaintances there.

[1] In July, 1875, the Admiralty had issued a circular to captains of British warships directing that a fugitive slave should not be received on board any of H.M. ships unless his life were in danger, and if in territorial waters he should be surrendered on legal proof of his condition. Immediately a storm of protest arose. The instructions defied Lord Mansfield's famous doctrine that a slave who entered British territory became free for ever, or they infringed the law that H.M. ships were British territory, wherever they might be found. The Admiralty issued a revised circular late in the year, but even this ordered that a fugitive slave was not be taken on board in territorial waters where slavery prevailed. The Government was challenged and escaped defeat in a party division by only 45 votes; but the fierce indignation of the country against the implied recognition of slavery made of this circular a dead letter.

[2] See page 225.

John Everett Millais John Bright Henry James
Sept. 30. 1875

"The Queen looked well and in good humour. As I passed, she said, smiling, 'I hope you are quite well, Mr. Bright.'

"The Duke of Cambridge shook me by the hand cordially. Rather a queer ceremony on the whole, whether more amusing or humiliating I have not been able to determine.

"House: walked up the House with my Bro. Jacob on his election for Manchester; Sir Thos. Bazley with us. Debate and division on 'Slave Circulars;' good speeches by Herschell and Sir W. Harcourt; majority 45 against us.

"[25th.] In train to Retford, Mr. Laycock, a farmer from Northumberland. Talk on wages and workmen. In his county, farm labourers 21/– per week in money; house and coals 4/–; potatoes for family 1/– per week: in all 26/– per week. Farm labourers formerly 14/– per week in money with same extras. Colliers rose 50% since 1871, and now fallen to 15% above the wages of that time. Farm labourers keep their 50% advance and no sign of reduction. Trades Unions of no permanent good to colliers.

"[March 6.] With Philip to Westminster Abbey. Saw the Queen on our way down by the Palace. From the Abbey to South Kensington Museum, and Patent Museum, where Philip was delighted with models of engines, etc. In the evening to the House. Philip in gallery for an hour; then took him to the House of Lords, where he saw the 'potentates in their gilded chamber.'

"[8th.] Lord Granville's: met Gladstone, Lowe, Hartington and Forster, to discuss course on 'Royal Titles Bill.'[1]

"[9th.] House: debate on 'Titles Bill.' House insincere and voting what it is secretly against.

"My old friend Thos. Thomasson of Bolton died last night at 9.20. He has been long one of the foremost of my friends, and I have received many kindnesses from him.

"[13th.] With dear Helen to Bolton, to the funeral of my old friend Thos. Thomasson. A small party; the funeral quiet and simple, as of one of our Society. The burial was at Turton Church, 5 miles from Bolton, and was without any Church service, after the manner of 'Friends.' . . . My old friends thus one by one pass away, and the longer we are in the world in one sense, the more solitary we become.

"[16th.] House: Royal Titles Bill. A large majority for, tho' almost all the House notoriously against it.

[1] Disraeli's Bill, whose chief purpose was to confer upon the Queen the title of Empress of India, had been introduced on February 17.

"[*17th.*] Dined with Sir F. Buxton and party, L. and L. Abinger, Mr. and Mrs. Ridley, Mr. Trollope, the author, and Mr. Froude, historian, and others.

"[*23rd.*] Westminster Meeting. Wedding of Theodore Harris and Gertrude Louisa Russell, daughter of Lord Chas. Russell, late Serjeant-at-Arms of the House of Commons. Curious and perhaps unique case of a marriage in a Friends' Meeting House between one of our members and the daughter of one of our oldest and highest aristocratic families. But it is a good family. The breakfast was at the Grosvenor Hotel. I was present. A party of 50. Lord Edwd. Russell a lively old man. Lord Arthur Russell and his wife were there.

"House: 3rd reading of Royal Titles Bill. Remarkable debate. Gladstone's speech serious and impressive, and Disraeli frivolous and mischievous, and must have been a sore humiliation to every thoughtful man in his party.[1]

"[*25th.*] Sir Chas. Trevelyan called on me to talk over Royal Titles Bill—his hostility to it very strong. Different titles for different parts of the Empire is an act of dismemberment and not of union. Disraeli's speech is more of madness than of statesmanship.

"Dined 80, Eccleston Square, with W. E. Forster. Listened to Ernest de Bunsen on modern prophecies, and on abstruse questions of ancient faiths.

"[*26th.*] Read Deuteronomy: many parts very noble in language and sentiment.

"[*April* 8.] To Mr. Theed, sculptor, and sat for an hour for bust. Then to Zoological Gardens: dined there. Club. Evening dined with Sir D. Marjoribanks, Park Lane. A grand house and a large party. My place between Mrs. Brand, the Speaker's wife, and Lady Cotterell, from Herefordshire. Long chat with C. P. Villiers. His criticisms as usual severe and not friendly on Mr. Gladstone, whom he charges with wishing to get back to the place of leader of the Liberal Party, etc.

"[*25th.*] Made some notes on question of Women's Suffrage Bill coming on to-morrow, but hope I may not have occasion to speak.

"[*26th.*] House: spoke on Women's Suffrage Bill. Good House.

---

[1] The outstanding features of the debate were Disraeli's castigation of Lowe (who had been most acidulated, indiscreet and inaccurate in opposition to the Bill, and never recovered from the humiliation), and the maiden speech of Joseph Cowen, of Newcastle. *The Times* and London society were as hostile as the Radicals; they regarded the whole thing as a vulgar ostentation. Disraeli, however, succeeded in pleasing both the Queen and the populace.

Speech considered very successful against the Bill, and division with majority of 87 against.

"Some of my relations will be angry, but I could not but speak my own convictions on the question.[1]

"[*27th*.] To dinner at 81, Eaton Square, Duke of Bedford's. Small party: Mr. Motley and his two daughters, Mr. Jowett from Oxford, Mr. Lecky, author of the 'History of Rationalism,' and his wife. Motley stronger in health. 'He could talk about his country but not about its administration,' of which he was greatly ashamed. Recent disclosures of corruption have much disgusted him.

"Mr. Jowett's gentle manner pleases me. Mr. Lecky, tall, pleasant and intelligent countenance, large eyes, manner modest and engaging.

"The Duke very friendly. His second son for the Army when education finished. I advised him to go to the House of Commons: I thought the more Russells there the better, as the breed is so good.

"[*29th*.] To dinner, 8, Grosvenor Crescent, with Sir C. Trevelyan. Fitzjames Stephen there, Lord Justice James, J. W. Pease, Laurence Oliphant, Sir W. Lawson and ladies, and Geo. O. Trevelyan and his wife.

"Read 'Life of Macaulay' last two nights till one o'clock.[2]

"[*May* 1.] House. Great dissatisfaction with the Proclamation of 'Empress.' It is a fraud on the House and may cause much dissension.

"Home early and finished 'Life and Letters of Macaulay.' An interesting work. Could find some fault with him and it. The attack on Mrs. Stowe needless and offensive. Her services to freedom should have saved her from this from Zachary Macaulay's son. It is curious how much we may be told about a man's life and opinions and not see a word which indicated any opinion on religion—except

[1] In 1858, when he was drawing up his own Reform Bill, Mrs. Pochin had asked him to insert in it a provision for women's suffrage. He told her he knew of no valid argument against it, but "in the present state of opinion" it would do harm to the cause of Reform to bring in the question and no good to the cause of Women's Votes. In 1867 he voted for J. S. Mill's amendment in favour of the feminine suffrage. But in 1871 he began to have doubts about the wisdom of that vote. He told Miss Sturge that women's votes would do no good to them and would tend to strengthen the party which had opposed every good measure for the last 30 years and add to the power of priestcraft. "I hope this view of the question may be a mistaken one, because it does not seem to me very unlikely that the suffrage will be granted to women." He still held that view in 1876. The "relations" whom he expected to be angry, headed by his sister, Mrs. McLaren, included three of his own daughters.

[2] Sir George Trevelyan's "Macaulay" had just been published.

the assertion that he was a 'Christian' to the electors of Leeds. My opinion of Macaulay much raised by reading his nephew's 2 vols.

"[3rd.] Lord Granville called. Asked me to move resolution on the Proclamation as not according to promises of Ministers. Hesitated and wished for time to consider it. Walk in Park; Club and House. Fawcett, Cowen and Dilke urged it upon me, but I declined. Not my forte—rather a legal question, and did not feel it in my line. They were all kind, and so I escaped.

"[4th.] Home at 11, and read translation of Ste.-Beuve's Essays on English Portraits.

"[5th.] Home early: read Ste.-Beuve on our poet Cowper—charming essay.

"[6th.] Dined at Fenton's Hotel, St. James's St., with Hugh Mason. W. Agnew there. He had bought a picture, Gainsborough's 'Duchess of Devonshire,' for 10,000 guineas!

"[8th.] Called at Agnew's and saw the costly picture. Much colour, but not a picture to my taste. There are many better of Gainsborough.

"House: smoking-room. Long chat with Sir H. Holland on Macaulay, his wife's uncle. He lamented his errors and obstinacy in the charges against Wm. Penn. Chat with Mr. Fawcett. Said he will not bring on Women's Suffrage Bill again in this Parliament: the friends of the Bill lukewarm; only one man on his side spoke in its support.

"Dined with Mr. Waddy, Q.C., at the House. Gave me curious anecdotes about the 'Claimant' at his trial. Sitting near him, heard his remarks to his counsel, showing what he was. M. A. Loader (witness) said Orton was about 9 months in England after his first voyage. Claimant said to Kenealy, his Counsel, 'Cross-examine her well on this; it was only 3 months.'

"Mrs. Jury, from Australia, was in Court, and saw him, but was not known to the general public. Next day Kenealy told him she was come, and would be a witness. He said, 'I know she is come, for I saw her in the Court yesterday,' showing that he knew her and was the Orton to whom she lent the money in Australia.

"[12th.] House: Irish Sunday Closing Bill. Spoke, and with some effect, I hope. A good division against the Govt.

"Morning: call from Lord Granville. Talk on Burials Bill and on part taken by Queen on Titles Bill, and on opinion of Duke of S. on India. Wise men there only give us 50 years of possession, etc.!

"[*30th.*] Morning: making notes for speech, which probably may not be spoken, on County Franchise Bill. House. Spoke on 'County Franchise' resolution. Dear Elizabeth and Sophie in the Ladies' Gallery. The question too large to be easily dealt with, but general conviction that the proposition is right and cannot be long resisted.

"Lowe opposed, and I spoke after him, which created some interest in the House.

"[*31st.*] Lunch with Goschen, to meet M. Léon Say, French Finance Minister. Mr. Speaker there, Judge Bramwell, Sir S. Northcote and others.

"With Sir W. V. Harcourt to Duchess of Argyll's garden party, Campden Hill. Fine day, large party, and pleasant. Met Lady Bell, widow of Sir Chas. Bell, 90 years of age—beautiful in her age, and intelligent.

"[*June* 1.] Professor Lister [1] called to talk on 'Vivisection.' Interesting man. His views against the Govt. Bill. Mr. Claflin, from Boston, U.S.A., called to take leave.

"[*5th.*] To Saffron Walden to stay the night with G. S. Gibson's family. A pleasant visit. His garden beautiful. In a small field adjoining, saw a singular sight—many skeletons lying exposed on the chalk, supposed to be of Saxon times, men, women and children. The soil, two to three feet in depth, being removed, the skeletons were found laid in hollow places in the chalk. Some trinkets were found on one of them. No history of the cemetery: all obscure.

"[*8th.*] Heard of the death of my old friend, A. W. Paulton, on the 6th inst. He has gradually sunk since I last saw him. He was confidential Secretary to the Anti-Corn Law League, and a great friend of Mr. Cobden. Our fellow-workers in the Free Trade cause are going, and few are now left of those most concerned in that great contest.

"[*14th.*] House: Permissive Bill. Speech intended, but no time for it; so did not speak or vote.

"[*15th.*] House: Education Bill. A bad Bill.[2]

[1] The future Lord Lister came of a Quaker family. The Vivisection Bill (in which the Queen took great interest) required every experimenter to hold a licence from the Home Secretary, and forbade the vivisection of an animal which had not been rendered insensible to pain.

[2] The best point in the Bill, introduced by Lord Sandon, was that it repealed the 25th clause of Forster's Act. The Church schools were benefited by a clause providing that the Parliamentary grant might exceed the amount of the voluntary subscriptions if it did not go beyond the total of 17*s*. 6*d*. per child. The worst

"[22nd.] Called on Mr. Gladstone, 33, Harley St.; then on Baroness Burdett-Coutts, on her invitation for next Wednesday to a reading by Mr. Irving,[1] the actor.

"Dined at Stafford House to meet Sir Sálár Jung, Minister of the Nizam of Hyderabad.[2] He is lame from an accident, and is wheeled about in a chair. He is man of active brain, of pleasant manners and address, and speaks English well. Had some conversation with him. Large party at dinner and much company afterwards. 3 Dukes and 3 Duchesses, Lord and Lady Salisbury, Disraeli, Rawlinson, Mr. Farrar, Russell, *The Times* famous correspondent, Lady Chesham, and crowds of whom I know nothing. A fine party—grand rooms and much music and plenty of light.

"[28th.] To Baroness Burdett-Coutts to hear Mr. Irving read *Macbeth*. Disappointed: manner and tone not natural.

"[29th.] Note from Duke of Sutherland, asking me to go with him and Sir Sálár Jung to Trentham, the Potteries, Liverpool, Dunrobin, Glasgow and Edinburgh. Wrote to decline: dare not undergo the excitement and fatigue, tho' much that is tempting in the invitation.

"[30th.] Mr. Haworth, of Southport, called to talk the Tichborne case over. Quite strong in his delusion. Proposed interview with Onslow, Biddulph, etc., to discuss, which I declined. Told me of case getting up against Lady Radcliffe, and advised him strongly against it.

"House: Home Rule debate and division.[3] Home after 2 o'clock.

"[*July* 1.] Home early, and read Shelley's *Queen Mab*. Fine poem, but infidel and blasphemous passages in it.

"[2nd.] Stafford House to see Duke of Sutherland, on his invitation.

point in the Bill was its failure to ensure compulsory attendance. At that time the percentage of attendance was less than 70. Another provision suspect to progressive minds permitted the dissolution of School Boards in districts where there were no Board Schools.

[1] The future Sir Henry Irving.

[2] Sir Sálár Jung (Mír Turáb Alí) supported the British cause during the Mutiny and by his exertions kept the Deccan quiet. He had introduced widespread reforms in the hitherto ill-governed dominion of the Nizam, and was now in England endeavouring to secure the restoration to Hyderabad of the province of Berar, which the British Government had annexed because of the failure of the Nizam to keep his treaty obligations. He failed in this, but obtained considerable personal esteem in this country.

[3] The annual debate raised by Mr. Isaac Butt. It was made notable on this occasion by the impassioned speech of an out-and-out Repealer, Mr. Patrick Smyth, who maintained the O'Connell tradition and poured vitriolic scorn on the milder proposals of the Home Rulers.

Partly agreed to go down to Trentham on Friday with him and Sir Sálár Jung.

"[6*th*.] Dined with Sir Sálár Jung, Piccadilly. Large party. Prince of Wales there. Prince held a 'Durbar' in Indian fashion. Scenes interesting. Indians introduced to him bearing presents, and then to us,—small phials of otto of roses, which we touched and returned. I sat within 3 of the Prince, and between Lord Northbrook and Lyon Playfair.

"[7*th*.] By 5.10 train to Trentham with Duke of Sutherland and Sir Sálár Jung. The Indians in saloon carriage. The Duke, myself and Mr. Grey in the Duke's own saloon carriage. Everything very comfortable—compass, aneroid, and gauge to show speed of train. Trentham at ½ past 9. Dinner.

"[8*th*.] To Stoke, to visit Minton's works and show-rooms: interesting. Thunder shower; morning very hot. Went over gardens and glass-houses after lunch. Dinner: several guests. Afterwards Bowling Alley for an hour or two.

"[9*th*.] Party to church. I spent 2 hours with Sir Sálár Jung, talking India and his particular expectations and claims. He is moderate and sensible, and I think his case is good. Afternoon, drove out; scenery very pleasing.

"[10*th*.] To Crewe and shown thro' the great engine and iron and steel works. Duke and his guest returned to Trentham. I came on home for a short visit.

"[12*th*.] Meeting. Afternoon, Prince Arthur, Duke of Connaught, came up to see our mills, and took coffee with us at 'One Ash.' Major Picard with him; also R. T. Heape and Mr. Willans, our friends and neighbours. The Prince is affable and pleasant.

"[13*th*.] 8.20 train to London. House: introduced my new colleague, Joseph Chamberlain.[1]

"[14*th*.] Deputation to Lord Derby and introduced them. His speech remarkable; gave much satisfaction.[2] Albert was there, and went with me to the House, and spent the evening with me at my lodgings.

"Mr. Illingworth and Mr. Wade, from Bradford, called to urge

[1] Mr. Dixon having resigned his seat, Mr. Chamberlain was elected unopposed, as Bright had been before him. He had contested Sheffield unsuccessfully at the General Election of 1874. Fresh from his immensely successful campaign for municipal reform and his mayoralty of three years, he entered the House of Commons with a reputation for extreme Radicalism.

[2] This is the first allusion in the diaries to the "Eastern Question." See page 375.

me to be present at uncovering of statue of Mr. Cobden in their town some time in the autumn. Partly consented.

"[15th.] Dined with Sir W. Millar, 1, Park Lane. Large party; dining-room hot. Dinners should be suspended at this season. All strangers to me, but evening pleasant. Col. Hoffman, U.S. Secretary of Legation, came in. Talk on American politics.

"[17th.] Reform Club: Club meeting, and spoke at it. House: Education Bill; spoke in favour of reducing punishment from 3 mos. to 14 days. Committee agreed. Severe punishments unwise and unjust.

"[18th.] Dined with W. Rathbone. A party of Liberal M.P.s. Conversation with Mr. Sullivan, M.P. for Louth, on Home Rule question. Suggested Irish and Scotch Bureaux or Committees for Irish and Scotch business, Bills prepared by them to be submitted to the House; thus give advantages of self-govt. modified only in accordance with interests of the United Kingdom. Walked home with Sir W. Lawson.

"[19th.] Dined with G. O. Trevelyan. Mr. and Mrs. Sidgwick there; talk on spiritualism.

"[20th.] Called on Sir Sálár Jung, and talk with him on his visit to Scotland, and his Indian affairs. House till 12 o'clock: discussion on Education Bill in Committee. Sandon offensive and dishonest.

"[21st.] Dined with Sir H. James, Wilton Place, to meet Mr. Blake,[1] Attorney-Genl. of Canada, a pleasant and sensible man. Present: Lord Hartington, F. Cavendish, Harcourt, Evelyn Ashley, and Chas. Villiers. Much talk about the 'Bravo' Inquest. It is curious and painful to find such a case made the subject for laughter and for something like coarse jests. Sir H. James is retained for Mrs. Bravo, and has 100 guineas per day for attending the inquest. This he told me.[2]

"Talk with Harcourt and Mr. Blake on extradition question (America) in which Canada is much concerned.

"[22nd.] By 4.10 train from Waterloo Station to Shepperton to

[1] Edward Blake, an Irishman, led the Canadian Liberals for some years. He afterwards entered British politics, was returned as Nationalist Member for South Longford in 1892, and took a prominent part in the parliamentary proceedings on the second Home Rule Bill.

[2] Mrs. Bravo was suspected of poisoning her husband. She had been intimate with Dr. James Manby Gully, of the water-cure, who is the original of "Dr. Gullson" in Charles Reade's "It's Never Too Late To Mend."

see W. S. Lindsay. There before ½ past 5. Pleasant evening on terrace looking on the river. Sir P. Colquhoun to dinner.

"[*23rd.*] Yesterday was terribly hot, and to-day is warm. To Shepperton Church. Mr. Govett bought the living, and, I suspect, buys his sermons. Pretty church, small congregation, mostly women; apparently no 'working people.' Service mostly unintelligible to me, except Litany, and sermon, which was dry and read without effect or impressiveness.

"River lovely: alive with small steam launches and pleasure boats till night. We sat on the terrace, and hardly any scene could be more lovely.

"[*24th.*] House: Education Bill Committee. I spoke earnestly against the course of the Govt. in permitting the dissolution of School Boards. Long debate till midnight.

"[*27th.*] House. Moved an amendment on Education Bill, and spoke strongly on treatment of Dissenters. No answer to my arguments and facts, but the vote against me.

"[*August* 1.] House: spoke in favour of release of Fenian prisoners.

"[*2nd.*] Education deputation to Lord Hartington.

"[*3rd.*] House: Education Bill.

"[*4th.*] By 10.10 train to Rochdale.[1]

"[*17th.*] Bernard Becker, from *World* newspaper, called to 'interview' me. Employed to write articles on 'distinguished men,' where they lived, and how, particulars likely to interest the public. I told him I was already too much written about and could do nothing for him. He said he would detain me only a few minutes; information wanted such as my favourite books, favourite studies, and something I forget about 'oratory.' I told him I had no favourite books and did not study, and, as to oratory, my speeches were published and open to all. I was now on the shelf, and was not before the public, etc. He apologized for his intrusion. I asked him to have some dinner as it was our dinner time, so he joined us at table; but he did not get much matter for the paper he is to write. He said Mr. Tennyson, the poet, did not object to furnish such information as they wanted. He thanked me for my 'hospitality,' and I hoped he would not think me uncourteous if I did not assist him in his labours.

"[*18th.*] Eli Johnson, U.S.A., called. Talk on Temperance

---

[1] Bright missed the maiden speech of Joseph Chamberlain, which was made this day (August 4) on the Report stage of the Education Bill.

question. He described modes of adulteration of spirits and wines and beer, and how to make them by chemical mixtures.[1]

"[*December* 4.] To Birmingham to Mr. Chamberlain's. Town Hall: great meeting. I spoke for an hour and 20 minutes with force and ease. Meeting unusually quiet—intent on subject of possible war, Turkey and Russia.[2]

"Jno. Morley, Editor of *Fortnightly Review*, at Chamberlain's; intelligent and pleasant.[3]

"[*25th, at Rochdale.*] Christmas Day comes with cold frost and threatenings of snow.

"[*27th.*] Meeting. Town Hall, to a meeting of Freeholders of Townships on question of the 'Common.'"[4]

[1] Bright spent some part of the following three months fishing in Scotland and holiday-making with the family in North Wales, where he received a visit from Chamberlain. In the meantime the Eastern Question had blazed up suddenly and fiercely. Bright's speech at the Manchester Reform Club, Gladstone's pamphlet on the Bulgarian atrocities, Baring's Report, Beaconsfield's speech at the Guildhall, and the Tsar's reply had followed each other in rapid procession. The stage was set for the Russo-Turkish War.

[2] This was the second of Bright's speeches during the winter on the Eastern Question. He had visited Manchester on September 21, and met Mr. Armitage, Mr. Robert Leake and Dr. Watts, who "asked me to come to evening party at the Reform Club on Monday, 10th month, 2, to which I consented, but with great reluctance." On October 2, therefore, he attended a "soirée" at the Club and put into solemn and memorable words his judgment of Beaconsfield and his plea for our neutrality. He denounced the Prime Minister's attitude as defiant of the people of England and heartlessly cruel to the people of Bulgaria and Servia. The country, he said, regretted the Crimean War. "We are not now anxious to go to war to defend the Turk, and we are not called upon, and do not intend, to go to war to attack the enemies of the Turk."

Between the Manchester and Birmingham meetings occurred Beaconsfield's fiery pro-Turk speech at the Mansion House. Against this warlike outburst Bright fulminated to his great audience: "Shall the might of England again be put forth to sustain so foul a tyranny as that which rules in Constantinople—a tyranny which is drying up realms to deserts, a tyranny which throughout all its wide range of influence has blasted for centuries past with its withering breath all that is lovely and beautiful in Nature and all that is noble and exalted in man?"

[3] John Morley's brief connexion with *The Morning Star* as its last editor (June to October, 1869) began after Bright had severed his connexion with the paper on joining the Gladstone Government. This appears to have been their first meeting.

[4] The common lay between "One Ash" and the town of Rochdale: the Bright Mills adjoined it.

On the sweltering August day of 1876 when the world learned of Disraeli's elevation to the House of Lords as Earl Beaconsfield, Bright was at Rochdale playing bowls on his brother's lawn at Green Bank. He made no note either of Disraeli's last speech in the Commons and his silent farewell to the House, or of his translation, or of the excitements of the succeeding weeks, when the flame of indignation against Disraeli's pro-Turk policy, lit by Gladstone's Bulgarian pamphlet, was fanned to a fierce blaze by Baring's detailed report on the atrocities. He kept these subjects for his speeches.

He did not return to London during the early development of the divisions in the Liberal Party on Eastern policy, and when he attended the House for the first time in the Session of 1877 (March 8) the outbreak of the Russo-Turkish War was only six weeks away.

Bright's position in the Eastern controversies, as the diaries show, differed from Gladstone's; for the logical issue of Gladstone's arguments would have been British intervention against the Porte. Bright, much as he hated the Turkish system, was for no intervention at all. Perhaps at this moment he stood closer to Lord Derby than to any other statesman, holding that "the greatest of British interests was Peace."

Before embarking on the troubled waters in which the Liberal ship strained so painfully that year, he had a pleasant week with Mrs. Bright in London. She had come up for Mr. Charles McLaren's [1] wedding to Miss Laura Pochin, and one of the diversions of the visit was a night in the Ladies' Gallery to hear the speech of Chamberlain on the Gothenburg licensing system,—the second he had made in the House since his election. Chamberlain's municipal experiences in Birmingham had engendered in him a keen interest in licensing reform, and in 1876 he had studied the Gothenburg system on the spot. [2] He ardently desired to see some such solution applied to licensing problems in England, and this was the burden of his song on March 13.

---

[1] Now Lord Aberconway.

[2] In the previous January Chamberlain had strongly advocated in the City Council of Birmingham the municipalization of the local liquor traffic. He argued that the first result of such a measure would be a reduction of 1,000 in the number of public-houses in the city. This was Bright's solution of the licensing problem. (See page 375.) Under the Gothenburg system of disinterested management, the local authorities contracted with a limited company, which administered the licensed houses and handed over the net proceeds of the business to the Treasury.

"[*March* 13, 1877.] House: dear Elizabeth in Gallery, to hear Mr. Chamberlain's fine speech on Gothenburg system of promoting temperance.

"[*17th.*] Dined with Sir W. V. Harcourt and his bride, who is a daughter of Mr. Motley, the American historian. Party of 12 at table. Walked back with Sir W. Lawson. The lady very thin; pleasant and intelligent; has been much in Europe.

"[*19th.*] To Lord Granville's to discuss return of Sir H. Elliot to Constantinople. Hartington, Gladstone, Gorst, Cardwell there.[1] Rumours that arrangement between our Government and Russia not completed, but difficulties not defined.

"[*21st.*] Dined with Lord Hartington at Devonshire House: a party of 22. Sat between Fredk. Leveson-Gower and Mr. Samuda. The latter is building a frigate for Japan, and asked me to go down to see the launch, which I should like to do.

"[*22nd.*] To the Temple, to call on my friend Sir David Dundas, now very ill. He was pleased to see me, and talked a little. Referred to our meeting 20 years ago in Scotland. Spoke of his love of books and reading, and quoted from Bacon. 'May God lead you by the hand;' to which I replied, 'Let us say that to each other.' I left him, saying 'Farewell,' to which he answered 'Farewell.' Shall probably not see him again.

"House. Evening, dined with Fras. Buxton, 15, Eaton Place; pleasant party. Read *Epic of Hades*, and greatly pleased with it.[2]

[1] Sir Henry Elliot, Ambassador at Constantinople, had incurred the wrath of sympathizers with the victims of Turkish persecution by a sentence in his letter covering Baring's report on the atrocities in Bulgaria. He said British interests were not concerned in the question whether ten or twenty thousand persons perished in the insurrection. This was literally true of material interests, and Elliot meant it in that sense. But it had the appearance of an inhuman indifference when read in the temper of righteous indignation that possessed the people at home. His recall was demanded, but he remained in office till Sir H. Layard succeeded him at the end of the year.

[2] Bright retained a great admiration for Lewis Morris's poem and frequently quoted from it. In the following July, when he used some lines in his speech at the unveiling of Cobden's statue at Bradford—

"For knowledge is a steep which few may climb,
    While duty is a path which all may tread,"

he said of the *Epic*, "It is another gem added to the wealth of the poetry of our language." Morris afterwards told him that in the day or two after this allusion 3,000 copies of the *Epic* were sold. In 1887, when Morris wrote his Jubilee Ode, he showed the draft to Bright, who read the words, "the rattling of the busy loom," and changed them to "the throbbing of the busy loom," thinking that an apter description. The change greatly pleased Morris.

"[*23rd.*] House: debate on Eastern question. Gladstone spoke at length, but occasionally under unusual excitement. Home 10 o'clock. Read Stigand's 'Life of Heinrich Heine;' interesting.

"[*24th.*] Dined with W. E. Forster, 80, Eccleston Square. Sir T. Wade, Minister in China, there; also Mr. White, Consul at Belgrade; Sir T. F. Buxton and his wife, Matthew Arnold and his wife and others; a pleasant party. The Eastern question discussed. Mr. Townsend of *The Spectator* was there; believed in war being unavoidable and necessary for the deliverance of population of Turkish Empire. He believed the negotiations concerning the Protocol had failed and were at an end. Home: read Heine till near 1 o'clock.

"[*26th.*] Sloane St., to dine with Sir C. Dilke; 'advanced' political party there.[1]

"[*April* 12.] House: Budget—no interest. Trade bad, revenue lessening, only expenditure growing. A rapid change from the last year of our Administration. Mr. Gladstone left a surplus of £6,000,000 —and now! Evening read Heine: very sad.

"[*17th.*] Talk with Mr. Bourke, Under-Secretary, Foreign Office. He said 'European Concert' never real, only a sham and pretence from beginning. Jealousies of Powers made it impossible.[2]

"[*19th.*] Called on my sister Priscilla at 'The Boltons.' Lunched with her. Arranged to go with her on Monday to the funeral of our poor friend, Mrs. Cobden, whose death occurred yesterday.

"House. Salford election result unfavourable, and unlooked for by both parties. A constituency below average intelligence, and much open to evil influences—those of drink especially.

"[*23rd.*] To Midhurst to the funeral of Mrs. Cobden. A small party. My dear Priscilla[3] there, always full of sympathy. The daughters in great trouble. Their life has had much of sorrow in it since the death of their father.

"[*26th.*] To 73, Harley St., to breakfast with Mr. Gladstone. Lord Granville and his bro., F. Leveson-Gower, there, Sir W. James, etc. Alfred Tennyson and his son came in as we finished breakfast.

[1] "I was engaged at this moment on an attempt to form a circle of friends who would be superior, from the existence with them of a standpoint, to the mere ordinary political world, and I began doing my best to meet frequently those whom I most liked—John Morley, Dillwyn, Leonard Courtney and Fitzmaurice, prominently among the politicians . . ." (Sir Charles Dilke's Diary.)

[2] Turkey had repudiated on the 10th the Protocol of London demanding the execution of reforms. Russia declared war on the 24th.

[3] Mrs. Duncan McLaren.

As we were introduced he said, 'I have often wished to meet you.' I referred to the last time we met; it was at the Bar of the House of Lords. He remembered it well, and also the subject of debate, and a foolish speech some peer was making—particulars of which I remember nothing.

"We talked of Russia and Turkey. He was not wishful for Turkish rule to be prolonged, but thought 'their religion was a very good religion,' —I suppose, or hope, as compared with other non-Christian religions.

"Mr. Gladstone, Lord Granville, and I went into another room and had a long talk on Eastern question, Granville not agreeing with Gladstone as to wisdom or necessity of proposing resolutions to the House. After Granville left I remained, and the conversation was serious. Gladstone burdened with sense of responsibility in connexion with his share in the Crimean War, and anxious to urge that sense of responsibility on the conscience of the nation. Declared he must act alone if his former colleagues and friends declined to act.

"House: Universities Bill. Home early: read *Epic of Hades* with renewed pleasure; also a Chapter in Matthew—in French.

"[*27th.*] To meeting at Lord Granville's; 15 or 16 present. Gladstone not well and not present. Long discussion, but nearly all unwilling to submit any resolutions to the House, and much regret expressed that Gladstone was so resolved to act alone. I was requested to see him and represent opinions of his friends.

"Went up to Harley St. and found him in bed. An hour of earnest conversation with him. Not surprised, but grieved at the conclusions of his friends. His soul full of the great subject of sufferings of Christians in Turkish provinces. Could not restrain himself. His conscience and some sense of responsibility made it imperative upon him to speak, and he had decided to give notice of resolutions, and wished me to see that it was done in conjunction with Mr. Goschen, to whom he had spoken on the subject.

"How I wished at this moment that this remarkable man had been clear of the tremendous mistake of the Crimean War! How it would have enabled him to have proclaimed true principles and policy in our foreign affairs and especially on this Eastern question! The 'notice' was given by Chas. Howard, M.P. for Cumberland, and we shall have a great speech—and perhaps a great debate.[1]

[1] Gladstone's four resolutions censured the Turks for the Bulgarian horrors; asserted that Turkey had lost all claim to moral or material assistance from Britain; declared the need for the autonomy of the provinces; and asked that through the

"Evening, dined with Sir C. Trevelyan, 8, Grosvenor Crescent. Mr. Trollope, the author of many novels, was there. He is rather loud and boisterous in his manner of speaking.

"Read *Nineteenth Century*: Gladstone's article on Montenegro, etc.

"[*28th.*] With Mr. Prideaux to see his invention for burning smoke and saving coal, at Betts and Co., capsule manfrs. The invention is simple and ingenious and seems to work quite satisfactorily.

"Dined with Grant Duff, 4, Queen's Gate Gardens. Dutch Minister there, Matt. Arnold, Jno. Morley of the *Fortnightly*, etc. Pleasant evening. Much talk of Turkish question, but without much result. Home: read *Contemporary Review* till one o'clock.

"[*30th.*] Mr. Peto, son of Sir Morton Peto, called. Have seconded his nomination as a candidate for Reform Club.

"[*May* 1.] Called on Lord Granville. Long talk on Mr. Gladstone's resolutions and difficulties caused by them. House. Committee on my clauses of the Irish Land Act. Evening read a touching story in verse written by Lady Granville's mother, describing some of the joys and sorrows of her life.

"[*2nd.*] To Devonshire House, City, to hear address from Mr. Spurgeon [1] to men of business. Noble and impressive address, fine voice and manner.

"Lord Granville's: Meeting of late Government on Gladstone's resolutions. Much discussion and great difficulties, which threaten to break up the Party, and may drive Lord Hartington to resign his leadership.

"[*3rd.*] Discussion and discord in lobbies on Mr. Gladstone's resolutions.

"[*7th.*] By 8.20 train to London. Found note from Lord Granville to say the Party difficulty removed by concession on the part of Mr. Gladstone, which was a great relief to me.

"House: much surprise, pleasure, and some disappointment among the foolish and extreme men. Gladstone's speech good in every

Concert of Europe the British Government should demand guarantees from the Turkish Government for justice and humanity. These very reasonable resolutions were regarded, even by the majority of the Liberal ex-Ministers, as untimely. Lord Hartington thought there should be no parliamentary action just then, and Lord Granville held with him. Only the Duke of Argyll supported Gladstone's position.

[1] The Rev. C. H. Spurgeon, at the Friends' Meeting House.

respect.[1] Home after 10. Read through Mr. Freeman's book on Turkey.[2]

"[8*th*.] Dined with Sir D. Marjoribanks, Brook House, Park Lane. A grand dinner and display and Lords and Ladies in great plenty. Marquis of Hamilton and his wife, Earl Grosvenor and his wife, Lord Dacre and his wife, Lord Cowper, Lord Lyttelton and others whose names I forget. The house is large, and on the landing is a marble figure of 'The daughter of Pharaoh and Moses,' of wonderful beauty.

"[9*th*.] Dined with Geo. O. Trevelyan and his wife. H. Strutt and his wife also there: he is the son of Lord Belper. A pleasant evening; better than a crowd, such as is often seen at London parties.

"[12*th*.] To breakfast at Lord Granville's—Present: Morley, Richard, McArthur, Hopwood, Chamberlain, Waddy and Lord Lansdowne—to consider the Burials Bill and amendments. Morley, always good and moderate, is disposed to compromise; the rest are against it. Compromise proposed is a surrender of the principle contended for.

"Billiards with my friend B. Dickenson and beat him. Home early and read till 11. *The Epic of Hades* gives me great pleasure.

"[14*th*.] John Pender called on deputation to Lord Salisbury on Railways in Nizam's Territory—to ask liberty for Nizam to borrow funds in England.

"[15*th*.] India Office, with deputation to Lord Salisbury; no result, as it would be necessary to take opinion of Indian Government House. Curious accident happened to me. On taking my usual seat on the Front Bench, my hat was placed on the table before me. Shortly after, I observed that the hat was gone, and it could nowhere be found.

---

[1] To avoid a Party split and the resignation of Lord Hartington, Gladstone agreed to drop all but the second of his resolutions. This did not prevent him from making the speech he would have made on all four. Chamberlain supported him vigorously. The division, after a five days' debate, gave a majority of 131 for the Government, which, through Mr. Cross, declared that it would preserve neutrality in the war unless Egypt, the Suez Canal, or Constantinople were threatened.

[2] E. A. Freeman, the historian, was a fervent supporter of Gladstone's Eastern views and an even more fervent hater of Turkish tyranny and cruelty. At the great meeting at St. James's Hall to which Carlyle's letter on "the unspeakable Turk" was read, Freeman declaimed the passionate words, "Perish the interests of England, perish our dominion in India, sooner than we should strike one blow or speak one word on behalf of the wrong against the right!"

Sent up home for a soft travelling hat in which I returned home afterwards.

"Dined with Mr. and Mrs. Goschen. Lord Lorne and the Princess Louise were there; Professor Huxley; Mr. and Mrs. Lewes (George Eliot, author of so many famous novels); Capt. Burnaby, author of the 'Ride to Khiva.' Took in Mrs. Lewes to dinner. She looks old and worn, but is very pleasant in talk, thoughtful and good. She asked me about oratory, and if orators are not often moved by something of an overmastering feeling under which they must speak, etc.

"We spoke of poetry, especially of Wm. Morris of *The Earthly Paradise*, and of Lewis Morris, of whose new poem *The Epic of Hades* she had not heard. In conversation she spoke against Women's Suffrage, as did Mr. Huxley, though he had once been disposed to favour it.

"Princess Louise sat near me and she joined in the talk. After dinner in the drawing-room, I had a long chat with her—on Balmoral, on Catholicism: she wondered any sensible person could accept it; on Tunbridge Wells and the beauty of the neighbourhood; on Mrs. Lewes's novels: she liked [Daniel] 'Deronda' better than 'Middlemarch,' but perhaps 'Adam Bede' was best. The Princess seems well and happy. Her manners are charming, her conversation intelligent.

"Burnaby just the man for the 'Ride to Khiva:' fine constitution and health, plenty of good spirits; talks against the Russians; thinks wars horrible—but how to be avoided?

"Walked down with Professor Huxley. His visit to America: Everybody should go to see its greatness and growth. Talked of Gladstone and his wonderful mental activity and power.

"The evening most pleasant and interesting.

"[16*th*.] Conference on 'County Franchise extension' in Exeter Hall: presided at it. Spoke ¾ of an hour. Many other speeches till 4 o'clock. Meeting from 12 to 4. Remarkable gathering; said to be 1,200 farm labourers present from the English counties and 1,200 other delegates. Evening, dined in Grosvenor St., 49, with Edmund Backhouse. Much tired with Exeter Hall, too much so to enjoy this evening party.

"[24*th*.] By Settle and Carlisle to Edinbro', to the house of John McLaren.[1]

"[25*th*.] To Newington House, to the marriage of my dear sister Priscilla's daughter Helen [2] to Dr. Rabagliati, of Bradford. Had to

---

[1] Afterwards Lord McLaren.　　　　　　　　　[2] Miss McLaren.

speak at wedding breakfast, and dear P. was much pleased—which was sufficient return for anything I could do.

"[27th.] Club to lunch. Interesting talk with Goldwin Smith on Canada. He thinks economic causes will force Canada into the American Union.

"Called on U.S. Minister, Mr. Pierrepont; dined with him and Mrs. P. Long and pleasant talk till after 11 o'clock, on public affairs chiefly. He sensible and gentlemanly,—she very pleasant.

"[28th.] Bernard Roth called this morning: long conversation on his preference for my dear child Lillie. Wrote to her at Street.

"[30th.] Dined with Lord Coleridge: pleasant party. Lord and Lady Selborne and daughter; Bishop of London (Jackson); Dean of Durham (Lake); Lady Cath. Petre. Took into dinner Miss Palmer, Lord Selborne's daughter; sensible and good. Pleasant talk on some books and poetry. Bishops and Deans do not appear much afflicted at the distractions of their Church.

"[June 1.] To Birmingham; Queen's Hotel. Mayor's dinner to Mr. Gladstone. Spoke, but audience apparently more pleased than myself. My friends well satisfied that I was there.[1]

"[4th.] To Kensal Green Cemetery, to funeral of J. L. Motley, American historian of Dutch Republic. His three daughters present; also Duke of Argyll, Lord Houghton, Mr. Lecky, Jno. Murray and many others. The Dean of Westminster read the service very impressively.

"[5th.] With Lillie to Academy exhibition for nearly 2 hours. Wm. Tallack came to talk with me on capital punishment for approaching debate. Evening to Mr. Pierrepont's to meet Gen. Grant. A crowded party.[2]

"[6th.] Dear Lillie with Bernard Roth, who asks her to accept

[1] Gladstone's lively note on this visit to Birmingham is quoted in Morley. (Book VIII, Chapter 4.) Bright responded to the toast of the Borough Members. One of them was the Mayor, Mr. Chamberlain. The great complaint of Mr. Chamberlain, said Bright in a chaffing passage, was that nobody was active enough for him. He had passed through "a great week" at Birmingham, but no doubt he would be looking round for more excitements next week. "Mr. Chamberlain looks through his eyeglass as if he was only waiting till I should resume my seat—and then he will be able to answer this charge."

[2] Goldwin Smith says of this visit, during which he met General and Mrs. Grant: "A curiously rustic couple they looked. . . . Grant was then touring under the auspices of politicians who wanted a third term for him, and thought it might be secured by presenting him to the world's homage. No showman could have had a worse lion." ("Reminiscences," page 344.)

him. This causes me great anxiety in my interest for my dear child.

"[*9th.*] To lunch with Lord Granville, to meet Gen. Grant. Pleasant chat with him, being next him at table. Talk on Mormon settlement and its industry, and beauty of Salt Lake City, 'The most beautiful city in the world,' said Gen. Grant.

"[*11th.*] Bernard Roth here to tea.

"[*12th.*] House, 9 in the evening! Capital punishment debate. Spoke at some length; case against it unanswerable. Dear Elizabeth in the gallery. Home about ½ past 2.

"[*16th.*] Dined at Kensington Palace with Lord Lorne and Princess Louise: 26 to dinner. Gen. Grant, U.S.A., and Mrs. Grant there. I sat between Mrs. Grant and Lady Wolseley. The party very pleasant.

"[*July 5.*] Dined with W. Cowper Temple, 15, Great Stanhope Street. Mr. Gladstone there, and Lord Selborne, and Lord Northbrook, and Mr. Browning, the poet; also Lord Lymington and Mr. Newton.

"[*10th.*] Dined with Mr. Childers. Met M. Waddington, member of the late French Cabinet; intelligent and pleasant man. Much talk of great interest on France, and some on war and sympathy of France with Egypt.

"[*12th.*] Sir Jos. Whitworth called. Spoke about his invention of a new kind of wheel for carriages—made of steel with flexible spokes, each one being a spring. House.

"At ½ past 5 to Garden Party, Marlborough House. The Queen there. She spoke to me, and seemed cheerful and in good spirits.

"The Prince I met in passing thro' the house. He stopped and talked a little. Afterwards he brought the Princess towards me in the garden and introduced me to her. She is very elegant and handsome, but to me has not a friendly manner,—rather cold, not genial. I spoke to Prince Leopold, whom I saw at Balmoral. He is wonderfully improved in health. There was a large party, some of whom I knew.

"Lady Waldegrave insisted on my going to Strawberry Hill— Saturday to dinner. The party was from 5 to 7 o'clock.

"Home about 8 o'clock; made notes for Bradford Statue speech, but much perplexed about it.[1]

"[*13th.*] Called on Sir Jos. Whitworth at Thomas's Hotel, Berkeley Square. Examined his models of instruments for measuring

[1] At the unveiling of Cobden's statue. See page 396.

the millionth part of an inch, etc. Also his new invention of steel wheels for carriages: very curious.

"[15*th.*] Called on Priscilla and took tea with them, and spent evening there. Read them 'Andromeda' from *Epic of Hades*.

"[17*th.*] Dined with Arthur Peel, 70, Eaton Place. Small party: Lord and Lady Jersey, Chas. Peel and Mrs. P., Mr. Campbell, son of 'plain John Campbell,' Lord Chancellor. After dinner, pleasant chat with Lady Jersey on London life, its risks and worries, and on the unwisdom and unhappiness of many marriages.

"Read Cobden Club book on mode of controlling expenditure by Foreign Govts.

"[18*th.*] Awake till 4 or 5 o'clock. Brain too active—will think and not rest."

4

English politics has produced no friendship more affectionate and constant than that of Cobden and Bright. They were alike enough for harmony, too unlike for boredom. An unerring public instinct has joined their names so closely that people rarely mention one without the other. The spiritual twinship which it divines is a very real thing. The militant Quaker and the loyal son of the Church did not always give the same values either to measures or to men; but in the realm of pure ideals they were utterly one.

Bright never spoke of Cobden, after his death, without deep feeling. The task he faced this July at Bradford bore heavily on him, for it was bound to be emotionally exhausting. Nevertheless, the address in which he celebrated his comrade-in-arms of the battle for Free Trade was a triumph distinguished even among his many triumphs. Its perfect fitness and simplicity gave it the true poetic quality. "I come to speak for a little while of my lamented friend. . . . He trod what he believed to be the path of duty, and trod it with a firm and unfaltering footstep. . . . When I look upon this statue . . . so like him, and so spotless, as was his name and character . . . I trust . . . that from this stainless marble and from those voiceless lips there may be taught a perpetual lesson to many generations of the intelligent and industrious men of this district of our country."

The speech consisted of a series of little aspects of the various but unchanging Cobden whom he had known in deeper intimacy than any other man. But all worked up into an heroic impression of the figure of the great Emancipator who removed the taxes from the people's food and hushed the cries of their hungry children, who opened the sluices of their trade and brought them out of stagnant squalor.

> "Why need we monuments supply
> To rescue what can never die?

Those who deserve statues most require them least," said Bright. This could not be Cobden's greatest memorial. "There is not a homestead in the country in which there is not added comfort from his labours, not a cottage the dwellers in which have not steadier employment, higher wages, and a more solid independence. This is his enduring monument."

"[*24th.*] To Bradford; dear Elizabeth with me. Alfred Illingworth met me at the train. Dinner party, more than 30 guests.

"[*25th.*] Breakfast party, more than 50 guests. Exchange room at 12.30; quite full. W. E. Forster, Chairman. My speech well received.

"At 3 o'clock, lunch with Mr. Jacob Behrens, President of the Chamber of Commerce, and near 100 of his friends. Another speech on Free Trade and higher duties of Chambers of Commerce. At ½ past 7, great meeting in St. George's Hall, Isaac Holden in the chair. I spoke for more than an hour on the Eastern question, Turkish war, and the foreign policy of the country. The day's work a heavy burden and a great relief when over.[1]

"[*26th.*] Visit to Saltaire to see the works and village built by the late Sir Titus Salt. Lunch in the office at the works. Afternoon, left Bradford after a visit to the Exchange Room to see the statue, which is good, and a fair likeness of my lamented friend. Home at 7.30.

"[*August 4, at Rochdale.*] Albert and Lillie left us to-day for London on their way to Switzerland, to spend two or three weeks with dear Mary at Villars-sur-Ollon. We are very quiet without them.

"[*21st.*] Goldwin Smith came to-day. Drove out with him on the old Todmorden road.

"[*22nd.*] Goldwin Smith returned to Ben Rhydding. Much pleasant talk with him on many subjects: Canada, States, India, the war, etc.

"[*23rd.*] Cyrus W. Field came and spent the morning on his way

[1] The statue of Cobden was presented to Bradford by Mr. G. H. Booth, an American citizen, who was partner in a Bradford business. He died before the scheme was completed, and it was carried out by his partners. The statue of Bright, by Bruce Joy, in the Houses of Parliament was presented by Mr. Andrew Carnegie.

to Hawarden. Full of information; much talk on States and Protection.

"[*September* 12.] Morning making notes for speech at Manchester. Town Hall Banquet for to-morrow. Dr. and Mrs. Roth came this afternoon from Harrogate.

"[13*th.*] Manchester Town Hall Banquet, and spoke for ½ an hour. Not much satisfied: time too short, and subject not definite enough. Bishop of Manchester a good 'stump orator;' earnest man— too earnest for a Bishop of a State Church.[1]

"[14*th.*] Dr. and Mrs. Roth left us for Liverpool.

"[25*th.*] Town Hall: Science and Art Classes in connexion with Co-operative Store. Spoke for an hour. Not well satisfied with myself and annoyed by the excessive compliments of the new Vicar of Rochdale, Mr. McClure.

"[27*th.*] Bernard Roth came on a visit this afternoon. Lillie and Sophie[2] have been to Leeds to attend Mr. Carter the dentist.

"[28*th.*] Mr. Courtney, M.P. for Liskeard, called and dined with us.[3]

"[*October* 2.] Mr. Clarke, of Bristol, here to ask me to attend [their 'Colston' dinner on Nov. 13. Did not accept or wholly refuse.

"[4*th.*] Bernard Roth returned to-day to London. His visit has been pleasant to us.

"[9*th.*] To Stancliffe, nr. Matlock, to visit Sir Joseph Whitworth. In Manchester, visited new Town Hall, a very fine and costly building. Dear Elizabeth with me to Stancliffe.

"[12*th.*] Left Stancliffe for home. Pleasant visit. On the 11th in the evening, my old friend Sir Joseph Whitworth gave me an interesting account of his early life and the sources of his success. His industry, anxiety to study; his resolve to instruct himself in everything

---

1 The banquet was held to celebrate the formal opening of the new Town Hall. In spite of his own dissatisfaction, Bright, who responded to the toast of the House of Commons, delivered a capital after-dinner speech. He made great play of the advancement of Manchester within half a century from government by a Borough Reeve ("a person . . . now as extinct as that almost fabulous bird, the dodo") to the stately dignity of a great municipality which had endowed itself with a new municipal palace. "What vast force there is—force of liberality and force of generosity—in freedom everywhere, and in municipal freedom wherever we see it!"

2 His youngest daughter.

3 The future Lord Courtney of Penwith had been successful in a by-election at Liskeard in the previous December, and had taken a prominent part in the debates on the Eastern Question.

connected with mechanics and machine-making. Referring to his conduct when young, he said, 'I was a very good lad, never a better,'—worked hard, studied, and conducted himself well. For many months he had lived on 5/2 per week for food. He is now very rich, has no children, wishes to leave or give much of his property for public uses.

"Lady Whitworth, his wife, is pleasant and well-looking. Their house is in every respect comfortable and elegant and of moderate size. The grounds are lovely.

"[*November 7.*[1]] J. Chamberlain, M.P., came. With him to meeting in the Town Hall. I was in the chair and spoke. The meeting very large and good.[2]

"[*8th.*] Mr. Chamberlain left us.

"[*23rd.*] To Hickleton Hall, nr. Doncaster, to visit Lord Halifax.[3] A pleasant party: Lord Ripon; Lord and Lady Selborne and daughter; Mr. Bodley, architect, and his wife; Hy. Wood and Capt. Ardagh; and Lord Devon.

"[*24th.*] A walk: roads and fields very wet.

"[*25th.*] Church: old and picturesque. Service as usual.

"[*26th.*] Walk with Lord Halifax. Pleasant talk with him and Lord Selborne on India and some public questions. Among them on Capital Punishment. Referred to Article of Church of England on that subject. Lord Selborne did not believe there was any such Article. Prayer Book sent for, and Article found among famous 39! A clergyman, Mr. Horley, once denied there was such an Article, and was astonished when I showed it to him. So much for the knowledge of the Articles of their Church exhibited by great Churchmen.[4]

"[*29th.*] To Ashton, to dine with Hugh Mason. A good party; Sir Arthur Cotton there. Much talk on India.

"[*30th.*] At noon left Ashton for Chatsworth. Day very wet and unpleasant. At the door of Chatsworth, met the Duke of Devonshire: very kind and cordial. The party almost all out. Found Lady

[1] After a visit to Street and a fortnight's jaunt in Somerset and Gloucestershire.
[2] A meeting to promote the better organization of the Liberal Party on the Birmingham model. "Mr. Chamberlain," said Bright, "is a juvenile member of Parliament in comparison with myself. He was a small boy, I suppose, when I first entered the House of Commons in the year 1843; but outside the House he has done great service in his own great town, and there, where he is best known, he is best and most appreciated."
[3] The Sir Charles Wood of the Palmerston era.
[4] Article XXXVII, Of the Civil Magistrates. ". . . The Laws of the Realm may punish Christian men with death, for heinous and grievous offences."

Edwd. Cavendish in the drawing-room. Chas. Howard, Fredk. Leveson-Gower (Lord Granville's bro.), Admiral Egerton and his wife and children, and others of the party—about 20—to dinner. I sat between the Duke's daughter, Lady Louisa Egerton, and his daughter-in-law, the wife of Lord Edward Cavendish. Conversation lively and pleasant, as it was in the drawing-room afterwards. Later in the smoking-room the war was freely discussed. Some officers of the party. (Lord Northbrook and daughter.)

"[*December* 1.] Sir Jos. Whitworth called and took me with him to lunch and sent me back afterwards.

"[*2nd.*] To church: no sermon, as 'Communion' to-day. Remained to see the sacrament administered. For the manner of it no sanction in the New Testament. About 12 or 13 persons partook of it; 9 women and 3 men. Of the whole number 7 came from Chatsworth. About 30 to dinner: guests come and go daily. Afternoon, a long walk in the woods, I mostly talking with the Duke and his daughter. Walked nearly 2 hours.

"[*3rd.*] To Manchester and home. Visit very pleasant. The family kind and liberal and good. The Duke is genial and modest in his manner, very kind and social; all regard him with great respect, which he well deserves. The ladies are intelligent and agreeable.

"[*11th.*] To Manchester Town Hall, meeting on India, the Mayor in the Chair. Sir A. Cotton spoke. I followed for an hour. The Bishop spoke briefly. The meeting good, and all passed off well.[1]

"[*25th.*] Christmas Day: cold; slight frost.

"[*26th.*] Heavy snow and storm.

"[*27th.*] More snow. Yesterday Bernard Roth returned to London, having been here since 22nd.

"[*29th.*] Reading 1st Vol. of Chas. Sumner's 'Life and Correspondence;' very good.[2]

5

Bright's interest in the development of the Eastern Question, his criticism of Beaconsfield's Imperialism, and his active concern about

---

[1] The meeting was convened by the Indian Association of Manchester to hear Sir Arthur Cotton on the Indian Famine question. Bright, with a great knowledge of Indian problems, produced a formidable array of statistical facts in support of Sir Arthur's proposals for irrigation. The great works in the deltas of the Godaveri, Kistna and Kaveri, achieved by Cotton's genius and energy, formed the model of irrigation schemes in India and the exemplar of their benefits.

[2] The "Memorial and Letters of Charles Sumner," by E. L. Pierce.

the distracted state of the Liberal Party continued unabated up to the middle of May, 1878. Then a thunderbolt fell which destroyed politics for him, drove him in upon himself and filled his world with woe.

His wife died very suddenly of apoplexy on May 13, during his absence in London.

They had been thirty-one years married. She had borne him seven children. They had built up an idyllic family life at "One Ash," and they remained lovers to the end. This sudden tragic snapping of the bond left him broken and numb. For months he lost all interest in public affairs, and desperately tried to avoid the selfish nursing of his sorrow by an intenser devotion to the concerns of his children.

During these months the war in the Near East came to an end, Beaconsfield went to Berlin and returned to make play with the resounding slogan invented by Lord John Russell a dozen years before, "peace with honour;" the Afghan War and the Zulu War were added to the rich harvest of Imperialism, and the Egyptian trouble peeped over the horizon; but Bright let it all pass without comment and almost without notice.

"[*January* 11, 1878, *at Manchester*.] Breakfast with B. Armitage and then to Town Hall to look over plans of the great scheme for supplying Manchester with water from Lake Thirlmere. Then to Victoria Park and called on my old friend Geo. Hadfield, now in his 91st year. Found him well and cheerful, his mind quite clear, and for an hour we conversed most pleasantly.

"His daughter was with him, and seems his guardian angel in his old age. This visit has given me real enjoyment, for Geo. Hadfield has been so good and true, and I have known him for so many years.

"[12*th*.] To Birmingham, and in the evening to meeting in the Town Hall. Spoke 50 minutes on War question.[1] Chamberlain

---

[1] Parliament had been summoned for an unusually early date, January 17, and the fact gave rise to some public uneasiness. Bright pointed to that feeling as an indication of the difference between the English attitude now and at the time of the Crimean War. Then "the public mind was filled with falsehoods . . . it became almost drunk with passion. . . . I met the night before last an old friend. . . He said, 'Do you recollect me twenty-three or twenty-four years ago? You know I walked down Market Street with you that day when you came out of the Town Hall where you had been hissed and hooted and maltreated . . . and when you were not allowed to pass down the street without gross insult.' Well, now a man may have an opinion in favour of peace and the dogs of war will scarcely bark at him."

spoke well on the same topic. Was his guest during my stay in Birmingham.

"[*16th.*] Dined at Devonshire House with Lord Hartington and old officials of the Party. Queen's speech read and discussed: difference of opinion as to meaning of it.

"[*17th.*] House: debate on Address. Some clouds dispelled, and rumours of intervention in War got rid of. Up to 132, Piccadilly, with my colleague, Chamberlain. Tea, and talk till near 12 o'clock.

"[*23rd.*] Home early and read Disraeli's 'Life.'

"[*24th.*] House: excitement from notice to increase military vote to menace or make war on Russia. Rumour that Lord Carnarvon and Derby have left Govt. Home 10 o'clock. Read 'Life' of Disraeli.

"Last night awake till after 4 o'clock. Mind occupied with War and the dangers ahead. At ¼ to 3 rose, lighted my candle, and in next room made notes of what had been passing in my brain, which may perhaps serve for some speech on the question of the day.

"[*25th.*] Govt. notice of 'Vote' for military expenses. Lord Carnarvon resigned; Lord Derby also, it is reported.

"[*26th.*] To Lord Granville's: consultation as to course of Govt.

"[*27th.*] At my door met the Duke of Teck. He shook hands with me and told me his name, for I did not recognize him, not having seen him for many years. He had called upon the Marquis Fortunato, who lodges above me, and who was out. I asked him the news. He said Beaconsfield had told the Princess Mary (his wife) that Lord Derby would stay in the Govt., but that he did not believe it. He had no news of the signature of the Treaty of Peace.

"The Duke is a good-looking man, and was very civil. Am sorry I did not invite him into my rooms.

"[*28th.*] H. Ashworth called to talk over the second edition of his book 'Cobden and the League.' He leaves to-morrow for Italy. He is 83 years of age: a fine old man.

"House: Northcote's statement moving vote of 6 millions for military expenses—War in the East of Europe, tho' no intervention intended! House excited.

"[*29th.*] At Lord Granville's at 12 o'clock; large meeting of late Govt. Discussion on 'Vote of Credit:' difficulty in coming to conclusion as to amendment to be moved. Hartington doubting the wisdom of direct opposition to the vote. Left them before decision arrived at. Evening, learned that Forster was to give notice of amendment, which I fear is a blunder. A leader should lead. Home before 8. Till midnight, notes for speech.

"[*30th.*] House: in first division of the session—Bill to allow prisoners to give evidence on their own behalf. Lord Hartington asked me to speak in debate to-morrow night. Home early: notes for speech.

"[*31st.*] House: Forster's speech solid and good, but he is not gifted with special power of public speaking. I spoke after 10 o'clock for an hour. House recd. it well. Some Tory members called out 'Poland,' to remind me of past ill deeds of Russia. This stirred me to quote 4 lines from some verses I attempted in my young days, which were recd. with great cheering from both sides. The Speaker has since asked me where I got the lines from, and I told him he would not find them in any of the books—leaving him to suspect that they were original.[1]

"Walked up home with Tom Johnson, of Manchester, who was in the Lobby.

"[*February* 1.] The debate continued. A curious incident happened. Sir Robt. Peel,[2] rather a wild man, referred to my speeches on the Crimean War—1854/56—and said their effect on him had been such that he had then resolved that he would never do anything to support the Ottoman power in Europe.

"[*3rd.*] Positive news to-day of signature of terms of Armistice

---

[1] Hansard has enshrined this, the only surviving record of Bright's youthful experiments in versification. The essential passage reaus:

"Mr. Bright: I have observed that English Ministers, for a very long time past, have generally, in their speeches in this House expressed sympathy with suffering and a hope that freedom might be extended to those who were oppressed and enslaved.

"An hon. Member: Poland!

"Mr. Bright: That is perfectly true with regard to Poland. When I was a boy, everybody in England, so far as I can remember hearing or reading, lamented the calamities which had befallen Poland. Lines come to my mind which have rested there from that time to the present moment. They refer to a battlefield—

'Where Poland sees her gallant sons,
Her first, her best, her bravest ones,
On the cold earth all gory lie,
For Poland breathe a prayer, and die.'

"Sir, surely I am saying nothing offensive to the character of anyone when I say that we may expect from every English statesman—I hope we may expect it if he belongs to the Party opposite, and I am sure we shall never miss it if he belongs to this Party—that in his speeches in this House and in his statesmanship he shall have regard to the sufferings of the oppressed, be they black or be they white, in every region of the globe."

[2] The second baronet.

and bases of Peace between Russia and Turkey. What a year of suffering for the poor people directly concerned in the War!

"[4th.] House: Gladstone opened—good and moderate. Hardy violent and coarse, as is his custom; but suits his party. Childers's speech very good. Home before 2 o'clock.

"[5th.] Letters and Petitions: 200 letters or more yesterday and to-day. House: presented 82 Petitions against Vote of Credit as a menace of War. Home at 1 o'clock; walked up with Mr. Chamberlain.

"[7th.] To Lord Granville's: consultation on Amendment; agreed to withdraw it. House: great excitement, telegram from Layard at Constantinople causing exaggerated alarm; afterwards contradicted by one from St. Petersburg. I spoke briefly during the exciting discussion.[1]

"To Mr. C. Dicey's to dine, and met Mr. Welsh, U.S. Minister, and his two daughters. Walked home with Mr. Hayward.

"[8th.] Vaughan called here; then I called on Mrs. Schwabe in Clarges St.[2] House: presented 160 Petitions against Vote of Credit. Debate on Vote. Mr. Gladstone's speech admirable—perfect. Division after midnight: 328–124.

"[12th.] House: Thirlmere Lake and Manchester Corporation Water Scheme. Some silly people opposed to it, but Bill read 2nd time.

"[14th.] House: discussion on war question. Govt. in mischief. Fleet at Constantinople and menacing attitude: much anxiety in many minds. Home before 12. Read Barclay for an hour.[3]

[1] Layard, whom Beaconsfield had sent as Ambassador to Constantinople in 1877, telegraphed a message, read in the House by Sir Stafford Northcote, stating that the Russians, in spite of the armistice, were advancing on Constantinople. Forster, who had moved the amendment to the Vote of Credit, precipitately withdrew it. But Bright's "brief" intervention in the discussion was the one demonstration of sanity during a scene of wild excitement: he said, in effect, that he did not believe the Ambassador. Within a few minutes Northcote was reading a dispatch from the Ambassador at St. Petersburg which, on the word of Prince Gortschakoff, informed the Government that all Russian troop movements had ceased at the Armistice, and that everything now being done was with the consent of Turkey.

[2] See page 407.

[3] While Bright solaced his evenings with Barclay's "Religious Societies of the Commonwealth," the British fleet was sent to Constantinople, great naval and military preparations were put in hand, and rowdy demonstrators smashed Mr. Gladstone's windows. The fleet was turned back, as Bright pointed out in his Manchester speech two months later, "partly to secure the continuance of Lord Derby in the Government." But eventually it did pass into the Sea of Marmora. Sir Stafford Northcote naïvely explained to the House that the purpose of this great naval display was to protect the lives and property of British subjects in those parts.

"[15th.] House: Burials Bill. Spoke in the debate. Not much to be said. Majority of 15 only against us.

"To 17, Hyde Park Terrace: a large party, 20 or more to dinner; among them Miss Helen Taylor (stepdaughter of Jno. S. Mill), Mrs. Garrett Anderson, Nelly Cobden, daughter of my lamented friend, and Constance Leese, daughter of my old friend Wm. Hargreaves. Walked home late with Mr. Hopwood, M.P., and Mr. Courtney, M.P.

"[17th.] Afternoon to my room: read St. Mark in French. Some passages seem more striking than our own version.

"[21st.] Mrs. Schwabe called with MS. of her intended volume with letters and notices of Mr. Cobden.[1] To Burnard, sculptor, to see his bust of me for Mr. Armitstead of Dundee. To Mr. Theed's to see his statue of Mr. Gladstone.

"[22nd.] J. Chamberlain called to talk over scheme for Govt. of King Edward's School.

"[March 4.] Our visit to Exton House,[2] Gurney Barclay's Brighton home, has been very pleasant. Met there the widow of the late Robt. Barclay, the author of the 'Inner Life of the Religious Societies of the Commonwealth,' and 3 of her daughters. She seems much cast down by her bereavement. House: Army Estimates, which do not interest me much.

"[5th.] House: speech on scheme for government of King Edward's Grammar School, Birmingham. Argument conclusive against a portion of the scheme, but votes contrary. Govt. and their party, as usual, against any proposition of a popular or liberal sort.

"[6th.] To 8, Chester St. Dined with Mr. Deichman and his wife (once Hilda Bunsen). Count Munster, German Minister, and his daughter there. Much political talk with the Count. He thinks the danger of war over, but has before much feared it.

"[13th.] This morning we walked up to Mr. Theed's studio to see the statue of Mr. Gladstone. Mine also, which I do not like, and wish, as I have always wished, I had not been persuaded to permit it to be made—not because I do not like it as a work of art.

"House: debate on Capital Punishment. Dear Elizabeth in the Gallery.

"[23rd.] From Waterloo Station to Street. Dear Helen and William at the station to meet me. Storm of wind and snow when between Templecombe and Glastonbury near 3 o'clock.

"[24th.] To Meeting. Stood by the grave of 'Uncle Joseph'—

[1] See page 407.   [2] March 2 to 4.

Joseph Clark whom we saw when last at Street. Afternoon: storm of wind and snow, like that of yesterday.

"[25th.] Walk to new works, not yet complete, for making leather board from waste leather and other substances. By 12.52 train to London: another storm of wind and snow in the afternoon between 4 and 5 o'clock.

"Hear of loss of *Eurydice*, with more than 300 men, off Isle of Wight yesterday afternoon, in the sudden squall about 4 o'clock, a very sad event.

"[28th.] House: Resignation of Lord Derby, Foreign Secy. 'Reserve Force' to be called out: alarm that war is intended.[1]

"[29th.] At Lord Granville's: meeting of former Cabinet. Much talk. Agreed to wait till 'Papers' produced. Walked down to the House with Mr. Gladstone.

"[31st.] To Holloway Meeting House, to see it, if desirable place for dear Lillie's wedding.[2]

"[*April* 1.] Wrote long letter to dear Mary on late letter from R. F. Curry. Called on Mr. Gladstone: talk on condition of affairs, war prospects, etc.

"[3rd.] Great deputation from 120 towns to Lord Hartington on the question of Peace or War. Lord Granville present: his speech very good. I was made to introduce the Deputation and to act somewhat as Chairman.

"Evening: dinner at Devonshire Club to Lord Hartington. I sat at his left hand, between him and Sir James Ramsden of Barrow. Lord Granville spoke with his usual success. Hartington returned thanks for the Club and himself. Mr. Gladstone also spoke, after loud calls for him, and I was forced to say something, but nothing satisfactory to myself, and (I should fear) not more to my audience. Walked up to my rooms with Sir Wilfrid Lawson.

"[4th.] House: Budget. Income Tax increase 2d., tobacco 4d. per lb. Speech good, but case for Govt. very bad.

"[5th.] At Lord Granville's at 2 o'clock: long discussion as to course in the House. No leaders, no followers. Agreed to have no

[1] Lord Derby had told Gortschakoff that the claim to amend the Treaty of San Stefano could not be admitted without reference to all the signatories. But Beaconsfield's determination to call out the Reserves and a proposal in the Cabinet for the forcible seizure of Cyprus proved too strong for his stomach. Lord Salisbury succeeded him at the Foreign Office.

[2] The romance indicated in the entries about Mr. Roth in 1877 now approached its culmination, and another was beginning.

amendment to the Address on Reserve Forces. Evidently some present have a policy so like that of Govt. as not to be easily distinguished from it. Mr. Gladstone always strong and earnest, but few up to his mark.

"Dined at T. Hankey's, 59, Portland Place: Duke of Bedford, Lord Lyons, Lord Hammond, Mr. Heathcote there; much talk on foreign affairs. Lord Lyons a sensible man, calm of temper and serious. Had he been at Constantinople, affairs might have been different.[1]

"[8th.] House: great speech from Mr. Gladstone. Home 10 o'clock and made notes for speech, perhaps for to-morrow.

"Letter from my dear girl at Nice telling me of her partial engagement with R. F. Curry. Gives me much anxiety, her health being so precarious.

"[9th.] Notes revised, but may not be used, as I feel indisposed to speak. House: debate. Did not speak. Home after 1 o'clock. Debate much against Govt., but votes with them.[2]

"[10th.] Home early, and read M. McColl's book, 'Three Years of the Eastern Question,' an excellent work on the question now causing us so much anxiety.

"[11th.] Read McColl's book and finished it. I wish every man in England could read it. Rumours to-day very gloomy and prospects of peace not more assuring.

"[12th.] Did not go to the House. Nothing important, and I am weary of spending so much time there without result. Evening: called on Dr. Roth in Wimpole St. Pleasant talk with him and Mrs. Roth.

"[15th.] Mr. Flower, of Stratford-on-Avon, called—spoke of dear Mary and his neighbour, R. F. Curry, and showed me a letter from his mother, Mrs. Collis.

"Rupert Potter called on difficulty in connexion with the proposed Memoirs of Mr. Cobden by John Morley, who refuses to go on with it unless Mrs. Schwabe gives up her intention of publishing a small volume on the same subject. It is suggested I may bring about a solution of the difficulty.[3]

[1] Lord Lyons, who was Minister at Washington during the negotiations about the *Trent,* had served at Constantinople for a short time before entering upon his famous embassy in Paris from 1867 to 1887.

[2] On a motion by Sir Wilfrid Lawson condemning the calling out of the Reserves as a war measure in time of peace.

[3] Mrs. Salis Schwabe and her husband had accompanied Cobden on his tour of Europe in 1846–47. Mrs. Schwabe's "Reminiscences of Richard Cobden" were not published till 1895 (Fisher Unwin).

"[19th, ta Rochdale.] Sunday School Union Conference, and presided at it. Spoke for ½ an hour. A very large meeting; Baillie St. Chapel much crowded.

"[20th.] With dear Elizabeth to Llandudno, 11, Gloddaeth Crescent, as usual.

"[22nd.] Thro' Gloddaeth Wood and round by Little Ormes Head. . . . Evening, read *Faery Queen*, Spenser.

"[26th.] Ormes Head, by lighthouse, and then back by little church, where we saw the little grave of our precious child.

"[30th.] Evening, to Manchester: great meeting in Free Trade Hall, at which I was Chairman, and spoke for an hour and 10 minutes, dissecting and condemning Govt. policy on Eastern question and in direction of War with Russia.[1] On coming out, at ½ past 10, crowds in the street, and some 'rowdies'—partisans of the Govt.—made a disturbance.

"[*May* 8.] Arthur Albright called, on Peace Conference; also Wm. Tallack on an article he has written for *Nineteenth Century*.

"[10th.] W. Tallack called on his article for *Nineteenth Century*, which I criticized severely. It is below my expectations. House: dined there. Counted out early when Kenealy rose to call in question the decision of Mr. Speaker on a former evening as to a question he had put or wished to be put to Home Secretary. Called at 19, Hobart Place, to ask after Sir W. Lawson and saw Lady L. He is very ill, I fear dangerously so—congestion of the lungs—tho' she did not seem aware of the seriousness of the attack.

"[12th.] Westminster Meeting. Thos. Hodgkin there and spoke. Dined with dear Priscilla in Onslow Gardens. Afterwards to J. W. Pease's in Kensington Palace Gardens. T. Hodgkin there. Home near 11 o'clock.

"[13th.] How can I write of this sad day? At 9.30, telegram from Albert telling me of his dear mother's illness: 'Come by the first train.' I felt that the great calamity had come. Her sweet letter of yesterday I had only just read, and now the end had come: I felt it at once. By 11 train for home; a sad journey. At Crewe, Albert on

---

[1] In this speech, referring to the naval measures and the orders for the dispatch of Indian troops to Malta (sent without the knowledge of Parliament and on the very day when it rose for a three weeks Recess at Easter), Bright declared that the Prime Minister's object was not to maintain any true British interests, but "to sustain that terrible oppression, that multitudinous crime which we call the Ottoman Government."

the station, pale and anxious. I saw the truth in his sad countenance. My precious wife was gone, and I was desolate.

"Home: cannot describe it now. Dear Helen with us; dear Philip home from Darmstadt on the 15th; only dear Mary absent of the children—she on her way home, but too late for the 16th, the day of the funeral. Cannot say much of that day. The kindness of our friends, the sympathizing crowds in the streets, the solemnity of the Meeting may be remembered, but cannot be written about. Dear Priscilla came down on the 14th and remained with us till the 22nd. Her presence was most comforting to us all.

"We have had many letters, probably more than 300, with many resolutions of meetings and public meetings, an expression, remarkable and most touching, of the sympathy felt for us.

"My dear children's kindness and tenderness has been a great solace to me. If much has been taken much is still left.

"[29*th*.] Dear Mary with us, better in health. Thankful for her.

"[31*st*.] Dear Helen and her sweet child left us this morning; we feel her going very much.

"[*June* 17.] Since last notes, have passed the time at home, often in great sadness, but solaced by the love and tenderness of my dear children. This morning left home for London with dear Mary, Lillie and Sophie, and reached my rooms in Piccadilly at 6 o'clock. After dinner I took dear Sophie to 64, Onslow Gardens, for the night with her aunt.

"[18*th*.] Afternoon drove over to Knott's Green [1] with M. and S., dear Lillie by train.

"[19*th*.] A quiet day here with our dear friends and relatives. Albert, Willie and Philip came in the evening, also Helen and William from Street; so all our family here, the place of the dear lost one only vacant.

"[20*th*.] The day fine. The Meeting at 11 o'clock; small and select. Dr. and Mrs. Roth and all their children, but one who is abroad, were here. Aunt Tilla and McLaren came over. The meeting solemn. Ann Fowler prayed, and spoke afterwards in her own very beautiful manner. My kind bro.-in-law, J. Gurney Barclay, read the 27th Psalm first of all. Then Bernard and Lillie made their declaration, speaking clearly and with right feeling. Nothing could

---

[1] The residence of his brother-in-law, Gurney Barclay, at Leyton, Essex, for the wedding of his daughter Lillie with Mr. Roth.

have been more satisfactory to us all than the proceedings at the meeting.

"When dear Lillie had spoken, I was sorely distressed. The feeling that she was leaving me, and that her precious mother was not with us, was too much for me, and my tears could not be restrained; and the reference to her in the certificate was very painful.

"At 1 o'clock sat down to breakfast—all abundant and beautiful. Dr. Roth rose and thanked our kind hosts for their great kindness. No other speeches; only J. G. B. acknowledged the thanks in a few kind words.

"At ¼ before 3 Bernard and Lillie left us for London Bridge Station on their way to Ventnor, in the Isle of Wight.

"The garden here lovely on this lovely day. Friends from Forest House and Woodford have called. Our hearts are touched with the kindness of our friends, and we can be glad that all has been arranged and has passed over just as the dear absent one would have approved.

"[23rd.] Did not go to Meeting, but spent the morning with my sweet girl Mary in the lovely garden and arbors at Knott's Green. Soon after 12, rain began to fall; then thunder came on and lightning. For 2 hours we had a storm of extraordinary force.

"The thunder was grand—almost incessant, and the flashes followed each other with startling rapidity. The rain was very heavy and the lawn looked like the surface of a lake disturbed with the wind. Such a storm I have rarely if ever known, and we seemed to be about the centre of it. In the afternoon we measured the fall of rain, and it was $3\frac{1}{10}$ inches in the space of 2 hours. The evening was calm, but the air was not much cooled.

"[24th.] Left Knott's Green, my dear children with me—Mary, Sophie and Philip—all feeling much the kindness of our friends and relatives, and how much all had passed as the dear absent one would have wished. To her, Knott's Green, after her own home, was perhaps the most loved place in the world, and she was much pleased that the marriage of our dear child should take place there or from there. How sad, how terribly sad to us that she was not with us!

"[25th.] Evening to dine at 64, Onslow Gardens, with dear Priscilla. R. F. Curry with us. Day intensely hot: 84 deg.

"[26th.] Curry here to breakfast and lunch. Dear Mary and he left me at 2 for Stratford-on-Avon. Very sad when they were gone. Evening to Onslow Gardens. Read the *Nineteenth Century* before going to bed. My rooms painfully quiet and solitary.

"[*29th.*] By 6.30 train from Paddington to Stratford-on-Avon; at 10.30 to Shottery Hall.

"[*July* 1.] Visit to Shottery Hall very pleasant. Mrs. Collis an admirable woman; Dr. Collis very active and doing good. They were very kind to me, and Mary is a favourite with them.

"[*11th.*] With dear Mary to Brighton, to see dear Lillie in her new home. Found her very happy.

"[*14th.*] Walk with J. H. Tuke. Conversation about my dear lost one: his reference to time long past, when he was one of her admirers; effect upon him of his then sore disappointment.

"[*August* 4, *at Inverness.*[1]] To Union St. Church, U.P. George Robson, minister. Good congregation and good minister—a little too much effort in his oratory. Streets almost crowded with people going to or coming from church. If the Christianity of Scotland were at all equal to the profession of it, what a country it would be! But may not this be said of all Christian countries? And do we not all fall sadly short of our outward profession?

"Last evening and to-day very sad. Two years ago my dearest one was here with me: same house and same rooms. Now, how changed! I cannot write what I have felt and suffered whilst here.

"[*12th.*] Yesterday and to-day, read 'Letters' of Thos. Erskine. Much interested in them: his life and character remarkable for piety and zeal. Some interesting letters from Thos. Carlyle to him,—one particularly so to me, as it refers to the sudden loss of his wife, and speaks of the solitary life of an old man so bereaved.

"There is a curious reference to my speeches in one of Erskine's letters. He did not take much part in public political affairs, and was disposed to doubt the sincerity of 'agitators,' and hoped rather than believed that the changes promoted would do much good. He does not blame me, but asks a question which I may ask myself, and expresses his good opinion or admiration of my speeches.[2]

"[*16th.*] Lord Colin Campbell, Duke of Argyll's son, and candidate for the County, is at Oban this evening meeting the electors. Mr.

---

[1] He spent the end of July and the first three weeks of August in Scotland with his daughter Sophie, and did some fishing.

[2] Thomas Erskine of Linlathen, the theologian, spiritual forerunner and personal friend of F. D. Maurice. He died in 1870, and his "Letters," in two volumes, with Reminiscences by Dean Stanley and Principal Shairp, had been edited by Dr. William Hanna and published in 1877.

Craig Sellar called on me, asking me to go to the meeting. I could not consent.

"[17th.] The Duke of Argyll wrote to ask us to go on board his yacht. He was going up the loch to trawl for fish. We went soon after 10, one of his boats and 4 men coming off for us. The trawling was not very successful, but some fish were taken, among them a fish called 'Whiff,' and some Norway lobsters, which I have not seen before. With the Duke were his daughter, Lady Mary, a nice girl, with a look of goodness in her countenance, and Mrs. Bromley, a cousin of the Duke's, and half-sister to Lady Granville. We lunched on board and came away about 3 o'clock. The Duke spoke with much feeling of his great loss, and of mine. His son Lord Colin, who is now a candidate for the County, and Lord Walter, another son, were on board for a short time during our stay. The day was very wet, but cleared up in the evening.

"[20th, at Glasgow.] Called on Mr. Maclehose, publisher, a fine, intelligent man. Pleasant conversation with him. He gave me a small parcel of books and pamphlets. Mr. Daglish, formerly M.P. for Glasgow, called on me in Mr. Maclehose's shop and asked us to go out to dine with him. Went with him 6 miles to his beautiful house in the country. Mr. Anderson, M.P., came also to dinner: a pleasant evening.

"[22nd, at Rochdale.] Conversation with the doctor [1] on health and prospects of my dear child Mary. His report and opinion on the whole satisfactory.

"[29th.] Dr. and Mrs. Meyhoffer left us after a visit of ten days; pleasant company. Dear Philip also left us this morning for London and Darmstadt. The house is very quiet and I have many times of loneliness and almost of melancholy.

"[30th.] Morning: endeavouring to make notes for my will. Very difficult, with 7 children and property engaged in business.[2]

"[September 3.] Engaged on my will and completed it. Must be copied and signed.

"[17th.] To Holker Hall, to call on Duke of Devonshire and his family.

"[18th.] To Holker: sale of 'shorthorns.' One cow sold for

---

[1] Dr. Meyhoffer, who had been attending Mary Bright during her stay in Switzerland.

[2] The business of John Bright and Bros. was shortly afterwards formed into a private limited liability company.

£2,660; one young bull, about a year old, for £1,750. A very interesting sight. A large attendance—500 or 600 people there.

"[20th.] R. F. Curry at 'One Ash.'

"[24th.] R. F. Curry left us this morning. His visit has been very pleasant.

"[30th.] Dear Mary's birthday—29. Have made a fair copy of my will, which has been some time preparing. Have signed it to-day at the office, Jesse Fessant and Fredk. Lye being witnesses. Dear Mary has read it and approves of it.

"[October 4.] To Manchester to meet Executive of 'Alliance' on Permissive Bill, or legislation in favour of Temperance. Met several of them at their offices, 44, Jno. Dalton St., Manchester; Ben. Whitworth, M.P., in the Chair.

"Discussion for nearly 3 hours. Explained my objections to their Bill, and what I should recommend in place of it. Interview very friendly, and I hope not without some useful result.

"Dear Helen and Lillie and Bernard arrived this evening—to stay over the wedding. Albert home from Paris.

"[7th.] Dr. and Mrs. Collis [1] and their daughter Ella [2] came to-day.

"[10th, at Southport.] Dear Mary's wedding day. The meeting house crowded. Ceremony as usual with 'Friends,' but curiously mixed up with 'Church.' Dr. Collis gave us a short prayer from his Church Catechism and, placing his hands on the heads of Mary and Richard, gave them an impressive benediction. The dear girl looked lovely, and the pair together very attractive. Wedding breakfast at ½ past 12; a beautiful and excellent repast. At 2.30, the new-wedded left us for Liverpool and London, and by 5 o'clock the whole party had left Southport for their homes.

"The great event over on the whole very comfortably. It is hard to lose such a daughter, in every way so choice and so good; but she goes with one who is worthy of her, as we believe, and who will care for her with tenderness and a constant love.

"[22nd, at Kelso.[3]] Yesterday heard of the death of my old friend James King on the morning of the 20th. The funeral is fixed for Thursday the 24th, and I leave here to-day for Carlisle and home to-morrow to attend it. This event has made me sad, for I have had no

[1] Dr. Collis was the Vicar of Stratford-on-Avon and stepfather of Mr. Curry.
[2] Now Mrs. J. Wiseman Keogh, wife of the British Consul-General at Nice.
[3] He had returned to the North for fishing on the Tweed.

more kind and true friend than Jas. King. He was my schoolfellow more than 50 years ago, travelled with me for 6 mos. in the Levant and in Italy, and has always been my neighbour and warm friend, as his father was my father's friend. I regret much that I did not call upon him before leaving home, tho' he was probably too ill to see any of his friends. My intended visits to Naworth Castle and to Brayton must now be postponed or given up.

"[*November 9, at Rochdale.*] House very quiet. Sophie at Brighton, Willie not returned from London, Albert at the meeting of the Town Council for election of Mayor of Rochdale; no mother and no daughters. My home become very desolate.

"[*26th.*] Jno. Morley, of the *Fortnightly Review*, came here this evening. He is writing a Memoir of Mr. Cobden, and comes to talk to me about it.

"[*27th.*] J. Morley left us.[1]

"[*December 9.*] House: debate on Afghan War. Mr. Whitbread spoke excellently in introducing the vote of censure on the Government.

"[*10th.*] House: debate continued. Mr. Gladstone a fine speech. Home at midnight.

"[*11th.*] My cold better; cough very troublesome.

"[*12th.*] Euston Hotel all day. Evening, a note from Mr. Gladstone, urging me to speak in the debate. Had to write to say it could not be in my present state.

"[*16th.*] Wrote a note to the Marchioness of Ely, sending message of sympathy to the Queen on sad news of the death of Princess Alice at Darmstadt.[2]

"[*18th.*] Recd. a nice note from Marchioness of Ely, with a message from the Queen.

"[*19th.*] Home by 11 train: snow lying heavy as we approached the North."

---

[1] "Mr. Bright, with an unwearied kindness for which I can never be too grateful, has allowed me to consult him constantly, and has abounded in helpful corrections and suggestions." (Preface to Morley's "Life of Richard Cobden," 1881.)

[2] The Princess Alice died of diphtheria, as also did one of her daughters. She was greatly beloved by the British residents in Darmstadt.

CHAPTER XVI

IRISH, BOERS AND FELLAHEEN

I

THE Midlothian Campaign of 1879 marked a new departure in British politics and the preparations for it a new phase of Bright's life—the last in which he was to share the responsibility of governing the country.

The four agitated years from 1879 to 1882 dug a gulf deep and broad between the old and the new conceptions in politics. Bright, Radical and progressive as he was, belonged distinctly to the old era. To those years the much abused label, "a time of transition," has been correctly applied. No doubt, every time in a mutable world is a time of transition; but within this period occurred not only a startling uprising of new issues and new men, but a subtle change in the temper of politics and a new alignment of minds which altered the very texture of parties—and of the Liberal Party especially. In a true perspective, the crashing controversies of 1900, of 1906, and of 1909–14, and their sequel in the past decade, were implicit in the chemical transformations of 1879 to 1882. On the one hand the Radical-Imperialism of Chamberlain and Dilke, and on the other the fermentation of the new ideas about State activity in Social Reform, seemed to a Victorian reformer dangerous vagaries from his ideal of liberation, pacification, non-intervention. They were alien theories cutting athwart his own conception of the evolution of a sturdy and independent society by means of free competition in industry and commerce conducted in an atmosphere of political and intellectual liberty and material peace.

In 1879, when Beaconsfield's Government was tottering, Bright had high hopes of his ideal and expressed them in a vigorous speech at Birmingham in April. The great Liberal victory of 1880 raised them higher. But they faded into despair as the Imperial chicken came home to roost from Ireland, from South Africa and from Egypt, as the decencies of Parliamentary life wore thin in the Irish disorders and the insensate Bradlaugh controversies, as the incompatibilities of Radicals and Whigs,

Imperialists and non-Imperialists, in the Party grew plainer and the tone of their disputes more strident.

The diaries (becoming fuller in his partial solitude) display Bright's reaction to the new spirit with a certain unconscious pathos. He is in his sixty-eighth year, more than a little lonely, losing his elasticity—no less a Radical than ever, leaping as keenly on infractions of liberty, reprehending as fiercely all deeds of militarism, as ardent in his admiration of Gladstone and his liberalizing policies; but set in his convictions of the relative importance of causes and the nature of the remedies for evils. It was inevitable that he should find circumstance less tractable as the years passed: in that he differed nowise from other men of his age. The difference was that the profundity of his convictions and a conscience perhaps even over-sensitive made him less tractable to circumstance than the commonalty of politicians.

He had joined the Government in 1868 out of regard for Gladstone. When the Midlothian campaign made Gladstone the only possible successor of Beaconsfield in 1880, for the same reason and under the same hard pressure he became a Minister again. Better, undoubtedly, for his physical ease and his peace of mind if he had resisted the pressure and remained a private member. But his association with the hapless Government, also undoubtedly, lends much interest to his diaries.

When the period opens, the Midlothian adventure is in preparation.

"[*January* 29, 1879.] To Hawarden, nr. Chester; dear Sophie with me. There at 5 o'clock. Mr. and Mrs. Gladstone, their daughter Mary, and Lord F. Cavendish and his wife.

"[30*th.*] A walk of two hours with Mr. Gladstone. Much talk on public affairs and on possibility of change of Govt. and on difficulty of new Govt. in connexion with old colleagues and with elements of trouble in the non-official portion of the Liberal Party. He has consented to become a candidate for Midlothian at the next election. I have doubted the wisdom of this, but his reasons are very strong, and he acts solely with a view to the public interest.

"[31*st.*] Another long walk and talk with Mr. G. Very interesting: his aims so unselfish and so noble, and his language so impressive.

"At lunch, Chas. Bateman, clergyman, St. John's, Hawarden, once a Moravian, and much of one even now. A man of great simplicity and goodness. Thinks 'Establishment' a great evil to the Church of England, in which I agree, and I suspect our host does not much differ from us.

"Mr. Gladstone's son,[1] Rector of Hawarden, and his curates, Mr. Lyttelton and Mr. Gamlin, spent an evening with us. The Rector and Mr. Lyttelton seem burdened with their labours, which are constant and heavy.

"W. H. Gladstone, M.P. for Whitby, and his pale and gentle-looking wife here this evening; also Lord Crewe,[2] who is a curious man, pleasant and gentlemanly, but eccentric in conversation. His memory seemed to run much upon bishops.

"[*February* 1.] Left Hawarden before 11 o'clock for Broughton Hall station on the way to Chester. Our visit has been most pleasant and refreshing. The circle at Hawarden one much to be admired. Mrs. Gladstone very kind and good to everybody. Mr. Gladstone's energy and industry an example I cannot imitate. I can only wonder at it and admire. Home at 4 o'clock.

"[*12th.*] To London, Euston Hotel. Dined with Lord Hartington and old officials of the Party at Devonshire House: a pleasant evening.

"[*13th.*] House: dull debate. Govt. and their friends do not look in good spirits. The bad news from Natal troubles them.

"[*14th.*] To my old lodgings at 132, Piccadilly.

"[*15th.*] Called on Lord Dufferin at St. George's Hotel, Albemarle St. Conversation for an hour and a half with him on his appointment, on Russian Tariff, and on 'purchase clauses' in Irish Land Act. He goes out as Minister to St. Petersburg. I called to interest him in the question of the Russian Tariff, and urged him to promote its reduction as a great means of improving political feeling between the two countries. He entered most cordially into my views, and will write to me from St. Petersburg when he has had time to make observations there. He told me he had urged the Irish Chief Secretary, Lowther, to carry my clauses in the Land Act into effect as the main hope of safety to Irish landlords. He said he was sitting at the feet of Tenterden at the Foreign Office to get up his facts for his new appointment. He mentioned to Disraeli his Reform Club banquet, which he hoped would make no difficulty. The Minister said, 'My dear Dufferin, I don't care where you dine.'

"There is great intelligence and quickness in Lord Dufferin. His manner is very pleasant. I reminded him of our meeting at Nice 22 years ago, and of his mother who was then with him. I think he was pleased with my visit and I hope some good may come from it.

[1] Rev. Stephen Gladstone.   [2] Uncle of the present Lord Crewe.

"[16*th*.] Evening, read Essays of Justin McCarthy, 'Con Amore' —mainly on German and French Literature. Afterwards Book of Judges and Ruth. The former very confused. I do not feel called upon to believe in all its horrors.

"[17*th*.] Called at Chesham House and saw Count Shouvaloff, Russian Minister here, on subject of Russian Tariff to show him how English opinion might be influenced favourably towards Russia by a change in their tariff and extension of trade between the two countries. He very friendly, but said he was no economist and did not know much about tariffs. Genl. Greig, their Finance Minister, was the man to consider the question; but he was going to St. Petersburg soon and would not forget what I had said to him. He asked me to dine with him that evening.

"Evening, dined with him: large party. French Minister, D'Harcourt there, and his wife and daughter, Lord and Lady Derby and 2 daughters, Lord and Lady Dufferin, Sir W. Harcourt and his wife, and others—22 or 24 at table. I took Lady Harcourt (Mr. Motley's daughter) in to dinner, and sat between her and Mlle. D'Harcourt, a favourable place for conversation. Miss D'Harcourt speaks English excellently, and there is much of gentleness in her countenance.

"Lord Derby, speaking to me on the Gladstone Govt., said we did so much in a short time that timid people were frightened, but what was done was 'magnificently right' in his view, with very slight exception. He referred to the many conversations he and I had had in the smoking-room of the House of Commons, and he said, 'And I learned a good many things from you.' He was very cheerful and friendly, and is, I suspect, more happy in Liberal than Tory companionship.

"Lord Dufferin is to dine at the Reform Club on Saturday.[1] I explained to him why I could not be at the dinner. The sadness of the past 9 months seemed to forbid my taking part in public festivities.

"[28*th*.] House: *India*—Mr. Fawcett. I spoke at the close of the debate, the first time for 10 or 11 mos. Voice rather hoarse. Came up in a cab with Geo. Trevelyan and nearly upset in passing thro' Storey's Gate.

"[*March* 2.] Afternoon, wrote letter to Genl. Greig, Finance Minister, St. Petersburg, on reduction of Russian Tariff as means of improving relations between England and Russia.

"[3*rd*.] Call from Mr. Crane, from U.S. Much talk on Free

[1] Lord Dufferin had just returned from his brilliant reign as Governor-General in Canada, and was about to become Ambassador at St. Petersburg.

Trade. Call from Mrs. Kay, widow of the late Jos. Kay,[1] with proofs of the volume of his letters on the Land question. Gave me particulars of her husband's illness and death, her eyes filling with tears as she spoke. She is the daughter of Hy. Drummond, who was Secy. to Lord Morpeth in Ireland.

"[7th.] House: Women's Suffrage resolution. Debate and division against: 217–103. Women's suffrage question going back in the House; its supporters are for the most part insincere.

"[8th.] Yesterday, the 7th, I posted the letter to Genl. Greig, Russian Finance Minister, suggesting that a more open trade with England would change the tone of English opinion and feeling towards Russia and promote and secure peace. Am not sanguine it will have any effect, but I have thought it my duty to do something in this direction. Perhaps it may bear some little fruit.

"[9th.] Late, read Whittier, his *Pennsylvania Pilgrims*, a charming poem. Am more and more impressed with the beauty and purity of his writings.

"[12th.] Evening, dined with Mr. Speaker. Sat between Mr. Lowe and Mr. Goschen. Talk on Egyptian affairs, which are much complicated.

"[13th.] To Mr. Ouless.[2] A large party there—too many for the artist. Generally not pleased with the portrait.

"[14th.] To Doré Picture Gallery, to Grosvenor Gallery, and to Mr. Theed's studio, to see statue of Mr. Gladstone for Manchester Town Hall. Evening, dined with Mr. Pender in Arlington St. Large party to meet Mr. Berry and others from Australia. Lord Derby, Granville, Gladstone, Lowe, Childers and others at the dinner. Fine pictures—Turner, Landseer and others—in Mr. Pender's house: formerly belonged to Edwd. Ellice, to Horace Walpole, and to Nell Gwynne of Charles the 2nd days. Home, with Lord Granville in his carriage, he going to South Audley St. since the fire at his house, Carlton House Terrace.

"[17th.] E. L. Pierce from Boston called. House: Mr. Pierce

---

[1] Joseph Kay was conspicuous among the land reformers, a disciple of Cobden, and an apostle of the "free land" movement, i.e., the free market for land which the abolition of settlement and entail would secure. The aim was the sub-division of land into smaller holdings and the breaking up of great estates.

[2] W. W. Ouless, then A.R.A. He became R.A. in 1881. Bright had given the first sitting for his portrait on June 13 of the previous year, and had paid many visits to the studio.

there. Dined with him at the House. He came up here and spent evening with us.

"[19th.] Mr. Berry, Minister of Province of Victoria, called. Long talk on their Constitutional difficulty, which has brought him over to the Colonial Office. He is a shrewd man, intelligent and pleasant in conversation. Lunched with Mrs. Schwabe, 8, Clarges St. H. Richard, M.P., there.

"[20th.] To Mr. Ouless: portrait finished.

"[25th.] Mr. Pearson, from Melbourne, called for an hour on political troubles in Victoria.

"[26th.] Mr. Haddon, Editor of *Argus*, from Melbourne, called to talk on Victoria politics. He is opposed to the views and objects of Mr. Berry and Mr. Pearson. Mrs. Kay called at 11. Gave her the proof sheets of her book, and, afternoon, sent her the short preface I had written out for it.

"Evening: dined with Cowper-Temple, 15, Great Stanhope St.— a very pleasant party: Mr. and Mrs. Gladstone and daughter, Harcourt and his wife, Lady Cowper, Lady Ripon, Lord Colin Campbell, Lord Strafford (Byng), Dr. Gunsberg—a great scholar who promised to send me his account of the Moabitish Stone; he is acquainted with 'Friends,' having married one of the Crosfields, of Liverpool.

"[27th.] House: debate on Zulu War. A very good speech from Sir C. Dilke.[1] Walked up home at 11 o'clock. My rooms very lonely: often very desolate when alone.

"[28th.] Letters. Wrote to John Donnelly, English College, Rome, on his wish to leave the Romish Church and to join 'Friends,' enclosing a letter from my dear friend J. B. Braithwaite.

"[April 1.] Dined with Mrs. Schwabe, No. 8, Clarges St.: family party—daughters and their husbands; among the latter Mr. Lockwood,[2] a lawyer of much promise. Sad news to-day of the death of Dr. Collis of Shottery Hall. Mrs. Collis is the mother of my son-in-law, Richd. F. Curry.

---

[1] This was accounted Dilke's finest speech in the House. He made it on a motion, of which he had given notice, regretting that the Government, having censured the proceedings of Sir Bartle Frere in South Africa, had not recalled him. He spoke to a full House for two hours and a half. Dilke himself thought he had made dozens of better speeches: "it was an easy speech to make—a mere Blue-Book speech."

[2] The promise was amply fulfilled. Lockwood became Q.C. in 1882, Recorder of Sheffield in 1884, and Lord Rosebery's Solicitor-General in 1894. He stood for King's Lynn in 1880, and for York in 1883, unsuccessfully, but was elected at York in the General Election of 1885.

"[*2nd.*] Richd. F. Curry called this morning—just come from Nice. Is gone on to Stratford. Mrs. Kay called: reported death of Sir U. Kay Shuttleworth, her nephew; report quite false, which it is a great relief to know. £5 to Fund for Widows of Soldiers killed in Natal.

"[*3rd.*] Jas. H. Tuke . . . with me to Mr. Ouless, who made a slight alteration in the portrait; but I do not think he has been successful with my likeness. A rumour, too true I fear, that Isaac Fletcher, M.P., has committed suicide at Morley's Hotel. Almost every day brings its sad story.

"[*4th.*] To lunch with Mrs. Drummond and Mrs. Kay, 18, Hyde Park Gardens. House: India Cotton Import Duties. To dinner with Mr. Smalley, of the *New York Tribune*. Mr. Welsh, U.S. Minister and his daughter there; also Professor Huxley and his wife (whom I took down to dinner); also Mr. Roundell and Sir C. Dilke, and Mrs. Procter, widow of 'Barry Cornwall.' She brought me to my lodgings in her carriage. Mrs. Huxley, intelligent and pleasant, seemed to me like one of our best kind of 'lady Friend.'

"[*7th, at Rochdale.*] Call on Thos. Short, a fine old man 92 yrs. of age, very cheerful, and much interested in public affairs and in his friends. A minister in our Society, once, I am told, Professor of Music at Cambridge—if there be such an office.

"[*16th.*] To Birmingham by 11 train; dear Lillie with me to Stafford; W. N. Molesworth[1] in the same carriage.

"To William Kenrick's, The Grove, Harborne, Birmingham. Dinner, and after to the Town Hall. Grand meeting—the Mayor in the Chair. I spoke for an hour on Russia, India, and England, and 'liberated my mind' on what has often pressed upon it recently and was most kindly received as usual.

"[*17th.*] Visited 3 of the Coffee Houses lately opened—very nice houses, and likely to be very useful in the Temperance cause. Called on Mr. Jaffray at the office of the *Daily Post*; then to The Arts Club for lunch and conversation with some of our friends.

"[*24th, at Rochdale.*] Mr. Rogers[2] here for a long talk. Mr. Cheney, a pleasant American, here: talk about movement of negroes from South to Kansas.

---

[1] Author of Molesworth's "History of England," published in 1874 by Chapman and Hall. He did much of his work in Bright's library at "One Ash," coming there almost daily for many months.

[2] Professor Thorold Rogers.

"[29th.] Mr. G. H. Bayley [1] (Southwark) called—talk about Mr. Rogers as a candidate for the Borough, and difficulty as to his expenses.

"[30th.] D. White called, on Freedmen's Mission work in Africa by coloured missionaries: could not undertake to go to a meeting on the subject.

"Devonshire Club to lunch with Jasper Moore and delegates from Roumelia: Lord Houghton, Goschen, Tracy and others there. Mr. Gerschoff only escaped being hanged by the ruffianly Turks: he is one of the delegates.

"[May 1.] Home early: notes for possible speech on Irish Land purchase clauses to-morrow.

"[2nd.] Letter from darling Sophie this morning gives me anxiety: is the last of my daughters to leave me? . . . Notes of speech written out. House: spoke on 'purchase clauses' of Irish Land Bill.

"[3rd.] Afternoon to Twickenham to York House to visit Grant Duff, M.P.

"[4th.] Day very fine. Afternoon, crossed the Thames and walked round Ham House: of historical interest. John Morley and Edwd. Dicey came. York House party separated. W. R. Grey and his wife, Mr. Morier (who is Minister at Lisbon),[2] Jno. Morley and E. Dicey: much pleasant conversation. Correcting speeches for new volume of Speeches. House: question to Northcote on Zulu War. Dined with Sir T. May, and met there Lady Russell and her daughter Lady Agatha. She spoke of the portrait of Lord Russell at the Reform Club, and is coming to-morrow to see it, when I am to meet her.

"Walked up with Sir W. Lawson, the evening lovely. Dean Stanley has sent me a volume of sermons and speeches during his American tour.

"[6th.] Dr. Cheney and Govr. Dingley and his wife, from U. States, called this morning. Much talk on English affairs and on American tariff.

"Lady Russell and her daughter Lady Agatha came to the Reform Club to see the portrait of Lord Russell lately put up in the hall of the

---

[1] Mr. Bayley afterwards represented North Camberwell in Parliament as a Liberal.

[2] Afterwards, Sir Robert Morier, Ambassador at St. Petersburg during the Penjdeh crisis. He had been Minister at Darmstadt at the time of the Franco-Prussian War. Bismarck, who held him in great aversion, brought false charges against him of betraying to Bazaine the movements of German troops. Morier, the close friend and confidant of Benjamin Jowett for forty years, was a diplomatist after Bright's own heart. He did a great deal for the improvement of the relations between England and Russia. Morier was a nephew of the author of "Haji Baba."

JOHN BRIGHT AND PROFESSOR THOROLD ROGERS IN THE GARDEN
OF "ONE ASH," ROCHDALE

Club. Went with them thro' the Club. The portrait is good. House at 9 o'clock: resolution on actions for 'Breach of promise.' Mr. Herschell's speech very good. Resolution carried by large majority. Home rather late: to bed after one o'clock.

"[8*th*.] To call on Edwd. Miall with a deputation to present an address to him on his 70th birthday. Found him rather feeble, but very pleasant. I spoke shortly on my long acquaintance with him and my high regard for him. Bought at Sampson Low's a copy of Milton for Nelly Cobden and of Whittier for Mrs. Grant Duff. House: but home early, before 10 o'clock.

"[12*th, at Rochdale*.] Dined with W. N. Molesworth and met Bishop of Manchester. Pleasant conversation. Bishop is fettered on some questions by his Church office, but he is a man of great sincerity, boldness, and of great wish to do good. He works very earnestly in his diocese.

"[13*th*.] With dear Sophie to Blackstone Edge—an hour's pleasant walk. Heard the cuckoo for the first time this year. Our thoughts much on the dear mother no longer with us in her favourite drive and walk.

"[15*th*.] Theodore Cash came in the evening.[1]

"[16*th*.] Drove on the old Todmorden road with dear Sophie and Theodore Cash. The morning was lovely. It was sad to ramble over the ground on which I have walked and lingered so often with the dear one who is no longer with us.

"[17*th*.] Theodore Cash left us in the evening to return to Torquay, and then to Berlin.

"[20*th, in London*.] Hy. Ashworth called; then Mr. Ghose, a native Indian lawyer; intelligent on Indian affairs. Then to Devonshire House: consultation on course to be taken on Irish University Bill. Lord Granville walked back with me, and we discussed some things in the career of Chas. Villiers for his speech at Wolverhampton when the statue of Villiers is to be uncovered.

"[21*st*.] Dined at Lord Aberdeen's, 31 Grosvenor Square, grandson of Lord Aberdeen, with whom I spent a week at Haddo in 1856.[2]

[1] John Theodore Cash, F.R.S. (who became dean of Aberdeen University), was the cause of the exclamation in the diary on May 2. He afterwards married Miss Sophie Bright.

[2] The seventh (and present) Earl of Aberdeen, who became Gladstone's Lord-Lieutenant of Ireland in 1886 and adhered to the Gladstonian Party throughout the Home Rule controversies. The dream of a visit to Haddo with his daughter came true in October.

His wife, daughter of Sir D. Marjoribanks. A large dinner party. Afterwards a larger party and much music, some very loud—too much noise for my taste. Invited to visit them at Haddo in the autumn. It would be pleasant to take dear Sophie there.

"[*June* 17.[1]] House: debate on Flogging: Army Discipline Bill. Spoke briefly for diminution of the punishment. Feeling of the House very strong and Government forced to yield.[2]

"[*23rd.*] Devonshire House: discussion on Irish University Bill.[3] Majority for 2nd reading: I could not go with them.

"[*24th.*] Dined with Jas. Caird, lately home from India on Famine Commission. Long talk on Indian affairs. He is in favour of independent Presidencies for India, the plan I suggested in 1858.

"[*25th.*] Call from Robt. Knight, of Calcutta. He is here to start a new weekly paper *The Statesman*, to give more attention to Indian affairs.[4]

"[*27th.*] Dined with J. Chamberlain at Star and Garter, Richmond. Fawcett, J. Morley, Lord Arthur Russell, F. Greenwood of the *Pall Mall Gazette*, and others there.

"[*28th.*] To Oxford, to Professor Rogers. In the evening dined Hall of Worcester College: a party of 20. Pleasant talk till 12 o'clock.

"[*29th.*] With Rogers to the Park. Called to see Museum— very interesting. Evening, dined with Prof. Max Müller, Hall of All Souls. Small party, very pleasant. Much conversation with Max Müller on Germany and Bismarck, whose character is a strange one.

"[*30th.*] Visited Bodleian Library and Ashmolean Museum. Wish I could have lingered for hours in them. To London by 12.5 train. My visit to Oxford was of extreme interest. Pleasure constantly saddened by thought of how much the dear one no longer here would have enjoyed what I saw. This feeling rose to my mind at every moment when I felt surprise and pleasure at the interesting objects before me. Professor Rogers and his family very kind.

"[*July* 1.] My Calcutta friend, Lalmohun Ghose, called to ask if I would attend a meeting for him to speak on Indian affairs and claims of natives to more consideration. Did not give any answer.

"[*2nd.*] Philip came from Darmstadt—much grown and very pleasant. Most welcome. Henry B. Adams, U.S.A., called. In-

---

[1] In the interim he had taken a trip in the Lake District with his daughter.
[2] See page 425.   [3] i.e., at a meeting of ex-Ministers.
[4] The Knight family retained the control of *The Statesman*, which became an important daily paper, until quite recent years.

teresting talk on America, her soil and vast produce: effects on England and on Europe in coming years.

"[*3rd.*] Mr. Pierce of Boston called; also Dr. Stillman of San Francisco. Then Mr. Chesson about proposed meeting for my Calcutta friend, Lalmohun Ghose, to speak on subject of his deputation to England. House: Home early: notes for speech to-morrow.

"[*4th.*] House: debate on Commission on Agricultural Distress. Spoke for nearly an hour, exposing shallow pretences of those who asked for inquiry, etc. Philip in the Gallery, and much enjoyed listening to the debate.

"[*5th.*] To Orpington and High Elms, to visit Sir Jno. Lubbock: Dr. Playfair, and Mr. and Mrs. Huxley and their daughter, Vivian and Digby in the train. A pleasant party.

"[*6th.*] Afternoon a long walk, mostly in the rain. Much conversation.

"[*7th.*] By 10 train to Charing Cross. This little visit has given me great pleasure. Lubbock, Huxley and Playfair represent the science of this country, and it would be difficult to find 3 men more pleasant to spend a day with. Mrs. Huxley and her daughter and Lady Lubbock and her daughter added much to the pleasantness of the party. Sir Jno. Lubbock showed us his nests of ants, and explained many of the peculiarities of his curious little friends.

"To-day is the anniversary of the death of my dear father 28 years ago.

"House: spoke briefly on Flogging in the Army. The contest very severe on this question.[1] In this is the secret of Disraeli's career and of his success—acting upon and with a party careful only of ends and regardless of means.

"House: discussion and division on Flogging in the Army.[2] Home before 2 in the morning.

"[*10th.*] With Mr. Pierce, of Boston, and Philip to Slough; then drove to Stoke Poges Church. Tomb of the poet Gray and a monument

[1] Irish obstruction began to make itself felt in the debates on the Army Regulation Bill. The Radicals (including Chamberlain) were as fiercely opposed for reasons of humanity to flogging in the army as Parnell and Biggar for reasons of politics. Lord Hartington, who did not feel so strongly about it, was induced to move on this day (July 7) for the abolition of flogging, but was defeated by a big majority. Sir Stafford Northcote vainly endeavoured to conquer the Irish "hold-up" by minor alterations of the rules of the House.

[2] Flogging was abolished in both Army and Navy by Gladstone's Government in 1881.

to him in adjoining field. Church and graveyard very picturesque. Then on to Beaconsfield. Church in which Burke was buried. Waller's tomb in the churchyard. Then on to the 'Gregories,' where Burke's house once stood—now entirely gone. Then on to the Jordans Meeting House, where Wm. Penn, his two wives and several of his children and Thos. Ellwood were buried. Then to Chalfont St. Giles, and called at the house where Milton is said to have lived when he left London during the time of the Plague. Returned to Slough and took the 5 o'clock train to London, spending nearly 6 hours in the drive. The day very fine, the country beautiful, the places we visited full of interest. The graves of Wm. Penn and his wife Guli had most interest for me: I wished to be alone that I might dwell on the goodness and loveliness of those whose mortal remains had been laid to rest in that quiet and secluded ground. My heart was full as I thought of the intense delight which this excursion would have given to her who is no longer with me. Now every pleasure permitted to me is clouded by this thought.

"Club: heard of excitement in the House among Irish members on course taken by the Speaker in connexion with their 'obstruction' of the business of the House. The subject is to be discussed to-morrow at the 2 o'clock morning sitting.

"[11th.] House: debate on Mr. Speaker's ordering notes to be taken of speeches of members. Did not vote. I thought Parnell's motion more right than Northcote's amendment and preferred not to record my opinion.

"Evening: dined with Ernest de Bunsen at Abbey Lodge. Grand Duke of Baden (Hereditary) there and Crown Prince of Sweden came after dinner. Good looking young man, intelligent and modest in manner. They were in the House on the Agricultural Distress Debate a week ago, and seemed pleased with my speech. The Baden Duke is interested in the land question.

"[17th.] Called 74, Eaton Square. Chat with Lady Cardwell. Anecdote of Mrs. Stonor, daughter of Sir R. Peel: Had long avoided introduction to Disraeli, but once found him next to her at dinner. He began conversation, and uttered fulsome praises of her father. She, disgusted, asked how he explained his conduct to him. Disraeli answered, in those days he was nobody and to bring himself into notice he attacked the greatest man in the country. Mrs. Stonor had more than once told this to Lady Cardwell.

"[18th.] Breakfast with W. G. Smalley of the *New York Tribune*, to meet Mr. Joseph H. Choate of New York. Also there, Professor

Huxley, Mr. Browning, Lord E. Fitzmaurice, Mr. Stedman, an American. House: Mr. Choate and wife into the galleries. Evening: dined with S. and Emma Winkworth, Holly Lodge. Professor Bryce and his sister there.

"[19*th*.] Geo. Howell [1] called this morning to talk over an Association for reform of Land Laws. Pleasant letters this morning from Albert, Helen, Mary and Sophie; but the dear Mother's letter wanting. Last night and this morning very sad about her. My loneliness seems to have little relief and the future affords no gleam of light.

"[21*st*.] To dinner with Lord and Lady Frederick Cavendish: a party of 12. Mr. and Mrs. Gladstone, Mr. Herschel, Sir H. James, Lord Edward Cavendish and his wife, Mr. and Mrs. Choate from New York. Afterwards Sir R. Phillimore and his wife and some others. Evening very lively and pleasant. Sophie enjoyed it much.

"[23*rd*.] 3 o'clock, to Willis's Rooms, a crowded meeting, of which I was Chairman. Lalmohun Ghose spoke for $\frac{1}{2}$ an hour admirably. I think no Englishman could have spoken better in language, matter, clearness and beauty of expression or force. I spoke after him for nearly an hour, and I hope with some effect. Mr. Fawcett spoke, and the meeting was over about 5 o'clock.

"[25*th*.] House: debate on Pardon to E. Galley, convicted of murder in 1836. Spoke in favour of pardon. Mr. Cross, Home Secretary, behaved foolishly, but was compelled to yield by general opinion of both sides of the House. Home with a cheerful feeling that mercy had prevailed over official harshness and cruelty. To bed at 2 o'clock."

2

Another urgent invitation to visit America reached Bright in August at Rochdale. He was, at the moment, entertaining E. L. Pierce of Boston, to evenings of talk and excursions to Blackstone Edge and the Roman road; and no doubt the pressure from the other side was reinforced by his guest. Mr. Pierce sailed from Liverpool in the *Parthia* on the 13th, and next day Bright sat down to deal with the message from President Hayes at Washington.

Ever since the Civil War he had been pressed by various people to go over; but even so long ago as 1863 he thought himself "getting too far on in life to cross the ocean" unless he could see some prospect of being useful and had some duty clear before him. This, however, was a rather

[1] The eminent Trade Union Leader.

different matter—an affair of high state: he was asked to be the President's guest at the White House. Doubtless the visit would have called forth great popular demonstrations. The prospect affrighted him:

"Wrote to the President of the United States thanking him for his invitation to be his guest if I would visit America; also to Mr. Evarts, Secretary of State, in answer to his kind letter. Explained why I cannot cross the Atlantic. I shrink from the excitement."

So, while his son William, bent on a tour of America, sailed for New York in the *Adriatic* on the 19th, Bright himself remained at Rochdale, enjoying the company of his youngest son Philip and his daughter Sophie, entertaining Mrs. McLaren, making up parcels of books for the library of the new workhouse, taking family parties for drives in the neighbour-hood, and receiving the pilgrims who, in increasing numbers, made their way to "One Ash." In September, having been made proud and happy by his daughter, Mrs. Roth, who presented him with a grandson on the 9th, he escaped North to fish in the Tweed, meeting at Kelso Mr. Bidder, the lawyer, son of the famous "Calculating Boy." At the beginning of October he was, with his daughter, the guest of Rupert Potter at Dalguise.

"[*October* 5.] Mr. J. E. Millais, the great painter, came up to lunch. His daughter Mary came also, with her uncle, Albert Gray. Our host would photograph us in his garden by an instantaneous process. Millais is a fine powerful man; talks loudly and is boisterous as a rough schoolboy, but much good sense evident in his quieter moments. He spoke to R. Potter about my sitting to him for a portrait, which he thinks he could do—tho' several painters have failed in attempting it.[1]

"[8*th*.] To Dunkeld. Called on the Duchess of Atholl: sensible and pleasant in conversation. Rupert Potter with me.

"[9*th*.] To Aberdeen, to the Imperial Hotel. A few moments after our arrival, the Provost and two other civic dignitaries came in to ask me to accept the Freedom of the City whilst in this neighbourhood. Told them I was going away to-morrow and came to Scotland for quiet and not for meetings and speeches, and begged them to excuse me. They were disappointed but courteous and kind, and hoped at some future time I might give them the opportunity of showing their respect and of enrolling my name on the list of the Citizens of Aberdeen.

"Dear Sophie and I walked about the grand granite streets of

---

[1] No painter produced a really satisfactory portrait of Bright. Only one sculptor succeeded—Albert Bruce-Joy.

this remarkable city,[1] admired its handsome buildings and its fine shops.

"[10*th.*] Carriage round the city. Saw and admired the beauty of its new streets, of their architecture and their granite. To old Aberdeen University. Met there Professor Geddes (Greek) who was most kindly, showed us round the venerable old place and the church, and went on with us to the old Bridge of Don. Afterwards saw Noel Paton's great picture 'The Man of Sorrows.' A fine picture, but I do not like the attempts to give us portraits of the Saviour, and do not subscribe to or for engravings of them.

"About 1 o'clock by train to Old Meldrum. Carriage from Haddo House [2] waiting for us. Haddo 6 miles off. Received most kindly. Found some company there. Ladies Dundas and Charteris, sisters of Earl Wemyss I believe. Lady Kintore and daughter. Afternoon on the lake, but the trout did not rise freely. The lake and wood lovely. This day: birthday of my dear daughter Helen and wedding-day of my dear child Mary.

"[11*th.*] Morning walk. Afternoon drive to Sich Castle—old ruin of the family. Beautiful valley, little river and lovely woods. Lady Aberdeen drove me home, by partly different road, but all picturesque and charming.

"[12*th.*] To Mathlich Church: building new since my former visit to Haddo in 1856, but same minister—now elderly and venerable. Afternoon long walk by lakes and in the park.

"[13*th.*] Fished River Ythan: water too low and no fish. Afternoon on one of the lakes, the new one. Some nice trout. At tea, a few tenants of the estate came. Pleasant conversation with them on farming affairs; but bad harvests have had ill effects on them. At dinner about 20: Marquis of Huntley and his wife, Lord and Lady Lovatt, Sir A. Gordon and his wife, W. S. Lindsay and Lady Harriet, his wife, the Provost of Aberdeen, Sheriff Thompson, and two Bailies of the city. After dinner Sophie played and sang in the drawing-room. Later in the smoking-room, warm discussion on Land Question. Lord Huntley hot for reform and changes, Mr. Lindsay opposing on the ground of injury to aristocratic order.

"[14*th.*] After 12, left Haddo for railway at Old Meldrum, and reached Inverness after dark. Our visit to Haddo has been very pleasant. Lord and Lady Aberdeen most kind. They are religious, good—everything about them shows the influence of good. They have prayers twice

[1] Afterwards his daughter's home for many years.   [2] Lord Aberdeen's seat.

daily—9 a.m. and 7 p.m. Lord Aberdeen reads a portion of Scripture and a prayer, and in the evening a hymn is sung by those present, servants included. They have one child, a boy of eight months old;[1] somewhat delicate I fear, and requiring and having great care shown to him. The house is large; the grounds are extensive and fine; woods full of beauty and of colour at this season. Lord Aberdeen is building a chapel close to the house, not to be consecrated, but for use for religious and other discourses and services. Lady Aberdeen most kind to my dear Sophie, who has enjoyed her visit greatly.

"[15th.] To Inverness. Town very pretty. Afternoon drive on the shore of Loch Ness.

"[16th.] Day wild and very cold. Provost and deputation up to offer me Freedom of Boro', but leaving to-morrow. Could not consent.

"[18th, at Rochdale.] Very pleasant to be at home again, but felt that one welcome was wanting. House very quiet, and sadness felt as I passed from one room to another and thought of the past and the present.

"[22nd.] To Meeting. Called on my old friend Oliver Ormerod.[2] Very ill and sinking. Saw him for a few minutes in his bed, looking old and feeble, but quite clear in mind and tranquil in spirit. Have known him from our schooldays when at W. Littlewood's school. His life has been one of great usefulness and devotion to well doing, especially in connexion with Sunday Schools and in all benevolent and religious work. His loss will be greatly felt in the town. My call seemed to please him and I am glad I was able once again to see him.[3]

"[23rd.] Mrs. Kemp[4] and her daughter called. Notes for speech at great meeting in Manchester on Saturday. Burdened with thoughts of it. Difficulty: what to say, and what not to say. Somewhat nervous and uneasy, for these very great meetings are hazardous and rarely quite satisfactory. I would give something considerable to be able to escape from it.

"[25th.] To Manchester. The great meeting in 'Pomona Palace.' Wonderful gathering of people: 20,000 in the hall, and probably double that number outside.

"Lord Hartington spoke ½ an hour. I followed for an hour. Whole audience seemed to hear perfectly. My speech severe on the Govt. but *just* I am quite sure, and I am satisfied with it. Home to

[1] The present Lord Haddo.
[2] A writer of books in the Lancashire dialect.
[3] Bright attended the funeral of Mr. Ormerod on November 7.
[4] The mother of Lord Rochdale.

dinner at 7. Our family party very pleasant, but I was somewhat tired with the day's anxiety and work.

"[29th.] Theodore Cash left us to-day. My dear child Sophie has accepted him and is engaged to marry him. Her friends and his approve of the match. For me it promises to leave me even more desolate; but I trust it may increase her happiness.

"[31st.] I left home at 11 for Birmingham. To the house of Mr. Collings,[1] the Mayor. After dinner to new Council rooms to a grand party of 1,000 people. More than half were teachers—men and women—of elementary schools in Birmingham. I spoke a short time to them; some others also. Afterwards music and dancing for those who liked the amusement. I met many of my friends, and the evening passed pleasantly. Home with the Mayor and his wife and daughter after midnight.

"[November 16.] To-day is my birthday—68. Very sad; one absent whose loving interest made my birthday more noticed.

"[20th.] Wm. Digby, from Wisbech, here. Has lived 9 years in Madras and was Secretary of the Famine Fund distribution. Now to be editor of the *Liverpool and Southport Daily News*. Much conversation on India. Intelligent and pleasant man.[2]

"[December 8.] This evening began to write a narrative of some of the incidents of my youth and life, believing that my children will take an interest in it.[3]

"[10th.] Letters: one to Lord Leigh, who has asked me to accept Commission of the Peace for Warwickshire. Have declined it, not liking some of the duties of the magistracy, and doubting if it is a system which should be maintained.

"[17th.] Yesterday and to-day, engaged in making some notes for speech at the meeting to-morrow to welcome Mr. Potter [4] on his return from United States.

"[18th.] Town Hall Meeting: T. B. Potter's speech on America very good, and interesting. I spoke for an hour, to show greatness and importance of U. States; wisdom of much of their policy. Urged Free Trade upon them and our Colonies, etc. Meeting very good and successful in every way.

[1] Jesse Collings, M.P.

[2] William Digby was one of the best-known Liberal journalists of his time. He held several editorships in England after his return from India.

[3] See page 1.

[4] T. B. Potter, M.P. for Rochdale.

"[*23rd.*] With Joe Cross [1] to Bolton, to see the fine spinning mill of the company with which he is connected. Afterwards to the new Town Hall and the large Market Hall. Afternoon we went to spend the evening and night at the house of my niece, Kate Thomasson, and her husband: they live next door. At dinner we had the pleasant company of my old friend Henry Ashworth and his daughter Eliza Leach.

"[*29th.*] Terrible news this morning of the breakdown of the Tay Bridge and of the loss of a train and passengers. Caused me much sadness all day—such desolation in homes and families in Dundee."

3

In a letter written in March to a correspondent in Devon, Bright said the Disraeli Government was "the worst we have had for more than fifty years." When the great year of 1880 dawned, its end was near, and the progress of the Midlothian campaign left no doubt about the verdict of the country when the issues should be put before it. Thus it was with the certainty of a great Liberal victory in view that he went down to Birmingham for the annual meeting with his constituents.

He was the guest of Mr. Arthur Chamberlain at Moor Green. Harcourt was there, with Muntz and Chamberlain, and they all spoke at the Town Hall banquet. "Harcourt clever and amusing," he notes; "my aim is rather to instruct than amuse." In the various meetings which followed, he instructed them on Irish Land and the reform of the County Franchise—destined to be the two chief domestic concerns of the new Parliament.

"[*January* 18, 1880.] To Meeting, morning. Afternoon, Matthew Knight, from Stockport, called and brought me a copy of the New Testament which formerly belonged to my ancestor John Gratton. It was sent to me by Maria Bradburn, the widow of the late Saml. Bradburn, of the Wash, near Chapel-en-le-Frith. He collected many old Friends' books, and wished this to be given to me.

"[*19th.*] To 'Store' Library, to seek for something in Hansard, 1860; but did not find it. It was a speech of Sir Stafford Northcote, in which he thanked the Lords for having rejected the Paper Duty Repeal Bill.

"[*28th.*] At Birmingham heard the sad news of the sudden death

---

[1] Joseph Cross married Bright's niece, Anne Frances Ashworth.

of my friend Henry Fowler, of Woodford. His wife and large family thus brought into deep grief. She, the dearest friend of her whose loss I mourn: her house and mine thus stricken and made desolate!

"[*30th.*] To Town Hall, Manchester. Dinner by the Mayor to the Judges—Lord Coleridge and Brett. Lord Derby there. Slept at the Town Hall. 50 or 60 persons at dinner. Mixed company as to politics.

"[*February* 10.] To Union Chapel, Islington, ½ past 7. Large chapel. Fine meeting. Spoke on 'Nonconformity' for ¾ of an hour. Felt feeble and stupid, but got thro' pretty well. Mr. Dale then read his lecture. Very good and well delivered. Afterwards to house of Mr. H. Allon, the Minister, to tea. Mr. Oakley, clergyman of Hoxton, and his curate, Mr. Ottley, there. The young curate has a look of goodness and purity in his countenance. Mr. Oakley very liberal and sincere.

"[*17th.*] Call from John Morley to talk over some points in his Memoir of my dear friend Cobden. He told me, what I before suspected, that Thomasson had given Mrs. Cobden £20,000 besides the £5,000 given to the subscription.

"House: Irish Boro' Franchise. I spoke late in the evening. Voice not good from cold still lingering about me.

"[*20th.*] House: Privilege case of Mr. Plimsoll. I spoke against Govt. resolution.

"[*21st.*] To Mr. Muller, 11, Notting Hill Terrace, to give him sitting for portrait he had made from photographs.

"[*23rd.*] With Rupert Potter to Mr. Millais for first sitting for my portrait; ¾ of an hour. He only expects to require 4 or 5 sittings. Very lively and pleasant man with great force in his art. House: Question of Privilege again. House in confusion from feebleness and blunders of Stafford Northcote, leader of the Tory Party.

"[*24th.*] Buckingham Palace Hotel to breakfast with Cyrus W. Field and his wife. Mr. Smalley and Chesson there. Mr. Sanford, late Minister U.S.A., to Belgium, came in. Conversation on the South and on Florida and its wonderful growth of oranges, etc. House: much talk of dissolution of Parliament. Home about 11 o'clock.

"[*26th.*] To Mr. Millais. Gave him an hour and a half. Progress; but he is not well satisfied. He finds the 'mouth' the difficult feature, as other artists have found it.

"[*27th.*] House: resolution on obstruction of Irish Members. Home early. Letters. Read a powerful pamphlet on Mr. Cowen's treason to his party—and to the Mr. Cowen of two or three years ago.[1]

"[*29th.*] Dined with Henry Adams and his lively and clever wife, 22, Queen Anne's Gate, Westminster. Sir R. Cunliffe there. Much talk till midnight on Canada, the States, England and Europe. Walked home with Sir R. Cunliffe to Hyde Park Corner. Afternoon read 'Penns and Penningtons,'[2] a record of noble lives and of much suffering; then Epistle to the Hebrews—impressive always.

"[*March* 1.] To Mr. Millais: sitting for portrait, 1¼ hours; progress made. Rupert Potter there photographing.

"[*4th.*] Ballot at Reform Club. My dear boy Willie elected: my friends very kind and gave him general support. With Mr. Millais this morning; he is satisfied with the promised success of his picture. Dined with Lord Selborne in Portland Place, No. 30. Lady Russell there; Mr. Balfour, who has married Duke of Argyll's daughter; and one of Tennyson's sons, who stammers; his wife is good and pleasant.

"[*5th.*] Call from Mr. Allen, Secy. to the Marriage Law Reform Socy. Asks me to speak at a meeting to promote Bill to legalize marriage with a deceased wife's sister, and have consented to do so. It is a question in which I take a great interest. My dear friend Cobden was much interested in it, two of his sisters having married Mr. Sale of Manchester.

"Writing notes for a speech on Sir W. Lawson's Temperance resolution this evening. House: debate. Spoke, but voice not good and not well satisfied with myself. Debate kept me from dining with Lord Granville. Home about one o'clock.

"[*6th.*] Dined with Mitchell Henry, M.P., at Stratheden House, Knightsbridge. Talk with Dr. Quain on Thos. Carlyle, and on the singular manner of his wife's death. She died in the carriage in which she was being driven in Hyde Park from the shock she received from her little dog being run over, tho' not killed, by another carriage. It is supposed she was driven twice round the park after her death, and before it was known she was dead.[3] When Disraeli offered Carlyle a baronetcy and a pension he declined, saying he had no one to leave his title to: he had enough to live upon, and he did not understand decorations.

[1] Mr. Joseph Cowen, the Newcastle Radical, almost the only public man in England who advocated Home Rule, was an ardent supporter of Beaconsfield's policy.

[2] Maria Webb's record of the families of William Penn and his wife Sulielma Springett, a descendant of the Penningtons, was published in 1867.

[3] Mrs. Carlyle died in 1866.

"[8th.] Called in George St., Hanover Square, to see lodgings. Announcement of dissolution of Parliament: a pleasant surprise. Shall get home for a month and possibly for a much longer time.

"With Mr. Millais for a sitting for the portrait.

"[11th.] To Mr. Millais, morning, for 1¼ hours. Lunched with Rupert Potter, and was photographed in aid of Mr. Millais for figure only. House: voted against flogging.

"[13th.] With Mr. Millais for an hour or more. With dear Sophie to 40, Dover St., Lady Stanley's, to large party of teachers of the London Board Schools. A very interesting party and a pleasant evening.

"[14th.] To Westminster Meeting. Afternoon called on Mr. Millais. He considers the portrait almost complete and requires no more sittings.

"[19th.] To Birmingham.[1] Much congratulation at stations on the way, especially at Stafford, where my nephew Chas. McLaren [2] is a candidate. To Mr. Chamberlain's house. Evening: Town Hall; speech to working men; grand meeting.

"[23rd.] Evening: two meetings in St. George's and All Saints Wards. Spoke on County Franchise and on cost and wickedness of recent wars.

"[24th.] Deputation of school teachers. Evening: great meeting in Cave's 'Repository,' a very large room. Spoke chiefly on Land question.

"[27th.] Meeting in Holder's Circus: large and unanimous—all the meetings have been so.

"[29th.] To three great open air meetings in playgrounds of the Board Schools—foretelling victory.

"[30th.] To Rochdale by 11.25 train: home before 4 o'clock.

"[31st.] Rochdale election: Potter v. Gamble. Great success; very large majority—2,000 for Potter. Pleasant to find our town so faithful to Liberal principles.

"[*April* 1.] To Manchester, and voted for my brother Jacob and Jno. Slagg, who were elected by very large majorities, as were the Liberal candidates for Salford. The Tory Government majority is gone.

"[7th.] To Meeting. Then to the Town Hall with Albert and my brother Thomas to vote for Mr. Leake and Mr. Agnew for this division of this county. At 11 this evening heard of their complete success, and of many other gains of the Liberal Party.

[1] From Rochdale. This was the opening of the General Election campaign.
[2] Now Lord Aberconway.

"[*8th.*] Deputation from students of Glasgow University asking me to become a candidate for office of Lord Rector of the University. Mitchell, Raeburn and Ferguson names of deputation. Have been asked same question on a former occasion and refused. Am now very unwilling, but am in difficulty about it. The purpose of the deputation and their friends being so good, I must send a reply in a day or two. Deputation dined with us. Election returns increasingly in favour of Liberal Party: their majority very large.[1]

"[*15th, at Llandudno.*] Rain and high wind from N.E. Day unpleasant. Evening, wrote many letters: one to Mr. Pierce, of Boston, U.S.A., on hearing of the death of his wife, and one to Mrs. J. S. Wright, of Birmingham, on hearing of the sudden death of her husband, J. S. Wright, M.P. for Nottingham. He has been one of my greatest friends in Birmingham. His removal will be a great loss, for his services to the town and to all good objects have been constant and remarkable. It is another lesson to teach us how frail is the tenure by which our lives are held."

4

The correspondence of Queen Victoria with Beaconsfield reveals the horrified alarm that assailed Conservative minds when the election results were complete. They could hardly believe that Fate had played them such a trick. Gladstone, resting after Midlothian, had no illusions about the immediate future, as Bright's diaries show. He knew what Midlothian meant. He could not accept service under any other leader, and he was conscious that the country would tolerate no other leadership than his.

The efforts to evade the inevitable which occupied a week of agitated negotiation were pathetic in their futility. The Queen, "shocked and ashamed" at the success of the man who had "done so much mischief," thought it "impossible to send for Mr. Gladstone." Beaconsfield encouraged her to grasp at straws—talked about a Hartington or a Granville Government, and kept up the pretence till Hartington and Granville, with gentle bluntness, had disabused her Majesty. Many days before this happened, Gladstone and Bright, in quiet talk at Hawarden, had taken a clear view over the course of probability, and even, as the sequel would seem to show, discussed the composition of the new Ministry.

[1] The Conservatives stood in a minority of 173 if the Liberal and the Irish vote were combined. The Liberal majority over all other parties in the House was 41.

The misgiving with which Bright gazed on the heritage left to their successors by "the worst Government in fifty years" was soon justified. The new Ministry encountered the earliest and the least of their difficulties in the liquidation of Lord Lytton's policy of partition in Afghanistan, costly as it was alike in life, in money, and in prestige. To realize the hopes of the Boers that a Liberal Government would reverse the annexation policy proved a troublesome task. To instrument the clauses of the Treaty of Berlin relating to Christian communities in European Turkey was another. In the actual workaday world of Parliament, to defeat Irish obstruction (with Parnell, dour, cold, determined, as the new leader of an Irish Party devoid of respect for the House and indifferent to the Constitution) and at the same time to counter the ingenuities of the "Fourth Party," brilliantly led by Lord Randolph Churchill, was in itself a labour of Hercules.

But all these were infinitesimal troubles compared with the spectre of murderous despair that stalked in Ireland. Land League, boycott, agrarian outrage; Irish intransigence, English ignorance and prejudice— the Government waded deep into the hideous welter before it had been six months in office. Ireland took charge of the Parliament of 1880 from the mad moment when the House of Lords rejected the Tenants Compensation Bill and tore out of the Government's hands the one weapon that might have enabled them to cope with the forces of rebellion. That folly threw Ireland utterly into the arms of the League. Forster's Coercion Act and its train of woe followed in a resistless and satanic syllogism.

Bright anxiously records the gathering tragedy in his diaries; in letters and speeches he gallantly defends his chief. He begins with a visit to Hawarden.

"[*April* 16.] Have been to Hawarden, to call on Mr. Gladstone and to lunch with them at the Rectory, as the Castle is in the hands of the painters. A pleasant walk of nearly an hour in the park, and afterwards much talk in the Library on the political situation.

"It is not likely he will take any office in a Govt. of which he is not the head, and only on the ground of the requirements of the public interests pressed upon him will he again accept the labours and cares of office. Spoke of many of our public men—their claims and their chances of usefulness; of the Govr. General of India, of Constantinople and the Embassy, of the Queen's book, 'Life of the Prince Consort,' and of a great misrepresentation of his course in respect of expenditure for fortifications, about which he had written to remonstrate or complain to Theo. Martin, who has written the book.[1]

"I told him I was struck with the spiteful way in which he was treated on more than one occasion. In regard to unjust attacks upon himself he speaks with great moderation and forbearance and makes allowance even for what he is obliged to condemn.

"He rejoices in the overthrow of the Govt. as a grand testimony against an evil policy and a demoralizing system of administration. He spoke of Disraeli as one of the most remarkable men in our Parliamentary annals. His courage and patience remarkable, and bringing weaker men to aid him in what they must at first have doubted or condemned.

"He is much pleased with his son's success in East Worcestershire and with the prospect of his son Herbert's election for Leeds, when he himself vacates the seat by selecting Midlothian as the constituency he will represent.[2]

"He remains quietly at Hawarden not to seem to interfere in the discussion in London, but will probably go up to Town early next week.[3]

"Our conversation very free and confidential, and to me very interesting. But I am pressed with a sense of the great anxiety and difficulty bequeathed by the Govt. which is condemned to their successors who are about to be appointed.

"I took tea with Mr. and Mrs. Gladstone and W. H. Gladstone and his gentle wife, who told me how she had accompanied him in his canvass and been present at so many of his meetings.

"Came away at ½ past 5. The black horse which took me to Queen's Ferry Station is named 'Tory.' He is 20 years old and very

---

[1] The question was of Gladstone's attitude towards the "compromise" on fortifications in 1860 (see page 250) when Palmerston, in the judgment of his colleague broke faith. Bright had been under no illusion at the time: he declared that the compromise was invented "to enable the Government to avoid the rock or get over the quicksand which this question has interjected into their midst." The transaction was a characteristic piece of Palmerstonian cynicism. Gladstone wrote an account of the matter as a reply to the statements in Sir Theodore Martin's book. It is printed as an Appendix to Vol. II of Morley's "Life."

[2] Mr. W. H. Gladstone was elected for Worcestershire. Gladstone himself had been placed at the top of the poll in both Midlothian and Leeds. He chose to sit for Midlothian, the scene of his great campaign, whereupon Leeds at the resulting bye-election returned his son Herbert (the late Viscount Gladstone) unopposed.

[3] The Queen sent for Lord Hartington. He told her that there could be no Government without Gladstone and that Gladstone would probably not accept any but the first place. He put the question and received the expected answer from Gladstone, who kissed hands as First Lord of the Treasury on April 23.

vicious—not in kicking, but in biting—and has to be muzzled when he is dressed in his stall!

"[*24th.*] To London by 3.10 train: to Euston Hotel.

"[*25th.*] Called at Lord Granville's at 2.30 to see Mr. Gladstone. Talk about new Govt. and distribution of offices. Later: again at Lord Granville's, on question of Dilke or Chamberlain joining the Govt.

"[*27th.*] Called on Mr. Gladstone. Granville came. Much talk on appointments. My colleague, Chamberlain, to be in the Cabinet.[1] Will be good for advice and for administration. Shows how by degrees the old exclusive system is breaking down. I wish his coming in would let me out. My head will not stand much excitement, and last night have slept badly; but I do not like to disappoint Mr. Gladstone and to appear so changeable on a matter of importance.

"[*28th.*] To Windsor this morning. Paddington Station at 1.10. Saloon carriage, 15 passengers: Dukes of Connaught, Westminster and Argyll, Marquesses of Hartington and Ripon, Earls Granville, Kimberley, Northbrook and Sydney, Lord Selborne, Gladstone, Childers, Harcourt, Forster and myself. Lunch at the Castle. The Queen gracious and kindly to me as she has always been. Her son, the Duke of Connaught, with her when I 'kissed hands.' Came back at 4. Very great crowds at Paddington and Windsor, and our friends very enthusiastic. The Duke of Argyll looks older and not in good spirits. Told me of the accident to his son and the Princess, so nearly fatal to her and so dangerous to both.

"Lord Ripon spoke to me on his appointment as Govr. General of India: said he felt very diffident about it. I told him I thought the place was too big for any man, but I hoped he would do what man could do.

"[*29th.*] Evening dined with W. Rathbone; Whitbread, M.P., Lord Ramsay, M.P., Mundella, M.P., Jos. W. Pease, M.P., and others there.

"[*May* 1.] Academy Dinner. Sat opposite to and near Prince of

---

[1] Bright curiously omits from the diary any reference to his own acceptance of the Duchy of Lancaster. The arrangement had probably been made provisionally at Hawarden on the 16th, when Gladstone noted in his journal: "Mr. Bright came over from Llandudno, and we spent nearly all the time in conversation on the situation. He is most kind and satisfactory." The story of the ultimatum delivered to the Prime Minister by Sir Charles Dilke—either Chamberlain or Dilke in the Cabinet or neither in the Government at all—is told in great detail in the "Life of Sir Charles Dilke" (Gwynn and Tuckwell). Lord Morley says that "Mr. Bright was desired to interfere, but the pair remained inexorable." Gladstone's letter to Chamberlain offering him the Board of Trade was dated April 27.

Wales, Prince Christian, Saxe-Weimar and Duke of Teck. Prince very friendly. I sat between Mr. Goschen and Lord Sydney. My portrait by Millais: do not much like it. Seems to want colour and face rather care-worn. Some people think it very good, as Lord Justice James and the Lord Chief Justice, who passed it with me.

"Speeches not much to hear. Mr. Gladstone fairly good. President [1] fluent and elegant, but given to somewhat excessive compliment. Bret Harte, American, read a short speech—not effective. 'He is a writer, not a speaker,' he said.

"[*2nd.*] Albert left me for home at 2.50. He has been here two or three days, partly on business. It is very pleasant to have him. But for business at home, I would have him as my secretary.

"[*3rd.*] Left Euston Hotel for lodgings, 10, George Street, Hanover Square, nearly opposite the church famous for fashionable weddings. The house is occupied by Mr. Columiati Meredyth, and promises me a comfortable home whilst in London. £8 8s. per week, including everything but food.

"Cabinet Meeting to-day: long discussion on India, Lord Lytton, and on South Africa and Bartle Frere. Difficulties left very serious and almost unmanageable.

"[*4th.*] Sir Barrington Simeon came as private secretary. Gave him some letters to answer. Hope he may be useful. He seems very well disposed.

"[*5th.*] Cabinet Meeting 2.30. Talk on home matters chiefly. Burials Bill, Land Purchase Bill, Game Laws, etc. Much pressing business and many difficulties. Walked up through the Park with Mr. Gladstone.

"Evening: Marlborough House to dine with Prince and Princess of Wales. A large party; 36 sat down to dinner, nearly all the Cabinet Ministers among them.

"Before Prince and Princess came in, the company stood in two rows —we on one side, ladies on the other.

"They came in; the Princess first, and bowed to those present as she passed. He shook hands with us as he passed and bowed to the ladies.

"At dinner the Prince and Princess sat opposite each other. She was between Duke of Cambridge and Duke of Argyll. I sat between Lord Kimberley and Mr. Chamberlain. Room and service very fine, table decorated, dinner very good. When ladies retired, cigarettes were introduced. In the drawing-room, pleasant talk. Lady Eliz. Campbell,

[1] Lord Leighton (then Sir Frederick Leighton).

daughter of the Duke of Argyll, told me she was to be married soon and was going to India, her husband having an appointment under Lord Ripon, the new Govr. General.

"The Prince came and asked me to be introduced to the Princess. She was most pleasant and I had a few minutes' conversation with her on the election and change of Govt., so sudden and so complete. She said, smiling, 'I am a Liberal.' She is remarkably pretty, her expression pure and sweet, elegant in figure and gracious and simple in manner. She looks as young as when I saw her several years ago at Mr. Gladstone's, and she seems even more healthy and robust.

"The Prince and Princess know how to receive their company and how to make the evening pass pleasantly.

"[13*th*.] Drawing Room, Buckingham Palace. Interesting and amusing sight. The Queen, evidently tired with the ceremony, left the conclusion of it to the Princess of Wales.

"[15*th*.] To Brighton to spend Sunday with dear Lillie, Bernard, and the famous Baby.

"[19*th*.] Heard this morning of the death of my dear old friend, Henry Ashworth, at Florence.[1] Roman fever said to be the cause of it. Am grieved to hear this sad news. He has been one of my best and oldest friends and he was in his 86th year, I believe. Dined with Mr. Gladstone in Downing Street. Large official party. Afterwards others came. Conversation with many, and home about 12.

"[20*th*.] House at 4. Affirmation, and took my seat. A good deal of excitement. Address. Answer moved by Albert Grey and Hugh Mason in good speeches.

"[21*st*.] House. Debate on question of admitting Mr. Bradlaugh, M.P. for Northampton, to take the oath. Passion of the Opposition. I spoke strongly on question in favour of consideration by Committee. But considerable section of House indisposed to moderation.

"To Spencer House, St. James's Place, to dine with Lord Spencer. Lords Cowper and O'Hagan there. Also Mr. Palles from Dublin and Shaw-Lefevre. Much talk on Ireland and Land Laws.

"[23*rd*.] Léon Say, French Minister, called before 11 o'clock. An hour's talk on French Treaty, Sugar Bounties question, Armaments and Eastern question. His countenance shows intelligence and force. He speaks fairly well in English. His call kept me from Westminster Meeting, which I much regretted.

[1] Henry Ashworth was a prominent member of the Anti-Corn Law League and an associate of Cobden and Bright in the great crusade of forty years before.

"[*24th.*] Deputation from Liverpool on appointment of magistrates. Lord Ramsay with them.

"[*June* 2.] Committee on Parly. Oath.[1] Bradlaugh gave evidence and made statement in defence of his claim to take the Oath and his seat. Showed much knowledge of the question and great skill in conducting his case—not a word too much and nothing omitted. His statement, in my judgment, unanswerable, and his opponents on the Committee are in difficulties, as I judge from private admissions to me of Mr. Walpole, Chairman, and Mr. Gibson, M.P. for Dublin University.

"Evening: University College Debating Society, annual meeting. Debate fairly good. After 10 o'clock I spoke for 40 minutes with great sense of freedom in favour of abolition of Capital Punishment. The Lecture Room much crowded: probably 800 persons present.

"[*3rd.*] House: long debate on Employers' Liability Bill—a Bill not much favoured by me. I think present law unjust and the Bill will extend the injustice, but I may submit to the opinion of my colleagues and of others.

"Evening: dined with Henry Adams, 22, Queen Anne's Gate. Small company: Mr. Lowell, U.S. Minister, Sir Francis Doyle, Mr. and Mrs. Lecky, Mrs. Proctor, Sir R. Cunliffe, M.P., and his wife. Mr. Lowell very pleasant, as indeed all the company I met there were. House: late. Did not leave till half-past 1 o'clock. To bed about 2.

"[*5th.*] Cabinet 2.30. Called before it on Mr. Gladstone to hear his plans for financial statement on Thursday next. It will surprise the country and I hope it will meet with general support.

"Cabinet. Budget. Irish Land Bill. Coming away I had some conversation with Lords Granville and Kimberley on American Fisheries Treaty and recommended them to send out some capable man to examine the question with a view to negotiation with U. States.

"Evening, dined with Léon Say, French Ambassador. A large party. Mr. Gladstone there. To dinner with the wife of the Military Attaché to the Embassy—a pleasant and intelligent lady speaking English remarkably well. Léon Say leaves on the 8th to take the office of President of the French Senate.

[1] The second Select Committee on the Bradlaugh case. The first had reported (by a majority of one) against Bradlaugh's claim to affirm. Bradlaugh then claimed the right to take the oath. The second Committee reported against this solution, but recommended that he should be permitted to affirm at his own risk. Sir Hardinge Giffard (afterwards Lord Halsbury), however, carried a motion of the whole House that he be allowed neither to make affirmation nor to take the oath.

"[*6th*.] Afternoon at home with some writing: notes for Bradlaugh Committee and draft letter for Mr. Gladstone to certain malcontents in the House on the question of the recall of Sir Bartle Frere.

"[*7th*.] Dear Helen called this morning. How nice and good she is! My dear children are now my only comfort.

"To Downing Street to Mr. Gladstone, and am to be there again to-morrow at ½ past 10 to consider some proposals of his Budget.

"Bradlaugh Committee. 3 hours' discussion. I gave my views and urged what I thought right on the question. Committee in confusion. Our Law officers as wrong, almost, as the Tories on the Committee. I fear that common sense will not prevail and that the House will suffer by the creation of a bad precedent.

"[*8th*.] Downing Street to Mr. Gladstone to discuss proposed changes in charges on licences to sell spirits, wines and beer. Mr. Childers there and officers from the Excise Department.

"[*10th*.] House: Mr. Gladstone's great speech on his Malt Tax Budget. The Tories excited and surprised. Several expressed their satisfaction.[1]

"33 years since my wedding-day—1847. What a change and how lonely I am.

"[*13th*.] Lunched with Lord Reay in Gt. Stanhope St. Lord and Lady Rosebery there. She is rich, and kind and generous in expression.[2] Laurence Oliphant and Chamberlain were there.

"[*14th*.] Bradlaugh Committee, from 1 to 7 o'clock. Not satisfactory. House: disorder, O'Donnell attacking and insulting new French Ambassador.[3]

"[*18th*.] Duchy office: appointed magistrates for Liverpool, Manchester, Salford and Oldham,—23 in all.

[1] The Budget, which secured "the freedom of the mash-tub," was popular, especially among the farmers. Gladstone took off the Malt Tax and put a duty of six shillings a barrel on beer. He increased the Income Tax from fivepence to sixpence to finance the first cost of the change.

[2] Lord Rosebery had married Miss Hannah Rothschild, the daughter and heiress of Baron Merger de Rothschild, of Mentmore, in 1878. She died in 1890.

[3] M. Challemel-Lacour, who had succeeded Léon Say, was disliked by the Church of Rome. Frank Hugh O'Donnell, an Irish Catholic member, asked an insulting question which Dilke answered with an absolute denial of its suggestions. O'Donnell moved the adjournment of the House in order to pursue the matter. This incident gave rise to a remarkable precedent. Gladstone, greatly indignant, moved that O'Donnell be not heard. Speaker Brand put the question, remarking that no such question had been put for 200 years.

"House: Sir W. Lawson's resolution on 'Local Option' in respect of the granting of licences to sell drink carried by a majority.

"[*21st.*] House: debate on Bradlaugh Oath question. I spoke about 11 o'clock. Much cheering on our side, with protests and excitement on the other. Spoke with a feeling of great freedom and a sense of success in favour of free election and absence of tests as to seats in Parliament.

"[*22nd.*] House: debate on Bradlaugh. Mr. Gladstone spoke admirably against jurisdiction of House in the case.

"Bigotry, passion and fanaticism prevailed. Majority of 45 against us. But we have probably not yet seen the end of this question.[1]

"[*23rd.*] By 12 train to Wheathampstead. Lunched with Lord Kilcoursie. My old friend C. H. Lattimore there. After lunch drove out with Lord K. to Brockett Park and the Hall, a large brick house, where Lord Palmerston died. Very pleasant to meet my old friend Lattimore.

"Club: chat with Mr. Leake and Thos. Ashton, and with Labouchere on the state of the Bradlaugh difficulty. Day very pleasant.

"[*24th.*] Bradlaugh liberated. To Lord Granville's to dinner: a party of 25. King of Greece there. Sensible and lively. Conversation with him on Greece and its condition and prospects. Speaks English very well: in great spirits at prospects of his country. Change of Govt. here given great satisfaction in Greece.

"[*25th.*] House: Irish Land Bill. Forster spoke admirably. Evening. Sunday closing of public houses. Resolution. Did not wish to vote, so kept away. Resolution too strong for me.

"[*26th.*] Cabinet 2 to 5 o'clock. Long 2 hours' discussion on Bradlaugh Oath case. Course to be announced in the House on Monday. Evening: dined with Mr. Chamberlain. Mr. Froude there. Talk with him on South Africa, Confederation, etc.

"[*28th.*] House: Mr. Gladstone gave notice of resolution in Bradlaugh case. It seems to have given general satisfaction to our friends.

"[*July* 2.] House: Bradlaugh Oath question. Division: 54 majority for Mr. Gladstone's resolution to admit members on affirmation. Afterwards, Irish Debate and home after 4 o'clock in the morning.

"Note from Miss Plowden, Ladies' Gallery. Went up to see her. Told me of the death of her father, aged 93. Referred to our acquaintance of years ago at Tulchan on the Spey. Said she always remained

[1] This was the day when Bradlaugh presented himself at the bar, refused to obey the order to withdraw, and was committed to the Clock Tower.

Liberal in her politics and reminded me of a conversation with her long ago, when I told her to take a *generous view* of all political questions and she would probably be right. She said it was this which made her *Liberal*, which, I understood, was not the view held by her family.

"[*3rd.*] House at 2 o'clock. Mr. Bradlaugh came to the Table and made the affirmation without objection. The storm is over, tho' prosecution is threatened by some fanatical outsiders.

"Card of invitation to dine at Windsor on Wednesday the 7th inst., so had to write to Lady Derby to ask to be excused, as royalty takes precedence of aristocracy. Weather showery.

"Cabinet meeting: discussion on Cape Colony and Bartle Frere, and on Irish Evictions Bill.

"[*7th.*] To Windsor. Dined with the Queen; Harcourt and Lord Hartington there also. The Queen, Princess Beatrice, Lady Paget and her daughter, Lady Abercrombie, Miss Stopford, Lord Zetland, and Sir H. Ponsonby. Queen talked and laughed during dinner—chiefly with Lord Hartington, who sat next to her. In the gallery she spoke to me and to others—friendly and cheerful. To me on *Atalanta* ship and its unhappy crew; on the accident to her daughter in Canada; but nothing political.

"[*17th.*] Cabinet: Greek Frontier question and probably naval demonstration. Explained my view of a better policy of absolute non-intervention—not yet possible for this country, I fear.[1]

"[*21st.*] Dined with Lord Kimberley in Lowndes Square. His boy of 20 a pleasant and good countenance. To bed: did not sleep till after 4 o'clock; heat great. Thinking of speech on 3rd reading of Irish Bill, but perhaps silence is best on a subject so difficult and inflammable.

"[*22nd.*] Call from F. Saunders, author of 'Convict Life.' Gave him £5 to help him to emigrate. Call from . . .; gave him 20/–. No work yet; comes to me to help him.

"[*26th.*] House: Irish Bill, 3rd reading. . . . Bill passed. Home late.[2]

"[*28th.*] By 10 train to Stratford-on-Avon. Walter Wren, late M.P. for Wallingford, and his wife in same carriage. College School:

---

[1] Sir Henry Layard was recalled from Constantinople and Mr. Goschen went out on a special mission to procure the fulfilment by Turkey of the clauses in the Treaty of Berlin relating to the emancipation of the Christian races. The Greek question arose over the failure to restore Thessaly and Epirus to Greece.

[2] The Compensation for Disturbance Bill. Its general object was to give greater security to tenants against vindictive or unreasonable eviction.

distributed prizes. Heard recitations—Greek, English and French. Philip in French better than any of the others. Afterwards gave the company a short speech, directed to the boys. All passed off pleasantly.

"[29th.] House: 'Hares and Rabbits' Bill,' to give tenants concurrent right to kill hares and rabbits, causes much interest and some anger among the sporting members.[1]

"[31st.] £10 to . . . of which £5 is given by Geo. Palmer, M.P.

"Cabinet, 2 o'clock: heard of Mr. Gladstone's illness. Could not be present with us. Dr. Andrew Clark was there. Mr. Gladstone sent to his bed, suffering from fever, temperature high and indication of very serious illness. His colleagues in great anxiety. Evening, 10 o'clock, went down to inquire. Saw his daughter. He was in bed quiet and not uncomfortable.

"[*August* 1.] To Downing St. at 10 to inquire as to his state. Fever somewhat abated. Left lung slightly congested.

"[2nd.] Accounts of Mr. Gladstone this morning somewhat better as to fever, but I am sorely anxious. Thos. Johnson called to bring me latest bulletin. Jacob called. Lalmohun Ghose called on Indian Memorial. Gen. Showers called and said much on Afghan difficulties. Am much disturbed with Mr. Gladstone's state and with anxieties of office. There seem only clouds and dangers about us.

"[3rd.] News from Afghanistan gives us much anxiety. Future difficult and dark.

"[4th.] Cabinet at 2.30. Discussion on Lords' rejection of Irish Bill—compensation for disturbance of tenants,[2] on Afghan news, and on business of session. Dined with T. B. Potter, 31, Courtfield Gardens. The French Ambassador, Challemel-Lacour, there; talk with him on the Greek question. French not for active interference. Mr. Gladstone much better to-day.[3]

"[6th.] Dined at 80, Eccleston Square, with W. E. Forster. M. Waddington, late French Premier, there. Walked with him after 11 o'clock to Reform Club. Talk on conduct of business in the French Chamber of Deputies. He is willing to write for me a memorandum

---

[1] The Ground Game Act was successfully piloted through the House by Sir William Harcourt. It gave the farmers, equally with the landlords, the right to kill and take ground game.

[2] The House of Lords threw out the Bill by 333 to 51. The division was taken on the previous day.

[3] There had been grave anxiety about Gladstone. He was 70, and the illness attacked him sharply; but his fine constitution threw it off and he was in the House again on August 28.

of their arrangements to assist in consideration of changes in ours. He is a very pleasant man in conversation, intelligent and frank—his English perfect, from his 4 years' residence at Cambridge in his youth.

"Sir Rutherford Alcock and his wife were at dinner, Mr. and Mrs. Dodson,[1] Herbert Gladstone and others. I sat between Mrs. Forster and Mrs. Dodson—a pleasant place for conversation.

"[10th.] House: spoke on 'Hares and Rabbits' Bill.'

"[11th.] House: same Bill; spoke again. Dined with Sir W. Harcourt in Grafton St. Some M.P.s there; also Lady Ripon, who is soon going to India to her husband, Lord Ripon. She is not robust, and I felt sorry for her.

"[12th.] Burials Bill. Spoke at some length. Full House, attentive, and our friends pleased. Division gave us majority of 179.

"[14th.] By 4 train from Victoria Station with Lord Granville to Dorking, and on to Holmbury to his brother's house. Mr. and Mrs. and Miss Gladstone, the Duke of Argyll, and his daughter Eva, Lord and Lady Granville, Mr. Lowell, the U.S. Minister, and myself formed the party, with F. Leveson-Gower, our host, and his son. Dinner and a pleasant evening. Mr. Gladstone looking much as usual and very cheerful. Conversation interesting.

"[15th.] To church, built by Mr. Street, architect, who lives near. Service 'high'—a performance, and not one of Christian simplicity. At lunch, Lord Arthur Russell and his amiable and sensible wife. Day fine; garden most inviting; pleasant walk before dinner. Evening much interesting conversation. Mr. Gladstone much more like himself.

"[16th.] Saw Mr. Gladstone in his bed. Talk with him about Burials Bill. He is anxious about the clause which mentions Convocation and change in the Church Burial Service. His regard for clergy great—far more, I think, than for the Church as an Establishment.

"[17th.] Dined with Duke of Argyll at Campden Hill. U.S. Minister there and Sir J. A. Macdonald and Tupper, Canadian Ministers, a son of Mr. Tennyson and his nice little wife—delicate, but looks good and gentle.

"The Duke's little daughters are like the girls in a Friend's family, intelligent and good—as, from father and mother, might be expected.

"[20th.] Duchy office: appointed magistrates at Warrington. House: 'Hares and Rabbits' Bill'—constant hostility of sporting party.

"[21st.] Cabinet at 12 o'clock. Mr. Gladstone present, the first

---

[1] Mr. Dodson was President of the Local Government Board, and had charge of the Employers' Liability Bill; he afterwards became Lord Monkbretton.

time since his illness. Discussion on Afghanistan and Russia, and on Turkey and Montenegro and Greece. Dined with the Ambassador of France. Diplomatic Corps there. Conversation afterwards with the Russian Ambassador—Prince Lobanoff, sensible and pleasant.

"[26th.] House: Irish Constabulary Estimate. Opposition of Irish Members. I spoke at some length on condition of Ireland. Obstruction from Irish Members. House sat all night, and till one o'clock at noon on the 27th. I went home at 2 o'clock and left the House to its labours.

"[27th.] To Mr. Ouless—final sitting. My bro.-in-law Vaughan there. He likes the portrait.[1]

"[31st.] Report on Burials Bill: read 3rd time. Home before 4 o'clock.[2]

"[September 1.] To Mr. Ouless, to meet my dear Priscilla to see the portrait. She made some suggestions, but likes the portrait.

"Duchy office: wrote a letter to the Queen on Duchy business. House. Evening, by boat to Greenwich, Trafalgar Hotel, with colleagues: dinner, a party of about 40. Amusing speeches by Lord Granville and Hartington. I had to speak, but do not succeed well in after dinner oratory, when serious or earnest talk is not wanted or expected.

"Returned by boat to Parliament Stairs. The evening very pleasant and the Ministerial fish dinner better than I expected.

"[4th.] Cabinet: discussion on giving up Kandahar. Opinion of the Queen.[3] Queen's Speech considered.

"[6th.] Cabinet at 2.30: Kandahar discussion; also Montenegro and Greek question.

"[7th.] House 1.30. Lords at 2 o'clock: curious old ceremony of Prorogation. I stood close behind the Speaker; on my right Childers

[1] He had given many sittings to Ouless for this portrait during the month.

[2] The Burial Act put an end to the long and dreary controversy in which Bright had so often spoken with indignation and passion. It permitted burials in churchyards either without religious ceremony or with such Christian rite as the persons concerned thought proper, and thus removed a classic grievance of the Nonconformists.

[3] "The Queen had written for the second time to Lord Hartington urging with great warmth that we should retain Kandahar." (Sir Charles Dilke's Diary.) Sir Frederick Roberts's march to Kandahar began on August 9 and ended on September 3, when the garrison was relieved, and Ayub Khan's army broken. The Cabinet had determined to evacuate the country, believing occupation to be both a danger and a gross expense to India. In this they were supported both by Sir Donald Stewart and Major Baring. They did not, however, rush the matter. The operation was postponed till the New Year.

and Gladstone.   Meeting of some of Cabinet in Mr. Gladstone's room on Kandahar: messages to and from the Queen.   By 5 train left London for home, after 4 mos. absence.   Home about 11 o'clock; found dear Mary and Dick there.

"[12th.]   To Meeting twice: small company.   Dear Priscilla with us in the morning.   We went there as children, and now as the oldest of those assembled.

"[30th.¹]   12 o'clock Cabinet: only Lord Spencer absent.   Much discussion on Turkish question, its difficulties and dangers, the chief cause of our meeting; also on condition of Ireland.

"[October 1.]   Called on Mr. Gladstone and walked thro' the Park with him to Lord Granville's.   Talk about work of coming session. Heavy questions before us: Land question, County Govt., London Municipal Govt., beside Irish question, which I think the most pressing.

"[10th, at Kelso.]   To U.P. Chapel: service far too long and tedious. Telegram last night for Cabinet on Monday; so left Kelso this evening at 7.40 for London.   Arrived at 6 o'clock in the morning.

"[11th.]   Cabinet postponed.   Called on Mr. Gladstone and Lord Granville: much talk on Turkish question and much uncertainty about it.

"[12th.]   Saw Lord Granville: news very satisfactory from Constantinople.   Turk gives up Dulcigno to the Montenegrins.²   Albert has been up, and is gone down to Cornwall for a holiday.   I return to Kelso this evening.

"[21st.]   About 10 o'clock, telegram from Albert saying that my 'stepmother' died this morning at 20 min. before 8 o'clock.   Proposed to go home by the train at 2.25.   Reached home by way of Carlisle and Bolton before 10 o'clock.

"[22nd.]   Called with Albert and saw the remains of the widow of my dear father.   She has outlived him 29 years and has died, we believe, in her 95th year.   Till within her last year, she said she had never had a doctor, her health having been so uniformally good.   She has been blind for several, probably for 9 or 10 years.   She has been an example of humility and patience and gratefulness to all of us, and it has been a pleasure to do anything to render her old age comfortable.

"My own dear Elizabeth for many years scarcely omitted a day to go

¹ He had taken ten days in Scotland fishing on the Awe.   Three days afterwards he went North again—on the Tweed at Kelso.

² As the result of the naval demonstration proposed by Lord Granville to the Concert of Europe and accepted by the Powers.

to see her, to chat with her and to cheer her in her solitude and blindness, and to render her any help in her power.

"[*November* 10.] Cabinet Council: discussion on Ireland—Coercion, Land Bill, etc. Evening: Club with Chamberlain, discussing difficulties before the Government.

"[13*th*.] Called on Mr. Gladstone: talk on Irish question, and my speech at Birmingham meeting on Tuesday next. By 2.45 train to Rochdale.

"[16*th*.] My birthday: have entered my 70th year. How much have I to look back upon—much to be thankful for, much to regret!

"To Birmingham, to Mr. Chamberlain's new house at Highbury. Town Hall meeting: spoke for an hour on Ireland chiefly. Much relieved in my mind. The thought of this meeting has been very burdensome for many days. I hope what I have said has done no harm: the Irish question one of great complexity and difficulty.[1]

"[17*th*.] With Chamberlain and Mr. Verney to London to Alexandra Hotel. Cabinet at 2 o'clock; interview with Mr. Gladstone earlier. The Irish difficulty becomes more pressing.

"[19*th*.] Cabinet: conversation with Mr. Gladstone before it. Difficulties very great. Lord Granville made a very useful suggestion. Discussion on Irish question: difference of opinion not removed.

"[27*th*.] By 4.15 train to Cheddington, for Mentmore,[2] Lord Northbrook and his daughter Lady Emma going down also. Small party: H. Calcraft [3]; Mr. James,[4] American novelist; F. Bassett, banker; Mr. Lacaita.

"[28*th*.] Afternoon, walked a mile to see race-horses that had won the Derby—Maccaroni, Lord Lyon, and two others.

"[29*th*.] Stag hunt, meet at Mentmore. Interesting if rather foolish. Many to breakfast—many farmers of the neighbourhood.

---

[1] The Irish situation had grown desperate. The Lord-Lieutenant (Earl Cowper) was pressing for the suspension of Habeas Corpus and the passing of an Arms Act to deal with disorder. Gladstone hesitated. In the meantime the prosecution of the Land League chiefs, including Parnell, had begun. Bright and Chamberlain were both opposed to coercion and resisted Forster's urgency for it. Uncertainty prevailed as to the course the Government would take. In these circumstances Bright made a speech at Birmingham in favour of appeasement, described and denounced the misgovernment of Ireland by Dublin Castle, condemned the system of land tenure and the absence of security for tenants, and dealt in no mincing words with the Peers for throwing out the Compensation Bill.

[2] Lord Rosebery's seat.

[3] Secretary of the Board of Trade.　　　　[4] The late Henry James.

Some scores mounted, but few in scarlet. The stag, let out of van near the house, went off lightly over the fields; 20 mins. later, dogs and horses and riders after him. The morning very fine—scene very lively. The stag is not to be killed—this is understood, and I hope the stag understands it.

"Left Mentmore: joined the 12 train from London at Cheddington Station. A very pleasant visit. Lord Rosebery very pleasant and intelligent and liberal; Lady Rosebery—sensible and kind. They have a nice girl about a year old, the joy of their house.

"The house is very large, on a plan devised by Sir Jos. Paxton 30 years ago. The central hall very large—full, much too crowded with furniture, as indeed the house is, of rare and costly kinds. Central hall, 3 lamps hang from ceiling or roof formerly in 'Bucentaur,' vessel of the Doge of Venice; chimney-piece from the house of Rubens, the great painter. Among other things is a writing-desk once belonging to Necker, the Finance Minister of Louis XVI of France. The curtains of the drawing-room were worked by ladies of Marie Antoinette. Many articles of furniture have a history—and many interesting portraits.

"[*December* 13.] To 132, Piccadilly, and engaged my old rooms. Cabinet Council at 3 o'clock. Ireland, of course. Adhered to-day for meeting of Parliament, and no objection to measures of repression if condition of country no better.[1] Evening: Mr. Hussey, great land agent, from Kerry, came and we had two hours talk on Irish question. Hussey is a 'refugee' driven for safety to England. He thinks no remedy but more proprietors—as I have thought and said for more than 20 years.

"Lodgings comfortable; size of the rooms gives a sense of freedom.

"[14*th*.] Cabinet Council: 3 hours' discussion on the lines of the proposed Irish Land Bill.

"[15*th*.] Duchy office: wrote to the Queen, giving her results of the Duchy for the year, and sending her £26,000 for the half year; in all £41,000.

"Evening to dine with Mr. Childers and his wife and daughter. After dinner, talk with him till 12 o'clock on scheme for buying farms for Irish tenants. He has a large scheme to expend in all 70 millions. My plan more simple and I think far more likely to be effective.

---

[1] Gladstone had conceded to Cowper and Forster an early meeting of Parliament to deal with Ireland, and January 6 was fixed. He himself was in favour of strengthening the penal provisions of the ordinary law rather than of special coercive measures. He found that both Bright and Chamberlain preferred the suspension of Habeas Corpus to the stringencies which he would have been prepared to propose.

"[17*th*.] Wrote Memorandum on Commission for Purchase of Farms in Ireland, for circulation among members of the Cabinet.

"[18*th*.] By 10 train for Rochdale. Bernard and Lillie and their fine boy there, and we went down together.

"[25*th*.] Christmas Day. Family party: Richard and Mary from Stratford; Bernard and Lillie and their boy from Brighton; Theodore Cash from London; Philip from Stratford-on-Avon; and Sophie from Ben Rhydding. A party of 10 at dinner, and continuing for some days. Very pleasant tho' the weather quite winterly.

"[30*th*.] Cabinet Council: long discussion on Habeas Corpus suspension—most unpleasant matter for discussion. I wish I could escape from official responsibilities. Am made very unhappy by the difficulties which surround the Govt. in connexion with Irish affairs.

"[31*st*.] Cabinet. Irish Land Bill discussed for about 3 hours. Nearer approach to agreement and to mode of dealing with the question."

5

The second session of the Parliament of 1880 was memorable for the foolish excitements of the Bradlaugh debates and the wild and exasperating disorder created by organized Irish obstruction. It was historically important because it brought to birth the great Irish Land Act. The Liberal Party remained fairly united all the year, though Chamberlain and Bright had both been doubtful about the Irish Coercion Bill and Morley in the *Pall Mall Gazette* fought openly and ardently against it. The real difficulties of the Party, as usual, arose rather from entanglements abroad than from differences about domestic policy. The steady application of Liberal principles disposed of the inherited bugbears of Kandahar and the Transvaal, but even they gave the Government a tremor as if by way of forewarning of the earthquake that was presently to rock it when the guns opened fire on Alexandria and murder walked in the glades of Phœnix Park.

This year Bright became seventy. An ever lonelier and a rather sad figure he seems when communing with himself in the shortening confidences of his diary. But he was still formidable in Parliament. The passionate hatred of the Parnellites testfiies of that. For forty years his had been one of the few voices raised in England on behalf of the native Irish, sympathizing with their grievances, understanding the economic and social basis of their woes perhaps better than most Irishmen, and always advocating measures of pacification and reform. But, radical as his views were, he was a Constitutionalist in the very roots of him. He saw in the new Irish policy of obstruction and chaos in Parliament, as well as in the illegalities of the Land League and their accompanying crimes, the foundering of his hopes of accommodation and peace. For him Parnell and his followers became "rebels," and, with his inborn forthrightness he told them so. The clouds that covered the political sky are reflected in the diaries. Gleams of domestic sunshine flash across the greyness now and then; but even they become rarer as relatives and the friends of a lifetime drop off one by one.

"[*January* 2, 1881.] Fog all day. Did not go out till near 5 o'clock. Read to-day some chapters of St. Matthew in French, and some of Broderick's new vol. on the Land question. Very quiet and very lonely all day. My condition is often one of a sense of desolation which time does not seem much to modify.

"[4th.] Cabinet: Queen's Speech.

"[14th.] Called on Mr. Gladstone to speak to him on the Lord Advocate [1] and his coming into Parlt. on the proposed retirement of his venerable father: this at his father's request. Mr. Gladstone was in bed, his cold keeping him there. Talk about business of the House and a suggestion of his to overcome obstruction of Irish insurrectionary party led by Mr. Parnell. Not an easy matter.[2] Also about Land Bill, in which I think he becomes more resolute.

"Evening dined with Lord Spencer to meet Dr. Macdonald from Dublin to talk over Irish Land question and the 'Longfield Lease,' a mode suggested by Judge Longfield. Fredk. Leveson-Gower there. With him to the House in his brougham. House disturbed; Irishmen noisy and interrupting. Have not spoken. Not well to-day, and much out of mood for speaking with sense of the great difficulty in making any progress in the House.

[1] John McLaren, a son of Duncan McLaren by a former marriage.

[2] Sir Charles Dilke thought a Coercion Bill unwise. "On January 14th," he wrote in his journal, "I had a full talk with Bright, trying to get him to go with me. Bright told me that the outrages had got much worse in Ireland since the middle of December, as for example that of firing into houses. He had come round a great deal in the coercion direction. He now distinctly favoured suspension of the Habeas Corpus Act—that is to say, did not unwillingly yield to it, like Chamberlain, but supported it almost willingly, and he evidently has been converted by Forster to the view that things had grown to be very bad, and that by locking up a small number of the chiefs the rule of law might be restored. I did not agree, but his opinion showed me how completely I was isolated." ("Life of Sir Charles Dilke," Vol. I, p. 362.)

"[16*th*.]   Evening to Buckingham Palace Hotel with dear Priscilla and McLaren.   Conversation on position of the Lord Advocate and the suggestion that his father should resign his seat in Parlt. to allow him to come in for Edinburgh.   McLaren very quiet as usual, and disposed to make a sacrifice for his son's interest.

"[17*th*.]   House: Irish debate; as usual Mr. Gladstone spoke with much force and impressiveness on the Irish question and obstruction in the House.   Albert returned from Paris and was under the gallery all the evening.   His appetite for Parlt. is very strong.

"[18*th*.]   House: Irish debate continued.   Great storm: wind, snow, frost—such a day rarely known in London.

"[19*th*.]   Great snow during the night; traffic suspended, streets deserted; very difficult to get to and from the House.   River traffic suspended by floating ice; railways blocked in many parts of the country; great inconvenience everywhere.   Dined with Mr. Speaker.   Mr. Chamberlain conveyed me there and back in his brougham.

"[22*nd*.]   Cabinet at 2 o'clock: subjects several—obstruction and how to meet it; Land Bill, when to be announced.   On latter subject my colleagues not wise in my opinion.   Evening dined with Harcourt. Courtney there, and Miss Rothschild.

"[24*th*.]   House: Irish Suspension of Habeas Corpus Act proposed by W. E. Forster in a powerful speech; debate followed.

"[25*th*.]   House: obstruction by Irish members; wrangle—and Mr. Biggar, M.P. for Cavan, was ordered to withdraw.   I left the House before 12 o'clock expecting the sitting to go on all night.

"[26*th*.]   House: sitting continued for 22 hours from 4 yesterday to 2 this day, when Irish opposition yielded.

"Called on Mr. Reece, Medical Hall, Piccadilly, for relief for the deafness which has lately troubled me.   He put a little warm almond oil in my ears at 3 o'clock and at 5 o'clock he syringed them with warm water, and then put in some preparation of Wright's Liniment.   Deafness has gone and am much relieved.   Mr. Reece is an interesting man. He showed me a new hand gas lamp, for carriages, etc., ingenious and useful.

"Dined with Mr. Chamberlain.   Party: Board of Trade people and engaged or concerned in shipping; Admiral, Capt., Sir E. Reed, M.P., Constructor of Ships, etc.

"This evening thaw began: hope it may continue.   We have had a very severe season; extraordinary quantity of snow and severe frost.

"[27*th*.]   House.   Spoke for 40 mins.   Our friends pleased.   Had not intended or prepared to speak, but Mr. Gladstone thought it might be well, so consented. Philip under the Gallery and well pleased.[1]

"[*28th.*] Introduced Jno. McLaren to the House—Lord Advocate, elected for Edinburgh. Great speech from Mr. Gladstone late this evening.

"[*February* 1.] Debate continued, and again thro' the night. Left the House at 2 o'clock, having spoken about 1 o'clock, briefly but satisfactorily to our friends.

"[*2nd.*] At 9 this morning the Speaker closed the debate and compelled a division on introduction of the Bill.[2] Was not present at this curious and unexpected scene. House met again at 12 and debate on Irish obstructive motion for adjournment till 6 o'clock. To a party

[1] Bright had, *pace* Dilke, unwillingly accepted the necessity for the Suspension Bill, but he could not endure the comparison which the Irish "rebels" were making between their Land League and his Anti-Corn Law League. He held up the crime and disorder promoted by the one against the orderly and constitutional methods of the other. The effectiveness of the contrast irritated the Home Rulers to execration of the man who had been of all Englishmen the most persistent and faithful advocate of Irish reform. It was on the next night that Gladstone made the famous declaration that "the steps of crime dog the steps of the Land League."

[2] This was the first time the "closure" was applied to a debate in Parliament. The House had been sitting continuously for 41 hours discussing the question whether Forster should be allowed to bring in the Bill—and that sitting began a whole week after he had risen to introduce it. The House had taken up the first reading debate again on Monday, the 30th. After twenty-four hours of it, on Tuesday afternoon, Speaker Brand determined to break a tradition in order to conquer obstruction. He told the Cabinet that if the debate had not ended by Wednesday morning he intended to put the question. The Deputy Speaker, Dr. Playfair, the Clerk of the House, Sir Erskine May, and the Leader of the Opposition, Sir Stafford Northcote, were informed. Mr. Biggar was on his feet when the Speaker took the chair on Wednesday morning at nine o'clock, told the House that its credit was threatened and its authority paralysed, asked for its support, and put the question. Leave was given, by 164 to 19, to introduce the Bill. Of course the question of "privilege" was raised. When Mr. Labouchere asked under what Standing Order the Speaker had acted, Mr. Brand replied that he had acted on his own responsibility from a sense of duty to the House. The sequel mentioned by Bright, the suspension and removal of thirty-seven Irish members, occurred during an attempt by Gladstone to move a resolution that, if the House voted by a majority of three to one that the state of public business was "urgent," the conduct of business should be under the control of the Chair until the Speaker himself determined it. The special cause of the rowdyism was the announcement by the Home Secretary (Harcourt) that Michael Davitt (then on ticket-of-leave) had been re-arrested that day and sent back to Portland. Davitt was convicted of treason-felony and sentenced by Cockburn to 15 years penal servitude, but had been released on licence in 1877 by Mr. Cross, Disraeli's Home Secretary.

at Mr. Gladstone's.   Met there for the first time the Duke and Duchess of Edinburgh.   She seems pleasant and sensible.   He was very courteous to me.

"[*3rd.*]   House: strange scene.   Irish Party, obstructing, objected to Mr. Gladstone speaking and defied the Chair.   Speaker 'named' the member obstructing, and finally Irish Members, 30 or more, were suspended during sitting by vote of the House, and were removed by the Serjeant-at-Arms—a strange and humiliating spectacle.   House, cleared of disturbing element, becomes calm.   Mr. Gladstone, in a speech of great force and beauty, moved resolutions to amend mode of procedure which, after debate, were carried at 2 o'clock with great cheering.   The House seemed relieved after the removal of Irish obstructives.

"[*6th.*]   Westminster Meeting.   Afternoon and evening, at home writing some notes for G. Barnett Smith (who persists in writing my 'Life') and some pages of my Memoir for my dear children.   Have reached as far as 1833—and my first foreign travel.[1]

"[*8th.*]   Dined with Francis Buxton, 15, Eaton Place.   Met there Lady Buxton, in days long past Catherine Gurney, and one of my dearest's great friends.   It was pleasant, tho' sad, to see her and to talk with her of old times.

"[*15th.*]   Cabinet.   Transvaal War: agreed to propose armistice, and to send Commissionaire to propose terms of settlement.   All most anxious to prevent further conflict and bloodshed.[2]   India Office: Argyll, Northbrook, Fawcett and Hartington.   Discussed whether Parly. inquiry useful on Indian affairs.

"[*18th.*]   House: Irish Bill.   Towards midnight, stormy debate. The Irish Members unruly and almost beyond control.   Parnell there. Proposed to except women from clause, alter word 'person;' and much violent oratory expended in praise of Irish women.   I left the House

---

[1] G. Barnett-Smith published "The Life and Speeches of John Bright," in 1882.

[2] Bright and Chamberlain pleaded in the Cabinet for the immediate restoration of the Transvaal to the Boers, who had expected that the Liberal Government would give effect to Gladstone's protests against the annexation of 1877.   Gladstone was inclined to that policy, but Lord Kimberley, the Colonial Secretary, ill-informed from the Cape, believed the Boers to be generally amenable to the British system and was convinced of the possibility of immediate African Federation.   When the Boers proclaimed their Republic at Heidelberg on December 16, Sir George Colley was in command of the British forces.   Natal had been invaded by Joubert, and the affair at Laing's Nek was fought on February 8.   Kruger proposed to Colley on the 12th that a Royal Commission should be sent out to investigate the facts, and it was Colley's telegram on this subject that the Cabinet now considered.

before 1 o'clock wearied with the disorder which it seemed impossible to suppress. We must be approaching some crisis or catastrophe.

"[*22nd.*] Cabinet 12: Land Bill. Great difference of opinion; extremes apparent. My opinion of Bill: it is too complex, and requires more strength in some particulars, especially as to tenure. Confidential talk with our Chief on our Bench as to Land Bill and difficulties and differences of the Cabinet.

"[*23rd.*] Sir T. F. Buxton called on Church Livings in parts of Norfolk—too many and too small either for work or stipend. Roger Fenton's two daughters called to tell me of difficulties. The youngest is partly engaged to be married, but the young man has at present no employment. Could have gone out to Ceylon, but the girl cannot leave her mother; so they come to me to advise them. A curious case. I wish I could help them, from sympathy with their family, my old friends.

"Miss Plowden has sent me a fine photo portrait of her venerable father.

"Wedding breakfast, 22, Hill St., Berkeley Square—my nephew Arthur W. Leatham [1] and Miss Kennard. Spoke after breakfast, and hope I contented the party. Speeches good for such an occasion. The bride very sweet-looking girl, and much admired—good-looking and looking good.

"[*24th.*] Cabinet at 12 o'clock. Mr. Gladstone not present. Last night, coming home from dining with the Prince of Wales, he fell on entering the garden at his house in Downing St. and cut his head severely. Will be some days away from work and the House.

"[*25th.*] House: 'Suspension' Bill read a third time. Division and some excitement.

"[*26th.*] Cabinet. Mr. Gladstone not there. Discussion on Irish Arms Bill. Decision to go on with Bill, contrary to my judgment. Evening dined at Lord Spencer's. After dinner 'pricked' for sheriffs. Selected them for the counties.

"To-day has been fine and very pleasant—a great relief after so much storm, snow, rain and not seldom fog.

"[*March* 1.] Bad news from the Transvaal. Sir Geo. Colley and many men of his force killed. Prospect of peace much further off. [2]

---

[1] Son of E. A. Leatham, M.P. for Huddersfield.
[2] Ill fortune dogged every step of the Government in South Africa. Lord Kimberley had agreed to send the Commission if the Boers would cease resistance. Colley forwarded this message to Kruger, but gave him only forty-eight hours to

"House: Arms Bill. Harcourt made a powerful speech in introducing it.

"Read the Duke of Argyll's article in *Contemporary Review* on 'The Unity of Nature:' interesting.

"[*2nd.*] By special train to Windsor: Lord Spencer, Sydney, Huntley in the carriage: Lunch at the Castle. Council: Spencer, Sydney and myself. Huntley and Sir A. Hobhouse sworn in as Privy Councillors.

"My interview with the Queen to 'prick' the Sheriff for Lancashire. The Queen very kind in manner. She spoke of the Transvaal disaster and evidently feels much grief at the loss of life; also of Mr. Gladstone and his recent accident.

"[*3rd.*] At 1 o'clock called on Mr. Gladstone; for an hour discussed the unhappy Transvaal question. I argued that the recent disaster should not interfere with measures for peace, that negotiations should go on as if it had not happened, that no operations for sake of vengeance should be adopted. Mr. Gladstone agreed with me. I said it would be impossible for me to consent to any measures of a vindictive character, or to the shedding of blood to restore the credit of British arms. Mr. Chamberlain holds the same view. Mr. Gladstone spoke on this subject as I hoped and expected.[1]

"House: Arms Bill. Remarkable speech from John Dillon; replied to by Sir W. Harcourt.

"[*5th.*] Cabinet at 2 o'clock. Discussion on Land Bill and the Transvaal troubles. Difficulties as to Land Bill: to meet again on

reply. Kruger did not receive the letter till five days later. Meanwhile, Colley occupied Majuba Hill, was attacked by the Boers on February 27, and lost the engagement and his own life.

[1] "On Wednesday, March 2, after a long interview between me and Chamberlain on the state of affairs, Chamberlain had an hour and a half with Bright, and got him to write a strong letter to Gladstone about the Transvaal, which we put forward as the ground for a proposed resignation, although of course the strength of the Coercion measures, the weakness of the Land measures, and the predominance of the Whigs in the Cabinet were the reasons which weighed chiefly with Chamberlain and myself. In the Transvaal matter, however, we should not be two but four, for Bright and Courtney must go out with us, and Lefevre might do so. On the other hand, we had reason to think that if the Whigs yielded to us on the Transvaal Kimberley would go. On the next day, Thursday the 3rd, Bright was sent for by Gladstone on his letter. Bright found him in entire harmony with our views. Kimberley at once gave in and telegraphed what he was told; so the difficulty was over before the Cabinet was able to meet, and we as far from resignation as ever." (Sir Charles Dilke, "Life," Vol. I, p. 368.)

Tuesday. On Transvaal affair, no member of the Govt. urging war for sake of recovering reparation to English arms. Terms of pacification the same as before last conflict on Majuba Hill on the 27th of this month.[1] Home early. Read Walpole's 'History.'[2]

"[8th.] Cabinet at 12. Discussion on Transvaal: action all in favour of peace; opinion, with some exception, in one direction.

"[9th.] Dined with Wm. Graham, 35, Grosvenor Place: a nice party. Duke of Argyll and his daughter, Lady Mary, there; Lady Selborne and daughter, Mr. Glyn, etc. After dinner to Clarence House. Duke and Duchess of Edinbro' very courteous and friendly. Large party, chiefly, I thought, Liberals. Some talk with Russian and American Ministers—with the latter on the Fortune Bay Fishery question.

"[10th.] House: Irish Arms Bill. Report, many divisions. Irish rebel party giving as much trouble as possible. Home before 12 o'clock. Day very mild. Have felt languid and tired for 3 or 4 days past; sometimes feel sensible that I am growing old.

"[11th.] Govt. outvoted on resolution on 'Preservation of Ancient Monuments' by Sir J. Lubbock.

"[12th.] Cabinet: long discussion on Transvaal negotiations. Talk unsatisfactory. War Dept. memorandum bad in every respect. Urged moderation and efforts for peace, with less success than I had hoped for. All will depend on judgment shown by men selected as commissioners: Hercules Robinson, Sir H. de Villiers, and Genl. Wood. It may be impossible for me to remain with the Govt. if a resolute attempt for peace is not made.[3]

"[13th.] Dined with Vaughan. Rumour of murder of Emperor of Russia. Late in the evening recd. copy of dispatch from Lord Dufferin from St. Petersburg confirming the rumour. The shocking event took place this afternoon in the street at St. Petersburg. An

[1] Chamberlain and Bright would have resigned their Ministries if the Government had yielded to the clamour that arose for the "vindication of British arms" after Majuba. Gladstone with difficulty brought the rest of the Cabinet round to their view. The Convention of Pretoria, which ended the war, included the provision for British "suzerainty" which was a fruitful source of trouble in the future.

[2] Sir Spencer Walpole's "History of England" was published 1878–80.

[3] Sir Frederick Roberts had been sent out to succeed Colley, and to fulfil the prophecy made to the Boers by Sir Garnet Wolseley that the Vaal would flow back to the Drakensberg before the British flag ceased to fly at Pretoria. General Roberts arrived at Cape Town to find that peace had been declared on March 22, and was recalled twenty-four hours after he landed.

explosive bomb was thrown at or under the Emperor's carriage. He alighted, when a second bomb was thrown, close to him. His legs were dreadfully wounded and broken. He was taken to his Palace and died within two hours.

"This terrible event has much affected me. The cruelty and wickedness of the act seem rather of the doings of fiends than of men.

"[*14th.*] Slept badly. The Russian tragedy continually disturbed me.

"[*15th.*] House. Sympathy with family of murdered Emperor of Russia. Mr. Gladstone's speech admirable. Afterwards had an interesting conversation with him on Transvaal conflict and chances of arrangement; also on question of Army organization and its difficulties. The Court, Duke of Cambridge and Sir Garnet Wolseley: correspondence and obstacles. Duke and old class of officers not in favour of reform and of changes now deemed needful by Secretary of War.

"[*17th.*] Cabinet at 2 o'clock. Discussion on Transvaal question and dispatch to Sir E. Wood. Aspect more favourable for peace: somewhat relieved by this.

"Last night an attempt to blow up with gunpowder part of the Mansion House. Supposed to be done by Irishman from America, whose name is known to the police, and whose coming and objects have been telegraphed from the States.

"[*19th.*] Cabinet at 2 o'clock: discussion again on Transvaal mischief. Did what I could in favour of peace, which seems near, but may not come yet: result too much in the hands of military commander to make one comfortable.

"Home early. Read Walpole's 'History' till 12 o'clock.

"[*20th.*] Called on Lord Kimberley on Transvaal. No further news. Suggested slight change in message he was about to send to Genl. Wood; introduced the word 'necessity' into it.

"[*22nd.*] Summoned to Cabinet at 2.30. Ministers together in Mr. Gladstone's room. Was afraid of bad news from Transvaal. Lord Northbrook told me all our propositions were accepted by the Boer leaders and we were met to sanction arrangement—a great relief to all of us.

"House: announcement made, with great cheering from one side, and I hope many opposite were ready to accept it in a friendly spirit.

"[*24th.*] Called in at Mr. Agnew's picture gallery in Old Bond Street; saw a most perfect engraved portrait of Mr. Gladstone from Millais's picture. Mr. Agnew thinks no engraving of equal beauty and quality has been done in England for 60 years past. House: debate on retention of Kandahar. Herbert Gladstone spoke well. House much interested in and pleased at his success.

"[*25th.*] House: Kandahar debate. Great speech from Lord Hartington.[1] Great division: 216 to 336. The Tory Party sorely trampled on in debate and in the division.

"[*April* 2.] Sixteen years to-day since the death of my dear friend Cobden. How often have I wished him here for his counsel and help! Cabinet at Lord Granville's house: Budget explained and discussed.

"[*4th.*] House: Budget. Speech of Mr. Gladstone interesting. Not much change; no means for a great or good Budget.

"[*5th.*] Dined at Mr. Gladstone's. Only 10 at dinner: Dr. Andrew Clark, Dean Church, Duke of Argyll. Party afterwards; among them Mr. Tennyson: looks very old, and complained of blindness. A weird-looking, tall old man.[2]

"[*7th.*] House: Mr. Gladstone brought in the Irish Land Bill— spoke 2¼ hours. Bill intricate, and not easy to explain. House apparently well satisfied. On our side it was received with great warmth. The Tories were quiet, and they and the Irish 'irreconcileables' seemed to be puzzled. The Bill too much for the former and too good for the latter. Albert and Geo. Hallett,[3] under the Gallery, were much pleased.

"[*8th.*] Resignation of Duke of Argyll announced in newspapers. Difference on Land Bill: cannot undertake to defend departure from rules of political economy. His withdrawal much regretted by his colleagues,—by me especially, as I have a great personal regard for the Duke.[4] Cabinet 2 o'clock. House: wrote a letter to the Duke of Argyll on his resignation of office.

[1] Gladstone said this was the best debating speech he ever heard in Parliament. Hartington refused to advance the Indian Frontier and insisted on the need for the unity of Afghanistan. This policy, involving the withdrawal of troops from Kandahar, Beaconsfield had described as a "policy of scuttle." Its wisdom was amply proved by events.

[2] Tennyson was then 72. He lived another eleven years, and outlasted Bright by three years.

[3] A medical man who married Bright's niece, Lilias Ashworth.

[4] The Duke of Argyll (Lord Privy Seal) resigned on the ground that the Bill transgressed the laws of political economy. This theory had been advanced by Mr. Bonamy Price, Professor of Political Economy at Oxford, and a member of the Duke of Richmond's Commission. It was of Bonamy Price that Gladstone, the day before, had said in a well-remembered phrase that he applied the principles of political economy, in all their unmitigated authority, to the people and circum-

"[16th.] Home: very quiet from day to day. Letters in the morning and 2 hours at billiards with my brother Thomas at Green Bank in the afternoon—our chief exercise, and very pleasant.

"[17th.] Dear Helen and her sweet child left us this morning for Bristol and home. Her nice boy, John, also gone back to school at York. Darling Helen!—she is so kind and good, and intelligent and loving, it is hard to part with her; and the sweet child has won the hearts of all in the house.

"Heard of the death of Disraeli—Lord Beaconsfield—which took place at ½ past 4 this morning. He has been ill for about a month, and with little belief in his recovery on the part of his doctors. His death will create a great interest in this country and elsewhere, but I do not think it will make any sensible difference in public affairs. His life has been devoted to the pursuit of his own personal ambition, and political principles and his Party have been made subservient to that end.

"His success shows what may be done by unworthy means, and to offer him as an example is to encourage other men to do evil. In his private life and character, I think he has been kind and generous where his main pursuit was not interfered with. I have had many friendly conversations with him, but not for some years past, and I have not spoken to him since he left the House of Commons.

"[26th.] To Mr. Gladstone, to consider Bradlaugh case, again coming on. House: spoke in debate on Oath and Bradlaugh. Division against us, and Bradlaugh not permitted to take the Oath. Scene in the House: Bradlaugh, removed by Serjeant, returned, and again removed. House adjourned to get rid of the difficulty for the day.[1] Home and to bed after 3 o'clock.

"[27th.] House. Bradlaugh Case again. Spoke to suggest way out of difficulty. Well received, and hope I was the means of doing something towards a settlement of this unpleasant business. Evening, dined at Fishmongers' Hall, London Bridge. Lord Hartington, good speech. I spoke on Irish question and on land losses in England and effects on home trades. Home with Lord Hartington in his brougham.

---

stances of Ireland, "exactly as if he had been proposing to legislate for the inhabitants of Saturn or Jupiter." The Bill, one of Gladstone's finest legislative conceptions, established the "three Fs"—fixity of tenure, fair rent and free sale.

[1] The Court of Appeal had held that a Member of Parliament could not "affirm," and that Bradlaugh, being unsworn, had vacated his seat. He was immediately re-elected for Northampton and reappeared on April 26 to take his place in the House.

Yesterday, 26th, funeral of Lord Beaconsfield at Hughenden, Buckinghamshire.

"[*30th.*] Academy Dinner. As usual, many speeches not very good. Millais's portrait of Disraeli not good, and not pleasant to look at.

"[*May* 1.] Afternoon: read over proof of G. Barnett Smith's Biography. Crossed out much trifling matter of no authority.

"[*5th.*] To Mr. Boehm's studio to sit for a bust for Lord Rosebery. Mr. Boehm very intelligent, very rapid and skilful in his work. Saw a beautiful monument of the unfortunate Prince Imperial, who was killed by the Zulus in South Africa, and other works of much merit.

"By train to Honor Oak Station, to attend the funeral of my old and valued friend Edward Miall. A large company and real mourners.

"I have known E. Miall since the year 1840 when he came to 'One Ash,' I believe the day before my dear Helen was born, to tell me of the paper, *The Nonconformist*, he was intending to bring out. I obtained for him a subscription of £80 in Rochdale, of which I gave £20. The paper has done great good, and the question of disestablishment of the Church occupies its present position mainly through the labour of its editor and proprietor, Mr. Miall.

"He had a great cause. He conducted it with singular ability and temper, and he worked on thro' or over all the obstacles in his path with a wonderful persistency and unflagging zeal. I regard him as one of the most remarkable men I have been connected with during my political life.

"[*6th.*] Duchy office: magistrates and other business. House: Irish labourers' condition. Spoke. Irishmen of the rebel party very angry. Simulated anger, I suspect, my advice being too honest and wise for their ruffianly objects and conduct. After midnight: Oaths Bill. Angry opposition of Tories. Spoke about 3 in the morning, but speech and reasoning useless with men inflamed with passion and bigotry. To bed at ½ past 3.

"[*8th.*] Read 'A Fool's Errand,' a story of Southern society after the American War of Secession: well written, and a striking picture of the evil slavery has left behind it.

"[*9th.*] House: Motion for monument to Disraeli in Westminster Abbey. Mr. Gladstone's speech admirable. I was not present. Could not vote for monument, and did not go to the House till the question was disposed of. Mr. Gladstone's magnanimity led him into the mistake of proposing the monument: the Party much against it. He, I suspect, has regretted it, and his position in regard to it has given him not a little annoyance and irritation.

"Land Bill debate: I spoke for an hour with ease. Our friends satisfied with what I said, and I hope I gave some help to the Bill.[1] Home late—bed at 3 o'clock.

"[10*th*.] House: debate on arrest of Mr. Dillon, M.P. Conversation with Mr. Daly, M.P. for Cork. Described great demoralization of farmers and others. Refuse to pay not rent only, but all debts. Shopkeepers in great difficulties; industry and trade damaged; mischief done by doctrines taught by Land League.

"[13*th*.] Duchy office: appointed some magistrates—and wrote a short official letter to the Queen. Cabinet at 2 o'clock. Talk on Tunis and French invasion, Irish Land Bill, and on Cyprus. House. Home before one o'clock. A day of sad memories. Three years since the great blow fell upon me—3 years without my dear and loved wife. How sore the trial has been!

"[14*th*.] To Mr. Boehm for bust. Evening, dined with Mrs. Drummond, 18, Hyde Park Gardens. Mr. Lecky, the author, there.

"[17*th*.] To Mr. Boehm's; dear Sophie with me. House: met Mr. McKenzie, late Prime Minister of Canada, in Dr. Playfair's room. Interesting talk on Canada and its affairs. He believes the next election will reverse the decision of the last, and that Free Trade views will prevail.[2]

"[19*th*.] Dear Sophie and Theodore Cash to Highgate, to look out for a home for them in the autumn. Mrs. Barber called. Her son killed in the Orange Free State, said to be by Boers. She in great grief, and asks Govt. aid to enable her to go out to Durban, Natal, to bring home her two small grandchildren. To Mr. Boehm, the sculptor, when the bust was considered finished. I do not know if the bust is better than Burnard's or Theed's. House: Land Bill, debate and division at 2 o'clock. For Bill 352; against 176. Great cheering on our side. Met two Americans at the House: Whitelaw Reid,[3] editor of the *New York Tribune*, and Professor Cattell, of a Pennsylvania University.

---

[1] In this speech Bright made his famous use of the theory of "prairie value." He said that if a map were made of Ireland stripped of everything the tenant had done and marking only what the landlord had done, it would be like an American prairie, "bare of house and barn, fence and cultivation."

[2] Alexander McKenzie had been Premier of Canada from 1873 to 1878, having led the campaign which defeated Sir John Macdonald over the Pacific Railway charter. An industrial slump had brought about the overthrow of McKenzie's Liberal and Free Trade Government in 1878. His forecast to Bright was not realized. The Conservative Party remained in power until the revival of Liberalism under the leadership of Sir Wilfrid Laurier gave it the resounding electoral victory of 1896.

[3] Afterwards U.S. Ambassador in London.

"[*20th.*] House: Irish wrangle on arrest of Catholic priest on motion of adjournment.

"[*24th.*] Breakfast with Americans in this house. Genl. Kilby Smith, Mr. Dorsheimer, Mr. Reid of the *Tribune*, Mr. Cox of the House of Representatives and his wife, and Mr. Russell Lowell, U.S. Minister here.

"Mrs. Barber, mother of an Englishman murdered by Boers in Orange Free State, to meet Donald Currie [1] on arrangement for bringing her grandchildren home from the Cape. She in great trouble. Am trying to help her. Mr. Currie very kind in the matter.

"House: debate on arrests in Ireland—Dillon and priest.[2] W. E. Forster defended the conduct of Irish Govt. The rebel Irish Party violent, and their conduct disgraceful.

"This morning heard of the death of my sister-in-law, wife of my brother Thomas. She died last evening at ½ past 10. A long illness— ill for 4 years. A great blow for Thomas. I intend to go down home to-morrow for a few days.

"[*29th, at Rochdale.*] Pleasant talk with my dear boys on the terrace. They are very kind, and very dear to me. My darling child Mary is over from Stratford. She seems almost nearer and dearer to me than any other of my children, and I often think she combines the good qualities and dispositions of her sisters—and they are all very nice and good.

"[*30th.*] By 11 train to London. House: squabble among the Irish Party—interesting and may do good.

"[*June* 1.] Called on Mr. Boehm for sitting for my bust. He promises me a nice bust of Mr. Gladstone in terra-cotta. No House to-day: the 'Derby day.'

"[*2nd.*] Dined with Lord Granville to meet Mr. Evarts,[3] from New York. A pleasant party: Duke of St. Albans, Lord Spencer, Kimberley, Jno. Morley, Mr. Thompson of the *Pall Mall Gazette*, and others.

"[*3rd.*] Dined with Sir W. Harcourt. Mr. Evarts and other

---

[1] Of the Castle Line.

[2] The arrest of Dillon (May 2) during the second reading debate on the Land Bill, was one of Forster's many errors. He made the free gift of a martyr to the Irish Party. Still less judicious was the incarceration of Father Sheeny, of Kilmallock (May 20), on a thin suspicion of "treasonable practices." He cost the Government dear in the animosity of the Irish peasantry. Mr. Gladstone procured Sheeny's release in September. But the damage was done.

[3] President Hayes's Secretary of State.

Americans there. To the House with Lord Hartington in his brougham. Left dinner party to listen to Irish debate!

"[*14th.*] House at 9: Sir W. Lawson on Licensing system. I spoke favourably towards him, but against any early Govt. action in the matter.

"[*22nd.*] Mr. Pierce from Boston breakfasted with me. House: Capital Punishment debate. Evening dined with Chamberlain to meet French Commissioner on Treaty negotiation. Prospects of Treaty not good.

"[*24th.*] Dined with Lyulph Stanley, 82, Harley St. An American, Mr. Butler, there: old man, intelligent. Told me of the anti-rent conflict in New York State 40 years ago. Walked home with Mr. Smalley of the *New York Tribune*. He came in, and had a long chat till ½ past 12.

"[*26th.*] Called on Duke of Argyll. He has been ill and is now not well—upstairs and on his couch. Pleasant talk with him. His daughter, Lady Evelyn, introduced me to Mr. Baillie Hamilton, her future husband. The Duke's daughters very nice and good.

"[*29th.*] Dined with Benchers of the Middle Temple in their fine old Hall, built 300 years ago. Sir H. James, Attorney-Genl., called for me, and I went with him. Dinner profuse. Sir H. Thompson, the great surgeon, and Sir H. James near me. Very pleasant talk.

"After dinner, dessert and wine in adjoining room and speeches. I spoke on complaint of Lord Houghton that House of Lords has nothing to do, showing that, being out of sympathy with Govt. and H. of C. and constituencies, it is not willing to do anything which the country wants.

"Noticed among the students many dark faces from India. Coming from the dining-hall, I was very much cheered by the mass of students. The Indians were very cordial in their greeting.

"The evening very pleasantly spent, beyond that of any other public or great banquet within my recent recollection.

"[*July* 4.] At Woking Station, heard the sad news of an attempt to murder President Garfield at Washington—dangerously wounded; his condition critical.[1]

[1] President James Abram Garfield, the twentieth president of the United States, had been elected in November, 1880, and inaugurated on March 4. As he was on his way on July 2 to Commencement at Williams College, a madman, Guiteau, an office-seeker, shot him. Garfield lingered till September 19, when he died of his wound.

"House: Land Bill. Late in the evening, the Tory rowdies were very offensive, causing delay and much disturbance in the House. The day very hot. Home at ½ past 1 o'clock.

"[*5th.*] Weather very hot, in London 92 degrees in the shade.

"[*6th.*] Dined with Serjeant Simon, M.P. for Dewsbury, a Jew. Sat by his wife at dinner. Interesting talk with her on the Jews and the Old Testament, on the Book of Esther, and the Psalms of David. A pleasant family.

"[*7th.*] House till 1 o'clock. Spoke on a clause in Land Bill—that which determines amount to be advanced to tenants purchasing their farms. Clause 19 of the Bill. Home about 2 o'clock.

"[*14th.*] Afternoon 5 o'clock Garden Party at Marlboro' House: great crowd of 'high society' there. The Queen, Prince and Princess of Wales, etc. Walked about with Lady Rosebery, Lord R. not having arrived. The Queen spoke kindly to me. She suffered from the sun—her forehead covered with perspiration, which was the condition of multitudes. The Prince and the always charming Princess shook hands with their company as they arrived.

"I told him I thought it was like an American reception having to shake hands with so many people.

"House: a rough night with the rebel Irish. Spoke shortly, condemning their conduct and language. House sat on till 4, and passed Emigration Clause so much opposed by the rebel lot.

"[*15th.*] Mr. Harrison, Philadelphia, called on project for removing remains of William Penn to Pennsylvania. I could not encourage him.[1]

"House: became ill and very sick. Club: still very unwell. Something eaten seemed as if unwholesome, or extreme heat disturbed me. Heat registered said to be 98 in the shade—rarely equalled in this country. Home 8 o'clock and did not go down to the House.

"[*16th.*] Very hot. After a good night feel much better. Afternoon to Mrs. Gladstone's, a small party to tea to meet the Crown Prince and Princess of Germany.[2] He is a pleasant and manly person. She still young, very nice and simple and kind in her manners, a great favourite with all who know her. Home early.

[1] William Penn was buried beside his first and second wives at Jordans, the Friends' Meeting House, at Chalfont St. Giles.

[2] Afterwards the Emperor Frederick III. He had married the Crown Princess Victoria of England in 1858. He succeeded to the throne in 1888 and died a few months later.

"[*21st.*] Last evening distressed to hear of death by suicide of E. G. Midgley of Keswick, grandson of my old friend, Jas. Midgley, of Spring Hill. Have heard no particulars of this sad event.

"[*23rd.*] Dined with Wm. Agnew. Mr. Burnand, Editor of *Punch*, and Mr. Tenniel, artist of *Punch*, there. A party full of talk and merriment—I think the most noisy dinner party I have known: but the *Punch* detachment were not noisy. Frank Holl,[1] a portrait painter of growing celebrity, was also there.

"[*25th.*] To Bowater's, to order clothes for the coming wedding.

"[*27th.*] Dined with Osborn Morgan, Judge-Advocate, 20, Bolton St. Met Archibald Peel and Lady Georgina Russell that was; pleasant to see them again. Sir R. Cunliffe walked home with me, and we talked politics and poetry till after 1 o'clock.

"[*28th.*] House: Land Bill—report. An hour in Dr. Playfair's[2] room with Professor March of Newhaven. Explained his discoveries in Rocky Mountains—fossils, etc.

"[*29th.*] House: debate on 3rd reading of Land Bill. Adjourned to 9 o'clock. Short debate and division—220 against 14. Tory Party almost absent, their leaders not wishing to face final division. Enthusiastic cheering for Mr. Gladstone.

"Morning. Dr. Thomas, of Baltimore, called on me. Very pleasant conversation. Before leaving me he knelt and offered a short prayer for me, referring to my long labours in public life and to the loneliness of my home since my sad loss.

"[*31st.*] Francis J. King, of Baltimore, came in. Interesting talk with him. Intelligent and good man. Much engaged as trustee of some large bequests of money for public purposes: £800,000 for University and £700,000 for Hospital in Baltimore, left by a Friend, J. Hopkins.[3] Reading poetry. Gray of the *Elegy*. Very interesting.

"[*August* 3.] House 12 o'clock: crowd outside in favour of Bradlaugh. Debate on his removal from the House, in which I spoke for a few minutes. Did not vote on approval of measures taken to exclude him.[4]

[1] Painted the portrait of Bright for the Reform Club.

[2] The Chairman of Ways and Means, afterwards Sir Lyon Playfair, an eminent scientist.

[3] The Johns Hopkins University and Hospital in Baltimore were inaugurated in 1876.

[4] Bradlaugh tried to force his way into the House, and was dragged out into Palace Yard by the police.

"Corrected proofs of 'Great Movements and How to Make Them' —on parts containing Repeal of the Corn Law and the taxes on the Newspaper Press.

"[*4th.*] Conversation with Mr. Gladstone on difficulty between Lord Advocate [1] and Sir W. Harcourt. Condemned course taken to get Lord Advocate out of his office—was very frank in my criticism of proposed change to force him to accept Scotch Judgeship.

"[*5th.*] Lord Advocate called. Wrote a note to Mr. Gladstone to accompany one from him.

"[*6th.*] Cabinet at Lord Granville's. To consider Lords' amendments to Land Bill. Agreed to restore most of the portions rejected by them. Evening: dined at the Mansion House. Speeches by Gladstone, Childers, Northbrook, Hartington. I was called on and forced to speak, and what I said seemed to please the company. The evening passed off very well. Lord Mayor McArthur performed the part of host with great propriety.

"[*10th.*] House: Lords' amendments of Land Bill. Unpleasant night: Irishmen violent and offensive.

"The Lord Advocate and his wife called. She in great trouble at the harsh treatment her husband has received from Harcourt and Mr. Gladstone.

"[*12th.*] 4, Camden Square, and called on Frank Holl, artist, to see his portrait of Capt. Sim, my old friend of the Reform Club, now 93 yrs. of age. The portrait excellent. Mr. Holl hoped to paint me some time soon, but I am weary of giving so much time to portrait painters who do not succeed with me.

"House: debate on French Treaty. J. K. Cross, of Bolton, and my colleague Chamberlain spoke excellently well. The Lords at their congenial work, destroying our Irish Land Bill and doing infinite mischief, I fear.

"[*13th.*] Cabinet at 12: consider Lords' amendment to Land Bill. Agreed to some changes, but to none of importance. Home early—to read.

"[*15th.*] To Clapham Common, to see a small house taken by Theodore Cash for the first home of him and my dear child after their marriage. It is called Lancaster Lodge, Bolingbroke Grove. House. Repairing injuries of Lords to Land Bill. Great excitement about

[1] John McLaren M.P., son of Duncan McLaren, and stepson of Bright's sister Priscilla McLaren. Apparently Sir William Harcourt did not like him and would not work harmoniously with him.

result. The Irish rebel party behaved very ill—furious at the prospect of the passing of the Bill.

"[*16th.*] Lords yielded to firmness of Govt. and House, and accepted our amendments of their amendments, and passed-the Land Bill." [1]

6

His first distraction after the end of the long session of 1881 was the wedding of his daughter Sophie to Theodore Cash at Torquay (August 24). During his visit to Scotland in September he received at Dalguise the proofs of Morley's "Cobden" for his revision. In October he was called back to London for the Cabinet meeting which decided to arrest Parnell. "No other course possible," he wrote. At the end of the month the "Cobden" appeared, with this dedication:

To the Right Honourable John Bright, this Memoir of his close comrade in the cause of wise, just and sedate government is inscribed with the author's sincere respect.

Bright immediately sent copies to his daughters and to some friends, including E. L. Pierce at Boston and a sturdy Cornish Liberal, Mr. Northy, of St. Columb, who had made of "the Tribune" his personal exemplar as well as his political pattern. Then he turned to a matter that roused in him a queer mixture of feelings, the celebration of his seventieth birthday.

"[*November* 3.] Evening: notes for speech at the coming meeting on my birthday, 16th inst. Difficult to select topic of speech. I am weary of speaking in public.

"[*7th.*] Am spending my time very quietly at home, but not without some subjects of anxious thought, both as regards public affairs and in connexion with position and prospects of my boys. Have written out a memo. on project of Limited Liability for our firm. Some difficulties in the way.

"[*9th.*] Did not attend banquet at Guildhall. Do not like great banquets when expected to speak.

"[*10th.*] Cabinet Council 2 o'clock: sat for 4 hours. House business, change of rules, local govt. for unions and counties, forces in Natal, possible arrangement with Russia on question of Afghanistan, etc.

[1] The Peers did not seriously challenge a fight with the Commons on this Bill. They passed the Second Reading without a Division, and the amendments made in Committee were passed with small hope of acceptance by the Government. When the House of Commons insisted, the House of Lords gave way.

"Mr. Gladstone spoke to me of Morley's 'Life of Cobden'; thought it very good, only scarcely enough said about Cobden's religious spirit.

"[*16th, at Rochdale.*] My birthday—3 score and 10. Birmingham deputation with address. Workpeople's meeting—with address. Town's meeting with address. Speech on the three occasions. Newspapers many columns of report. My friends all very kind. For myself, do not feel that all they say is deserved. Indeed I often think the more a man is honoured by his friends, neighbours and countrymen, the more he should be humbled, for he knows more of his life and motives than others know, and, knowing so much, he will have less ground for applauding himself. I have some presents, and letters very many. Lord Granville sent me a copy of Milton in 2 Vols. printed by Baskerville. Goldwin Smith, selection from Wordsworth.[1]

"[*29th, after a visit to the Tweed.*] To Carlisle and home. 42 years to-day since I left Carlisle, 2 days after I was first married, going with my precious wife to spend a few days at the Lakes.

"[*December* 3.] Every day occupied with letters. I have no rest from them. I suppose I must have had 300 letters since my birthday.

"[*8th, at Llandudno.*] Board School, Lloyd Street.[2] Procession, bands, flags, etc., etc. in the little town. Ceremony and short speech soon over. W. Rathbone, M.P. for the County of Carnarvon, there; always kind and sensible. Evening meeting: several speeches. Too much laudation of my poor self, but real kindness shown to me by all. I spoke for over an hour; speech rather discursive—educational, political and personal,—but well received. On the whole, the meeting very pleasant. Mr. Roberts, M.P., and Mr. Davies, M.P., were there and spoke briefly.

"[*9th.*] With Philip to visit the little grave on the mountain, and spent some sad minutes there. A beautiful wreath and an exquisite bouquet of flowers were on the grave, placed there by the hands of Mrs. Williams, the wife of our friend Thos. Williams, of Mostyn St. Drove round the mountain, calling to look at the lighthouse, in which Philip was interested. From the Great Ormes Head drove to call on poor Mrs. Hughes, the crippled invalid, for several years the object of interest

[1] Goldwin Smith's recollection is different: "He asked me whom I thought the greatest of Englishmen, and answered his own question by naming Milton, because Milton was so great at once as a man of letters and as a citizen. On his seventieth birthday, when his friends were sending him presents, I got a copy of the Baskerville Milton, printed at Birmingham, for which Bright was then member, and wrote his own words on the fly-leaf." ("Reminiscences," by Goldwin Smith, p. 240.)

[2] Bright laid the foundation-stone.

to my dear Elizabeth. Took her a little gift of tea and sugar, and provided her with coals for the winter. She is cheerful and resigned in her sad condition.

"Afternoon, drove over to Conway, to call on Saml. Roberts, an old minister, who has written to me occasionally for some years past: has taken an active interest in public affairs.

"[12th.] To Manchester. Dined at the Town Hall to meet 3 Princes—Dukes of Edinbro' and Albany and Prince Christian. Sat between Lord Houghton and Sir F. Bramwell. The Princes modest and pleasant in their manner. I did not go with them to the Free Trade Hall, not caring much for their question—musical education, and not wishing to be called upon to speak.[1]

"[16th.] To Salford, Hope Hall, to dine with Mr. Grafton, M.P., to meet Lord Hartington. Bishop of Manchester and his wife there; also Professor Green, Owen's College, Mr. Lord, Indian merchant. A large house; good pictures and engravings. Large family—8 daughters and 2 sons. Dinner very good; conversation pleasant. Sir Ughtred Shuttleworth of the company. Very pleasant evening.

"[19th.] Walter Wren (late M.P. for Wallingford) came to stay the night. A remarkable man; a cripple, walking with difficulty with two sticks—illness of the spine. Very successful as a teacher of young men working for examinations as a passport to offices in the public service.

"[25th.] *Christmas Day.* Evening, music in the drawing-room. Dear Sophie played and sang. Albert, Willie, Philip and Theodore sang some beautiful hymns. They made me very sad; they brought back so painful a remembrance of the past.

"[28th.] Meeting this morning: only 6 present—3 on each side of the house. But numbers and voices are not needed for the true object which leads to a place of worship. Why should not all places, and especially our homes, be places of worship? Evening: Notes for speech for Jany. 3.

"[*January* 3, 1882.] By 11 train to Birmingham. To Highbury, Mr. Chamberlain's house. Evening to the Town Hall: great meeting. Mr. T. Avery, the Mayor, in the Chair—a man much respected in the town; allied to the Conservative Party, but friendly to me, and generally supporting me in the Boro. I spoke an hour and ten minutes, chiefly on the Irish question. Meeting well satisfied.

[1] The Duke of Edinburgh was an ardent musician. He founded the Royal Orchestral Society and occasionally played a first violin at its concerts.

"[4th.] At noon left Highbury for Gilbertstone to visit R. Tangye.[1] Evening a large party of Birmingham friends; pleasant company, only that I was much tired with so much talking.

"[5th.] A large party to breakfast—60 present. Dinner party at 2 o'clock. Evening to Town Hall—great meeting of Ward Committees. Spoke for ¾ of an hour. Very weary, and my head rather feeble. From meeting to Highbury and spent late evening with Chamberlain and a few friends.

"[6th.] By 9.30 train to London. Mr. Chamberlain with me. Cabinet Meeting, 2 o'clock: discussion on 'Rules of the House,' with conversation on condition of Ireland.

"[19th.] Much interested in reading 'Memorials,' etc., of Caroline Fox, of Falmouth. Charming book, records of a mind intelligent and good.[2]

"[27th.] Cabinet at 2. Discussion on County Govt. Bill: many difficulties. Dined at Brooks's Club in St. James's St. Small party invited by Algernon West and Mr. Hamilton. Mr. Gladstone there, Lord Enfield, Mr. Goschen. Pleasant evening.

"[30th.] Sad letter this morning telling of death of my old friend Henry Crosfield of Liverpool [3] by his own hand: distressing melancholia and sudden impulse. He lived for 3 days and explained circumstances and his feelings. Great shock to his friends, and great loss to many. How uncertain everything seems to me. Apparently in robust health so recently, and now gone, and in a way so sudden and shocking!

"Cabinet 2 to 6 o'clock: consideration of proposed changes of rules of the House. Mr. Speaker and Sir Erskine May were present for consultation and advice.

"Dined at the Reform Club with John Morley, Chamberlain, Sir A. Lyall, Mr. Brett, M.P.,[4] and Lord Reay.

---

[1] Sir Richard Tangye, the eminent engineer, of the Cornwall Works, Birmingham; a Cornishman and an ardent Gladstonian.

[2] See page 331. The "Journals" of Miss Caroline Fox deserve Bright's eulogy. They record the lives of the Fox family, describe their friends, their literary tastes, and characterize the visitors to Penjerrick, all with a simple and perfectly irresistible charm. Miss Fox is said to have invented the word "polytechnic" in naming the scientific society which she and her sister, Anna Maria Fox, helped to found, now known as the Royal Cornwall Polytechnic.

[3] He was Auditor of the London and North-Western Railway Company. His daughters were schoolfellows and close friends of Bright's daughters.

[4] Mr. R. B. Brett, Hartington's private secretary, succeeded his father, the first Lord Esher, in 1899. Mr. Brett sat in the 1880 Parliament for Penryn and Falmouth.

"To Piccadilly with Mr. Wren in his brougham. Then an hour in opening and reading some F.O. dispatches and some letters and to bed at 1 o'clock. Did not sleep till 4 o'clock: too much thinking; the sad end of my poor friend H. Crosfield pressing upon me, and perplexities public and private. Activity of the brain seems the great obstacle to sleep.

"[*February* 1.] Cabinet 2 o'clock: discussion on business of the House, especially on subject of Grand Committees to relieve House from Committees on Bills.

"Anxious discussion on crisis in Egypt—contest between 'Notables' and the Minister—and on foreign control of finances.

"Evening: Cabinet Dinner at Mr. Gladstone's. All the Ministers present. After dinner, 2 hours on Basuto difficulty, South Africa, and on proposed boundaries arrangement in Asia, Persia and Afghanistan, and as to an arrangement on boundaries with Russia. I sat next to Mr. Gladstone at dinner: proposed to him to suggest question in the House on the Bradlaugh business. He thought my idea good. Must think more of it.

"[5*th*.] Afternoon, called on Mr. Gladstone. Found him resting on a sofa, reading one of the reviews.

"Conversation on the Bradlaugh question, and my proposal of questions to Bradlaugh before any action of privation of his seat in the House. He quite approves, and will support me in it. Suggests I should see Lord R. Grosvenor to-morrow about it. I proposed to see Mr. Speaker, which he approved. (I called at the Speaker's house, but he was not in and I could not see him.)

"Mr. Gladstone spoke very freely about his prospects. He seems much resolved to quit office during this year. I showed him the difficulty of it, and what should be done before he doffs his harness: the question of the Land, the County Suffrage, and the distribution of seats.

"He did not think he was especially bound to continue thro' these great questions, tho' his zeal in regard to them had not slackened. He will summon a Cabinet for Tuesday at 12 to settle the course on the Bradlaugh debate, approving of my suggestion.

"[6*th*.] Dined with Mr. Gladstone: Parly. dinner; about 40 present. Speech [1] read before dinner. After dinner, large evening party. Talked with many people. A son of Prince Bismarck was present.

"[7*th*.] Cabinet at 12: discussion on Bradlaugh. My proposed amendment not agreed to, so I am free from the burden of a speech.

[1] i.e., the Queen's Speech at the opening of the session.

House at 4 o'clock: Bradlaugh again. Majority refused to allow him to take the oath. Address in answer to the 'Speech.' J. F. B. Firth seconded in an appropriate and excellent speech. Home midnight.

"[8*th*.] House at 1 o'clock. Northcote a long speech, feeble and cavilling, answered by Mr. Gladstone in one of his finest speeches. Afterwards P. J. Smyth on 'Repeal'—interesting and eloquent; and then O'Connor Power,[1] very good.

"Mr. Gladstone suggested that I should speak on 'Repeal' in answer to some things said in the debate. Must consider the matter before to-morrow. Dined with Lord and Lady Selborne, 30, Portland Place. Met there Sir Arthur Hobhouse and his wife and Goldwin Smith and his wife; a pleasant evening. Talk on Spiritualism and dreams and on dogs. I spoke of our pet dogs at home, and when I got to my rooms I found a letter from Albert telling me of the death of our dear old dog 'Tyke,' who has been a great favourite with us for 10 years. The news made me quite sad. We all had a great affection for our poor old friend.

"[11*th*.] Called on my old friend C. P. Villiers, who is ill, 39, Sloane St.; did not see him, but was glad to hear that he is better.

"Cabinet at 2 o'clock: discussion on dealing with certain corrupt boros whose writs have not been issued; on proposed new rules of procedure; and on Channel Tunnel. Astonished at objection of some and at terrors which, to me, are ridiculous and purely imaginary.

"[14*th*.] House: speech from Mr. Sexton in defence of Irish Land League—2¼ hours. Clever, but false in much of it. Division early, and then House counted out.

"[15*th*.] Dr. Lyman Abbott, U.S.A., called—editor of *Christian Union*. Intelligent. Talk on 'Civil Service' and American Tariff, the evil of which he clearly sees. House: debate on Address. Evening, dined with Lord Rosebery at Lansdowne House—a large party, mostly Scotchmen.

"[16*th*.] To House with Lord Carlingford. He spoke in touching language of his desolate condition since the loss of his wife, and asked me to visit him at his house near Bath.

"[19*th*.] Night disturbed by cough and irritation of air passages. Could not go to Meeting.

"[20*th*.] Night again disturbed; cough very troublesome; did not go out to-day. From this to Friday the 24th indoors, troubled with cough; gradually mending. My dear Sophie came and spent some

[1] P. J. Smyth and J. O'Connor Power were orators in every sense of the word. O'Connor Power lived in Rochdale at one time.

hours with me on two or three days. Theodore also came and prescribed for me. This week indoors has not been unpleasant. I bear solitude better than many, and inside the house finds me sufficient employment. Books are good companions. I have been reading Milton. Lord Rosebery has sent me 2 vols. of his poems, edited by Professor Masson. The industry of Masson is wonderful, and there is much in connexion with particular poems of the great master which is very curious and interesting.

"[27th.] To Windsor to a Council: Mr. Gladstone, Lord Spencer, Lord Sydney there. The Queen seemed very well and pleasant. She 'pricked' the Sheriff of Lancashire—a curious old ceremony. Lunch in the saloon carriage on our way back to Paddington. Meeting of Liberal Party in Downing St., very large and very harmonious. House: Mr. Gladstone—great speech on Lords' Land Act Committee.[1] Division gave us a majority of 133. Tactics of Tories very bad. Home 10 o'clock.

"[28th.] Cabinet hastily called at 4 o'clock to consider if arrangement possible with Lords' Committee. Letter from Lord Cairns inviting Forster to give evidence before the Lords' Committee. House: debate on writ for Meath in place of Michael Davitt. Home early. Read 'Life' of Fredk. Douglas, the American coloured orator.

[March 6.] Better night, but weary of London and the House and the insolence and worry of the Opposition.

"[9th.] House: division on resolution condemning House of Lords and its Committee on Irish Land Act.[2]

"[11th.] Called on Mr. Boehm, sculptor, to give him a short sitting to finish my bust.

"[22nd.] Woodford: marriage of Rachel J. Fowler to Geo. H. Fox, of Falmouth. Large and pleasant party. Day very cold.

"Evening: dined with G. Shaw-Lefevre. Pleasant party. Much talk with Mrs. Moulton, wife of Mr. Moulton, a barrister, I think one of the Cambridge Senior Wranglers.[3]

[1] The appointment by the House of Lords of a Select Committee to inquire into the working of an Act passed only six months before was an unprecedented piece of petulance. No members of the Government would serve on the Committee and the Cabinet refused to allowed Forster to give evidence before it. Gladstone moved and carried in the House of Commons a resolution condemning the conduct of the Peers. The Act was, indeed, working very well. The Land Courts were full of business, and the No Rent Manifesto had completely failed.

[2] The House carried the resolution by a majority of 68.

[3] J. Fletcher Moulton, afterwards Lord Moulton.

"[23rd.] Lord Granville called on motion of Lord Redesdale to prevent atheists sitting in either House of Parliament. House: Vote for Prince Leopold. Offensive speeches by Healy, and Storey, M.P. for Sunderland.[1]

"[24th.] House: Committee on Tariffs debate; Chamberlain spoke admirably in opposition to it.

"[29th.] Dined with Wm. Rathbone, M.P.: a large party. A pleasant chat with Sir J. Lubbock's daughter, recently married to Sydney Buxton. (Mr. Gibson, M.P. for Dublin University, and a Tory of a strong colour, speaking of Mr. Forster, Secretary for Ireland, said he considered him a man of extraordinary physical courage, and that his temper was remarkable. This was at the dinner at Mr. Chamberlain's the other day.)[2]

"[30th.] House: I opened the adjourned debate on the Closure resolution. Spoke for ¾ of an hour—close argument, with some plain things about the Irishmen at the close. House very friendly. Division at 2 o'clock. Govt. Majority 39.[3]

"[*April* 27.] To Windsor, to attend wedding of Prince Leopold. Church and the ceremony. Lunch. Evening dinner. After dinner, drawing-room. Some conversation with Duke of Connaught, Prince of Wales, and the Queen—all very friendly. The Queen spoke of her visit to Mentone and of the kind attention of Thos. Hanbury.[4]

"[28th.] Evening party at Marlboro' House, Prince of Wales. Many there. King of Holland there. He spoke with me yesterday at Windsor.

"[29th.] Academy dinner: quite a string of Royalties. Too many

[1] The additional allowance to Prince Leopold (Duke of Albany) who was about to marry. Radical members objected strongly to the traditional form of these grants, and demanded that the principles on which provision was made for members of the Royal Family should be definitely settled, so that applications to the House of Commons might be avoided. The marriage allowance to the Duke of Albany produced a minor Cabinet crisis. Dilke walked out without voting, and the Queen resented his action. Although Chamberlain voted with the Government as a member of the Cabinet which proposed the grant, he strongly supported Dilke and was prepared to resign if Dilke were forced out of office.

[2] Forster had taken his life in his hands a month before by making a tour through County Clare, one of the most disturbed parts of the country. In King's County at Tullamore he harangued a crowd from a window and lectured them on the moral cowardice of their crimes.

[3] The Government majority was brought down by a combination of Parnellites with Conservatives against the resolution.

[4] The owner of "La Mortola," Ventimiglia, which the Queen frequently visited.

speeches and the dinner over late. Talk with Sir F. Leighton and the Prince afterwards. The Prince very free and pleasant. Many persons of note there as usual.

"[*May* 7.[1]] Heard this morning of the dreadful murder last evening in Dublin of Lord F. Cavendish and Mr. Burke—a crime scarcely equalled in our modern years. On Friday last, I sat with Lord Frederick, just appointed Secretary to the Lord-Lieutenant of Ireland, in a Committee of the Cabinet to discuss clauses of new Prevention of Crime Bill. He sat next to me on my left hand, and on parting I wished him a pleasant voyage across the Channel. The sea was more merciful than the cruel and wicked men who murdered him and Mr. Burke a little more than 24 hours afterwards.

"This crime has created a great sensation. He was greatly liked in the House of Commons. He was amiable, intelligent, and liberal— a man very popular on all grounds. The sympathy for his family and for his desolate wife deep and universal.

"To Mr. Gladstone's at 3 o'clock. All Ministers who were present very sad. Discussion on appointments necessary, and on course to be taken in the House.

"[*8th*.] House adjourned after a few remarks from Mr. Gladstone, Northcote and Forster.

"[*9th*.] Committee on Prevention of Crime Bill in Privy Council room. House: Ballot Bill read a second time.

"[*10th*.] Cabinet at 12. Settled clauses of Bill after much discussion. Mr. Gladstone, as usual, for moderation.

"[*11th*.] Funeral of Lord F. Cavendish at Chatsworth. I did not attend it, wishing to avoid danger of fresh cold, and being required to attend the Queen's Drawing Room—not a pleasant duty on a day of so great and general sorrow.

1 Parnell had been released on parole from Kilmainham on April 10 to attend the funeral of his nephew in Paris. While he was at liberty he communicated the proposals of an Arrears Bill through O'Shea to Gladstone. Gladstone was sympathetic, but could not vote for the Bill as it stood. It was introduced by Mr. Redmond on the 26th, two days after Parnell had returned to prison. Within the next few days Lord Spencer succeeded Lord Cowper as Viceroy and the Cabinet decided to release Parnell and the two other members of Parliament who were under arrest. Forster immediately resigned the Chief Secretaryship. Lord Frederick Cavendish was appointed in his place. In what was apparently a more friendly atmosphere than Englishmen had breathed in Dublin for many a day, Lord Frederick and Lord Spencer arrived in Dublin on the afternoon of Saturday, May 6. In the evening he was stabbed to death, and his Under-Secretary with him. Within a few hours the fires of hate blazed more furiously than ever.

"Drawing Room: usual ceremony and display. Spoke to Chinese Minister. He said no Drawing Rooms in his country. Thought the ceremony very pretty. Princess of Wales so gracious; she is quite a model. The American Minister, Mr. Lowell, thought they had too little ceremony in his country—if we had somewhat too much.

"Evening: 9 o'clock, House. Sir W. Harcourt introduced Prevention of Crime Bill for Ireland. His speech, in my view, too severe. No conciliation in it, and not calculated to soothe Irish members, some of whom spoke with great passion against it. The 'Rebel party' in great difficulty—in peril from Fenian ruffians in Ireland, and not daring to be moderate in the House.

"I spoke shortly in answer to an attack from Mr. Chaplin. Home after 2 o'clock; to bed at 3, nervous and unhappy from difficulties on every side. Great relief if I could escape from responsibilities of office. Very weary of its duties and irritations.

"[12th.] F. M. Edge called to talk about Fenians in the States, some of whom he knew when in America. Summer seems to have begun yesterday. My cough much less troublesome. House. Home before midnight.

"[13th.] Cabinet at 12. Egypt a difficulty, and occupied some time. By 5.40 train to Brighton. Found dear Lillie and the 'new baby' well. Mr. Dodson with me in the train, so the journey passed in pleasant chat. This day 4 years my precious Elizabeth was taken from me. How many sad days have passed—and now how great is my loneliness and my loss! Time is not a remedy, and there is no cure.

"[15th.] Midnight. Mr. Gladstone brought in the Arrears Bill. Warm discussion on letter of Parnell to O'Shea on prospect of something like a truce between Parnell and his adherents and the Govt. on Irish affairs. Forster justly bitter against Parnell, and scarcely considerate enough of his old colleagues. Home ½ past 2.

"[16th.] Excited discussion on subject of supposed arrangement with 'Irish Party': occupied all afternoon from 2 to 7 o'clock. Dined with Lady Stanley in Dover St. Talk with Mr. Froude on condition of South Africa. Coming out, met Lord Granville, who walked with me to my lodgings, discussing Prevention of Crime Bill.

"[19th.] Dined with Sir Charles Forster: large party, and a crowd afterwards. Took Lady O'Hagan down to dinner. She is one of the Townley heiresses from Burnley. Much talk on Ireland. She says Catholic clergy and curates have abandoned teachings of their Church in connecting themselves with the Land League and its counsels.

Evidently she is much distressed at the state of things in Ireland. Afterwards talk with Dr. Quain and Lord Cork on Ireland, now the chief subject of conversation. N.-West Riding Election: Mr. Holden returned by good majority of more than 2,000 votes.

"[31*st*.] Cabinet Council: Egypt and Zulus the subjects of discussion. By 6.30 train to Birmingham. The Mayor, Mr. Avery, met me at the station. Called to see building of new Central Free Library. Fine building; large collection of books; good pictures; interesting in every respect.

"[*June* 1.] Sir Henry Parkes and daughter, from New South Wales, to breakfast. Town Hall at 12. A large meeting: all seated, very quiet. I spoke for an hour on Libraries and Books—with anecdotes and quotations from some poets. To Library: opened formally by the Mayor. Evening: banquet in the Council rooms—6 o'clock to 11. Some good speeches. I had spoken in the morning and had little to do in the evening but to listen. Dear Mary came in from Stratford. It is a real pleasure to see her, and to find her so well and cheerful. Many seemed pleased with my speeches, and some were anxious to know more of Janet Hamilton, and would send for the book I had mentioned.[1]

"[5*th*.] Friday last, conversation with Mr. Goschen on offer made him to join the Govt., which he has declined. Mr. Goschen requested me to see him. Difficulty was to his objection to County Household Suffrage. He also fears Liberal Party going too fast and too far. Also doubts Mr. Gladstone as to concessions to Irish Party on Irish Legislature: he evidently timid and going backward rather than forward in his political opinions. Did not succeed in convincing him.

"This evening reported my interview to Mr. G. in his room at the House. He told me of his hope that Mr. Whitbread would take War Office—that Mr. Childers might become Chancellor of the Exchequer, and suggested I should see Whitbread and encourage him to consent; but did not meet him during the evening. Home rather late. To bed after 2 o'clock and did not sleep well.

"[6*th*.] House: Irish Crimes Bill. Conversation with Mr. Gladstone in his room at the House. Difficulty in making the changes

---

[1] "Poems and Essays of Janet Hamilton" was published in 1880 by Maclehose, Glasgow, publisher to the University. Janet Hamilton was born in 1795 at Carshill, Shotts, N.B., and died in 1873. She could not write until she was 50 and became blind at 60.

in the Cabinet he contemplates. Mr. Whitbread not willing to take office: health not good.

"[8*th*.] To Elliott and Fry—photographed. Called on the Misses Cobden. Sorry to hear that Nelly is still ill, and not able to leave her room. Conversation with Annie about her approaching marriage with Mr. Sanderson. Told her I must give her a wedding present. She said she should like me to give her a copy of Milton's poems.

"House: Crime Bill, no real progress. Irish disposed to obstruct and prospect of progress unsatisfactory. News from Ireland bad. Mr. Burke and a soldier escort with him shot this afternoon near the town of Gort.

"[9*th*.] To Conduit St., to see Munkacsy's great picture of Christ before Pilate. Much force in the figures and fine colour. The head of the one figure superior, I think, to anything I have before seen. There is gentleness, but perhaps, as is usual, too little force; but there is a light and purity about it very striking.

"House: Crime Bill. Much talk and slow progress. Home before one o'clock.

"[10*th*.] 35 years ago—our wedding day. What memories this date recalls!

"Dined with Lyulph Stanley, 82, Harley St. Small party. His fine old mother, Lady Stanley, there; also Lord Arthur Russell and his wife, and Mr. Blunt and his wife, Lady Anne, who is a granddaughter of Lord Byron. Talk with Mr. Blunt about Egypt—his enthusiasm in favour of Arabi Pasha, and of Egyptian reform and independence.

"Geo. Howard, M.P., of the little party. He walked down with me, and came in to talk Ireland with me till 1 o'clock.

"[11*th*.] Westminster Meeting. B. Braithwaite spoke with much earnestness. Poor, kind Mrs. Reynolds there, daughter of Elizabeth Fry. She seemed quite glad to meet me again. We spoke about Llandudno where we last met, but my dear Elizabeth not now with us. The thought made me very sad.

"Dined with J. Chamberlain, 72, Princes Gate. Talk on Ireland. Captn. O'Shea, M.P., there, Jno. Morley, and Jesse Collings. The two last bitter and unreasonable on Irish question and the conduct of Govt. Home near 1 o'clock."

7

In the summer of 1882 came the crash which had been threatening for several months—ever since the revolt of Arabi against the Khedive

Tewfik in the previous autumn. It was a puckish fate that led a
Liberal Government into one of the most emphatic acts of imperialism
in history, the establishment of British overlordship in Egypt. The
situation which brought about the joint demonstration of the. French
and British fleets before Alexandria (May 15) was, like the other international imbroglios of the Government, an inheritance from the Dis-
raelian régime—the direct consequence of the dual French and British
control set up in 1879 as the sequel of the Treaty of Berlin. A political
crisis in France, the fall of Gambetta and the succession of de Freycinet
at the moment of the military crisis in Egypt, completed the irony.
England was left to deal alone with the events which followed upon
Arabi's rebellion.

Bright watched the development of the trouble with intense anxiety.
He did not mean to be dragged as a Minister into compliance with
warlike policies which he had spent his life in denouncing. It gave
him infinite pain to break with Gladstone, as his hesitations prove; and
he disliked intensely the sensation of divorce from his colleague Chamberlain. But his path was clear. As soon as Admiral Seymour's guns
fired on the forts at Alexandria, he resolved to resign.

"[*May* 19.] Cabinet summoned so could not give the promised
sitting to Frank Holl. Cabinet: Egypt. Great difficulty. Past
arrangements not wise, and now position almost beyond remedy.
French Govt. uncertain and hard to act with.[1]

"[*20th.*] House. Cabinet in Mr. Gladstone's room. Egypt:
warm discussion and great difference of opinion. Very anxious on
this question, and doubts as to my position in regard to it. Crime Bill
labouring thro' Committee.

"[*21st.*] House. Cabinet in Mr. Gladstone's room. Egypt:
discussion less warm, but much difference of opinion. Mr. Gladstone
moderate and wise as usual. My anxiety somewhat relieved by more
moderate tone. House: Crime Bill. Evening: dined with Theodore
Fry at 22, Queen Anne's Gate. Very pleasant party: Justice Fry,
Jos. Pease, Waterhouse, and their wives, mostly Friends or connected
with Friends, except Mr. Cohen and his daughter, Jews.

"[*22nd.*] To 4, Camden Square, to Frank Holl's, to sit for my

---

[1] Arabi's revolt against Tewfik had started the train of events which led to the
bombardment of Alexandria and Bright's resignation. The French and English
fleets had appeared before Alexandria on May 15. On June 10 occurred the
military riots in which 200 Europeans were killed.

portrait. It will be the one to be painted for my friends in Birmingham to be given to me or to my children.

"House: Egypt. Afterwards Crime Bill. Amendment carried to extend the alien clause to England. Feeling in the House so strong that Govt. was forced to accept it.

"[23rd.] To Frank Holl's for the portrait. Called in York Place, Baker St., No. 14, to inquire for a good photo of my dear friend, Mr. Cobden, for his portrait in the cheap edition of his Life by Jno. Morley.[1] His daughter Jane gave me a photo, tho' not so good as I wished to find.

"House: Crime Bill. To dinner with Geo. Trevelyan and his wife, 40, Ennismore Gardens; no other company. Returned to the House at 9 o'clock: Crime Bill. I spoke on the 'Alien Clause,' and urged the conspiracy between Irish in America and in Ireland as justifying the adoption of the Clause.

"[24th.] To dine with Mr. Mundella, Elvaston Place, Queen's Gardens: a pleasant party. When some of the guests were gone, the talk was of poetry and of Whittier. I had to read some short pieces, which seemed to give much satisfaction. Mr. Rathbone brought me home in his carriage. My friends almost burden me with their kindness. Read till 1 o'clock.

"[25th.] Westminster Meeting—solemn. Club. Called on Edwin Lawrence, and my old friend, his pleasant wife. Afterwards called on our new baronet, Sir Joseph W. Pease, and took tea with them, and walked home with him thro' the Park, accompanied by the Manager of the North-Eastern Railway. The day lovely, and the Park offering its pleasant recreation to crowds of the London population.

"[27th.] Read in *Time*, a magazine sent me by Sir Arthur Otway, M.P., an article on 'Cobden and Bright'—review of Morley and Barnett Smith's biographies, very friendly. Also a very touching little poem, called *The Prince*.

"Talk with Lord Hartington on Egypt and its difficulties. Does not see his way out of them. Perhaps we may come to grief in or thro' them. I spoke quite frankly: could be no party to invasion or occupation of Egypt. Any mode out of the mess would be better than occupation and war on or with Turkey, and perhaps quarrel with France. Time and patience might solve the problem.

"[28th.] Cabinet meeting in Mr. Gladstone's room: answer to question from the Sultan's secretary to Lord Dufferin.

[1] A shilling (abridged) edition of the great biography was published this year.

"[29th.] Mr. Wilfred Blunt called. Long conversation. An enthusiast on Egyptian affairs. Wishes our Govt. to take sides with Arabi Pacha and National or Reform Party.

"News from Ireland bad. Murder of Lord Clanricarde's agent, Mr. Blake, and his servant.

"[*July* 1.] House at 12. Found that a party of Irish members had been suspended for the sitting, about 9 o'clock.[1] Later another lot were suspended and the Bill passed Committee.

"Club. Home before 12. During the afternoon, Cabinet met in Mr. Gladstone's room. Egypt an anxious question. Conference doing better. French acting reluctantly or refusing to act. I suspect they are wiser than we are, tho' their conduct is marked by weakness, and I fear with some insincerity.

"Decided, if needful, to sit thro' the night and into Sunday in order to get thro' the Bill as printed, not including new clauses. Our Chief agreed to this very unwillingly, but all turned out well, and the Bill was thro' Committee at 8 o'clock.

"[2nd.] Cabinet at 2 o'clock. Egypt very critical. Opposed strongly measures which I think tending to force and war. Am nearing the point when I must decide whether I can retain my place in the Govt. To leave it may be hurtful to it; to keep with it may be hurtful to myself.

"Discussion on language of O'Donnell, M.P. for Dungarvan, spoken on Saturday last. Spoke late in the evening on 'urgency' for Arrears Bill.

"[4th.] House 2 o'clock. 'Urgency' carried by great majority. Crime Bill through Committee, about 20 Irishmen of the 'Rebel party' leaving the House.

"Conversation with Mr. Gladstone on the Egyptian difficulty in his room. He referred to suggestion from two of our colleagues, Hartington and Childers, to which he could not assent. I explained to him my views. The position is very critical, but last advices from Constantinople[2] somewhat more favourable.

"[6th.] House: Arrears Bill. Spoke before dinner at Mr. Gladstone's suggestion. My friends satisfied, and some difficulties in some

---

[1] Dr. Playfair, the Chairman of Committees, was severely criticized for naming and suspending sixteen members, some of whom were not guilty and others not in the House. The incident occurred during a sitting which Irish obstruction had prolonged to thirty hours.

[2] Where the representatives of the Concert of Europe were meeting.

minds removed. Division 2 o'clock. Home by 3 o'clock. A pleasant morning for a drive from the House.

"[*7th.*] The day on which my dear father died, 31 years ago. To Frank Holl: another sitting for the portrait.

"House: found much excitement on a clause in the Crime Bill touching power of domiciliary visits by night. Opposition to concession proposed by Mr. Gladstone. Debate excited, and several speeches against Govt. from our side of the House. I spoke shortly on behalf of the concession, but on a division Govt. defeated by majority of 13. It is said 21 votes from our side went against us. Crimes Bill read a third time at ½ past 12.

"In Mr. Gladstone's room: long and private conversation. He much disturbed at the adverse vote of the House, and explained what he proposed to say to the Cabinet to-morrow, and to the House on Monday. He is carrying a heavy burden, and would gladly escape, if it were possible.

"[*8th.*] Cabinet at 12 to 3.30. Yesterday's division. Arrears Bill, as to tenant-right being counted as an asset in allowing claim to receive State aid to pay arrears of rent.

"Egypt. Contended against eagerness of War and Navy Departments to organize forces and ships for 'operations'—that is war—in Egypt. Mr. Gladstone firm against extravagant proposals generated in the atmosphere of the 'Services.' Painful to observe how much of the 'jingo' or war spirit can be shown by certain members of a Liberal Cabinet.

"Home before 9 o'clock, and read till near 12. Milton's essay on 'Unlicensed Printing' in the vol. given me by Mr. Willis, Q.C., M.P. for Colchester.

"[*10th.*] Received a note from Mr. Gladstone on my conversation with him as to my leaving the Govt. on the Egyptian question. News from Alexandria very disquieting to me. Bombardment of forts imminent: may hear of it to-morrow.

"Conversation with Mr. Gladstone in the Lobby. He very anxious, and finds no adequate support where he has most right to look for it. I am distressed at the thought of being compelled to separate from him. But how can I even seem to take part in a policy and proceedings at variance with all the teaching of my public life?

"Jacob up home with me, and walked on to his house in Norfolk St.

"[*11th.*] Sad news from Alexandria: War and bombardment of forts. What I have so much feared has come at last.

"In great trouble. Did not go down to the House in the afternoon. Wrote a letter to Mr. Gladstone asking him to accept my resignation. Wrote 3 copies of it, finding it not easy to say what I wished. Did not send it to him.

"Evening, House: Arrears Bill. Was on Treasury Bench as usual with Mr. Gladstone. No conversation on the subject which troubled us both, except his complaint of the way in which everyone seemed to lose his head: projects of laying telegraph wires all along Suez Canal, as if various preparations for great war were necessary.

"Wrote to Albert and to Helen and Mary telling them of my intended withdrawal from the Govt.

"Home by ½ past one o'clock.

"Much troubled all day. Great regret at my position. Shall be blamed by many, but cannot accept the responsibility of War which I deem unjust and unnecessary.

"There seems not a single friend of mine with whom I can consult. Must rely on my own judgment, which I hope will not mislead me.

"[12*th*.] House: debate on Egypt. Did not hear much of it. Arrears Bill in Committee. Felt quite unable to take my usual place on the Treasury Bench.

"Wrote a new letter to Mr. Gladstone asking him to accept my resignation, intending to give to him in the House. During the afternoon I recd. a letter from him suggesting I might take further time for deliberation, as more favourable news of truce might change view of circumstances.

"To this I wrote a short reply, and enclosed my letter of resignation to him, that he might see to what conclusion I had come, but consenting to wait till to-morrow when perhaps I could see him.

"Conversation with some of our friends in the House who are sorely distressed at what has occurred. They saw my difficulty and urged me not to leave the Govt., the result of which they thought would be very injurious.

"Dined this evening with Serjeant Simon and a pleasant party. Home with Sir H. James, Attorney-Genl., who urged me not to resign: said 'it would soon be the end of all things' as far as the Govt. was concerned.

"My perplexity very great. Duty seems to call both ways. Can I help in arresting further mischief, and in hope of this can I remain in office? It is hard that to such a question I should have difficulty in coming at once to a decisive conclusion.

"Recd. this evening a nice letter from my dear child at Street, who is always so sensible and so good.

"[13th.] Cabinet at 12. Egypt and the sad news from Alexandria. Took almost no part in the discussion. The case has gone beyond my range, and counsel from me of no avail. I felt that I had no longer any concern in the decision of those who are still my colleagues.

"At 11 o'clock, Lord Granville called upon me. Mr. Gladstone had shown him my letter and he suggested I should see Mr. Gladstone and talk over the difficulties of the position. He was evidently in real trouble—spoke of my kindness to him, and of the influence I had in the Cabinet. Our short interview was distressing to both of us.

"The tone of the conversation at the Cabinet convinced me that I could do nothing more—that with the members of the Cabinet on the Egyptian question I must silently consent to much that I must condemn, or be in constant conflict with them, and that there was nothing for me but to retire. I have therefore written a final letter to Mr. Gladstone asking him to accept my resignation, which I must give him in the course of the evening.

"To Marlboro' House garden party only for a short time. A large number of people there. The Queen and Prince walked round, moving to all the visitors, and the Queen speaking to many of them. I was not in the front and was not noticed in the crowd.

"House: Arrears Bill, but could not take my old seat on the Treasury Bench, or take part in the discussion of the clauses. Spent the evening in the Lobby or News Room, and on the Terrace. Home at 12 o'clock.

"After the Cabinet, went up to Camden Square and gave another sitting to Mr. Holl for my portrait.

"[14th.] Sent Sir Barrington Simeon to Mr. Gladstone with my letter, and recd. a note in reply asking me to go down to see him at 1.30. Went and met him at the corner of the Athenæum Club and walked down with him to his house in Downing St. He then explained his views—to me somewhat strange and unexpected. He urged as if all that has been done in the Egyptian case was right, and even persuaded himself that he is fully justified in the interest of Peace. I made little reply, but gave him no expectation that my view coincided with his or had in any degree changed. I took lunch with him and his daughter Mary, and came away, he going to the House.

"This evening he sent me up a letter or memorandum repeating what he had said during our conversation, and the contents of it much surprised me. He seems to have the power of convincing himself that what to me seems glaringly wrong is evidently right, and tho' he regrets that a crowd of men should be killed, he regards it almost as an occurrence which is not to be condemned, as if it is one of the incidents of a policy out of which he hopes for a better order of things. He even spoke of our being able to justify our conduct in the great day of account. His letter this afternoon explains his views.[1]

"Dined this evening with Mr. Davies, M.P. for Anglesea, and with his pleasant and intelligent wife and their nice daughters. These are good people and I am glad to be acquainted with them.

"[15th.] Up late—1 o'clock a.m. Wrote what I hope is a final letter to Mr. Gladstone, insisting on my retirement from the Cabinet and my office as Chancellor of the Duchy of Lancaster. I have no option. I could not bear the remorse of being connected with the policy in which the Govt. is involved, and this I have told him in reply to the attempted justification he has sent to me.

"Dined with Lord Aberdeen, 37, Grosvenor Square. Large party afterwards. Many M.P.s there. Much expression of regret at my resignation, but general approval given. Took down to dinner Lady Katherine Bannerman. Pleasant conversation on War question; she wholly against war on Christian grounds. Cannot understand how men can engage themselves to fight in any case at the command of any man. Mentioned to me remarkable case of 'conversion' of her step-daughter when quite a child, whose temper and conduct underwent suddenly a singular and most happy change. I promised to send her a copy of 'Dymond's Essays' and to call upon her. Lady Aberdeen asked me to give her a copy of my published speeches, which I engaged to send to her.

"[17th.] To Frank Holl's, for the portrait. House: found a kind note from Mr. Gladstone. Spoke shortly on my resignation.

---

[1] Lord Morley gives this letter almost fully ("Gladstone," Vol. III, p. 84). He adds: "The correspondence closed with a wish from Mr. Gladstone: 'Believe in the sore sense of practical loss, and the (I trust) unalterable friendship and regard with which I remain, etc.' When Bright came to explain his resignation in Parliament, he said something about the moral law, which led to a sharp retort from the Prime Minister, but still their friendship did appear to remain unalterable, as Mr. Gladstone trusted that it would." Sir Charles Dilke wrote in his Memoir (Vol. I, p. 471): "After the sitting (of the Cabinet on July 18) Lord Granville told me that Mr. Gladstone's letter to Bright about his resignation was far from pleasant in tone, and had put an end to a very long friendship. Morley, in his 'Life of Gladstone,' states the contrary, but he is wrong." Bright's diaries show that Lord Morley was right and that there was no basis whatever either for the reported statement of Lord Granville or for Dilke's assumption.

House very quiet and friendly, cheering when I rose, and when I sat down.

"In my old seat 2nd bench below the gangway, the House seems more pleasant to me this evening than any other this session. Members most friendly, regretting my leaving the Govt. but expressing their sense of my right action.[1]

"[18th.] To breakfast with my old friend Cyrus W. Field, of New York, in Queen Anne's Mansions. Club: not down to the House. Met Sir Thos. Bazley: very pleasant to see him so well in his 86th year. To dine at Lady Lefevre's—nice party. Lord Aberdare, G. Shaw-Lefevre and his wife, Mr. H. Ward and his wife,[2] who gave me the 4 vols. of the English Poets. Home in Lord Aberdare's carriage. Friendly letters from Lord Selborne, Lord Northbrook and Sir W. V. Harcourt.

"[19th.] Many letters to-day, very friendly from Lord Carlingford and Lord Halifax. . . . Dined with R. K. Causton, 3, Clanricarde Gardens: large party. The lady of the house[3] attractive and clever. Will send me 'Claudius,' a book of the times of Domitian, which she has written. Home with Napier Higgins—successful lawyer—in his carriage.

"[21st.] Duchy office, perhaps for the last time. Mr. Engleheart quite sad at the prospect of my retirement. He is an admirable public servant, and has been most helpful to me. House: Arrears Bill, 3rd reading; majority for, 108. Home: found a very kind letter from Lord Spencer on my quitting the Govt. I know no public man of whom I have a higher opinion. He is liberal and honourable to a remarkable degree. Spoke to Mr. Gladstone during the division. He was friendly and pleasant.

"[24th.] Did not go to the House: did not wish to hear Mr. Gladstone make poor excuses for the evil policy he has been driven into.

"[25th.] By 9.30 train from Victoria Station for Osborne, Isle of Wight. Special train: Kimberley, Carlingford, Sydney, Childers, Morier, Minister at Madrid, and Lennox Peel with us. Portsmouth: crossed to Cowes in *Fire Queen*, light boat; sea quite smooth. Osborne by 1 o'clock. Waiting and sauntering in passages and room till near

[1] Sir Charles Dilke was taken into the Cabinet to fill Bright's place.

[2] Mr. and Mrs. Humphry Ward had come to London from Oxford in the previous year on his appointment as a leader writer of *The Times*.

[3] Now Lady Southwark—a daughter of Sir Thomas Chambers, Q.C., Recorder of the City of London.

two. Then lunch. About 20 sat down. Duchess of Atholl there: spoke of Dunkeld and my visit to her about 2 years ago.

"After lunch, Childers first, and then I, went into the Queen's room. She was alone. I took the Duchy seals from the box, and said I was sorry to have to give them up. She said, 'And I am very sorry to have to receive them.' I said I thought she would understand my difficulty, and how impossible it was for me to take any other course. She replied that she quite understood it. She hoped I was well, and I thanked her for the kindness she had always shown me. I bowed to her; she returned it; and I left the room.

"The Queen looked well and young. She was most courteous and kind. This probably final visit or interview has passed as pleasantly as could be looked or wished for. Left Osborne at ½ past 3, and reached London soon after 6.

"[26th.] A party of Americans from Boston came by appointment, 25 in number,—workpeople of Mr. Jordan, of Boston, who came with them. Giving them an excursion to London and Paris. Very interesting company; anxious to see me, of whom, it seems, they had heard in their own country. I spoke to them, perhaps 15 or 20 minutes. They seemed much pleased, as did Mr. Jordan. On leaving I shook hands with each of them.

"By 1 o'clock train for Stratford-on-Avon. Sir Robert Cunliffe, M.P., in the same carriage; also an interesting old gentleman who smoked a curious German pipe which he bought in the Black Forest 60 years ago! Stratford at 5 o'clock. Evening 7 o'clock to the College,[1] with dear Mary and Dick. Supper with the boys—very abundant and much enjoyed. After supper, prizes given by me, and spoke a short address to the boys: not much at my ease, but seemed satisfactory to my audience. Later, concert given by the boys; some things amusing and clever.

"[*August* 5.] To Frank Holl's to finish portrait. This is my last sitting. Hope the result will be thought satisfactory. Holl tells me he has spent £10,000 on a new house at St. John's Wood and has paid for it out of one year's income from his portrait painting!

"[8th.] House, after a fortnight's absence. Arrears Bill, Lords' amendments. Some concessions made, not important, and Bill sent up to the Lords. It is expected they will pass it on Thursday.

"[9th.] House: debate on conduct of Dr. Playfair on suspension of Irish members some weeks ago. Dined with Lord Granville: small

[1] Trinity College School.

party. Dutch Minister and another Dutchman, Lord Dalhousie, Mr. Grenfell and W. E. Forster and Stuart, one of our Foreign Ministers; very pleasant evening.

"Read 'Judaism and Rome'—interesting but sad details of human wrongs and suffering.

"[*11th.*] By 12 Midland train to Manchester and home.[1]

"[*September* 14.] News to-day confirming that of yesterday of battle in Egypt. This Christian nation is killing crowds of Egyptians from whom we have recd. no injury or threat of harm.[2]

"[*22nd, at Windermere.*] The 3 days very fine. These excursions full of pleasure mingled with not a little of sadness. My mind oppressed with memories of companions no longer here. They are not with me but my love for them remains not diminished, but deepened, and made more solemn.

"[*October* 8, *at Kelso.*] Dined at Main House with Mr. Bidder and his nice family; one son and 4 daughters there, all clever and well taught. The mother a comely and sensible person. One girl, Bertha, I think, has much of the singular talent of her grandfather who was famous for his power of calculation of figures. He was called 50 years ago, 'the Calculating Boy,' and excited much public interest.

"[*16th.*] River up; no fishing. Called in on Alfred Denison. His fishing machinery extensive—29 rods standing in one corner of his room; in one box probably more than 1,000 salmon flies. He has a library of works on Fishing, of 2,500 vols., and is now publishing a catalogue of them.

"[*27th, in London.*] House till after midnight; my friends there very cordial and kind. Mr. Engleheart called this morning. Would like to be made a C.B.,—an honour which I think he merits, tho' why men should covet it is rather a puzzle to me.

"[*31st, at Leamington.*] Called on an old friend, Jno. Harding, now 80 years of age and feeble. He received me very cordially. I looked over his pictures and praised some of them, which I think are good. I dined with him, a pleasant neighbour, Mr. Alcock, coming in. The dinner consisted of a fine roast goose. The poor bird might

---

[1] Bright now took full advantage of his release from the responsibilities of office. He spent most of the remaining months of the year either at home, receiving visits from members of his family, or in the Lake District or on the Tweed, and his daily entry in the notebook becomes for the most part a mere record of movements.

[2] The Battle of Tel-el-Kebir, fought on September 13. Arabi Pasha was captured on the 14th, and Sir Garnet Wolseley occupied Cairo.

have been vain could it have heard the praises lavished upon it. Mr. Alcock drove me to the station.

"Going up to Mr. Harding's, I called in Clarendon Square to look upon No. 20, the house in which I spent many weeks in the year 1841 with my sweet young wife, and where she died on the 10th of Sept. in that year. The house is now not occupied, and I could not get in; but I lingered outside, dwelling with much sadness on the grief which, tho' so long past, is often present with me.

"[*November* 3.] Long and singular letter from Valentine Durrant, author of 'Cheveley Novels,' asking for help; his wants too great for my means. House till after midnight: spoke on proposal for all members to enter protests on the Journals of the House when debate closed by the new rule.

"[6*th*.] Letter from Albert telling me of his engagement to Edith Shawcross.

"[16*th*.] My birthday. How fast the years run on as they become few!

"[17*th*.] Evening with the Alfred Tylors, 22, Queen Anne's Gate. My dear Willie has engaged himself to his daughter Isabella M. Tylor. A pleasant evening: the young people very happy, and the parents of the young lady very kind. I much hope this unexpected event may prove all I could wish for in regard to my dear boy.

"[27*th*.] House: debate on 'Grand Committees.' Bad news from Dublin: murders of members of secret societies.

"[29*th*.] Dined with H. Yates Thompson, 26, Bryanston Square. Small party: Sir H. Thompson, eminent surgeon, Col. Lyttleton—home from Egypt, Madame Novikoff—Russian. Walked home with Lyttleton. He is the brother of Lady Frederick Cavendish; talk about her and her sore trouble.

"[30*th*.] Letter from my nephew, Walter McLaren, telling me of his marriage engagement. The matrimonial fever seems very prevalent in our family circle.

"[*December* 29, *at Llandudno*.] Drove to the lighthouse: the wind so strong, did not go round the Head. Visited the little church, and the *little grave*; 18 years have passed since that sad time.

"Geo. Dixon and R. W. Dale from Birmingham came over to discuss question of members' usual meeting. Agreed not to hold the meeting at present, especially as I am expected to be in Birmingham at Whitsuntide. This is a relief to me. Our Birmingham affairs just now are rather 'mixed,' and the future is not very clearly seen."

CHAPTER XVII

REFORM AND THE HOUSE OF LORDS

I

CLOSE as was the agreement between Bright and Chamberlain in domestic politics, it did not bridge the chasm that separated their ideas of foreign policy. Chamberlain had never shared Bright's non-intervention principles. In the General Election of 1859, when a young man of 23, he had supported Dyke-Acland, who stood as a "Liberal-Conservative" against Bright and Scholefield in Birmingham. They had, it is true, acted together on Majuba. But the division between them on Imperialism in general was fundamental.

The rift reached the surface over Egypt. Chamberlain in a speech at Ashton cast scorn upon "the ignoble doctrine of non-intervention." Bright thought it Palmerstonian stuff, and would have none of it. "I can have no part in it, and shall denounce it when I am forced to speak upon it," he wrote to Dixon. "I do not want to assail the Government, or to get into open conflict with my colleagues; still less to create any difficulty with my friends in Birmingham. And yet how to escape it I cannot see if I stand on the same platform with Mr. Chamberlain at this moment." He protested strongly in a letter to Gladstone against the execution of the sentence of death pronounced by a court martial on Arabi Pasha. Gladstone seemed inclined to let things take their course. "I value your reputation almost as my own," said Bright, "and hope it may have no stain upon it in connexion with the fate of Arabi and his supporters in the Egyptian revolution." Counsels of moderation were heeded: Arabi went into exile in Ceylon instead of standing against a wall.

When Whitsuntide came and the visit to Birmingham, the mutations of politics had shifted the emphasis from Egypt back to England. The demands of the British democracy for reform and the new situation in Ireland were now paramount over the grievances of the Fellaheen,

493

and the weight of the speeches made by Bright and Chamberlain rested upon home and not upon foreign affairs.

Two days before going to London for the opening of the session of 1883, Bright made his will. The other personal event of importance that spring was his acceptance of the Freedom of Glasgow.

"[*February* 13, 1883.] *Signed my will*: witnesses, Geo. Kale, carpet manager, and Fredrk. Lye, a clerk in our office. Some relief that this duty is performed. It has caused me much thought and some anxiety. My daughters Helen and Mary are acquainted with contents of the Will, and are satisfied with it. I intend that Albert shall see it.

"[16*th*.] Lady Stanley's: party of teachers of Board Schools. Pleasant conversation with many of them on their great work. Their zeal and their enthusiasm very interesting to witness. 56 years this day since I left school in the year 1827. How time has passed!

"[17*th*.] Dined with Sir W. Harcourt. After dinner he. read to me telegrams from Dublin of the informer Carey's evidence on the murders in the Phœnix Park last summer.[1]

"[22*nd*.] House: speech of W. E. Forster on Irish Crime, and charges against Parnell and the ruffians who act with him and for him. Home after midnight.

"[24*th*.] Dined with Mrs. Drummond: Sir Leopold McClintock, Arctic explorer, one of the party.

"[25*th*.] Home afternoon and evening, making some notes for Glasgow University speech; subject difficult—too much matter crowding upon me.

[1] On the morning of February 17, James Carey, instead of standing in the dock with the other prisoners charged with complicity in the Phœnix Park murders, appeared in the witness-box as Queen's Evidence, saved his own neck, got five men hanged and three sent to penal servitude for life, and revealed to a horrified world the secret story of the murder society known as the "Invincibles." The Government sent Carey to South Africa for his own safety, but the Invincibles had marked him down. He was shot dead before he could land at Cape Town. O'Donnell, who killed him, was brought to England and executed at Newgate. There was no connexion between the Invincibles and the Land League, and in his terrible indictment of Parnell (mentioned in the next extract quoted) Forster specifically acquitted him of responsibility for their crimes. But the Land League had stood by and watched iniquities committed upon landlords and upon tenants who did not obey its orders, without lifting a finger even to prevent murder. Parnell was crushed. He refused to reply that night. Next day he rode off on the assertion that the House of Commons had no jurisdiction over him: he was responsible to Ireland only.

"[*March* 3.] A week of fine weather, very cheerful. At the Club, looked up some historical facts which may be useful for the Glasgow speech. Home: read several of Mr. Robertson's sermons (of Brighton). Some very striking.

"[8*th*.] Home 12 o'clock. Streets so slippery, had to leave my cab in Jermyn St. and to walk home. Some snow last night, and frost to-day; difficult for omnibus and cab horses, poor things.

"[9*th*.] Engaged on notes for Glasgow speech. House: time wasted by needless talk. Conversation with Geo. Trevelyan on Irish affairs and difficulties. Spoke to Mr. Gladstone. He seems cheerful. His holiday at Cannes has been of great service to him.

"[10*th*.] Dined with Mr. Chamberlain. Lords Kimberley and Sudeley there; Sir W. Wedderburn; Yates of the *World* paper there: rather surprised to meet him.

"[13*th*.] Malcolm McColl came in about proposed degree at Glasgow. A man of great activity of mind. There is another Malcolm McColl, also a clergyman, whose speeches and doings are often attributed to the other, who is wishful to have the degree that he may be distinguished from the one who bears his name but is not of the same character. It is a curious reason for desiring to be made LL.D. of Glasgow University. Wrote to-day to W. N. Molesworth to ask if he would like to have the degree conferred on him.

"[16*th*.] Last evening, at 3 min. past 9, heard explosion at Govt. offices in Parlt. St.—dynamite; supposed Fenian outrage.[1]

"[21*st*.] To Glasgow by Midland train from Bolton. Albert with me: a good journey. At ½ past 4 met, at the St. Enoch Station, by Mr. Tennant and the Lord Provost. A small dinner party at Mr. Tennant's.

"[22*nd*.] To St. Andrew's Hall: a very fine room and a great audience. First ceremony: admitting to degree of LL.D. I was first 'capped,' as the ceremony is called. After others had been 'capped,' I took the Chair and began my speech. The hall is good to speak in; the audience was attentive; and I spoke with ease and freedom—and the whole passed off better than I had feared.

[1] At the Local Government Board Offices. This outrage and the dynamite campaign of the following year were the result of the propaganda of violence conducted by Patrick Ford in the *Irish World* of New York, who called upon Irishmen to lay the cities of England in ruin. The Explosive Substances Bill, to which Bright refers on April 9, was a drastic measure, carried through both Houses in a single day. It provided terrible penalties for dynamite conspirators.

"Afterwards, to the house of Dr. Caird, the Principal, where a University Court was held, at which I was supposed to preside—only six present—to appoint some examiners.

"Then to a Hall in the College, where we had an elegant lunch, and I had to thank those present for drinking my health.

"Evening a dinner party of 20 at Mr. Tennant's house.

"[23rd.] At 1 o'clock to City Hall to receive Freedom of the City. A large meeting, the Lord Provost in the Chair. His speech very good, only far too complimentary. The 'Freedom' is given in a box of silver-gilt, of beautiful workmanship.

"I spoke for half an hour or more, apparently to the satisfaction of the audience. Lord Rosebery was there and spoke well, paying me some compliments. Afterwards, to the Council Rooms to another elegant lunch, the Lord Provost presiding, where I had again to return thanks.

"Evening: went by train to Helensburgh, down the Clyde, to dine with the Lord Provost. A party at table of 28. His house most elegantly decorated and furnished. Returned by special train soon after 10 o'clock.

"[24th.] With Mr. Tennant to Mr. Annan, the photographer, to sit for a portrait to be grouped with some of the students. Then called on Mr. Maclehose, publisher and bookseller, a fine elderly man in a large and very beautiful shop. He gave me 3 vols. of poetry— David Gray, Hedderwick, and Stoddart.

"This morning Albert went home by 10.14 train. I left Glasgow at 12, Mr. Tennant and the Lord Provost coming to the station; a crowd of kind friends also there.

"On to Coatbridge, where Janet Hamilton, poetess and essayist, lived and died. Mr. Wright met me, and went with me to see the remaining daughter of Janet Hamilton, who repeated to me her mother's beautiful ballad, *Effie*. We then visited the drinking fountain, a memorial of the remarkable woman who had lived and died in a small house of two rooms just opposite and overlooking the park.

"At the station was a crowd of men anxious to see me, and scores of them got on the step of the carriage to shake hands with me before the train left the station. Mr. Wright was very kind. I took tea with him and his brother and sister.

"Much pleased with my visit to Coatbridge. The place where Mrs. Hamilton lived and worked and wrote and died should not be forgotten.

"Edinbro' at 4 o'clock and drove to Newington House, where I found my dear sister Priscilla better than I had expected.

"[*26th.*] By 10.30 train, Midland, and reached home before 9 o'clock. A crowd at the station to see me off. The Scotch are very political and very Liberal, and they seem all to be my friends.

"[*27th.*] The weather has been very severe for 3 weeks past, and my cold seems unwilling to leave me. But my Glasgow expedition has passed off well, and I feel greatly relieved now my duty is discharged. I have endeavoured to speak the truth on great questions, and hope some minds have been stirred to consider how far a true patriotism can be dissociated from an observance of the moral law.

"[*28th.*] To Carshalton: marriage of my dear boy Willie. A large party. The church crowded. Canon Farrar officiated in a manner satisfactory and impressive. The bride—Isabella McIvor Tylor, daughter of Alfred and Isabella Tylor, of Shepley House, Carshalton. Was sorry the marriage was at the church, but did not feel bound to interfere with the wish of the bride in this matter. She is a good girl, and my son may well be content with his prospects. About 50 sat down to the wedding breakfast. The day passed pleasantly. At ½ past 3 the 'happy pair' left us on their way to Dover.

"[*April 5.*] House: Budget. Childers's speech very good and clear. In the Lobby, Professors Stewart and Browne, from Boston for Liberia, as teachers for the Africans. They are coloured. Pleasant and intelligent.

"Some of my friends from Birmingham,—W. Kenrick, R. Chamberlain, Powell Williams and F. Schnadhorst, on the 'celebration' arrangements.[1] They propose banquet, Town Hall; great meeting Bingley Hall; and Mayor's breakfast. Also to invite Mr. Gladstone and Lord Hartington, to which I objected. They have too much to do, might not wish to seem to slight me, and yet could not reasonably be expected to come. I urged that they should not be troubled. I remonstrated with them as doing too much on my behalf and as making their kindness oppressive to me.

"Some interest and alarm created by arrest of explosion conspirators in London and Birmingham.

"[*7th.*] Club: spoke in answer to attacks on proposed Channel Tunnel.

"[*9th.*] With Philip, walk round the Serpentine—good exercise. House: new Bill on Explosives—new crime and new law.

[1] The celebration of his 25th year as Member for Birmingham.

"[10th.] Dined with Willie and his wife: their rooms or *flat* in Victoria Street not so inviting as a *house* would be.

"[12th.] House at 12. Standing Committee on Law: Criminal Appeal Bill. A new method of getting thro' business of the House, and likely to be very useful. Home early. Read J. C. Dyer's memoirs of himself; his youth in America very interesting; would make a pleasant book, useful for young people.

"[17th.] To Mrs. Müller's, 86, Portland Place: evening party before wedding of my nephew, Walter McLaren, and Eva Müller, fixed for to-morrow. A large party and a handsome supper provided.

"[18th.] Westminster Meeting: Wedding very nice and quiet and simple. Bevan Braithwaite spoke most acceptably. To lunch at 86, Portland Place, and saw the newly-married pair off at 3.30 for Canterbury. Dined with Lord Reay in Gt. Stanhope St.: a very pleasant party. Among guests, Lord Thurloe, whose opinions on Land question very advanced: thinks many great estates and few landowners a serious peril to the nation.

"[26th.] Grand Committee on Criminal Appeal Bill. Spoke shortly in favour of Bill and condemning irregularity and severity of sentences. House: Affirmation Bill—remarkable speech from Mr. Gladstone.

"[27th.] House: 'Local option' resolution of Sir Wilfrid Lawson carried by increased majority. Dined with Sir Jas. Caird, but returned to the House to vote.

"[28th.] Dined at Devonshire Club in honour of Jno. K. Cross, M.P. for Bolton, who has accepted office as Under-Secretary for India. Had to speak, as usual. Lord Hartington in the Chair. A pleasant evening.

"[29th.] Read some of 'John Inglesant.'

"[30th.] Notes for speech at 'Liberation' meeting; not easy to satisfy myself.

"[*May* 1.] House till 7. Then to dine with Jno. Pender in Arlington St. Dinner party nearly all artists of eminence. Sat next to Mr. Sant. House full of costly pictures. House old and interesting. Horace Walpole lived here and wrote many of his letters in it. My old friend Edwd. Ellice lived in it before Mr. Pender.

"[2nd.] Evening, to Tabernacle, to meeting of Liberation Society. I was Chairman. A remarkable meeting as to size and quality. I spoke about an hour, criticizing course of Church, and especially of its Bishops, on important public questions. Many marks of appreciation and friendship on the part of my friends. Mr. Illingworth and Dick Peddie came with me in a 4-wheel cab to the Reform Club. As Mr. Illingworth was about to pay the cabman, the latter was unwilling to receive his fare, evidently from his sympathy with us, and, turning to me, he said, 'I am a Christian, and I hope we shall meet above.' I regret I did not ask his name. Mr. Illingworth prevailed upon him to take the amount of his fare. The incident seemed to me worthy of being remembered. I thought it remarkable and very touching.

"A great dinner, at the Aquarium this evening, of the new National Liberal Club—near 2,000 in number. Mr. Gladstone's speech in defence of the policy of the Govt. He was, I learn, recd. with great enthusiasm. I was not present, being engaged at the Liberation meeting.[1]

"[8th.] A note from Mr. Gladstone, asking me to dine with him this evening, and to breakfast with him on Thursday to meet Mr. Hutton of the *Spectator*, whose article on my Liberation speech he refers to. I am engaged to dine elsewhere, but I hope to breakfast with him on Thursday. Dined with Lady Lefevre, 41, Seymour St. Lord Eversley there, in his 90th year. A very remarkable man, tall, handsome, in good health, cheerful and active in mind. As Mr. Shaw-Lefevre he was Speaker of the House of Commons.[2]

"[9th.] Called on Dr. Andrew Clark to consult him on giddiness and discomfort. Nothing important, he said; advised a return to the living recommended to me 10 years ago; gave me a prescription in case I should not be better in a few days.

"[10th.] To breakfast with Mr. Gladstone at 10. Small party: Professor Blackie from Edinbro', Mr. Hutton of the *Spectator*, Mr. Stanton, earnest clergyman from East of London. Talk on many subjects—Church, perhaps, chiefly—my recent speech, and question of disestablishment, etc. After breakfast, spoke to Mr. Gladstone in favour of pension for Wm. Pengelly, of Torquay,[3] and of C.B. for Mr. Engleheart of the Duchy Council. Mr. Gladstone apparently in good health.

"[24th.] Law Committee: obstruction by Lord R. Churchill, and Govt. business impossible with such men.

[1] The foundation-stone of the Club building in Whitehall Place was not laid till November 4, 1884.

[2] From 1839 to 1857. Lord Eversley died at 96 in the year 1888.

[3] The eminent scientist who directed the work of the British Association Committee in the exploration of Kent's Cavern.

"[*30th, at Rochdale.*] Albert's wedding, Water St. Unitarian Chapel. Streets crowded and much friendship shown. Ceremony very simple, and all conducted in a manner very becoming. To Foxholes to breakfast, or dinner. Party near 70 present. Some short speeches, appropriate. I said a few words, which my children seemed to like. Albert and his bride left at 4 o'clock and went to Rowsley in Derbyshire.

"[*June 5.*] Remained at home till the 4th of June, and then to London. Our parlourmaid, Mary Storey, very ill, dangerously so, suffering from diphtheria. Dr. Blackley, from Manchester, to see her, along with Tom Hayle, our young doctor, and a nurse obtained from the Manchester Infirmary. I left home with much uneasiness at the poor girl's state, and with much fear as to the result of her sore illness. Grand Committee on Criminal Code.

"[*6th.*] Notes for speech at Birmingham: difficult to fix upon anything.

"[*7th.*] Heard this morning a good account of the invalid at 'One Ash.' A great relief to me.

"[*8th.*] Evening at home, considering notes for my Birmingham speeches. Read a note from Sir F. Bramwell suggesting that I should give evidence before the Channel Tunnel Committee. I could give them no facts—only arguments to meet the childish fears of the military witnesses."

2

On June 13, Bright had represented Birmingham in the House of Commons for exactly twenty-five years, and the City celebrated the anniversary in several days of festivity.

This occasion acquired a more than local and personal notoriety. Both Bright and Chamberlain made speeches which reverberated loudly in Downing Street, in the House of Commons, and at Windsor. Bright accused the Conservatives in Parliament of deliberate obstruction and of allying themselves for this purpose with the Irish members, whom he described once more as "rebels" who broke their oath of allegiance by association with the enemies of the country. Northcote raised the question of "privilege," and there was a debate (on the 18th). Bright had no difficulty in rebutting the charge that he had infringed Parliamentary rule or transgressed privilege. The incident evoked a characteristic ratiocination from Gladstone which Lord Morley gives in full ("Gladstone," Book VIII, Chap. 8).

Chamberlain's adventure was far more serious. He had declared at the Bingley Hall meeting for manhood suffrage, equal electoral districts, payment of members, and disestablishment of the Church. He had spoken of the "so-called" rights of property. He had pointed out that representatives of royalty were not there to do honour to Mr. Bright—and that they were not missed!

This was Jacobinical language, said Lord Salisbury. It introduced "a new, a sinister, a most terrible feature in our constitutional history." The Queen, who had mildly disapproved of Chamberlain's "They toil not, neither do they spin" speech, was really angry about this one. It tried Gladstone almost as high. He had to make explanations to Sir Henry Ponsonby: and it offended his doctrine of Cabinet responsibility. Chamberlain was asked to modify his tone in a forthcoming speech to the Cobden Club. Instead, he declared that Radicals would not be bribed to silence by places. It was almost a Cabinet crisis. In the end Dilke smoothed it over.

"[*June* 11.] In saloon carriage to Birmingham to Small Heath Station. Met by the Mayor and Mr. Geo. Dixon and a crowd of friends. Presented with a Gold Medal to commemorate the week's celebration. Procession formed. From 1 o'clock to near 5 going thro' the great town; crowds everywhere. Streets full, windows full, flags, handkerchiefs, music, shouting, cheering.

"At Aston public offices, at window to see the procession pass. The whole affair extraordinary from multitude of people, and from their excitement and enthusiasm. The good order everywhere admirable.

"To 'The Dales,' Geo. Dixon's house. Small party, not more than 8 to dinner.

"[12*th*.] At 'The Dales,' quiet all day. Two or three friends up to breakfast. The garden lovely. Small party again to dinner.

"[13*th*.] Quiet day. Evening: great meeting in Bingley Hall. Estimated 20,000 there. More than 150 Addresses from clubs and towns presented, deputation passing before me on the platform. Mr. Dixon spoke briefly; then Mr. Dale; then myself for about 50 minutes. Afterwards Chamberlain—strong 'Radical' speech as to Reform Bill required. Costly present of service silver and glass exhibited. I am alarmed at the cost and beauty of presents.

"[14*th*.] Quiet day. Evening: banquet in the Town Hall: Mayor in the Chair. Lord Granville spoke to my health. I spoke for nearly an hour, and with great freedom and acceptance by my friends.

"[15th.] Mayor's breakfast in Council Rooms. I spoke for nearly an hour on Suez Canal and Channel Tunnel, urging moderation in dealing with the French on the Canal question and reason in dealing with the proposed railway under the Straits of Dover. After breakfast uncovered statue to our lost friend J. S. Wright, in heavy rain. Then meeting in Town Hall, where I spoke shortly in presenting the statue to the Mayor and Corporation of Birmingham. Called on my old and kind friends Wm. Middlemore and Henry Manton, the former old, the latter recovering from long and severe illness. Called at *Daily Post* office.

"[16th.] Breakfast with Committee of Junior Liberal Club; 30 present. Conversation-speech, political, and advising young men, for 45 minutes. Then to Snow Hill Station. Again saloon carriage for Stratford. Many friends to see me off, with cheers from a goodly company on the platform. Pleasant to be at Stratford again after such a week, much relieved in my mind, and much impressed with the wonderful kindness of the troops of friends I have seen during the days I have spent in Birmingham.

"[18th.] Ten train, same saloon carriage, to London. Letters alarmingly numerous. One informed me that Stafford Northcote would move in the House that I was guilty of a breach of privilege in remarks at the close of the banquet speech on Thursday last. The charge was ridiculous, but he made it, and I had to reply. The charge was absurd, and failed. It was childish, and was thought so by men of his own party.

"[20th.] Dined 52, Green St., with Mrs. Agar Ellis, whom I met at Chatsworth some years ago. She is separated from her husband: quarrel about bringing up of her 3 daughters—whether Catholic with her, or Protestant with him.

"Small party. Lord and Lady Lathom—she, daughter of late Lord Clarendon, so had much pleasant talk with her. Mr. Chaplin, M.P., Lady Churchill, Mr. Petre, and Mr. Grenfell. Mrs. Ellis told me she painted at South Kensington to help her means of living. She had high connexions and is, I think, a daughter of the late Lord Camoys.

"[28th.] The Lords have thrown out Marriage Bill: a monstrous cruelty to hundreds of families in this country. The Bishops have done it. Their day will come.

"[29th.] To breakfast with G. W. Smalley of the *New York Tribune*. Mr. Howell and Mr. Robinson, Americans, there; also

Lord Reay, Lyulph Stanley, and Geo. Trevelyan. Much pleasant conversation—States, Ireland, Emigration, etc.

"[*July* 3.] Dined with F. Leveson-Gower in South Audley St. Mrs. Jeune there, Duchess of Leeds, and Lady Dorothy Nevill, who is amusing and intelligent as in past years.

"[4*th.*] Exeter Hall: Meeting of East India Association; paper on Land Banks in India by Sir W. Wedderburn. As Chairman I spoke briefly in introducing the subject of the meeting. Hope the plan may do good to the suffering ryots of India.

"[6*th.*] Dined at the National Liberal Club with my dear boy Willie: a party of 8 and very pleasant. Mr. Thorndyke Rice, of *North American Review,* there. House: voted against Woman Suffrage, a proposition to which I am much opposed. Walked up with Mr. Leake about 1 o'clock; a lovely night.

"[10*th.*] Bought salmon rod, winch, and lines and flies, and sent them to my son-in-law, Richd. Curry, at Stratford, for his Scotch excursion; cost £6.0.0. Dined with Sir Jas. Caird. Met Sir Richd. Meade, late resident at Hyderabad and other native Indian Courts. He seems to have sympathy for Indian people.

"[11*th.*] Call from Lalmohun Ghose from Calcutta on proposed meeting to support Lord Ripon and his liberal policy.[1]

"[12*th.*] Mr. Chesson and Mr. Ghose called on the proposed India meeting. Willie called. Went with him to the Fishery Exhibition: extensive and interesting.

"[18*th.*] Afternoon, to Norwood College for the Blind. Witnessed exercises of the students—races, drill, gymnastics. Meeting in a large tent and a crowded audience. Duke of Westminster presided: his new and young wife with him, very nice and kind-looking, both apparently very happy.[2] I spoke for 20 minutes, urging the claim of the College to public support. My audience seemed pleased. I then gave the prizes to the students, boys and girls. The scene and the ceremony were very interesting. The Duke handed diplomas to those entitled to them. I have rarely spent an afternoon more pleasantly.

[1] Lord Ripon, who had succeeded Lord Dufferin as Viceroy in 1880, was prosecuting a policy of administrative reform and encouragement of the native population, and developing local government. In the Ilbert Bill, of which he was the real author, he gave district magistrates in the provinces the same jurisdiction over Europeans as they already had in the Presidency towns—a policy foreshadowed by Macaulay's action many years before in the Mofussil.

[2] *née* the Hon. Catherine Cavendish, daughter of Lord Chesham.

"[*20th.*] Dined 37, Wimpole St., with Mr. and Mrs. Jeune. Lady Ely there, whom I met at Nice long ago. She is often in attendance on the Queen, but how greatly changed in appearance.

"My speech at the Blind College seems to have pleased many people. I hope it will have increased the interest of the public in the condition of blind children.

"[*28th.*] L. Ghose called on India meeting; also Lord Provost of Edinbro'. Revising proofs for Cassell and Co. Not pleasant work. Obscurity better than this notoriety.

"[*29th.*] Afternoon, read 'Ben Hur: a Tale of the Christ,' an interesting American work.[1]

"[*August* 1.] India Meeting, Willis's Rooms; myself Chairman. Spoke easily and to my own fair satisfaction. Other speeches very good: case well treated, audience very crowded, and most attentive. Meeting will, I think, do much good. Evening, dined with Sir C. Forster, M.P. A large party. M. Waddington, French Minister, there. Speaking to me, he said, 'You know why I have come, and what it means—goodwill and peace.' I said we were all pleased to see him here again He brought me up here in his carriage, and was very friendly. Of the party, Mr. Gladstone, the Lord Chancellor, Childers, Chamberlain, Carlingford, Mr. Speaker, and others. I sat between the Speaker and Sir Thos. Brassey.

"[*2nd.*] Called on Bruce Joy, sculptor, and on Haines, photographer, in connexion with the Birmingham statue, which I wish were not to be proceeded with. The model seems very good.

"[*6th.*] Dined with Mr. Childers, 117, Piccadilly. Small party: French Minister, M. Waddington, Cardinal Howard, and Geo. Trevelyan. The Cardinal is a tall powerful man, more like a Life-Guardsman, as he formerly was, than a priest. Talks a great deal, and when others are talking, and does not give the impression of the character one would like to see in the eminent Christian professor. He more corresponds with one's idea of a dignitary of a political institution. He was dressed in a long coat and in red stockings. Perhaps it is wrong, but I always feel a dislike of these high priests of Rome. I have a sense that they are insincere, and the representatives of a system injurious to religion and to freedom.

"[*7th.*] Called on Miss M. R. Darby Smith, of Philadelphia, descendant of Jas. Logan, secretary and friend of William Penn. A remarkable woman; traveller; has lived much in Europe; is acquainted

[1] General Lew Wallace's popular romance had been published in 1880.

with many persons of note; has notes from and photographs of many of them.

"[8*th*.] Read interesting book from Miss Darby Smith—her recollections of Countess Guiccioli or Boissy, the friend of Lord Byron, and of Count Waldeck, who lived to be 110 years old. Both narratives very interesting. Yesterday and to-day, rain; anxiety about the weather and the crops.

"[9*th*.] Reading Memoirs of Sir J. Bowring. Interesting: a life of wonderful activity; travel; many languages; recollections of many men of eminence.[1]

"[10*th*.] Called on Madame de Novikoff at Holloway's Hotel, Down St. Long conversation on politics and political persons. Spoke of her 'Life' of Scobeloff, the Russian General. I said I did not like such men, who delight in war. She was rather shocked, and said he was a generous man, and gave some particulars.

"Asked her how she could leave her husband and son. She said her husband knew she was 'cracked about England,' and he did not object to her coming here for 3 or 4 months.[2]

"Dined with David Ainsworth, 25, Pont St., M.P. for Cumberland. Dr. Collier, eminent Unitarian minister from New York, there. A large man; good head and handsome face; from Yorkshire and a blacksmith by trade, which he followed for some years in the States. He thinks Protection is breaking down, but some arguments influence artisan class. Mrs. Ainsworth much against the 'Women's rights' ideas as to suffrage. Evening, read, till 2 o'clock, F. Seebohm's remarkable book on ancient land arrangements in this country.

"[14*th*.] Home early and finished reading F. Seebohm's interesting book on 'English Village Communities,' a work of much research and labour. Read also pamphlet on wheat supply from India—a great question, demanding attention of the Govt.; of great interest for India and for England.

"[15*th*.] To Mr. Mayall, the photographer, in Bond St. Sat for

[1] Bowring, whose high-handed conduct in Hong-Kong preluded the second Chinese War and had received Bright's severest censure, was nevertheless a personality of great interest to him. Bowring was a Free Trader whose advocacy of tariff for revenue only (in the *Westminster Review*) long ante-dated the Corn Law campaign. He said he knew 200 languages and could speak 100. He certainly had a deep acquaintance with over forty, and was one of the greatest linguists who ever lived.

[2] The confidante of many English politicians. Gladstone corresponded with her largely during the Eastern crisis.

several photos by the electric light. The light intense, and the heat from it considerable. A young lady artist made notes of my complexion —colour of hair, eyes, eyebrows—to enable her to colour the photo portraits. The whole process rather amusing.

"[*28th.*] To Birmingham, to the house of my friend Wm. White, Mayor this year.

"[*29th.*] Breakfast at Cobden Coffee House, which I opened. A large party and some interesting speeches on the Temperance movement. Afterwards, at 1 o'clock, Town Hall meeting. I spoke for near an hour on Temperance and proposals for legislation upon it. Lunched with the Mayor and came home the same evening.

"[*September* 27.¹] Lady Lawson came home to-day. A family of 8 children, six at home. Eldest son home from Oxford; two sons at Harrow; 4 daughters, and one very young boy at home. A pleasant and very lively party; the mother handsome and healthy, a model in her house. Sir Wilfrid had some talk on Temperance question. He is very liberal, and in most things to be admired. He might have been brought up among Friends.

"[*October* 17.] To Leeds, to John Barran, M.P., Chapel Allerton Hall. Evening to meeting and conversazione in Town Hall. Spoke very briefly.

"[*18th.*] Town Hall meeting, Reform. Was in the Chair. Spoke for an hour or more on Reform and mode of proceeding.²

"[*19th.*] Breakfast party at Mr. Barran's. Home by train at one o'clock. Mr. Barran very kind; his wife very kind and sensible. Two daughters add much to the charm of the house. Weather unfavourable; much rain.

"[*31st, at Kelso.*] Fast day here. Did not go down to the river.

¹ At Brayton, Carlisle, the residence of Sir Wilfrid Lawson, after a fortnight in Scotland.

² The Leeds Conference sounded the first note of advance in the new campaign which ended with the enfranchisement of the agricultural labourer in the Act of 1884. Bright was in his element in a battle for Reform, and he made history at Leeds. Foreseeing that the House of Lords would resist any scheme which could satisfy democratic ambitions, he put forward in embryo the policy of a limited veto which, twenty-eight years later, was embodied in the Parliament Act. The Crown could not now reject a Bill sent up to it. Why, he asked, should not the power of the Peers be limited in the same way? "Why not enact that if the Peers have rejected a Bill once and it has been considered in a subsequent session by the Commons, and, after due deliberation, has been again sent up to the Peers, then the Peers must pass it on and it will receive the Royal assent and will become law?" This was the germ of the Parliament Act.

Did not wish to offend any of those who think the day should be kept as Sunday is kept in Scotland.

"[*November* 27, *at Llandudno.*] Very fine day. Walked up to the little church on the Great Ormes Head to see the little grave. Stood where his dear mother and I have so often stood, and where our hearts have been bowed with sorrow. Now I am alone. The sorrow is there still, but there is none to share it with me. The walk was soothing, for the morning has been lovely.

"[*December* 1.] Pleasant day. Called upon poor Mrs. Hughes and took some supplies of tea and sugar, etc. Her cheerfulness and resignation unchanged. She has been 19 years confined to her bed. To visit her is a lesson from which all may learn.

"[19*th.*[1]] Home comfortable, tho' lonely. The dogs gave me a warm reception, not barking, but manifesting their sympathy in their doggish manner."

3

In an age of universal suffrage, when the citizen finds it more diffi-cult to avoid the franchise than to attain it, the fierce resistance aroused by the mild and cautious Franchise Bill of 1884 seems wellnigh incomprehensible. Bright had during many years pleaded hard for such a measure. It did but extend to the dwellers in the country a degree of citizenship already enjoyed for seventeen years by the dwellers in towns. It brought two millions of voters on to the rolls—all rate-payers or occupiers with as large a "stake in the country" as their means would allow them to possess. But they included a large proportion of agricultural labourers. The labourers on the land had hitherto been voteless, "dumb driven cattle." Gladstone's offence was that he pro-posed to raze the last citadel of feudalism and to complete the slow revolution which in fifty years transformed Parliament from a mirror of the land-owning classes into a reflection, more or less accurate, of all the social strata.

He held counsel with Bright while preparing the Bill, and produced a plan large and democratic enough to satisfy the old Radical, whose

---

[1] Returning from a visit to Yorkshire. First to Mr. Isaac Holden, M.P., at Oakworth House, Keighley, where he had made a speech at luncheon, given away prizes at the Mechanics' Institute, and received an address from the Liberal Association. Then to Gawthorpe Hall, Sir U. Kay Shuttleworth's place, where the Chancellor of the Exchequer (Childers) and other Liberal politicians had gathered.

earnest support weighed heavily in the struggle with the House of Lords at the end of the year.

"[*January* 26, 1884, *at Rochdale.*] Mr. Blake Wirgman, an artist, here to take a portrait of me in the Library for the use of the *Graphic* paper. Sat at least 3 hours, and was rather tired. I wish I had finished with photographers, artists, sculptors and interviewers and newspaper people. They have given me not a little trouble—and will not leave me 'obscure.'

"[*29th.*] By 11 train, for Birmingham at 3.10. To Highbury, Mr. Chamberlain's house, and with him to the Town Hall after an early dinner. Great meeting; very satisfactory.

"[*30th.*] Some of our friends to breakfast. Evening to Town Hall, 'Forward Club' meeting. My speech chiefly on Land question, with some criticism of the American Mr. George, author of a book, 'Progress and Poverty.' [1]

"[*February* 5, *in London.*] Felt dull, and unwilling to go down to the House. First news there of defeat of Baker Pacha. If true, very serious for the Govt. Will the Egyptian blunder destroy the Govt. and break up the Party, as I told Lord Hartington I thought it would? [2]

"[*11th.*] House: Bradlaugh Case. Disgraceful scene. Bradlaugh much more of a gentleman that many of his opponents. [3] Home before one o'clock.

"[*12th.*] House: Vote of Censure. Great speech from Mr. Gladstone in defence of Egyptian policy. Northcote's speech moderate and somewhat feeble.

"[*18th.*] Dined with Sir W. Harcourt: small party; Mr. Gladstone, Hartington and Geo. Trevelyan from the House. I sat between Mr. Gladstone and the Duchess of Manchester. Some confidential

---

[1] "Progress and Poverty," the first of Henry George's series of treatises on the theory of the Single Tax, appeared in 1879.

[2] The disaster to Colonel Valentine Baker, who, having relieved Suakim, was overwhelmed on February 4 by the Mahdi's forces while attempting to relieve Tokar. Gordon was at this time on his way to Khartoum, with instructions to evacuate the Soudan. He entered the town on the 18th.

[3] Bradlaugh walked up to the table, supported by Labouchere and Burt, and proposed to administer the oath to himself. Northcote moved to exclude him, and he voted in three divisions in order that, by suing him for penalties, the Attorney-General might bring the issue into the Law Courts again. He then took the Chiltern Hundreds and was re-elected for Northampton by an increased majority. Bradlaugh did not, however, succeed in taking his seat in this Parliament.

talk with Mr. G. on Franchise Bill and redistribution prospects; also on the unhappy Egyptian business.

"[21st.] House: Bradlaugh exclusion again. Tory Party persist in their scandalous course. Dined with Lord Granville: large party. M. Waddington, French Minister, there; also M. Clemenceau, Member of the French Chamber—a very pleasant man, interesting in conversation and character. Lord Bramwell sat next to me at dinner; sensible and amusing; his conversation instructive.

"[24th.] Westminster Meeting morning; large meeting. Afternoon, home quiet, reading. In the evening, *Paradise Regained*, always with increasing pleasure.

"[25th.] Speaker's retirement.[1] Was not present. Dined with Lord Northbrook, Admiralty. Lord Morley,[2] G. O. Trevelyan, Napier Sturt there. Home with Mrs. Trevelyan in her brougham. Talk after dinner on Free Land. Good sense on this once formidable and forbidden topic.

"[26th.] House: new Speaker chosen. Mr. Whitbread proposed Arthur Peel, M.P. for Warwick; Wm. Rathbone seconded. Arthur Peel spoke and accepted. Mr. Gladstone and Northcote spoke. The whole passed off well. The new Speaker's speech very good. Whitbread very good.

"This morning at 1 o'clock, explosion at Victoria Station: supposed dynamite and Fenian plot. Much damage done, but no one killed.[3]

"[28th.] Franchise Bill. Mr. Gladstone's speech very good. Bill large and complete and satisfactory.[4]

"[*March* 9.] Wrote to Augustine Jones, of the Friends' School, Providence, Rhode Island. My bust placed in their lecture hall. Read Salvation Army book and *Paradise Regained*, and Romans in French Testament.

[1] Sir Henry Brand, the first Lord Hampden.
[2] The 3rd Earl of Morley, Gladstone's Under-Secretary for War. He became Chairman of Committees in the House of Lords in 1889.
[3] The explosion at Victoria was part of a scheme for wrecking four railway stations, the other three being Paddington, Charing Cross and Ludgate Hill. The bomb went off at Victoria only. A man named Daly, formerly a Fenian, and Egan in whose house he had lodged at Birmingham, were tried at Warwick Assizes. Under the provisions of the Explosive Substances Act, Daly was sentenced to penal servitude for life and Egan for twenty years.
[4] The Bill extended the household and lodger franchises from the towns to the counties and increased the number of electors from three millions to five millions.

"[10*th.*] Dined with Sir C. Forster, M.P. Home with Lord Crewe in his carriage. What a funny man he is! Rather weak.

"[11*th.*] Dined with Francis Buxton. His wife is a daughter of Lord Lawrence. Albert Grey and his wife there. Chat with daughter of Lord Portsmouth, Lady Rosamund Christie; intelligent and very pleasant young lady—her mother's daughter, evidently.

"[12*th.*] Dined with Mrs. Drummond, a remarkable old lady, widow of Thos. Drummond, Secy. in Dublin long ago, and much esteemed there. Came away with Sir Arthur Otway, M.P.

"[13*th.*] To Theberton, Suffolk, to the funeral of my old friend and colleague, T. Milner Gibson, who died at Algiers 3 weeks ago.[1] Theberton is near Saxmundham, and is 95 miles from London. A small party from London; a large congregation at the church and round the grave. The two sons of my old friend were there, the younger much distressed. Came back to town by 8 o'clock.

"[16*th.*] Called on Mrs. Milner Gibson. Spoke of my old friend, her late husband. She has joined the Catholic Church and is mostly in Paris. My visit seemed to please her much. Evening, dined with Vaughan. Read them some of the Lancashire dialect, 'Visit to the Great Exhibition.'[2]

"[18*th.*] Read some of new 'Life' of George Fox by A. C. Bickley: the book dedicated to me.

"[19*th.*] Dined with Chamberlain. Sorry to meet there Lord Wolseley. I abhor the profession of the soldier. He is a lively and smart fellow, but does not give the impression of much weight. His opposition to the Channel Tunnel is not a proof of much good sense. Met there also Sir James F. Stephen, the judge, a man of power, but not of sentiment or imagination, and not likely to take the merciful side of a question. Home after 12 o'clock.

"Mr. Escott, editor of the *Fortnightly Review*, there.[3] Is engaged on a History of the House of Commons. I suggested that 'Curiosities of English Legislation' would make an interesting book. He may say something of this in his work.

"[21*st.*] Evening, to meeting of Friends' Institute, Devonshire House, at which I took the Chair and spoke on Libraries and Debating Societies: a large meeting and pleasant evening.

[1] See page 90.
[2] By Oliver Ormerod, whose death is referred to on page 430.
[3] T. H. S. Escott was the second editor of *The Fortnightly Review*, having succeeded John Morley in November, 1882.

"House: Motion to banish Bishops from the House of Lords by Mr. Willis. Debate very interesting. Willis spoke well, Fowler of Wolverhampton admirably. Majority against motion 11: immense Liberal cheering. The Bishops will have some unpleasant reading furnished by this debate. It points to some things to come.

"[22*nd*.] Dined with G. Shaw-Lefevre in Bryanston Square. M. Waddington, French Minister, there. I took down to dinner Mrs. Walter, wife of John Walter, chief proprietor of *The Times* newspaper. She has been in the States and spoke most favourably of Americans, men and women.

"[23*rd*.] Notes for speech on the Franchise Bill. Lord Hartington has asked me to speak to-morrow evening after Lord John Manners, who is to open the debate, and to move an amendment of which he has given notice. I may be ready if opportunity is convenient. Finished reading new 'Life' of Geo. Fox by A. C. Bickley. Very interesting, the latter part especially so.

"[24*th*.] House: Debate, 2nd reading of Franchise Bill. Spoke for an hour, defending the Bill and answering Lord Jno. Manners, dealing especially with question that Ireland should be fairly treated, and maintaining rights conferred and guaranteed by the Act of Union.[1]

"[25*th*.] Dined at Indian (Northbrook) Club: many natives of India there. Lord Reay, Chairman. Spoke with ease and freedom; most kindly recd. by all present. Speech very satisfactory to myself —from my heart full of sympathy for the young Indians present.

"[26*th*.] Dined with Mrs. Jeune, 37, Wimpole St. A large party: Lord and Lady Selborne, Mr. and Mrs. Goschen. I sat between these two ladies. The U.S. Minister was there, Mr. Lowell, Sir H. Mayne, Mr. Reeve of the *Edinburgh Review*, Lady Stanley and others.

"Morning: called on Lady Dorothy Nevill, 45, Charles St., Berkeley Square, a pleasant and very amusing lady. Long chat—an hour or more. Conservative, but thinks their party very stupid on many occasions. In the room, portraits of the Walpole family, to which she belongs.

"[*April* 9.] Up before noon and much better.[2] Many of my friends have called to inquire after me, and paragraphs most unneces-

---

[1] Lord John's amendment was a demand for the production of a Redistribution Scheme along with the Bill—the flank attack afterwards pressed further by the Lords. Ireland played a large part in the debates. Bright argued strongly that Ireland was entitled by the Treaty of Union to a fixed quota of representatives, which could not be diminished without Ireland's consent.

[2] He had suffered for a fortnight from congestion of the lungs.

sarily numerous have been in the newspapers. I have had many presents of flowers, grapes and strawberries, and ought to feel grateful for the sympathy shown me by so many of my friends and acquaintances. My dear girls Mary and Lillie have been here most of the week, and their loving and most kind attention has been a great help to me. No father has more choice and devoted daughters than I have.

"[14th.] Lord Granville called this evening; a pleasant chat with him for half an hour. He was in trouble for the loss, I think, of his sister. We talked of the prospects of the Party, which I fear will suffer greatly from the difficulties in Egypt.

"[15th.] Dear Helen came at 6 o'clock—her company very grateful to me.

"[16th.] To-day we posted more than 100 notes of thanks to my many friends who have called upon me during my recent illness. The newspapers will not permit us to take our occasions of illness with the quiet which obscurity has formerly secured us. A daily paragraph is a daily intrusion, and I wish it could be avoided.

"[17th.] Yesterday we recd. the sad news of the death at Cannes of my brother-in-law, Hadwen Priestman. His singular kindness has much endeared him to all his family and friends.

"[19th.] Calls this morning from Genl. Showers, Indian officer, Newman Hall, Sir Wm. Dunbar, Bart., Sir James Caird, Chas. P. Villiers, M.P. Pleasant conversation with each of them. My son-in-law, Wm. Clark, came last evening to remain here with dear Helen till Monday the 21st.

"[20th.] Calls to-day from Mr. Childers and W. E. Forster. Talk about the coming Budget with the Chancellor of the Exchequer. Forster abrupt and amusing as usual. Weather still cold: still a prisoner here.

"[25th.] Mr. Chamberlain called: talk on questions now pressing on the Govt., Egypt especially.

"[26th.] Dear Helen left me this morning for Bristol and Street. Dear Sophie came in her place. Mr. Gladstone called for ½ an hour—on Egypt, and the Franchise Bill. His great anxiety to force the Bill on. His resolution not to go further in the Soudan or to send a force to Khartoum; impossible at this season. He is looking well—but sees the difficulties which beset his Govt. Egypt is the only ground of the danger.[1] This morning I had a drive round the Regent's Park in Mr.

---

[1] Gordon was beleaguered in Khartoum. The Cabinet, first stunned by Gordon's light-hearted project for appointing Zubair to succeed him as Governor-General of

W. Miller's carriage: exactly a month since I was out last. The day pleasant.

"[*June* 26.] House: 3rd reading of Franchise Bill; no division. A memorable evening.

"[*July* 4.] Calls from Edwd. L. Pierce and his brother Henry, from Boston; also from Henry Roth, from Queensland; also from Mrs. Miller of Lancaster Gate. House: business obstructed by Tories. Home early: read 'Anti-Slavery Sketches'—interesting story of Anti-Slavery agitation and war. A good book for the 4th July reading.

"[8*th.*] Calls: from Mr. Bunting, of the *Contemporary Review*, asking me to write an article on position of House of Lords. Refused to do so, but gave him my opinion—to limit their power of veto to one occasion of Bill from the House of Commons. From Wm. Stigand, Consul at Ragusa. Also from Sir John Gorrie: wishes to be Commissioner in region of New Guinea.

"[9*th.*] To wedding party, 46, Eaton Square. My niece, Beatrice Leatham, the bride. Evening, read *North American Review*.

"[10*th.*] J. Andrews,[1] New York and Mentone, called. My grandson, John B. Clark, tells me that he has passed his matriculation exam. for London University. He sends me honey, the yield of the industry of his own bees."

4

In a desperate effort to force the Government to dissolve, the House of Lords on July 8 had rejected the Franchise Bill. From the introduction of the Bill onwards the Conservative Party had devoted itself to "tactics." Too wary to offer direct opposition to the extension of the vote to the agricultural labourers, it attacked on the flank. In a fine frenzy of democracy, it refused to accept Franchise unaccompanied by Redistribution. Gladstone was quite prepared for Redistribution, and intended to propose it; but he said quite reasonably that to tack the two things together would give the Opposition and the Peers the excuse they needed for throwing out suffrage unless they could have the particular kind of redistribution they favoured.

When the Bill went to the Upper Chamber, the "die-hards" had their way. Despite the warnings of such enlightened Conservatives

---

a province it desired to evacuate, was now alarmed by the outcry at home for a relief expedition, and paralysed by its own dissensions. At a meeting on April 7, six Ministers had voted for an autumn expedition and five against.

[1] Son-in-law of Cyrus W. Field.

as Lord Randolph Churchill in the House of Commons and the Dukes of Argyll and Marlborough and Lord Jersey in the House of Lords, the amendment of Lord Cairns (a demand for the two schemes together) was carried by a majority of 59.

Gladstone, denying the right of the Peers to force a dissolution on this issue, summoned a meeting of the Liberal Party at the Foreign Office on the 10th, and announced that he proposed to call an Autumn Session and re-submit the Bill. Goschen, the only Liberal who had voted against the Government in the House of Commons, now objected to an agitation against the House of Lords. Bright replied to him. "A hereditary House of Parliament," he said, "is not and cannot be perpetual in a free country. The Crown, so popular in the country and so important in our system, has long ago given up its absolute veto. It would be to the great advantage, in my opinion, of the House of Lords if some limit were placed upon their veto."

"[*July* 10.] Foreign Office: meeting of Liberal Party. Mr. Gladstone's speech excellent on Parly. crisis. I was called on and forced to speak quite unprepared. Our friends kind, and recd. what I said with great apparent favour. House: acrimonious debate, Tories and Irish behaving badly. Dined with Willie and his wife. Their constant kindness is quite a comfort to me. Evening, late, read part of 'Gaythorne Hall,' a story sent me by Mr. Fothergill, whom I do not know.

"[16*th*.] Mr. Escott, of the *Fortnightly Review*, called; talk about his proposed book on History of House of Commons. Dined with Mr. Childers, 117, Piccadilly. Mrs. Luttrell of Dunster with me to dinner. Evening party. Conversation with several. Company not too large, and very pleasant. Lord Houghton; Lord Spencer on Ireland; Lady Mary, Duke of Argyll's nice daughter; Mrs. Grant Duff; Mrs. Walpole, an extreme old Tory, as she calls herself; and others.

"[18*th*.] House: talk with Lord Hartington on Manchester meeting. Ministers will not join in any assault upon the Lords; not wise at this stage of the conflict forced upon them, in which I concur; but others cannot be prevented from speaking out on this constitutional question. Conversation with Captain O'Shea[1] on Ireland, Parnell, Davitt and the future.

"[21*st*.] Great Reform procession passed my windows. Dear

[1] The petitioner in the Parnell Divorce case.

Sophie and Kivor[1] and her two sisters here; also Kate Thomasson and her nice daughter, and our Cousin Esther Albertson from America; and Robt. Fox of Falmouth and Bernard here to see the procession. Crowd enormous. Stood 3 hours at the window. Cheering extraordinary and continuous, which I recd. with such courtesy as I could show the multitude.[2]

"[*22nd.*] Dr. Jas. Taylor, from Edinbro', called: interesting conversation with him. D. Anderson, from *Daily Telegraph*, called, to ask my opinion of the procession of yesterday! Mr. Woodall, M.P., called to ask me to go to Leek to open Mr. Nicholson's Library, etc. Could not consent. Dined with Mr. Bryce, M.P., at 35, Bryanston Square. Met Mr. Villard, son-in-law, and W. P. Garrison, son of Lloyd-Garrison, and spent a very pleasant evening. Interesting conversation on America, Germany and this country.[3]

"[*24th.*] Mr. Stigand called. Also Riley, an Irish bricksetter, very friendly to me. He called 3 times when I was ill. He said he prayed for me every night when I was ill. By 12 train home; found all well.

"[*26th.*] To great meeting, Pomona Gardens, Manchester. To Wm. Agnew's, Summerhill. Met there Lord Hartington and Sir Henry James, Attorney-General. With them to the meeting. Philip with me. Meeting very great. Hartington's speech strong and good. I spoke easily, tho' to so great an audience. I was Chairman, and felt the office and the speaking no burden. Spoke briefly to a smaller meeting on the same premises, and home by a late train to Rochdale.

"[*August* 2.] To Birmingham, to Geo. Dixon's at 'The Dales.'

"[*4th.*] Great procession thro' the town to Soho Pool. Fine day; concourse of people very great. Looked on the vast throng from an elevated spot: a sight of great interest and wonder. Evening, to

[1] Kivor was Mrs. William Leatham Bright: her second name was "McIvor," and this was an abbreviation of it

[2] The procession included numbers of agricultural labourers who had come to London to "demonstrate." Estimates of the crowd at the Hyde Park meetings varied between 50,000 and 100,000.

[3] Henry Villard, the owner of the *New York Evening Post*, then edited by E. L. Godkin, who said of him that he was the most disinterested newspaper proprietor he had ever known. Godkin having taken his paper, *The Nation*, into the office of the *Evening Post*, W. P. Garrison was put in charge of it. Bryce was now busy writing "The American Commonwealth." It was in 1884 that he gave the lecture at Oxford which discussed so memorably the distinction between rigid and flexible constitutions and foreshadowed the classic presentation in his great book of the contrasts between the American and British systems.

Bingley Hall. I was Chairman and spoke for an hour. My voice not so good and clear as usual. Chamberlain spoke well—very strong against the Lords for a member of the Govt. The day's proceedings very satisfactory.[1]

"[5th.] Called on Wm. Middlemore, a fine old man, most liberal and just; also on Mr. Jaffray at the office of the *Daily Post*. At dinner the Mayor, also Richard Tangye, Powell-Williams, Osler and Griffiths: a very pleasant evening.

"[9th, at Street.] My grandson Roger left us for York, where he is at the Friends' School. His eyes were red and the parting was not very easy. I gave him half a sovereign, as one source of comfort.

"[12th, at Cheltenham.[2]] Drove to Colesburn, to call on Mr. Elwes, a Liberal squire, which is a scarce personage in this district. A small garden party of pleasant people. Among them Lord Bathurst and Mr. Taylor, formerly of Wigan, at whose house we called on our return—a very large and fine mansion with costly pictures and furniture, but with no occupant except Mr. Taylor and his servants.

"[27th, at Rochdale.] Edwd. L. Pierce came home. (28th.) Drive with him on the Old Todmorden Road. (29th.) Drive by Simpson Clough. (30th.) Left us for Leeds. He is a wonderful talker: seems to have seen almost everything. His activity and inquiry incessant. Our talk on America and this country interesting.

"[September 18.[3]] Left Tulchan for Stratford-on-Avon to attend the funeral of Mrs. Collis, the mother of my son-in-law, Richard F. Curry. She died on the 16th at Bray in Ireland where she has lived since leaving Shottery Hall, nr. Stratford-on-Avon. Richard and dear Mary have spent their holiday with her. She apparently in good health till the day before their intended departure, when she became suddenly ill. An excellent and charming woman to her family. Her death is an irreparable loss.

"From Advie Station to Boat of Garten, Mr. Bruce, M.P., brother of Lord Elgin, with me. At Boat of Garten, Duke of Sutherland asked me to enter his superb private carriage, in which I travelled with him to Perth. Robt. Spencer, M.P., was there, and Capt. Shaw (Fire

---

[1] Bright again propounded and discussed his proposal to solve the Lords question by giving the Upper House a suspensory veto only.

[2] Where he had gone to visit his brother-in-law, Edward Leatham, at Miserden Park, Cirencester.

[3] After a visit to Cassencary (to stay with Sir James Caird) and to Tulchan Lodge.

Brigade`; [1] also Mr. Webb, of the L. and N.W. Railway Works, Crewe. The Duke thought some reform of the House of Lords was necessary. To Carlisle alone. Quiet and pleasant journey. At County Hotel met Jas. Cropper, M.P.

"[*19th.*] Breakfasted with him and Mr. Moon, Chairman of the L. and N.W. Railway, the latter a man of some original views. He ordered for me a carriage thro' to Birmingham, which was a favour which I valued.

"Richard and Mary and his 3 brothers and sisters came from Dublin after my arrival. They brought with them the coffin of their dear mother.

"[*20th.*] Funeral at small old church at Clifford, 2 miles from Stratford. The vault is the one in which Admiral Curry was buried. The company not very large, but the occasion very solemn. Some relatives present from Dorset and Devonshire. My boy Philip was present, and returned to London after the funeral.

"[*26th, at Rochdale.*] Message from Albert from Blackpool, with sad news of the sudden death of Mr. Shawcross, his father-in-law, taken ill at midnight, died at noon; complaint of the heart supposed cause.

"Mr. Henbury came over from Dolgelly to discuss Chinese affairs with me, but no light discovered. The French proceedings are atrocious, but we have done so much wrong that we are out of court and cannot publicly condemn or advise them. [2]

"Albert and Edith came here this evening from Blackpool; she greatly distressed.

"[*29th.*] Funeral of my neighbour and friend, W. T. Shawcross. Many carriages and large attendance. Great regret at his loss felt and expressed.

"[*October* 2.] On the Tay. 1 fish 13½ lbs.; day not favourable. At dinner, Provost and Baillies of Dundee deputation asking me to visit Dundee to accept Freedom of the Boro'. Compelled to decline it,

---

[1] The famous chief officer of the London Fire Brigade.

> "Oh, Captain Shaw,
> Type of true love kept under!
> Could thy Brigade
> With cold cascade
> Quench my great love, I wonder?"
> —*Iolanthe.*

[2] The Egyptian difficulty produced a crop of little enterprises by France in many parts of the world which wounded British feelings.

not wishing to speak in public; have refused so many urgent invitations to Meetings in Scotland.

"[10*th*, *at Kelso*.] Evening to hear the 'Jubilee Singers' from Nashville, Tennessee, U.S.A. A crowded audience much pleased.

"[11*th*.] To Edinbro', Newington House. Evening, to Duncan's[1] evening party, to meet missionaries going to India.

"[13*th*.] To Kelso, from a pleasant visit to my dear sister Priscilla, and her venerable husband, now near completing his 85th year.

"[20*th*.] Left Kelso for home. Fishing again proved disappointing, but Kelso and the Tweed and boats and pleasant company not to be thought little of. A pleasant time.

"[23*rd*.] House of Commons met,[2] but I was not present.

"[25*th*.] Mr. Leech, of Bowden, here. He wishes to publish all my published letters and has collected more than 100 of them. He brought over his MS. copies of the letters, and I looked over many or several of them. They will make a good octavo volume, and Mr. Leech thinks it will find many readers.[3]

"[28*th*.] To 132, Piccadilly; entered on my lodgings on the 3rd floor. Moderate rate, £5.5.0 per week up to June next, the price paid by Mr. Hulse who has preceded me. Rooms very comfortable and quiet, being so high above the street. Mrs. Leech, granddaughter of my old friend Henry Ashworth, called; wishes her son to get into the Diplomatic service. Club to dinner, not going to the House: weary of Irish debates.

"[29*th*.] Calls this morning: Mr. Stewart, from Canada, with letter of introduction from J. G. Whittier; also from P. Bigelow, son of John Bigelow, formerly U.S. Minister to France. Evening: reading Mr. Mull's volume on amendments of the text of *Paradise Lost*.

"[*November* 1.] By 4.45 train to Oxford, visit to Geo. Brodrick, Warden of Merton College. Met there Chas. Roundell and his wife, H. James, American novelist, and Lady Sarah Spencer. At dinner, Edwd. Tylor and his wife.

"[2*nd*.] A long walk with Brodrick and Roundell and James. Called on Edwd. Tylor.[4] Afternoon, Mr. Jowett of Balliol called

---

[1] A son of Duncan McLaren, his brother-in-law, by a former marriage.

[2] For the Autumn Session which settled the dispute with the House of Lords, passed the Franchise Bill and began Redistribution.

[3] "The Public Letters of Rt. Hon. John Bright," edited by H. J. Leech, was published in 1885.

[4] Professor of Anthropology at Oxford.

upon me. He has the countenance of a good man. Burdon Sanderson, professor, of the party. He spoke highly of J. Theodore Cash, the husband of my dear Sophie. Evening Chapel, but could scarcely hear anything of the singing, intoning and preaching. Sat up late for two nights with Mr. James. Conversation on America interesting.

"[3rd.] Called on Dean Liddell. Visited Hall, Library and Cathedral. Oxford a city of rare interest.

"[4th.] Dined with Lady Stanley of Alderley, 40, Dover Street: a pleasant and lively party. Interesting conversation with Lady Airlie, now a widow, and very sad. Intelligent on public questions, and on matters affecting the land and laws dealing with owners and occupiers of land. She invited me to visit her at her house in Forfarshire during next autumn. Mackenzie Wallace there. He came with me, and we talked Russia and Egypt and India till 2 in the morning. Intelligent man and conversation very interesting.[1]

"[5th.] Club. Evening dined with S. Morley, 34, Grosvenor Street: large party of members of the House. Morley a generous and good man. Three of his sons there, superior young men, in the foot-steps of their father. Home in Lord Chas. Bruce's carriage.

"[6th.] Miss Booth, of the Salvation Army, called to speak of the persecution of her friends and herself in Switzerland. She is young, 25 years old; has a sweet countenance; dressed simply and in black. Her conversation interesting and impressive, her faith great. There is a goodness about her which is charming and attractive. What would not anyone part with to be like her in goodness and faith and service to the Christ in whose cause she gives up her life? I gave her a copy of 'Ben Hur, or a Tale of the Christ.' She seemed pleased to receive it. She told me of a conversation in Geneva which must have been of the nature of a miracle. In going away she said, 'I am sure you will pray for us.' I said I hoped God would bless their labours and their cause. All their family whose education is completed are working in the Salvation Army.

"House: 2nd reading of Franchise Bill. Mr. Gladstone's speech conciliatory.

"[7th.] House: Franchise Bill. Dear Mary in the Ladies' Gallery. Division at 1 o'clock—372–232; 140 majority. We came up with Geo. O. Trevelyan.

"[8th.] Twenty years to-day since we lost our dear boy. How

[1] The future Sir Donald Mackenzie Wallace had first published his classic work, "Russia," in 1877.

many sad anniversaries we have as we grow older! Afternoon to Dorking, to Nedley, to visit Mrs. Drummond. A nice party there: Kegan Paul, the publisher, Mr. Gibbs, once tutor to the Prince of Wales, and a son of Sir R. Collier, and his wife, and F. Cheetham, M.P.

"[9th.] Walk to the top of Box Hill; the country and the view of unsurpassable beauty. Called on Mr. Dixon. His house large and almost palatial, his conservatory very fine; Victoria Regia and Loe there. His brother is my friend Geo. Dixon of Birmingham.

"[14th.] Franchise Bill: 3rd reading—no division.

"[16th.] My birthday—73 years old. I ask myself how I have lived so long? To Wandsworth Meeting—small and quiet.

"[18th.] Dined with the 'Eighty Club;' about 120 present. I spoke $\frac{3}{4}$ of an hour on the mode of redistribution of seats and was well received, and treated with much attention. A vote of thanks was moved by Mr. Lyttelton and seconded by Mr. Asquith in very good speeches.

"[19th.] Dined with Chamberlain. A very good party: Froude, Carlyle's friend, there. Also Mr. Buckle, the new and young editor of *The Times*—a pleasant man. He sat next to me and we had a good deal of conversation. Also Mr. Taubman, who has been much in Africa, on the Niger, and is connected with a trading company doing much with the natives, and apparently on good principles—treating them honestly and gaining their confidence.[1]

"[20th.] Met Lord Rosebery and his wife in the street. She is to send her album for me to write my name in it: autographs are much in request just now. Wrote to Mr. Gladstone on the subject of grouping boroughs in the new Bill, advising against it, and sending him a letter from Mr. Page, of King's Lynn, on the subject.

"Dined with Sir C. Forster, M.P. Mr. Storey and Mr. Burt, and my old friend C. P. Villiers, there; also Miss Tennant[2]—an old acquaintance of mine from her childhood. She writes and paints, and 'must do something.' She said she had made £350 this year by writing and painting. She is now making a portrait of Mr. Burt, M.P. She

---

[1] Captain Goldie Taubman (afterwards the Rt. Hon. Sir George Taubman Goldie, K.C.M.G.) had founded the United African Company in 1879. He had the foresight to realize the coming partition of Africa. His enterprise became the National African Company in 1882, and, when Bright met him, he had purchased all the French interests in the basin of the Lower Niger. The company had 400 treaties with native chiefs and administered a vast region extending from the Gulf of Guinea to the Sahara. It received a charter as the Royal Niger Company in 1886, and the territory was finally transferred to the Crown in 1900.

[2] Dorothy Tennant, later Lady Stanley.

brought me up home in her mother's brougham. Her enthusiasm and energy are remarkable.

"[*24th.*] Call from Nestorian Christian and his son from Persia. Story of the cruelties practised on the Christians by the followers of Mahomet.

"[*27th.*] Forty-five years this day since my marriage at Newcastle. What a time and what changes! Received a short letter from Mr. Gladstone from Windsor on the prospects of the arrangement of the Parliamentary Seats Bill.

"[*29th, at Rochdale.*] To London by Midland, 12 o'clock train. Passengers an American, connected with Arnold Constable and Co., strongly in favour of Free Trade; also Mr. Valdez, merchant of Bogota, Colombia, resident in London, conducting business for his firm in Bogota. Very intelligent, and gave me much information about his country, its produce and exports, etc. His boy, 10 years old, could quote passages of my speeches, which have been much read in his house!

"[*December* 1.] Foreign Office meeting, Liberal Party. Mr. Gladstone's speech on the Bill for distribution of seats. No discussion. Scheme well received. House. Bill brought in. Singular sight. After months of contest, all calm and all apparently agreed. 3 months of agitation has had its effect. The Opposition no longer opposes.

"[*4th.*] House: Redistribution Bill read a second time. Mr. Courtney's long speech against the Bill, and in favour of a new mode of voting not easy to be understood. Mr. Gladstone's answer amusing and clever.[1]

"[*31st.*] Sad news this morning of the death of Alfred Tylor at Carshalton. His daughter is the wife of my son Willie. The loss to the family will be grievous. He was a man of much intelligence, and of eminent kindliness of disposition, always willing to help those who needed help. His kindness to Willie has been singular and constant. To-day, too, we hear of the death of James Tweedale, one of our workmen, who has been in the employ of our firm for 61 years. A man of many good qualities, industrious, trustworthy, of admirable temper, and much respected by all who knew him. He was at his usual work yesterday and died during the night.'

[1] Courtney, who had been Secretary to the Treasury, resigned on December 1, after hearing the proposed terms of the Redistribution Bill at the F.O. meeting on the ground that it contained no provision for Proportional Representation, the cause which he had more closely at heart than any other. Gladstone said, in the speech which amused Bright, that Courtney's proposal, "though certified as simple enough, was in truth a *pons asinorum* which very few members would be able to cross."

CHAPTER XVIII

HOME RULE AND THE END

I

"I SPOKE for an hour with ease and freedom," says Bright, recording the annual meeting of his constituents at Birmingham in January, 1885. Those who heard him in his prime declared that the measured and mellow eloquence of his old age, charming and finished as it was, quite lacked the electrical magic of the orations on the Crimea and America and India. None are left who listened to these, but personal testimony can be given to the effect of his later speeches on ardent youths in the 'eighties. He seemed to them very wise, very authoritative, very benign—and, until the keen sword of racial and religious strife sliced through the body of the Liberal Party, very modern and very·radical. And there is no doubt that now, at 73, he still looked forward to triumph for the principles of peaceful democracy founded in political equality, freedom of speech and thought, freedom of trade and individual liberty. His correspondence of the time betokens an undimmed zest in all these causes.

But the shadows were soon to descend. The last Ministry in which he served expired within six months of the Birmingham meeting, notwithstanding the administration of successive doses of oxygen—the recruiting of Campbell-Bannerman to the Irish Office, the bringing of Lord Rosebery into the Cabinet, and Shaw-Lefevre, the Radical, as Postmaster-General. Difficulties crowded on. Should Ireland have another draught of coercion, or a Land Bill—or both? Or should the scheme of a Central Council, fathered by Bright and Chamberlain, be tried? How to pacify the raging country when it heard of Gordon's death? How to reconcile the taxpayers to a huge Budget of expenses on expeditions that had failed?

The crisis that came on the Budget might have come on any question. The Government was moribund. "When the same heart hath two mortal wounds given it together, it is hard to say which of them killeth." Bright, however, had no hesitation in attributing the death-blow to the policy of military adventure in which he had resolutely declined to share.

"[*January* 29, 1885.] By 11 train to Birmingham. To Mr. Chamberlain's at Highbury. Evening, Town Hall: fine meeting. Mayor, Mr. Martineau, in the Chair. I spoke for an hour, with ease and freedom. Chamberlain followed. Some parts not so judicious as I could have wished.[1]

"[30*th.*] At Highbury. Large dinner party of our political friends and pleasant evening.

"[*February* 5.] Snow. Ground well covered for the first time this winter. News of Fall of Khartoum: difficulties of Government seem to increase.[2]

"[15*th.*] To Meeting. A young lady Friend (Bell) from Ireland present. Address and prayer remarkable. Her countenance as I spoke with her after the meeting reminded me much of that of Miss Booth, General Booth's daughter, of the Salvation Army. Their faith seems to give a singular sweetness and purity to the countenance.

"[24*th.*] Willie called. Long talk about his affairs, and proposal of his becoming a candidate for Division of Westminster! Lalmohun Ghose called to discuss his being a candidate for the Boro' of Greenwich. Club: dined with Chas. Harrison there.[3] Home early—made some notes for the Ripon banquet to-morrow.

"[25*th.*] Ripon banquet. Too many speeches. My turn very late at 11.30. Wished not to speak, but Lord Kimberley, Chairman, urged it.

"[27*th.*] Vote of censure: Govt. majority 14.[4]

"[*March* 2, *at Brighton.*] To London. Sir R. Peel with me in same carriage. Much talk on position of parties. He and his friends

[1] Nearly all Chamberlain's indiscretions of 1885 are now enshrined in law or practice. They were: Abolition of plural voting, manhood suffrage, payment of members, graduated income tax, power of local authorities to acquire land, breaking up of great estates as a first step in land reform.

[2] Khartoum had fallen and Gordon died on January 26. The news reached England on February 5.

[3] Brother of Frederick Harrison. Charles Harrison was then fifty. Ten years later he took his seat in Parliament for the first time as a Member for Plymouth. At his death in 1897 he was Vice-Chairman of the London County Council, of which he had been a member from the first.

[4] Votes of censure on the conduct of the Soudan affair were moved in both Houses. Assailed by the Opposition for doing too little and by the Radicals for doing too much, the Government just scraped through with their lives against a miscellaneous assortment of Conservatives, Liberals and Parnellites.

greatly annoyed at arrangement of Seats Bill. He thinks Conservative Party almost destroyed: next Parliament fatal to them.

"Dined with Mrs. Gladstone. After dinner sat for ½ an hour or more with Mr. Gladstone, who is ill with cold and hoarseness. Long talk on Egypt. He said he had suffered torture during the continuance of the difficulty in that country. The sending Gordon out was a great mistake—a man totally unsuited for the work he undertook. Mr. Gladstone never saw Gordon; he was appointed by Ministers in Town, and Gladstone concurred, but had never seen him. Mr. G. very friendly to me; tells me how much he wishes I was with him in the Cabinet. I am very sorry for his troubles. I have not made them, and would have saved him from them, if he had been strong enough to have taken my advice.

"[4*th*.] Dined with Lord Rosebery at Lansdowne House. Count Bismarck from Berlin and Lord Carrington the only other guests.

"[5*th*.] Dined again with Lord Rosebery. Mr. and Mrs. Gladstone there; also Count Herbert Bismarck, one of the Rothschilds, Edwd. Hamilton, and Count Munster, German Minister, here.

"Much interesting conversation on Colonies and Federation. Mr. Gladstone agreed with me that the wisest plan is to leave Colonies much as they are.

"Rosebery's view different, but I think quite wrong. I condemned the sending of Australian soldiers to Egypt, but Gladstone defended this; the result may show who is right in this.

"[8*th*.] Dined with Vaughan, my brother-in-law. After dinner some visitors came in; among them Lord and Lady Grantley. She is American, talks freely, and is amusing.[1]

"[10*th*.] Dined with Sir James Caird: a pleasant party. Three Americans. Mr. and Mrs. Brooks from Boston. An intelligent and interesting couple.

"[18*th*.] Dined with Mr. Speaker: a mixed company of members. I sat between my old friend C. P. Villiers and W. E. Baxter of Montrose.

"[21*st*.] Dined with Lord Ripon: large party. Mr. and Mrs. Gladstone there. He seemed in good spirits; she, I thought, anxious and sad. Talk with Lord Ripon on Russian scare and Afghan boundary difficulty.[2] Lord Dalhousie brought me up in his carriage.

[1] Lady Grantley was Miss Katherine M'Vickar, daughter of W. H. M'Vickar, of New York.

[2] The boundary dispute arose out of the Russian annexation of Turcoman territory, which had brought the Tsar's forces close to the borders of Afghanistan. A

"[*22nd.*] Snow this morning. Indoors. 2 o'clock, to lunch with Dalhousie. His 3 nice little boys with us; his wife upstairs with twins. So his family grows. The 3 boys came and gave me a kiss when they left the table.

"Long talk with him on Egypt and on Ireland. I suggested a mode of dealing with Irish question. Ireland; 32 Counties, 32 County Boards; 64 representatives to a Central Council in Dublin for internal affairs, excluding Army, Navy, Import Duties, Church, perhaps Police, but leaving to it Education, Local taxation and Control.

"The question a great difficulty, but some solution must be found.[1]

"[*24th.*] Dined with Lord Dalhousie. Small party. Lord Camperdown, C. Parker, M.P., Caine, M.P., and Crawford, Secretary to the Lord Advocate. Much talk on Egypt; every one distressed with present state of things and the Govt.

"[*25th.*] Dined with Sir J. Pease. Large party and luxurious table. Mrs. Ritchie, daughter of W. M. Thackeray, there; pleasant talk with her about her father. Herself a writer of merit. David Dale, of Darlington, home with me. An hour's talk on public questions; intelligent man and influential in his district.

"[*26th.*] Called on Mr. Theed, sculptor, to see a bust of Elizth. Fry, which is going to the Friends' School, Providence, Rhode Island. The bust is from the fine engraving of Richmond's portrait; the cap upon it is from one of my dear mother's, and has been lent to the sculptor by my dear sister Margaret.[2] The bust is very good; the marble spotless and perfect. Called on Mr. Hutchinson, dentist, 46, Brook St. Evening: read Pitt's speech against Peace with France.

"[*April* 23.] Am greatly troubled at the prospect of war with Russia.[3] Our Govt. seems afflicted with madness.

"Mr. Chamberlain called and had a talk on Russian question. I

joint British and Russian Commission having been appointed to delimit frontiers, there was now acute difference of opinion about its instructions. Lord Ripon had returned from India in November.

[1] Chamberlain had discussed a National Council scheme with Parnell in January. In May Gladstone told Lord Granville that his opinions were "strong in favour of some plan for a Central Board of Local Government in Ireland on something of an elective basis."

[2] Mrs. Samuel Lucas.

[3] The collision between Russian and Afghan troops at Penjdeh, on March 30, created intense excitement in the country. Gladstone had used grave language in the House of Commons, and was preparing to ask for a Vote of Credit for contingent warlike operations.

had asked him, in a note, 'Could he stand another war?' He said he thought he could not, but I have no confidence in politicians however liberal their pretensions, who regard War as one of the common accidents of political life, and consider bloodshed, if under the name of War, as not specially guilty.

"We spoke of Gladstone. I referred to the Crimean War and the horrid events in Egypt and the Soudan. He thought there would be no war with Russia with Gladstone at the head of the Government, which I heard with much satisfaction.

"[24th.] Mr. Gladstone called, and we had a long conversation almost entirely on Russia. He is most anxious for peace, but he seems to fix upon some point, in my view of no importance, and to persuade himself that it is so important that even war may justly depend upon it. It is amazing to me that a mind so powerful can involve itself in difficulties so unnecessarily. That he is most anxious to avoid war I am certain, and he is looking to some mode of extrication by mediation and arbitration, probably thro' the old German Emperor, tho' what there is to arbitrate about I cannot discern.

"The old Emperor should tell the two parties to go home—to regret the incident which brought them before him, and not to get up ill blood about trifles.[1]

"[*May* 1.] Conversation this morning with Mrs. Plowden. She was well acquainted with Sir P. Lumsden at Simla, where he was deemed a fool, wholly unfit for a position of great responsibility. Astonishment at Simla when he was appointed to be the head of the Afghan Boundary Commission.

"I wrote to Mr. Gladstone telling him this, and showing him how often the Govt. is led wrong by its servants abroad—gave him cases of Bowring, Bartle Frere, Lord Stratford de Redcliffe and Beauchamp Seymour. He sent me an interesting little note in reply.[2]

"[2nd.] This week I have given 6 sittings to Mr. J. Adams Acton for a bust ordered by my old friend Isaac Holden. The sittings were

[1] Gladstone moved on April 27 for a credit of eleven millions, of which six and a half were for preparations to meet the possible difficulties on the Afghan frontier.

[2] Sir Peter Lumsden was, according to Dilke, "sending the most violent telegrams." Lord Granville wrote: "Lumsden was a bad appointment, and I for a moment wished to recall him. But it would be condemned here as an immense knock-under." The crisis subsided suddenly. On May 2 it was announced that Russia accepted arbitration. Some trouble arose about the choice of arbitrator, and the proposal was not pursued. Sir J. West Ridgeway succeeded Lumsden and eventually delimited the frontier quite peaceably.

tedious; I hope it is the last of such engagements. I have been indoors nearly all the week, and am not well.

"[*3rd.*] This evening, Dr. Dudgeon called, at the suggestion of my dear kind boy Willie, who met him at the Zoological Gardens. . . . Pulsatilla, and advised me to go down home, and to go to Llandudno for a week or two. I hope to take his advice and to leave for home on Tuesday.

"[*13th.*] Anniversary of the day of my great sorrow. Seventeen years have passed since the heavy stroke fell on me.

"[*14th.*] W. C. Plowden at 'One Ash,' wishing to be a candidate for our County Division, but I think he will not be chosen.[1] His rival, Col. Schwabe, has the advantage of being better known in the district.

"[*June* 6.] Dined with Mr. Gladstone. The Queen's Birthday dinner; about 40 present. I sat between Lord Aberdeen and Lord Hampden, the late Speaker. The Prince very courteous. Asked me if I had received his letter. I thanked him for it. He said he would like a reply as an autograph. The eldest son, Albert Victor, is pleasant-looking, modest and sensible. Have thus met the future Kings of England. I hope they may live to reign and to see days of prosperity and peace.[2]

"[*8th.*] Frederick Rous, nephew of our old friend Lydia Rous,[3] from Canada, called. I am to get him an order for the House for to-morrow. A soaking rain this morning. Dined this evening with Lord Granville: a pleasant party."

2

From Lord Granville's dinner-party Bright went down to the House to listen to the debate on an amendment to the Budget. No crisis was expected immediately. The Parliamentary managers thought the debate would go over to the next day. But the division bells rang that night while Liberal members were scattered all over London. Within a few hours their Government no longer existed.

The actual machinery of its defeat is merely a matter of Parliamentary curiosity. The expenditure of the year had reached 100 millions, a

---

[1] He was not chosen, but later entered Parliament as Liberal member for Wolverhampton.

[2] Prince Albert Victor, Duke of Clarence, however, died of influenza in January, 1892.

[3] She was governess to the Bright children. If the girls were disobedient she stamped on their toes!

figure then thought alarming. Childers faced a deficit of 15 millions, including the 11 millions of the Vote of Credit, and the Navy Estimates were up 3 millions as the result of Stead's "big navy" agitation of the previous autumn. The Chancellor proposed to raise the Income Tax from 6*d.* to 8*d.*, to add a little to the Succession Duties, to raise the Beer Duty by two shillings a gallon, and to suspend the Sinking Fund.

The higher Beer Duty was unpopular with the Radicals; both Chamberlain and Dilke had threatened to resign on this point. Sir Michael Hicks-Beach fastened on it as the vulnerable point. He moved that the Beer and Spirit Duties should not be increased without a commensurate increase in the Wine Duty, and that no addition should be made to the Estate Duty without provision for further grants from the Treasury for local purposes. He carried it by 12 votes.

It was, of course, a sham fight. Gordon and Ireland brought down the Government, not the hostility of the "Trade," pronounced as that was. The majority against Ministers was a combination of Conservatives and Parnellites—the first Parliamentary expression of the manœuvres of Gavan-Duffy and Lord Carnarvon towards a Conservative-Irish entente.

The Government minority was only a minority because of the absence of some seventy Liberal members. Yet the distracted Ministry, torn with dissensions and fatigued by the labours of more than five Sisyphean years, resigned without a regret. The dissolution was postponed till the redistribution of seats had been accomplished. During the months while Bright rested at "One Ash," or wandered about Scotland throwing a fly here and there, Lord Salisbury's first Government came into being.

"[*June* 8.] House, and voted in the fatal division. Government defeated on their Budget by majority of 12 against them. Resignation to-morrow certain. Thus, after 3 years, my foretelling is proved correct—that the bombardment of Alexandria would destroy the Government. Blood may be shed without danger to an Administration, but to attempt to provide money for it in some honest way may be, and in this case is, fatal.

"[*26th, at Rochdale.*] Fine day, but east wind. Began to cut grass in the small field before Albert's house; good crops of grass.

"Call to-day from Mr. Butlea, a tall and very black man from Canada, over here with a troup of negro singers. He was a slave in Maryland, and escaped by help of Friends and the 'underground railway' a few years before the great war. Gave him £2 towards the funds of the singing party. They send missionaries out to Africa.

"[*July* 1.] Left home for London, very unwillingly. In Piccadilly soon after 6 o'clock. Dined with Mr. Chamberlain, a large party and a pleasant evening.

"[*2nd.*] Mr. Rantoul called, introduced by J. G. Whittier from Boston.

"[*3rd.*] To lunch with my sister-in-law, Selina, and met Rebecca Smith, the granddaughter of my Uncle John Wood, the brother of my dear mother. She is an intelligent woman, refined and pleasant in conversation, and is here for a change, for her health has not been good.

"[*6th.*] House: division on Bradlaugh case. The day very hot.

"[*7th.*] 34 years to-day since the death of my dear father. My own age has nearly reached his—only 3 years short of it.

"[*16th.*] Dined with Mr. Agnew. Sat next to Mr. Du Maurier, one of the *Punch* artists, intelligent and very pleasant.

"[*18th.*] Dined at Reform Club. Small party invited by my brother-in-law, W. H. Leatham. Ernest de Bunsen one of the guests.

"[*23rd.*] T. G. Darton called. Agreed with him to bring out a new edition of Dymond's 'Essays on Morality.' Cost will be about £150. Geo. Palmer and Joseph Pease and myself to give a guarantee of £50 each towards the whole cost.

"[*25th.*] J. B. Braithwaite gave me a copy of his poem, *Paul the Apostle*. He said he was not aware that he had any poetic power about him till he began this poem.

"Evening to dine with Vaughan; a small party. A young man, Mr. Riley,[1] who has lived some weeks with the monks on Mount Athos: interesting details of their condition and lives.

"[*26th.*] By 10.5 Midland train to Manchester and home. To-day and yesterday very hot. Cooler after reaching Derby.

"[*27th.*] By early train back to London to meet attack by Philip Callan, an Irish member, on my speech on Friday, the 24th, at the banquet to Lord Spencer, late Viceroy of Ireland. House: Callan's speech. My answer much cheered. Lord Hartington strongly supported me. Vote 154 to 23. Rebel party did not gain anything by this move.[2]

---

[1] Mr. Athelstan Riley, afterwards a well-known member of the London School Board and a protagonist of the religious education controversies. He published his "Athos, or the Mountain of the Monks" in 1887.

[2] The banquet to Lord Spencer given to mark the sense of his success in Ireland and the disapproval of Lord Randolph Churchill's attacks on his régime, was attended

"[*August* 24.] Left home for Manchester and Perth. Arrived at 7.30, British Hotel.

"[*25th*.] By 9.30 train to Grantown. In the train 2 canoes and their owners. Much pleasant talk with them. They were going down the Spey from Kingussie. To the small farm-house where my dear sister and McLaren are lodging, 1½ miles from the town, and close to the Spey.

"[*26th*.] Excursion with McLaren and Agnes,[1] his *doctor* daughter, down the Strath to Advie. Met John McPherson, so often with me when fishing the Spey. Called at his house. His nice daughter gave us some rich milk, and our call was very pleasant. Crossed the bridge at Advie and returned to Grantown. Four miles up, we met the canoes coming down. Had a chat with the canoe-ers and watched them rapidly going down the river.

"[*29th*.] Drive to Bouskeid, the beautiful house and grounds of the Barbours. Nothing more lovely can, I think, be seen in Scotland. The old lady most pleased to see me. She said her husband, now old and feeble, had politically brought up his sons or family on my speeches— which he so much approved of!

"[*September* 1.] Drive to and thro' Glen Tilt. Nothing more charming perhaps in Scotland. Only open to public and carriages during special hours. The Duke of Atholl will find this restriction not maintainable for very long. Public opinion will change many things in connexion with landowners' privileges or pretensions.

"[*3rd*.] At Cassencary, with my friends Sir James and Lady Caird. Found there Mr. McCulloch from near Reigate, Sir H. Edwards, M.P. for Weymouth, and Mr. Goodheard and his little wife, the daughter of my host. With Lady Caird and her daughter and Sir James to Newtown Stewart. Visited the Town Hall in course of building.

"[*4th*.] Drive down the shore; stroll by the rocks on the coast. Mr. Hume, son of my old friend Joseph Hume, so long M.P. for Montrose, came this morning. He has been 36 years in India, and is busy on measures favourable to the natives. Mr. Hume consulted Caird

by about 300 members of both Houses. Lord Hartington presided. Bright condemned in good round terms the alliance between the "Irish rebels" and the new Ministry. Mr. Callan brought up the question of "privilege," and gave Bright the opportunity, eagerly accepted, of repeating (with interest) in the House what he had said outside.

[1] The daughter of Duncan McLaren by a former marriage.

and myself as to means of conveying accurate information of Indian affairs and native Indian opinion to English newspapers by telegraphic dispatches furnished gratuitously by Association in India. His information very extensive, and his conversation interesting. He is a vegetarian for 8 years past; seems in admirable health, and full of energy. He seems a worthy son of a worthy father.

"[*17th.*] My dear boy Philip left me this morning for Liverpool. He sails to-day in the *Adriatic* for New York with J. J. Tylor. He goes on business, and I hope he may return by the end of the year. I am very sorry to part with him.

"[*28th.*] Hear this morning of the arrival of the *Adriatic* at New York. Pleasant to think that my dear boy Philip has had a fair passage —exactly 9 days.

"[*October* 10.] Left Bath for Street.[1] At Glastonbury station a great crowd with a band and flags come to meet me.

"[*12th.*] To Crispin Hall, a handsome building built by William and Helen for the use of the village and Workmen's Club. 4 o'clock business meeting: to hand over lease to Workmen's Committee. Evening, crowded meeting, perhaps 1,000 present. I spoke for an hour and quarter. Meeting eager to hear and intelligent to understand. The proceedings of the day passed off pleasantly. I felt more comfortable after my speech, for of late I have been much indisposed to speak in public.

"Helen's dear children very nice and good. They will, I hope and I believe, grow up to do credit to their parents whose example is admirable.

"[*15th.*] To Hawarden Castle. A drive with Mr. and Mrs. Gladstone, afternoon. Evening: Lord Dalhousie, Spencer, and Alfred Lyttelton, and the wife of the latter. Edwd. Hamilton of the party.

"[*16th.*] Drive with Mrs. Gladstone. Called upon her two sons, W. H., and Stephen, who is rector of Hawarden. Talk about Disestablishment of the Church. He thinks Church better if not allied with the State; has no fear of change. An earnest and good man.

"[*17th.*] Conversation with Mr. G. on public affairs. He is in good health, but feels the weight of impending questions, especially of the Irish question, on which he would act if any hope of reconciliation with the discontented portion of the Irish people. Left Hawarden at 11 and home at half-past two. Found here a nice long letter from my dear boy Philip.

[1] Mrs. Curry had been unwell and he had visited her at Bath.

"[*November* 4.] To Birmingham, Midland train, to Geo. Dixon, 'The Dale's, Augustus Road.[1]

"[*5th.*] Town Hall: great meeting. Jno. Jaffray in the chair. Spoke an hour and a quarter with ease and effect. Reception most friendly.

"[*6th.*] Called on Richd. Tangye; then at *Daily Post* office for a chat with Mr. Bunce. Then called on Jaffray. Evening with Alfred Osler to a meeting in the Priory Rooms. Spoke for an hour: pleasant evening.

"[*7th.*] Home.

"[*11th.*] Great meeting, Circus. Spoke for an hour and 10 minutes in place of T. B. Potter, absent owing to the death of his wife at Cannes. Meeting very good.

"[*16th.*] My birthday—74. How my life has passed on to almost old age! And how much have I had that I ought to be grateful for. To Birmingham to Geo. Dixon's.

"[*17th.*] Meeting in Ada St. School, on behalf of Mr. Broadhurst's[2] candidature. He is hard pressed by a great brewer, and by publicans and parsons of the Church.

"[*18th.*] Spoke at two crowded meetings in Exchange Division— an hour each speech.

"[*19th.*] To Bath to see my dear child Mary. Found her somewhat better, but weak and confined mostly to her bed.

"[*21st.*] Returned to Birmingham, and in the evening spoke at Town Hall meeting.

"[*22nd.*] Afternoon, Indian deputation came to 'The Dales' to tea. Interesting talk with them for two hours.

"[*23rd.*] Town Hall: meeting to present portrait of Arthur O'Neill to the Mayor. Spoke shortly on Chartist movement 40 years ago. New Liberal Club to lunch, and came away at 3.30 for Manchester and home.

"[*25th.*] News of the great success in Birmingham yesterday— 7 Liberals elected, and one for Aston, which is part of Birmingham. During the week, election news disappointing,[3] but not difficult to

---

[1] For the opening of the election campaign. Birmingham now voted for the first time in "divisions," and returned 7 members instead of 3.

[2] Henry Broadhurst: he was a stone-mason and became Under-Secretary for Home Affairs later.

[3] The Liberals did very badly in the towns, except Birmingham and Glasgow. The counties turned the scale: the agricultural labourers, voting for the first time,

account for it. Egypt and policy of late Govt. is sufficient explanation of failure. Rochdale has done well, but the Lancashire boroughs very badly.

"[*December* 7.] To Birmingham, to G. Dixon's. Town Hall meeting to receive delegates from India. Presided at the meeting and spoke on India question after delegates had spoken. Unpleasant time for me, for I suffered from toothache nearly all the evening. The meeting good.

"[8*th*.] Left Birmingham and came to Alderley Edge, and spent the night there with my Bro. Jacob and his family.

"[9*th*.] Home. Wish I had not to leave it so often. Weather very cold. Frost.

"[16*th*.] T. Shearman, U.S.A., called to talk Free Trade. He seeks information to aid him in promoting Free Trade in his country.

"[17*th*.] Suffering from cold and toothache. I did not go to Birmingham to the banquet to the 8 Birmingham members. Am sorry to be absent, tho' the duty of attending has been a burden to me.

"[29*th*.] This is Mr. Gladstone's birthday—76."

3

The next six months were among the most painful of Bright's later life. The year 1886 had hardly begun before the Home Rule kite was flying. He watched its ascent with misgiving. As Gladstone's Irish plans took shape he found his leader leaping away in a direction which to him seemed full of peril. Conversation between them was free and candid as ever, and their personal relations remained quite friendly; but Bright, protagonist of Irish liberties as he had always been, believed an Irish Parliament would be an English as well as an Irish disaster. This was fundamental. Once Gladstone had determined upon setting up a separate legislature in Dublin, the die was cast for his colleague. What the separation cost Bright may be judged from the tone of misery in which his entries on the subject are cast, and from the fierceness of the mental struggle that tore him before he decided that it was his duty to vote against the second reading of the Bill and to ally himself with the Liberal Unionists.

"[*January* 4.] T. Watson, M.P., called this morning to talk over his going to the House on its meeting. Jonathan Hogg and T. Pim supported the party which had given them the franchise. But the Liberal majority, not counting the Home Rulers, was only 85. Parnell's solid and formidable party of 85 cancelled it out.

from Dublin to dinner. Called to discuss Irish question, and, much alarmed at rumours of Mr. Gladstone's views on a Parlt. in Dublin,[1] are seeking interviews with English Members of influence and urging the evils of Home Rule, and of any concessions to Parnell and his party beyond such local government arrangements as may be given to Great Britain. They left me for Leeds after much interesting conversation.

"[8th.] Note from Mr. Gladstone, asking me to second nomination of Mr. Peel as Speaker of the new Parlt.

"[11th.] To London. Euston Hotel.

"[12th.] House, 2 o'clock. Seconded the nomination of Mr. Peel for the Chair in a very short speech which was well received. The whole proceedings satisfactory. Peel spoke with great dignity.

"[13th.] Called upon Gladstone. Not much talk with him. Down to the House with him. He will speak in debate on the Address.

"[23rd.] Week of snow and frost. Winter severe. Last year almost no snow or frost. This week Mr. Bright Morris, artist, has been here making a portrait of me for Albert, and at his request. His work so far promises to be successful.

"[30th.] At home all this week. Govt. defeated;[2] resignation. House not sitting, so remain at home very quiet. Weather not pleasant.

"[February 1.] To-morrow my dear boy Philip is to leave New York on his way home. He will have been nearly 6 months away and has much enjoyed his trip.

"[28th.] My dear boy Philip reached home to-day from New York by the steamer Adriatic. A great pleasure to see him. His visit to the States has, I hope, been of great service to him. He has enjoyed it greatly.

"[March 9.] H. of Commons. Division on question of Welsh Church—a sign of the new order of things which is coming upon the country.

---

[1] The publication in the *Leeds Mercury* and *The Standard* of the announcement that Mr. Gladstone proposed a Home Rule Parliament as a solution of the Irish problem took place a week before Christmas.

[2] On Mr. Jesse Collings's famous "three acres and a cow" amendment to the Address (Jan. 27) the Government were beaten by a majority of 79. Lord Salisbury resigned immediately, and Gladstone two days later undertook to form a Government. Lord Morley mentions as an "ominous circumstance" that 76 Liberals were absent from the division, "including among them the imposing personality of Mr. Bright;" and, in connexion with the refusals Gladstone encountered in the task of making up his Ministry, "Most lamented among all the abstentions was the honoured and trusted name of Mr. Bright."

"[10th.] Engaged rooms at the Alexandra Hotel. Small but very comfortable; 5 guineas weekly with some extras. Some invitations to dinner—from Geo. Howard, Lord Rosebery and Mrs. F. Buxton. Called on Lord Hartington at Devonshire House, having recd. a letter from him. An hour's talk on the great Irish question. He very reasonable, and his course greatly to his credit. He wished me to see Mr. Goschen to discuss the difficulties before us.

"[12th.] Jno. Taylor called asking me to preside at Temperance Conference during the summer, to which I could not consent. Hodgson Pratt called to ask me to succeed Lord Shaftesbury as Chairman or President of his Peace and Arbitration Society, to which I have not consented. He gave me interesting information on his efforts to form Committees in Paris, Berlin, and other cities in favour of the Peace movement.

"Evening dined with Mr. Gladstone. Lord Northbourne and his son Walter James there; also Admiral Egerton and Sir Chas. Forster, M.P. Mr. Gladstone much better. Conversation at dinner on Wales and the Welsh Church division in the House. After dinner much private talk with Mr. Gladstone on Ireland. His object is to settle the Land question, which I rather think ought *now* to be considered as settled. On the question of a Parlt. in Dublin, he wishes to get rid of Irish representation at Westminster, in which I entirely agree with him, if it is possible.[1]

"Lord Northbourne insisted on bringing me up here in his brougham. He suggested that Belfast might be made a Free City, which I told him I thought was not practicable.

"[16th.] Dined with Geo. Howard, Kensington Palace Green. Pleasant party. John Morley, M.P., new Irish Secretary, there; Wilfrid Blunt and his wife, who is a granddaughter of Lord Byron; Mr. James, the American writer; Lady Airlie, sister of Mrs. Geo. Howard. Much talk on Ireland and Mr. Gladstone's supposed plans. Lady Airlie brought me home in her carriage.

"Among the guests was Sir H. Ponsonby, the Queen's secretary, always sensible and pleasant.

"[17th.] House. Long talk with Chamberlain on his difficulties and resignation in connexion with Mr. Gladstone's proposed Irish policy. I think his view is in the main correct and that it is not wise

[1] Mr. Gladstone unfolded his dual plan of Home Rule Bill and Land Bill to the Cabinet next day.

in him to adopt or support the intended measures.[1]   Dined with Lord Rosebery at Lansdowne House, Berkeley Square: a party of 30.   Very pleasant evening.   Talk with our host, and with my old friend C. P. Villiers.

"[18*th*.]   Geo. Dixon called to discuss Irish question.   His view agrees with mine and Chamberlain's.

"This is Albert's birthday: 38 years ago, he was born in Wimpole St.   On that day the Park guns were fired on the birth of the Princess Louise, and to-day I heard them again on the occasion of her birthday. How changed is the world to me since that now distant but not forgotten time!

"[19*th*.]   House: voted in favour of H. Richard's motion to prevent war without consent of Parlt.

"[20*th*.]   Downing St.   Long interview for 2 hours with Mr. Gladstone at his request.   He gave me a long memorandum, historical in character, on the past Irish story, which seemed to be somewhat one-sided, leaving out of view the important minority and the views and feelings of the Protestant and loyal portion of the people.

"He explained much of his policy as to a Dublin Parlt. and as to Land purchase.   I objected to the Land policy as unnecessary.   The Act of 1881 has done all that was reasonable for the tenants: why adopt the policy of the Rebel Party and get rid of landholders, and thus evict the English garrison, as the rebels call them?   I denied the value of the security for repayment.   Mr. G. argued that his finance arrangements would be better than the present system of purchase, and that we were bound in honour to succour the landlords, which I contested.   Why not go to the help of other interests in Belfast and in Dublin?

"As to a Dublin Parlt. I argued that he was making a surrender all along the line.   A Dublin Parlt. would work with constant friction, and would press against any barrier he might create to keep up the unity of the 3 Kingdoms.

"What of a volunteer force, and what of import duties and protection as against British goods?   He would not object, but any armed force must be under officers appointed by the Crown; and he did not think duties as against England would be imposed.

"Mr. G. is in favour of excluding all Irish representation from the Imperial Parlt.   Thinks Irish members in Dublin and at Westminster

[1] Chamberlain and Trevelyan had announced their resignation at the Cabinet meeting of the 13th, but it was held up for a fortnight.

not possible. Irish members think they could not supply representatives for both Houses.

"I told him I thought to get rid of the Irishmen from Westminster, such as we have known them for 5 or 6 years past, would do something to make his propositions less offensive and distasteful in Gt. Britain, tho' it tends to more complete separation.

"I told him how anxious and alarmed many of his friends were, and quoted what Mr. Paget, Agnew, Rathbone and others said. Many would vote out of regard for him, many fearing a dissolution of Parlt. possible, but few would like his great schemes. I said I was as much against his Land purchase as against the Dublin Parlt., and suggested that he should lessen the amount to be advanced by showing that only voluntary sale was contemplated, and that if the offer made by the Govt. was at a moderate or low figure, the landlords' demand would not be so great as rumour had imagined.

"I thought he placed far too much confidence in the leaders of the Rebel Party. I could place none in them, and the general feeling was and is that any terms made with them would not be kept, and that, thro' them, I could not hope for reconciliation with discontented and disloyal Ireland.

"Our interview lasted for 2 hours. The conversation very free and open. Mr. Gladstone was cheerful and earnest. He has given incessant attention to this great question for 2 months past. He spoke of the authority of Lord Bessborough, Lord Monk, and Lord Spencer and Sir Robt. Hamilton, and is resolved to go on. He does not understand the course and object of Mr. Chamberlain, and hinted at correspondence with him which would show how much he had changed his ground. He said this question should not be made a great party question involving a struggle in the constituencies, and that if he failed he should retire and leave others who thought themselves capable of doing it to undertake the settlement of the Irish difficulty. He was very friendly, and said how much he relied on such assistance as I could render him.

"I came away not wholly without some sense of relief, but still burdened with a feeling that so great a question has not in my time been before us. If it be disposed of in any satisfactory manner, it can only be thro' the energy and the resolution of a Minister in whom the nation has learned to place a confidence quite unusual between a political party and its leader.

"We must now wait. Of the result I am not confident, and will not therefore speak further.

"[21*st*.] To Westminster Meeting and afterwards to Reform Club—much conversation on Irish question·

"[23*rd*.] Club: long talk with Mr. Labouchere on Ireland. He is intimate with Parnell and others of the Irish Rebel party.

"[27*th*.] To Mr. Adams's studio to see statue in clay of Cobden, to be erected at Stockport. Suggested some alterations.

"Deputation of Ulster Liberals on Mr. Gladstone's supposed Irish policy. The fears very pressing upon them. I tried to console them as far as I could.

"Dined at Reform Club: Edwd. Leatham's party to Club Committee and a few others. Trevelyan, Campbell-Bannerman and Mundella there. The 'out' Trevelyan strong against Gladstone's views; the 'ins' professing to be warmly for.

"[29*th*.] House. Conversation with Lord Hartington, Sir Henry James, and Sir W. Harcourt on Irish question. Anxiety great. I much fear that Mr. Gladstone has led himself and his Party into a difficulty which cannot be measured.

"[30*th*.] Dined with Sir Chas. Forster, M.P. M. Waddington, French Ambassador, there; Sir Hussey Vivian, M.P., there, strong against Mr. Gladstone's Irish policy. Lord Monson thought the Lords were very hostile, which I do not doubt. To Bruce Joy for statue.[1] Casts of my hands taken.

"[31*st*.] Great anxiety on Irish question in the House and thro' the Party.

"[*April* 1.] Mr. Schnadhorst[2] and Mr. Harris from Birmingham at Reform Club. Long conversation on political position here and in Birmingham. Dined with Fras. Buxton: small and pleasant party. Much talk on Irish question; much anxiety and no definite result.

"[2*nd*.] To Bruce Joy's studio to sit for the Birmingham statue.

"[3*rd*.] To Home Office to see Mr. Childers[3] as to opening telegrams in the hope of discovering something as to an American, Mr. Nourse, who has disappeared. Mr. Rantoul, from Mass., accompanied me, but permission not granted, which I think unreasonable.

[1] There are three of these statues. The original is in the Birmingham Art Gallery, and the others in Albert Square, Manchester, and in the Houses of Parliament. The last-named was given by the late Andrew Carnegie and replaced one by Alfred Gilbert, R.A., the cost of which was subscribed after Bright's death: his family disliked the Gilbert statue and it was removed.

[2] The National Liberal Federation declared on May 5 in favour of Gladstone's policy.

[3] Then Home Secretary.

JOHN BRIGHT
From the statue by A. Bruce Joy in the Birmingham Art Gallery

"Conversation with Mr. Childers on Irish question and Govt. He is miserable and the Govt. in a very unpleasant and unsafe condition. He urged me to call on Mr. Gladstone, which I did, on leaving him.

"Only a short time with Mr. G. He seems weary and not so brisk and eager as when I saw him a fortnight since. He insisted upon it that there was no Cabinet difficulty, only the ordinary differences as to details. This I know not to be accurate. I know that two of his chief colleagues are entirely against his Irish policy, but he seems obstinately determined to go on with it. He suggested I should see him at the House on Monday evening.

"Lady Wolverton wrote asking me to go to Coombe Wood, Kingston-on-Thames, for to-morrow to meet Mr. and Mrs. Gladstone. Engagements prevent this, which is perhaps fortunate. A note from Mrs. Gladstone asks me to dine on Tuesday. In my present position as to the Irish question, would rather not. It is difficult to oppose a Minister on a critical question and to associate with him and frequent his table.

"This morning I told him I thought he could not carry his Bill, but I do not see how he is to escape the danger he has placed himself in. I am grieved to see the peril to himself, and to the Party, and to Ireland. There is a certain wilfulness in all this not usual with him, and it does not promise any good.

"Evening, dined with Sir Harry Verney, 4, South St., Park Lane: a large party. I took down to dinner Mrs. Ponsonby, a widow, daughter of Lord Dunsany, a very sensible and nice lady, living mostly in Ireland. Our conversation on the Irish question. She very reasonable and just in her estimation of Irish people, but condemns the tyrannous action of the Nationalists.

"M. Waddington, French Ambassador, and his American wife were there, and Mrs. Green, the widow of Mr. Green, the writer of the 'History of the English People.' Lady Verney lies on her couch, a victim of rheumatism. She reminded me of poor Mrs. Hughes of Llandudno. She is very quick and intelligent, and her conversation is interesting. The party very pleasant.

"[5th.] Seth Low, from Brooklyn, New York, called. Procedure Committee: progress slow. Dined with Bernard at Reform Club.

"My old friend W. E. Forster died to-day after a long illness. I called on Friday to ask after him. He was out for a drive with his wife, and had been rather better for a few days; but his recovery has long

539

been doubtful. He was a remarkable man, and has done good service in Parlt. Much regret expressed at the loss we have sustained.

"[8*th*.] House crowded. Mr. Gladstone on Irish Govt. scheme. Spoke 3 hours and 20 minutes. Measure complex and of doubtful character. Great excitement.

"[9*th*.] Chamberlain spoke. Scarcely so good as I expected.

"[12*th*.] House. R. Churchill spoke well, and with less than his usual eccentricities, in opposition to Irish Bill. Dined with Mr. and Mrs. Gladstone. He very cheerful and well.

"[13*th*.] Dear Sophie called. Willie also. It is very pleasant to have my dear children here during the session. Letter last night from dear Priscilla, with sad account of the illness of her venerable husband. Fear his end is not far off. Have written to her this morning. Am grieved to think of her anxiety.

"[16*th*.] Mr. Gladstone's Irish Land scheme and speech. Speech overdone, and scheme, in my judgment, not a wise one.

"[17*th*.] Spent an hour with Florence Nightingale, 10, South St., Park Lane. Talk on India in which she takes great interest. Her countenance is full of intelligence and benevolence. She is an invalid and was reclining on her couch. She is a sister of Lady H. Verney, who is also an invalid and on her couch. Dined with Mr. Agnew, M.P.: a good company. Woolner, sculptor, one of the party, and Mr. Hook, an eminent painter of sea-pieces.

"[26*th*.] Letter this morning from dear Priscilla. Her venerable husband evidently sinking. She asks me to write to him. But at noon I recd. a message from Charles that his father had 'passed quietly away' at $\frac{1}{4}$ past 11 this morning. A remarkable life has closed—his age 86—a life of continuous, devoted and honourable labour and service to Edinbro', to Scotland, and to the whole country. Dear Priscilla will be in great sorrow.

"[30*th*.] To Edinbro' by Midland train.

"[*May* 1.] The funeral of my brother-in-law, Duncan McLaren: public funeral. Many thousands of people in the streets as the procession passed through.

"[13*th*.] Anniversary of my great sorrow and loss.

"A note from Mr. Gladstone [1] asking me to go up to town to see him, but did not go till the following day.

---

[1] Bright's reply to Gladstone (Rochdale, May 13) is printed by Lord Morley ("Gladstone," Vol. III, p. 327). He had "not been able to bring myself to the point of giving a vote in favour of your Bills. I am grieved to have to say this. . . .

"[14th.] By Midland train. Rivers flooded in Derbyshire: near Matlock, line under water, but went thro' it without damage.

"Evening, Reform Club. Mr. Whitbread came up. Long conversation with him. He supports Mr. Gladstone, but is anxious to get him out of his trouble with his Irish Bills. Could the Bill be read a second time and then withdrawn? Difficulty great. No solution possible at the moment. Long talk with Mr. Caine [1] on same subject. He considers the Irish Bill as good as dead.

"[15th.] Club. Evening to Alexandra Hotel to pay my bill and take some things left there to the Euston Hotel, where I have taken excellent rooms on the 2nd floor. Up to Easter, paid at Alexandra Hotel 5 guineas per week for rather small rooms with 6/6 daily for fire, lights and attendance, being in all more than 7 guineas weekly. After Easter, charge for same rooms 14 guineas, and extras 2 gs., in all 16 guineas. Euston Hotel: two large rooms together, well furnished, weekly cost, including fire, lights, attendance, £6.10.0. The saving is considerable.

"[17th.] Gave letter to Mr. Whitbread on crisis on Irish policy of the Govt. Spoke to Chamberlain whose anxiety is very apparent. Showed him the letter to Whitbread. Talk with Harcourt in his room. He says a dissolution of Parlt. will follow the defeat of the Irish Bill. I condemned it as a wicked policy, leading probably to greater confusion and difficulty.

For thirty years I have preached justice to Ireland. I am as much in her favour now as in past times, but I do not think it justice or wisdom for Great Britain to consign her population, including Ulster and all her Protestant families, to what there is of justice and wisdom in the Irish Party now sitting in the Parliament at Westminster."

[1] This was the day of the meeting of dissentient Liberals at Lord Hartington's house, when Chamberlain finally came out for open opposition to the Bill. W. S. Caine, who had won the Barrow by-election (April 6) on a Unionist programme, acted during this crisis as an unofficial "Whip" for the dissentients. "Much depended on Mr. Bright, both in the country and in the House," writes Mr. John Newton in his biography of Caine. "He was so distressed by his acute differences from his old leader that he could not bring himself to attend the debates, but remained in the Reform Club, where Mr. Caine reported to him each evening after dinner the progress of events. In the early stages of the controversy Mr. Bright's tendency was merely to abstain from voting. He would not speak against the Bill; neither would he vote against. But as the temperature of the discussions gradually rose, he steadily moved from that position into the opposing camp, and at last felt it his duty, though with infinite reluctance, to vote against. By this time Mr. Caine was a warm advocate of opposition; no half measures would satisfy him, and he poured his views into Mr. Bright's ears day by day. . . ." ("W. S. Caine, A Biography," pp. 151-152.)

"[20*th*.] Heard of the death of my old friend John Holgate [1] yesterday morning—a man of great religious faith; of the Plymouth Brethren Society or Church.

"Club: dined there with Albert, and put Philip's name as a candidate for the Club. House: long conversation with Geo. Dixon on the situation, and particularly as to the condition of politics in Birmingham. Conversation with Lord Hartington. Some rumours of arrangement in the air, but nothing likely to take effect."

4

On the 27th Gladstone called a meeting of the Liberal Parliamentary Party at the Foreign Office. The invitation was to Liberals who were "in favour of the establishment of a legislative body in Dublin for the management of affairs specifically and exclusively Irish"—in other words, to the supporters of the principle of the Bill. "Many," says Lord Morley, "thought this discrimination a mistake." Bright was among the many. He put down under date, May 27:

"Meeting at Foreign Office: section of the Party willing to support the Government. The language of the invitation prevents my being present. Adherents of the Government on Irish policy only expected to attend."

As he made no record of his further part in the proceedings that led to the formation of the Unionist Party, it may be appropriate to recall shortly what happened. He did not attend the critical meeting of the dissentients on May 31 in Committee Room 15, when the fate of the Bill was determined. But he sent a letter which, by general admission, decided the policy of the group and the course of events on Home Rule. It was addressed to Chamberlain:

My present intention is to vote against the Second Reading, not having spoken in the debate. I am not willing to leave my view of the Bill or any Bills in doubt. But I am not willing to take the responsibility of advising others as to their course. If they can content themselves with abstaining from the division I shall be glad. They will render a greater service by preventing the threatened dissolution than by compelling it, if Mr. Gladstone is unwise enough to venture upon it. You will see exactly where I am. A small majority for the Bill may be almost as good as its defeat and may save the country from the heavy sacrifice of a General Election. I wish I could join you, but I cannot now change the path I have taken from the beginning of this unhappy discussion. . . . If you think it of any use you may read this note to your friends.

---

[1] A much respected solicitor in Rochdale who had charge of Bright's legal matters.

Chamberlain's invitation to the meeting had asked for the attendance of those Liberals "who, being in favour of some sort of autonomy for Ireland, disapproved of the Government Bills in their present shape." Bright did not approve of any sort of autonomy that would have been recognized by either Irish or English Home Rulers as autonomous. At the meeting the question was, as Lord Morley says, "whether they should content themselves with abstention from the division, or should go into the lobby against the Government. If they abstained, the Bill would pass, and an extension of the Party schism would be averted. . . . The Chairman" (Chamberlain) "opened in a neutral sense. It seems to have been mainly the moral weight of Mr. Bright that sent down the scale. . . . This letter was afterwards described as the death-warrant of the Bill and of the administration."

While his leaven worked thus in the political body, Bright was at his lodgings, writing to his daughters about his marriage settlements, drawing cheques for all his children under those settlements, and attending to his private concerns in general. These are the only topics of his diary. But on the day following the meeting, Caine having communicated its result to him, he wrote to tell Chamberlain of his surprise at the decision and at the influence his letter was said to have exercised upon its hearers:

For my note was intended to make it more easy for you and your friends to abstain from voting in the coming division. If I had thought I should do harm I should have said something *more* or *less*. Even now, if it is not too late, I could join you in abstaining if we could save the House and the country from a dissolution which may for the Liberal Party turn out a catastrophe the magnitude of which cannot be measured. For myself I have no anxiety, but I care for the Party and for its objects and for the country.

But it was too late. There could be no going back upon such a decision so taken. He wrote again to Chamberlain on June 5: "I see nothing more that can be done. . . . I am not sure that the fear of dissolution will not after all carry the second reading. I shall regret it, but the discussions between now and October or February will, I hope, more effectually kill the Bill. But I believe no Parliament is needed and I shall not support one." Two days later the Bill was already dead. Bright fulfilled his resolve to vote against the Government, and 92 other Liberal members went with him into the Opposition lobby.

"[*May* 28.] Evening, 40, Dover St. School Board Teachers' party at Lady Stanley's. Large party and pleasant. Conversation with Cardinal Manning, always most friendly. Asked me to come to lunch with him. His feeling against Irish Bills. Thought if the authorities of his Church in Ireland had been more decided, say 7 years ago, much trouble might have been avoided.

"This morning, with dear Helen to the Indian and Colonial Exhibition: very interesting show of products of the outlying countries connected with England.

"[29*th*.] Club. W. Kenrick, M.P., Birmingham, called to press me to speak in the Irish debate on Monday. Am not fixed in my mind, but may say something.

"Queen's Birthday dinner at Mr. Gladstone's; 40 present—very many who are in opposition on Irish Bills.

"I sat between Lord Hartington and Chas. Villiers. The *young* Prince, the future King, sat on the other side of Hartington.

"[*June* 3.] Midnight note from Vaughan telling me of the death of his dear wife last night. He is in sore distress.

"[4*th*.] To Glos'ter Terrace. Found Vaughan in great trouble, scarcely able to speak and in tears. Remained with him to dinner. Funeral fixed for Thursday the 10th. Coming away he said my visit had done him good.

"[7*th*.] House. Great debate on Irish Govt. Bill. Great excitement. Bill defeated by 340 votes to 311. Home by 2 o'clock.

"[8*th*.] Wrote to Mr. Richards, Wadham College, Oxford, accepting degree of D.C.L. to be conferred on the 30th inst. Would rather decline it but fear to be rude when kindness and good feeling intended.

"[10*th*.] Funeral of Mrs. Vaughan, the wife of my bro.-in-law, Jas. Vaughan, at Willesden Church. The day very wet. To-day is the anniversary of my marriage in 1847—39 years since. Parlt. to be dissolved on the Irish question.

"[11*th*.] By Midland 10.10 train home. Pleasant journey, all alone; day fine. Met Albert at Manchester on the station.

"[12*th*.] Wrote to Mr. Jaffray, consenting to be candidate for Central Division, Birmingham.

"[17*th*.] Col. Schwabe, M.P., here to dinner. He retires from County Division, rejected by partisans of Mr. Gladstone.

"[20*th*.] Meeting, morning. Discussion as to the proposal to read a chapter of Scripture at opening of Meetings. Appeared to be acceptable; no objection offered.

"[27*th*.] Most lovely day. Meeting, morning. Evening, making notes for Birmingham speech on Thursday next. Material far too great. This week much troubled with letters and messages on election matters. My opinion asked by so many Liberal voters in difficulty as to their votes.

"[28*th*.] To Manchester and Oxford; long journey. Edward Tylor and dear Kivor met me at the station. Drove to Prof. Max Müller's house. A small garden party, among them Prince and Princess Christian: call there to see her, as she had a message for me. It was from the Queen, who wished her to tell me how much satisfaction she had in what I had said in connexion with the Irish question, and desired that I should know it.

"The Queen is much against what is proposed, but the Princess said, 'You know, the Queen is very brave,' meaning that she submits to what in her position is necessary. I asked her to thank the Queen for her kind remembrance of me, and to say how much I was glad that anything I had said had given her satisfaction.

"To E. Tylor's house—Willie and Kivor there. To Balliol to dine with the Vice-Chancellor, Mr. Jowett. Large party, among them the Lord Chancellor. I sat between his wife Lady Herschel, and Lady Camilla Wallop, daughter of Lord Portsmouth: all his daughters are nice. After dinner we walked from the Common Hall, in which we had dined, across the Green to the Vice-Chancellor's house and drawing-room. Had some conversation with Burdon Sanderson, Professor of Physiology. He spoke most kindly of my son-in-law, Theodore Cash.

"[30*th*.] To breakfast with Mr. Herbert Richards, Senior Proctor of Wadham College, and walked in the charming garden of the College. At noon to the Sheldonian Theatre. It was crowded. The new doctors were called in, in their order—the Lord Chancellor first. I followed him, and then the rest—in all, I think, 6 or 7. We stood in a space like a pathway fronting the Vice-Chancellor, who sat a good way above us. The Latin Orator, Mr. Palgrave, spoke or read a short Latin speech in commendation of each of the new doctors; and, one by one, after his eulogium, we walked up a few steps to the Vice-Chancellor, shook hands with him and took our seats. To me he was specially complimentary, for he introduced into the usual formal address of admission the words 'patria et libertatis,' which was thought remarkable, and which I thought very kind.

"Then we had essays or papers read, some in English, others in Latin and Greek. After these, the Newdigate Prize Poem—on the death of Savonarola, the great Italian reformer.

"I thought it good, and it was listened to with great attention.

"Afterwards thro' the street in our crimson gowns to All Souls for lunch; 160 present at it. In the garden, the Princess again spoke to me, repeating what she said yesterday. I spoke to her son and wished him success in his studies. At lunch, sat between Mrs. Max Müller and Lady Dashwood.

"After lunch to the Masons' Garden Party. Very many there. Pleasant talk with several, the Professor of Chinese among them.

"Evening dinner party at E. Tylor's. Sat next to Mr. Brodrick, Warden of Merton College—a good man and pleasant. The day very fine. All passed off well: even my doctor's gown seemed to fit me, with all its colour. All very kind.

"[*July* 1.] With E. Tylor into the great Museum, to see Genl. Pitt-Rivers's collection now being placed there. He came in for a short time.

"Left Oxford about 11. Dear Kivor with me for Birmingham, she going on to Stoke, where Willie went yesterday on his election business. Mr. Johnson, Mr. Dixon and others met me at the station. My election has been unopposed, and I was again one of the Members for Birmingham. To 'The Dales,' Mr. Dixon's house. He came up in the evening to dine, with Dr. Dale and Mr. Osler.

"To the Town Hall: a great meeting. Mr. Jaffray in the Chair. I spoke for an hour and 40 minutes; voice good, and speech well received.[1] Tickets of admission had been sent to all voters in the Central Division. Mr. Dixon and Osler with us.

"[*2nd.*] Day very hot. Remained at 'The Dales.' Evening, Jas. H. Tuke and his wife came up to dinner. Talk on Ireland till 10 o'clock, and much on emigration.

"[*3rd.*] By 11.38 train for Bath; journey very hot; train good. Richd. Curry, my good son-in-law, met me. Found my dear Mary better than I expected.

"[*4th.*] Indoors or in small garden all day. Much talk with my dear child, who is not convinced that I am right on the Irish question.

"[*5th.*] By 5.50 train to London. Club. Much political conversation. Interest in returns of polling. Results so far against the Govt.—that is, Mr. Gladstone and his Bills.

"[*11th.*] I have been sorely burdened with letters and telegrams on election matters, asking my opinion on candidates and votes, and

[1] "The heaviest and most telling attack came from Mr. Bright, who had up to now in public been studiously silent. Every word, as they said of Daniel Webster, seemed to weigh a pound." (Morley, "Gladstone," Vol. III, p. 342.)

wishing me to write or telegraph in favour of particular candidates. The result of the contests is heavily against the Govt. and their resignation is expected.[1]

"[*August* 13.] Great cessation of letters since the elections over.[2]

"[30*th*.] To Perth, to see cattle sales. Sheep and lambs sold. Butchers the purchasers. Sheep unconscious of their fate, and of the character of the men taking so much interest in them. Went to the Pullar's great Dyeing Works, and to lunch with Jas. Pullar. A luxurious house. His little German wife very attractive in countenance and language.

"[*September* 18, *at Cassencary Creetown*.] Visit to Sir Jas. Caird. A pleasant visit of 8 days. Called on Miss Maxwell at Cardoness, and met there Gertrude Leatham, from Heath. Very glad to see her. Drove to Ed. Maxwell's, a large and good house on the Cree. Called also on Walter McCullagh, a fine old man over 80 years. Visit most pleasant. Weather good: only one wet day.

"[28*th*.] Fished Red Gorton water. Got one fish 18 lbs. Sent it to Sir Jas. Caird. I fished with Mr. McLean, once a Java merchant. The day cold and I was very tired with 6 hours on the river.

"[30*th*.] Fishing Red Gorton water, got 2 fish, 20 lbs. One to dear Helen. Dined with Mr. McLean at Battleby; a nice house and a pleasant party.

"[*October* 1.] To Birnam House, Dunkeld, to Sir John Everett Millais. Fished upper water and got 5 fish—24, 20, 16 lbs. and two smaller grilse. Sent off the fish to Lillie, 24 lbs., and to Mrs. Shawcross 20 lbs., and to T. Smithson 16 lbs. Dined at Birnam House with a pleasant party and slept there.

"[2*nd*.] Fished: only one fish 20 lbs. Sent to my bro.-in-law, Vaughan.

"[10*th*.] To Darnick, village near Melrose, to lunch with Andrew Heiton, who lives in the old town at Darnick. Singular and interesting place, some hundreds of years old, with dates of over 300 years on portion of the walls and furniture; the whole in ancient character. Mr. Heiton is an architect at Perth; comes here for holidays. In one room, curious ancient arms and armour. Sir Walter Scott frequently here, visiting Mr. Heiton's old uncle 80 to 100 years ago.

"[13*th*.] To Hawick, to lunch with my old friend Walter Wilson

[1] The final returns gave: Gladstonian Liberals, 191; Liberal Unionists, 78; Conservatives, 315; Parnellites, 86.

[2] He now went to Scotland for his fishing.

at Orchard House. He is in his 91st year, blind for 4 years. Cheerful and much pleased with my visit. His family consists of his wife, intelligent and very pleasant, his daughter and granddaughter. Most affectionate surroundings for him. His conversation interesting on the political past and present. He has been a very useful man, is a Friend, and my visit to him has been very instructive and very pleasant.

"Miss Yule, a friend of Lady Caird, has called on me. Long talk on public affairs and on India. Her father, Col. Yule, is one of the Indian Council in London. She seems infected with military 'Jingoism,' and is Conservative, and condemns Mr. Gladstone—but a clever woman.

"[*19th.*] To Clovensford to call on W. Thomson and to see his vineyard. Very large glass-house and quantities of grapes, which he grows chiefly for the London market. A clever man and interesting, full of information on gardening and vine-growing. Eight miles from Melrose. It is 14 years since *we* visited his vineyard. How sad the change![1]

"[*November* 16*th.*] My birthday. Many letters and much kindness from family, relatives and friends. 75 years!!

"[*December* 7.] Meeting and banquet of 'Unionist' Party in London. A letter from me to Lord Hartington read at the meeting.

"[*18th.*] This evening my poor dog *Ferran* died after a week's illness. This has caused quite a grief in our household. He was a charming companion. He came from Glencoe, Scotland.

"[*23rd.*] News of resignation of Lord Randolph Churchill, Chancellor of the Exchequer. Difficulty for the Govt. Leader of the House not easy to find; but that Churchill should have been leader is an astounding fact.

"[*28th.*] Letter from dear Sophie saying that Theodore is appointed Professor of 'Materia Medica,' University of Aberdeen. Very pleasant news."

5

On New Year's Day of 1887 he opens the last chapter of his diary. The entries continue till September. Then he writes no more.

Born nine years before the death of George III, Bright lived to witness and to record the Jubilee of Queen Victoria, and to lay at her feet the tribute of one small but eminent group of her subjects, the Friends.

[1] At the end of the month he returned to Rochdale and then spent the usual holiday at Llandudno.

One of the best passages in this final bit of his forty years' journal describes the scene at Windsor when the silver-haired Queen and the silver-haired Quaker spoke together for the last time.

His tenancies of office had been short and the offices themselves not such as to place him in constant touch with the Throne. But his relations with the Queen were those of mutual liking and respect, as the diaries attest. They had no common ground in political philosophy. She who made of the later Disraeli her personal confidant and saw in him the pattern of statesmanship, who hung bravely on to the last shreds of Prerogative, could have found few links of political sympathy with the Lancashire cotton-spinner whose life had been devoted to the propaganda of Radical policies, the faithful Achates of her pet aversion Gladstone, and the comrade and colleague of the terrible author of the doctrine of ransom.

Yet an affinity stronger than political diversities and constitutional prepossessions attracted them. There was not a pin to chose between them in their conception of the domestic virtues and their views of the sanctity of family life. To Bright, the little woman whom he saw in the palaces of Windsor, Osborne, Balmoral, was more than a great Queen, his sovereign, better than the symbol of an Empire about which he had very definite and unimperial opinions. She was a lonely widow, a very human person, whose life had been devastated as his own, a devoted mother, an upholder of the old virtues. And he to her was more than the Radical politician, the popular orator, the anti-militarist who cut across all her ideas of political propriety, national glory and imperial strength. He was the embodiment of that sturdy, intelligent, decent-living middle-class upon which rested the security of the Throne throughout her long reign—an exemplar of conscience and sincerity in private and public life. He opened for her a window into a world from which she was shut off. When, in the winter of 1888, he took to his bed at the beginning of his last long illness, the Queen's message to him was among the earliest and the most sympathetic of the hundreds that poured into "One Ash" from every part of the world.

Bright's views of Monarchy were those of the broad, practical, common-sense men of his era. He declined to spare time for academic speculations about the mere forms of the State. He believed that Democracy could develop to an ample liberty within the framework of the Constitution. "Keep to the old ways," he once wrote to a correspondent; "I am in favour of the Constitution which has come down from our forefathers with such amendments as circumstance and our experience seem to warrant." In 1872 some one, who had been told that the English Republicans would elect Bright as their first President, wrote to ask him if he would accept the post! His answer is a neat example of his gentle but effective way with cranks: "Your Republican friend," he said, "must not be a very desperate character if he proposes to make me his first President, though I doubt if he can be a friend of mine. As to *opinions* on the question of Monarchy or Republicanism, I hope and believe it will be a long time before we are asked to give our opinion; our ancestors decided the matter a long time since, and I suggest that you and I should leave any further decision to our posterity. Now, from your letter I conclude you are willing to do this, and I can assure you I am not less willing."

The brief diary of 1887 includes, besides the account of his last interview with the Queen, that of his last meeting with Gladstone. Amid all the tragedies wrought in English life by the poisonous acridity of the Irish quarrel, hardly any was more poignant than the separation of these two. They had spent a quarter of a century in personal intimacy and public collaboration. Theirs was one of the friendships that Cicero counts among the rarest. The snows of man's winter had whitened their noble heads and long toil for the public good had furrowed their brows together. Now, with bitter pain for both, they parted.

Even the acute and irreconcilable difference about Home Rule did not destroy their friendship altogether. As he sank towards his end, Bright asked his eldest son to write to Gladstone and say that "he could not forget your unvarying kindness to him and the many services you have rendered to the country." And Gladstone replied, that Bright had been "little absent from his thoughts of late." "My feelings towards him are entirely unaltered by any of the occurrences of the last three years. . . . I have never felt separated from him in spirit. I heartily pray that he may enjoy the peace of God on this side the grave and on the other."

Yet it would be untrue to deny that the virus did work mischief. They who had met in constant communion on the great enterprises of their common faith for twenty years and more now ceased to meet. Between the election of 1886 and Bright's death in 1889 their one encounter was the casual meeting in the street somewhat wistfully recorded by Bright on the evening of February 24. Two letters passed afterwards—in June when the "Parnellism and Crime" articles added another drop of poison to the chalice. And that was all. Bright's last word rings like a knell: "I grieve that I cannot act with you as in years past, but my judgment and conscience forbid it. If I have said a word that seems harsh or unfriendly, I will ask you to forgive it." He did not, indeed, say many words of any sort in this last year of his political life. But, just as his letter to Chamberlain had brought the Unionist Party to birth, and as his speech at Birmingham had ensured for it a Parliamentary existence, so now a vote in the House of Commons prevented it from dissolving into its disparate elements. Ireland seethed with discontent and erupted in outrage. Mr. W. H. Smith proposed on March 22 that the Coercion Bill should take precedence over all other business. Mr. Morley moved an amendment asking the House to refuse a Coercion Bill while no security had been taken against abuse of the Law by exaction of excessive rents in Ireland. The debate went on till the 25th. "Mr. John Bright," wrote Lord George Hamilton, "took no part in the discussion, but a great deal depended on the action which he personally took. If he had abstained from voting, or voted against the Government, the Unionist coalition would have been practically broken up. On the other hand, if he, in order to avert Home Rule, voted for a procedure which was so contrary to his previous professions, the coalition would receive fresh source of strength and cohesion. When the division bell rang, Mr. Bright, who was sitting close by Gladstone, without a moment's hesitation walked straight into the Government lobby."

Almost his last political utterance, in a letter to a correspondent in November, was a protest against Gladstone's insistence on "an impossible legislation for Ireland." "Mr. Gladstone stops the way," he wrote. ". . . His followers still have faith in him and are anxious to return him to power. They are furious because the Conservatives are in office, and blame me and others for keeping them there. They seem blind to the fact that Mr. Gladstone put them in office. . . . We cannot allow Mr. Gladstone to go back to office with his Irish policy, and are willing to support a Government which the constituencies have by a great majority placed in power. I prefer to join hands with Lord Salisbury and his colleagues than with Mr. Parnell and his friends the leaders of Irish rebellion."

The diaries have made it plain that, apart from his constitutional dislike of the separate Parliament, his attitude towards the Nationalist movement had been much influenced by the "rebel" character of the policy which came into force when Parnell ousted Isaac Butt from the leadership. It offended his deep-seated belief in law and order, progress by discussion, the Parliamentary conception of government. It is significant that "Parnellism and Crime" had a profound effect upon his mind. His course would have been no different if *The Times* had never published Pigott's forgeries; but their appearance under the auspices of *The Times* confirmed and intensified his preconceived opinions of the wickedness and ugliness of the Irish Party's conduct. When, in the Parnell Commission in February, 1889, Sir Charles Russell dramatically exposed the miserable author of these libels and the wretch, fleeing to Madrid, blew out his brains to avoid arrest, John Bright was lying *in extremis* at Rochdale and in less than a week he was dead.

He pencils the first note in his little book for 1887 at Rochdale, where Mr. and Mrs. Bernard Roth and their two boys have been on a visit. He remarks on the severity of that winter—which preceded one of the most glorious summers in history. He records his usual January dinner with Mr. Armitage at Salford, when he is called upon to reply to the toast of his health and speaks "for ¾ of an hour" to a company of forty friends, who receive him with much kindness. A Swedenborgian (Mr. Broadfield) dines and chats with him at "One Ash," is "intelligent, amiable and evidently very sincere," must therefore have a book for a present, and gets a work on "Judaism Before and After the Birth of Christ," "sent me from America by the author of it." On February 8, he goes to London and takes up quarters at the Alexandra Hotel, Hyde Park Corner.

"[*February* 11, 1887.] House at 11 o'clock for the division on Parnell's amendment to the Address; majority 108.[1]

"[*14th.*] Call from J. Bevan Braithwaite on Peace address from Friends to public and to ministers of all the Churches, and on a proposed deputation to foreign Govts. I supported the first but opposed the second. Interesting conversation. His information and reading and learning very remarkable and admirable.

"[*15th.*] Dined with Sir Henry James. Small party: Duke and Duchess of St. Albans, Lady Airlie and daughter, and Lord Rowton, who was Disraeli's private secretary. He told me he had found an interesting letter from me to Disraeli on the Reform question which would be historical.[2]

"[*16th.*] Dined with Lord Coleridge, Lord Chief Justice; a party of 20 or more. I sat next to Mr. Phelps, U.S. Minister, a good man

[1] The Liberal Unionists voted for the Government in a body on Parnell's anti-Coercion amendment.
[2] See page 298.

for his office. Some judges of the party: Lord Bramwell, Sir J. Bacon, lately retired at the age of 88, a man of a pleasant countenance, and others; also Lord Napier of Magdala, who spoke in favour of England and English Govt. in India.

"Speaking of the late Sir Sálár Jung, Regent of Hyderabad, he said he was the only native of India under whom an Englishman or gentleman could serve without a sense of humiliation.[1]

"[*22nd.*] Westminster Meeting House. Peace meeting. Wm. Jones spoke very well for an hour. Then I spoke for nearly an hour on our war policy, and said some things which will not be pleasant to the members of the 'honourable profession of arms.'

"[*24th.*] Called on Mrs. Baden-Powell, who wrote to me some time ago. Saw the canaries and sparrows in the house. They have also a beehive in the drawing-room!

"Walking along Piccadilly, I met Mr. Gladstone. Had not seen him since the defeat of his Irish Bill last year. We stopped and shook hands. I remarked we had been far apart for some time. He said, 'I hope we may before long be nearer together again,' which I doubted, or feared, we might not be. I asked after his family. His son Herbert is in India, but is soon expected home. Herbert told him how good in India had been the influence of Lord Ripon's Govt. Mr. Gladstone took his glove off to shake hands with me as indicating more cordiality and feeling. We met at 1.30 just opposite the house where one of the Rothschilds lived—I think the house where Lady Rosebery's mother lived.

"[*March* 1.] Left 'Life' of Geo. Fox and autobiography of Stanley Newman and 'Book of Discipline' with Lady Airlie, 47, Grosvenor St. Sent Dymond's 'Principles of Morality' to Lady Caird—promised to her at Cassencary.

"[*8th.*] Called at 18, Clifford St., Bond St., and engaged lodgings there—3½ guineas *weekly*. Coals not included. Writing 21 letters to-day—very burdensome.

"[*20th, at Brighton.*] Meeting. Afternoon, called on Willie Barclay and at Exton House: met Lord and Lady Lymington there—daughter of the late Edward Pease.

"[*April* 1.] House: great division 2 o'clock on the morning of 2nd. Speaker closed debate. 'That the question be now put' carried by majority of 110. Mr. Gladstone and Opposition and their Irish allies rose and left the House, beaten and disgusted.

[1] See page 382. Sir Sálár Jung had died at Hyderabad in February, 1883.

"[*3rd.*] Afternoon with W. Miller to meeting of the Salvation Army at their hall in the Edgware Road; perhaps near 1,000 present. 'Genl.' Booth there, and his daughter Eva. The proceedings interesting and less extravagant than often described to be. Several spoke shortly, inviting others to join the Army and 'to be saved.' Christ was always willing to receive and to save. Genl. Booth spoke with much feeling and effect. His daughter charming in appearance and her part in the service attractive and important. I found my eyes moist under the urgent entreaties of her father and herself. Am glad to have had an opportunity of being present on this occasion. We had a little conversation with them after the service.

"With W. Miller to his house, 55, Lancaster Gate, to tea with his family. Afterwards to 40, Glos'ter Terrace, to dinner with my bro.-in-law Vaughan.

"[*7th, at Rochdale.*] Monthly meeting. Friends present agreed to a Minute offered by Thos. Emmott [1] of Oldham and J. J. Sparkes of Rochdale, restoring my dear Sister Priscilla to her membership in the Society, from which she was separated long, long ago, on her marriage with Duncan McLaren. [2] Friends showed much kind feeling during the discussion.

"[*16th.*] To Bradford, Victoria Hotel, to visit my dear Sister Priscilla, who has been there for 7 weeks in a long illness. She is better, but not well enough to remove. Spent 2 hours with her. John (Lord) McLaren was with us part of the time.

"[*28th.*] Dined with Sir Jno. Pender in Arlington St. Lord Derby there, and Lord Wemyss, late Lord Elcho. Artists of note: Long, Faed, Davis, Herkomer and others. Pleasant party.

"[*30th.*] Academy dinner. Sat next to Mr. Huxley and opposite Sir G. O. Trevelyan. Sir John Millais nearly opposite. Before dinner met Archbishop of Canterbury and Bishop of Peterboro' and talked on Oaths Bill. Showed them how 3 political Articles had been placed in their Church Articles by politicians and statesmen, and not by good bishops or pious men,—Oaths, War, and Capital Punishment. I think the Church dignitaries agreed with me. After dinner, with Prince of Wales and Duke of Cambridge. Both very friendly. They like my course on the Irish question, the Duke, I think, especially. The dinner was pleasant and the speaking good, only some blamed the Archbishop for writing a long sermon and reading it at the dinner!

"[*May* 4.] Dined at Athenæum Club. Small house-dinner, 12

[1] Father of the late Lord Emmott.　　　[2] See page 94.

in number: Norman Lockyer; Cumin, Education Depart.; Welby, Treasury; Sir G. Dasent; Thursfield, of *The Times*; Moncrieffe and others.

"[*8th.*] Westminster Meeting. Dinner with Mrs. Tylor. Called on Duke of Argyll. Tea with them. Duchess very pleasant.

"[*12th.*] J. B. Braithwaite called to ask me to go to Windsor on the 16th, to introduce to the Queen Friends presenting an Address. Could not well refuse to so good a man, tho' would have much preferred to decline the invitation.[1]

"[*13th.*] Anniversary of the day of the greatest sorrow of my life —9 years.

"[*14th.*] Dined with Geo. Dixon, Stoke Lodge. Hobhouse, Caldwell, Kenrick there. Much talk with Caldwell on opinion in Scotland on Irish question. Major Sanderson, North of Ireland member, great opponent of Parnell gang in Parlt., called, and some interesting talk with him.

"[*16th.*] To Windsor with a deputation from Friends to present an Address to the Queen: J. B. Braithwaite, Richard Littleboy, Stafford Allen and others. Lunch at the Castle. Friends were first introduced. I presented the Address to the Queen, who stood with members of the Court about her. I said a few words. I was there to introduce a deputation representing the Society of Friends, who were numerically but a small section of our population, but for whom I might say that they were as fervent as any portion of our people in wishes and prayers for the prolongation and prosperity of Her Majesty's reign. The Queen recd. the Address and gave me her reply. J. B. B. and R. Littleboy kissed the Queen's hand.

"I mentioned Stafford Allen as the nephew of William Allen, who was a friend of the Duke of Kent, whose name was not unknown to the Queen.

"Before going in, Sir H. Ponsonby told me the Queen wished me to see her after the deputation had been recd.

"I afterwards went into the Queen's Cabinet where she was alone. I was recd. with a pleasant greeting and smile.

"The Queen told me she was pleased with my course on the Irish question, and I thanked her for the message she had sent me by the Princess Christian when I was at Oxford on the 30th June last year. She spoke sorrowfully of the course of Mr. Gladstone and thought his mind strangely diverted in the line he has taken on Irish affairs.

[1] On the occasion of the Queen's Jubilee.

"She said she was going down to Scotland for a rest, when I remarked that I was afraid she suffered from the duties and anxieties of the time. She spoke of her gratification at the kind reception she had met with in the City, and at the kindness shown to members of her family at Liverpool, Manchester, Saltaire and Newcastle.

"She was very kind and shook hands with me at the beginning and end of the interview.

"Came back to London with Newman Hall, and pleasant conversation with him. We are in agreement on the Irish question. Dined at the Reform Club with my friend E. L. Pierce, of Boston.

"[*17th.*] With Mr. Pierce to the American Exhibition. An extraordinary display of horsemanship, interesting and amusing. Prince Henry of Battenberg and his wife, Princess Beatrice, in the box with us. With them to see the tents of the Indians who form the Corps of Riders, etc.

"Going into one of the tents, I stumbled and fell, coming down with my nose on a step above so violently that a stream of blood burst forth and for the moment I was almost stunned. I was helped into the tent, bleeding a good deal. I rested for a time and the bleeding ceased, and we came to my lodgings in a cab. I look as if I had recd. a severe blow, but no ill consequences have followed.

"[*June* 1, *at Rochdale.*] Presided over Meeting of Sunday School Conference of Baptist Churches held in the Baillie St. Chapel. Spoke for ½ an hour, suggesting some directions for usefulness to teachers. Chapel crowded. Speeches good, and I hope the meeting will be of use.

"[*7th.*] Heard this evening of the death of my old friend Geo. Crosfield, who died from injuries caused by fire in his bedroom. A grievous case. I have recently called upon him at Lancaster Gate.

"[*8th.*] At the office, posting up the private ledger. Am less competent at figures than in former years.

"[*11th.*] To London. Dined with Mrs. Jeune, 37, Wimpole St. Pleasant party. Lady Stanley, 80th year, *young* and fair and lively and intelligent as ever; Lord and Lady Carnarvon; Edwin Arnold [1] of the *Light of Asia*, and his wife, and Mr. Smalley, of the *New York Tribune*.

"[*14th.*] Dr. Edmunds called—am to second him as a candidate for Reform Club. Mahomedan Lawyer from Bombay called with letter from Lord Reay. His name is Budroodeen Tyabjce, a good-

[1] Editor of the *Daily Telegraph*.

looking man, speaking English perfectly. Afternoon called on Isabella Crosfield to condole with her on the sad death of my old friend, her husband. Great grief. Death from fire in bedroom. He in very weak health, and severe burning and shock were fatal. House. Saw Mr. Raikes on Post Office appointment. Spoke to Mr. Goschen on proposed Irish light railway from Galway to Clifden.

"[15*th*.] Dined at Middle Temple banquet. Great company. Prince of Wales and his son, Duke of Cambridge, Lord Chancellor, Lord Chief Justice and many judges and great lawyers there. The banquet in the fine old Hall. Grand Ball at the Reform Club, but did not go to it. Home 11 o'clock.

"[17*th*.] House. Voted in division in Crimes Bill Committee. Irishmen left the House disgusted at their failure.[1] Club. Conversation with Mr. Wilson, writer of *The Times* articles against the Parnell conspiracy. Has done much to expose, and I hope to break down, the criminal gang in Parlt. and in Ireland.[2]

"[21*st*.] Jubilee Day. We saw the procession from the front of Devonshire House. Interesting event. The Queen looked cheerful and happy.

"[28*th*.] Sittings to Frank Holl for portrait for Reform Club. Very tedious work.

"[*July* 1.] Dined with Sir Jas. Caird. Edwd. Atkinson, from Boston, there. His knowledge of economic questions very remarkable. Also Col. Stewart, a great traveller in Central Asia.

"[7*th*.] Dined with my nephew, Chas. McLaren,[3] 45, Harrington Gardens. Dear Priscilla there, Judge Sterling, and others. Tea with Blennerhasset, Hans Place. Met Lady Russell and pleasant party.

"[8*th*.] House. Division, 3rd reading of Crimes Bill. Ireland. Meeting of India Association. Interesting discussion, concluded by

[1] On June 10, the Government had carried the famous "guillotine" resolution, providing that if the Bill was not through Committee within a week the Chairman should put the remaining clauses without amendment or debate.

[2] The "Parnellism and Crime" articles attracted little attention till, on the morning of April 18, the day fixed for the second reading of the Crimes Bill, *The Times* published in facsimile the letter, forged by Pigott, in which Parnell purported to excuse himself for his public denunciation of the Phœnix Park murders and to express the opinion that "Burke got no more than his deserts." Despite Parnell's repudiation of the letter, it was at this time generally held to be genuine, on the ground that *The Times* would not have published such a document without being certain of its authenticity.

[3] Now Lord Aberconway.

a short speech from me on India question, chiefly on employment of natives in Indian Administration.

"[*9th.*] Call from Mr. Humphry Ward, who proposes to write a Biography of me for Cassell & Co. Long conversation with me.

"[*13th.*] Dined with Lord Monkbretton, 6, Seymour Place. Met Mr. Lecky, historian, there. Talk about Ireland. Henry Reeve there, editor of Greville's Memoirs. Sir C. Russell there after dinner, and many others. To F. Holl's studio from 11 to 4 o'clock, and lunched with him.

"[*14th.*] House till one in the morning, but no division (on) Irish Land Bill, Parnellites not daring to vote against it.[1]

"[*15th.*] To Holl—another sitting. Portrait nearly finished. Do not like it. All attempts seem destined to failure.

"[*16th.*] With Philip to Mr. Holl's to see the portrait. Dined at 74, South Audley St., with Mr. Quilter, M.P. The whole party were Unionist in politics, and the conversation was interesting. Mr. Quilter has a small gallery and many excellent pictures. One, a Spanish group by John Phillips, I admired much.

"[*17th.*] To Argyll Lodge, Putney, to visit my old friend Sir James Brunlees. He is not strong, and I fear I shall not see him on a Scotch river during the coming autumn.

"[*18th.*] To Town with Sir J. Brunlees. Dined with Sir Henry James at 28, Wilton Place: Honble. Arthur Elliot, M.P., Lady Dorothy Nevill, and Lady Hayter. Small party; much gossip.

"[*21st.*] Westminster Meeting. Wedding: Adelaide Spencer Bell and Middleton Fox. Large attendance. Bevan Braithwaite and Ann Fowler spoke beautifully, and Thos. Hodgkin. I signed the certificate. Occasion very interesting. Ann Fowler's words brought tears into my eyes in remembrance of the past. Reform Club: dined with Philip and two Americans, Genl. Hawley[2] and Mr. F. C. Penfield.[3]

"[*26th.*] John (Lord) McLaren called. Pleasant chat with him. Humphry Ward called. He is engaged by Cassell & Co., the great publishers, to write a Life of me. The proposition is not pleasant to

---

[1] Lord Cadogan's Land Bill which, after much vacillation on the part of the Government about the revision of judicial rents, carried out the provisions of the measure introduced by Parnell in 1886 and then rejected by the full Unionist majority.

[2] Senator for Connecticut, and a distinguished figure in the Civil War.

[3] Afterwards U.S. Consul-General in London and U.S. Minister in Vienna.

me, for it involves trouble and lays me open to a charge or suspicion of vanity. I am against biographies and portraits and statues. They are troublesome and are soon forgotten, and of no influence in the future. I have been and am a victim of the habit of my time to commemorate the ordinary labours of ordinary lives. Dined with Mr. Phelps, the American Minister, at 31, Lowndes Square; a party of 20 Americans and English. I sat between the U.S. Minister at Madrid and one of his countrymen whose name I forget. Conversation pleasant. Madrid Minister once a Confederate,—now loyal as any other American, and was grateful to me for the part I had taken in the great American conflict.

"Conversation with M. Waddington, French Ambassador. Had visited Mr. Gladstone at Dollis Hill a month ago. In talk with Mr. G., found him absorbed in Irish question. Former occasions they could discuss other subjects: he would always rise to Homer or some other literary topic. But now Homer failed, and only Ireland now—always Ireland. He thought, while as brilliant as ever in respect of language, that his judgment was impaired. One idea had got full possession of him—he has become a victim of what the French call *l'idée fixe*. M. Waddington thought the Home Rule policy led inevitably to the break up of the Empire.

"Speaking of France, M. Waddington thought Boulanger not a man of genius or likely to lead, and that the President, M. Grévy, had shown wisdom and firmness in refusing to have a Govt. in which he was a member.

"I recd. many compliments and expressions of kindness from Americans present. They said no other man in Europe would be received with so much enthusiasm of welcome as I should if I crossed the Atlantic.

"[28*th.*] To Street, Somerset. Dear Helen at the station.

"[29*th.*] Meeting.

"[30*th.*] Drive by Sedgemoor. Road hilly; sun very hot; views fine. Flower show in Capt. Butt's field; not crowded, but interesting. Mr. Plumptre, Dean of Wells, came over to see me. Pleasant talk on Dante and Milton and Hymns.[1]

"[31*st.*] Drive to Wells. Visited the Cathedral. On our way called on Mr. Freeman, historian and professor. Quiet, retired residence —house with many books, fitting for its master.

"[*August* 3.] Returned to London after a most pleasant visit.

[1] Edward Hayes Plumptre, the translator of the *Divina Commedia*, had been appointed Dean of Wells in 1881.

William so sensible, Helen so active and so good; the children, all of them, well brought up and promising well.

"[*4th.*] Dined 32, Dover St., with Mr. [name illegible] and General Cameron, the last survivor of Lincoln's Cabinet. He is in his 89th year, very thin, but healthy, clear in mind and cheerful in conversation. Believes in the American Tariff as the height of wisdom!

"[*5th.*] Greenwich, dinner to Lord Hartington, and was Chairman. 50 M.P.s by boat and from Greenwich. The party most pleasant.

"Had to propose Toast of the Queen—dislike Toasts as encouraging drinking, but I recommend water instead of wine. Spoke at some length—my audience apparently much satisfied. Hartington and Chamberlain spoke well. Sir H. James asked me to give him notes of my speech, which I did.

"[*8th.*] Dined with Mrs. Jeune, 39, Wimpole Street. Lymingtons, Chamberlain, Ashley, Sir James Stephen there. Recd. note from Mr. Buckle, Editor of *The Times*, apologizing for a bad report of my speech at the Greenwich dinner on Friday night.

"[*10th.*] Long talk with C. P. Villiers at the Reform Club, mainly on Irish affairs. Speaks well and clearly as ever tho' is said to be in his 86th year. Evening dined with Chamberlain, a party of 8; Hartington, Drummond Wolff there—interesting discussion on Egypt; I thought Wolff's remarks very sensible, and his sympathy is real for the wretched population of Egypt.

"[*26th.*] To London for Division on proclamation of Irish Rebel League.

"[*September 7.*] Rochdale to Perth—British Hotel.

"[*8th.*] To Grantown and Tulchan Lodge. Lord Ronald Gower in the train—pleasant talk with him. Pleasant party at Tulchan Lodge—Sir Henry James and his niece among them.

"[*15th.*] Left Tulchan for Aberdeen. Probably I may never see the Valley of the Spey again. How many pleasant weeks I have spent at Tulchan Lodge, enjoying Mr. Bass's friendship and hospitality!

"[*17th.*] To lunch with Principal Geddes at Old Aberdeen.

"[*19th.*] With Principal Geddes over Marshal College—Dr. Stevenson with us. Met Professor Struthers—saw much of his Anatomical Museum, and of his work."

So abruptly ends Bright's own story of his life from day to day. The rest has been told by Mr. Trevelyan in a chapter of infinite grace and needs no re-telling here. A few facts only will suffice. He fell ill in May, 1888, rallied towards the end of the summer, but relapsed so seriously in November that his children were called together and his worldly affairs set in order.   It was then that he sent to Gladstone the message printed on p. 550.   He lingered, gradually weakening, through Christmas into the spring, cheered and pleased by the company of his grandchildren who sat in his room when he felt well enough to have them there and to shower on them the abundant gentle love he felt for little children.   His dog, Fly, stayed with him always.

On a lovely spring morning, March 27, 1889, his heart ceased to beat.   The next evening they carried him in his coffin down to the drawing-room.   Lying there, with the rays of his reading lamp shining on his splendid head, "he looked exquisite," one of his daughters said; "his face refined and pure, with a look of majesty on it, and perfect peace."

Upon this serene nobility the mill-workers came all day to gaze, passing by in a continuous procession to take their farewell of the man who had counted for so much in their lives alike as wage-earners and as citizens.   They buried him beside his wife in the little graveyard of the Friends' Meeting House.   An immense concourse of people saw him pass for the last time through the streets of Rochdale.   The multitude was silent; only the clatter of the horses' hoofs on the paved streets broke the stillness; but the mourning family were conscious of a universal sorrow, intensely felt in this his home, coming to them in great waves from every corner of the world where men spoke the language he had spoken.   The affection of the English people for John Bright transcended the bitterness of the time.   While his name in these brief days was on all men's lips they held a truce of God.

INDEX

INDEX

A

Abbotsford, visit to, 346

Abbott, Dr. Lyman, on J. B. Gough, 169 (note); talk on American tariff with, 475

Aberdeen, Bright at, 428–9

Aberdeen, Lord, forms a Ministry, 131 (note); Irish Catholics given posts, 143; and the Eastern question, 159; frank speech with, 164 (and note), 165; Bright's view of, 165–6; changes in his Ministry, 173; surrenders seals of office, 183; on Cabinet resignations of Palmerston's government, 187; the Queen's regard for, 192; why he did not resign before Crimean War, 195 (note); on Gibson's motion of censure, 196; Court interview with, 198; on Gladstone's mission to Ionian Islands, 235; the situation discussed with, 238

Aberdeen, 7th Earl of, invites Bright to Haddo, 424; invitation accepted, and visit to, 429

Abolitionist movement, Bright and, 309 (note)

Abro, Mr., 32, 33

Ackworth School, schooldays of father and son at, 2, 5–7

Acton, J. Adams (sculptor), sittings to, 526

Adams, Mr., statue of Cobden, 538

Adams, Charles Francis (U.S. Minister), thanks Bright, 257; meetings with, 271, 272, 278, 280, 284, 308, 311

Advertisement Duty repealed, 141; debate on, 148

Affirmation Bill, Gladstone's speech, 498

Afghan boundary dispute, 524 (and note)

Afghan frontier, vote of credit to meet possible difficulties on, asked for and defeated, 526 (note), 528

Afghan War, debate on, 414

Afghanistan, grave news from, 446; evacuation determined on but postponed, 448 (note)

Agnew, William, buys "Duchess of Devonshire" by Gainsborough, 380; and an engraving of Gladstone from picture by Millais, 460; celebrities at dinner party given by, 468

Agricultural Labourers' Union, and the franchise, 371

Airlie, Lady, invites Bright to visit her, 519

Alabama affair, 261, 281; settlement delayed, 340 (note)

Albany, Duke of, 472

Albert, Prince Consort, at battue at Lord Salisbury's, 91–2; at opening of Great Exhibition, 123; illness of, 149; charges against rebutted, 157; and American Civil War, 252; esteem for Cobden, 336

Albert Edward, Prince of Wales, talks with Bright, 321, 395; critically ill, 348; visit to India, 372, 373; requests autograph of Bright, 527

Albert Victor, Prince (Duke of Clarence), Bright meets, 527; death of, 527 (note)

Alexander II, Tsar, assassination of, 459

Alexandra, Princess (afterwards Queen), introduction to, 441

Alexandria, visit to, 35–6; bombardment of, 482, 485

Alice, Princess, death at Darmstadt, 414

Allen, Stafford, accompanies Friends' deputation to the Queen, 555

Alliances, Bright on, 167

Allon, (Dr.) H., entertains Bright to tea, 433

Alma, battle of the, 177 (note)

Amberley, Lady, 326; influence of J. S. Mill on, 372

America, "Claims Convention" rejected by Senate, 340; an invitation to visit, declined, 341 (note), 427

American affairs, discussed in Rome, 223, 224

American Civil War, Bright's attitude, 252 *et seq.*; Liberals and, 254; end of, 289

American Exhibition, visit to, 556

André, M., gives Bright lessons in French, 206

"Angel of Death" speech, Bright's, 189–90

Anti-Corn-Law Circular, 63

Anti-Corn Law League formed, 53; objects of, 57; and Peel's Budget, 65; campaign fund of, 69, 72, 79; disbanded, 79; liquidation of, 80

Antwerp, visit to, 13

Appian Way, drive on, 222

Arabi's revolt against Tewfik, 481, 482 (note); capture of, 491 (note); exiled, 493

Arch, Joseph, questions discussed with, 371; elected M.P., 371 (note)

Argyll, Duchess of, 305; garden party at Campden Hill, 381

Argyll, Duke of, and American Civil War, 252; introduces Bright to Garibaldi, 275; meetings with, 304, 369; visit to, 350; fishing with, 412; resignation on Land Bill question, 461; warns Lords against rejection of Franchise Bill, 514

Army Discipline Bill, debate on, 424

Army Regulation Bill, Irish obstruction on, 425 (note)

Arnold, Dr., on Democracy and Aristocracy, 91

Arrow, seizure of: war follows, 211

Art, Bright's reactions to works of, 227

Arthur, Prince, Duke of Connaught, 333, 335; visits the Bright mills, 383

Ashantee War, Cabinet meetings on, 357, 358

Ashburton, Lord, 214

Ashley, Hon. Evelyn, Kenealy's complaint against, 366, 368; dines with Sir H. James, 384

Ashley, Lord, Bright's controversies on factory legislation with, 75–6; and oath of allegiance, 158 (note)

Ashworth, Miss Anne Frances (niece), 432 (note)

Ashworth, G. L., death of, 355

Ashworth, Henry, and Ferrand's outburst, 67; death of, 441

Ashworth, Miss Lilias, marries George Hallett, 461 (note)

Ashworth, Thomas, visits the Continent, 13

Asiatic cholera, outbreak of, 177 (note)

Athens, visits to and impressions of, 17, 24–5, 42–4; becomes capital of Greece, 26 (note); during the revolutionary war, 26 (note)

Atlantic telegraph scheme, 257; promoters of, 272

Australia, granted constitutional government, 113

Austria, and naval power in Black Sea, 190, 196 (note)

Avery, Mr., Mayor of Birmingham, opens Central Free Library, 480

B

Babojee, Rungor, meeting with, 126

Backhouse, James, garden and grounds visited, 374

Backhouse, John Church, 205

Baden, Grand Duke of, interest in land question, 426

Bagehot, Walter, 324

Baker, Col. Valentine, overwhelmed by Mahdi forces, 508 (note)

Balaklava, battle of, 177 (note); unfounded rumours of battle at, 195

Balkan question, opposing views of Disraeli and Gladstone on, 375–6

Ballot, established in Canadian municipal elections, 132; mode of voting in Massachusetts demonstrated, 135; Bright's speech on votes by, 308 (note)

Ballot Bill, second reading, 478

Bancroft, John, Houses of Parliament visited by, 172

Bancroft, Samuel (cousin), visits Bright, 127

Bank of England, visit to, 147

Bannerman, Lady K., views against war, 488

Barclay, J. Gurney, marriage of, 83; his house at Knott's Green, 409

Barclay, Robert, death of, 152; "Apology for True Christian Divinity" by, 351

Baring, Major Evelyn (1st Earl Cromer), report on Eastern question, 386 (note), 387

Baring, Sir F., resolution for prosecution of War carried, 197 (note)

Barker, Benjamin (agent to British and Foreign Bible Society), 29

Barker, H., tribute to, 38

Barker, H. R., entertains Bright, 27

Barlow, Mrs., 269

Barnett-Smith, G., "Life and Speeches of Bright" by, 456 (and note)

Barrett, Michael, execution of, 322 (note)

Bateman, Rev. Charles, view on establishment, 416

Bazley, (Sir) Thomas, and cotton cultivation in Africa, 122

Beaconsfield Church, visit to, 426

Beaconsfield, Lord (*see also* Disraeli), pro-Turk speech at Mansion House, 386 (note); and the Berlin Treaty, 401; death of, 462; funeral at Hughenden, 463

Beales, Edmund (president of Reform League), 294

Becker, Bernard, unsuccessful attempt to interview Bright, 385

Bedford, Duke of, 379

Behrens, Jacob, 397

Beirut, in quarantine at, 31

Belgian Neutrality, Treaty of, difficulty *re* interpretation of, 343 (note)

Bell, Lady (widow of Sir Charles), Bright and, 381

Bell, Miss Adelaide, wedding of, 558

Bell, Mr. (consul at Algiers), 207

Bellini dies of cholera, 46

"Ben Hur" (Lew Wallace's) read by Bright, 504

Ben Rhydding, taking the waters at, 87, 88, 204

Benezet, Mlle, mistress of Friends' School at Nîmes, 209, 210

C

T